Classification of map
according to reduced sca
and standard of distance

JN092669

Scale (1km Grid)
Scale (2km Grid)
) Scale (2km Grid)

Symbols Used
Explanatory Notes

- H Honzon (main Deity)
- Address
- Parking (capacity)
- A Access
- Phone
- S Temple Lodging (shukubō)
- Public Phone

寺

80-1 Ido-kita-yashiki, Kokufu-chō, Tokushima City
Free of charge (30)
A About 20 min. walk from JR Tokushima Line Kou Stn.
☎ 088-642-1324 S None

It is believed that Kūkai dug the well here in one night with just his staff and the name of this temple comes from this legend. The hut over the well is called *higiri daishi* meaning that if one makes a wish on a specific day then that wish will come true.

NOTE: Tourist Information (see green boxes)

These describe various unique and famous sites, as well as local cultures around Shikoku that might be of interest. This is a limited list of what Shikoku has to offer; however, it is our hope that you will visit such places and feel the local features of each area. By doing so, you will truly enrich your experience while in Shikoku.

Explanatory Notes

Oka-goten 岡御殿
O Open C Closed
F (Entrance) Fee
Picture Explanation

Shikoku pilgrimage route

What is most important is not reaching the goal, but the journey itself. The warm hearts of the people you meet and the beautiful nature of Shikoku you see will perfectly complement your action of doing the pilgrimage.

The Shikoku pilgrimage route, which is also called "HENRO" consists of eighty-eight "official" temples and numerous other sacred sites located around the island of Shikoku. It is believed that the founder of Shingon Buddhism in Japan, Kōbō Daishi (Kūkai) (774-835) trained or spent time at some of these places, thus he plays a central role in this pilgrimage. Although there are references to people making this pilgrimage from around the 12th century, it did not become popular among the general public until the first guidebooks were published in the late 17th century. Today, hundreds of thousands of people from around the world make this pilgrimage by bus, by car, by bicycle, on foot etc. They come for different reasons: to remember a relative or friend who has passed away, to get away from work and responsibilities in regular life, to enjoy the outdoors, or to have time to be alone. Despite the motive, all people are welcomed regardless of nationality, age, gender, social status, religious affiliation, cultural background, but it is important to remember that this is a religious journey, not a stamp rally or backpacking trail. The path, sites, objects and people that make up the pilgrimage should be treated with respect. As you follow the footsteps of those who have made the pilgrimage before you, please consider those who come after you. If you are thinking of embarking on some or all of this pilgrimage, do not worry because most likely other pilgrims, temple staff, and the local people will support you on your journey.

Legend

Words in Italic are the original Japanese.
The information in this book is accurate as of May 2024.

Pilgrim Facilities

2 elevation — One of the 88 Temples (Washrooms Available) *(fudasho)*

88 — Inner Sanctuary *(Okunoin)* or Related Sites of 88 Temples

12.3km — Distance to the next temple (Elevation & distance map Route)

P — Parking

Rest hut *(kyūkeisho)*

2 — One of the 20 other temples (Washrooms Available) *(bekkaku)*

卍 ⛩ — Related temples and shrines *(bangai)*

★ — Related hut and monument etc

▲ — Old Stone Path Marker

Walking Route

At times, the walking route merges with traffic roads.

125 — Distance from Temple No. 1 Pilgrim Route (Elevation & Distance Map)

△140 Height (unit: meter) — Pilgrim Route *1

Shikoku-no-michi (ENV) *2

Shikoku-no-michi (MLIT) *2

12.3km — Distance between Sections

Tourist Facilities

Washrooms are available.

Sightseeing Point *(midokoro)*

Park *(kōen)*

Campsite *(camp-jō)*

Noted Historic Places or Spots *(meisho)*

Hot Spring / Public Bath *(onsen / furo-ya / sentō)*

Michi-no-eki (Road Station) *3

Public Facilities

Washroom *(toire)*

Post Office *5 *(yūbin-kyoku)*
(available on Sundays, see pg10)

Police Station *(keisatsu/kōban)*

Museum / Pavilion *(hakubutsukan/pabilion)*

◎ — City (Town) Office *4 *(shiyakusho / yakuba)*

H.S. — High School
J.H.S. — Junior High School *(gakkō)*
E.S. — Elementary School

Hospital / Clinic *(byōin)*

Prefectural Boundary

City or Town Limit

Traffic Facilities

All roads are paved except Unpaved road.*

Interchange, Kōchi — Expressways *(kōsoku-dōro)*

55, Tunnel with Sidewalk — National Roads *(kokudō)*

29 — Main Regional Roads *(kendō)*

Route Number 220 — Regional Roads

Other Roads

Unpaved road *

Station *(eki)*, Awa-Kawabata — Japan Railways *6 (Yellow Station: All Ltd Exp stop)

Kawaramachi — Private Railways

Bus Route

Bus Stop *6 *(basu-tei)*

Taxi: Phone

Commercial Facilities

There is not a big difference between ryokan and minshuku, and business hotels and hotels.

■ Lodging & (Phone or OTA website)
(4,000 – 10,000 yen in urban areas) *7

M Minshuku *(minshuku)*
Small type of Japanese-style lodging run by families. Includes breakfast and dinner. Futon with shared bath.

R Ryokan *(ryokan)*
A more traditional Japanese-style type of accommodation than at a minshuku. Includes breakfast and dinner. Futon with shared bath.

GH Guesthouse
No meals. Bed or futon with shared bath.

BH Business Hotel
It is a hotel with small self-contained rooms. Bed with private bath.

H Hotel
Similar to a typical Western-style hotel. No meals. Private bath.

★ Recommended Lodging

M -----, 088-123-4567

Accommodation in case of without meals, and less than 4500yen are in italics.

Restaurant / Café

Gasoline Station
washroom - only for use in emergencies

Laundromat *(coin laundry)*

Supermarket / Store / Drugstore

Convenience Store *5

7-Eleven	FamilyMart
LAWSON	Others

There are washrooms in supermarkets and convenience stores. You can use a credit card for shopping.

Almost all signage around Shikoku is written only in Japanese, so this book shows the signs in both English and Japanese. You can point to the Japanese name (written in green) when asking for direction to prevent any confusion.

Ex. 徳島市 (Tokushima city)

*1 Except along principal routes (elevation & distance map route), path markers might be difficult to find. It may be easy to get lost in the mountains.

*2 The "Shikoku no Michi" route is a walking course around Shikoku which, at times, makes use of the pilgrim trail allowing one to visit the various temples along the route and to experience Shikoku. There are two routes: 1) The Ministry of Environment route for those interested in nature and 2) The Ministry of Land, Infrastructure and Transport route for those interested in history and culture. This route is very confusing as it occasionally overlaps with the Pilgrim Route.

symbol on path marker

*3 These facilities often display materials describing the local area, as well as sell food products and souvenirs. In most cases, staff are on duty from 9:00am-5:00pm.

*4 A washroom is available, as well as a tourist section where one can receive assistance. There are also washrooms in community centers and public halls listed on the maps. (Open: Weekdays 9:00am-5:00pm)

*5 Equipped with ATMs. see pg 10 on map. Post offices without an ATM are not listed.

*6 The time schedule of useful train stations and bus stops has been included on the maps. A new time schedule comes out every March for trains and every 2-3 years for buses, however, there is not a large degree of change so the noted time gives you a general idea.

*7 OTA (Online Travel Agent) are travel companies that operate on the Internet. There are some lodging facilities part of OTA which you can only reserve online, so the name of the OTA is listed instead of the phone number. Ex: (Henro House), (airbnb), (booking.com)

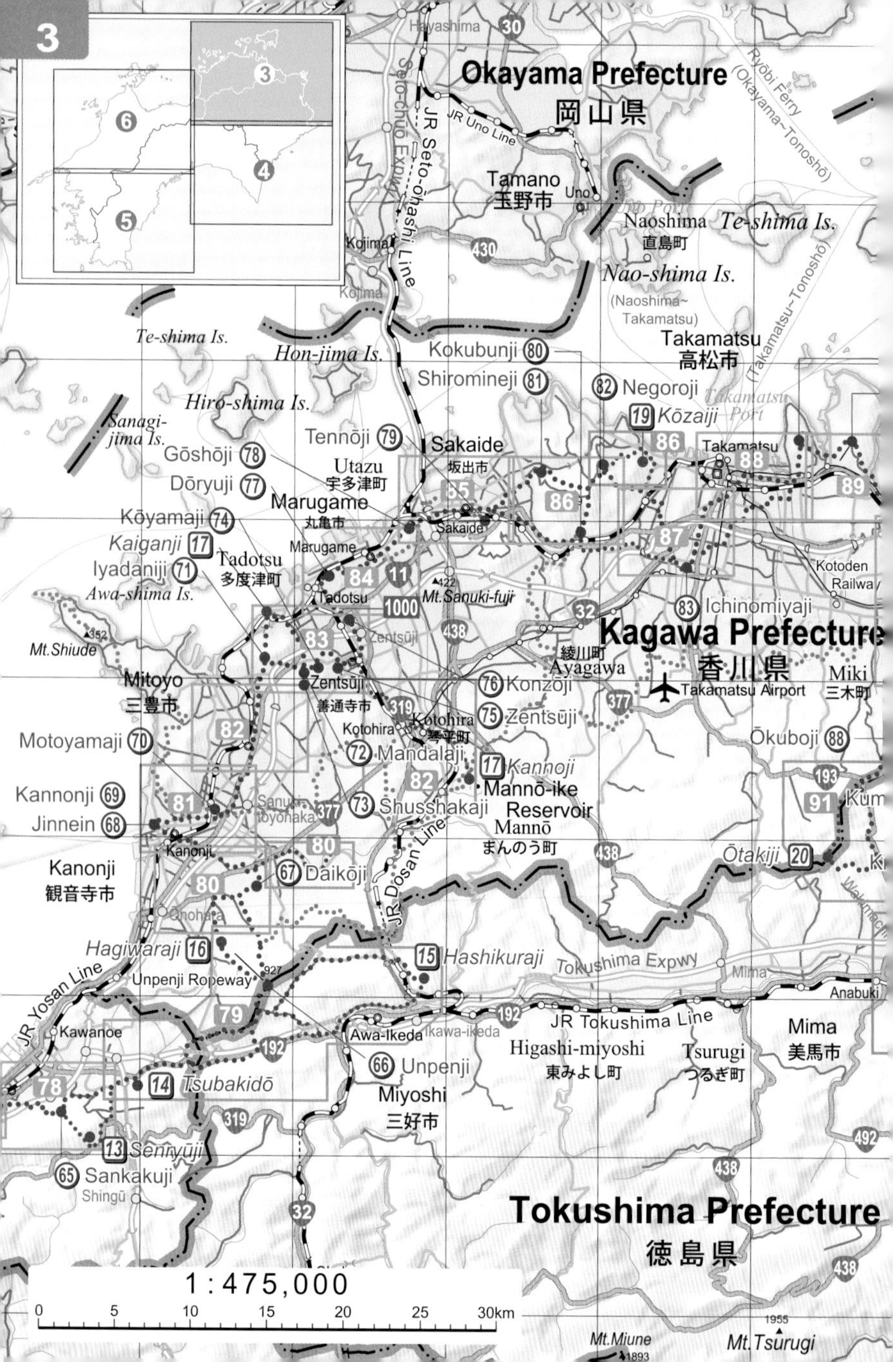

Okayama Prefecture
岡山県
Kagawa Prefecture
香川県
Tokushima Prefecture
徳島県
JR Uno Line
JR Seto-ōhashi Line
Seto-chūō Expwy
Tamano
玉野市
Uno
Naoshima
直島町
Nao-shima Is.
Te-shima Is.
Ryōbi Ferry (Okayama~Tonoshō)
(Naoshima~Takamatsu)
(Takamatsu~Tonoshō)
Takamatsu
高松市
Kojima
Hon-jima Is.
Hiro-shima Is.
Sanagi-jima Is.
Kokubunji 80
Shiromineji 81
82 Negoroji
19 Kōzaiji
Takamatsu Port
Tennōji 79
Sakaide
坂出市
Utazu
宇多津町
Gōshōji 78
Dōryuji 77
Marugame
丸亀市
Kōyamaji 74
Kaiganji 17
Iyadaniji 71
Tadotsu
多度津町
Awa-shima Is.
Mt.Sanuki-fuji
Mt.Shiude
Kotoden Railway
83 Ichinomiyaji
Mitoyo
三豊市
Zentsūji
善通寺市
76 Konzōji
75 Zentsūji
綾川町
Ayagawa
Takamatsu Airport
Miki
三木町
Kotohira
琴平町
Motoyamaji 70
72 Mandalaji
17 Kannoji
Mannō-ike Reservoir
Ōkuboji 88
Kannonji 69
Jinnein 68
73 Shusshakaji
Mannō
まんのう町
Kanonji
観音寺市
67 Daikōji
Ōtakiji 20
JR Dosan Line
Onohara
Hagiwaraji 16
15 Hashikuraji
Tokushima Expwy
Unpenji Ropeway
JR Yosan Line
Kawanoe
Awa-Ikeda
JR Tokushima Line
Higashi-miyoshi
東みよし町
Tsurugi
つるぎ町
Mima
美馬市
Anabuki
14 Tsubakidō
66 Unpenji
Miyoshi
三好市
13 Senryūji
65 Sankakuji
Shingū
1:475,000
0 5 10 15 20 25 30km
Mt.Miune
Mt.Tsurugi

3
Legend
86 Shidoji — One of the 88 temples
3 Jigenji — One of the 20 other temples
100 — Distance from Temple No. 1
Pilgrim Route (walk)
Shikoku-no-michi
Interchange
Expressways
Route Number 55
National Roads
Main Regional Roads
Other Roads
Prefectural Boundary
Station
Japan Railways
Station
Private Railways
Tsunami Inundation Forecast Zone (2021)
provided by Ministry of Land infrastracture and Transport (without Kagawa Pref)
to Himeji
10km
10km
Shōdo-shima Is.
Shōdoshima 88 Temples Sites
Shōdoshima
小豆島町
Seto Inland Sea
Shikoku-orange Ferry (Niihama, Tōyo - Ōsaka, Kōbe 9hrs)
Jumbo Ferry (Kōbe - Takamatsu 4:45 hr)
84 Yashimaji
85 Yakuriji
86 Shidoji
87 Nagaoji
Sanuki さぬき市
7 Jūrakuji
6 Anrakuji
5 Jizōji
4 Dainichiji
3 Konsenji
2 Gokurakuji
1 Ryōzenji
Hyōgo Prefecture
兵庫県
Awaji-shima Is.
Awajishima-minami
Minami-awaji
南あわじ市
Naruto Kaikyō Strait
Naruto-kita
Tsuda-sangawa
Tsuda-higashi
Higashi-kagawa
東かがわ市
Takamatsu Expwy
JR Kōtoku Line
Shirotori-ōuchi
Hiketa
90-a
90-b
91
92
93-a
93-b
1100
Taisanji 1
Itano
板野町
Naruto
Naruto 鳴門市
Ikenotani
17
18
19
28
Tokushima Airport
Matsushige 松茂町
8
9
10
上板町
Kamiita
Aizumi
藍住町
Kitajima
北島町
Tokushima
Awa
阿波市
Ishii 石井町
Kamojima
Yoshinogawa
吉野川市
Tokushima
Tokushima 徳島市
Nankai Ferry (Wakayama - Tokushima: 2:10 hr)
Yoshino River
17 Idoji
16 Kannonji
15 Kokubunji
14 Jōrakuji
13 Dainichiji
Komatsushima
小松島市
100
20
22
23
24-a
24-b
Fujiidera 11
Dōgakuji 2
Shōsanji 12
Sanagōchi
佐那河内村
21
Onzanji 18
Tatsueji 19
Ocean Tōkyū Ferry to Tokyo
to Kyūshū
Kamiyama
神山町
Jigenji 3
Katsuura
勝浦町
25-a
25-b
Naka River
Anan
阿南市
Anan
26
Kamikatsu
上勝町
Kakurinji 20
Tairyūji 21
Tairyūji Ropeway
Byōdōji 22
27
Kuwano
Aratano
I-shima Is.

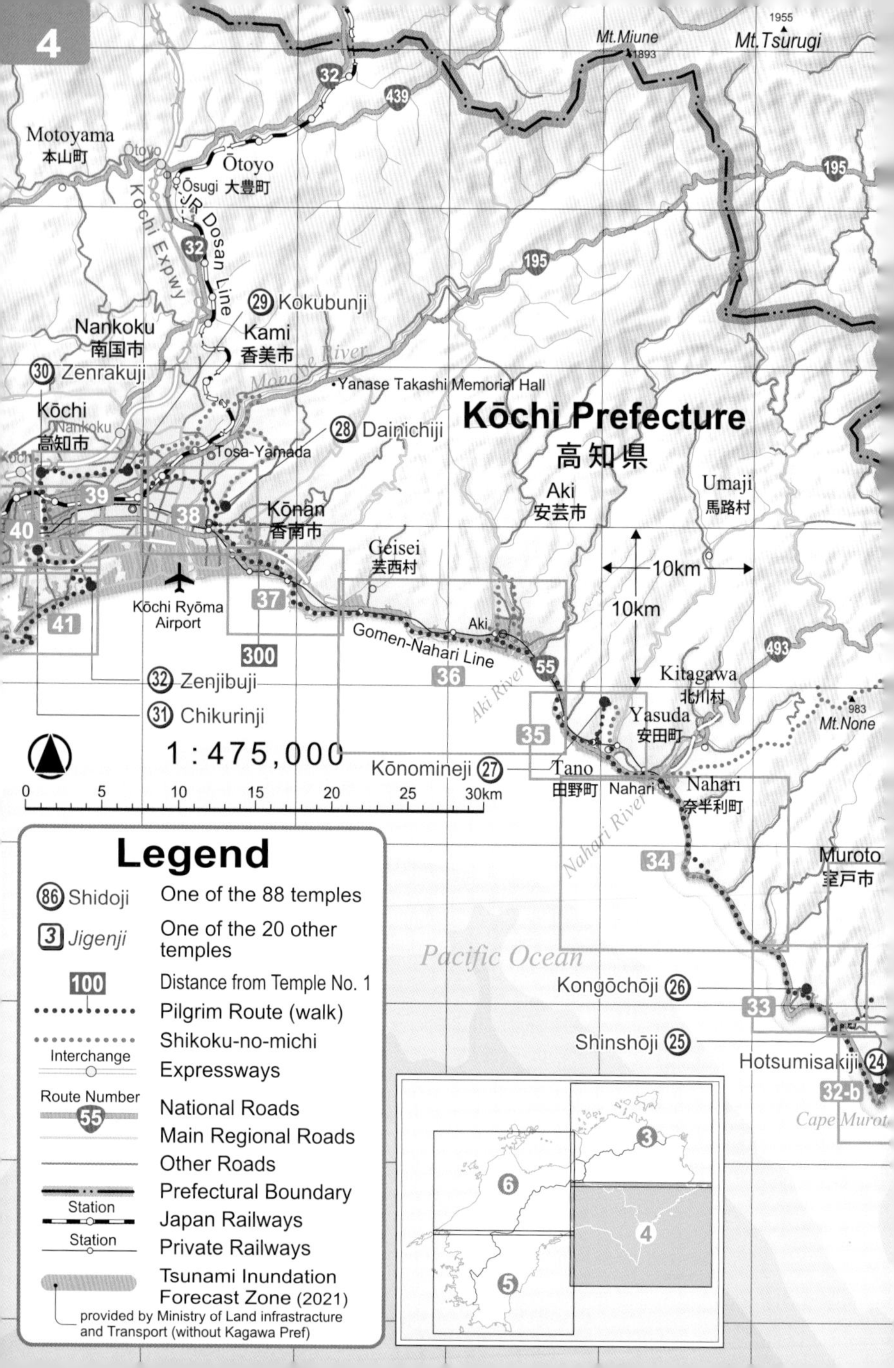
4
Mt.Miune 1893
1955
Mt.Tsurugi
Motoyama
本山町
Ōtoyo
大豊町
Ōsugi
JR Dosan Line
Kōchi Expwy
29 Kokubunji
Nankoku
南国市
Kami
香美市
30 Zenrakuji
Yanase Takashi Memorial Hall
Kōchi
高知市
28 Dainichiji
Kōchi Prefecture
高知県
Tosa-Yamada
Kōnan
香南市
Aki
安芸市
Umaji
馬路村
Geisei
芸西村
10km
10km
Kōchi Ryōma Airport
Aki
Gomen-Nahari Line
300
Aki River
Kitagawa
北川村
32 Zenjibuji
31 Chikurinji
Yasuda
安田町
Mt.None
983
1:475,000
Kōnomineji 27
Tano
田野町
Nahari
Nahari
奈半利町
Nahari River
0 5 10 15 20 25 30km
Muroto
室戸市
Pacific Ocean
Kongōchōji 26
Shinshōji 25
Hotsumisakiji 24
Cape Muroto
Legend
86 Shidoji One of the 88 temples
3 Jigenji One of the 20 other temples
100 Distance from Temple No. 1
Pilgrim Route (walk)
Shikoku-no-michi
Interchange
Expressways
Route Number
National Roads
Main Regional Roads
Other Roads
Prefectural Boundary
Station
Japan Railways
Station
Private Railways
Tsunami Inundation Forecast Zone (2021)
provided by Ministry of Land infrastracture and Transport (without Kagawa Pref)

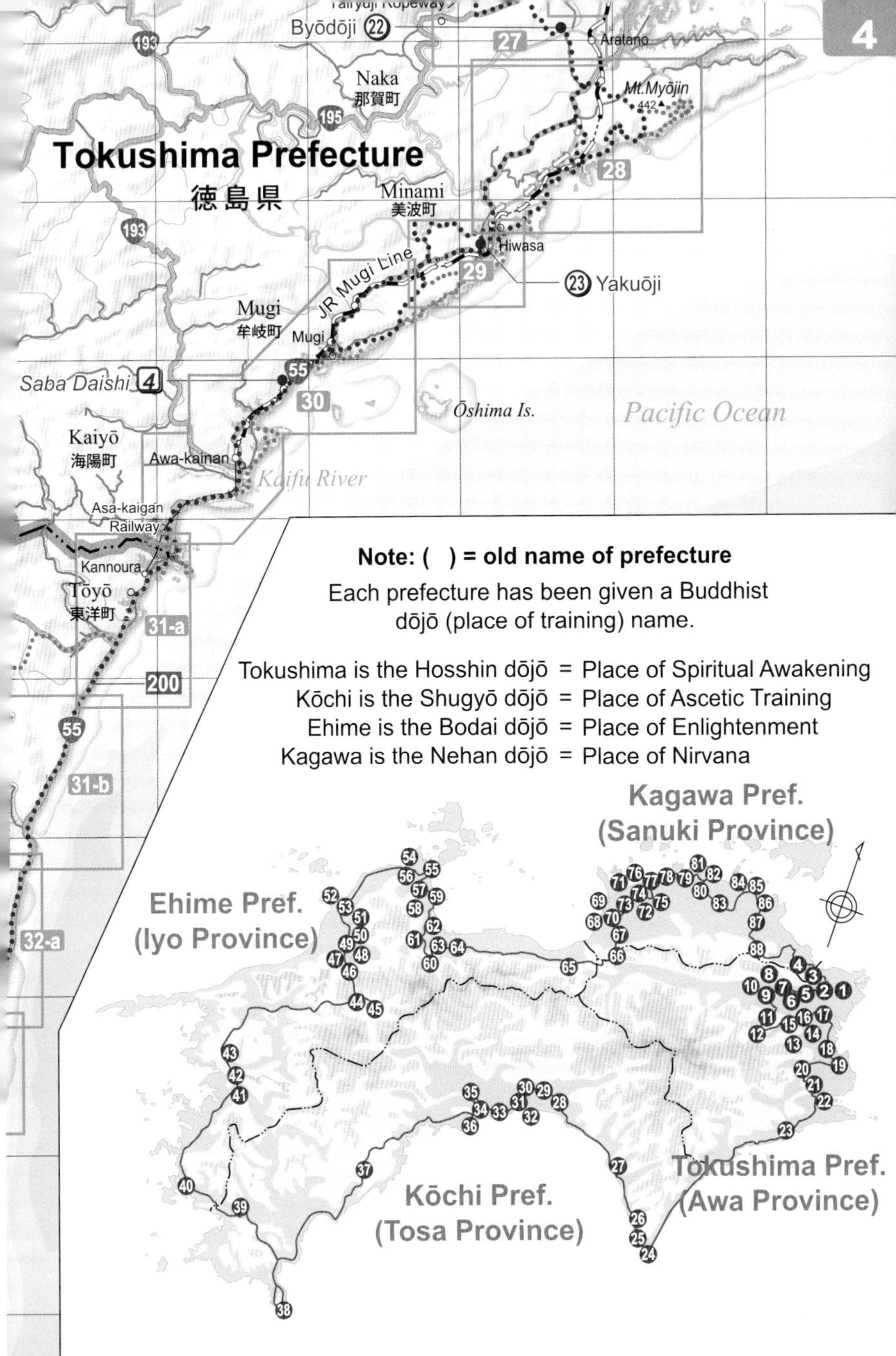

4
Byōdōji 22
193
27
Aratano
Naka
那賀町
Mt.Myōjin
442
195
Tokushima Prefecture
徳島県
28
Minami
美波町
193
Hiwasa
JR Mugi Line
29
23 Yakuōji
Mugi
牟岐町
Mugi
55
Saba Daishi 4
30
Ōshima Is.
Pacific Ocean
Kaiyō
海陽町
Awa-kainan
Kaifu River
Asa-kaigan
Railway
Kannoura
Tōyō
東洋町
31-a
200
55
31-b
32-a
Note: ( ) = old name of prefecture
Each prefecture has been given a Buddhist dōjō (place of training) name.
Tokushima is the Hosshin dōjō = Place of Spiritual Awakening
Kōchi is the Shugyō dōjō = Place of Ascetic Training
Ehime is the Bodai dōjō = Place of Enlightenment
Kagawa is the Nehan dōjō = Place of Nirvana
Kagawa Pref.
(Sanuki Province)
Ehime Pref.
(Iyo Province)
Kōchi Pref.
(Tosa Province)
Tokushima Pref.
(Awa Province)

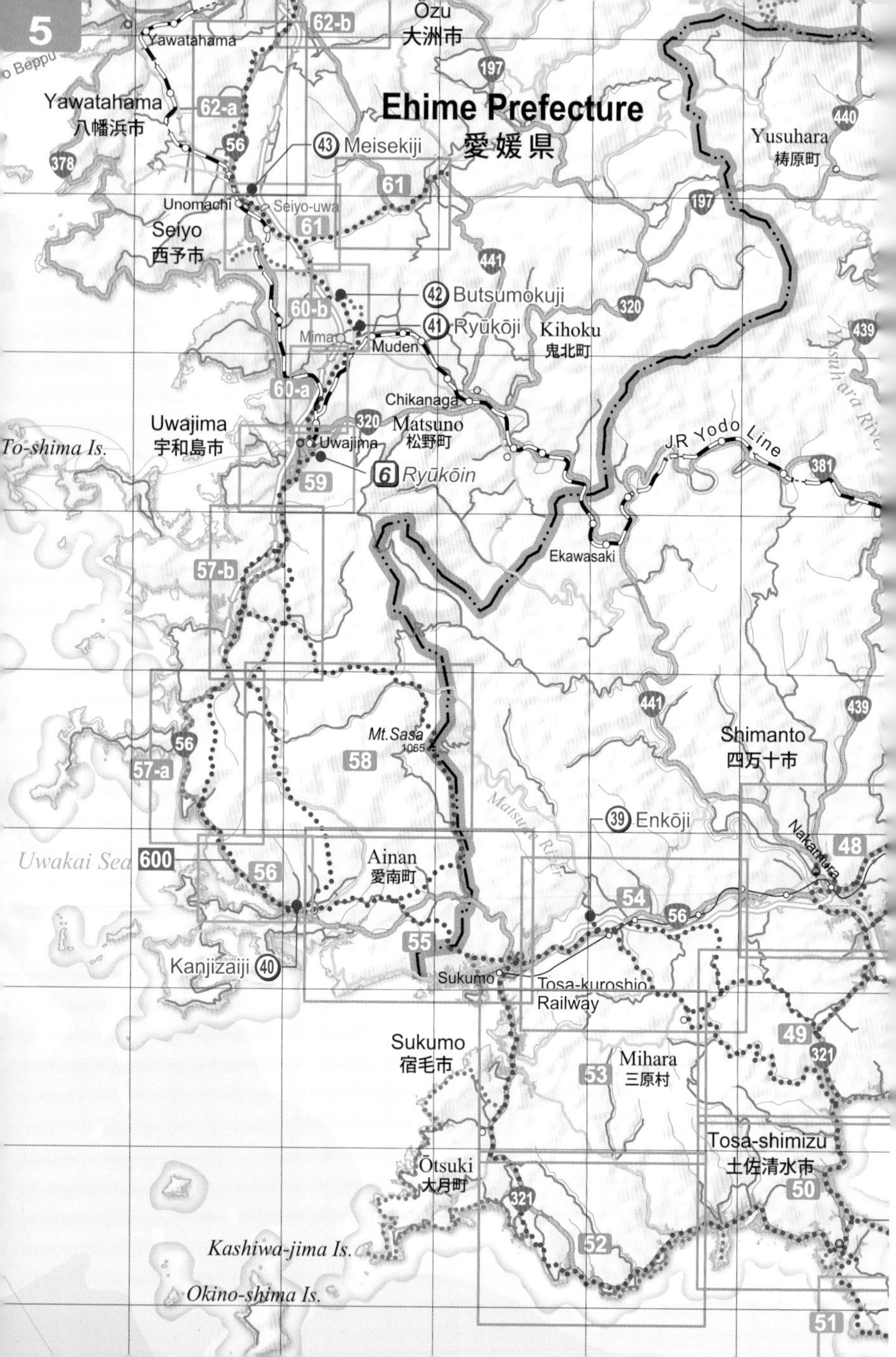
5
Ozu
大洲市
Yawatahama
to Beppu
Yawatahama
八幡浜市
62-a
62-b
Ehime Prefecture
愛媛県
43 Meisekiji
Unomachi
Seiyo-uwa
Seiyo
西予市
61
42 Butsumokuji
41 Ryūkōji
Mima
Muden
Kihoku
鬼北町
Yusuhara
梼原町
60-b
60-a
Chikanaga
Uwajima
宇和島市
Uwajima
Matsuno
松野町
6 Ryūkōin
59
To-shima Is.
JR Yodo Line
Ekawasaki
Yusuhara River
57-b
57-a
Mt.Sasa
1065
58
Shimanto
四万十市
Matsuda River
39 Enkōji
Nakamura
48
Uwakai Sea
600
56
Ainan
愛南町
54
55
Kanjizaiji 40
Sukumo
Tosa-kuroshio
Railway
49
Sukumo
宿毛市
Mihara
三原村
53
Tosa-shimizu
土佐清水市
Ōtsuki
大月町
50
52
Kashiwa-jima Is.
Okino-shima Is.
51
197
440
378
441
320
439
381
321

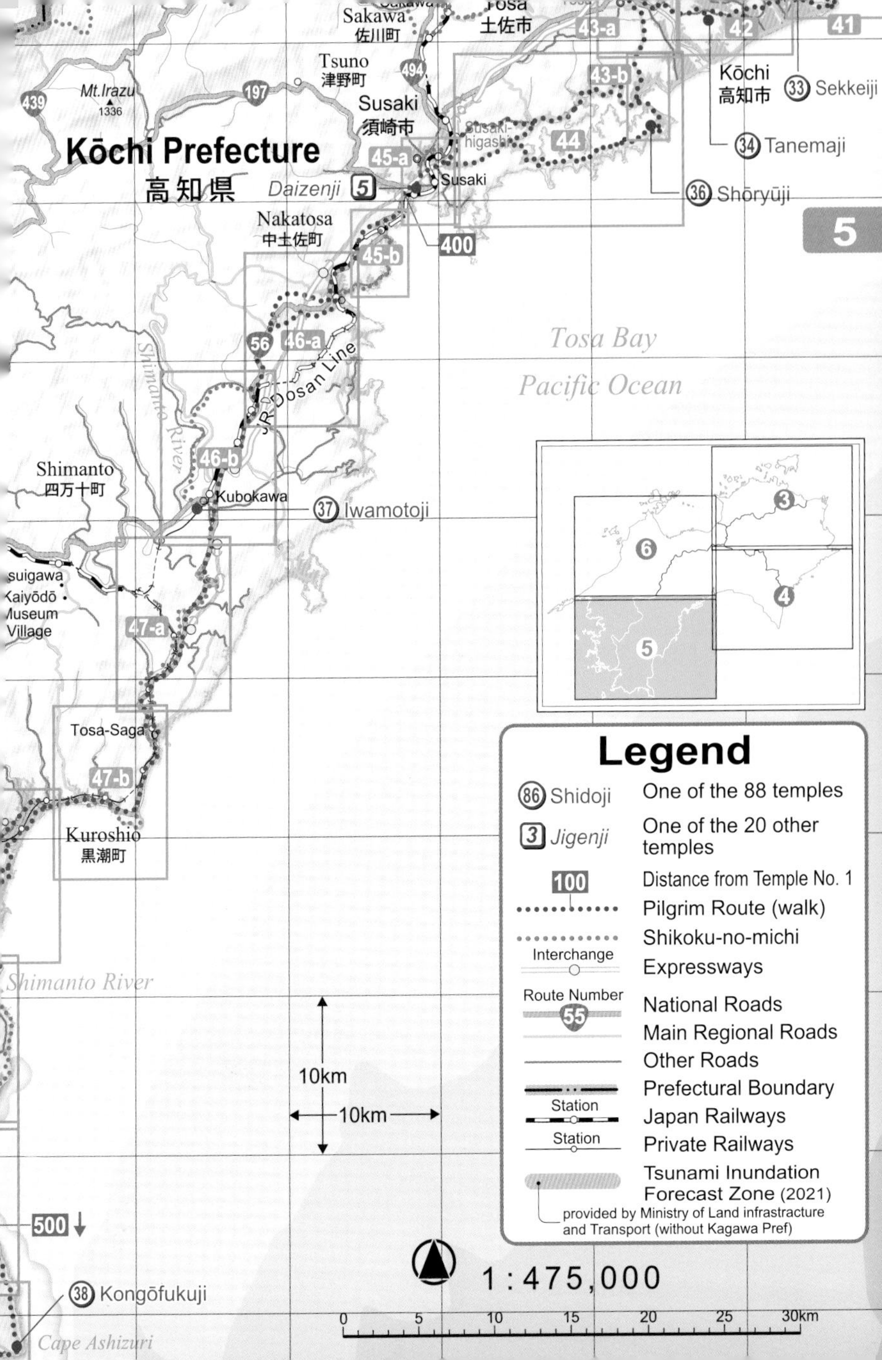

Sakawa
佐川町
Tosa
土佐市
43-a
42
41
Tsuno
津野町
494
Kōchi
高知市
33 Sekkeiji
Mt.Irazu
1336
197
439
Susaki
須崎市
43-b
Susaki-higashi
44
34 Tanemaji
Kōchi Prefecture
高知県
45-a
Susaki
Daizenji 5
36 Shōryūji
5
Nakatosa
中土佐町
400
45-b
Tosa Bay
Pacific Ocean
56
46-a
JR Dosan Line
Shimanto River
46-b
Shimanto
四万十町
Kubokawa
37 Iwamotoji
3
6
4
5
suigawa
Kaiyōdō
Museum
Village
47-a
Tosa-Saga
47-b
Kuroshio
黒潮町
Legend
86 Shidoji
One of the 88 temples
3 Jigenji
One of the 20 other temples
100
Distance from Temple No. 1
Pilgrim Route (walk)
Shikoku-no-michi
Interchange
Expressways
Route Number
55
National Roads
Main Regional Roads
Other Roads
Prefectural Boundary
Station
Japan Railways
Station
Private Railways
Tsunami Inundation Forecast Zone (2021)
provided by Ministry of Land infrastructure and Transport (without Kagawa Pref)
Shimanto River
10km
10km
500
38 Kongōfukuji
Cape Ashizuri
1:475,000
0 5 10 15 20 25 30km

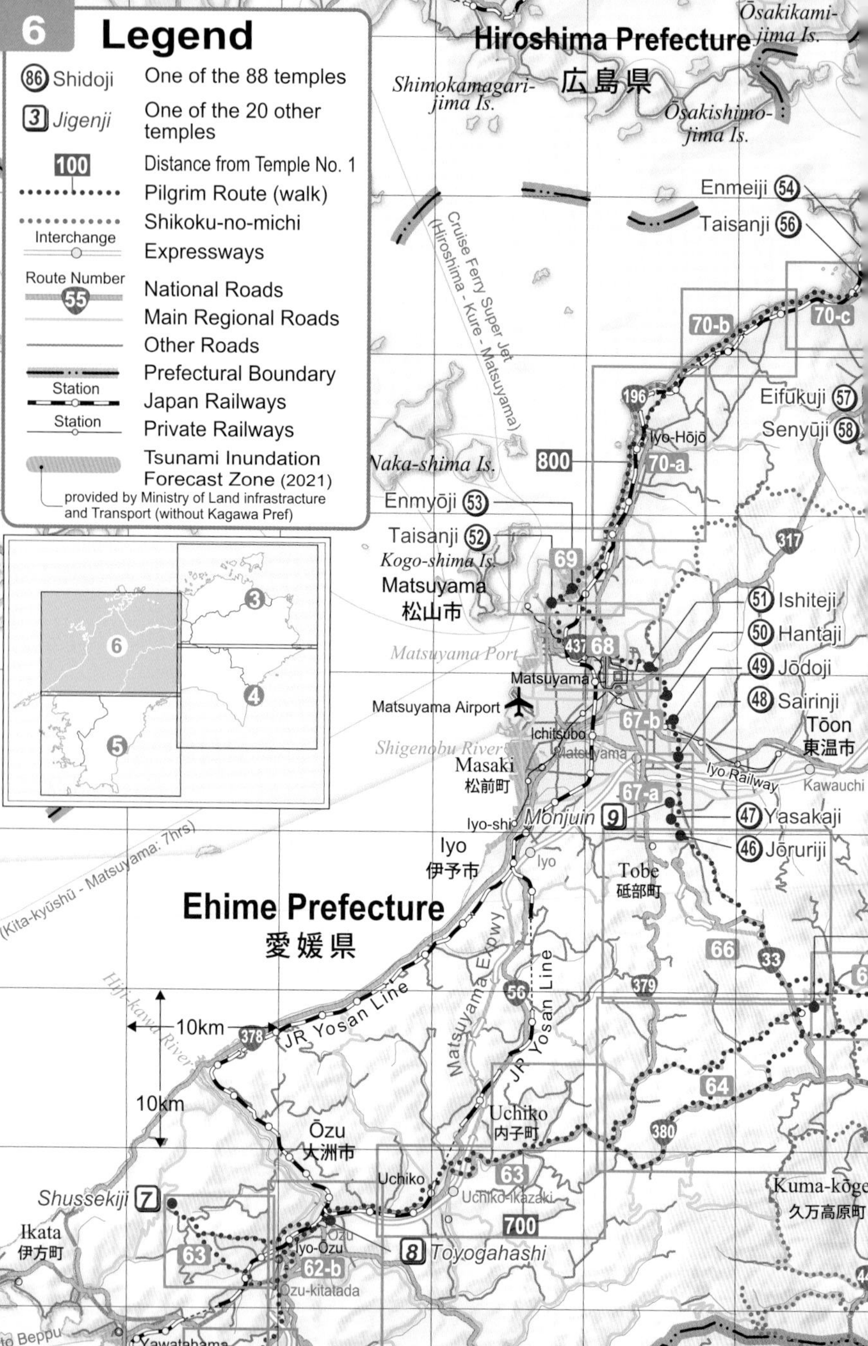

Legend
86 Shidoji One of the 88 temples
3 Jigenji One of the 20 other temples
100 Distance from Temple No. 1
Pilgrim Route (walk)
Shikoku-no-michi
Interchange
Expressways
Route Number
National Roads
Main Regional Roads
Other Roads
Prefectural Boundary
Station
Japan Railways
Station
Private Railways
Tsunami Inundation Forecast Zone (2021)
provided by Ministry of Land infrastructure and Transport (without Kagawa Pref)
Hiroshima Prefecture
広島県
Ōsakikami-jima Is.
Shimokamagari-jima Is.
Ōsakishimo-jima Is.
Enmeiji 54
Taisanji 56
Cruise Ferry Super Jet (Hiroshima - Kure - Matsuyama)
70-b
70-c
Eifukuji 57
Senyūji 58
Iyo-Hōjō
Naka-shima Is.
800
70-a
Enmyōji 53
Taisanji 52
Kogo-shima Is.
69
Matsuyama
松山市
51 Ishiteji
50 Hantaji
49 Jōdoji
48 Sairinji
Tōon
東温市
Matsuyama Port
68
Matsuyama
Matsuyama Airport
Ichitsubo
67-b
Shigenobu River
Masaki
松前町
Iyo Railway
Kawauchi
67-a
Iyo-shi
Monjuin 9
47 Yasakaji
46 Jōruriji
Iyo
伊予市
Iyo
Tobe
砥部町
(Kita-kyūshū - Matsuyama: 7hrs)
Ehime Prefecture
愛媛県
Matsuyama Expwy
JR Yosan Line
66
Hiji-kawa River
10km
10km
JR Yosan Line
Uchiko
内子町
64
Ōzu
大洲市
Uchiko
63
Uchiko-ikazaki
700
Kuma-kōgen
久万高原町
Shussekiji 7
Ikata
伊方町
63
Iyo-Ōzu
Ōzu
62-b
8 Toyogahashi
Ōzu-kitatada
to Beppu
Yawatahama

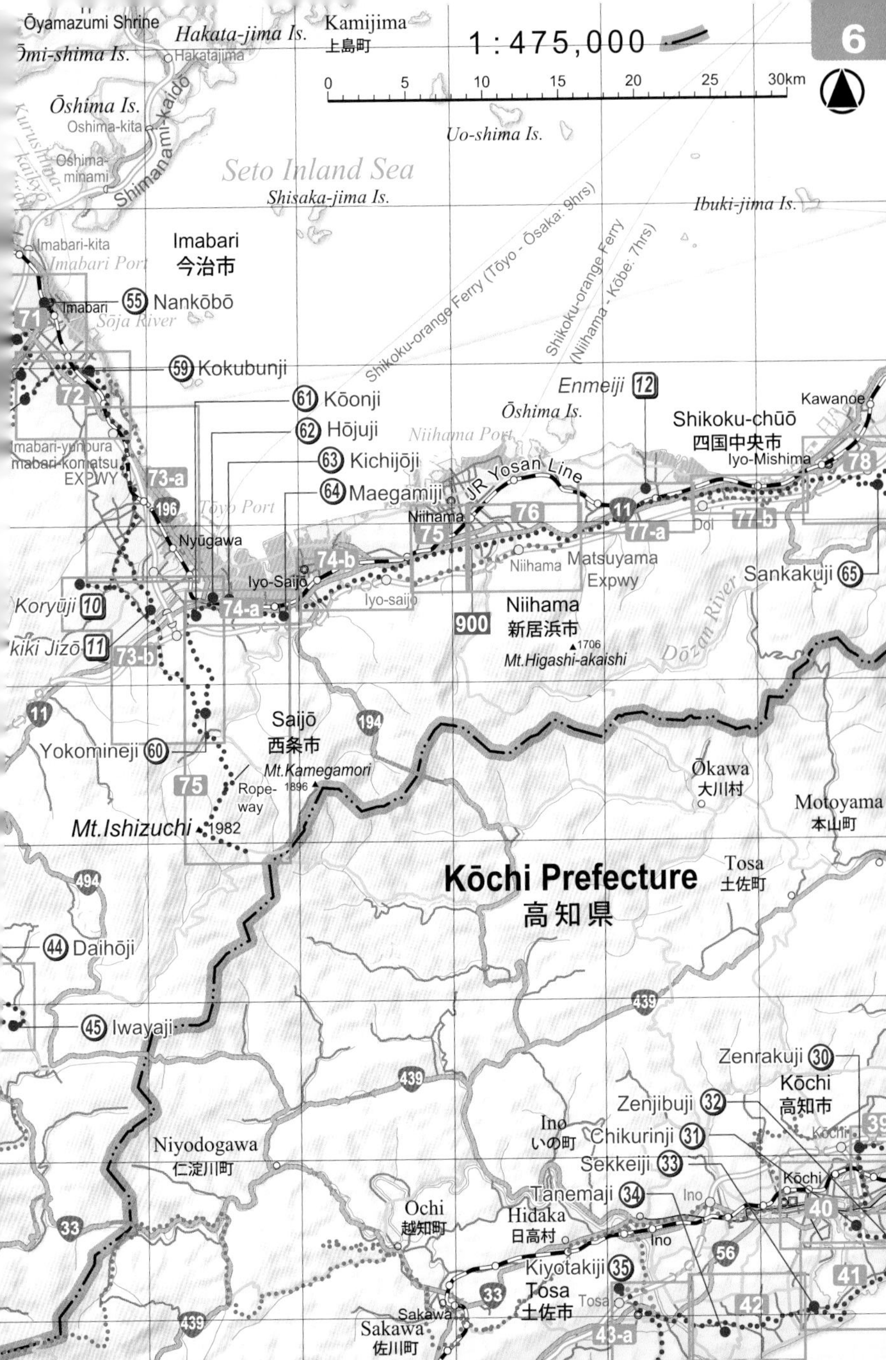

1:475,000
0 5 10 15 20 25 30km
Ōyamazumi Shrine
Ōmi-shima Is.
Hakata-jima Is.
Hakatajima
Kamijima
上島町
Ōshima Is.
Oshima-kita
Oshima-minami
Shimanami-kaidō
Uo-shima Is.
Seto Inland Sea
Shisaka-jima Is.
Ibuki-jima Is.
Imabari-kita
Imabari Port
Imabari
今治市
Imabari
55 Nankōbō
Sōja River
Shikoku-orange Ferry (Tōyo - Ōsaka: 9hrs)
Shikoku-orange Ferry (Niihama - Kōbe: 7hrs)
59 Kokubunji
61 Kōonji
62 Hōjuji
63 Kichijōji
64 Maegamiji
Enmeiji 12
Ōshima Is.
Niihama Port
Shikoku-chūō
四国中央市
Kawanoe
Iyo-Mishima
JR Yosan Line
Tōyo Port
Nyūgawa
Niihama
Iyo-Saijō
Iyo-saijō
Niihama
Matsuyama Expwy
Doi
Sankakuji 65
Koryūji 10
kiki Jizō 11
Niihama
新居浜市
1706
Mt.Higashi-akaishi
Dōzan River
Saijō
西条市
Mt.Kamegamori
1896
Yokomineji 60
Rope-way
Mt.Ishizuchi
1982
Ōkawa
大川村
Motoyama
本山町
Kōchi Prefecture
高知県
Tosa
土佐町
44 Daihōji
45 Iwayaji
Zenrakuji 30
Kōchi
高知市
Zenjibuji 32
Chikurinji 31
Sekkeiji 33
Tanemaji 34
Kiyotakiji 35
Ino
いの町
Niyodogawa
仁淀川町
Ochi
越知町
Hidaka
日高村
Tosa
土佐市
Sakawa
佐川町

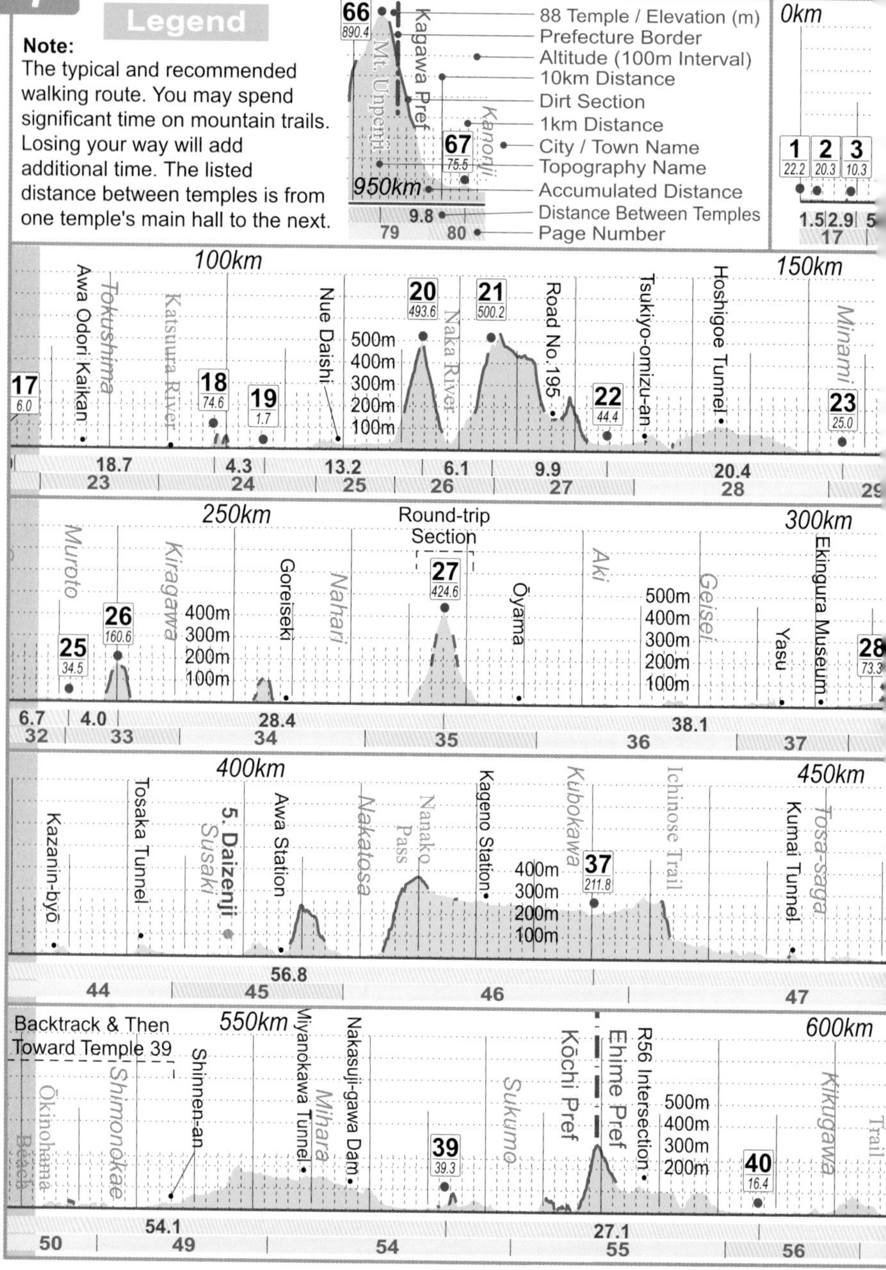

Legend
Note:
The typical and recommended walking route. You may spend significant time on mountain trails. Losing your way will add additional time. The listed distance between temples is from one temple's main hall to the next.
66
890.4
Mt. Unpenji
Kagawa Pref
Kanonji
67
75.5
950km
9.8
79
80
88 Temple / Elevation (m)
Prefecture Border
Altitude (100m Interval)
10km Distance
Dirt Section
1km Distance
City / Town Name
Topography Name
Accumulated Distance
Distance Between Temples
Page Number
0km
1
22.2
2
20.3
3
10.3
1.5
2.9
17
100km
150km
17
6.0
Awa Odori Kaikan
Tokushima
Katsuura River
18
74.6
19
1.7
Nue Daishi
500m
400m
300m
200m
100m
20
493.6
Naka River
21
500.2
Road No. 195
22
44.4
Tsukiyo-omizu-an
Hoshigoe Tunnel
Minami
23
25.0
18.7
4.3
13.2
6.1
9.9
20.4
23
24
25
26
27
28
250km
Round-trip Section
300km
Muroto
25
34.5
26
160.6
Kiragawa
400m
300m
200m
100m
Goreiseki
Nahari
27
424.6
Ōyama
Aki
500m
400m
300m
200m
100m
Geisei
Yasu
Ekingura Museum
28
73.3
6.7
4.0
28.4
38.1
32
33
34
35
36
37
400km
450km
Kazanin-byō
Tosaka Tunnel
5. Daizenji
Susaki
Awa Station
Nakatosa
Nanako Pass
Kageno Station
Kubokawa
400m
300m
200m
100m
37
211.8
Ichinose Trail
Kumai Tunnel
Tosa-saga
56.8
44
45
46
47
Backtrack & Then Toward Temple 39
550km
600km
Ōkinohama Beach
Shimonokae
Shinnen-an
Miyanokawa Tunnel
Mihara
Nakasuji-gawa Dam
39
39.3
Sukumo
Kōchi Pref
Ehime Pref
R56 Intersection
500m
400m
300m
200m
40
16.4
Kikugawa
Trail
54.1
27.1
50
49
54
55
56

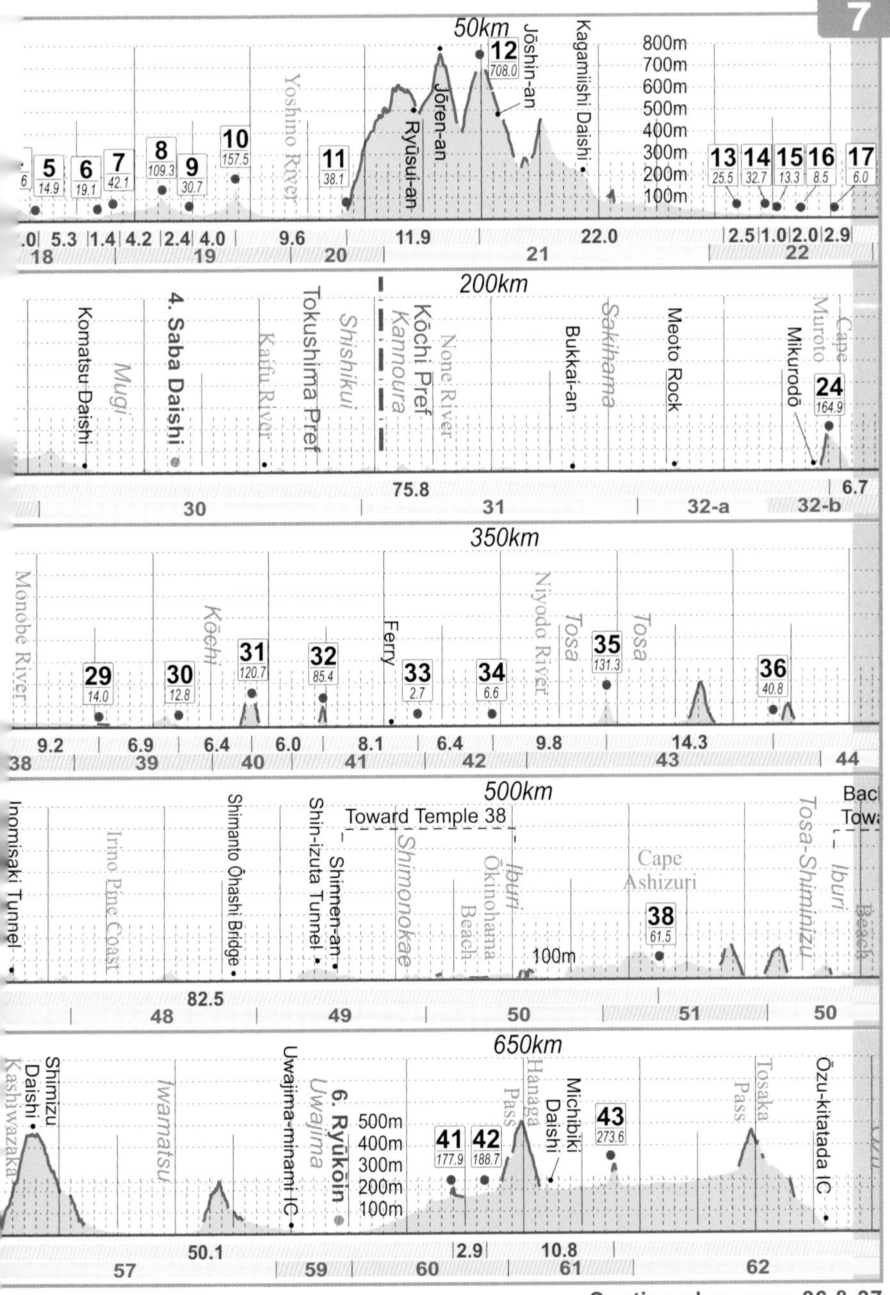
50km
12
708.0
Jōshin-an
Kagamiishi Daishi
Jōren-an
Ryūsui-an
Yoshino River
800m
700m
600m
500m
400m
300m
200m
100m
5
14.9
6
19.1
7
42.1
8
109.3
9
30.7
10
157.5
11
38.1
13
25.5
14
32.7
15
13.3
16
8.5
17
6.0
5.3
1.4
4.2
2.4
4.0
9.6
11.9
22.0
2.5
1.0
2.0
2.9
18
19
20
21
22
200km
Komatsu Daishi
Mugi
4. Saba Daishi
Kaifu River
Tokushima Pref
Shishikui
Kōchi Pref
Kannoura
None River
Bukkai-an
Sakihama
Meoto Rock
Mikurodō
Muroto
Cape
24
164.9
75.8
6.7
30
31
32-a
32-b
350km
Monobe River
Kōchi
Ferry
Niyodo River
Tosa
Tosa
29
14.0
30
12.8
31
120.7
32
85.4
33
2.7
34
6.6
35
131.3
36
40.8
9.2
6.9
6.4
6.0
8.1
6.4
9.8
14.3
38
39
40
41
42
43
44
500km
Inomisaki Tunnel
Irino Pine Coast
Shimanto Ōhashi Bridge
Shin-izuta Tunnel
Shinnen-an
Toward Temple 38
Shimonokae
Ōkinohama Beach
Iburi
100m
Cape Ashizuri
38
61.5
Tosa-Shimizu
Iburi
Beach
82.5
48
49
50
51
50
650km
Kashiwazaka
Shimizu Daishi
Iwamatsu
Uwajima-minami IC
6. Ryūkōin
Uwajima
500m
400m
300m
200m
100m
41
177.9
42
188.7
Hanaga Pass
Michibiki Daishi
43
273.6
Tosaka Pass
Ōzu-kitatada IC
50.1
2.9
10.8
57
59
60
61
62

Continued on page 36 & 37

Kōbō Daishi (Kūkai) (774-835)

弘法大師「空海」

He is one of the most well-known figures in Japanese history and is accredited with many great deeds. Throughout Japan, one often hears his name and one can visit the many places that he is said to have visited during his lifetime. He became the 8th Patriarch of Shingon Buddhism and actively spread the teachings of this new religion in Japan. As well, he is accredited with founding the Shikoku pilgrimage and so, people today believe that this route is a journey which follows his footsteps. However, people also believe that Kōbō Daishi accompanies pilgrims as they make the pilgrimage as shown by the phrase, dōgyō ninin (same practice, two people).

This Sanskrit mark ["yu"] represents Miroku Bosatsu and Kūkai (see pg 13)

Biography

774 : Born into the Saeki clan, a declining aristocratic family, at Temple no. 75, Zentsūji in Kagawa prefecture.

788 : Began to study the Chinese classics under the direction of his uncle.

791 : Entered university in Nara
About two years later, he left school, became a monk and spent time as a wandering ascetic.

797 : Committed himself to Buddhism and wrote “Indications of the Goals of the Three Teachings” (Sangō Shiiki) in which he compares Buddhism with Confucianism and Taoism. He argues for the superiority of Buddhism.

797- 804 : It is assumed that he lived as a traveling ascetic. During this time, he might have visited Mt. Kōya for the first time as well as have spent time in training at Temple no. 21, Tairyūji and a cave (Mikurodō) at Cape Muroto in Shikoku.

804 : Left for China with the plan to stay for 20 years to study Esoteric Buddhism.

806 : Returned to Japan after have becomeing the 8th Patriarch of Esoteric Buddhism. During his time in China, he studied under the previous Patriarch, Keika (Hui-kuo, 746-805) at a temple called Shōryūji.

809 : Was allowed to leave Kyūshū and come to Kyōto to reside at Takaosanji (later known as Jingoji). He stayed here until 823.

810 - 813 : Acted as administrative head of Tōdaiji in Nara.

816 : Received permission from the Emperor Saga (786-842) to use Mt. Kōya.

819 : The formal consecration of Mt. Kōya.

821 : Directed the reconstruction of the Mannō-ike reservoir.

823 : Moved the Headquarters to Tōji Temple in Kyōto.

824 : Was officially appointed administrative head in charge of the construction of Tōji Temple in Kyōto.
828 : Opened the School of Arts and Sciences (Shugei shuchi-in) in Kyōto open to all students, regardless of their social status or economic means.
835 : Entered a state of eternal meditation (nyūjō) at Mt. Kōya.
921 : Received the honorary name of Kōbō Daishi from Emperor Daigo (885-930)

However, Kūkai is often called by the more familiar term, "O-Daishi-san", which demonstrates how close he is to the hearts of the people. It is not known whether or not, Kūkai actually founded the Shikoku pilgrimage; however, pilgrims throughout the centuries who have traveled this route believe that the benevolent Kūkai will always be there for comfort and protection.

Useful Information

Different ways of doing the pilgrimage

Some people travel around Shikoku on foot, by bicycle, by motorcycle, by car, by bus, by public transportation, by some other method or by combining different methods. There is no set rule as to how one should make the Shikoku pilgrimage; however, walking is the traditional and recommended style because originally this act was for ascetic training. Everyone is welcome to come to Shikoku and complete part or all of the route according to the amount of money and time one has available.

By foot (about 25km/day)

You need to be in good physical health. This is the most traditional way to make the pilgrimage; however it also takes the most time and money. Some parts of the route involve climbing up steep mountain paths while other parts are on asphalts roads; however, by walking, one can enjoy nature to a fuller degree and be able to have closer contact with the local people and other walking henro. For mental and physical well-being, it is very important for walkers to not follow a strict schedule, but to allow for some flexibility. If one plans to visit the 20 *bekkaku* as well, then the entire distance will be about 1,300km; if not, it will be about 1,140km. The average time to walk the entire pilgrimage is between 40-50 days.

Advice

For walking pilgrims, it is imperative to keep the backpack as light at possible. Ideal weight for males: 4-5kg; for females: 3-4kg. If carrying sleeping gear and cooking gear, then do not go over 8-10kgs. Unexpected events, such as getting lost or bad weather, might happen so do not expect your pilgrimage to always go according to plan. Most people walk about 25km a day, so one should practice walking for long distances before coming on this pilgrimage. If some physical problem occurs, such as blisters or fatigue, stop and take care of the problem immediately. If you use your outdoor gear before the pilgrimage, you can prevent any possible trouble while on the route.

By car

Rental cars are available at large train stations and/or airports. Traveling by car allows you come at any time of the year and to visit sites or inns far from the pilgrimage route, but it is necessary to know the traffic rules of Japan. Be careful not to get in an accident for that will drastically affect your travel plans. You could use a smartphone or computer that has navigational abilities. It will take approximately ten days to complete the entire pilgrimage route by car.
Cost: from 140,000 yen (not including the price of the rental car)

Other ways: bicycle, motorbike, public transportation….

Information: Rental bike and baggage storage https://cycleshikoku.com/

Weather

March, April, May, October and November are the best months for weather and good temperatures. The route along the Seto Inland Sea has the least amount of rainfall and the route along the Pacific Ocean has the most. There is not much difference in temperature between the Seto Inland Sea side and Pacific Ocean side. Plan according to the season. Walking pilgrims must consider that summer is very hot and humid and there are many mosquitoes, that during the fall there is a danger of being caught in a typhoon and that in the winter, more clothing will be needed which will add weight to your pack.

Temperature, precipitation, hours of sunshine (according to month)

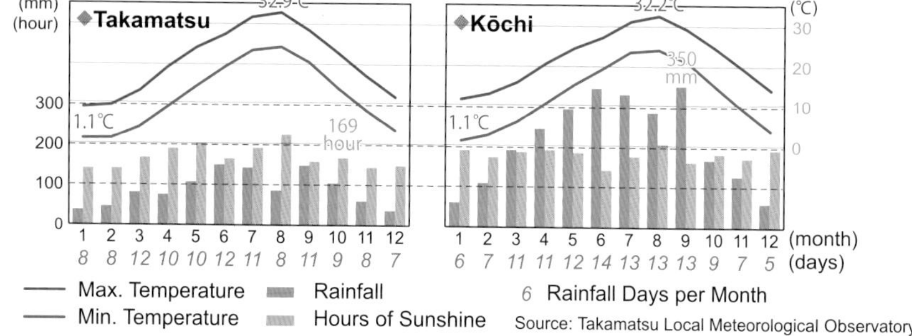
(mm)
(hour)
◆Takamatsu
32.9℃
1.1℃
169 hour
300
200
100
0
1 2 3 4 5 6 7 8 9 10 11 12
8 8 12 10 10 12 11 8 11 9 8 7
◆Kōchi
32.2℃
350 mm
1.1℃
(℃)
30
20
10
0
1 2 3 4 5 6 7 8 9 10 11 12 (month)
6 7 11 11 12 14 13 13 13 9 7 5 (days)
Max. Temperature
Min. Temperature
Rainfall
Hours of Sunshine
6 Rainfall Days per Month
Source: Takamatsu Local Meteorological Observatory

Lodging

There are many types of accommodation and, in some cases, dinner and breakfast are provided but if you want meals, you must make a reservation. If you choose to have meals plan your walking time properly because the times for breakfast and/or dinner are usually fixed. Arrive at a ryokan or minshuku before 5pm. If you are going to be late for some reason, make sure to call the place that you have reserved. If you have to cancel suddenly or do not show up, then you will most likely have to pay a cancellation charge. The price for a one-night stay should be around 4000 yen (no meals) to 8000 yen (with two meals), and for most places except minshuku and ryokan you should be able to use a credit card.

Places to stay along the pilgrim path are listed throughout this book. For big cities, priority has been given to list cheap places first. If the inn is far from the pilgrim path, call the owner and ask if pick-up service is possible. You will be refused a room if a place is fully booked. In this case try to arrange with the owner of a place with an available room to pick you up or take public transportation or a taxi to the nearest city and find a place. If you cannot find a place to stay, ask someone for assistance.

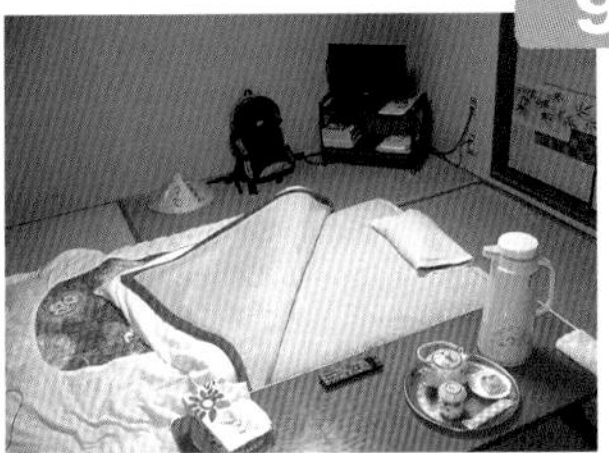
Minshuku

Many places have washing machines, so ask if you can use them. If not, ask if there is a laundromat (coin laundry) nearby, but the instructions might be in Japanese. Note: do not put your towel in the water when having a bath. NOTE: The henro community is supported by the goodwill of many people so please be mindful of what you say and do.

Shukubō

Temples offer two meals and a shared bath, but some temples will only accept individuals if a group is staying. The worship service (otsutome) in the main hall is held either in the morning or early evening. Guests are encouraged to attend. The price for a one-night stay including two meals is between 6000 and 9000yen.

Low cost accommodation : Points of concern regarding foreign henro

The recent increase of non-Japanese walking the Shikoku pilgrimage is a good thing, but one needs to be apprehensive about possible trouble between those who sleep outdoors – something quite predominant now - and the local people in Shikoku. We must work together to make sure this does not evolve into a social problem.

All land is owned by someone, so sleeping without permission on someone's property, other than official camp grounds, is not allowed. And even if permission is granted, people in the neighborhood who do not own the land, might feel uneasy about strangers putting up tents near their homes. To the local people it is like having a new stranger appear every day. Unfortunately, there is a lot of self-assertive information on the Internet of people staying the night at someone's home or at a hut. And so, other people who see this information visit such places. If there is a visitor, then the landowner will have to work extra to provide the place to stay. Some kind, selfless local people who have repeatedly offered support to pilgrims have felt this to be a burden and have stopped doing so.

Remember that if there is no other option but to sleep outdoors, please very sensitive to your surroundings. If you use a zenkonyado or tsuyado, please show your gratitude by leaving a donation. Expecting to stay for free somewhere is taking too much for granted.

How to get around

Other than road signs for cars, there are very few signs in English marking the route, so it is necessary to rely on markers written in Japanese.

38番札所
金剛福寺
Kongofukuji Temple
遍路道
大日寺
88
大窪寺
88 km
ALFREDO ALVAREZ PEREZ
ALFONSO ARIAS BALBOA

Signs, like the ones above, have been placed the pilgrimage in numerical order, so unless you are very familiar with the roads/paths in Shikoku do not attempt to go in reverse order.

Where to Start

There is no rule stating where one must start or finish the pilgrimage, but many start at Temple 1, Ryōzenji in Tokushima prefecture and proceed in order clockwise ending at Temple 88, Ōkuboji in Kagawa prefecture. Some go in reverse order. Others complete the route one prefecture at a time while some visit a few temples each weekend etc. Where and how you complete the Shikoku pilgrimage is up to you.

Meals

In the cities there are many convenience stores and restaurants, but their numbers drop dramatically in the countryside so plan accordingly. Make sure to carry food when climbing mountains. Tap water is safe to drink. Throughout Shikoku there are vending machines, which accept 1000 yen bills. Convenience stores are open all-year-round and have a wide variety of food and personal items such as band-aids, lotion, insect repellent, batteries etc. Supermarkets have more variety and are cheaper, but they close once a week. In the evening fresh food at supermarkets is usually discounted.
At family-run inns breakfast and dinner are usually Japanese-style with fish, rice and soup. If you have dietary or religious restrictions or allergies please tell the owner when you make a reservation and it might be possible to have food items changed.

Typical Dinner at an inn

Public Transportation

In most cases you can get really close to most temples by using trains and buses. If you want to use public transport see the time schedules listed throughout this book. In some places in Shikoku, trains and buses run very infrequently, so make sure to get the most recent timetable at public information centers (see pg 97) to prevent any problems along the journey. Feel free to ask staff there in English about travel logistics. Some use trains when temples are spaced far apart. When riding the train, buy a ticket from a machine to where you want to go. When riding a bus, ① Enter through the rear door. ② Take a seiri-ken (numbered ticket) if there is a machine. ③ When you want to get off, press the button to inform the driver. ④ Pay the fare on the price chart that matches the number on the seiri-ken. ⑤ The fare box will give change and it will change bills. ⑥ Put the exact fare and ticket into the fare box. ⑦ Exit through the front door.

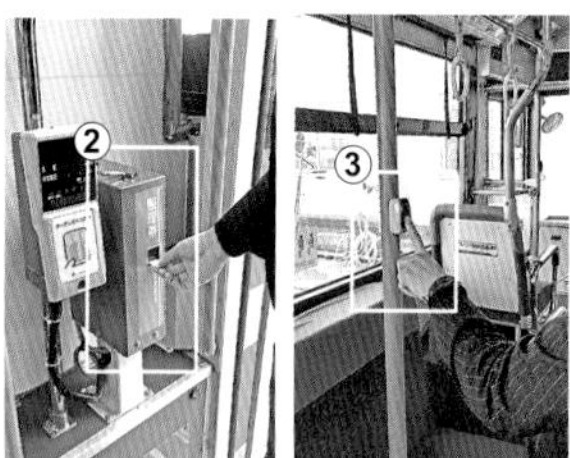
②
③

④
⑥
⑤

Safety / Health Care

Shikoku is a relatively safe place for walking travelers when compared to other places in the world. The rate of theft is low, but one can be caught up in bad weather or an accident, become a victim of a crime, or become ill. There is no guarantee that your journey will be completely free of some mishap. Remember that when you decide to embark on this pilgrimage, you are responsible for your own actions. WARNING: There are reports of thefts so do not carry more than is necessary and do not leave your valuables unattended.

- A general guide by the Japan National Tourism Organization (JNTO)
  https://www.japan.travel/en/plan/
- A useful website for when you need medical care in Japan: **Medical information**
  https://www.jnto.go.jp/emergency/eng/mi_guide.html
- Apps for **Safety tips**
  Earthquake Early Warning, Tsunami, Volcano and Weather information

JNTO

Medical information

Safety tips

Money Planning

Budget for around 450,000 yen if you intend to walk the entire route and stay at an inn or temple every night. This estimate does not include travel expenses to get to and from Shikoku. The total amount will depend on the individual and how the pilgrimage is carried out. Refer to this "Estimate Cost Summary" chart and "Cost Calculator": http://shikokuhenrotrail.com/shikoku/planningCost.html

There are many places such as convenience stores, restaurants, and accommodation facilities where a credit card can be used, but in most cases they can not be used at small family-run inns or stores. In Shikoku, there are several places where you can withdraw money using an overseas cash card, debit card or credit card. For example: post office or convenience stores like 7-Eleven, FamilyMart and Lawson.

① Post Office: Japan Post Bank, ② 7-Eleven Stores, ③ FamilyMart Stores, ④ Lawson Stores

	VISA	PLUS	Master Card	Maestro	Cirrus	American Express	Diners Club	JCB	China Unionpay	DISCOVER
⊠ ⊠	✓	✓	✓	✓	✓	✓		✓	✓	✓
7-Eleven	✓	✓	✓	✓	✓	✓	✓	✓	✓	✓
FamilyMart	✓	✓	✓	✓	✓	✓ *1		✓	✓	✓ *1
LAWSON	✓	✓	✓	✓	✓			✓	✓	

Japan Post Bank: https://www.jp-bank.japanpost.jp/en/ias/en_ias_index.html
Seven Bank: https://www.sevenbank.co.jp/oos/adv/intlcard02/en/
FamilyMart: https://www.enetcom.co.jp/intl/en/ & (same of Japan Post Bank)
Lawson: https://www.lawsonbank.jp/international/en/

① Operating hours will be slightly different, but they should be open on weekdays from 9:00am-5:30pm, Saturdays 9:00am-12:30pm. Yellow symbols ⊠ are usually open on weekdays from 9:00am-18:00pm, Saturdays 9:00am-17:00pm, Sundays 9:00am-12:30pm.

②, ③, ④ ATMs can be used any day of the week 24 hours a day.

③ There are two types of FamilyMart ATMs: E-net and Japan Post Bank.

Japan Post Bank

7-Eleven

FamilyMart

Lawson

By following the directions on the screen, it is quite easily to withdraw Japanese yen.

Post Office Sign & ATM Screen ▶

郵便局

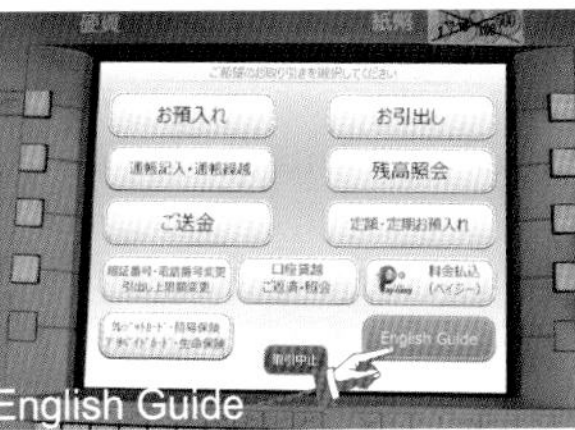
お預入れ
お引出し
ご送金
残高照会
English Guide

*1: American Express, and Discover cards are not available at E-net ATM.

Proper etiquette at a temple

Note: The following steps are recommended, but are not compulsory.

1 Main gate 山門
To ward off evil spirits.
Stand to the left of the gate, put your hands together and bow once.

2 Wash basin 水屋
To purify oneself.
Wash your hands and mouth here. Then put the *wagesa* around your neck and mala over your left wrist.

3 Bell tower 鐘楼
Rung to mark one's arrival.
Ring the bell once. It is considered bad luck to ring when leaving. Some temples have limited hours for ringing the bell so please adhere to any rules.

4 Main hall 本堂
The statue of the main deity is enshrined here.
Light one candle and three sticks of incense. Ring the bell once. Place the name-slip *(osame-fuda)* and copied sutra *(shakyō)* in the box. Place a donation in the offertory box, put your hands together and recite the sutras.

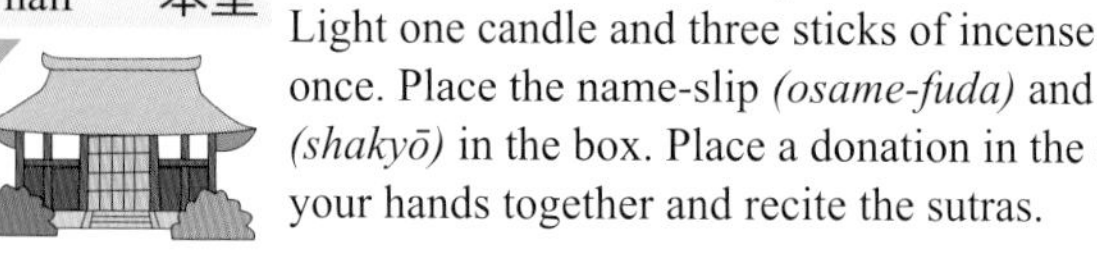

At the main hall, it is common to begin reciting in order the Heart Sutra, then continue with the *Gohonzon Shingon* and *Gohōgō* sutras. However, it is all right to pray silently. Later on, you might start reciting the sutras when you get used to hearing them.

In the 5th century before Buddhism was brought to Japan, a Chinese high priest, Hsuan Chuang (602-664), visited India and received the Heart Sutra *(Hannya Shingyō)* which is used in Japan now. Chuang selected Chinese characters which have the same sound as the original Sanskrit, so it is said that in Japan, the *Hannya Shingyō* is an all-encompassing sutra that gives no regard to the religious affiliation of the person reciting it.

5 Daishi hall 大師堂
A statue of Kōbō Daishi is enshrined here.
Worship in the same way as at the main hall.

6 Temple office 納経所
Receive the temple stamp in your pilgrimage book.
(Fee: 500yen , Open: 8:00am~5:00pm at most temple)

7 Main gate 山門
Face the main gate and bow once.

Order of Sutra Reading

1. Place the palms of your hands together and hold your hands in front of your chest with your thumbs facing toward you. This is called *gasshō*. Bow once and say, *"uyauyashiku mihotoke wo reihai shi-tatematsuru."* Do this two more times. I have come to reverently worship the Buddha.
2. Recite the *Kaigyōge* 開経偈 sutra once.
   Words spoken at the beginning of reciting sutras that praise Buddhism.

mu jō jin jin mi myō hō　　hyakusenman gō nan sō gū
無 上 甚 深 微 妙 法　　百 千 万 劫 難 遭 遇
ga kon kenmontoku ju ji　　gan ge nyo rai shin jitsu gi
我 今 見 聞 得 受 持　　願 解 如 来 真 実 義

3. Recite the *Hannya Shingyō* once.

HANNYA SHIN-GYŌ (Heart Sutra) 般 若 心 経

NOTE: Various English versions can be found on the Internet.

Title: Bussetsu Maka Hannya Haramitta Shin-gyō 佛説摩訶般若波羅蜜多心経

kanjizai bosatsu, gyō jin hannya hara mitta ji, shōken gōun kai kū, do issai kuyaku,
観自在 菩 薩 行 深 般 若 波羅蜜多時 照 見 五蘊 皆 空 度一切 苦 厄
sharishi, shiki fu i kū, kū fu i shiki, shiki soku ze kū, kū soku ze shiki, ju sō gyō shiki
舎利子 色 不異空 空不異 色 色 即 是 空 空 即 是 色 受想 行 識
yakubu nyo ze, sharishi, ze shohō kū sō, fushō fumetsu, fuku fujō, fuzō fugen, ze ko kū
亦 復 如 是 舎利子 是 諸 法 空 相 不 生 不 滅 不垢不浄 不増 不 減 是故空
chū, mu shiki, mu ju sō gyō shiki, mu gen ni bi zetsu shin ni, mu shiki shō kō mi shoku
中 無 色 無受想 行 識 無 眼 耳鼻 舌 身 意 無 色 聲 香 味 觸
hō, mu gen kai, nai shi mu i shiki kai, mu mu myō yaku, mu mu myō jin, nai shi mu rō
法 無 眼 界 乃 至 無意 識 界 無 無 明 亦 無 無 明 尽 乃 至 無 老
shi, yaku mu rō shi jin, mu ku shū metsu dō, mu chi yaku mu toku, i mu sho toku ko,
死 亦 無老死尽 無 苦 集 滅 道 無 智 亦 無 得 以無 所 得 故
bodai satta, e hannya hara mitta ko, shin mu kei ge, mu kei ge ko, mu u ku fu, on ri issai
菩提 薩埵 依 般 若 波羅 蜜多 故 心 無 罣 礙 無 罣 礙 故 無 有恐怖 遠離一切
tendō mu sō, kukyō nehan, san ze sho butsu, e hannya hara mitta ko, toku a noku tara
顛倒 夢 想 究竟 涅槃 三 世 諸 佛 依 般 若 波羅 蜜多 故 得 阿 耨 多羅
san myaku san bo dai, ko chi hannya hara mitta, ze dai jin shu, ze dai myō shu, ze mu
三 藐 三 菩 提 故 知 般 若 波羅 蜜多 是 大 神 呪 是 大 明 呪 是 無
jō shu, ze mu to dō shu, nō jo issai ku, shin jitsu fu ko, ko setsu hannya hara mitta shu,
上 呪 是 無 等 等 呪 能 除 一切 苦 真 實 不 虚 故 説 般 若 波羅 蜜多 呪
soku setsu shu watsu, gya tei gya tei, hara gya tei, harasō gya tei, bo ji sowaka.
即 説 呪 日 羯 諦 羯 諦 波羅 羯 諦 波羅僧 掲 諦 菩提薩婆訶

Back title: Hannya shin gyō. 般 若 心 経

4. Recite the *Gohonzon Shingon* mantra 3 times. (see pg 12, 13)
   Sanskrit words that differ according to the main deity.
5. Recite the *Kōmyō Shingon* 光明真言 mantra 3 times.
   A powerful and almighty sutra that can remove all misfortune.
   on a bo kya bei ro sha nō ma ka bo dara ma ni handoma jinbara harabari taya un
6. Recite the *Gohōgō* (name of Kōbō Daishi) 御宝号 3 times.
   Na mu dai shi Hen jō kon gō
   南 無 大 師 遍 照 金 剛
7. Recite the *Ekoumon* 廻向文 sutra once.
   A wish that one's good deeds may spread to all things in the world.
   gan ni shi ku doku fu gyū o issai ga tō yo shu jō kai gu jō butsu dō
   願 以 此 功 徳 普 及 於 一切 我 等 与 衆 生 皆 共 成 仏 道

Say *"arigatō gozaimasu"* (thank you) with hands in the *gasshō* position and bow once.

NOTE: The format of prayers is not fixed, so you can do as much or as little as you like; however, at least the *Hannya Shingyō* (step 3) and *Gohōgō* (step 6) should be included. This procedure should be carried out at both the main hall and Daishi hall, but omit step 4 when at the Daishi hall. Please stand to the left or right of the hall so that you do not block the way for other worshipers.

Oaths and Precepts

Pilgrims participate in ascetic training by following the path that Kōbō Daishi walked and during this time, some of them decide to follow the three oaths and obey the ten precepts noted below. The local people willingly give gifts *(osettai)* to pilgrims and one is humbled by such selfless actions and learns the true meaning of saying "Thank you". We ask that you strive to maintain the beautiful nature of Shikoku and treat with respect the pilgrim facilities run by the friendly people of Shikoku.

Pilgrim Oaths (三信条)

During my pilgrimage,

1. I will believe that Kōbō Daishi will save all living beings and that he will always be with me.
2. I will not complain if things do not go well while on the pilgrimage, but consider such experiences to be part of ascetic training.
3. I will believe that all can be saved in the present world and I will continually ask to be able to achieve enlightenment.

Ten Precepts (十善戒)

1. 不殺生 *fusesshō* I will not harm life.
2. 不偸盗 *fuchūtō* I will not steal.
3. 不邪淫 *fujain* I will not commit adultery.
4. 不妄語 *fumōgo* I will not tell a lie.
5. 不綺語 *fukigo* I will not exaggerate.
6. 不悪口 *fuakuku* I will not speak abusively.
7. 不両舌 *furyōzetsu* I will not cause discord.
8. 不慳貪 *fukendon* I will not be greedy.
9. 不瞋恚 *fushin-ni* I will not be hateful.
10. 不邪見 *fujaken* I will not lose sight of the Trut

On the sedge hat *(sugegasa)* is written the Sanskrit character for Kūkai and the 4 phrases of enlightenment (*shiku no satori* 四句の悟り) which teaches how humankind can obtain enlightenment and become a Bodhisattva.

迷故三界城 *[mayou ga yue ni sangai no shiro]*

(Being lost is due to the three large worlds of desire)

We constantly suffer because we are lost due to worldly desires.

悟故十方空 *[satoru ga yue ni juppō wa kū nari]*

(With enlightenment, 10-thousand skies will appear)

However, by doing such acts as a pilgrimage, the heart will be cleansed and one will be freed from the world of suffering.

本来無東西 *[honrai tōzai nashi]*

(Originally there is no East and West)

In this free world, if one discards oneself, continues in devoted practice and receives favor from Kōbō Daishi, all enemies will disappear and a peaceful society will arise.

何故有南北 *[izukunika nanboku aran]*

(Why is there a North and South?)

By not attaching ourselves to things and throwing away all desires, suffering and distress will disappear. A vast world will open up in front of oneself-the world of enlightenment.

Basic Information on Buddhist Statues

Introduction to the Main Deities of the 88 temples **S** Mantra (Shingon)

Due to the integration of Buddhism with the indigenous Japanese religion of *Shintō,* various different deities emerged. Inside the main hall of each temple, there is a statue of the main deity which is considered to be the central religious figure of each site. The most common deities along the Shikoku pilgrimage route are described below. It is said that originally Buddhist statues were made to represent the teachings of the scriptures in an easy-to-understand form. Nyorai, Boddhisattva, and Myōō tend not to have a gender in particular, but Tenbu are clearly either male or female.

Nyorai Statues（如来像）

These are enlightened beings, which are called Buddha (butsuda), and hold the highest position of all statues. In principal, they do not hold anything nor wear any accessories on their body.

Shaka Nyorai 釈迦如来 **S** nomaku sammanda bodanan baku

This represents Shakamuni who at the end of training achieved enlightenment and became a Nyorai. With his encompassing power, this being can save all humankind.

Amida Nyorai 阿弥陀如来 **S** on amirita teisei kara un

This Buddha lives forever and the light it gives forth shines to all people throughout the world and for those who believe in Amida Nyorai will be able to go to the Land of Paradise.

Yakushi Nyorai 薬師如来 **S** on korokoro sendari matougi sowaka

This figure is considered to be a Buddha of healing and people pray for cures from sicknesses. A unique feature is that he holds an apothecary jar in his left hand.

Dainichi Nyorai 大日如来 **S** on abiraunken bazara dadoban

He has a crown upon his head and other accessories and is said to be a model of a young Shakamumi. Within the teachings of Mikkyō, he is considered to be the greatest Nyorai.

Shaka Nyorai

Amida Nyorai

Yakushi Nyorai

Dainichi Nyorai

Boddhisattva (Bosatsu) Statues（菩薩像）

These beings try to save all people while training under Nyorai. These statues have accessories such as crowns, necklaces and earrings. As well, they carry in their hands objects that will fulfill the wishes of the people.

Jūichimen Kannon Bosatsu 十一面観音菩薩 S on maka kyaronikya sowaka

This being has 11 faces some with angry expressions, some with merciful expressions, and some with smiling expressions. They will guide people to being saved.

Senju Kannon Bosatsu 千手観音菩薩 S on bazara tarama kiriku

This statue has one thousand arms with an eye on the palm of each hand. It can reach out and save all according to what people wish for.

Jizō Bosatsu 地蔵菩薩 S on kakakabi sammaei sowaka

After the death of Shakamuni and until the appearance of Miroku Bosatsu, these beings have the role of saving people. They are believed to be the guardian deity of children, pregnant women and travelers, and they often appear in folktales as someone who brings good fortune to those who are honest and kind.

Shō Kannon Bosatsu 聖観音菩薩 S on arorikya sowaka

This being wears accessories such as a crown with a small Buddha in the front. In his left hand, he holds a lotus flower which symbolizes the Buddha mind.

Kokuzō Bosatsu 虚空蔵菩薩 S nobo akyasha kyarabaya on arikya maribori sowaka

This being wears a crown with 5 Buddhas engraved within. It is the Buddha which has the power to differentiate the truth.

Batō Kannon Bosatsu 馬頭観音菩薩 S on amirito dohamba unpatta sowaka

This being has a horse head and it eats the worldly desires of humankind just as ravenously as a horse eats fodder.

Jūichimen Kannon Bosatsu

Senju Kannon Bosatsu

Jizō Bosatsu

Shō Kannon Bosatsu

Kokuzō Bosatsu

Batō Kannon Bosatsu

Monju Bosatsu

Miroku Bosatsu

Monju Bosatsu 文殊菩薩 S on arahasha nou

This being can give one the power to properly judge things. In his right hand, he holds a sword, in his left hand, a lotus flower and roll of sutras.

Miroku Bosatsu 弥勒菩薩 S on mai tareiya sowaka

It is believed that this being will appear 56 million years after the death of Buddha and save all humankind. At that time, this being will become a Nyorai.

Myōō Statues（明王像）

They are considered to be a god created through Mikkyō and are a messenger to Nyorai. In the right hand is a jeweled sword used to destroy delusions and evil desires and in the left hand, a rope used to discipline restless minds. They have a fiery expression believed to scare away evil.

Fudō Myōō

Fudō Myōō 不動明王

This being remains stalwart and unmovable *(fudō)* able to block the various tricks of evil.

S nomaku sammanda bazaradan senda makaroshada sowataya untarata kamman

Deva Statues（天部像）

In most cases, these beings were created from the gods of Brahamanism as a protective god for Myōō, Bosatsu and Nyorai.

Four Heavenly Kings 四天王 S on beishiramandaya sowaka (Bishamon-ten, No.63)

The four figures below are the Kings, which are said to protect people from evil that comes from all directions. (north, south, east and west).

Jikoku-ten (east)　Zōchō-ten (south)　Kōmoku-ten (west)　Tamon-ten (Bishamon-ten) (north)

Kongō Rikishi

Left: Un-gyō
Right: A-gyō

Kongō Rikishi 金剛力士

These figures, also called Niō-zō, stand on the left and right of the temple gate and watch those that enter.

Pilgrim Attire and other items

You can use any or all of the following; however, if one wears the white vest, people will recognize and welcome you as a pilgrim. People will assist you in your journey and you can have more chances to talk with the local people. You can buy all of these things at Temple 1, Ryōzenji and at many temples and stores along the route.

By wearing the pilgrim attire, you fulfill one of the "three mysteries" *(sanmitsu 三密)*, namely acts, words and thoughts, that are integral parts of the ascetic training within Mikkyō Buddhism.

Staff

❶ sedge hat (sugegasa / 菅笠) (¥1,500 - ¥3,000)

It is useful to block the rain or sun. It is not necessary to remove one's hat when worshipping at a sacred site, whether inside or outside, or when talking with a priest.
The Sanskrit mark should face forward.

❷ white vest (hakui / 白衣・白装束) (¥2,000 - ¥3,500)

The white clothing worn by the pilgrim represents purity and innocence, however in the past it also held the meaning of a death shroud, symbolizing that the pilgrim was prepared to die at any time (recent Interpretation).
Some people receive the temple stamp on an extra vest. This becomes a family treasure and is later put on the deceased before cremation.

❸ bag (Zudabukuro / 頭陀袋) (¥1,500 - ¥4,000)

Things necessary for the journey, such as sutras, pilgrimage book, etc are put in here.

1
6
4
5
3
2
7

Hakui

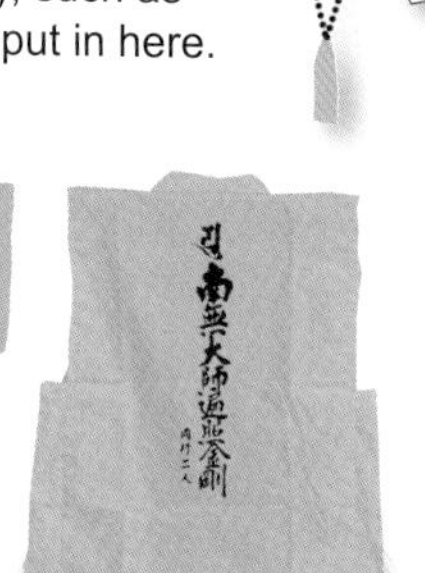
南無大師遍照金剛

Oizuru 笈摺

❹ mala (juzu / 数珠)

(¥3,000 - ¥15,000)

To the Japanese, this is a very familiar religious object. If one holds this with one's hands together, it is said that the illusions of one's mind will disappear and one will obtain merit.

pilgrimage book

(nōkyōchō / 納経帳) (¥2,000 - ¥3,500)

This acts as proof that you have visited each temple. Take it to the temple office after finishing worshiping at each site.
Fee: 500 yen per temple.
(scroll-1000yen)

Nōkyōchō

nameslips (osame-fuda / 納札)

(white: ¥100 / 200 Sheet)

You write your name, address, date, and wish on this. It is placed in the nameslip box at the both the main hall and Daishi hall. As well, it is given to those you receive gifts from.

The color of the nameslip depends on the number of times one has done the pilgrimage:

1-4 times:	white
5-7 times:	green
8-24 times:	red
25-49 times:	silver
50-99 times:	gold
100+ times:	brocade

Ex:
brocade nameslip.

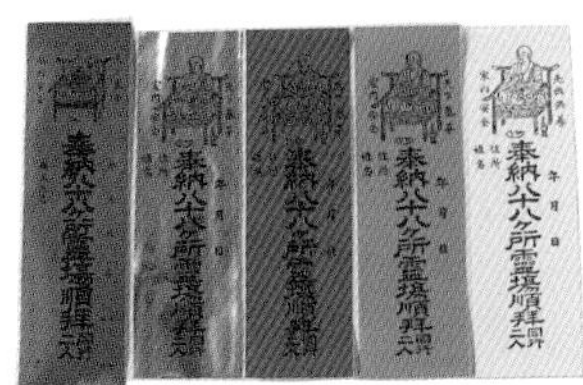

❺ bell (Jirei / 持鈴)

(¥4,000 —)

You should ring the bell after reciting each sutra.

❻ stole (wagesa / 輪袈裟)

(¥1,500 - ¥3,500)

The stole is part of the attire that a priest wears; however, this has been adapted for traveling. Take it off when going into a washroom and when eating meals.

❼ staff (kongōzue / 金剛杖) (¥1,500 - ¥3,500)

It is said to be the embodiment of Kōbō Daishi which guides pilgrims. Formerly, it seems to have been used as a grave marker for pilgrims who passed away while on the pilgrimage route.

Rules:

1. When you stop for a rest, make sure the staff is taken care of before yourself.
2. When you reach a place to stay, wash the end of the staff and, when you stay at an inn, place it in the room alcove *(tokonoma)*.
3. There is a belief that Kōbō Daishi might be sleeping under a bridge, so do not tap the staff when going over any bridge.
4. The end of the staff will fray over time. Do not cut it with a knife, however using a stone or other blunt object is allowed.

Access to Shikoku

As of May, 2024 (All prices noted are in Yen)

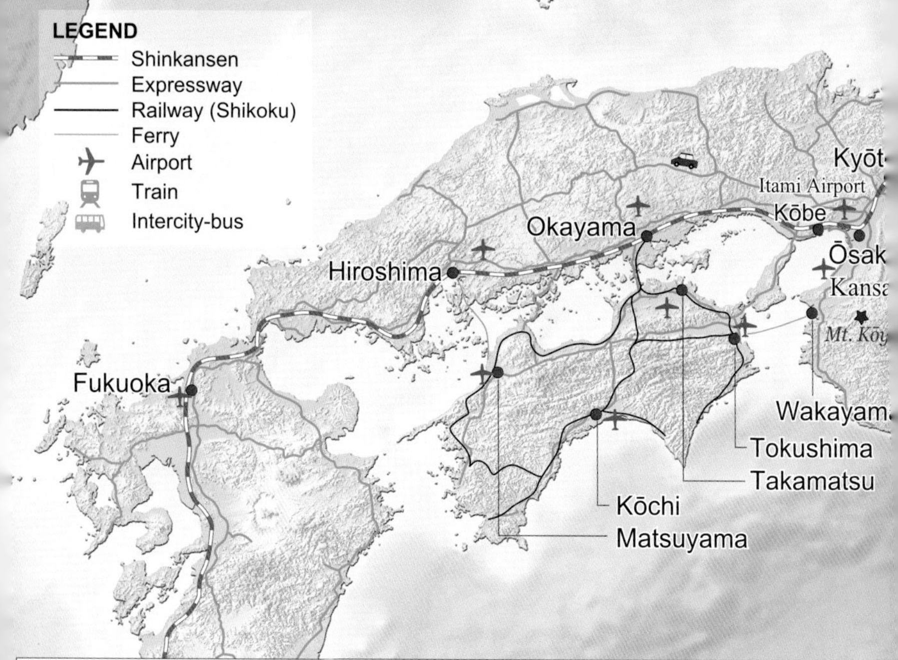

LEGEND
Shinkansen
Expressway
Railway (Shikoku)
Ferry
Airport
Train
Intercity-bus

Kyōto
Itami Airport
Kōbe
Okayama
Ōsaka
Hiroshima
Kansai
Mt. Kōya
Fukuoka
Wakayama
Tokushima
Takamatsu
Kōchi
Matsuyama

Kansai International Airport (KIX) to Tokushima Station

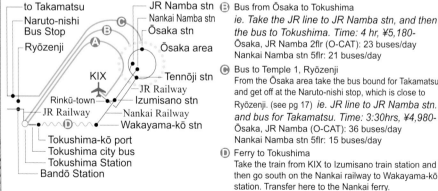

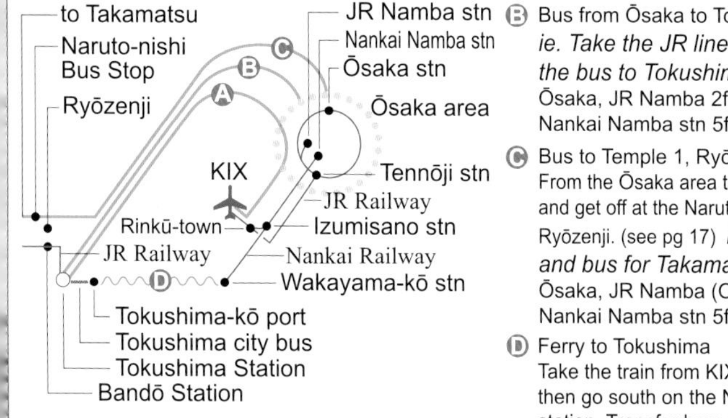
to Takamatsu
Naruto-nishi Bus Stop
Ryōzenji
C
B
A
KIX
Rinkū-town
JR Railway
D
Tokushima-kō port
Tokushima city bus
Tokushima Station
Bandō Station
JR Namba stn
Nankai Namba stn
Ōsaka stn
Ōsaka area
Tennōji stn
JR Railway
Izumisano stn
Nankai Railway
Wakayama-kō stn

Ⓑ Bus from Ōsaka to Tokushima
ie. Take the JR line to JR Namba stn, and then the bus to Tokushima. Time: 4 hr, ¥5,180-
Ōsaka, JR Namba 2flr (O-CAT): 23 buses/day
Nankai Namba stn 5flr: 21 buses/day

Ⓒ Bus to Temple 1, Ryōzenji
From the Ōsaka area take the bus bound for Takamatsu and get off at the Naruto-nishi stop, which is close to Ryōzenji. (see pg 17) *ie. JR line to JR Namba stn. and bus for Takamatsu. Time: 3:30hrs, ¥4,980-*
Ōsaka, JR Namba (O-CAT): 36 buses/day
Nankai Namba stn 5flr: 15 buses/day

Ⓓ Ferry to Tokushima
Take the train from KIX to Izumisano train station and then go south on the Nankai railway to Wakayama-kō station. Transfer here to the Nankai ferry.
ie. Nankai rlwy to Wakayama-kō, ferry and local bus to Tokushima stn. Time: approx 4hrs. ¥2,710-
Departure ferry times from Wakayama to Tokushima.

2:40	5:30	8:35	10:35	13:40
16:20	19:10	21:50		

Ⓐ Bus from KIX to Tokushima (Depart from T1 and T2)
Time: approx. 3hrs, ¥5,000-

T1	9:52	12:07	16:07
T2	10:05	12:20	16:20

* To ride an intercity bus you must buy a ticket at the departure terminal before boarding.

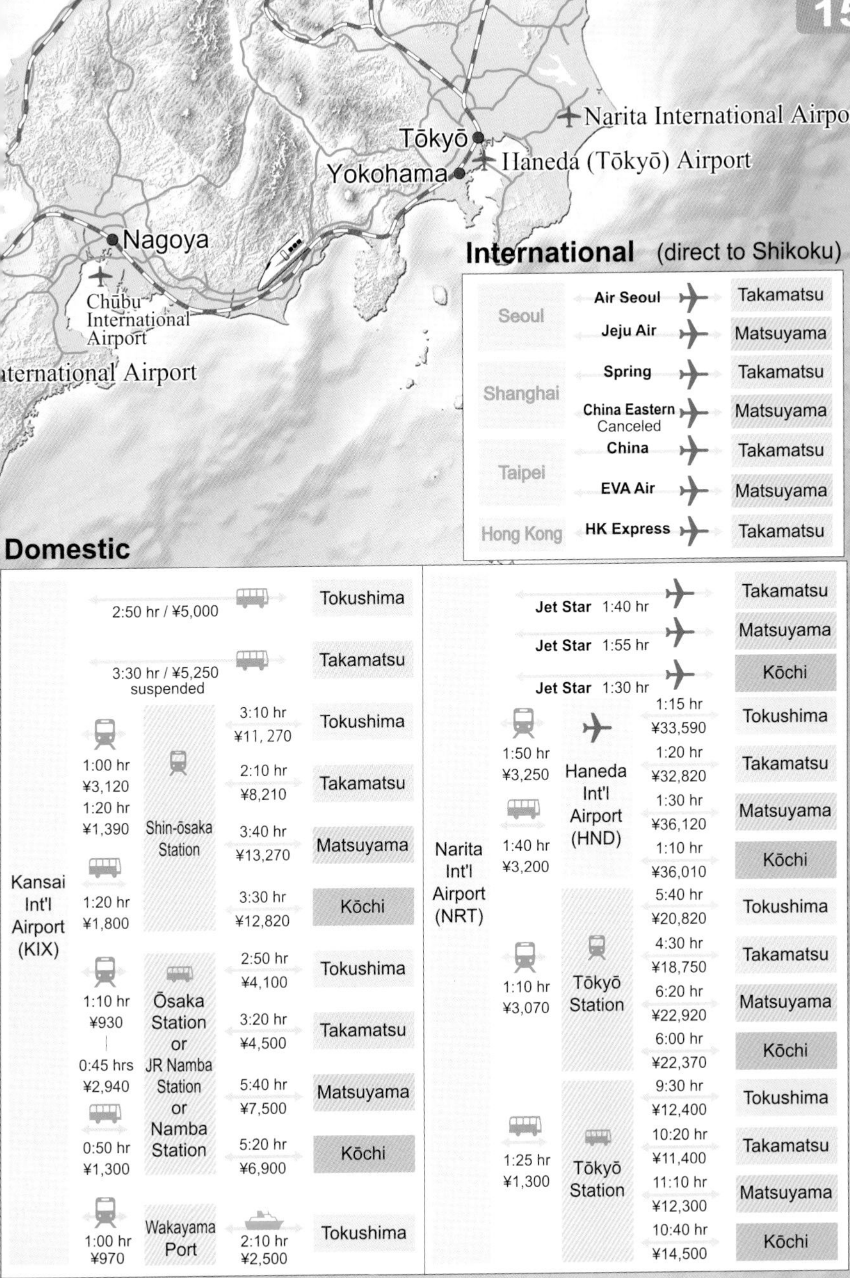

Narita International Airport
Tōkyō
Haneda (Tōkyō) Airport
Yokohama
Nagoya
Chūbu International Airport
ternational Airport

International (direct to Shikoku)

From	Airline	To
Seoul	Air Seoul	Takamatsu
	Jeju Air	Matsuyama
Shanghai	Spring	Takamatsu
	China Eastern Canceled	Matsuyama
Taipei	China	Takamatsu
	EVA Air	Matsuyama
Hong Kong	HK Express	Takamatsu

Domestic

From	Access	Via	Time / Fare	To
Kansai Int'l Airport (KIX)			2:50 hr / ¥5,000	Tokushima
			3:30 hr / ¥5,250 suspended	Takamatsu
	1:00 hr ¥3,120 / 1:20 hr ¥1,390 / 1:20 hr ¥1,800	Shin-ōsaka Station	3:10 hr ¥11, 270	Tokushima
			2:10 hr ¥8,210	Takamatsu
			3:40 hr ¥13,270	Matsuyama
			3:30 hr ¥12,820	Kōchi
	1:10 hr ¥930 / 0:45 hrs ¥2,940 / 0:50 hr ¥1,300	Ōsaka Station or JR Namba Station or Namba Station	2:50 hr ¥4,100	Tokushima
			3:20 hr ¥4,500	Takamatsu
			5:40 hr ¥7,500	Matsuyama
			5:20 hr ¥6,900	Kōchi
	1:00 hr ¥970	Wakayama Port	2:10 hr ¥2,500	Tokushima

From	Access	Via	Time / Fare	To
Narita Int'l Airport (NRT)			Jet Star 1:40 hr	Takamatsu
			Jet Star 1:55 hr	Matsuyama
			Jet Star 1:30 hr	Kōchi
	1:50 hr ¥3,250 / 1:40 hr ¥3,200	Haneda Int'l Airport (HND)	1:15 hr ¥33,590	Tokushima
			1:20 hr ¥32,820	Takamatsu
			1:30 hr ¥36,120	Matsuyama
			1:10 hr ¥36,010	Kōchi
	1:10 hr ¥3,070	Tōkyō Station	5:40 hr ¥20,820	Tokushima
			4:30 hr ¥18,750	Takamatsu
			6:20 hr ¥22,920	Matsuyama
			6:00 hr ¥22,370	Kōchi
	1:25 hr ¥1,300	Tōkyō Station	9:30 hr ¥12,400	Tokushima
			10:20 hr ¥11,400	Takamatsu
			11:10 hr ¥12,300	Matsuyama
			10:40 hr ¥14,500	Kōchi

Fare included LTD Express Reserved Seat. Bus terminals are adjacent to train stations.

Railway/Bus Route Map

If you have limited time, need to take a break, or the weather is bad, feel free to use public transportation; however, be aware that trains and buses can run very infrequently, so plan accordingly. Train stations and bus stops will be listed on the detailed maps.

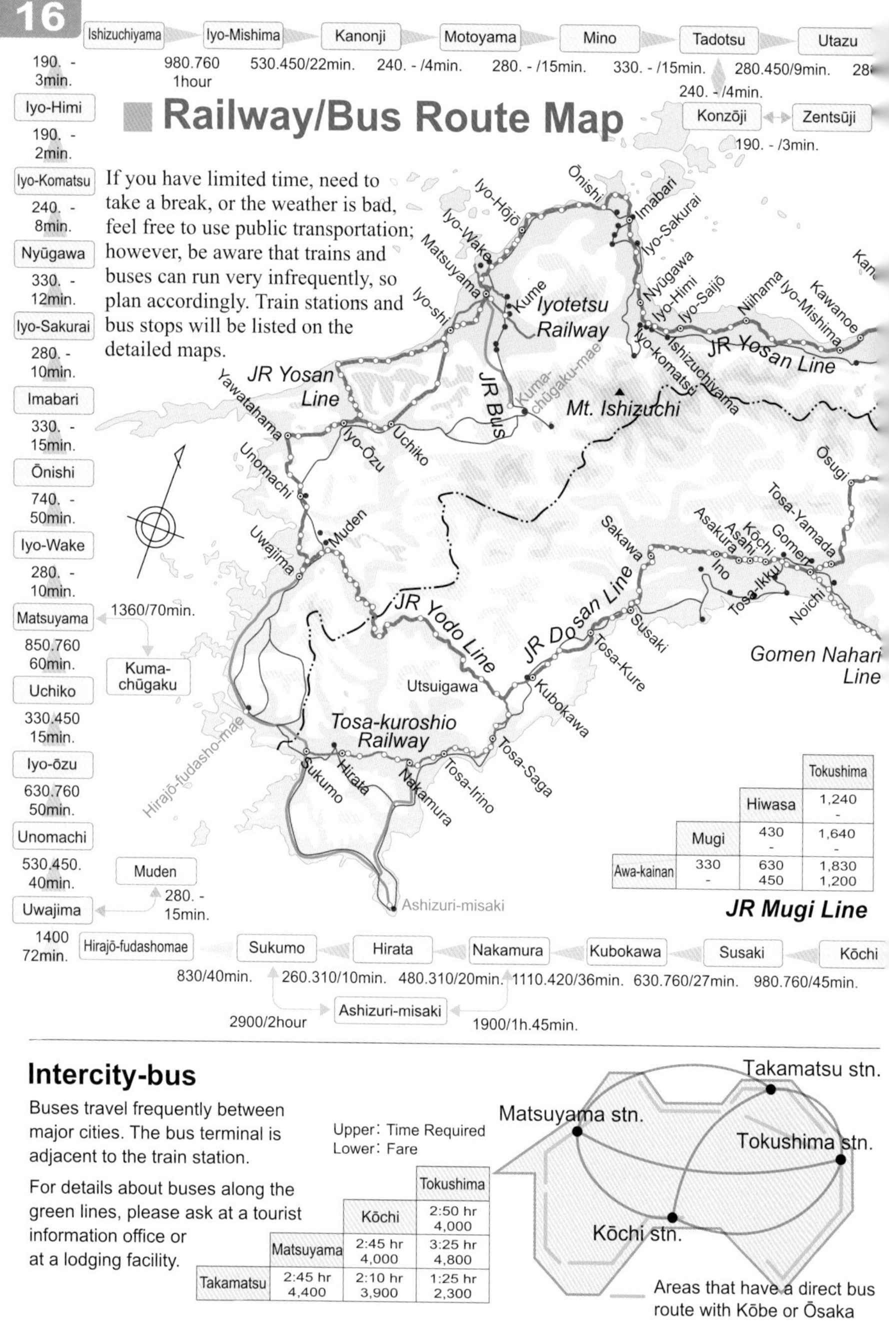

Ishizuchiyama
980.760
1hour
Iyo-Mishima
530.450/22min.
Kanonji
240. - /4min.
Motoyama
280. - /15min.
Mino
330. - /15min.
Tadotsu
280.450/9min.
Utazu
240. - /4min.
Konzōji
Zentsūji
190. - /3min.
190. -
3min.
Iyo-Himi
190. -
2min.
Iyo-Komatsu
240. -
8min.
Nyūgawa
330. -
12min.
Iyo-Sakurai
280. -
10min.
Imabari
330. -
15min.
Ōnishi
740. -
50min.
Iyo-Wake
280. -
10min.
Matsuyama
1360/70min.
Kuma-
chūgaku
850.760
60min.
Uchiko
330.450
15min.
Iyo-ōzu
630.760
50min.
Unomachi
530.450.
40min.
Muden
280. -
15min.
Uwajima
1400
72min.
Hirajō-fudashomae
830/40min.
Sukumo
260.310/10min.
Hirata
480.310/20min.
Nakamura
1110.420/36min.
Kubokawa
630.760/27min.
Susaki
980.760/45min.
Kōchi
2900/2hour
Ashizuri-misaki
1900/1h.45min.
Iyo-Hōjō
Ōnishi
Imabari
Iyo-Wake
Iyo-Sakurai
Matsuyama
Kume
Iyotetsu
Railway
Nyūgawa
Iyo-Himi
Iyo-Saijō
Niihama
Iyo-Mishima
Kawanoe
Iyo-shi
Iyo-komatsu
Ishizuchiyama
JR Yosan Line
JR Yosan
Line
Yawatahama
JR Bus
Kuma-
chūgaku-mae
Mt. Ishizuchi
Iyo-Ōzu
Uchiko
Unomachi
Ōsugi
Tosa-Yamada
Muden
Uwajima
Sakawa
Asakura
Asahi
Kōchi
Gomen
Ino
Tosa-Ikku
Noichi
JR Yodo Line
JR Dosan Line
Susaki
Tosa-Kure
Gomen Nahari
Line
Utsuigawa
Kubokawa
Tosa-kuroshio
Railway
Hirajō-fudasho-mae
Sukumo
Hirata
Nakamura
Tosa-Irino
Tosa-Saga
Ashizuri-misaki

	Mugi	Hiwasa	Tokushima
Hiwasa			1,240 -
Mugi		430 -	1,640 -
Awa-kainan	330 -	630 450	1,830 1,200

JR Mugi Line

Intercity-bus

Buses travel frequently between major cities. The bus terminal is adjacent to the train station.

For details about buses along the green lines, please ask at a tourist information office or at a lodging facility.

Upper：Time Required
Lower：Fare

	Matsuyama	Kōchi	Tokushima
Kōchi			2:50 hr 4,000
Matsuyama		2:45 hr 4,000	3:25 hr 4,800
Takamatsu	2:45 hr 4,400	2:10 hr 3,900	1:25 hr 2,300

Takamatsu stn.
Matsuyama stn.
Tokushima stn.
Kōchi stn.
Areas that have a direct bus route with Kōbe or Ōsaka

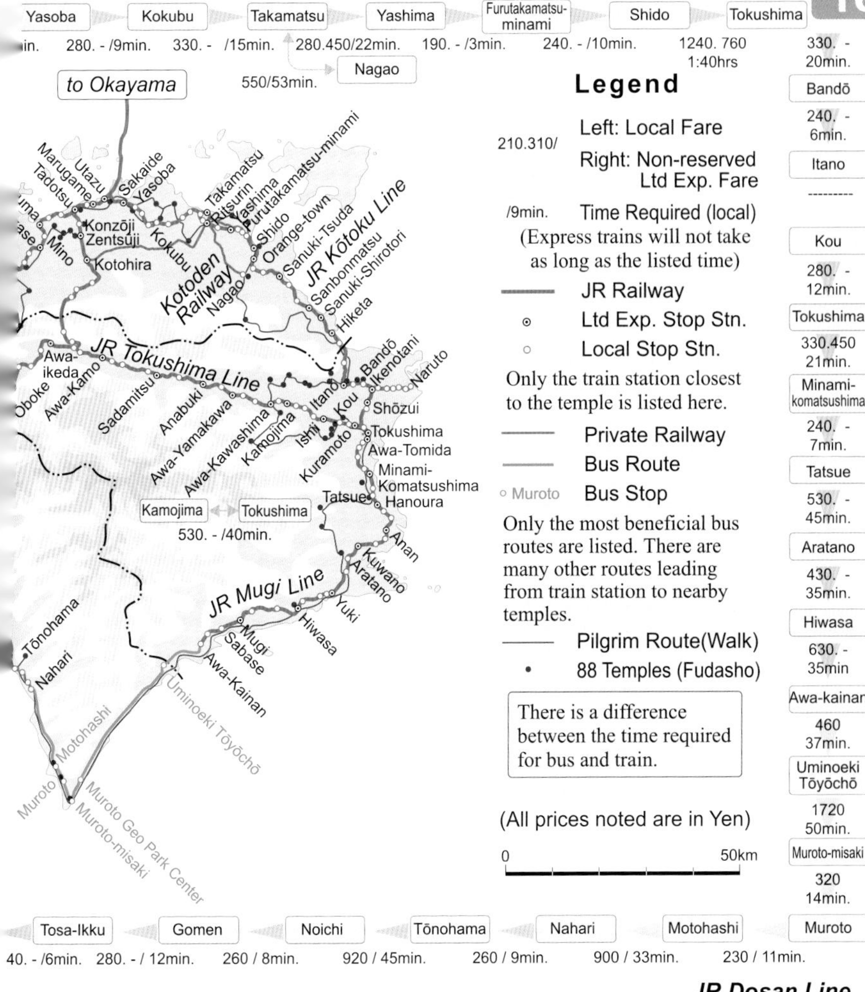
Yasoba
Kokubu
Takamatsu
Yashima
Furutakamatsu-minami
Shido
Tokushima
in. 280. - /9min.
330. - /15min.
280.450/22min.
190. - /3min.
240. - /10min.
1240. 760
1:40hrs
Nagao
550/53min.
to Okayama
330. -
20min.
Bandō
240. -
6min.
Itano

Kou
280. -
12min.
Tokushima
330.450
21min.
Minami-komatsushima
240. -
7min.
Tatsue
530. -
45min.
Aratano
430. -
35min.
Hiwasa
630. -
35min
Awa-kainan
460
37min.
Uminoeki Tōyōchō
1720
50min.
Muroto-misaki
320
14min.
Muroto
Legend
210.310/
Left: Local Fare
Right: Non-reserved Ltd Exp. Fare
/9min.
Time Required (local)
(Express trains will not take as long as the listed time)
JR Railway
Ltd Exp. Stop Stn.
Local Stop Stn.
Only the train station closest to the temple is listed here.
Private Railway
Bus Route
Muroto
Bus Stop
Only the most beneficial bus routes are listed. There are many other routes leading from train station to nearby temples.
Pilgrim Route(Walk)
88 Temples (Fudasho)
There is a difference between the time required for bus and train.
(All prices noted are in Yen)
0
50km
Marugame
Tadotsu
Utazu
Sakaide
Yasoba
Takamatsu
Ritsurin
Yashima
Furutakamatsu-minami
Shido
Orange-town
Sanuki-Tsuda
JR Kōtoku Line
Sanbonmatsu
Sanuki-Shirotori
Hiketa
Konzōji
Zentsūji
Mino
Kotohira
Kokubu
Kotoden Railway
Nagao
Awa-ikeda
Awa-Kamo
Oboke
JR Tokushima Line
Sadamitsu
Anabuki
Awa-Yamakawa
Awa-Kawashima
Kamojima
Ishii
Itano
Kou
Bandō
Ikenotani
Naruto
Shōzui
Tokushima
Awa-Tomida
Kuramoto
Minami-Komatsushima
Tatsue
Hanoura
Kamojima
Tokushima
530. - /40min.
Anan
Kuwano
Aratano
Yuki
Hiwasa
JR Mugi Line
Mugi
Sabase
Awa-Kainan
Umінoeki Tōyōchō
Tōnohama
Nahari
Motohashi
Muroto
Muroto Geo Park Center
Muroto-misaki
Tosa-Ikku
Gomen
Noichi
Tōnohama
Nahari
Motohashi
Muroto
40. - /6min.
280. - / 12min.
260 / 8min.
920 / 45min.
260 / 9min.
900 / 33min.
230 / 11min.

JR Yosan Line

5,830 2,420	5,170 2,420	3,960 2,200	3,190 1,860	2,310 1,860	1,240 1,200	Takamatsu
4,730 2,420	3,,960 2,200	2,750 1,860	1,830 1,200	1,240 1,200	Kanonji	
3,630 2,200	2,750 1,860	1,830 1,200	740 760	Iyo-Saijō		
3,190 1,860	2,010 760	1,080 760	Imabari			
2,010 1,200	1,080 760	Matsuyama				
1,080 760	Iyo-Ōzu					
Uwajima						

Upper: Local Fare
Lower: Fare of Non-reserved Ltd Express

JR Dosan Line
Tosa-kuroshio Railway

						Takamatsu
					Zentsūji	850 760
				Kōchi	2,750 1,860	3,190 1,860
			Susaki	980 760	3,630 2,200	4,400 2,200
		Kubokawa	630 760	1,640 1,200	3,960 2,200	4,730 2,420
	Nakamura	1,110 420	1,740 1,180	2,750 1,620	5,070 2,620	5,840 2,840
Sukumo	630 310	1,630 420	2,260 1,390	3,270 1,620	5,590 2,620	6,360 3,050

3 Konsenji 三番 金泉寺

- H Shaka Nyorai
- 66 Ōdera-kameyama-shita, Itano Town
- Free of charge (10)
- A About 10 min. walk from JR Kōtoku Line Itano Stn.
- ☎ 088-672-1087 S None

Founded by Gyōki. Kūkai later repaired the buildings and gave the temple its present name. The gold well *(Konsen)* beside the Daishi hall is why this temple was called Konsenji. If you can see your face in the reflected in the well water, you will live a long life. By the temple office, have a look at the huge stone that the warrior Benkei lifted in 1185.

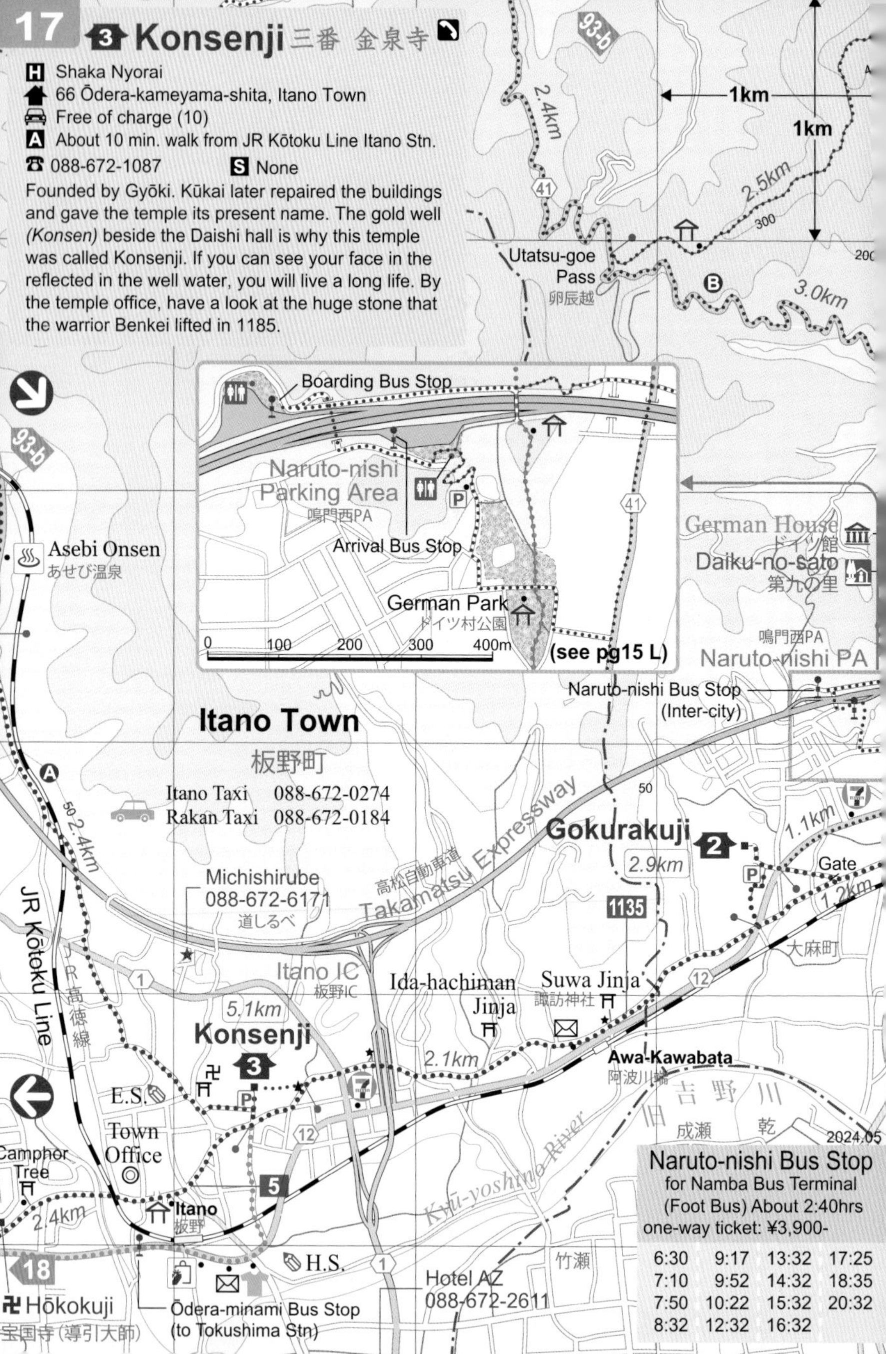

93-b
2.4km
1km
1km
41
2.5km
300
Utatsu-goe Pass
卵辰越
B
3.0km
200
Boarding Bus Stop
Naruto-nishi Parking Area
鳴門西PA
Arrival Bus Stop
German Park
ドイツ村公園
0 100 200 300 400m
(see pg15 L)
German House
ドイツ館
Daiku-no-sato
第九の里
鳴門西PA
Naruto-nishi PA
Naruto-nishi Bus Stop (Inter-city)
Asebi Onsen
あせび温泉
Itano Town
板野町
Itano Taxi 088-672-0274
Rakan Taxi 088-672-0184
A
50 2.4km
50
Takamatsu Expressway
高松自動車道
Gokurakuji
2
2.9km
1.1km
Gate
1.2km
1135
大麻町
Michishirube
088-672-6171
道しるべ
JR Kōtoku Line
JR高徳線
Itano IC
板野IC
1
Ida-hachiman Jinja
Suwa Jinja
諏訪神社
12
5.1km
Konsenji
3
2.1km
Awa-Kawabata
阿波川端
旧吉野川
成瀬
乾
E.S.
Town Office
Camphor Tree
5
Kyū-yoshino River
2.4km
Itano
板野
H.S.
竹瀬
18
Hōkokuji
宝国寺(導引大師)
Ōdera-minami Bus Stop (to Tokushima Stn)
Hotel AZ
088-672-2611

2024.05

Naruto-nishi Bus Stop
for Namba Bus Terminal (Foot Bus) About 2:40hrs
one-way ticket: ¥3,900-

6:30	9:17	13:32	17:25
7:10	9:52	14:32	18:35
7:50	10:22	15:32	20:32
8:32	12:32	16:32	

1 Ryōzenji 一番 霊山寺

H Shaka Nyorai
126 Bandō, Ōasa-chō, Naruto City
Free of charge (100)
A About 15 min. walk from JR Kōtoku Line Bandō Stn.
☎ 088-689-1111 S None

Founded by Gyōki (668-749), Kūkai later came and prayed for the farmers who were suffering from natural disasters and the spread of sickness. The characters for this temple come from a sacred mountain (ryōzen) in India where Buddha gave sermons on Buddhism.

2 Gokurakuji 二番 極楽寺

H Amida Nyorai
12 Dannoue, Ōasa-chō-hinoki, Naruto City
Free of charge (40)
A About 15 min. walk from JR Kōtoku Line Awa-Kawabata Stn.
☎ 088-689-1112 S None

This temple was founded by Gyōki; however Kūkai carved the statue of Amida Nyorai - the deity of light. In ancient times, it is said that this light reached the sea and prevented the fisherman from catching fish, so a small hill was built in front of the image. On the grounds, there is a large cedar tree, called "Chōmei-sugi" which is said to give one a longer life. People also come here to pray for an easy childbirth.

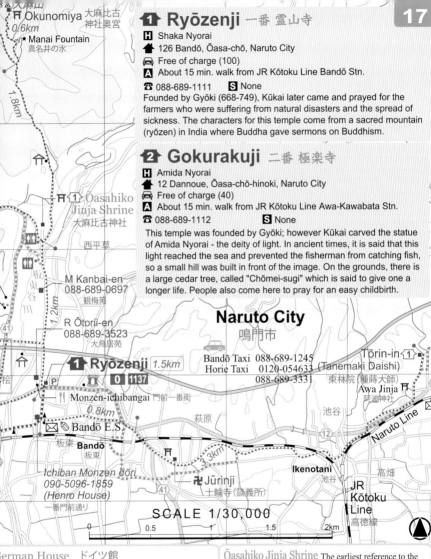

Okunomiya 大麻比古神社奥宮
0.6km
Manai Fountain 真名井の水
1.8km
1 Ōasahiko Jinja Shrine 大麻比古神社
西平草
板東谷川
M Kanbai-en 088-689-0697 観梅苑
1.2km
R Ōtorii-en 088-689-3523 大鳥居苑
41
1 Ryōzenji 1.5km
0 1137
Monzen-ichibangai 門前一番街
0.8km
Bandō E.S.
板東 Bandō 板東
225
Ichiban Monzen dōri 090-5096-1859 (Henro House) 一番門前通り

Naruto City 鳴門市

Bandō Taxi 088-689-1245
Horie Taxi 0120-054633 088-689-3331

Tōrin-in 1 (Tanemaki Daishi) 東林院(種蒔大師)
Awa Jinja 阿波神社
池谷
萩原
12
Naruto Line
3.3km
Jūrinji 十輪寺(談義所)
41
Ikenotani 池谷
高畑
JR Kōtoku Line 高徳線

SCALE 1/30,000
0 0.5 1 1.5 2km

German House ドイツ館

O 9:30am-4:30pm
C 4th Mon. F ¥400-

To commemorate the friendly exchange between the German prisoners of war and the local people between 1917 and 1920 in this area, this building was constructed in 1972 Inside there is a display room with a model of the camp, and various photos, artifacts, and explanations describing the life of the Germans.

Ōasahiko Jinja Shrine 大麻比古神社

The earliest reference to the establishment of this shrine is in a book called Engishiki written in 905. Many people believe that by visiting and praying here one will be protected while on the road and be able to ward off any misfortune associated with age or direction. Large crowds visit here at New Year's.

1 Taisanji 一番 大山寺

H Senju Kannon Bosatsu

Ōyama Kanyake Kamiita Town

☎ 088-694-5525

A By bus bound for Kajiyabara from Tokushima Stn. or Itano Stn. Get off at Kanyake Bus Stop, about 5km walk.

This temple was founded in the 6th century. Kūkai deemed this site to be optimal for training in Mikkyo Buddhism, built various buildings, and enshrined the statue of Senju Kanzeon received from his teacher in China. The present temple buildings are from the 19th century. Based on a legend from 400 years ago a chikara mochi (strength / rice event) event is held every January during which people attempt to carry an extremely heavy rice cake for as long as possible.

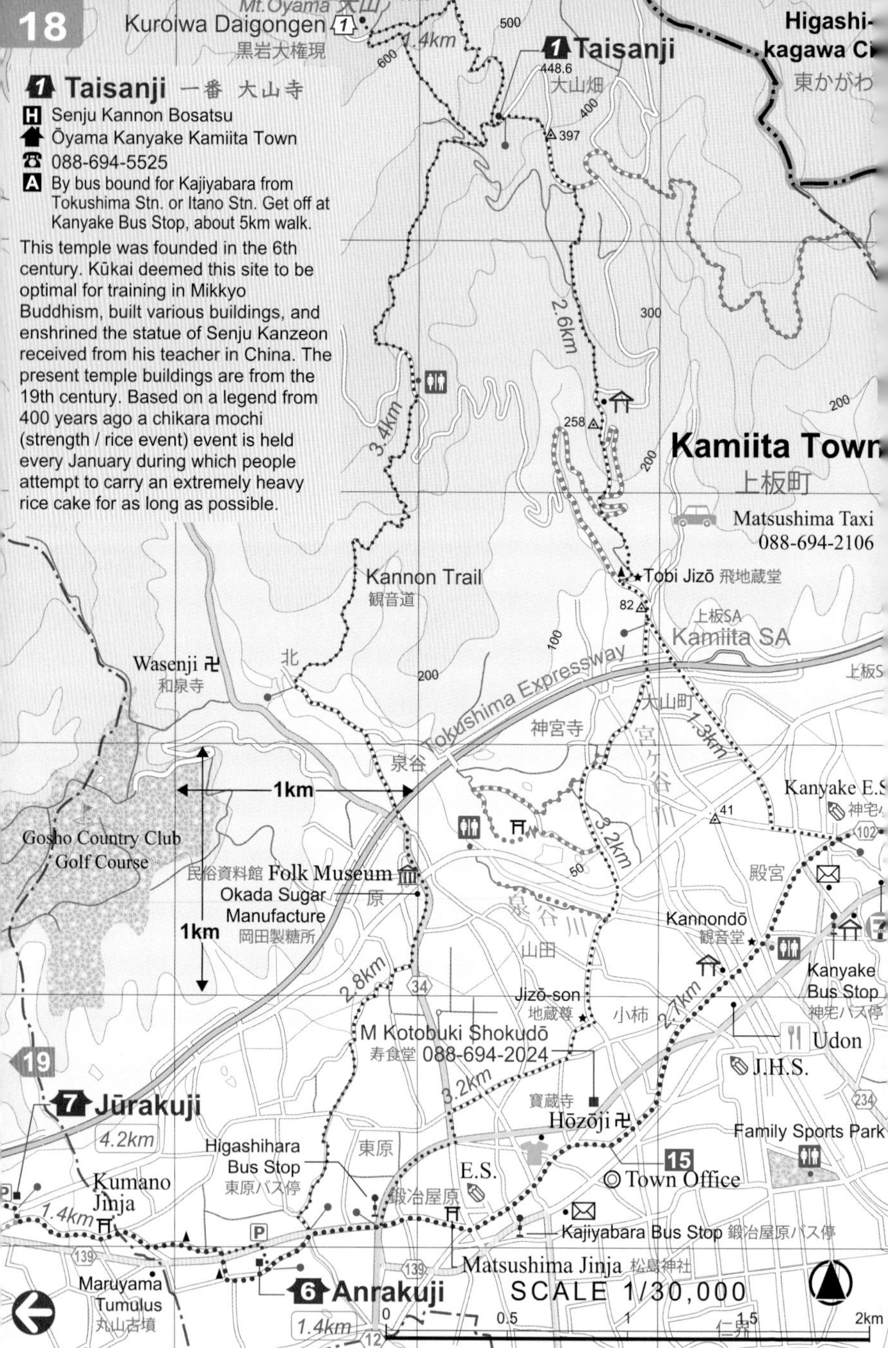

Mt.Oyama 大山
Kuroiwa Daigongen
黒岩大権現
1.4km
1 Taisanji
448.6
大山畑
397
Higashi-kagawa Ci
東かがわ
2.6km
3.4km
258
Kamiita Town
上板町
Matsushima Taxi
088-694-2106
Tobi Jizō 飛地蔵堂
82
Kannon Trail
観音道
上板SA
Kamiita SA
Wasenji 卍
和泉寺
北
Tokushima Expressway
大山町
神宮寺
1.3km
宮ケ谷川
泉谷
1km
Kanyake E.S
神宅小
102
41
Gosho Country Club Golf Course
3.2km
民俗資料館 Folk Museum
Okada Sugar Manufacture
岡田製糖所
原
殿宮
泉谷川
Kannondō
観音堂
山田
Kanyake Bus Stop
神宅バス停
2.8km
34
Jizō-son
地蔵尊
小柿
2.7km
Udon
M Kotobuki Shokudō
寿食堂 088-694-2024
J.H.S.
19
3.2km
234
7 Jūrakuji
4.2km
寶蔵寺
Hōzōji 卍
Family Sports Park
Higashihara Bus Stop
東原バス停
東原
15
E.S.
Town Office
Kumano Jinja
鍛冶屋原
1.4km
Kajiyabara Bus Stop 鍛冶屋原バス停
139
Matsushima Jinja 松島神社
Maruyama Tumulus
丸山古墳
6 Anrakuji
1.4km
SCALE 1/30,000
0
0.5
1
1.5
2km
12

4 Dainichiji 四番 大日寺

☎ 088-672-1225 S None

H Dainichi Nyorai 5 Kurotani, Itano Town Free of charge (50)

A By bus bound for Kajiyahara from Tokushima Stn.or Itano Stn. Get off at Rakan Bus Stop, about 45 min. walk.

ūkai carved a statue of Dainichi Nyorai here and is said to have founded iis temple. Throughout its history, this temple went through a continual ycle of disuse and reconstruction. The main hall and Daishi hall are onnected via a walkway and 33 Kannon statues are on display.

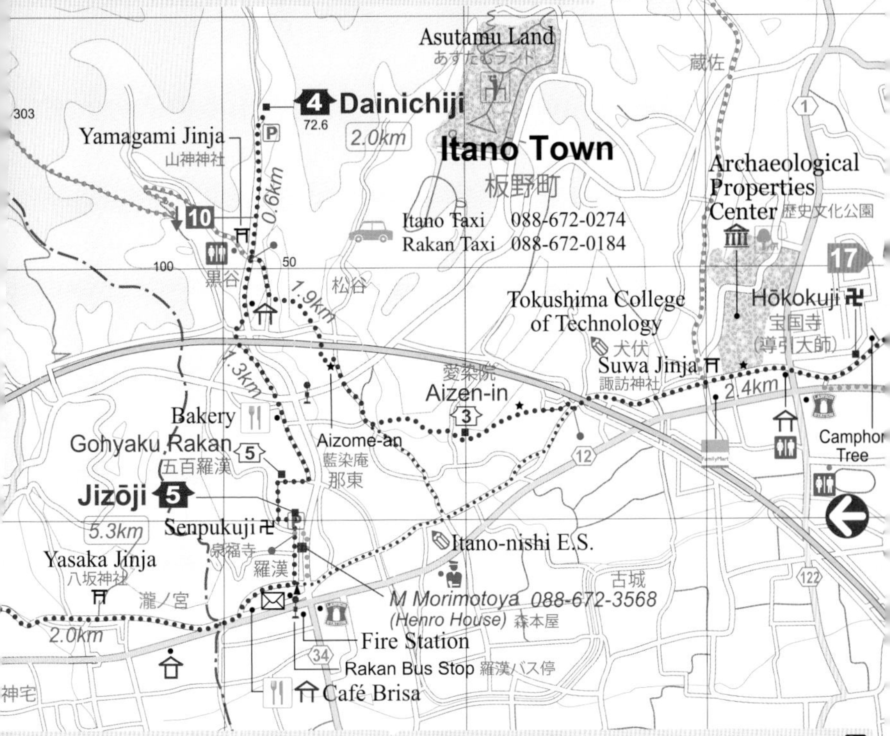

93-b
Takamatsu Expressway
高松自動車道
Hard to find the trail due to bushes
Asutamu Land
あすたむランド
蔵佐
303
4 Dainichiji
72.6
2.0km
Yamagami Jinja
山神神社
0.6km
Itano Town
板野町
Archaeological Properties Center 歴史文化公園
10
Itano Taxi 088-672-0274
Rakan Taxi 088-672-0184
100
50
黒谷
松谷
1.9km
17
Tokushima College of Technology
犬伏
Hōkokuji
宝国寺
(導引大師)
1.3km
愛染院
Aizen-in
3
Suwa Jinja
諏訪神社
2.4km
Bakery
Gohyaku Rakan
五百羅漢
5
Aizome-an
藍染庵
那東
12
Camphor Tree
Jizōji 5
5.3km
Senpukuji
泉福寺
Itano-nishi E.S.
Yasaka Jinja
八坂神社
羅漢
古城
瀧ノ宮
M Morimotoya 088-672-3568
(Henro House) 森本屋
2.0km
Fire Station
34
Rakan Bus Stop 羅漢バス停
122
神宅
Café Brisa

6 Anrakuji 六番 安楽寺

H Yakushi Nyorai ☎ 088-694-2046

Hikino, Kamiita Town S Available

Free of charge (80)

A By bus bound for Kajiyahara from Tokushima Stn. or Itano Stn. Get off at Higashibara Bus Stop, about 10 min. walk.

In the past people used the hot spring water in this vicinity to cure illnesses. In 811, Kūkai carved a statue of Yakushi Nyorai and founded this temple. On the temple grounds, there are 33 types of deity statues and an upside down pine tree said to ward off misfortune (yakuyoke no sakamatsu), which was planted by a hunter after his father was cured of an illness.

5 Jizōji 五番 地蔵寺

H Shōgun Jizō Bosatsu ☎ 088-672-4111 S None

5 Rakan-hayashi-higashi, Itano Town

Free of charge (30)

A By bus bound for Kajiyahara from Tokushima Stn. or Itano Stn. Get off at Rakan Bus Stop, about 5 min. walk.

Until the late 16th century many military leaders prayed to the main deity, which was carved by Kūkai, because they believed it would help them win battles. They also gave a lot of support to the temple so it grew in size. There is a huge 800-year-old gingko tree between the main hall and Daishi hall, and there is a well, where you can hear the sound of a single drop of water hitting the water surface, beside the main hall. The "Gohyaku (500) Rakan" hall behind the temple contains 200 wooden statues of arhats, which are enlightened disciples of Buddha (Fee: 200 yen).

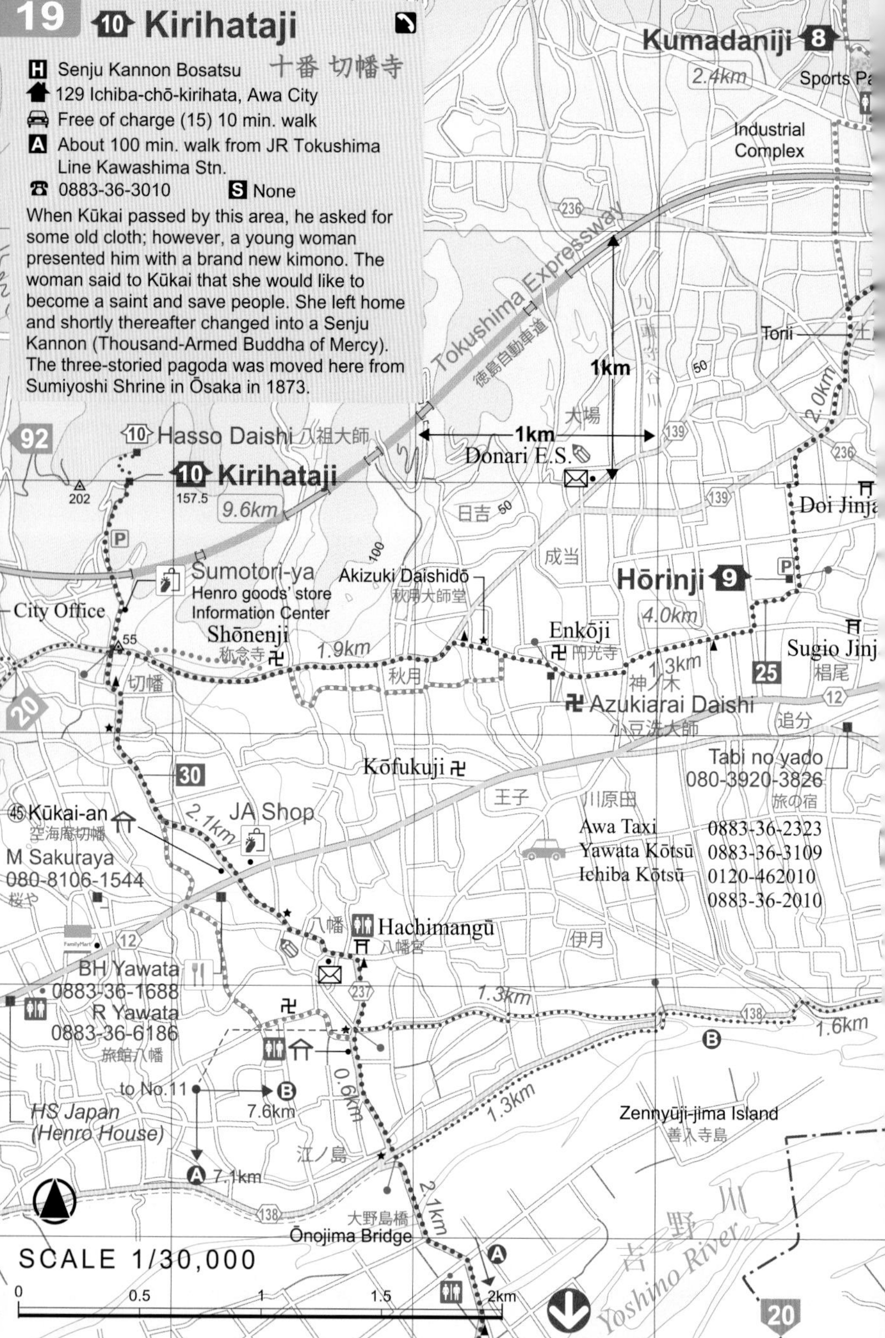
19
10 Kirihataji
十番 切幡寺
Senju Kannon Bosatsu
129 Ichiba-chō-kirihata, Awa City
Free of charge (15) 10 min. walk
About 100 min. walk from JR Tokushima Line Kawashima Stn.
0883-36-3010
None
When Kūkai passed by this area, he asked for some old cloth; however, a young woman presented him with a brand new kimono. The woman said to Kūkai that she would like to become a saint and save people. She left home and shortly thereafter changed into a Senju Kannon (Thousand-Armed Buddha of Mercy). The three-storied pagoda was moved here from Sumiyoshi Shrine in Ōsaka in 1873.
Kumadaniji 8
2.4km
Sports Pa
Industrial Complex
Tokushima Expressway
徳島自動車道
1km
1km
Torii
2.0km
大場
Donari E.S.
92
10 Hasso Daishi 八祖大師
10 Kirihataji
202
157.5
9.6km
日吉
Doi Jinja
成当
Sumotori-ya
Henro goods' store
Information Center
Akizuki Daishidō
秋月大師堂
Hōrinji 9
4.0km
City Office
Shōnenji
称念寺
1.9km
Enkōji
円光寺
Sugio Jinj
相尾
1.3km
神ノ木
切幡
秋月
25
20
Azukiarai Daishi
小豆洗大師
追分
Kōfukuji
Tabi no yado
080-3920-3826
旅の宿
30
王子
川原田
45 Kūkai-an
空海庵切幡
2.1km
JA Shop
Awa Taxi 0883-36-2323
Yawata Kōtsū 0883-36-3109
Ichiba Kōtsū 0120-462010
0883-36-2010
M Sakuraya
080-8106-1544
桜や
八幡
Hachimangū
八幡宮
伊月
BH Yawata
0883-36-1688
R Yawata
0883-36-6186
旅館八幡
1.3km
1.6km
to No.11
7.6km
0.6km
1.3km
HS Japan
(Henro House)
Zennyūji-jima Island
善入寺島
江ノ島
7.1km
2.1km
大野島橋
Ōnojima Bridge
吉野川
Yoshino River
SCALE 1/30,000
0
0.5
1
1.5
2km
20

Goshono-sato
御所の郷
M Okudaya (Henro House)
080-8721-5615 越久田屋
4.2km
Jūrakuji
Gosho Jinja
御所神社
Kannon-an
観音庵
Gosho E.S.
Donari IC
土成IC
3.7km
山分
Gosho-ōhashi Bridge
御所大橋
Tabi no yado
080-3920-3826
旅の宿
57 Donari
土成
Hiraimizu Daishi
平井水大師
Mehiki Daishi
目引大師
City Office Branch
History Museum
土成歴史館
Miyagochi-Tani River
Awa City
阿波市
318
Oe Taxi (Donari) 088-695-2006
Marunaka
北二条
柿原
二条
Awa-chuō Bridge
阿波中央橋
2.2km
GH Channelkan
(Henro House)
0883-24-7059
チャンネルカン
知恵島
E.S.
Yoshinogawa City
吉野川市

7 Jūrakuji 七番 十楽寺

H Amida Nyorai
58 Donari-chō-takao, Awa City
Free of charge (30)
A By bus bound for Kajiyahara from Tokushima Stn. or Itano Stn. Get off at Higashihara Bus Stop, about 25 min. walk.
☎ 088-695-2150 S Available

In order for Kūkai to obtain the 10 pleasures *(jūraku)* in Buddhist paradise, he gave this temple this name. To the left of the Main Hall is a statue of Jizō Bosatsu which is believed to cure eye problems. As well, there are another 70 Jizō Bosatsu figures for the memorial of children who died before birth or at a infant age *(mizuko)*.

8 Kumadaniji 八番 熊谷寺

H Senju Kannon Bosatsu
185 Donari-maeda, Donari-chō, Awa City
Charge (30)
A By bus bound for Kajiyahara from Tokushima Stn. or Itano Stn. Get off at Higashihara Bus Stop, about 90 min. walk.
☎ 088-695-2065 S None

Kūkai carved a large statue of Senju Kanzeon Bosatsu and placed smaller similar statues inside it. This event marked the founding of this temple. In 1687, the Main gate was built about 200m away. As well, in the gardens, there is a pine tree which looks like a dragon. *(garyū no matsu)*

9 Hōrinji 九番 法輪寺

H Shaka Nyorai
198-2 Donari-chō-tanaka, Awa City
Free of charge (50)
A About 90 min. walk from JR Tokushima Line Kamojima Stn.
☎ 088-695-2080 S None

Kūkai learned that there was a white snake living in a valley nearby that protected Buddhists, so he carved a statue of Shaka Nyorai and founded this temple. The main deity is made in the Nehan style (see pg 32-b) and is the only one along the Shikoku pilgrimage. In the main hall, many straw sandals (waraji) have been hung by people wishing for a cure of some sort of leg ailment.

Mini Shikoku 88-temple pilgrimage routes

ミニ四国八十八ヶ所

Throughout Japan there are many smaller versions of the 88-temple Shikoku pilgrimage route. Some take a few hours to complete, some take about a week. Those on the islands in the Inland Sea are called "Shima Shikoku" and play an important part in the lives of the local people.

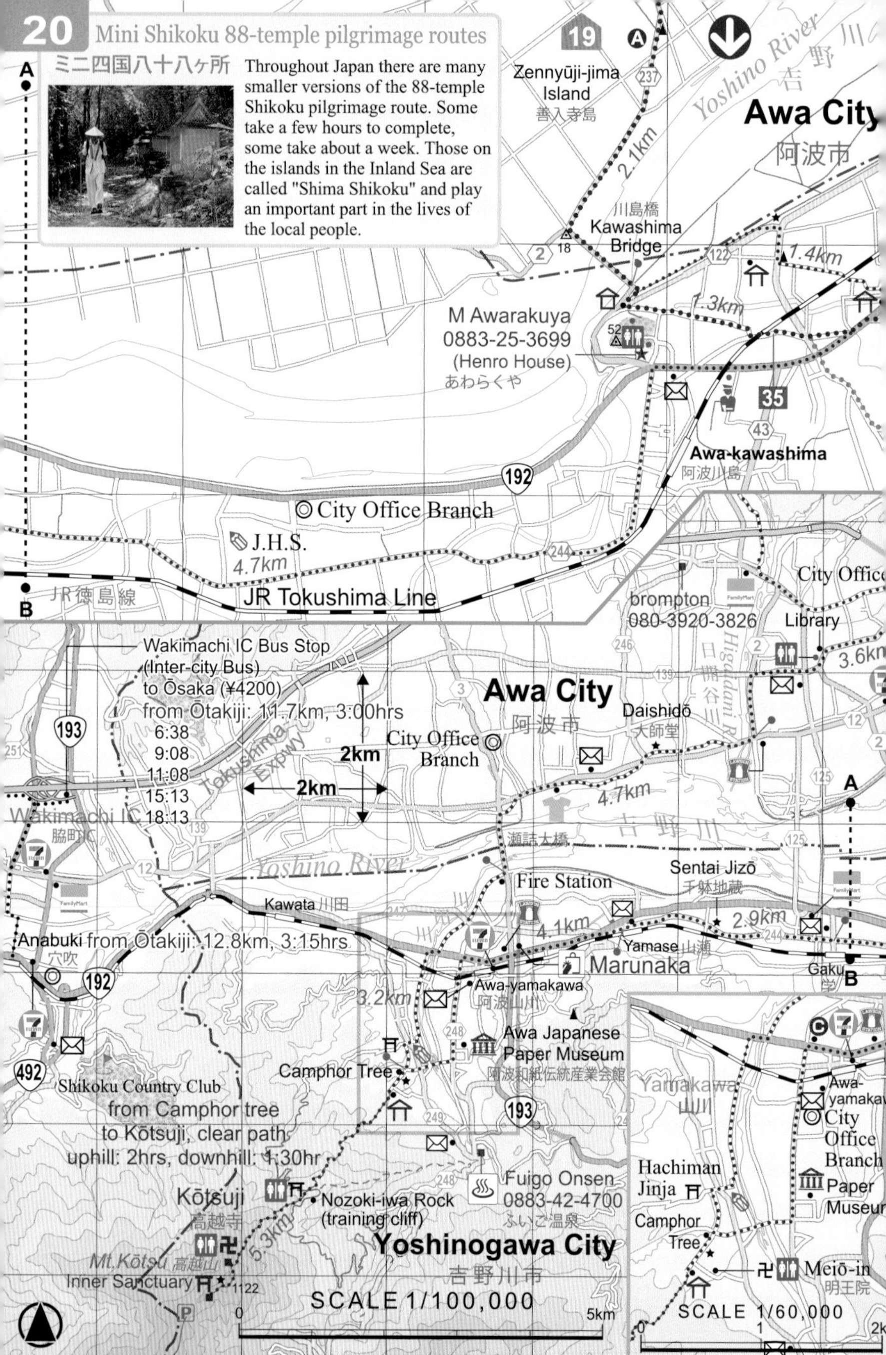

19
Zennyūji-jima Island
善入寺島
Yoshino River
吉野川
Awa City
阿波市
2.1km
川島橋
Kawashima Bridge
1.4km
1.3km
M Awarakuya
0883-25-3699
(Henro House)
あわらくや
35
Awa-kawashima
阿波川島
192
City Office Branch
J.H.S.
4.7km
JR徳島線
JR Tokushima Line
brompton
080-3920-3826
City Office
Library
3.6km
Higadani R.
日開谷川
Wakimachi IC Bus Stop
(Inter-city Bus)
to Ōsaka (¥4200)
from Ōtakiji: 11.7km, 3:00hrs
6:38
9:08
11:08
15:13
18:13
193
Tokushima Expwy
2km
2km
Awa City
阿波市
Daishidō
大師堂
City Office Branch
Wakimachi IC
脇町IC
4.7km
瀬詰大橋
吉野川
Yoshino River
Fire Station
Sentai Jizō
千躰地蔵
Kawata 川田
4.1km
2.9km
Anabuki from Ōtakiji: 12.8km, 3:15hrs
穴吹
Yamase 山瀬
Marunaka
Gaku
Awa-yamakawa
阿波山川
3.2km
Awa Japanese Paper Museum
阿波和紙伝統産業会館
492
Camphor Tree
Shikoku Country Club
from Camphor tree to Kōtsuji, clear path
uphill: 2hrs, downhill: 1:30hr
Kōtsuji
高越寺
Nozoki-iwa Rock
(training cliff)
Fuigo Onsen
0883-42-4700
ふいご温泉
5.3km
Yoshinogawa City
吉野川市
Mt.Kōtsu 高越山
Inner Sanctuary
1122
SCALE 1/100,000
0
5km
Yamakawa
山川
Awa-yamakawa
City Office Branch
Paper Museum
Hachiman Jinja
Camphor Tree
Meiō-in
明王院
SCALE 1/60,000
0
1
2km

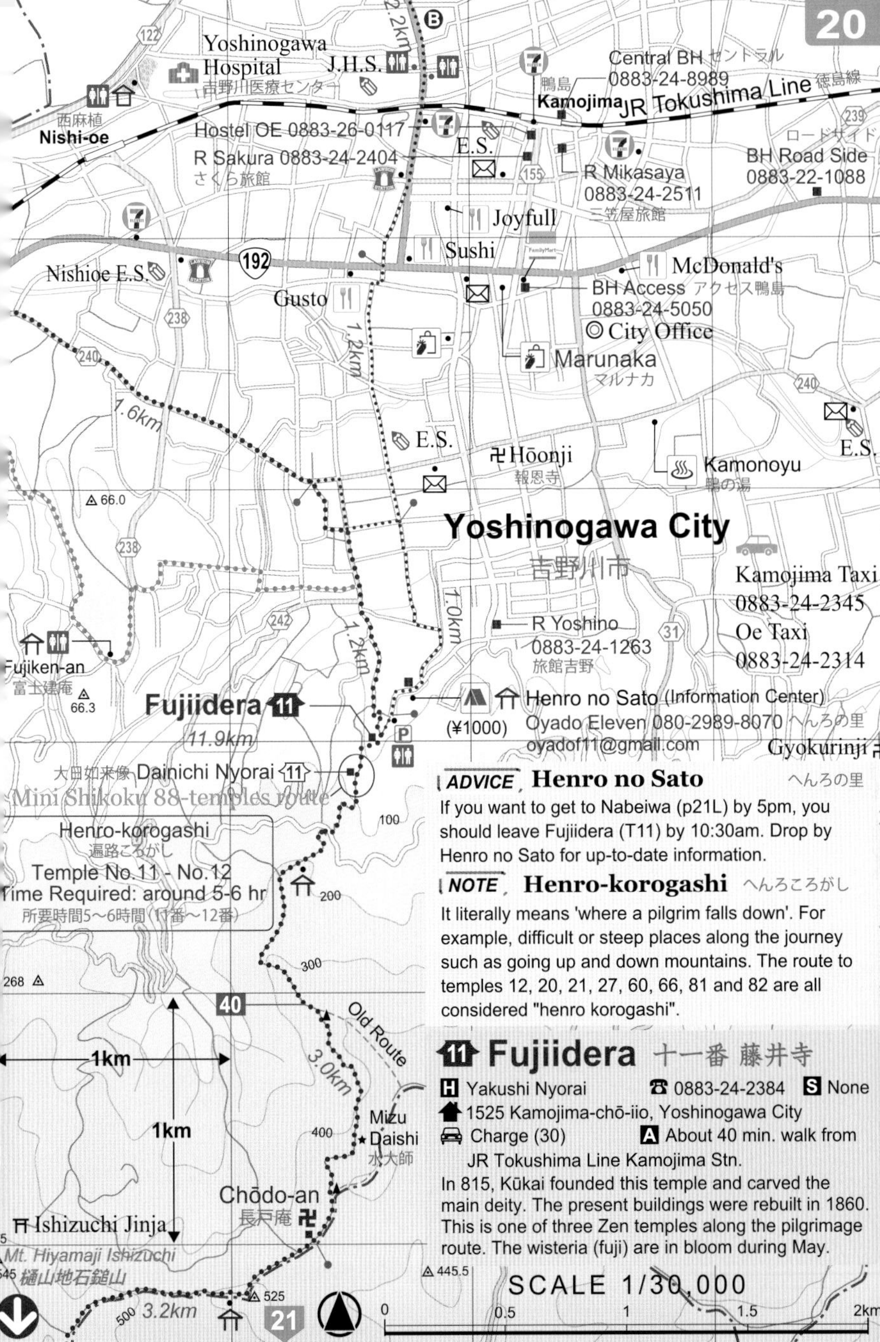

Yoshinogawa Hospital
吉野川医療センター
Yoshinogawa J.H.S.
Central BH セントラル
0883-24-8989
鴨島
Kamojima
JR Tokushima Line 徳島線
西麻植
Nishi-oe
Hostel OE 0883-26-0117
R Sakura 0883-24-2404
さくら旅館
E.S.
R Mikasaya
0883-24-2511
三笠屋旅館
ロードサイド
BH Road Side
0883-22-1088
Joyfull
Sushi
Nishioe E.S.
Gusto
McDonald's
BH Access アクセス鴨島
0883-24-5050
City Office
Marunaka
マルナカ
1.6km
1.2km
2.2km
E.S.
Hōonji
報恩寺
Kamonoyu
鴨の湯
E.S.
66.0
Yoshinogawa City
吉野川市
Kamojima Taxi
0883-24-2345
Oe Taxi
0883-24-2314
1.0km
1.2km
R Yoshino
0883-24-1263
旅館吉野
Fujiken-an
富士建庵
66.3
Fujiidera
11.9km
Henro no Sato (Information Center)
(¥1000)
Oyado Eleven 080-2989-8070 へんろの里
oyadof11@gmail.com
Gyokurinji
大日如来像 Dainichi Nyorai
Mini Shikoku 88-temples route
Henro-korogashi
遍路ころがし
Temple No.11 - No.12
Time Required: around 5-6 hr
所要時間5～6時間（11番～12番）
100
200
300
268
40
Old Route
3.0km
1km
1km
Mizu Daishi
水大師
400
Chōdo-an
長戸庵
Ishizuchi Jinja
Mt. Hiyamaji Ishizuchi
樋山地石鎚山
445.5
525
3.2km
500
21
SCALE 1/30,000
0
0.5
1
1.5
2km

ADVICE **Henro no Sato** へんろの里

If you want to get to Nabeiwa (p21L) by 5pm, you should leave Fujiidera (T11) by 10:30am. Drop by Henro no Sato for up-to-date information.

NOTE **Henro-korogashi** へんろころがし

It literally means 'where a pilgrim falls down'. For example, difficult or steep places along the journey such as going up and down mountains. The route to temples 12, 20, 21, 27, 60, 66, 81 and 82 are all considered "henro korogashi".

11 Fujiidera 十一番 藤井寺

H Yakushi Nyorai ☎ 0883-24-2384 S None

1525 Kamojima-chō-iio, Yoshinogawa City

Charge (30) A About 40 min. walk from JR Tokushima Line Kamojima Stn.

In 815, Kūkai founded this temple and carved the main deity. The present buildings were rebuilt in 1860. This is one of three Zen temples along the pilgrimage route. The wisteria (fuji) are in bloom during May.

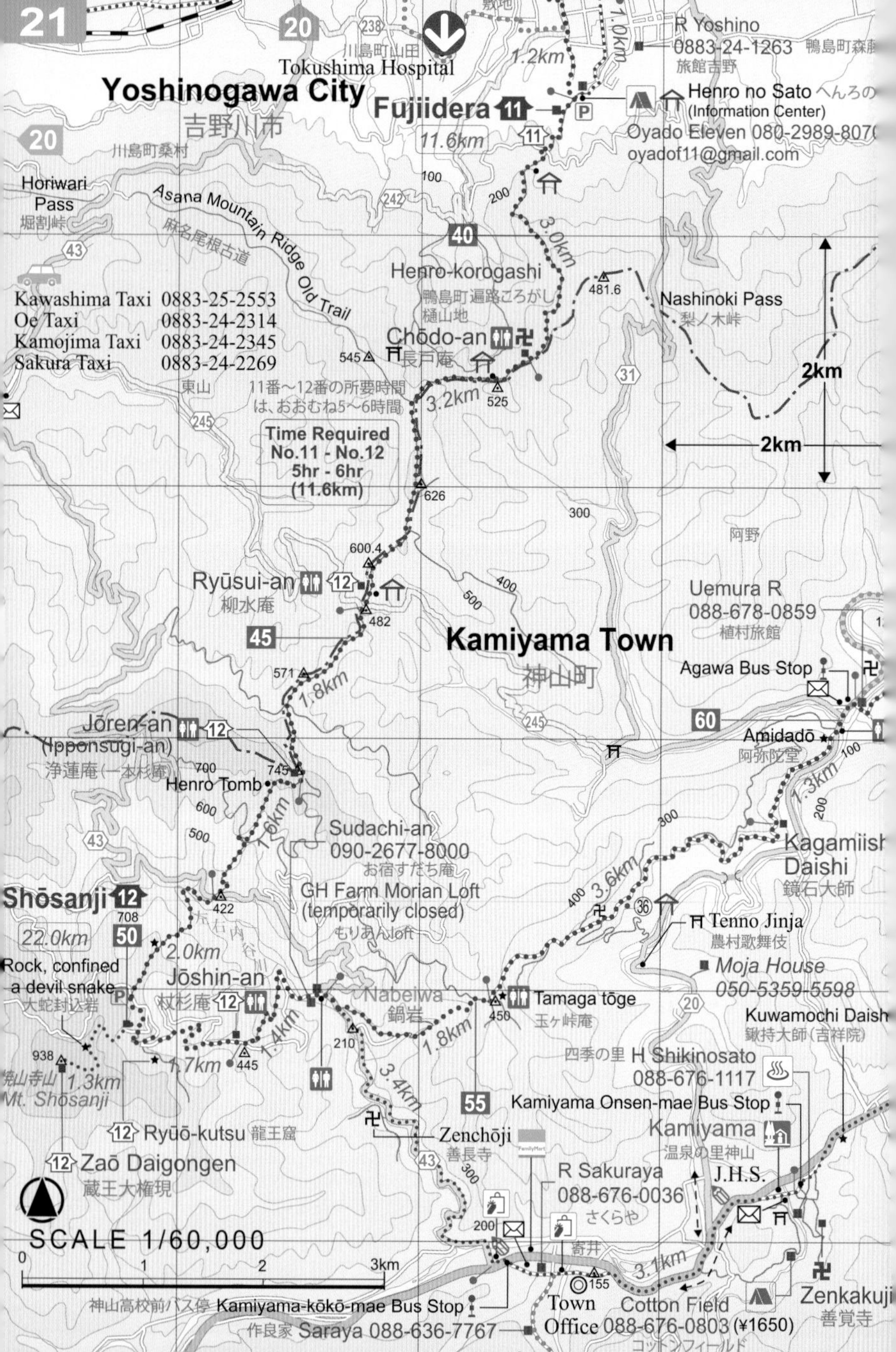

21
Tokushima Hospital
川島町山田
Yoshinogawa City
吉野川市
川島町桑村
Fujiidera 11
11.6km
1.2km
1.0km
R Yoshino
0883-24-1263
鴨島町森藤
旅館吉野
Henro no Sato へんろの
(Information Center)
Oyado Eleven 080-2989-8070
oyadof11@gmail.com
Horiwari Pass
堀割峠
Asana Mountain Ridge Old Trail
麻名尾根古道
3.0km
Henro-korogashi
鴨島町遍路ころがし
樋山地
481.6
Nashinoki Pass
梨ノ木峠
Kawashima Taxi 0883-25-2553
Oe Taxi 0883-24-2314
Kamojima Taxi 0883-24-2345
Sakura Taxi 0883-24-2269
Chōdo-an
長戸庵
545
525
3.2km
2km
東山
11番～12番の所要時間は、おおむね5～6時間
Time Required
No.11 - No.12
5hr - 6hr
(11.6km)
626
300
阿野
600.4
400
500
Ryūsui-an
柳水庵
482
Uemura R
088-678-0859
植村旅館
Kamiyama Town
神山町
571
1.8km
Agawa Bus Stop
Jōren-an
(Ipponsugi-an)
浄蓮庵(一本杉庵)
700
745
Henro Tomb
Amidadō
阿弥陀堂
100
1.3km
200
600
1.6km
Sudachi-an
090-2677-8000
お宿すだち庵
Kagamiishi Daishi
鏡石大師
GH Farm Morian Loft
(temporarily closed)
もりあんloft
3.6km
Shōsanji 12
422
708
22.0km
2.0km
Tenno Jinja
農村歌舞伎
Rock, confined a devil snake
大蛇封込岩
Jōshin-an
杖杉庵
Nabeiwa
鍋岩
Moja House
050-5359-5598
Tamaga tōge
玉ケ峠庵
450
1.4km
1.8km
Kuwamochi Daishi
鍬持大師(吉祥院)
938
445
210
焼山寺山
Mt. Shōsanji
1.3km
1.7km
四季の里 H Shikinosato
088-676-1117
3.4km
Kamiyama Onsen-mae Bus Stop
Kamiyama
温泉の里神山
Ryūō-kutsu 龍王窟
Zenchōji
善長寺
Zaō Daigongen
蔵王大権現
R Sakuraya
088-676-0036
さくらや
J.H.S.
SCALE 1/60,000
0 1 2 3km
200
寄井
3.1km
155
神山高校前バス停 Kamiyama-kōkō-mae Bus Stop
Town Office
Cotton Field
088-676-0803 (¥1650)
コットンフィールド
Zenkakuji
善覚寺
作良家 Saraya 088-636-7767

童学寺 Dōgakuji 2
Ishii Town
石井町
新童学寺
Dōgakuji Tunnel
641m
20
2.0km
100
13番への最短ルート
Shortest Route to Dainichiji
Tokushima Country Club
85
2.9km
70
NEW-TA
088-679-8898
(¥500)
123
Hanotsuji Jinja
Higashi-Tokushima Golf Course
1.0km
2.8km
21
E.S./J.H.S.
Kanshōji
観正寺
入田町
1.8km
Oyasuminashi-tei
おやすみなし亭
22
A
Karuizawa ¥1000
088-678-0981
軽井沢
2.2km
3.4km
Mini Shikoku 88-temples route
65
2.1km
3.7km
100
広野小 E.S.
0.9km
2.3km
200
Konji Waterfall 建治の滝
(Waterfall training)
Sun-pia Golf Club
12 13
22.0km
Public Hall
13
Konjiji
建治寺
Hirono Bus Stop
Tokushima City
徳島市
Shortest Route to Dainichiji
2.7km
13番への最短ルート
3.6km
200
300
495
西龍王山
408
東龍王山
Kamiyama Forest Park
神山森林公園
B
Akui River
鮎喰川
70
.6km
Ōzakura Tunnel
大桜峠
5.4km
207
200
12 13
25.9km
21
to Dainichiji
13番へ
11.2km
9.9km
(Road No.207)
142
12 13
24.6km
250
4.0km
209
Gokumon Pass
獄門峠
160
Yorii Kankō
088-676-0345
Tsubame Kankō
088-678-0224
1.7km
立見峠
215
Orono
鬼籠野
218
3.3km
196
438
新府能トンネル
Weeping cherry blossom section
(late March to early April)

2 Dōgakuji 二番 童学寺

- H Yakushi Nyorai
- Ishii-Jōnouchi, Ishii Town
- 088-674-0138
- A About 25 min. walk from Shimoura Stn.

This temple was given the name of "child - learning - temple" because a young Kūkai spent time studying and learning calligraphy here.

12 Shōsanji 十二番 焼山寺

- H Kokuzō Bosatsu
- 318 Shimobun, Kamiyama Town
- Charge (80) 10 min. walk
- 088-677-0112
- S None
- A By bus bound for Kamiyama-kōkō-mae from Tokushima Stn. Get off at the last stop, about 2 hrs walk.

Kūkai visited here to carry out ascetic training; however, according to legend, a large serpent set fire to the entire mountain *(shōsan)*. While chanting Pure Word *(Shingon)* mantras, Kūkai climbed the mountain under the protection of Kokuzō Bosatsu and confined the dragon into a cave. This cave, which remains today, can be found on the way to the inner sanctuary.

Tokushima Bus (Kamiyama Line)

Blue: Mon - Fri　　2022.10

Stop	Fare											
Kamiyama-kōkō-mae		6:41	7:12	7:51	8:32	10:36	12:51	14:41	15:47	17:31	18:02	19:16
Kamiyama Onsen-mae	¥190	6:47	—	7:57	—	10:42	12:57	14:47	—	17:37	—	19:22
Agawa	¥410	—	7:28	—	8:46	—	—	—	16:03	—	18:18	—
Ichinomiya-fudasho-mae (pg22L)	¥780	7:14	—	8:24	—	11:09	13:24	15:14	—	18:04	—	19:49
Tokushima Station (pg23L)	¥1000	7:49	8:24	9:04	9:44	11:44	13:59	15:49	16:59	18:39	19:14	20:21

16 Kannonji 十六番 観音寺

☎ 088-642-2375
S None

H Senju Kannon Bosatsu 49-2 Kokufu-chō-kanonji, Tokushima City

Free of charge (10) A About 20 min. walk from JR Tokushima Line Kou Stn.

Founded in 741. Kūkai later came, carved, enshrined a statue of Senju Kannon. During the 19th century a woman pilgrim was drying her hakui, which had gotten wet in the rain, over a fire, but the flames caught on the pilgrim coat and she burned herself severely. In the past, she had hit her mother-in-law so this was a punishment of her action. She repented of her bad deed and presented the temple with a painting of this incident with the fire. Between the main gate and the Daishi hall there is a statue of a Yonaki (evening/cry) Jizō, which is said to make children stop crying at night.

15 Kokubunji 十五番 国分寺

☎ 088-642-0525
S None

H Yakushi Nyorai 718-1 Kokufu-chō-yano, Tokushima City

Free of charge (10) A By bus bound for Yorii-naka from Tokushima Stn. Get off at Kokubunji-mae Bus Stop, about 10 min. walk.

Founded by Gyōki. It is one of the provincial temples *(kokubunji)* of Tokushima; however, it was burnt to the ground by the troops of Motochika Chōsokabe (1538-1599) during the 16th century. In 1741, it was rebuilt as a temple belonging to the Zen Sōtō sect. To the left of the main gate, one can see the foundation stones of a seven-storied pagoda. The entire temple grounds have been designated as a noted prefectural historical site.

14 Jōrakuji 十四番 常楽寺

☎ 088-642-0471
S None

H Miroku Bosatsu 606 Kokufu-chō-enmei, Tokushima City

Free of charge (10) A By bus bound for Yorii-naka from Tokushima Stn. Get off at Jōrakuji-mae Bus Stop, about 5 min. walk.

Founded by Kūkai in 815, it is the only temple along the Shikoku pilgrimage route which has Miroku Bosatsu as its main deity. It is said that if a diabetic prays and drinks the boiled leaves from the yew tree beside the main hall that the person will be cured. As well, the scenery of the temple grounds is very unique and at times, mist can be seen rising from the rocks.

13 Dainichiji 十三番 大日寺

☎ 088-644-0069
S temporarily closed

H Jūichimen Kannon Bosatsu 263 Ichinomiya-chō-nishichō, Tokushima City

Free of charge (20) A By bus bound for Yorii-naka from Tokushima Stn. Get off at Ichinomiya-fudasho-mae Bus Stop.

Kūkai visited this area, constructed a shrine and participated in ascetic training. At this time, Dainichi Nyorai appeared and as a result, he carved a statue of Dainichi and founded this temple. Dainichiji takes care of the administration of the locally, well-known Ichinomiya shrine located across the street.

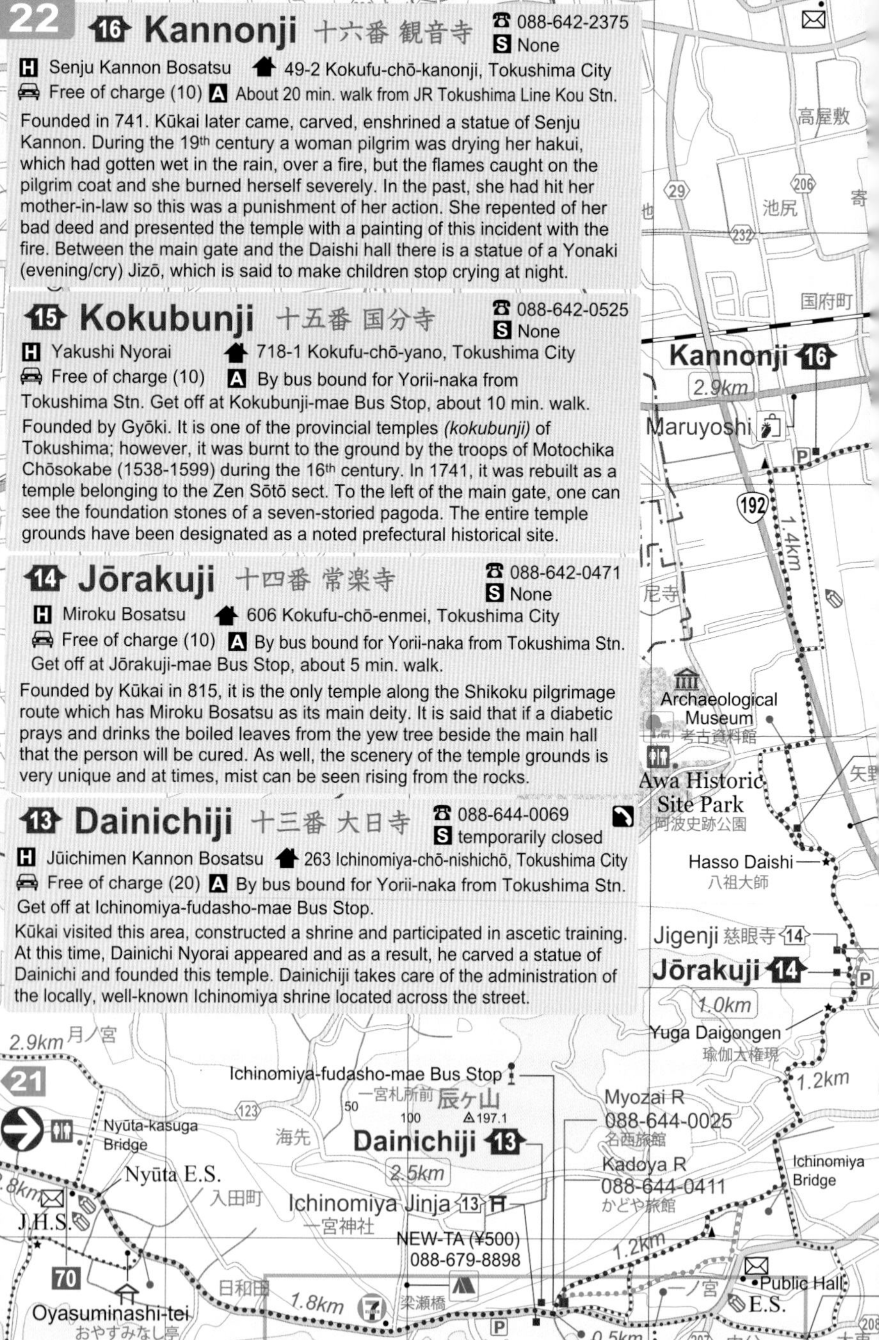

高屋敷
池尻
国府町
Kannonji 16
2.9km
Maruyoshi
1.4km
尼寺
Archaeological Museum
考古資料館
Awa Historic Site Park
阿波史跡公園
Hasso Daishi
八祖大師
Jigenji 慈眼寺 14
Jōrakuji 14
1.0km
Yuga Daigongen
瑜伽大権現
1.2km
2.9km 月ノ宮
21
Ichinomiya-fudasho-mae Bus Stop
一宮札所前
辰ヶ山
197.1
Nyūta-kasuga Bridge
海先
Dainichiji 13
2.5km
Nyūta E.S.
入田町
2.8km
J.H.S.
Ichinomiya Jinja 13
一宮神社
NEW-TA (¥500)
088-679-8898
Myozai R
088-644-0025
名西旅館
Kadoya R
088-644-0411
かどや旅館
Ichinomiya Bridge
1.2km
70
Oyasuminashi-tei
おやすみなし亭
日和田
1.8km
染瀬橋
一ノ宮
Public Hall
E.S.
0.5km
中分
大東

Idoji 17
Idoji-guchi
Bus Stop
井戸寺口バス停
M Matsumotoya
088-642-3772
松本屋
18.7km
80
29
2.1km
1.7km
1.2km
Naka-akui
Bridge
中鮎喰橋
Joyfull
Kyoei
Self Inn
088-676-2818
Church
Kuramoto
1.6km
Akui
鮎喰
JR Tokushima Line
JR徳島線
Kou
府中
Abe
Marunaka
Community Center
Tenguhisa Museum
天狗久資料館
Ōmiwa Jinja
大御和神社
Kokufu E.S.
R Uroko-rō
088-642-4337
鱗楼
Kami-akui
Bridge
Kami-akui
Bus Stop
Drugstore
E.S.
H.S.
Kyoei
1.1km
1.8km
192
E.S.
J.H.S.
Univ
Hospital
Kuramoto
Park
蔵本公園
2.8km
1.3km
1.8km
Ramen
Hōkokuji
法谷寺
加茂名町
23
Akui River
Mt.Bizan
290
眉山
203
Jizōin
地蔵院
70
Cemetery
15 Kokubunji
2.0km
Fukuya
福屋
1km
1km
Jizō-goe Route 地蔵越
Mountain (140m)
route. Same time
required as city route.
140
Bizan Country Club
Golf Course
SCALE 1/30,000
0 0.5 1 1.5 2km
2.6km
75
207
長谷
13
Dainichiji
21
208
A
5.4km
SCALE 1/60,000
B
Tokushima City
徳島市
Kokufu Taxi 088-642-1163
Sakae Taxi 088-642-3334
Akui Taxi 088-642-1050
Anzen Taxi 088-631-4988
Hachiman Onsen
八万温泉
13 Kuninakaji
国中寺
J.H.S.

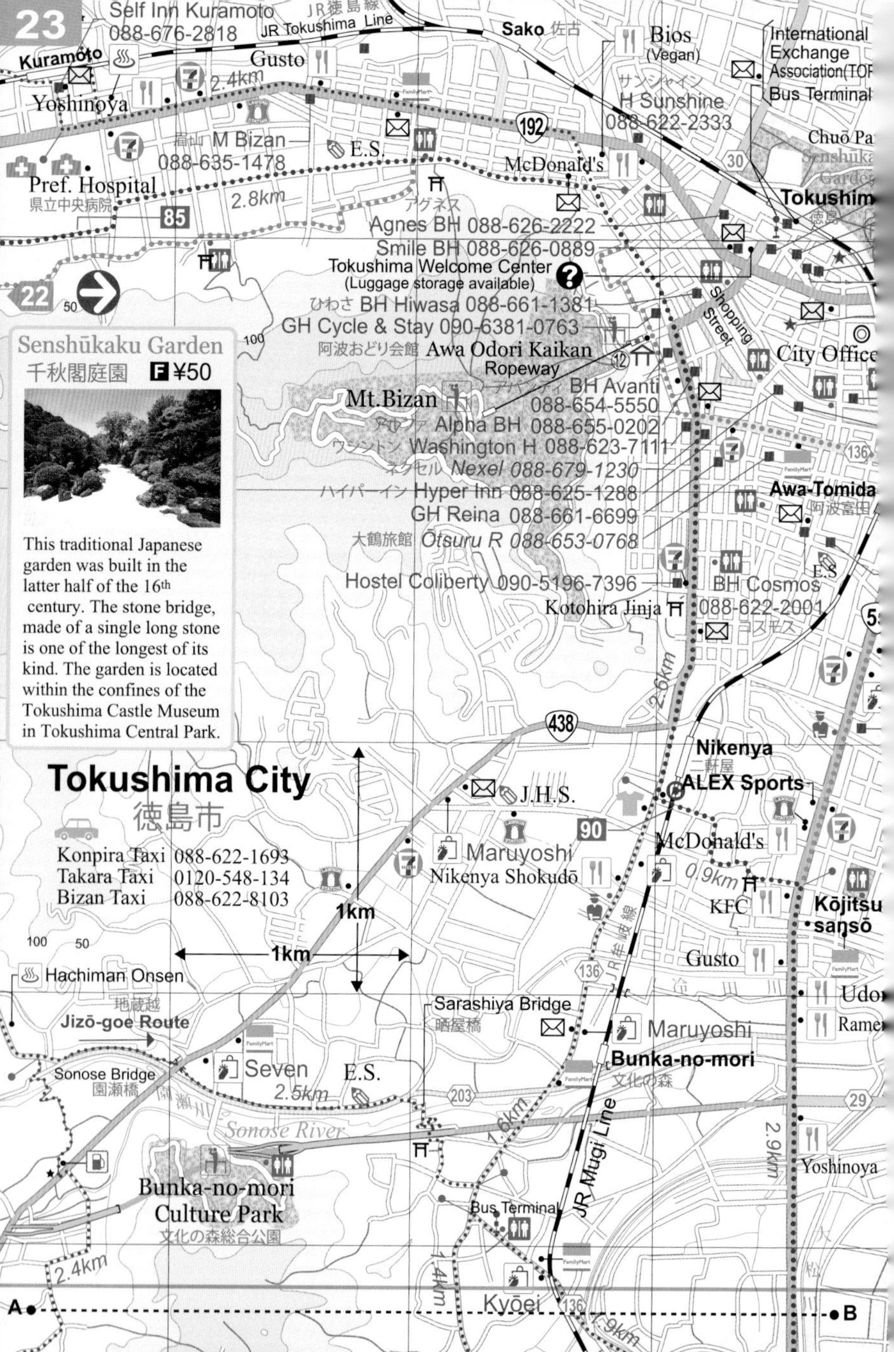
23
Self Inn Kuramoto
088-676-2818
JR徳島線
JR Tokushima Line
Sako 佐古
Bios
(Vegan)
International
Exchange
Association(TOP
Bus Terminal
Kuramoto
Gusto
2.4km
Yoshinoya
サンシャイン
H Sunshine
088-622-2333
眉山 M Bizan
088-635-1478
E.S.
192
Chuō Pa
Pref. Hospital
県立中央病院
McDonald's
30
2.8km
85
アグネス
Agnes BH 088-626-2222
Smile BH 088-626-0889
Tokushima
徳島
Tokushima Welcome Center
(Luggage storage available)
22
ひわさ BH Hiwasa 088-661-1381
GH Cycle & Stay 090-6381-0763
Shopping Street
阿波おどり会館 Awa Odori Kaikan
City Office
Ropeway
Senshūkaku Garden
千秋閣庭園 F ¥50
This traditional Japanese garden was built in the latter half of the 16th century. The stone bridge, made of a single long stone is one of the longest of its kind. The garden is located within the confines of the Tokushima Castle Museum in Tokushima Central Park.
Mt.Bizan
アバンティ BH Avanti
088-654-5550
アルファ Alpha BH 088-655-0202
ワシントン Washington H 088-623-7111
ネクセル Nexel 088-679-1230
ハイパーイン Hyper Inn 088-625-1288
GH Reina 088-661-6699
大鶴旅館 Ōtsuru R 088-653-0768
136
Awa-Tomida
阿波富田
E.S
Hostel Coliberty 090-5196-7396
BH Cosmos
088-622-2001
コスモス
Kotohira Jinja
2.6km
438
Nikenya
二軒屋
ALEX Sports
Tokushima City
徳島市
J.H.S.
90
Konpira Taxi 088-622-1693
Takara Taxi 0120-548-134
Bizan Taxi 088-622-8103
Maruyoshi
Nikenya Shokudō
McDonald's
0.9km
KFC
Kōjitsu sansō
1km
1km
Gusto
Hachiman Onsen
136
Udon
Ramen
地蔵越
Jizō-goe Route
Sarashiya Bridge
晒屋橋
Maruyoshi
Bunka-no-mori
文化の森
Sonose Bridge
園瀬橋
Seven
E.S.
2.5km
203
29
Sonose River
1.6km
JR Mugi Line
2.9km
Yoshinoya
Bunka-no-mori
Culture Park
文化の森総合公園
Bus Terminal
2.4km
1.4km
Kyōei
136
1.9km
A
B

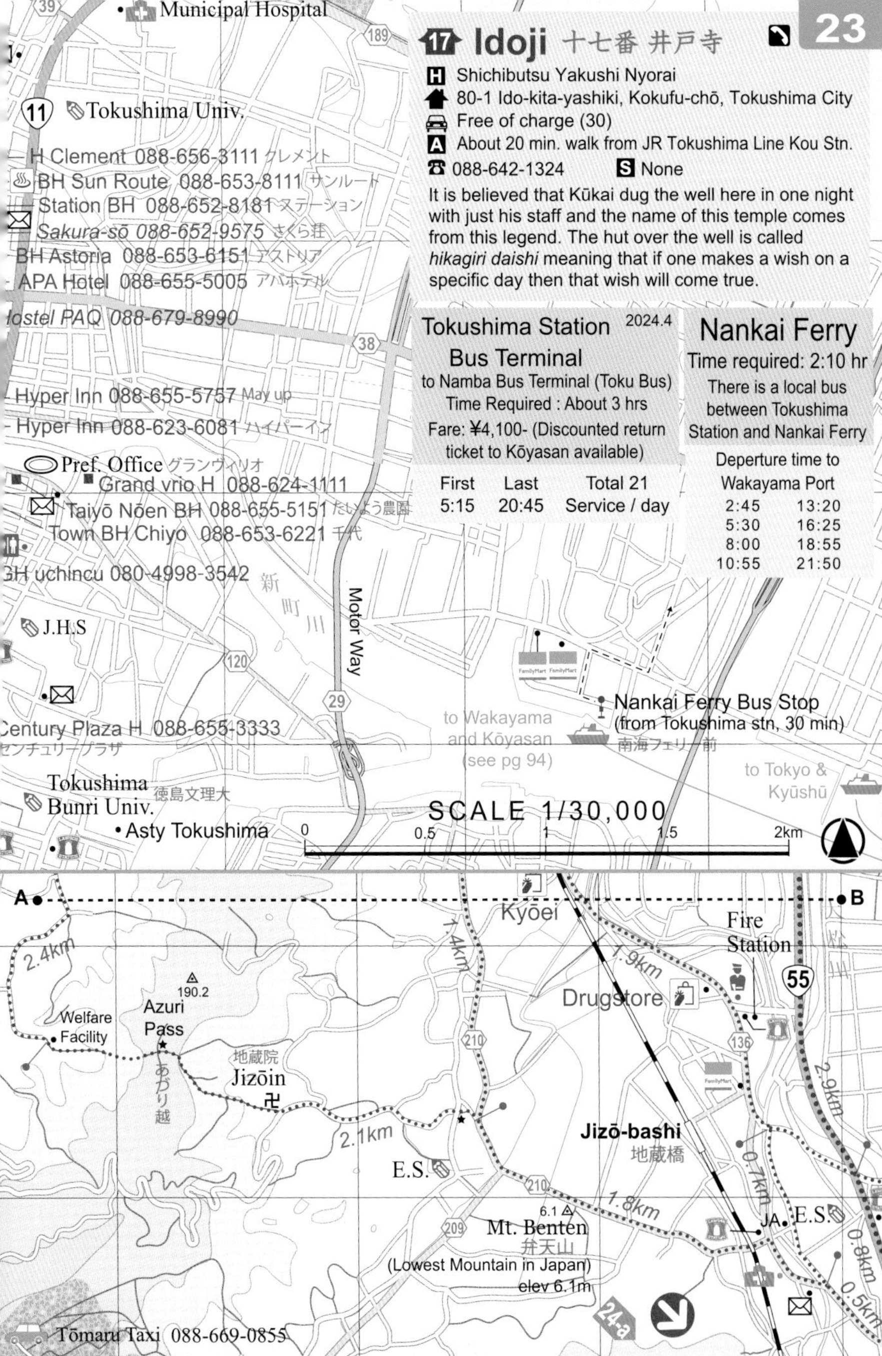

23
17 Idoji 十七番 井戸寺
Shichibutsu Yakushi Nyorai
80-1 Ido-kita-yashiki, Kokufu-chō, Tokushima City
Free of charge (30)
About 20 min. walk from JR Tokushima Line Kou Stn.
088-642-1324
S None
It is believed that Kūkai dug the well here in one night with just his staff and the name of this temple comes from this legend. The hut over the well is called hikagiri daishi meaning that if one makes a wish on a specific day then that wish will come true.
Tokushima Station Bus Terminal 2024.4
to Namba Bus Terminal (Toku Bus)
Time Required : About 3 hrs
Fare: ¥4,100- (Discounted return ticket to Kōyasan available)
First 5:15
Last 20:45
Total 21 Service / day
Nankai Ferry
Time required: 2:10 hr
There is a local bus between Tokushima Station and Nankai Ferry
Deperture time to Wakayama Port
2:45 13:20
5:30 16:25
8:00 18:55
10:55 21:50
Municipal Hospital
Tokushima Univ.
H Clement 088-656-3111 クレメント
BH Sun Route 088-653-8111 サンルート
Station BH 088-652-8181 ステーション
Sakura-sō 088-652-9575 さくら荘
BH Astoria 088-653-6151 アストリア
APA Hotel 088-655-5005 アパホテル
Hostel PAQ 088-679-8990
Hyper Inn 088-655-5757 May up
Hyper Inn 088-623-6081 ハイパーイン
Pref. Office グランヴィリオ
Grand vrio H 088-624-1111
Taiyō Nōen BH 088-655-5151 たいよう農園
Town BH Chiyo 088-653-6221 千代
GH úchincu 080-4998-3542
新町川
J.H.S
Motor Way
Century Plaza H 088-655-3333
センチュリープラザ
Tokushima Bunri Univ.
徳島文理大
Asty Tokushima
Nankai Ferry Bus Stop
(from Tokushima stn, 30 min)
南海フェリー前
to Wakayama and Kōyasan (see pg 94)
to Tokyo & Kyūshū
SCALE 1/30,000
0 0.5 1 1.5 2km
A B
Kyōei
Fire Station
Drugstore
1.4km
1.9km
2.4km
190.2
Azuri Pass
あづり越
Welfare Facility
地蔵院
Jizōin
2.1km
E.S.
Jizō-bashi
地蔵橋
0.7km
1.8km
6.1
Mt. Benten
弁天山
(Lowest Mountain in Japan)
elev 6.1m
JA.
E.S.
2.9km
0.8km
0.5km
24-a
Tōmaru Taxi 088-669-0855

18 Onzanji 十八番 恩山寺

☎ 0885-33-1218　S None

H Yakushi Nyorai　40 Onzanji-dani Tano-chō, Komatsushima City　Free of charge (20)

A By bus bound for Kayahara from Tokushima Stn. Get off at Onzanji-mae Bus Stop, about 15 min. walk

Founded by Gyōki. Originally this temple was off limits to women *(nyonin kinsei)*; but, when Kūkai was training here his mother, Tamayori Gozen, came to visit. She could not proceed past the gate, so Kūkai performed an esoteric rite for 17 days and was able to successfully stop this restriction and bring her on to the temple grounds.

19 Tatsueji 十九番 立江寺

☎ 0885-37-1019　S Available

H Enmei Jizō Bosatsu　Charge (40)

13 Wakamatsu Tatsue-chō, Komatsushima City

A About 5 min. walk from JR Mugi Line Tatsue Stn.

In 815, Kūkai stayed here and carved a statue of Jizō. This is one of the spiritual checkpoint *(sekisho)* temples. In 1803 a woman called Okyō from Shimane Prefecture, who, after killing her husband, came with her lover to Shikoku to make the pilgrimage. When she reached this temple, her hair got entwined in the bell rope. She called for help and asked for repentance. This hair is on display to the right of the Daishi hall. The paintings on the ceiling of the main hall were done by the Tōkyō University of the Arts in 1977.

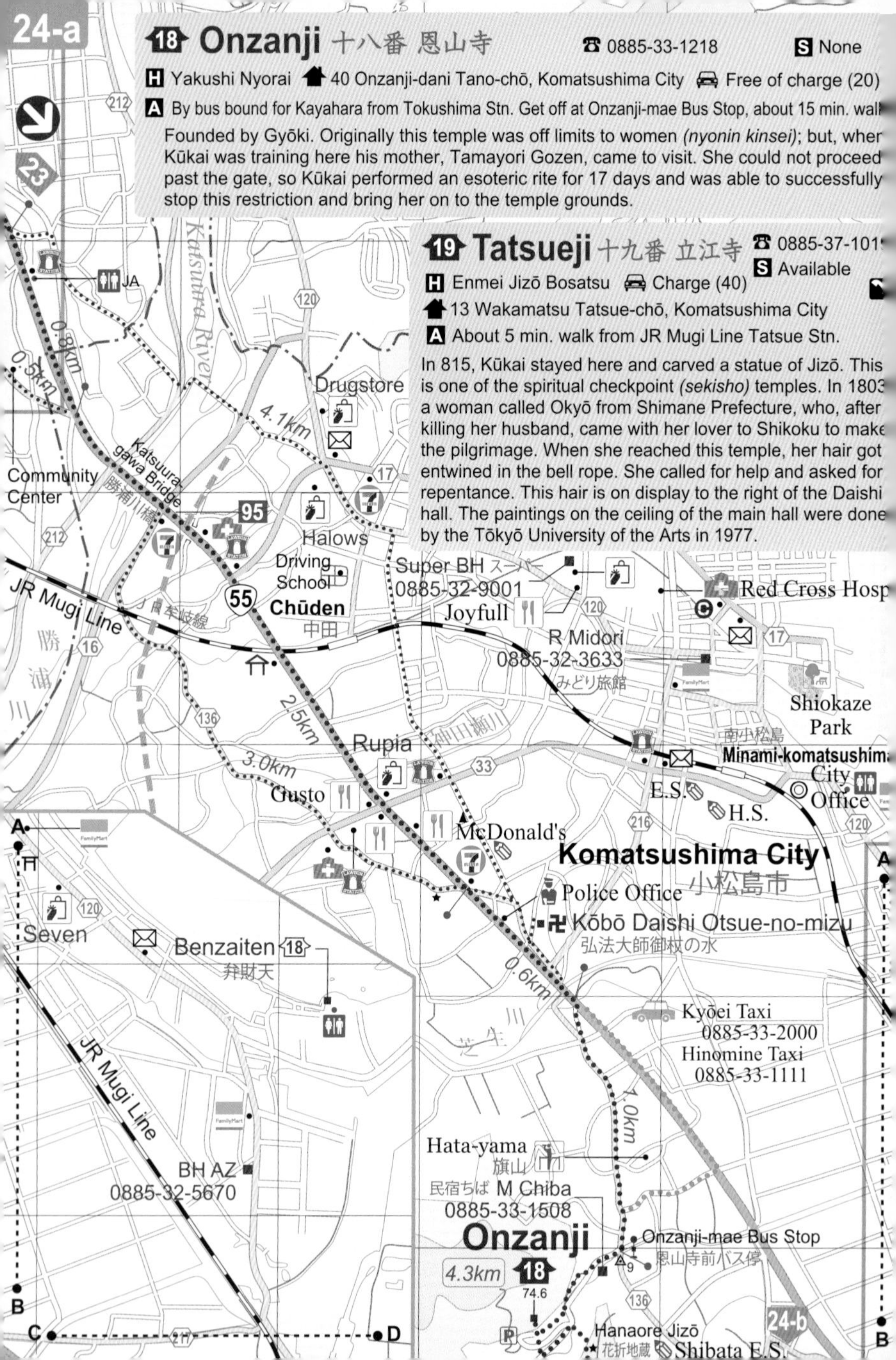

23
JA
Katsuura River
0.8km
0.5km
4.1km
Drugstore
Community Center
Katsuura-gawa Bridge
勝浦川橋
95
Halows
Driving School
55
Chūden
中田
JR Mugi Line
JR牟岐線
勝浦川
Super BH スーパー
0885-32-9001
Joyfull
Red Cross Hosp
R Midori
0885-32-3633
みどり旅館
Shiokaze Park
南小松島
Minami-komatsushima
City Office
2.5km
神田瀬川
Rupia
3.0km
Gusto
E.S.
H.S.
McDonald's
Komatsushima City
小松島市
Police Office
Kōbō Daishi Otsue-no-mizu
弘法大師御杖の水
Seven
Benzaiten
弁財天
0.6km
Kyōei Taxi
0885-33-2000
Hinomine Taxi
0885-33-1111
JR Mugi Line
1.0km
Hata-yama
旗山
民宿ちば M Chiba
0885-33-1508
BH AZ
0885-32-5670
Onzanji
Onzanji-mae Bus Stop
恩山寺前バス停
4.3km
18
74.6
Hanaore Jizō
花折地蔵
Shibata E.S.
24-b
A
B
C
D

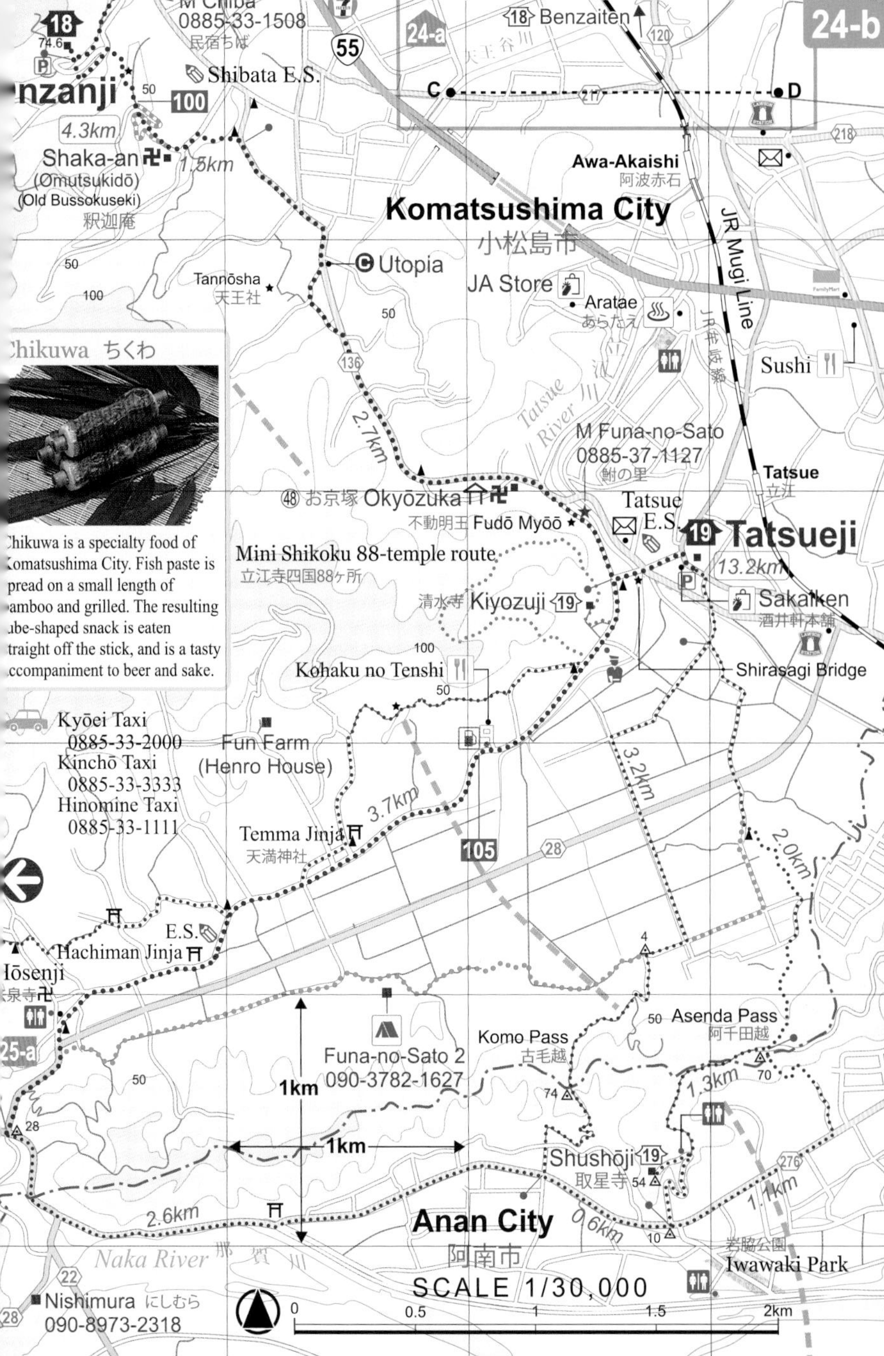
24-b
M Chiba
0885-33-1508
民宿ちば
Benzaiten
Shibata E.S.
24-a
C
D
nzanji
100
4.3km
Shaka-an
1.5km
(Ømutsukidō)
(Old Bussokuseki)
釈迦庵
Awa-Akaishi
阿波赤石
Komatsushima City
小松島市
JR Mugi Line
Utopia
Tannōsha
天王社
JA Store
Aratae
あらたえ
Sushi
Tatsue River
M Funa-no-Sato
0885-37-1127
鮒の里
Tatsue
立江
2.7km
48 お京塚 Okyōzuka
不動明王 Fudō Myōō
Tatsue E.S.
19 Tatsueji
13.2km
Mini Shikoku 88-temple route
立江寺四国88ヶ所
清水寺 Kiyozuji
Sakaiken
酒井軒本舗
Kohaku no Tenshi
Shirasagi Bridge
Chikuwa ちくわ
Chikuwa is a specialty food of Komatsushima City. Fish paste is spread on a small length of bamboo and grilled. The resulting tube-shaped snack is eaten straight off the stick, and is a tasty accompaniment to beer and sake.
Kyōei Taxi
0885-33-2000
Kinchō Taxi
0885-33-3333
Hinomine Taxi
0885-33-1111
Fun Farm
(Henro House)
3.2km
3.7km
Temma Jinja
天満神社
105
2.0km
E.S.
Hachiman Jinja
Hōsenji
宝泉寺
25-a
Asenda Pass
阿千田越
Komo Pass
古毛越
Funa-no-Sato 2
090-3782-1627
1km
1km
1.3km
2.6km
Shushōji
取星寺
1.1km
0.6km
Anan City
阿南市
Naka River 那賀川
岩脇公園
Iwawaki Park
SCALE 1/30,000
0 0.5 1 1.5 2km
Nishimura にしむら
090-8973-2318

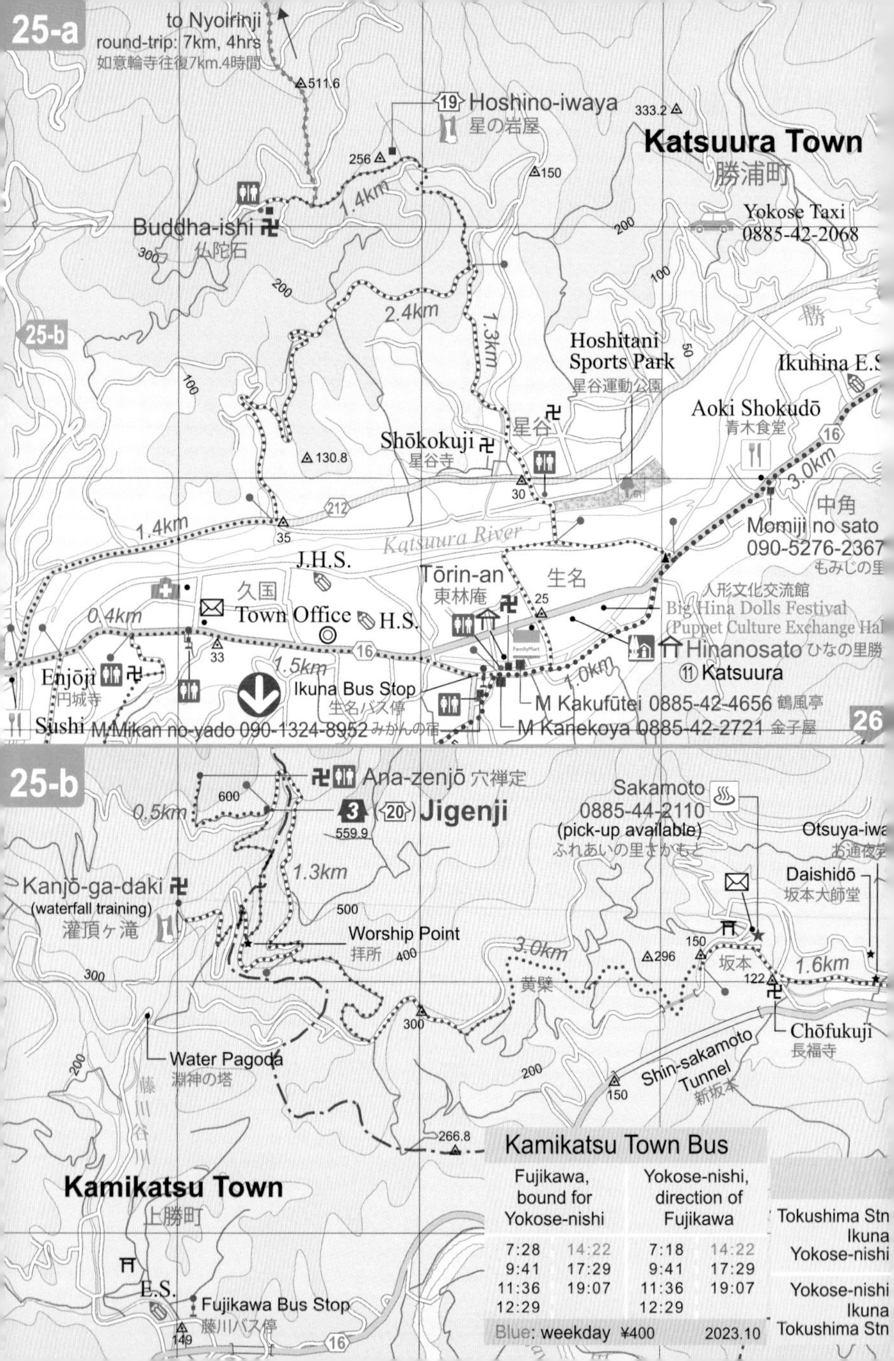
25-a
to Nyoirinji
round-trip: 7km, 4hrs
如意輪寺往復7km.4時間
511.6
19 Hoshino-iwaya
星の岩屋
333.2
Katsuura Town
勝浦町
256
150
1.4km
Buddha-ishi
仏陀石
300
200
Yokose Taxi
0885-42-2068
200
100
25-b
2.4km
1.3km
Hoshitani
Sports Park
星谷運動公園
50
Ikuhina E.S.
100
Aoki Shokudō
青木食堂
星谷
Shōkokuji
星谷寺
16
130.8
3.0km
30
212
中角
1.4km
35
Katsuura River
Momiji no sato
090-5276-2367
もみじの里
J.H.S.
Tōrin-an
東林庵
生名
久国
人形文化交流館
Big Hina Dolls Festival
(Puppet Culture Exchange Hall)
25
Town Office
H.S.
0.4km
Hinanosato ひなの里勝
16
1.5km
33
1.0km
11 Katsuura
Enjōji
円城寺
Ikuna Bus Stop
生名バス停
M Kakufūtei 0885-42-4656 鶴風亭
Sushi
M Mikan no-yado 090-1324-8952 みかんの宿
M Kanekoya 0885-42-2721 金子屋
26
25-b
Ana-zenjō 穴禅定
600
0.5km
3 20 Jigenji
559.9
Sakamoto
0885-44-2110
(pick-up available)
ふれあいの里さかもと
Otsuya-iwa
お通夜岩
1.3km
Kanjō-ga-daki
(waterfall training)
灌頂ヶ滝
Daishidō
坂本大師堂
500
Worship Point
拝所
400
3.0km
296
150
坂本
1.6km
黄檗
122
300
300
Chōfukuji
長福寺
Water Pagoda
淵神の塔
200
200
Shin-sakamoto
Tunnel
新坂本
150
藤川谷川
266.8
Kamikatsu Town
上勝町
E.S.
Fujikawa Bus Stop
藤川バス停
149
16

Kamikatsu Town Bus

Fujikawa, bound for Yokose-nishi		Yokose-nishi, direction of Fujikawa	
7:28	14:22	7:18	14:22
9:41	17:29	9:41	17:29
11:36	19:07	11:36	19:07
12:29		12:29	

Blue: weekday ¥400 2023.10

Tokushima Stn
Ikuna
Yokose-nishi

Yokose-nishi
Ikuna
Tokushima Stn

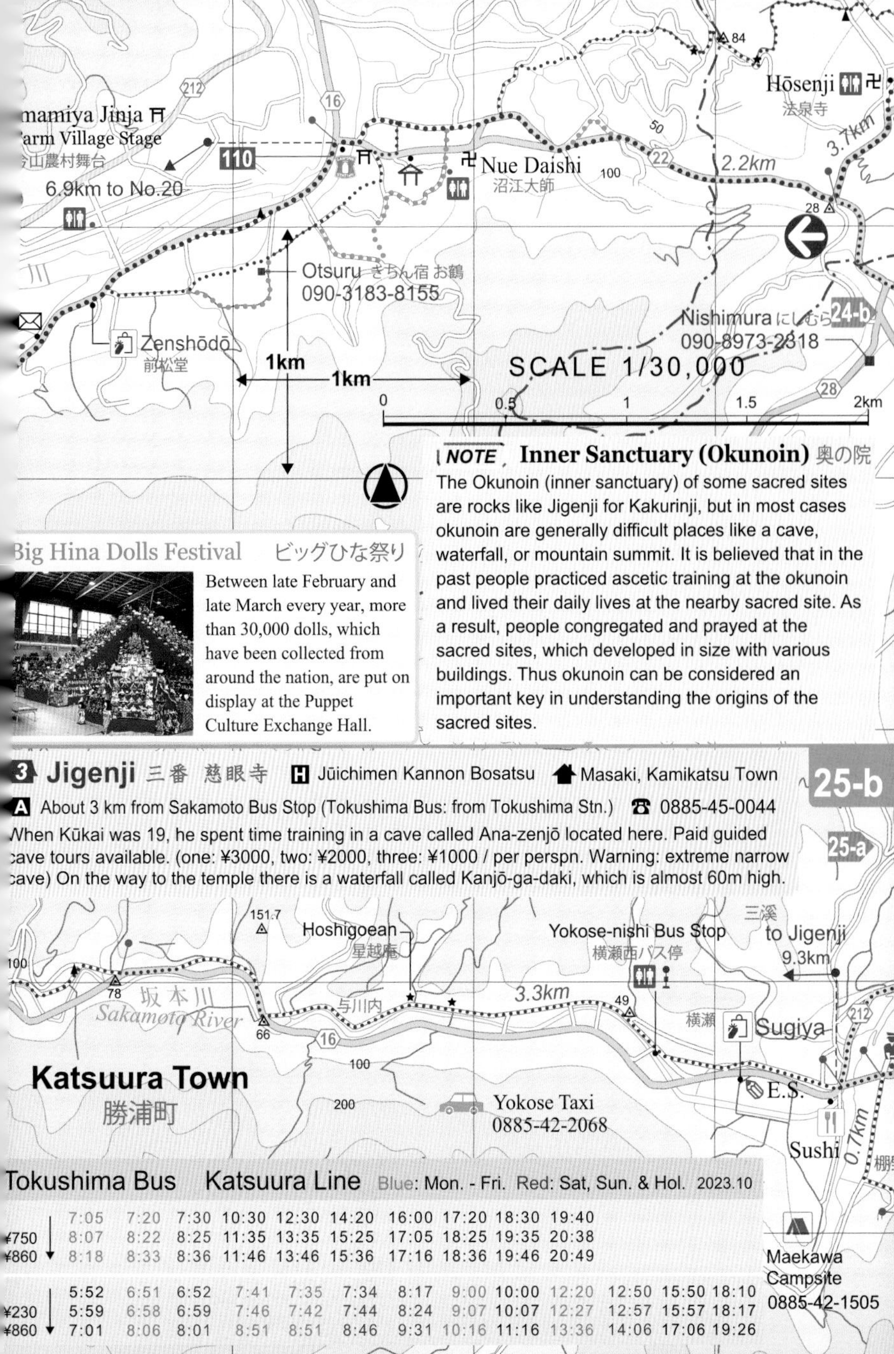

mamiya Jinja
Farm Village Stage
谷山農村舞台
110
6.9km to No.20
Nue Daishi
沼江大師
Otsuru きちん宿 お鶴
090-3183-8155
Zenshōdō
前松堂
1km
1km
Hōsenji
法泉寺
2.2km
3.7km
Nishimura にしむら
090-8973-2318
24-b
SCALE 1/30,000
0
0.5
1
1.5
2km
25-b
25-a
Hoshigoean
星越庵
151.7
78
66
49
坂本川
Sakamoto River
与川内
3.3km
Yokose-nishi Bus Stop
横瀬西バス停
三溪
to Jigenji
9.3km
横瀬
Sugiya
E.S.
Sushi
0.7km
Katsuura Town
勝浦町
Yokose Taxi
0885-42-2068
Maekawa
Campsite
0885-42-1505

Big Hina Dolls Festival ビッグひな祭り

Between late February and late March every year, more than 30,000 dolls, which have been collected from around the nation, are put on display at the Puppet Culture Exchange Hall.

NOTE Inner Sanctuary (Okunoin) 奥の院

The Okunoin (inner sanctuary) of some sacred sites are rocks like Jigenji for Kakurinji, but in most cases okunoin are generally difficult places like a cave, waterfall, or mountain summit. It is believed that in the past people practiced ascetic training at the okunoin and lived their daily lives at the nearby sacred site. As a result, people congregated and prayed at the sacred sites, which developed in size with various buildings. Thus okunoin can be considered an important key in understanding the origins of the sacred sites.

3 Jigenji 三番 慈眼寺

H Jūichimen Kannon Bosatsu — Masaki, Kamikatsu Town

A About 3 km from Sakamoto Bus Stop (Tokushima Bus: from Tokushima Stn.) ☎ 0885-45-0044

When Kūkai was 19, he spent time training in a cave called Ana-zenjō located here. Paid guided cave tours available. (one: ¥3000, two: ¥2000, three: ¥1000 / per perspn. Warning: extreme narrow cave) On the way to the temple there is a waterfall called Kanjō-ga-daki, which is almost 60m high.

Tokushima Bus Katsuura Line

Blue: Mon. - Fri. Red: Sat, Sun. & Hol. 2023.10

↓	7:05	7:20	7:30	10:30	12:30	14:20	16:00	17:20	18:30	19:40
¥750	8:07	8:22	8:25	11:35	13:35	15:25	17:05	18:25	19:35	20:38
¥860 ↓	8:18	8:33	8:36	11:46	13:46	15:36	17:16	18:36	19:46	20:49

↓	5:52	6:51	6:52	7:41	7:35	7:34	8:17	9:00	10:00	12:20	12:50	15:50	18:10
¥230	5:59	6:58	6:59	7:46	7:42	7:44	8:24	9:07	10:07	12:27	12:57	15:57	18:17
¥860 ↓	7:01	8:06	8:01	8:51	8:51	8:46	9:31	10:16	11:16	13:36	14:06	17:06	19:26

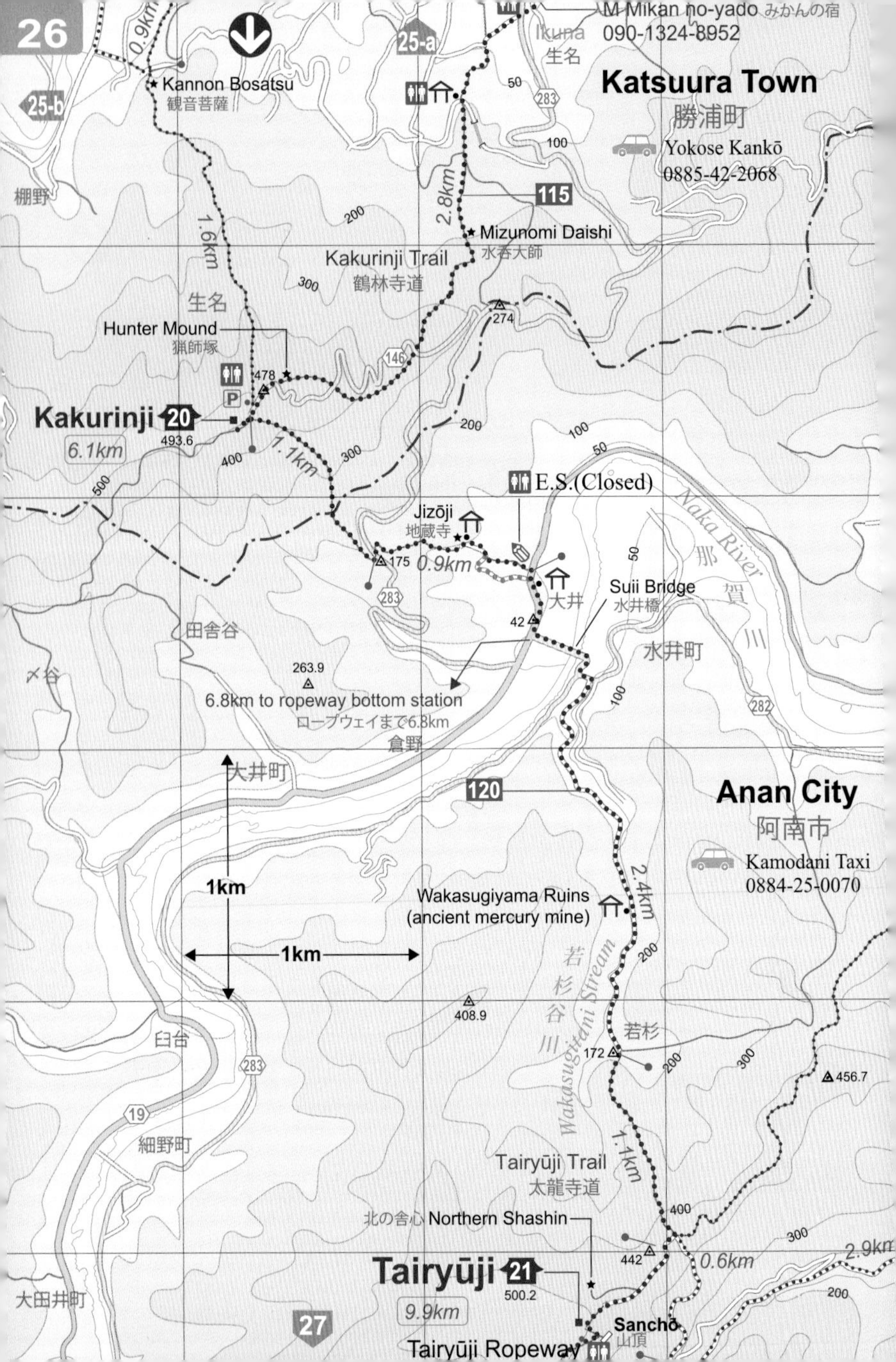

25-a
25-b
M Mikan no-yado みかんの宿
090-1324-8952
Ikuna
生名
Kannon Bosatsu
観音菩薩
0.9km
Katsuura Town
勝浦町
Yokose Kankō
0885-42-2068
115
2.8km
Mizunomi Daishi
水呑大師
Kakurinji Trail
鶴林寺道
1.6km
棚野
生名
Hunter Mound
猟師塚
478
274
146
Kakurinji
20
493.6
6.1km
1.1km
E.S.(Closed)
Jizōji
地蔵寺
175
0.9km
283
Naka River
那賀川
Suii Bridge
水井橋
大井
42
水井町
田舎谷
メ谷
263.9
6.8km to ropeway bottom station
ロープウェイまで6.8km
倉野
282
大井町
120
Anan City
阿南市
Kamodani Taxi
0884-25-0070
1km
1km
Wakasugiyama Ruins
(ancient mercury mine)
2.4km
若杉谷川
Wakasugitani Stream
408.9
臼台
若杉
172
456.7
283
19
細野町
1.1km
Tairyūji Trail
太龍寺道
北の舎心 Northern Shashin
442
0.6km
2.9km
Tairyūji
21
500.2
9.9km
大田井町
27
Sanchō
山頂
Tairyūji Ropeway

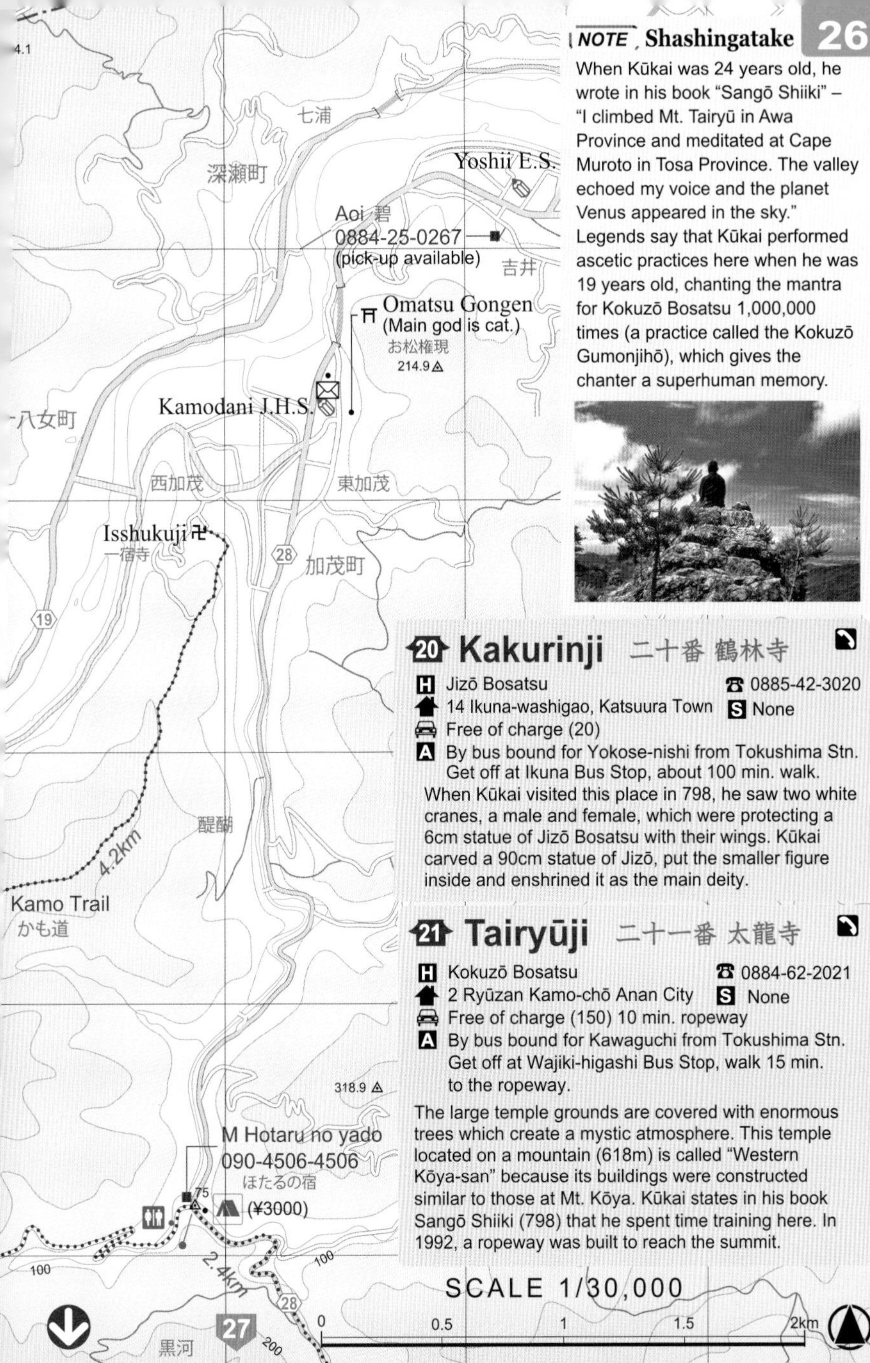

七浦
深瀬町
Yoshii E.S.
Aoi 碧
0884-25-0267
(pick-up available)
吉井
Omatsu Gongen
(Main god is cat.)
お松権現
214.9
Kamodani J.H.S.
八女町
西加茂
東加茂
Isshukuji
一宿寺
28
加茂町
19
醍醐
4.2km
Kamo Trail
かも道
318.9
M Hotaru no yado
090-4506-4506
ほたるの宿
75
(¥3000)
100
2.4km
100
28
27
200
黒河
SCALE 1/30,000
0
0.5
1
1.5
2km

NOTE Shashingatake

When Kūkai was 24 years old, he wrote in his book "Sangō Shiiki" – "I climbed Mt. Tairyū in Awa Province and meditated at Cape Muroto in Tosa Province. The valley echoed my voice and the planet Venus appeared in the sky." Legends say that Kūkai performed ascetic practices here when he was 19 years old, chanting the mantra for Kokuzō Bosatsu 1,000,000 times (a practice called the Kokuzō Gumonjihō), which gives the chanter a superhuman memory.

20 Kakurinji 二十番 鶴林寺

H Jizō Bosatsu ☎ 0885-42-3020
14 Ikuna-washigao, Katsuura Town S None
Free of charge (20)
A By bus bound for Yokose-nishi from Tokushima Stn. Get off at Ikuna Bus Stop, about 100 min. walk.

When Kūkai visited this place in 798, he saw two white cranes, a male and female, which were protecting a 6cm statue of Jizō Bosatsu with their wings. Kūkai carved a 90cm statue of Jizō, put the smaller figure inside and enshrined it as the main deity.

21 Tairyūji 二十一番 太龍寺

H Kokuzō Bosatsu ☎ 0884-62-2021
2 Ryūzan Kamo-chō Anan City S None
Free of charge (150) 10 min. ropeway
A By bus bound for Kawaguchi from Tokushima Stn. Get off at Wajiki-higashi Bus Stop, walk 15 min. to the ropeway.

The large temple grounds are covered with enormous trees which create a mystic atmosphere. This temple located on a mountain (618m) is called "Western Kōya-san" because its buildings were constructed similar to those at Mt. Kōya. Kūkai states in his book Sangō Shiiki (798) that he spent time training here. In 1992, a ropeway was built to reach the summit.

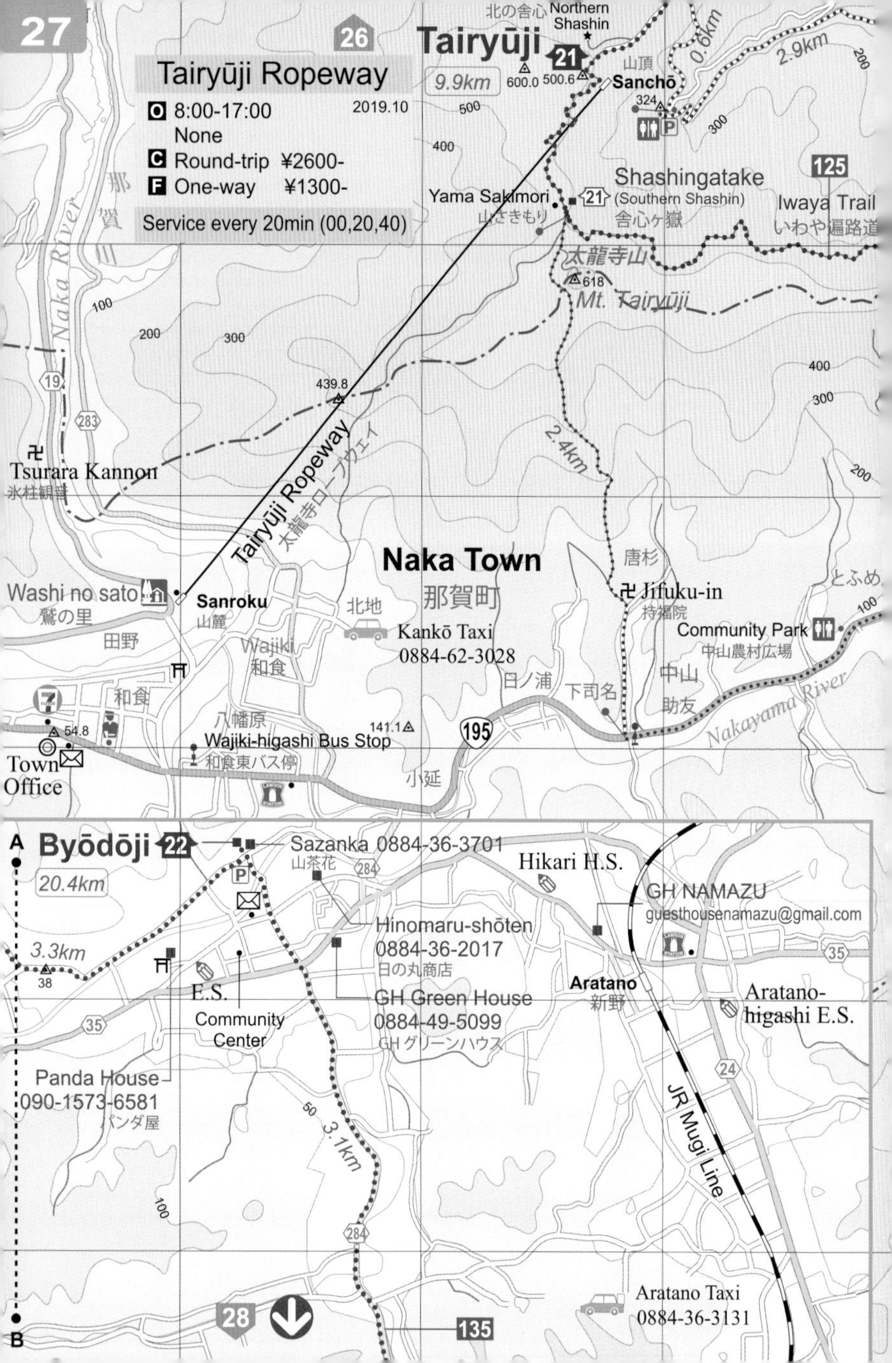

26
Tairyūji
21
9.9km
北の舎心 Northern Shashin
Sanchō
山頂
600.0
500.6
324
0.6km
2.9km
Tairyūji Ropeway
8:00-17:00
None
Round-trip ¥2600-
One-way ¥1300-
2019.10
Service every 20min (00,20,40)
Yama Sakimori
山さきもり
Shashingatake
(Southern Shashin)
舎心ヶ嶽
125
Iwaya Trail
いわや遍路道
太龍寺山
618
Mt. Tairyūji
那賀川
Naka River
19
283
439.8
Tairyūji Ropeway
太龍寺ロープウェイ
2.4km
Tsurara Kannon
氷柱観音
Naka Town
那賀町
唐杉
Jifuku-in
持福院
とふめ
Washi no sato
鷲の里
Sanroku
山麓
田野
北地
Wajiki
和食
Kankō Taxi
0884-62-3028
Community Park
中山農村広場
日ノ浦
下司名
中山
助友
Nakayama River
和食
八幡原
54.8
141.1
195
Wajiki-higashi Bus Stop
和食東バス停
Town Office
小延
Byōdōji
22
20.4km
Sazanka 0884-36-3701
山茶花
284
Hikari H.S.
GH NAMAZU
guesthousenamazu@gmail.com
3.3km
38
Hinomaru-shōten
0884-36-2017
日の丸商店
35
E.S.
Community Center
GH Green House
0884-49-5099
GHグリーンハウス
Aratano
新野
Aratano-higashi E.S.
35
24
Panda House
090-1573-6581
パンダ屋
3.1km
JR Mugi Line
284
Aratano Taxi
0884-36-3131
28
135
A
B

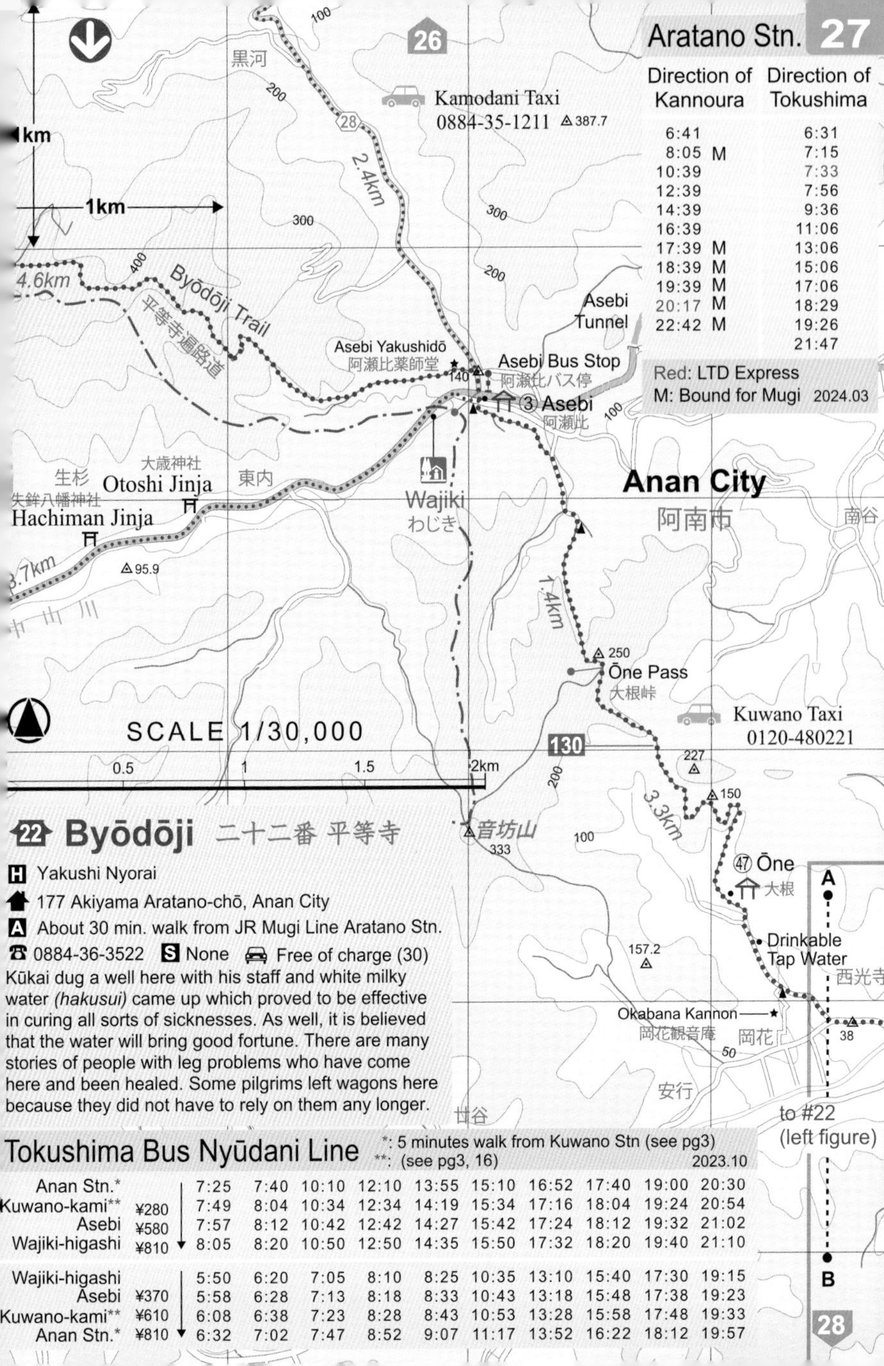

1km
1km
26
黒河
Kamodani Taxi
0884-35-1211
387.7
28
2.4km
4.6km
Byōdōji Trail
平等寺遍路道
Asebi Yakushidō
阿瀬比薬師堂
140
Asebi Bus Stop
阿瀬比バス停
③ Asebi
阿瀬比
Asebi Tunnel
大歳神社
Otoshi Jinja
生杉
矢鉾八幡神社
Hachiman Jinja
東内
Wajiki
わじき
95.9
3.7km
Anan City
阿南市
南谷
1.4km
250
Ōne Pass
大根峠
Kuwano Taxi
0120-480221
130
227
150
3.3km
音坊山
333
⑰ Ōne
大根
Drinkable Tap Water
西光寺
157.2
Okabana Kannon
岡花観音庵
岡花
38
安行
廿谷
A
B
to #22 (left figure)
28
SCALE 1/30,000
0.5
1
1.5
2km

Aratano Stn. 27

Direction of Kannoura		Direction of Tokushima
6:41		6:31
8:05	M	7:15
10:39		7:33
12:39		7:56
14:39		9:36
16:39		11:06
17:39	M	13:06
18:39	M	15:06
19:39	M	17:06
20:17	M	18:29
22:42	M	19:26
		21:47

Red: LTD Express
M: Bound for Mugi 2024.03

22 Byōdōji 二十二番 平等寺

H Yakushi Nyorai

177 Akiyama Aratano-chō, Anan City

A About 30 min. walk from JR Mugi Line Aratano Stn.

☎ 0884-36-3522 S None 🚗 Free of charge (30)

Kūkai dug a well here with his staff and white milky water *(hakusui)* came up which proved to be effective in curing all sorts of sicknesses. As well, it is believed that the water will bring good fortune. There are many stories of people with leg problems who have come here and been healed. Some pilgrims left wagons here because they did not have to rely on them any longer.

Tokushima Bus Nyūdani Line

*: 5 minutes walk from Kuwano Stn (see pg3)
**: (see pg3, 16)
2023.10

Stop	Fare										
Anan Stn.*		7:25	7:40	10:10	12:10	13:55	15:10	16:52	17:40	19:00	20:30
Kuwano-kami**	¥280	7:49	8:04	10:34	12:34	14:19	15:34	17:16	18:04	19:24	20:54
Asebi	¥580	7:57	8:12	10:42	12:42	14:27	15:42	17:24	18:12	19:32	21:02
Wajiki-higashi	¥810	8:05	8:20	10:50	12:50	14:35	15:50	17:32	18:20	19:40	21:10

Stop	Fare										
Wajiki-higashi		5:50	6:20	7:05	8:10	8:25	10:35	13:10	15:40	17:30	19:15
Asebi	¥370	5:58	6:28	7:13	8:18	8:33	10:43	13:18	15:48	17:38	19:23
Kuwano-kami**	¥610	6:08	6:38	7:23	8:28	8:43	10:53	13:28	15:58	17:48	19:33
Anan Stn.*	¥810	6:32	7:02	7:47	8:52	9:07	11:17	13:52	16:22	18:12	19:57

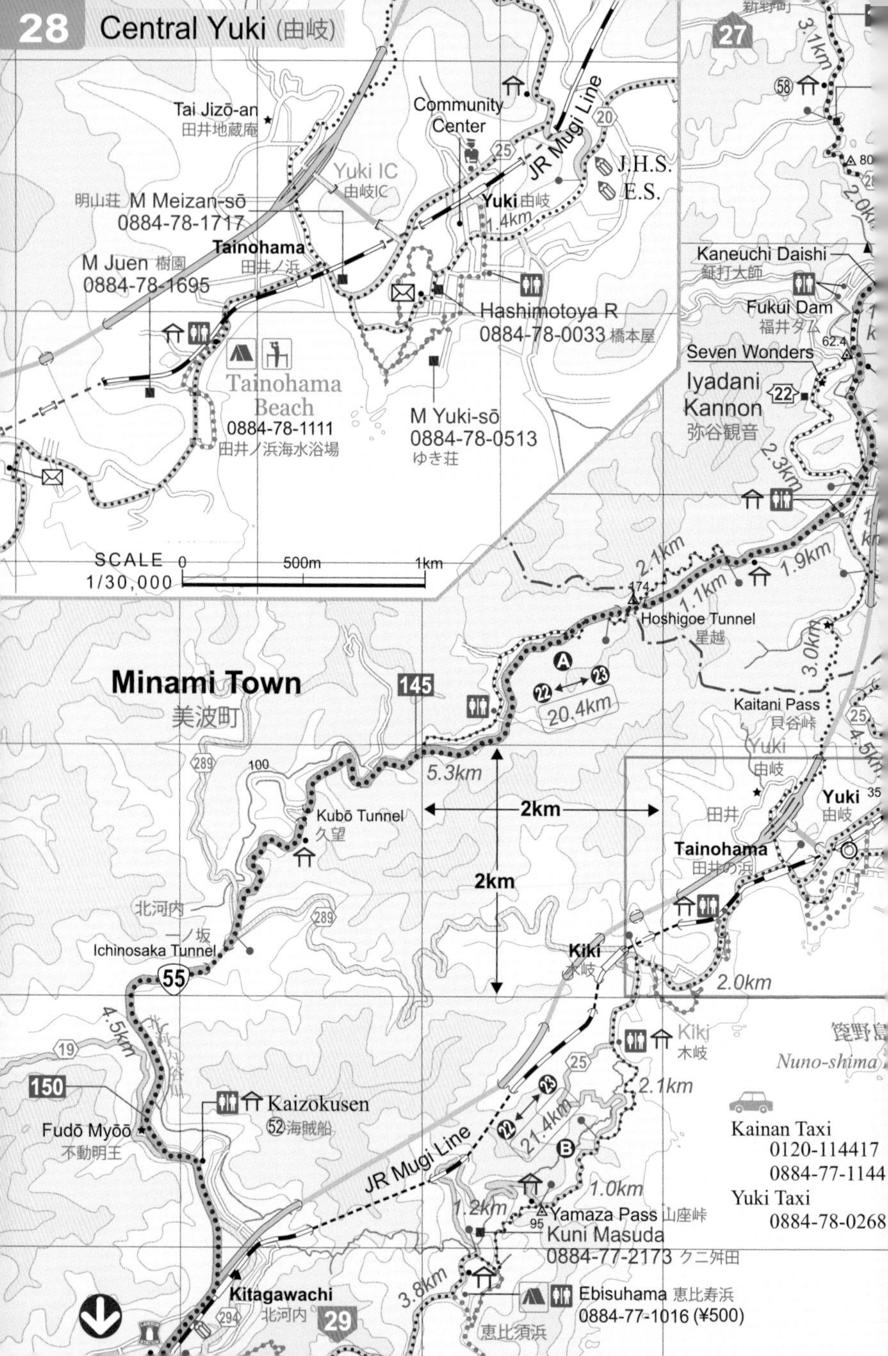

Tai Jizō-an
田井地蔵庵
Community Center
JR Mugi Line
J.H.S.
E.S.
Yuki IC
由岐IC
明山荘 M Meizan-sō
0884-78-1717
Yuki 由岐
1.4km
Tainohama
田井ノ浜
M Juen 樹園
0884-78-1695
Hashimotoya R
0884-78-0033 橋本屋
Tainohama Beach
0884-78-1111
田井ノ浜海水浴場
M Yuki-sō
0884-78-0513
ゆき荘
SCALE 1/30,000
0
500m
1km
Kaneuchi Daishi
鉦打大師
Fukui Dam
福井ダム
Seven Wonders
Iyadani Kannon
弥谷観音
2.3km
2.1km
1.1km
1.9km
Hoshigoe Tunnel
星越
3.0km
Kaitani Pass
貝谷峠
20.4km
Minami Town
美波町
5.3km
2km
2km
Kubō Tunnel
久望
北河内
一ノ坂
Ichinosaka Tunnel
4.5km
Yuki
由岐
Tainohama
田井の浜
Kiki
木岐
2.0km
Kiki
木岐
Nuno-shima
2.1km
21.4km
Kainan Taxi
0120-114417
0884-77-1144
Yuki Taxi
0884-78-0268
Fudō Myōō
不動明王
Kaizokusen
52 海賊船
JR Mugi Line
1.0km
1.2km
Yamaza Pass 山座峠
Kuni Masuda
0884-77-2173 クニ舛田
3.8km
Ebisuhama 恵比寿浜
0884-77-1016 (¥500)
Kitagawachi
北河内
恵比須浜

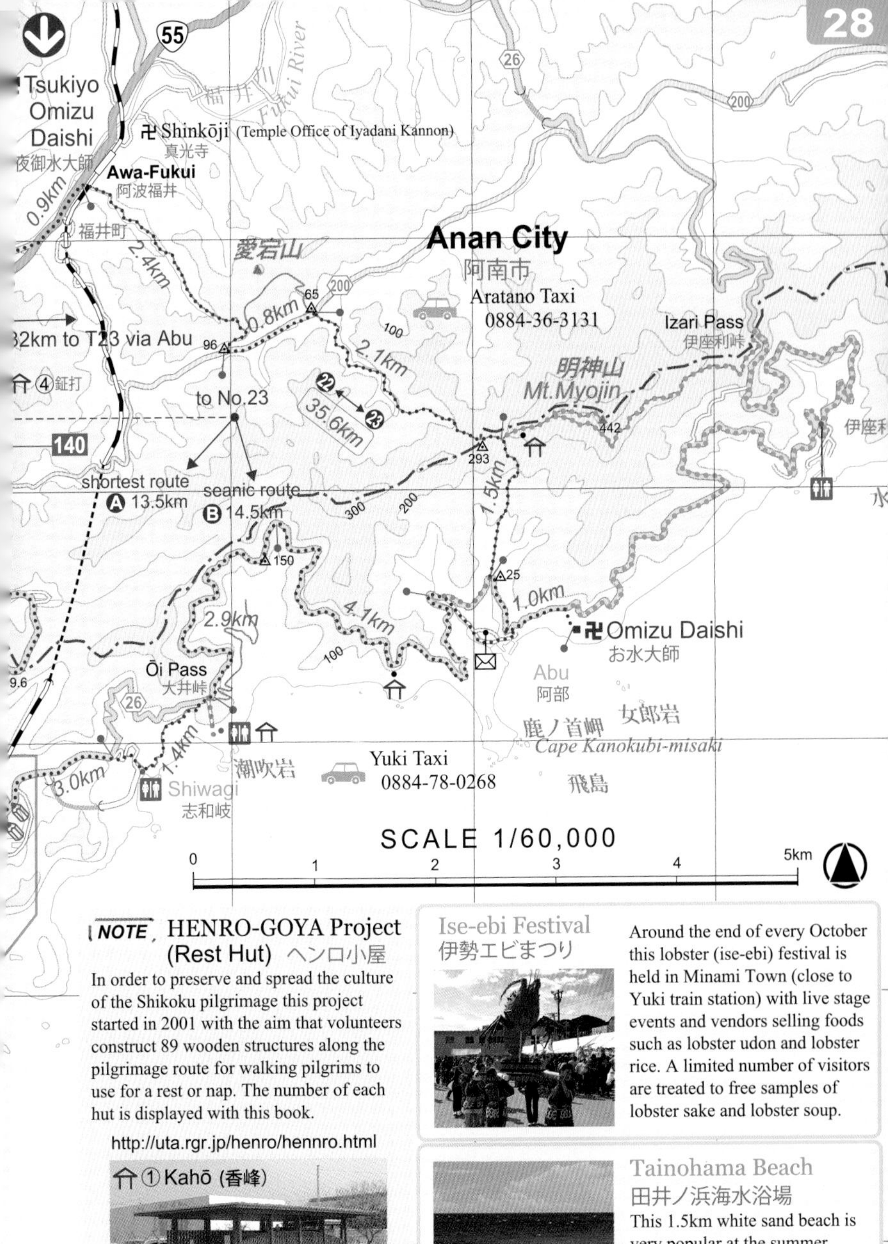

55
Fukui River
福井川
Tsukiyo Omizu Daishi
夜御水大師
Shinkōji (Temple Office of Iyadani Kannon)
真光寺
Awa-Fukui
阿波福井
0.9km
福井町
2.4km
26
200
Anan City
阿南市
Aratano Taxi
0884-36-3131
愛宕山
65
0.8km
96
32km to T23 via Abu
④鉦打
to No.23
2.1km
22 ↔ 23
35.6km
Izari Pass
伊座利峠
明神山
Mt.Myojin
442
293
伊座利
140
shortest route
A 13.5km
seanic route
B 14.5km
300
200
1.5km
150
25
1.0km
2.9km
4.1km
100
Omizu Daishi
お水大師
Abu
阿部
Ōi Pass
大井峠
26
鹿ノ首岬
Cape Kanokubi-misaki
女郎岩
3.0km
1.4km
Shiwagi
志和岐
潮吹岩
Yuki Taxi
0884-78-0268
飛島
SCALE 1/60,000
0 1 2 3 4 5km

NOTE HENRO-GOYA Project (Rest Hut) ヘンロ小屋

In order to preserve and spread the culture of the Shikoku pilgrimage this project started in 2001 with the aim that volunteers construct 89 wooden structures along the pilgrimage route for walking pilgrims to use for a rest or nap. The number of each hut is displayed with this book.

http://uta.rgr.jp/henro/henrro.html

① Kahō (香峰)

Ise-ebi Festival 伊勢エビまつり

Around the end of every October this lobster (ise-ebi) festival is held in Minami Town (close to Yuki train station) with live stage events and vendors selling foods such as lobster udon and lobster rice. A limited number of visitors are treated to free samples of lobster sake and lobster soup.

Tainohama Beach 田井ノ浜海水浴場

This 1.5km white sand beach is very popular at the summer months during which time sea turtles often come and lay their eggs on the beach.

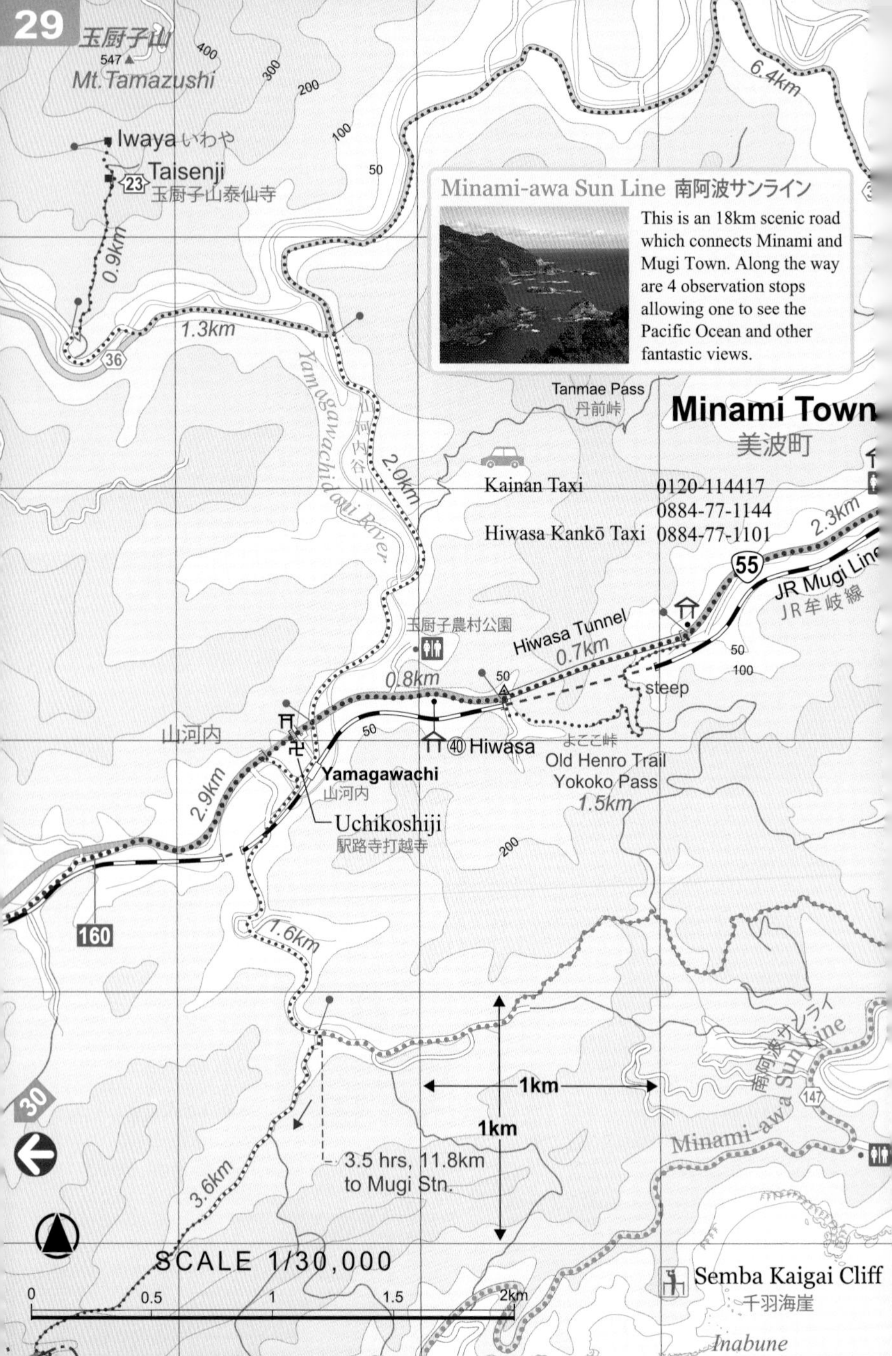

玉厨子山
547
Mt.Tamazushi
400
300
200
100
50
Iwaya いわや
Taisenji
23
玉厨子山泰仙寺
0.9km
1.3km
36
6.4km
Minami-awa Sun Line 南阿波サンライン
This is an 18km scenic road which connects Minami and Mugi Town. Along the way are 4 observation stops allowing one to see the Pacific Ocean and other fantastic views.
Tanmae Pass
丹前峠
Minami Town
美波町
Yamagawachidani River
山河内谷川
2.0km
Kainan Taxi 0120-114417
0884-77-1144
Hiwasa Kankō Taxi 0884-77-1101
2.3km
55
JR Mugi Line
JR牟岐線
玉厨子農村公園
Hiwasa Tunnel
0.7km
0.8km
steep
山河内
40 Hiwasa
よこご峠
Old Henro Trail
Yokoko Pass
1.5km
Yamagawachi
山河内
Uchikoshiji
駅路寺打越寺
2.9km
160
1.6km
1km
1km
3.5 hrs, 11.8km to Mugi Stn.
3.6km
南阿波サンライン
Minami-awa Sun Line
147
SCALE 1/30,000
0
0.5
1
1.5
2km
Semba Kaigai Cliff
千羽海崖
Inabune
30

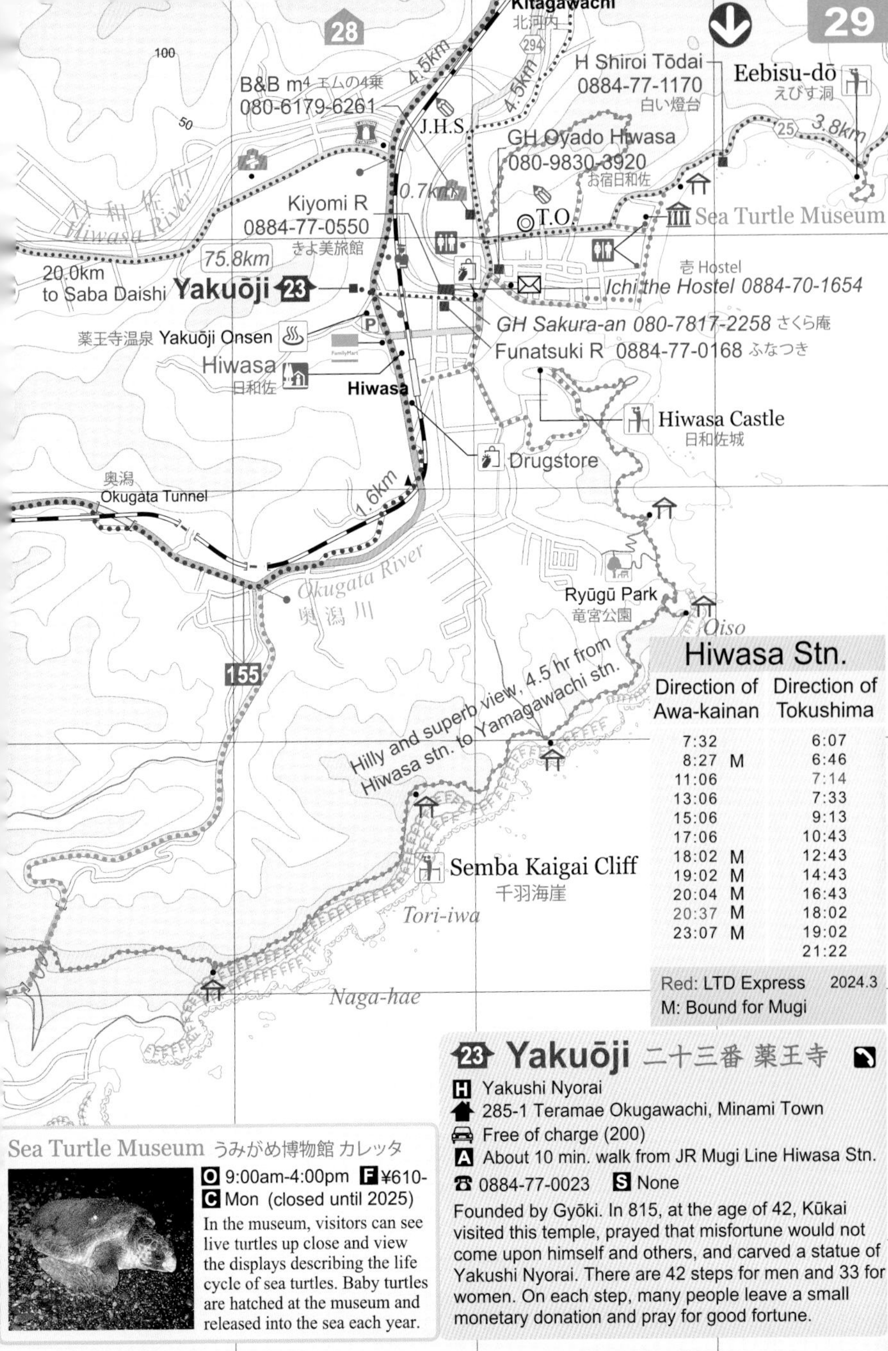
29
28
Kitagawachi
北河内
294
H Shiroi Tōdai
0884-77-1170
白い燈台
Eebisu-dō
えびす洞
25
3.8km
4.5km
4.5km
B&B m4 エムの4乗
080-6179-6261
J.H.S.
GH Oyado Hiwasa
080-9830-3920
お宿日和佐
0.7km
T.O.
Sea Turtle Museum
日和佐川
Hiwasa River
Kiyomi R
0884-77-0550
きよ美旅館
75.8km
20.0km
to Saba Daishi
Yakuōji 23
壱 Hostel
Ichi the Hostel 0884-70-1654
GH Sakura-an 080-7817-2258 さくら庵
Funatsuki R 0884-77-0168 ふなつき
薬王寺温泉 Yakuōji Onsen
Hiwasa
日和佐
Hiwasa
Hiwasa Castle
日和佐城
Drugstore
奥潟
Okugata Tunnel
1.6km
Okugata River
奥潟川
Ryūgū Park
竜宮公園
Oiso
155
Hilly and superb view, 4.5 hr from Hiwasa stn. to Yamagawachi stn.
Semba Kaigai Cliff
千羽海崖
Tori-iwa
Naga-hae
100
50

Hiwasa Stn.

Direction of Awa-kainan	Direction of Tokushima
7:32	6:07
8:27 M	6:46
11:06	7:14
13:06	7:33
15:06	9:13
17:06	10:43
18:02 M	12:43
19:02 M	14:43
20:04 M	16:43
20:37 M	18:02
23:07 M	19:02
	21:22

Red: LTD Express 2024.3
M: Bound for Mugi

23 Yakuōji 二十三番 薬王寺

H Yakushi Nyorai
285-1 Teramae Okugawachi, Minami Town
Free of charge (200)
A About 10 min. walk from JR Mugi Line Hiwasa Stn.
☎ 0884-77-0023 S None

Founded by Gyōki. In 815, at the age of 42, Kūkai visited this temple, prayed that misfortune would not come upon himself and others, and carved a statue of Yakushi Nyorai. There are 42 steps for men and 33 for women. On each step, many people leave a small monetary donation and pray for good fortune.

Sea Turtle Museum うみがめ博物館 カレッタ

O 9:00am-4:00pm F ¥610-
C Mon (closed until 2025)

In the museum, visitors can see live turtles up close and view the displays describing the life cycle of sea turtles. Baby turtles are hatched at the museum and released into the sea each year.

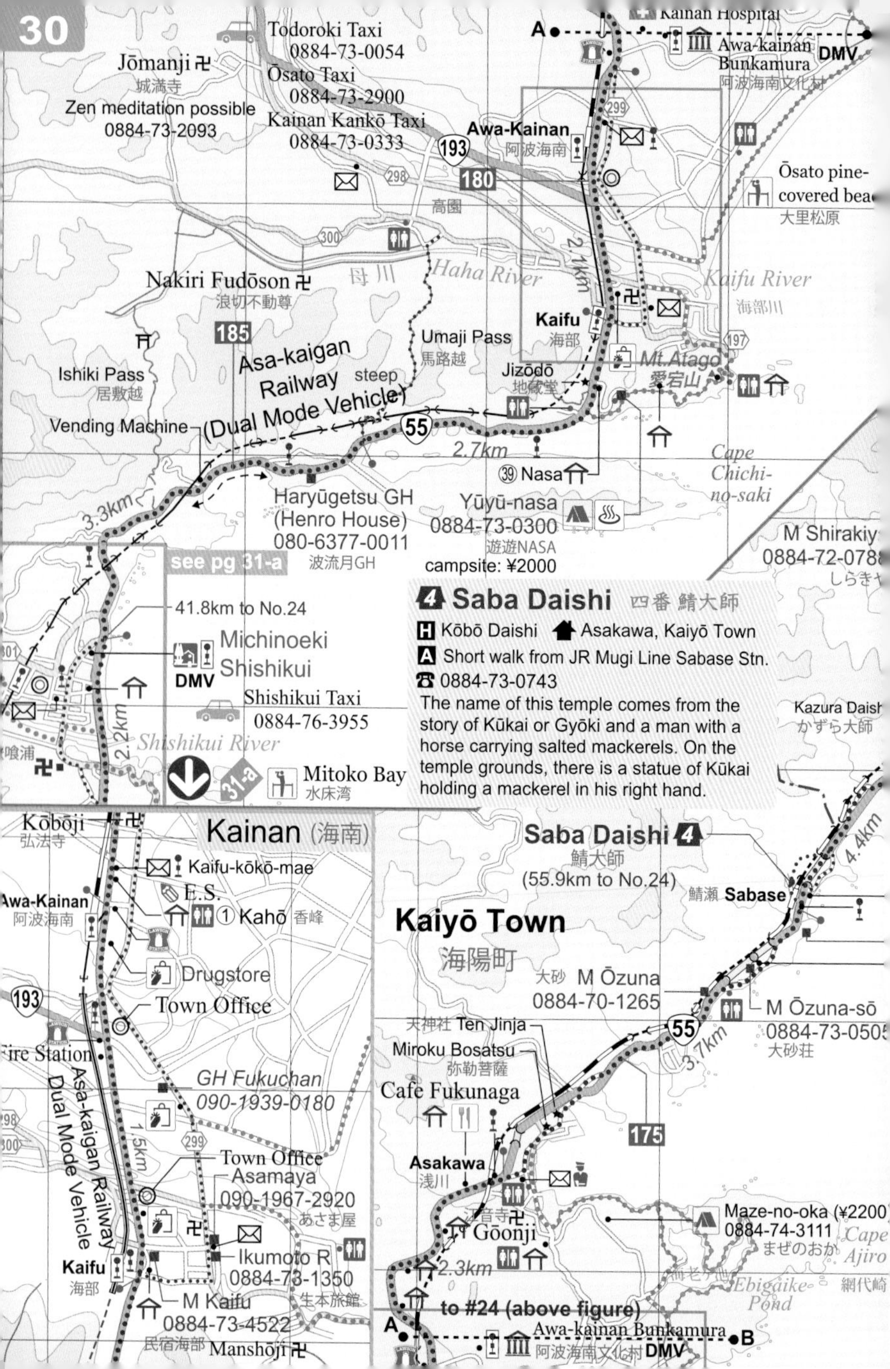

Todoroki Taxi
0884-73-0054
Ōsato Taxi
0884-73-2900
Kainan Kankō Taxi
0884-73-0333
Jōmanji 卍
城満寺
Zen meditation possible
0884-73-2093
Kainan Hospital
Awa-kainan Bunkamura
阿波海南文化村
DMV
Awa-Kainan
阿波海南
Ōsato pine-covered bea
大里松原
高園
Nakiri Fudōson 卍
浪切不動尊
母川 Haha River
2.1km
Kaifu River
海部川
Kaifu
海部
Umaji Pass
馬路越
Mt.Atago
愛宕山
Ishiki Pass
居敷越
Asa-kaigan Railway (Dual Mode Vehicle)
steep
Jizōdō
地蔵堂
Vending Machine
2.7km
Cape Chichi-no-saki
㊴ Nasa
Haryūgetsu GH
(Henro House)
080-6377-0011
波流月GH
Yūyū-nasa
0884-73-0300
遊遊NASA
campsite: ¥2000
3.3km
M Shirakiya
0884-72-0788
see pg 31-a
41.8km to No.24
Michinoeki Shishikui
DMV
Shishikui Taxi
0884-76-3955
2.2km
Shishikui River
Mitoko Bay
水床湾
4 Saba Daishi 四番 鯖大師
Kōbō Daishi
Asakawa, Kaiyō Town
Short walk from JR Mugi Line Sabase Stn.
0884-73-0743
The name of this temple comes from the story of Kūkai or Gyōki and a man with a horse carrying salted mackerels. On the temple grounds, there is a statue of Kūkai holding a mackerel in his right hand.
Kazura Daishi
かずら大師
Kōbōji
弘法寺
Kainan (海南)
Kaifu-kōkō-mae
E.S.
① Kahō 香峰
Awa-Kainan
阿波海南
Drugstore
Town Office
Fire Station
GH Fukuchan
090-1939-0180
1.5km
Asa-kaigan Railway Dual Mode Vehicle
Town Office
Asamaya
090-1967-2920
あさま屋
Ikumoto R
0884-73-1350
生本旅館
Kaifu
海部
M Kaifu
0884-73-4522
民宿海部
Manshōji 卍
Saba Daishi 4
鯖大師
(55.9km to No.24)
鯖瀬 Sabase
4.4km
Kaiyō Town
海陽町
大砂 M Ōzuna
0884-70-1265
M Ōzuna-sō
0884-73-0505
大砂荘
天神社 Ten Jinja
Miroku Bosatsu
弥勒菩薩
3.7km
Cafe Fukunaga
Asakawa
浅川
Maze-no-oka (¥2200)
0884-74-3111
まぜのおか
Cape Ajiro
網代崎
Gōonji
2.3km
Ebigaike Pond
to #24 (above figure)
Awa-kainan Bunkamura
阿波海南文化村 DMV

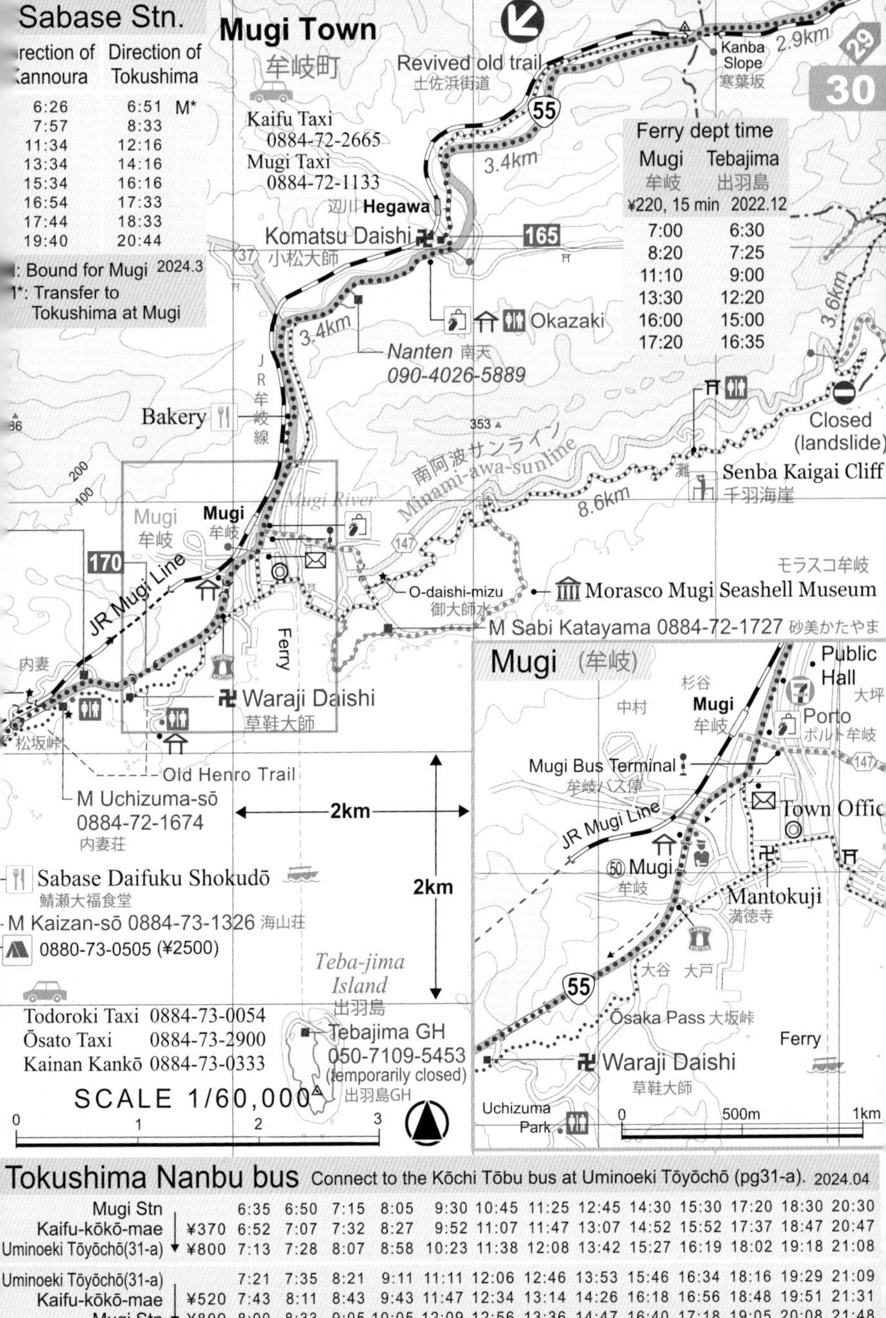

Mugi Town
牟岐町
Kaifu Taxi
0884-72-2665
Mugi Taxi
0884-72-1133
Revived old trail
土佐浜街道
Kanba Slope
寒葉坂
2.9km
29
30
55
3.4km
辺川 Hegawa
Komatsu Daishi
小松大師
165
37
3.4km
Okazaki
Nanten 南天
090-4026-5889
JR牟岐線
Bakery
353
南阿波サンライン
Minami-awa-sunline
3.6km
Closed (landslide)
Senba Kaigai Cliff
千羽海崖
8.6km
Mugi 牟岐
Mugi 牟岐
Mugi River
170
JR Mugi Line
147
O-daishi-mizu
御大師水
モラスコ牟岐
Morasco Mugi Seashell Museum
M Sabi Katayama 0884-72-1727 砂美かたやま
Ferry
内妻
Waraji Daishi
草鞋大師
松坂峠
Old Henro Trail
M Uchizuma-sō
0884-72-1674
内妻荘
2km
2km
Sabase Daifuku Shokudō
鯖瀬大福食堂
M Kaizan-sō 0884-73-1326 海山荘
0880-73-0505 (¥2500)
Teba-jima Island
出羽島
Todoroki Taxi 0884-73-0054
Ōsato Taxi 0884-73-2900
Kainan Kankō 0884-73-0333
Tebajima GH
050-7109-5453
(temporarily closed)
出羽島GH
SCALE 1/60,000
0 1 2 3
Mugi (牟岐)
Public Hall
大坪
杉谷
中村
Mugi 牟岐
Porto
ポルト牟岐
Mugi Bus Terminal
牟岐バス停
147
JR Mugi Line
Town Offic
50 Mugi
牟岐
Mantokuji
満徳寺
大谷 大戸
55
Ōsaka Pass 大坂峠
Ferry
Waraji Daishi
草鞋大師
Uchizuma Park
0 500m 1km

Sabase Stn.

Direction of Kannoura	Direction of Tokushima	
6:26	6:51	M*
7:57	8:33	
11:34	12:16	
13:34	14:16	
15:34	16:16	
16:54	17:33	
17:44	18:33	
19:40	20:44	

M: Bound for Mugi 2024.3
M*: Transfer to Tokushima at Mugi

Ferry dept time

Mugi 牟岐	Tebajima 出羽島
¥220, 15 min	2022.12
7:00	6:30
8:20	7:25
11:10	9:00
13:30	12:20
16:00	15:00
17:20	16:35

Tokushima Nanbu bus

Connect to the Kōchi Tōbu bus at Uminoeki Tōyōchō (pg31-a). 2024.04

Mugi Stn		6:35	6:50	7:15	8:05	9:30	10:45	11:25	12:45	14:30	15:30	17:20	18:30	20:30
Kaifu-kōkō-mae ↓	¥370	6:52	7:07	7:32	8:27	9:52	11:07	11:47	13:07	14:52	15:52	17:37	18:47	20:47
Uminoeki Tōyōchō(31-a)	¥800	7:13	7:28	8:07	8:58	10:23	11:38	12:08	13:42	15:27	16:19	18:02	19:18	21:08
Uminoeki Tōyōchō(31-a)		7:21	7:35	8:21	9:11	11:11	12:06	12:46	13:53	15:46	16:34	18:16	19:29	21:09
Kaifu-kōkō-mae ↓	¥520	7:43	8:11	8:43	9:43	11:47	12:34	13:14	14:26	16:18	16:56	18:48	19:51	21:31
Mugi Stn	¥800	8:00	8:33	9:05	10:05	12:09	12:56	13:36	14:47	16:40	17:18	19:05	20:08	21:48

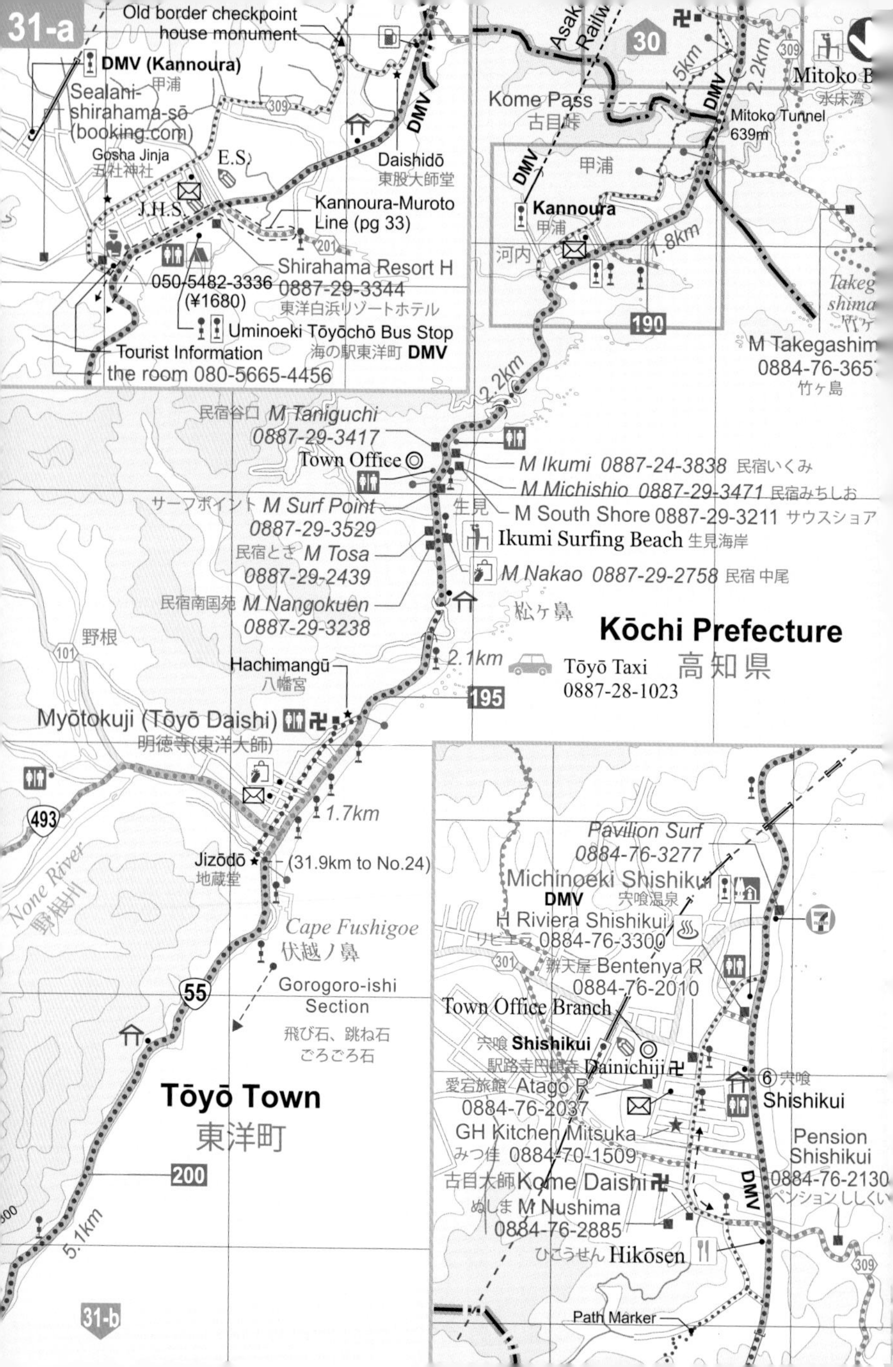
Old border checkpoint house monument
DMV (Kannoura)
甲浦
Sealani-shirahama-sō (booking.com)
Gosha Jinja
五社神社
E.S.
J.H.S.
Daishidō
東股大師堂
Kannoura-Muroto Line (pg 33)
Shirahama Resort H
0887-29-3344
東洋白浜リゾートホテル
050-5482-3336
(¥1680)
Uminoeki Tōyōchō Bus Stop
海の駅東洋町 DMV
Tourist Information
the room 080-5665-4456
30
Kome Pass
古目峠
Mitoko Tunnel
639m
1.5km
2.2km
Mitoko B
水床湾
Kannoura
甲浦
河内
1.8km
190
M Takegashim
0884-76-3657
竹ヶ島
2.2km
民宿谷口 M Taniguchi
0887-29-3417
Town Office
M Ikumi 0887-24-3838 民宿いくみ
M Michishio 0887-29-3471 民宿みちしお
サーフポイント M Surf Point
0887-29-3529
生見
M South Shore 0887-29-3211 サウスショア
Ikumi Surfing Beach 生見海岸
民宿とさ M Tosa
0887-29-2439
M Nakao 0887-29-2758 民宿 中尾
民宿南国苑 M Nangokuen
0887-29-3238
松ヶ鼻
Kōchi Prefecture
高知県
野根
2.1km
Tōyō Taxi
0887-28-1023
Hachimangū
八幡宮
195
Myōtokuji (Tōyō Daishi)
明徳寺(東洋大師)
493
1.7km
Jizōdō
地蔵堂
(31.9km to No.24)
None River
野根川
Cape Fushigoe
伏越ノ鼻
Gorogoro-ishi Section
飛び石、跳ね石
ごろごろ石
55
Tōyō Town
東洋町
200
5.1km
Pavilion Surf
0884-76-3277
Michinoeki Shishikui
DMV
宍喰温泉
H Riviera Shishikui
リビエラ 0884-76-3300
301
辨天屋 Bentenya R
0884-76-2010
Town Office Branch
宍喰 Shishikui
駅路寺円頓寺 Dainichiji
愛宕旅館 Atago R
0884-76-2037
GH Kitchen Mitsuka
みつ佳 0884-70-1509
古目大師 Kome Daishi
ぬしま M Nushima
0884-76-2885
ひこうせん Hikōsen
⑥宍喰
Shishikui
Pension Shishikui
0884-76-2130
ペンション ししくい
309
Path Marker
DMV

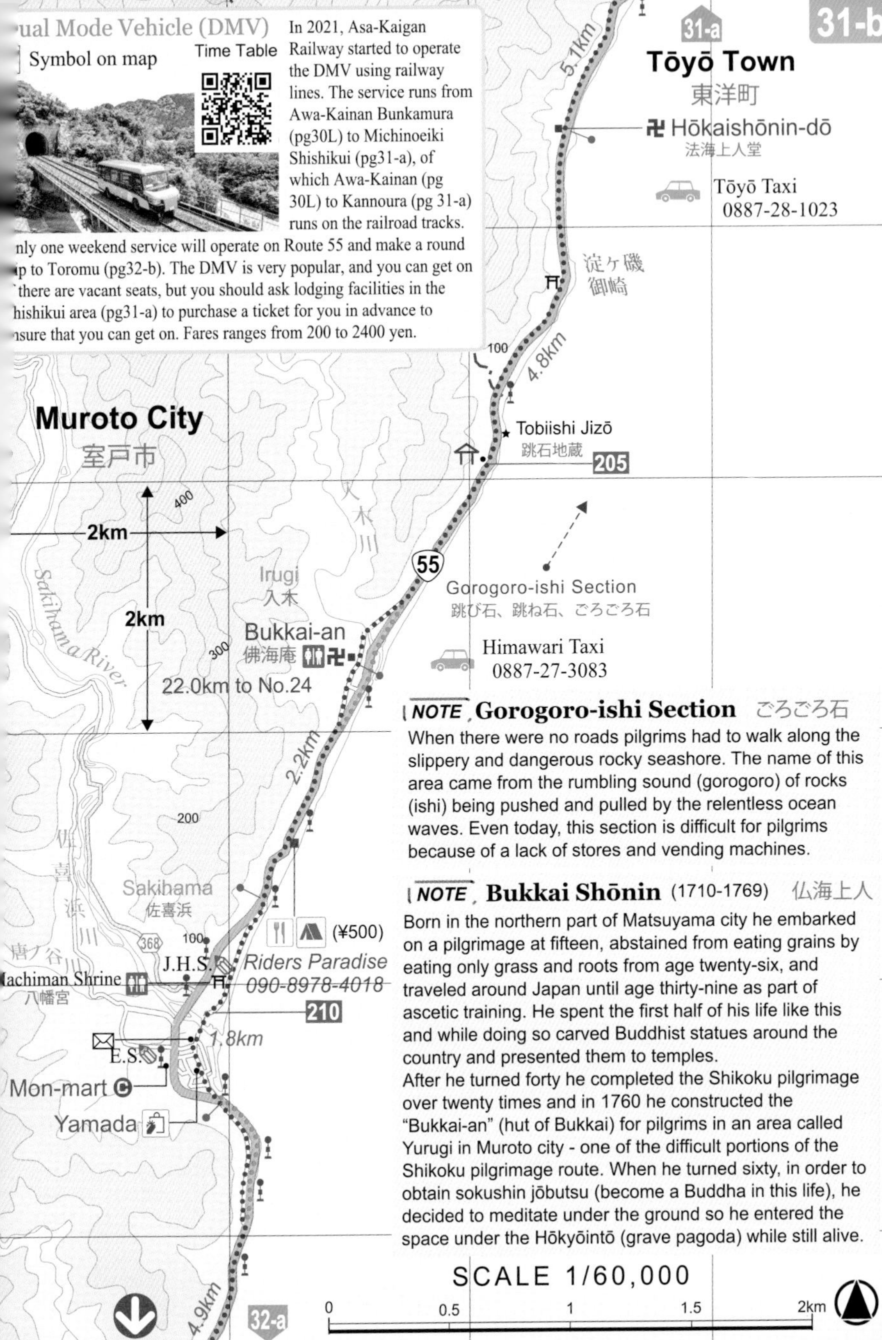
31-a
Tōyō Town
東洋町
Hōkaishōnin-dō
法海上人堂
Tōyō Taxi
0887-28-1023
5.1km
淀ヶ磯
御崎
100
4.8km
Tobiishi Jizō
跳石地蔵
205
Muroto City
室戸市
400
2km
2km
55
大木川
Irugi
入木
Gorogoro-ishi Section
跳び石、跳ね石、ごろごろ石
Sakihama River
300
Bukkai-an
佛海庵
22.0km to No.24
Himawari Taxi
0887-27-3083
2.2km
200
佐喜浜川
Sakihama
佐喜浜
368
100
唐ノ谷
(¥500)
J.H.S.
Riders Paradise
090-8978-4018
Hachiman Shrine
八幡宮
210
1.8km
E.S.
Mon-mart
Yamada
4.9km
32-a
SCALE 1/60,000
0
0.5
1
1.5
2km

Dual Mode Vehicle (DMV)

Symbol on map

Time Table

In 2021, Asa-Kaigan Railway started to operate the DMV using railway lines. The service runs from Awa-Kainan Bunkamura (pg30L) to Michinoeiki Shishikui (pg31-a), of which Awa-Kainan (pg 30L) to Kannoura (pg 31-a) runs on the railroad tracks. Only one weekend service will operate on Route 55 and make a round trip to Toromu (pg32-b). The DMV is very popular, and you can get on if there are vacant seats, but you should ask lodging facilities in the Shishikui area (pg31-a) to purchase a ticket for you in advance to ensure that you can get on. Fares ranges from 200 to 2400 yen.

NOTE Gorogoro-ishi Section ごろごろ石

When there were no roads pilgrims had to walk along the slippery and dangerous rocky seashore. The name of this area came from the rumbling sound (gorogoro) of rocks (ishi) being pushed and pulled by the relentless ocean waves. Even today, this section is difficult for pilgrims because of a lack of stores and vending machines.

NOTE Bukkai Shōnin (1710-1769) 仏海上人

Born in the northern part of Matsuyama city he embarked on a pilgrimage at fifteen, abstained from eating grains by eating only grass and roots from age twenty-six, and traveled around Japan until age thirty-nine as part of ascetic training. He spent the first half of his life like this and while doing so carved Buddhist statues around the country and presented them to temples.

After he turned forty he completed the Shikoku pilgrimage over twenty times and in 1760 he constructed the "Bukkai-an" (hut of Bukkai) for pilgrims in an area called Yurugi in Muroto city - one of the difficult portions of the Shikoku pilgrimage route. When he turned sixty, in order to obtain sokushin jōbutsu (become a Buddha in this life), he decided to meditate under the ground so he entered the space under the Hōkyōintō (grave pagoda) while still alive.

32-a 24 Hotsumisakiji

Kokuzō Bosatsu 二十四番 最御崎寺

4058-1 Muroto-misaki-chō, Muroto City ☎ 0887-23-0024

Free of charge (40) 5 min. walk S Available

A By bus bound for Kannoura from Nahari Stn., and vice versa. In either direction, get off at Muroto-misaki Bus Stop, about 30 min. walk.

In 807 Kūkai, who had returned from China, founded this temple by carving a statue of Kokuzō Bosatsu as the main deity. Many temple artifacts are stored in the Hōmotsukan building. One of the seven mysteries of Muroto is a “Kane-ishi” on the temple grounds. It is believed that the noise when you hit this rock with a small rock will reach the spirits of those who have passed away. This temple is known informally by the local people as Higashi-dera (Eastern temple) and Kongōchōji is known as Nishi-dera (Western temple).

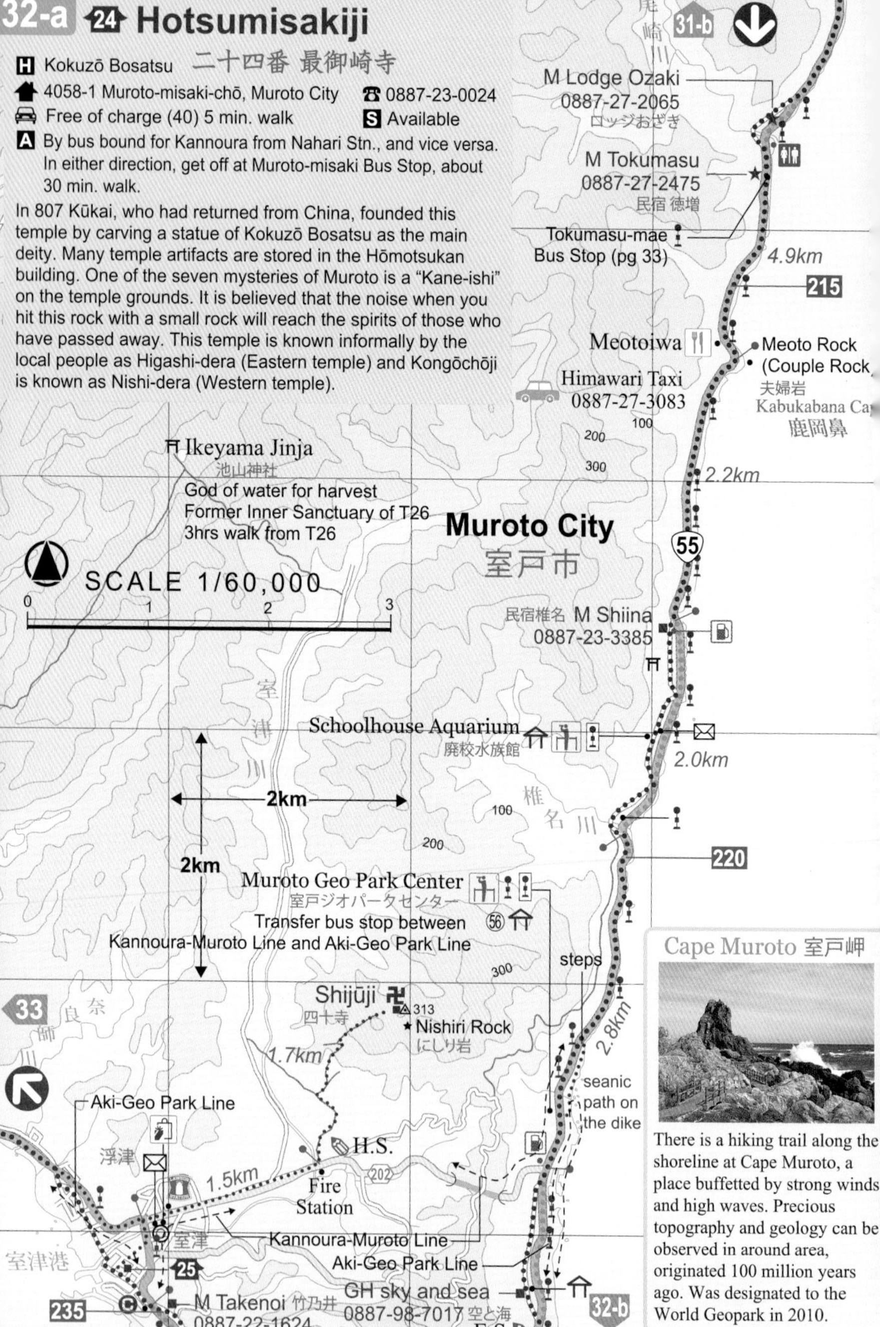

31-b
尾崎川
M Lodge Ozaki
0887-27-2065
ロッジおざき
M Tokumasu
0887-27-2475
民宿 徳増
Tokumasu-mae Bus Stop (pg 33)
4.9km
215
Meotoiwa
Meoto Rock (Couple Rock)
夫婦岩
Kabukabana Ca
鹿岡鼻
Himawari Taxi
0887-27-3083
100
200
300
2.2km
Ikeyama Jinja
池山神社
God of water for harvest
Former Inner Sanctuary of T26
3hrs walk from T26
Muroto City
室戸市
55
SCALE 1/60,000
0
1
2
3
民宿椎名 M Shiina
0887-23-3385
室津川
Schoolhouse Aquarium
廃校水族館
2.0km
2km
2km
椎名川
100
200
220
Muroto Geo Park Center
室戸ジオパークセンター
Transfer bus stop between Kannoura-Muroto Line and Aki-Geo Park Line
56
steps
300
33
奈良師川
Shijūji
四十寺
313
Nishiri Rock
にしり岩
2.8km
1.7km
seanic path on the dike
Aki-Geo Park Line
浮津
H.S.
1.5km
Fire Station
202
室津
室津港
Kannoura-Muroto Line
Aki-Geo Park Line
25
235
M Takenoi 竹乃井
0887-22-1624
GH sky and sea
0887-98-7017 空と海
32-b
E.S.

Cape Muroto 室戸岬

There is a hiking trail along the shoreline at Cape Muroto, a place buffetted by strong winds and high waves. Precious topography and geology can be observed in around area, originated 100 million years ago. Was designated to the World Geopark in 2010.

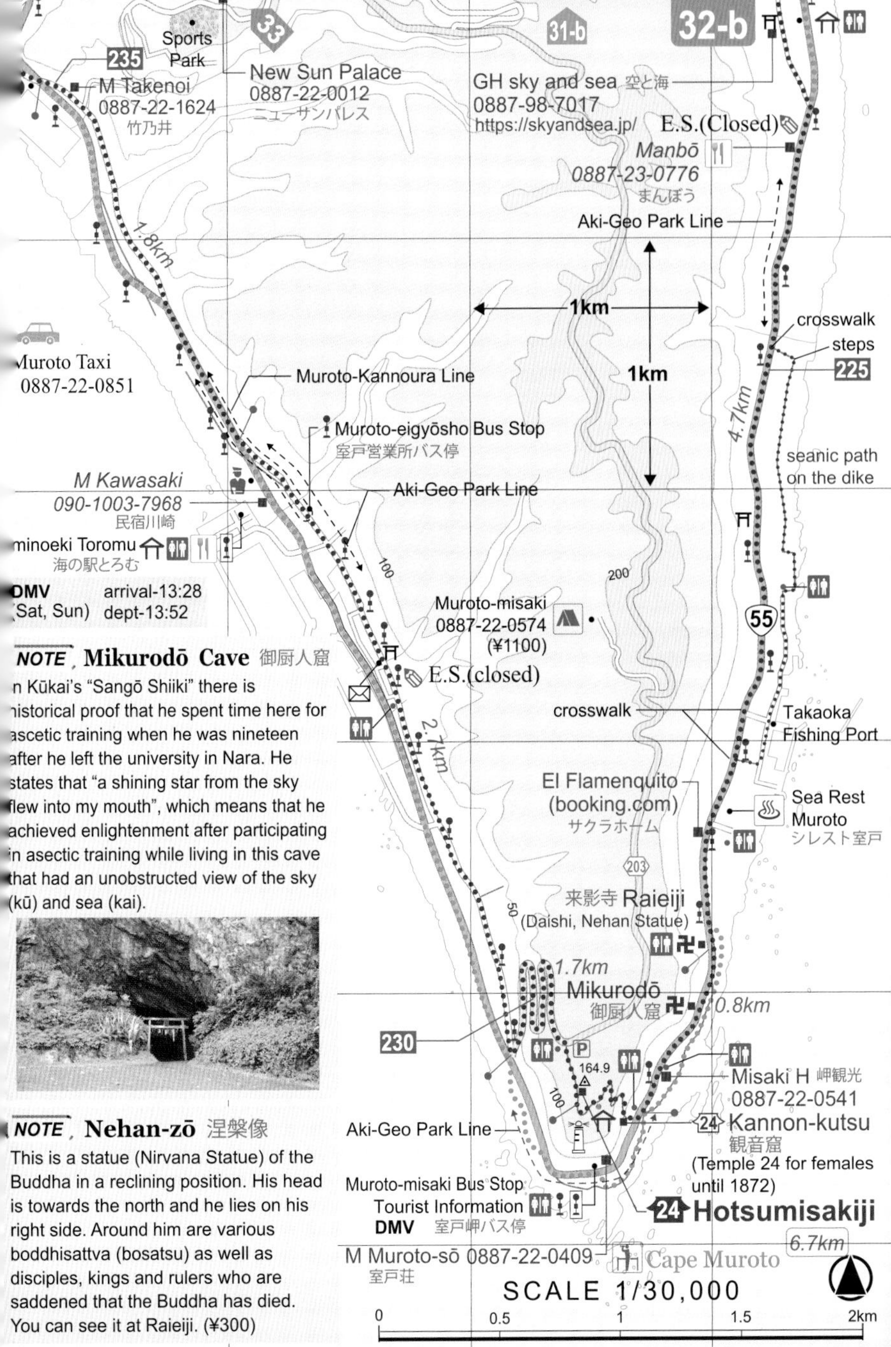

32-b
31-b
33
235
Sports Park
New Sun Palace
0887-22-0012
ニューサンパレス
M Takenoi
0887-22-1624
竹乃井
GH sky and sea 空と海
0887-98-7017
https://skyandsea.jp/
E.S.(Closed)
Manbō
0887-23-0776
まんぼう
Aki-Geo Park Line
1.8km
1km
1km
crosswalk
steps
225
Muroto Taxi
0887-22-0851
Muroto-Kannoura Line
4.7km
Muroto-eigyōsho Bus Stop
室戸営業所バス停
seanic path on the dike
M Kawasaki
090-1003-7968
民宿川崎
Aki-Geo Park Line
minoeki Toromu
海の駅とろむ
100
200
DMV arrival-13:28
(Sat, Sun) dept-13:52
Muroto-misaki
0887-22-0574
(¥1100)
55
E.S.(closed)
crosswalk
Takaoka Fishing Port
2.7km
El Flamenquito
(booking.com)
サクラホーム
Sea Rest Muroto
シレスト室戸
203
来影寺 Raieiji
(Daishi, Nehan Statue)
50
1.7km
Mikurodō
御厨人窟
0.8km
230
164.9
100
Misaki H 岬観光
0887-22-0541
Aki-Geo Park Line
24 Kannon-kutsu
観音窟
(Temple 24 for females until 1872)
Muroto-misaki Bus Stop
Tourist Information
DMV 室戸岬バス停
24 Hotsumisakiji
6.7km
M Muroto-sō 0887-22-0409
室戸荘
Cape Muroto
SCALE 1/30,000
0
0.5
1
1.5
2km

NOTE **Mikurodō Cave** 御厨人窟

In Kūkai's "Sangō Shiiki" there is historical proof that he spent time here for ascetic training when he was nineteen after he left the university in Nara. He states that "a shining star from the sky flew into my mouth", which means that he achieved enlightenment after participating in asectic training while living in this cave that had an unobstructed view of the sky (kū) and sea (kai).

NOTE **Nehan-zō** 涅槃像

This is a statue (Nirvana Statue) of the Buddha in a reclining position. His head is towards the north and he lies on his right side. Around him are various boddhisattva (bosatsu) as well as disciples, kings and rulers who are saddened that the Buddha has died. You can see it at Raieiji. (¥300)

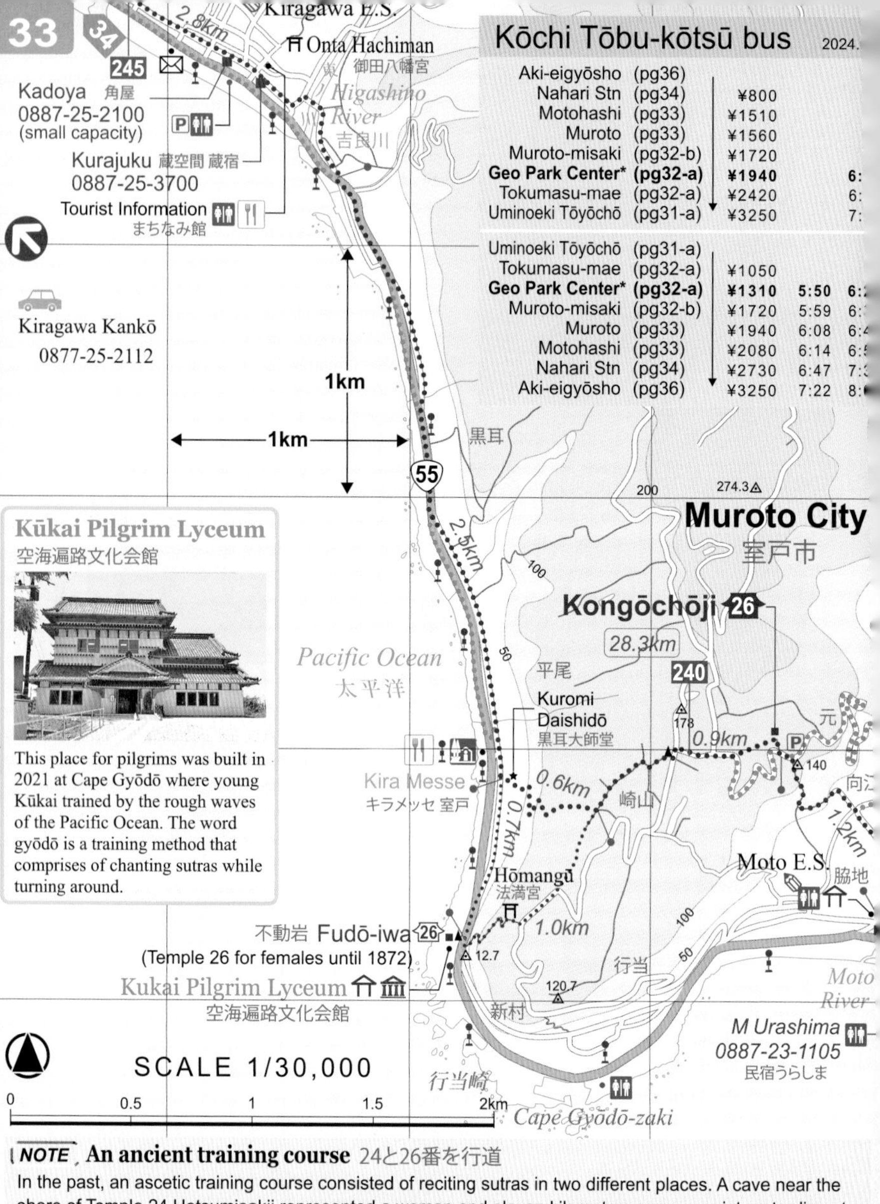
34
2.8km
Kiragawa E.S.
Onta Hachiman
御田八幡宮
Higashino River
吉良川
245
Kadoya 角屋
0887-25-2100
(small capacity)
Kurajuku 蔵空間 蔵宿
0887-25-3700
Tourist Information
まちなみ館
Kiragawa Kankō
0877-25-2112
1km
1km
55
黒耳
200
274.3
Muroto City
室戸市
100
2.5km
Kongōchōji 26
28.3km
Pacific Ocean
太平洋
50
平尾
240
Kuromi
Daishidō
黒耳大師堂
178
0.9km
140
元
Kira Messe
キラメッセ 室戸
0.6km
崎山
0.7km
1.2km
Hōmangū
法満宮
Moto E.S.
脇地
不動岩 Fudō-iwa 26
(Temple 26 for females until 1872)
12.7
1.0km
100
行当
50
Kukai Pilgrim Lyceum
空海遍路文化会館
120.7
新村
Moto River
M Urashima
0887-23-1105
民宿うらしま
SCALE 1/30,000
0
0.5
1
1.5
2km
行当崎
Cape Gyōdō-zaki

Kōchi Tōbu-kōtsū bus 2024.

Aki-eigyōsho	(pg36)			
Nahari Stn	(pg34)	¥800		
Motohashi	(pg33)	¥1510		
Muroto	(pg33)	¥1560		
Muroto-misaki	(pg32-b)	¥1720		
Geo Park Center*	**(pg32-a)**	**¥1940**		**6:**
Tokumasu-mae	(pg32-a)	¥2420		6:
Uminoeki Tōyōchō	(pg31-a)	¥3250		7:

Uminoeki Tōyōchō	(pg31-a)			
Tokumasu-mae	(pg32-a)	¥1050		
Geo Park Center*	**(pg32-a)**	**¥1310**	**5:50**	**6:**
Muroto-misaki	(pg32-b)	¥1720	5:59	6:
Muroto	(pg33)	¥1940	6:08	6:4
Motohashi	(pg33)	¥2080	6:14	6:5
Nahari Stn	(pg34)	¥2730	6:47	7:
Aki-eigyōsho	(pg36)	¥3250	7:22	8:

Kūkai Pilgrim Lyceum
空海遍路文化会館

This place for pilgrims was built in 2021 at Cape Gyōdō where young Kūkai trained by the rough waves of the Pacific Ocean. The word gyōdō is a training method that comprises of chanting sutras while turning around.

NOTE An ancient training course 24と26番を行道

In the past, an ascetic training course consisted of reciting sutras in two different places. A cave near the shore of Temple 24 Hotsumisakji represented a woman and eleven kilometers away, a point protruding at the shore near Temple 26 Kongōchōji represented a man. At each of the training spots a ritual fire (goma) would be lit, hand mudras would be done, and sutras would be recited. If one walked around in a circle at both spots, it was as if one was doing ascetic training for the Diamond and Womb Realm – the two great doctrines of Mikkyō Buddhism. Thus, because of this system both temples maintained a rule of not allowing women on their temple grounds until 1872.

2.0km
to Ikeyama Jinja
Iwaya River
Motohashi Bus Stop
元橋バス停
Iwato Jinja
Ikeyama Jinja
岩戸神社・池山神社
Narashi River
55
1.6km
Monument, prohibited to females
女人結界標石
Hatagoya
旅籠屋 0887-23-0858
Muroto J.H.S.
Minato Kankō Taxi 0887-23-2200
Chūō Taxi 0877-22-0530
1.0km
1km
Shinshōji 25
4.0km
太田旅館 Ōta R 0887-22-0004
(no Wifi available)
冨士 BH Fuji 0887-22-0205
235
Aki-Geo Park Line
Sunshine
E.S.
City Office
Muroto Bus Stop
室戸バス停
M Takenoi 竹乃井
0887-22-1624
32-b
1.5km
Kannoura-Muroto Line
Sun Palece
0887-22-0012
サンパレス
203
Sports Park
202
2.1km
H.S.
Fire Station
32-a

30	7:10	8:10	8:50	9:30	9:50	10:25	11:45	12:30	13:15	13:35	14:20	15:15	17:00	17:50	18:40	19:30	20:08
59	7:43	8:46	9:26	10:06	10:26	11:01	12:21	13:06	13:51	14:11	14:56	15:51	17:36	18:26	19:12	19:59	20:37
2	8:14	9:19	9:59	10:39	10:59	11:34	12:54	13:39	14:24	14:44	15:29	16:24	18:09	18:59	19:45	20:29	21:07
45	8:30	9:34	10:07	10:47	11:14	11:49	13:02	13:47	14:39	14:59	15:37	16:39	18:17	19:12	19:58	20:41	21:14
56	8:41	9:45	10:18	10:58	11:25	12:00	13:13	13:58	14:50	15:10	15:48	16:50	18:28	19:23	20:09	20:51	21:24
07	**8:52**	**9:56**	**10:29**	**11:09**	11:36	**12:11**	**13:24**	**14:09**	**15:01**	15:21	**15:59**	**17:01**	**18:39**	**19:34**	**20:20**	21:00	**21:33**
17		10:08				12:28		14:21				17:13		19:44			
45		10:39				12:59		14:52				17:44		20:13			

		7:35	8:40	9:33	10:03				12:20	12:28			14:55		16:31		18:13
		8:05	9:10	10:03	10:33				12:50	12:58			15:25		17:01		18:43
44	7:12	**8:19**	**9:19**	**10:19**	10:49	**11:25**	12:00	**12:35**	13:25	**13:45**	**14:29**	**15:21**	**15:44**	**16:30**	**17:18**	17:57	**18:57**
53	7:21	8:28	9:28	10:28	10:58	11:34	12:09	12:44	13:34	13:54	14:38	15:30	15:53	16:39	17:27	18:06	19:06
02	7:30	8:37	9:37	10:37	11:07	11:43	12:18	12:53	13:43	14:03	14:47	15:39	16:02	16:48	17:36	18:15	19:15
13	7:41	8:55	9:55	10:55	11:25	11:54	12:29	13:07	14:01	14:13	15:05	15:50	16:13	17:06	17:54	18:31	19:30
46	8:14	9:28	10:28	11:28	11:58	12:27	13:02	13:40	14:34	14:47	15:38	16:23	16:46	17:39	18:27	19:04	20:00
20	8:51	10:05	11:05	12:05	12:35	13:04	13:39	14:21	15:11	15:24	16:15	17:07	17:30	18:16	19:00	19:37	20:33

26 Kongōchōji 二十六番 金剛頂寺

☎ 0887-23-0026
S Available

H Yakushi Nyorai 523 Moto-otsu, Muroto City Charge (20) 3 min. walk

A By bus bound for Kannoura from Nahari Stn., and vice versa. In either direction, get off at Motohashi Bus Stop, about 50 min. walk.

In 807 when Kōbō Daishi arrived at the place and founded this temple a tengu arrived and engaged in a debate with Kōbō Daishi. The tengu lost the argument, was told to never appear again, and was confined to Cape Ashizuri. There are pictures on the walls of the Daishi hall that illustrate this story. In 1872 the law prohibiting women from visiting this temple was abolished.

25 Shinshōji 二十五番 津照寺

☎ 0887-23-0025 S None

H Kajitori Enmei Jizō Bosatsu Parking in port (Free of Charge) 3 min. walk

2644 Murotsu, Muroto City A By bus bound for Kannoura from Nahari Stn., and vice versa. In either direction, get off at Muroto Bus Stop, about 10 min. walk.

Kōbō Daishi founded this temple in 807 and carved a statue of Enmei Jizō Bosatsu, a deity which is also called Kajitori Jizō (Helmsman Jizō). Fishermen pray to it for protection while at sea.

35

Coastal Terrace 海岸段丘

The Muroto region has a typical coastal terrace topography, and is one of the components of the Geopark. No. 24 is located at an altitude of 165m, and No. 26 is 161m, but they are flat areas on terrace. This terrace are distributed over a wide area, and agriculture is also carried out there.

No. 26
GSI

Oka-goten 岡御殿

O 9:00am-4:30pm C Tue. F ¥500

This was completed in 1844 as a lodging facility for a feudal lord during the Edo period (1603-1867). The building, constructed in a residential architectural style called shoin-zukuri, and furniture are preserved in perfect condition.

Kiragawa Antique Street 吉良川の町並み

The main streets in Kiragawa are the same as they were in the late 19th and early 20th century. The narrow, maze-like roads, the white plaster walls, the tile roofs, and the rock walls have served to protect the homes from strong winds and rain.

Nahari Stn.

Direction of Gomen

5:53	15:01
6:24	16:03
7:03	17:12
8:55	17:48
9:50	18:32
10:56	19:09
12:32	20:06
13:20	21:01
13:51	21:47
14:01	23:00

Blue: Mon - Fri 2024.03

Central Nahari / Tano

2.5km
260
Nahari 奈半利
1.9km
Rental Bikes
Tourist Information
土佐湾 Tosa Bay
太平洋 Pacific Ocean
Daishidō Goreiseki 御霊跡 (14.2km to No.27)

田野駅屋 Tano-eki-ya
Misono 旅の宿美園 0887-38-2224 (Henro House)
Monet's Garden モネの庭 Marmottan
田野 Tano
Tanotano Onsen
大師堂 Daishidō
493
2.4km
2.5km
E.S.
Town Office
Takadaya 高田屋 (Cultural Property)
J.H.S.
Sunshine
Nahari
BH Nahari 0887-38-5111 ホテルなはり
Town Office
Oka-goten 岡御殿
Marunaka
E.S.
55
Nahari Stn. Bus Stop (pg 33) 奈半利駅バス停
Tano Town 田野町
1.9km
Nahari River 奈半利川
Bakery
GH Yorozuya (booking.com) 0887-30-1909 よろずや
Nahari Town 奈半利町
Hachimangū
自販機 Vending Machine
Yoshida

SCALE 1/30,000
0 500m 1km

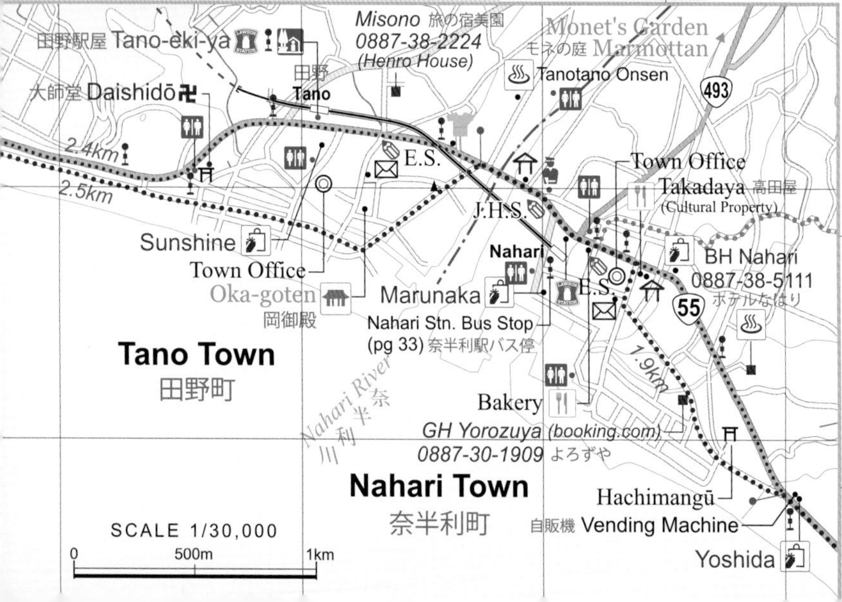

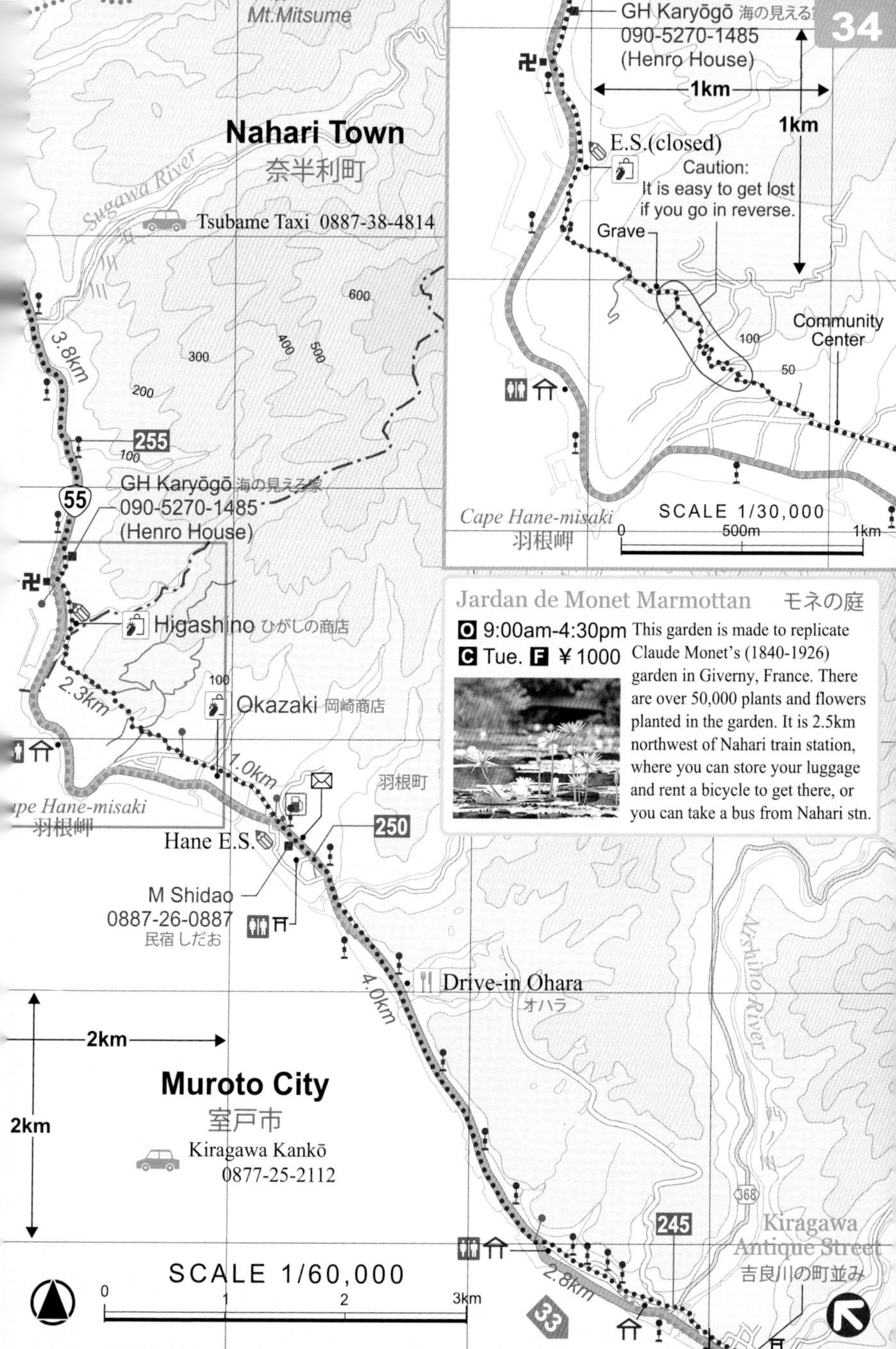
Mt.Mitsume
Nahari Town
奈半利町
Sugawa River
Tsubame Taxi 0887-38-4814
3.8km
255
55
GH Karyōgō 海の見える家
090-5270-1485
(Henro House)
Higashino ひがしの商店
Okazaki 岡崎商店
2.3km
1.0km
Cape Hane-misaki
羽根岬
羽根町
Hane E.S.
250
M Shidao
0887-26-0887
民宿 しだお
Drive-in Ohara
オハラ
4.0km
Nishino River
2km
2km
Muroto City
室戸市
Kiragawa Kankō
0877-25-2112
368
245
Kiragawa
Antique Street
吉良川の町並み
2.8km
33
SCALE 1/60,000
0
1
2
3km
GH Karyōgō 海の見える家
090-5270-1485
(Henro House)
1km
1km
E.S.(closed)
Caution:
It is easy to get lost
if you go in reverse.
Grave
Community
Center
100
50
Cape Hane-misaki
羽根岬
SCALE 1/30,000
0
500m
1km

Jardan de Monet Marmottan　モネの庭

O 9:00am-4:30pm
C Tue. F ¥1000

This garden is made to replicate Claude Monet's (1840-1926) garden in Giverny, France. There are over 50,000 plants and flowers planted in the garden. It is 2.5km northwest of Nahari train station, where you can store your luggage and rent a bicycle to get there, or you can take a bus from Nahari stn.

36

Aki City
安芸市

Ōyama 大山

3.1km 2.9km 1.1km 2.5km

Observatory 浜千鳥公園

275

Cape Ōyama-misaki 大山崎

Ōyama 西ノ浜 大山

Namura River

Shimoyama 下山

Tosa-kuroshio Railway Gomen-Nahari Line 土佐くろしお鉄道

Tōnohama Stn.

Direction of Gomen		Bound for Nahari	
6:02	15:10	5:38	14:45
6:33	16:12	6:09	15:37
7:11	17:21	6:39	16:36
7:45	17:57	7:20	17:30
9:04	18:41	8:13	18:06
9:58	19:18	9:34	18:49
11:05 A	20:14	10:42	19:42
12:42	21:09	11:53	20:23
13:29 A	21:56 A	12:50	21:33
14:00	23:09 A	13:38	22:47

Blue: Monday - Friday
A: Bound for Aki 2024.03

Ioki Hire	0120-652050
	0887-35-2050
Geiyo Taxi	0887-34-1122
Tani Taxi	0120-100417
	0887-35-2121
Maruwa Taxi	0120-502404
Cattleya Taxi	0887-35-3515

ADVICE 手ぶらで27番を往復

If you stay at an inn in the Tōnohama area, ask the owner if can leave your pack there while you walk to Temple 27 and back. Or ask at the shop Kōnomine.

Cycling Road サイクリングロード

There is a 14.5km scenic cycling road from Aki (p36) to Yasu (p37), which until 1974 was a railway line. It is not the traditional pilgrimage route, but it is very safe and easy to walk.

NOTE Sekishoji 関所寺

These are believed to be spiritual checkpoint temples (No.19 Tatsueji, No.27 Kōnomineji, No.60 Yokomineji and No.66 Unpenji) where one's spiritual motives are examined by Kōbō Daishi. If one is deemed unworthy to be doing the pilgrimage, then one will not be able to continue. See pg24-A for the story about Tatsueji.

Yaku-doshi (Unlucky year) 厄・厄年・厄除け

This is a "year of misfortune" when there is a high chance that something bad might occur. For men, this is during the 25th, 42nd and 61st year. For women, it is 19th, 33rd and 37th year. For children, it is 13th year. One theory for the number of 88 along the pilgrimage route is the total of the "most criticial years" for 42 (men), 33 (women) and 13 (children). By doing the pilgrimage, one will void any possible misfortune. And the number of steps in temples often follows these numbers. You may see stairs where someone put a coin on each step.

27 Kōnomineji 二十七番 神峯寺

H Jūichimen Kannon Bosatsu — 2594 Tōnohama, Yasuda Town — Charge (30) 10 min. walk

A About 90 min from Gomen-Nahari Line Tōnohama Stn. ☎ 0887-38-5495 S None

This temple, considered to be the "sekishoji" (spiritual checkpoint temple) of Kōchi prefecture, is located at the end of a very steep road. On the grounds is a beautiful garden and by the temple bell, "Kōnomine no mizu" (the water of Kōnomine) flows out between the rocks. A woman, who had a severe illness, saw Kūkai in her dream. He told her to drink this water and after she did so was cured.

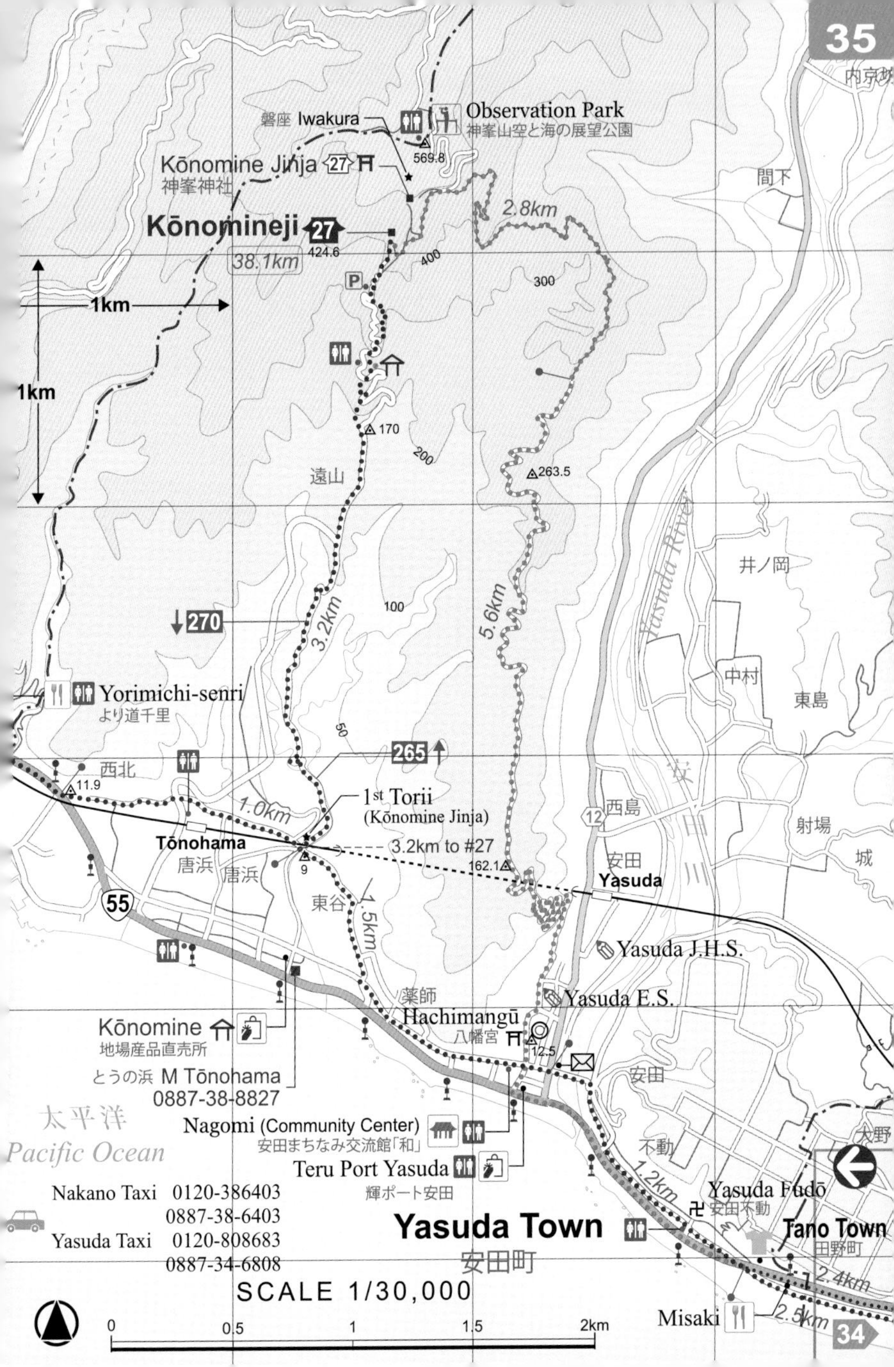

Observation Park
神峯山空と海の展望公園
磐座 Iwakura
569.8
Kōnomine Jinja 27
神峯神社
Kōnomineji 27
424.6
38.1km
2.8km
400
300
1km
1km
170
200
遠山
263.5
間下
井ノ岡
Yasuda River
270
3.2km
5.6km
100
50
中村
東島
安
田
川
Yorimichi-senri
より道千里
265
西北
11.9
1st Torii
(Kōnomine Jinja)
西島
射場
1.0km
Tōnohama
3.2km to #27
安田
城
唐浜
唐浜
9
162.1
Yasuda
55
東谷
1.5km
Yasuda J.H.S.
Yasuda E.S.
薬師
Kōnomine
地場産品直売所
Hachimangū
八幡宮
12.5
安田
とうの浜 M Tōnohama
0887-38-8827
太平洋
Pacific Ocean
Nagomi (Community Center)
安田まちなみ交流館「和」
不動
大野
Teru Port Yasuda
輝ポート安田
1.2km
Yasuda Fudō
安田不動
Nakano Taxi 0120-386403
0887-38-6403
Yasuda Taxi 0120-808683
0887-34-6808
Yasuda Town
安田町
Tano Town
田野町
2.4km
SCALE 1/30,000
Misaki
2.5km
34
0
0.5
1
1.5
2km

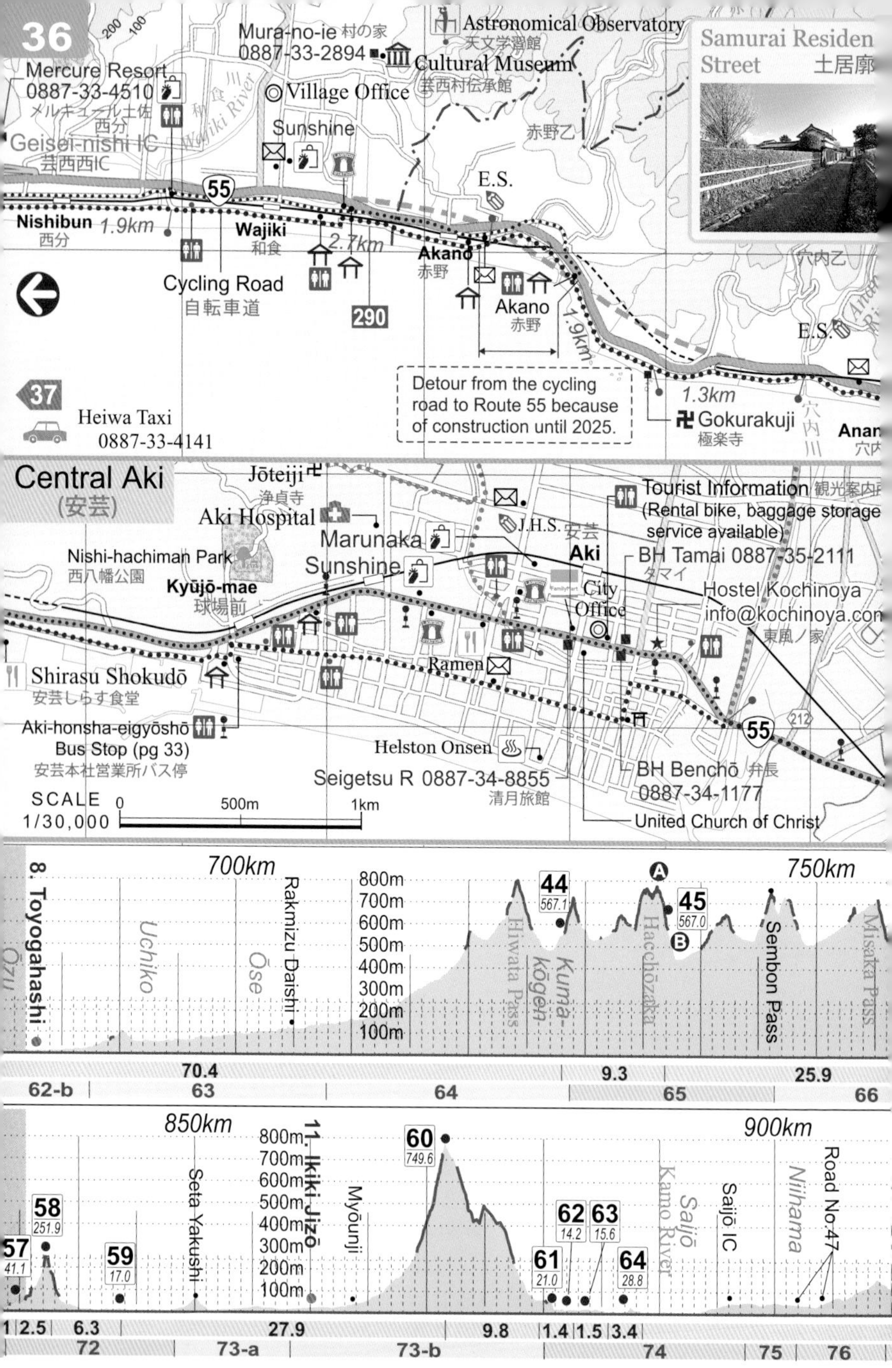
Mura-no-ie 村の家
0887-33-2894
Astronomical Observatory
天文学習館
Cultural Museum
芸西村伝承館
Samurai Residen
Street 土居廓
Mercure Resort
0887-33-4510
メルキュール土佐
西分
Village Office
Wajiki River
Geisei-nishi IC
芸西西IC
Sunshine
赤野乙
E.S.
55
Nishibun
西分
1.9km
Wajiki
和食
2.7km
Akano
赤野
穴内乙
Cycling Road
自転車道
290
Akano
赤野
1.9km
E.S.
37
Detour from the cycling road to Route 55 because of construction until 2025.
1.3km
Heiwa Taxi
0887-33-4141
Gokurakuji
極楽寺
Anan
Central Aki
(安芸)
Jōteiji
浄貞寺
Aki Hospital
Marunaka
J.H.S. 安芸
Tourist Information 観光案内
(Rental bike, baggage storage service available)
Nishi-hachiman Park
西八幡公園
Sunshine
Aki
BH Tamai 0887-35-2111
タマイ
Kyūjō-mae
球場前
City Office
Hostel Kochinoya
info@kochinoya.com
東風ノ家
Shirasu Shokudō
安芸しらす食堂
Ramen
Aki-honsha-eigyōshō
Bus Stop (pg 33)
安芸本社営業所バス停
Helston Onsen
212
55
Seigetsu R 0887-34-8855
清月旅館
BH Benchō 弁長
0887-34-1177
SCALE
1/30,000
0
500m
1km
United Church of Christ
8. Toyogahashi
Ōzu
700km
Uchiko
Ōse
Rakmizu Daishi
800m
700m
600m
500m
400m
300m
200m
100m
44
567.1
Hiwata Pass
Kuma-kōgen
A
Hacchōzaka
45
567.0
B
750km
Sembon Pass
Misaka Pass
70.4
9.3
25.9
62-b
63
64
65
66
850km
11. Ikiki Jizō
60
749.6
900km
57
41.1
58
251.9
59
17.0
Seta Yakushi
Myōunji
61
21.0
62
14.2
63
15.6
64
28.8
Saijō
Kamo River
Saijō IC
Niihama
Road No.47
1
2.5
6.3
27.9
9.8
1.4
1.5
3.4
72
73-a
73-b
74
75
76

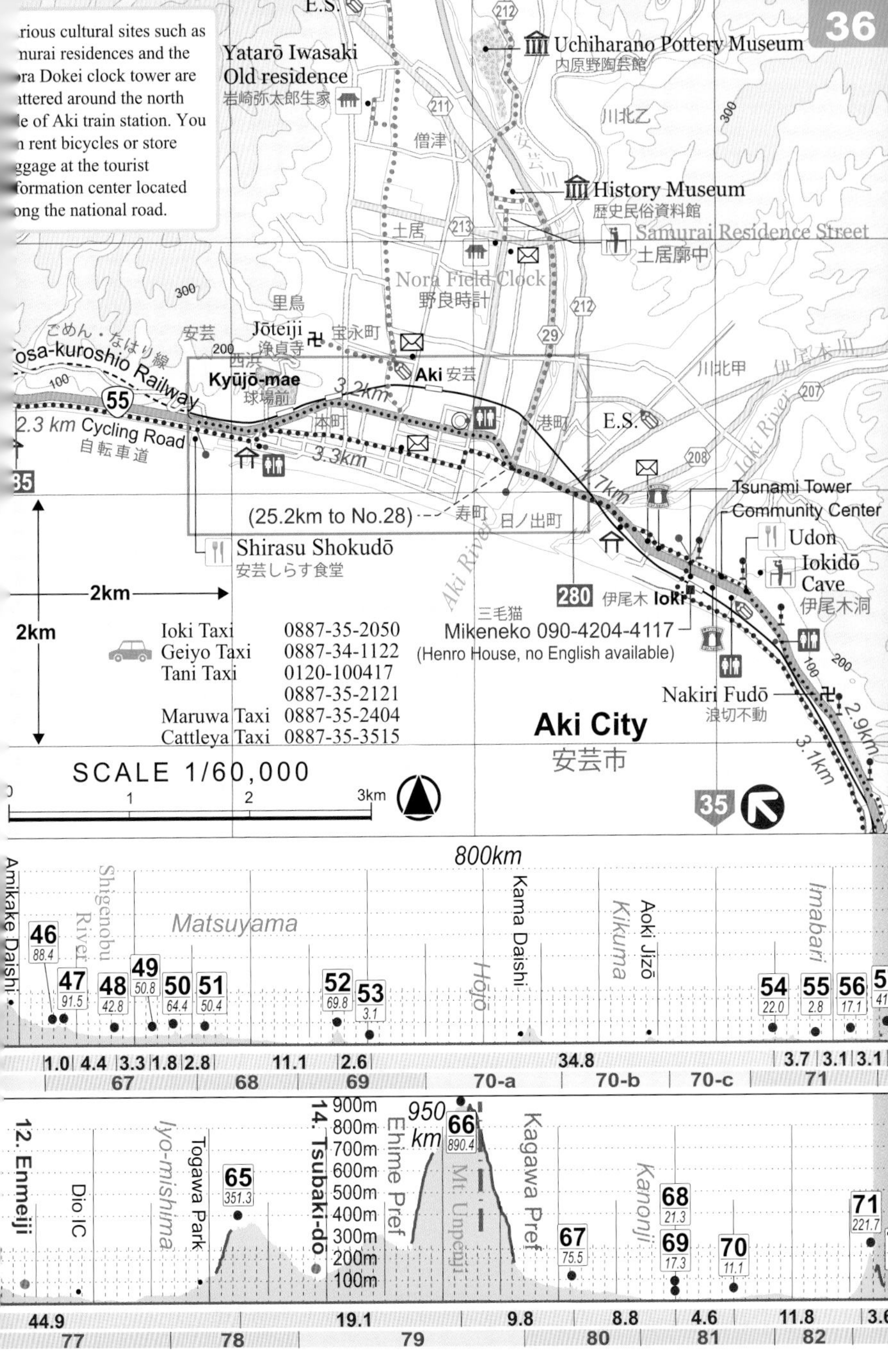
...rious cultural sites such as ...murai residences and the ...ra Dokei clock tower are ...attered around the north ...le of Aki train station. You ...n rent bicycles or store ...ggage at the tourist ...formation center located ...ong the national road.
Yatarō Iwasaki Old residence
岩崎弥太郎生家
Uchiharano Pottery Museum
内原野陶芸館
History Museum
歴史民俗資料館
Samurai Residence Street
土居廓中
Nora Field Clock
野良時計
Jōteiji
浄貞寺
Tosa-kuroshio Railway
ごめん・なはり線
Kyūjō-mae
球場前
Aki 安芸
2.3 km Cycling Road
自転車道
3.2km
3.3km
1.7km
(25.2km to No.28)
Shirasu Shokudō
安芸しらす食堂
Tsunami Tower
Community Center
Udon
Iokidō Cave
伊尾木洞
280 伊尾木 Ioki
三毛猫
Mikeneko 090-4204-4117
(Henro House, no English available)
Nakiri Fudō
浪切不動
2.9km
3.1km
Aki City
安芸市
Aki River
Ioki River
2km
2km
Ioki Taxi 0887-35-2050
Geiyo Taxi 0887-34-1122
Tani Taxi 0120-100417
0887-35-2121
Maruwa Taxi 0887-35-2404
Cattleya Taxi 0887-35-3515
SCALE 1/60,000
800km
Amikake Daishi
Shigenobu River
Matsuyama
Hōjō
Kama Daishi
Kikuma
Aoki Jizō
Imabari
46 88.4
47 91.5
48 42.8
49 50.8
50 64.4
51 50.4
52 69.8
53 3.1
54 22.0
55 2.8
56 17.1
1.0 4.4 3.3 1.8 2.8 11.1 2.6 34.8 3.7 3.1 3.1
67 68 69 70-a 70-b 70-c 71
12. Enmeiji
Dio IC
Iyo-mishima
Togawa Park
65 351.3
14. Tsubaki-dō
Ehime Pref
950 km
66 890.4
Mt. Unpenji
Kagawa Pref
67 75.5
Kanonji
68 21.3
69 17.3
70 11.1
71 221.7
44.9 19.1 9.8 8.8 4.6 11.8
77 78 79 80 81 82

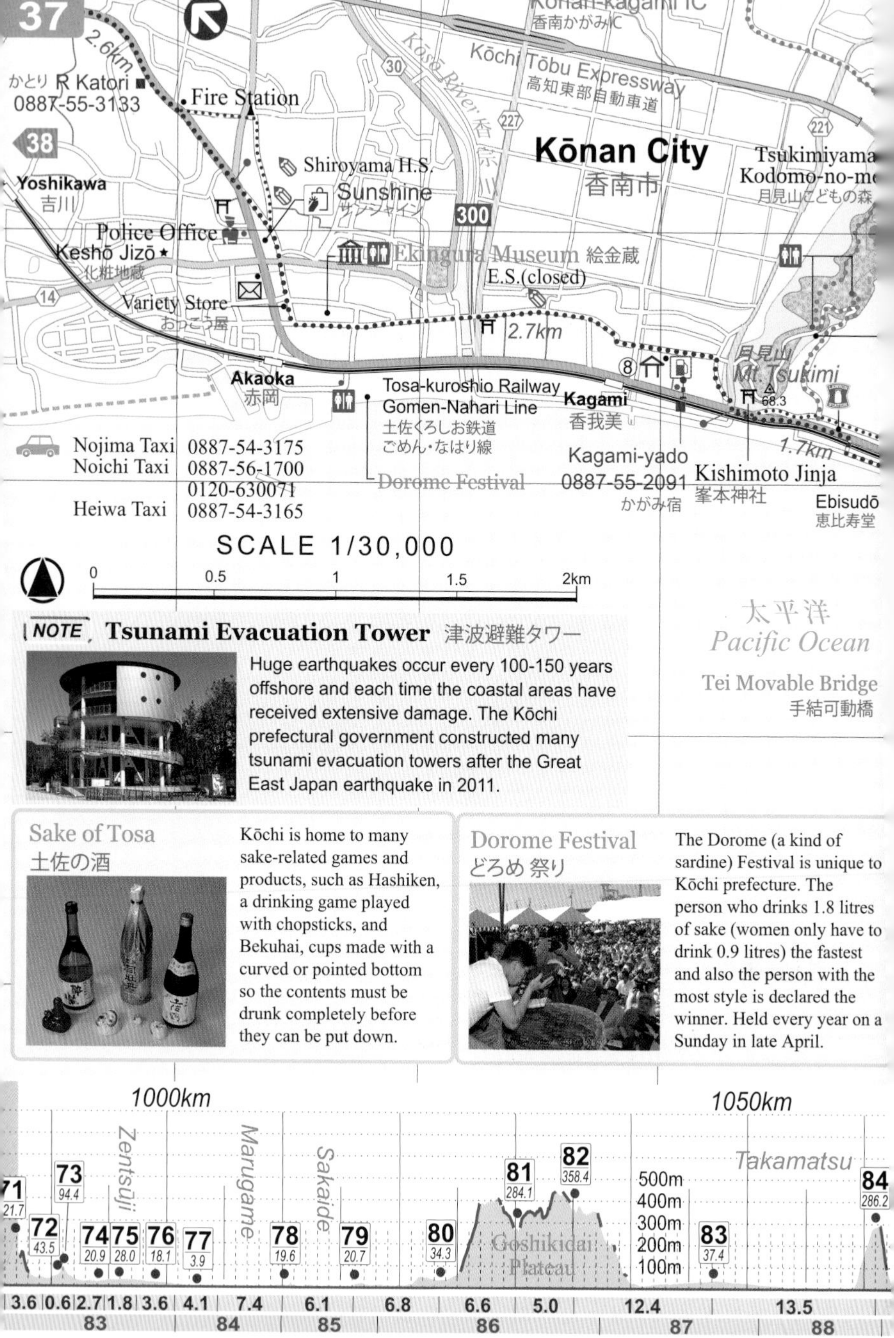
37
2.6km
かとり R Katori
0887-55-3133
Fire Station
38
Shiroyama H.S.
Sunshine
サンシャイン
Yoshikawa
吉川
Police Office
Keshō Jizō
化粧地蔵
Ekingura Museum 絵金蔵
E.S.(closed)
14
Variety Store
おっこう屋
2.7km
Kōnan-kagami IC
香南かがみIC
Kōso River 香宗川
Kōchi Tōbu Expressway
高知東部自動車道
30
227
300
221
Kōnan City
香南市
Tsukimiyama
Kodomo-no-m
月見山こどもの森
月見山
Mt. Tsukimi
68.3
8
Akaoka
赤岡
Tosa-kuroshio Railway
Gomen-Nahari Line
土佐くろしお鉄道
ごめん・なはり線
Kagami
香我美
1.7km
Nojima Taxi 0887-54-3175
Noichi Taxi 0887-56-1700
0120-630071
Heiwa Taxi 0887-54-3165
Dorome Festival
Kagami-yado
0887-55-2091
かがみ宿
Kishimoto Jinja
峯本神社
Ebisudō
恵比寿堂
SCALE 1/30,000
0
0.5
1
1.5
2km
太平洋
Pacific Ocean
Tei Movable Bridge
手結可動橋
NOTE
Tsunami Evacuation Tower 津波避難タワー
Huge earthquakes occur every 100-150 years offshore and each time the coastal areas have received extensive damage. The Kōchi prefectural government constructed many tsunami evacuation towers after the Great East Japan earthquake in 2011.
Sake of Tosa
土佐の酒
Kōchi is home to many sake-related games and products, such as Hashiken, a drinking game played with chopsticks, and Bekuhai, cups made with a curved or pointed bottom so the contents must be drunk completely before they can be put down.
Dorome Festival
どろめ祭り
The Dorome (a kind of sardine) Festival is unique to Kōchi prefecture. The person who drinks 1.8 litres of sake (women only have to drink 0.9 litres) the fastest and also the person with the most style is declared the winner. Held every year on a Sunday in late April.
1000km
1050km
Zentsūji
Marugame
Sakaide
Takamatsu
Goshikidai Plateau
500m
400m
300m
200m
100m
71
21.7
72
43.5
73
94.4
74
20.9
75
28.0
76
18.1
77
3.9
78
19.6
79
20.7
80
34.3
81
284.1
82
358.4
83
37.4
84
286.2
3.6
0.6
2.7
1.8
3.6
4.1
7.4
6.1
6.8
6.6
5.0
12.4
13.5
83
84
85
86
87
88

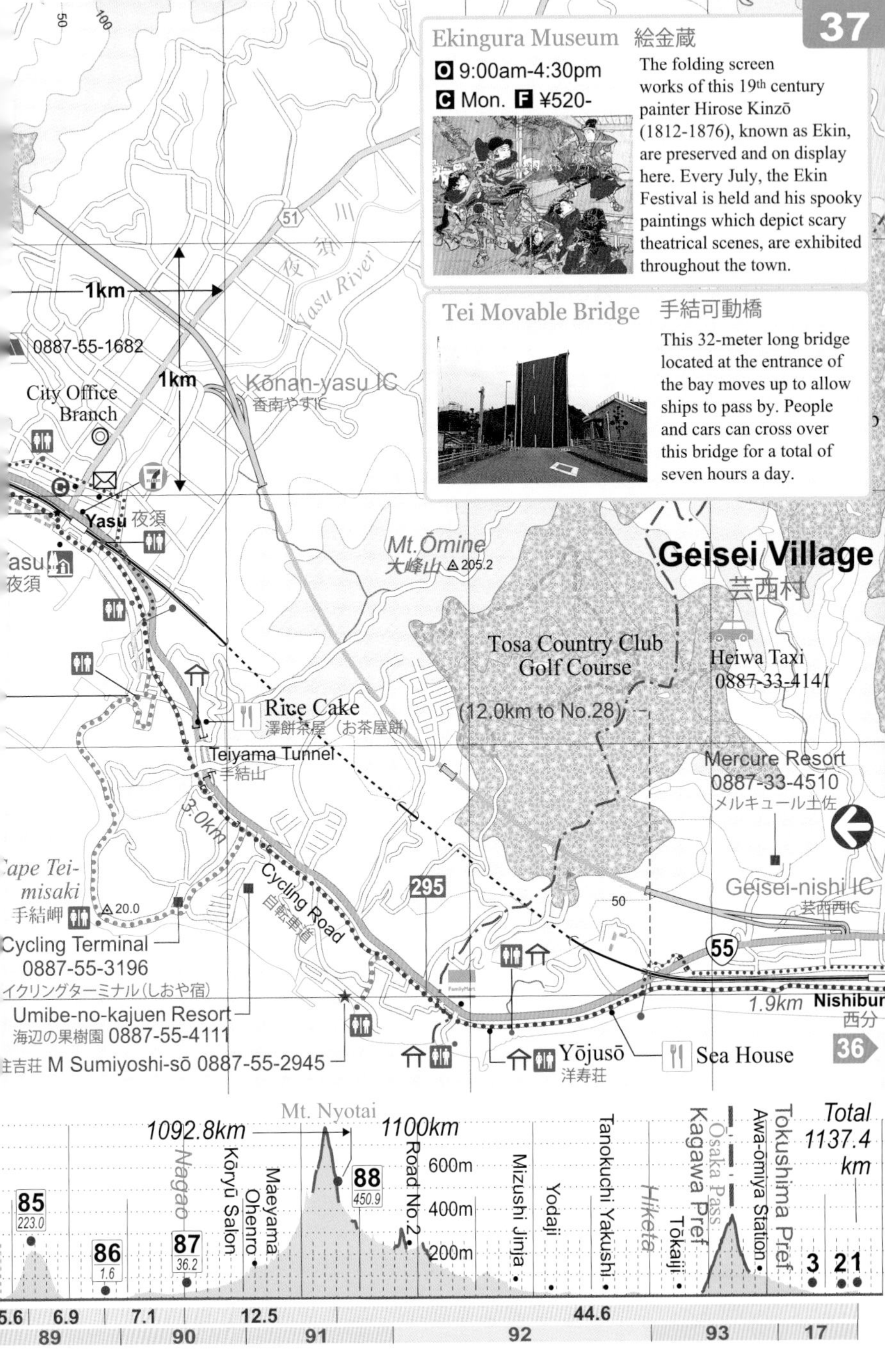
Ekingura Museum 絵金蔵
O 9:00am-4:30pm
C Mon. F ¥520-
The folding screen works of this 19th century painter Hirose Kinzō (1812-1876), known as Ekin, are preserved and on display here. Every July, the Ekin Festival is held and his spooky paintings which depict scary theatrical scenes, are exhibited throughout the town.
Tei Movable Bridge 手結可動橋
This 32-meter long bridge located at the entrance of the bay moves up to allow ships to pass by. People and cars can cross over this bridge for a total of seven hours a day.
1km
1km
0887-55-1682
City Office Branch
Kōnan-yasu IC
香南やすIC
Yasu River
夜須川
51
Yasu 夜須
Yasu
夜須
Mt.Ōmine
大峰山 205.2
Geisei Village
芸西村
Heiwa Taxi
0887-33-4141
Tosa Country Club Golf Course
(12.0km to No.28)
Rice Cake
澤餅茶屋（お茶屋餅）
Teiyama Tunnel
手結山
3.0km
Mercure Resort
0887-33-4510
メルキュール土佐
Cape Tei-misaki
手結岬
20.0
Cycling Road
自転車道
295
Geisei-nishi IC
芸西西IC
50
55
Cycling Terminal
0887-55-3196
サイクリングターミナル（しおや宿）
Umibe-no-kajuen Resort
海辺の果樹園 0887-55-4111
住吉荘 M Sumiyoshi-sō 0887-55-2945
Yōjusō
洋寿荘
Sea House
1.9km
Nishibun
西分
36
Mt. Nyotai
1092.8km
1100km
Total 1137.4 km
600m
400m
200m
85
223.0
86
1.6
87
36.2
88
450.9
Nagao
Kōryū Salon
Maeyama Ohenro
Road No.2
Mizushi Jinja
Yodaji
Tanokuchi Yakushi
Hiketa
Tōkaiji
Kagawa Pref
Ōsaka Pass
Awa-ōmiya Station
Tokushima Pref
3
2
1
5.6
6.9
7.1
12.5
44.6
89
90
91
92
93
17

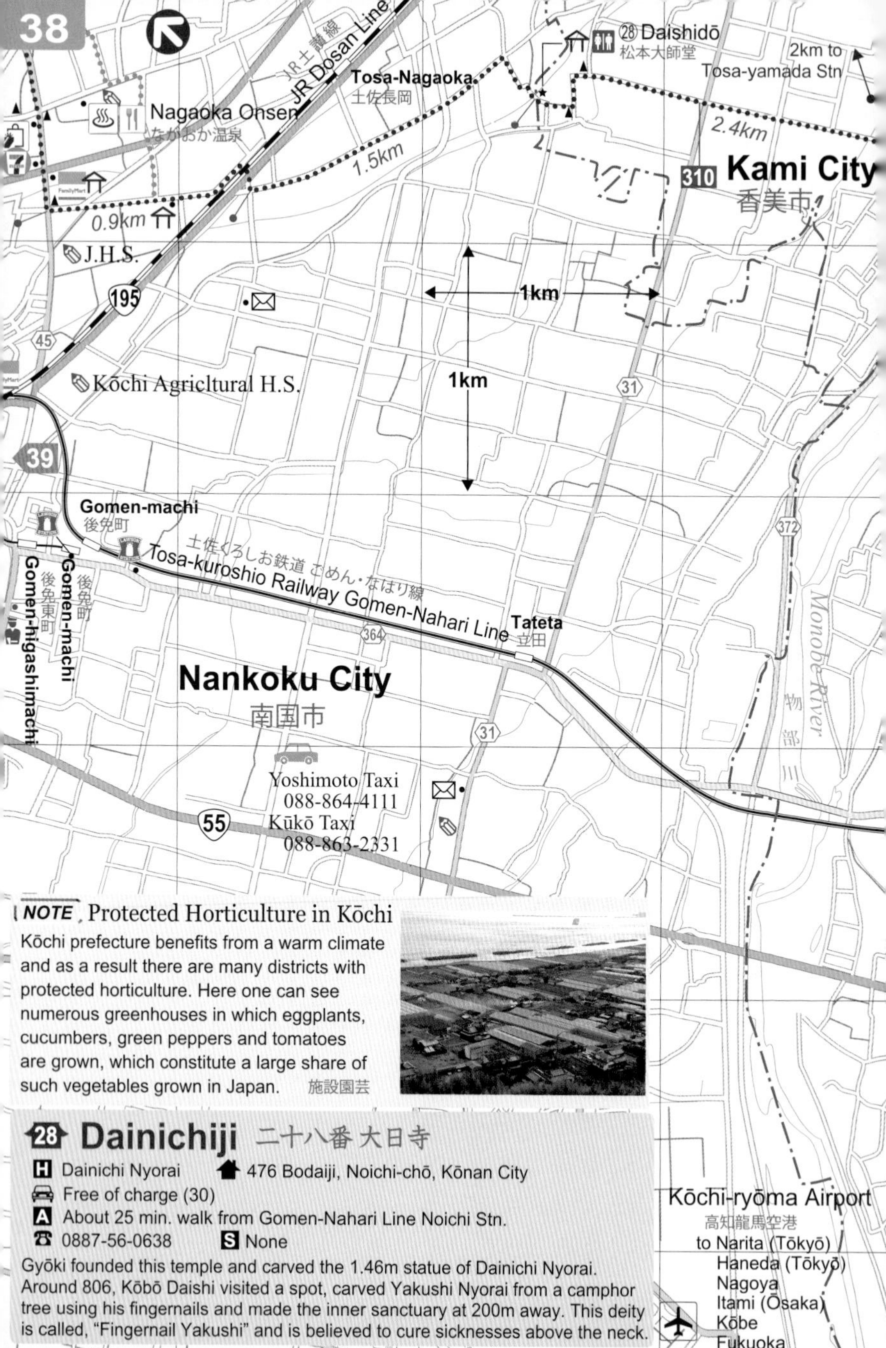

㉘ Daishidō
松本大師堂
2km to Tosa-yamada Stn
Tosa-Nagaoka
土佐長岡
JR Dosan Line
JR土讃線
Nagaoka Onsen
ながおか温泉
1.5km
0.9km
2.4km
310
Kami City
香美市
J.H.S.
195
45
1km
1km
Kōchi Agricltural H.S.
31
39
Gomen-machi
後免町
Gomen-machi
後免町
Gomen-higashimachi
後免東町
土佐くろしお鉄道 ごめん・なはり線
Tosa-kuroshio Railway Gomen-Nahari Line
Tateta
立田
364
372
Monobe River
物部川
Nankoku City
南国市
31
Yoshimoto Taxi
088-864-4111
Kūkō Taxi
088-863-2331
55
Kōchi-ryōma Airport
高知龍馬空港
to Narita (Tōkyō)
Haneda (Tōkyō)
Nagoya
Itami (Ōsaka)
Kōbe
Fukuoka

NOTE Protected Horticulture in Kōchi

Kōchi prefecture benefits from a warm climate and as a result there are many districts with protected horticulture. Here one can see numerous greenhouses in which eggplants, cucumbers, green peppers and tomatoes are grown, which constitute a large share of such vegetables grown in Japan. 施設園芸

28 Dainichiji 二十八番 大日寺

H Dainichi Nyorai
476 Bodaiji, Noichi-chō, Kōnan City
Free of charge (30)
A About 25 min. walk from Gomen-Nahari Line Noichi Stn.
☎ 0887-56-0638
S None

Gyōki founded this temple and carved the 1.46m statue of Dainichi Nyorai. Around 806, Kōbō Daishi visited a spot, carved Yakushi Nyorai from a camphor tree using his fingernails and made the inner sanctuary at 200m away. This deity is called, "Fingernail Yakushi" and is believed to cure sicknesses above the neck.

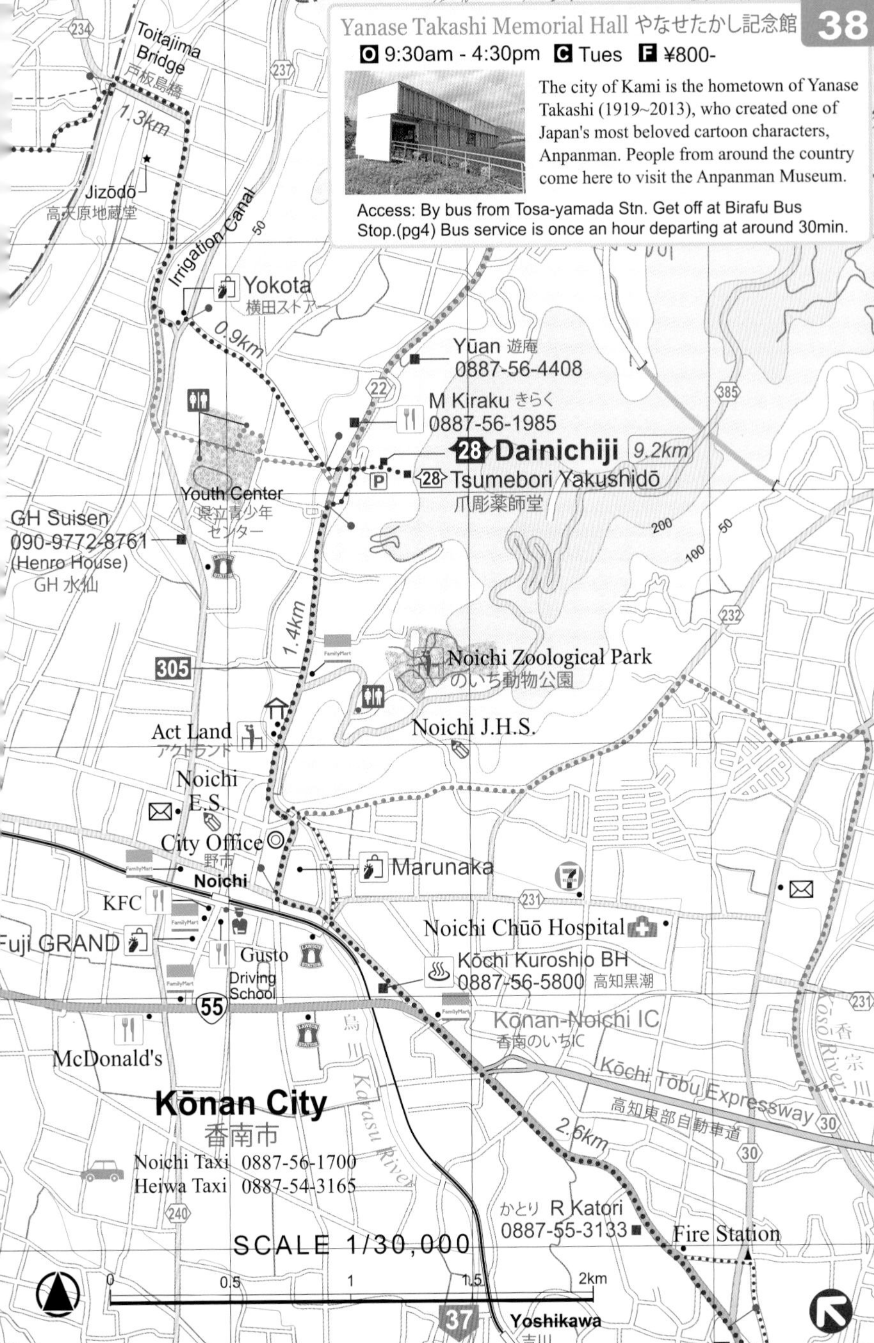

Yanase Takashi Memorial Hall やなせたかし記念館
O 9:30am - 4:30pm C Tues F ¥800-
The city of Kami is the hometown of Yanase Takashi (1919~2013), who created one of Japan's most beloved cartoon characters, Anpanman. People from around the country come here to visit the Anpanman Museum.
Access: By bus from Tosa-yamada Stn. Get off at Birafu Bus Stop.(pg4) Bus service is once an hour departing at around 30min.
Toitajima Bridge
戸板島橋
1.3km
Jizōdō
高天原地蔵堂
Irrigation Canal
Yokota
横田ストアー
0.9km
Yūan 遊庵
0887-56-4408
M Kiraku きらく
0887-56-1985
28 Dainichiji 9.2km
28 Tsumebori Yakushidō
爪彫薬師堂
Youth Center
県立青少年センター
GH Suisen
090-9772-8761
(Henro House)
GH 水仙
1.4km
305
Noichi Zoological Park
のいち動物公園
Act Land
アクトランド
Noichi J.H.S.
Noichi E.S.
City Office
野市
Marunaka
Noichi
KFC
Fuji GRAND
Gusto
Driving School
Noichi Chūō Hospital
Kōchi Kuroshio BH
0887-56-5800 高知黒潮
Kōnan-Noichi IC
香南のいちIC
McDonald's
Kōchi Tōbu Expressway
高知東部自動車道
Kōnan City
香南市
Karasu River
Koso River
2.6km
Noichi Taxi 0887-56-1700
Heiwa Taxi 0887-54-3165
かとり R Katori
0887-55-3133
Fire Station
SCALE 1/30,000
0 0.5 1 1.5 2km
Yoshikawa
吉川

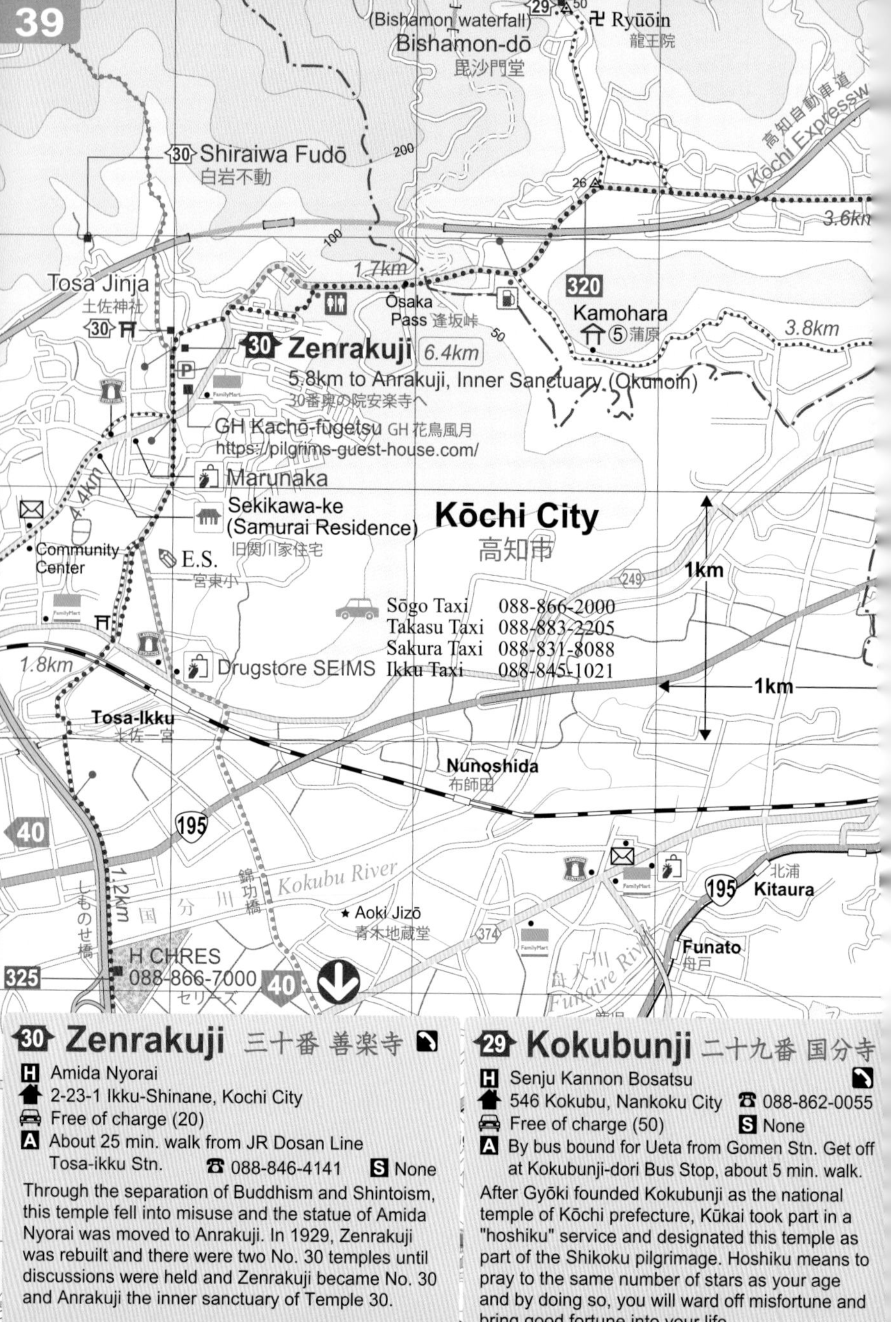

39
(Bishamon waterfall)
Bishamon-dō
毘沙門堂
29
Ryūōin
龍王院
高知自動車道
Kōchi Expressw
Shiraiwa Fudō
白岩不動
30
200
100
26
3.6km
1.7km
320
Tosa Jinja
土佐神社
Ōsaka Pass 逢坂峠
Kamohara
⑤蒲原
50
3.8km
30 Zenrakuji 6.4km
5.8km to Anrakuji, Inner Sanctuary (Okunoin)
30番奥の院安楽寺へ
GH Kachō-fūgetsu GH 花鳥風月
https://pilgrims-guest-house.com/
Marunaka
4.4km
Sekikawa-ke
(Samurai Residence)
旧関川家住宅
Kōchi City
高知市
Community Center
E.S.
一宮東小
249
1km
Sōgo Taxi 088-866-2000
Takasu Taxi 088-883-2205
Sakura Taxi 088-831-8088
Ikku Taxi 088-845-1021
1.8km
Drugstore SEIMS
1km
Tosa-Ikku
土佐一宮
Nunoshida
布師田
40
195
1.2km
しものせ橋
国分川
錦功橋
Kokubu River
Aoki Jizō
青木地蔵堂
374
北浦
Kitaura
Funato
舟戸
H CHRES
088-866-7000
セリーズ
325
40
舟入川
Funaire River

30 Zenrakuji 三十番 善楽寺

H Amida Nyorai
2-23-1 Ikku-Shinane, Kochi City
Free of charge (20)
A About 25 min. walk from JR Dosan Line Tosa-ikku Stn. ☎ 088-846-4141 S None

Through the separation of Buddhism and Shintoism, this temple fell into misuse and the statue of Amida Nyorai was moved to Anrakuji. In 1929, Zenrakuji was rebuilt and there were two No. 30 temples until discussions were held and Zenrakuji became No. 30 and Anrakuji the inner sanctuary of Temple 30.

29 Kokubunji 二十九番 国分寺

H Senju Kannon Bosatsu
546 Kokubu, Nankoku City ☎ 088-862-0055
Free of charge (50) S None
A By bus bound for Ueta from Gomen Stn. Get off at Kokubunji-dori Bus Stop, about 5 min. walk.

After Gyōki founded Kokubunji as the national temple of Kōchi prefecture, Kūkai took part in a "hoshiku" service and designated this temple as part of the Shikoku pilgrimage. Hoshiku means to pray to the same number of stars as your age and by doing so, you will ward off misfortune and bring good fortune into your life.

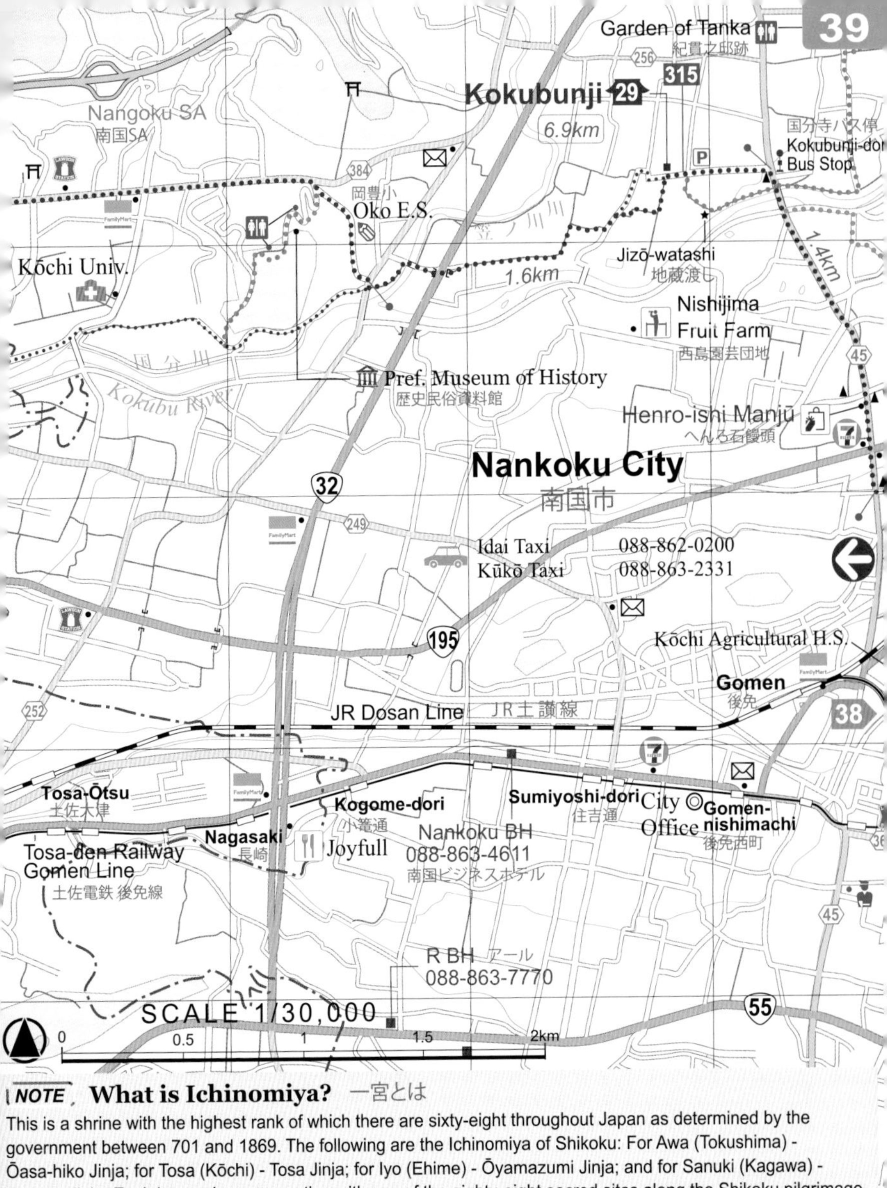
Garden of Tanka
紀貫之邸跡
Kokubunji 29
6.9km
315
Nangoku SA
南国SA
国分寺バス停
Kokubunji-dori Bus Stop
岡豊小
Oko E.S.
Kōchi Univ.
1.6km
1.4km
Jizō-watashi
地蔵渡し
Nishijima Fruit Farm
西島園芸団地
Kokubu River
Pref. Museum of History
歴史民俗資料館
Henro-ishi Manjū
へんろ石饅頭
Nankoku City
南国市
Idai Taxi 088-862-0200
Kūkō Taxi 088-863-2331
Kōchi Agricultural H.S.
Gomen
後免
38
JR Dosan Line
JR土讃線
Tosa-Ōtsu
土佐大津
Kogome-dori
小篭通
Sumiyoshi-dori
住吉通
City Office
Gomen-nishimachi
後免西町
Nagasaki
長崎
Joyfull
Nankoku BH
088-863-4611
南国ビジネスホテル
Tosa-den Railway Gomen Line
土佐電鉄 後免線
R BH アール
088-863-7770
SCALE 1/30,000
0
0.5
1
1.5
2km

NOTE **What is Ichinomiya?** 一宮とは

This is a shrine with the highest rank of which there are sixty-eight throughout Japan as determined by the government between 701 and 1869. The following are the Ichinomiya of Shikoku: For Awa (Tokushima) - Ōasa-hiko Jinja; for Tosa (Kōchi) - Tosa Jinja; for Iyo (Ehime) - Ōyamazumi Jinja; and for Sanuki (Kagawa) - Tamura Jinja. Each has a close connection with one of the eighty-eight sacred sites along the Shikoku pilgrimage.

Shinbutsu-bunri (separation ordinance of Buddhism and Shintoism) 神仏分離

In 1868, the government in their push towards nationalism considered Shintō the true religion of Japan and ordered the separation of Buddhism and Shintō. As a result, various temples and precious artifacts were destroyed as part of the haibutsu kishaku (destroy Buddhism) movement. This continued until 1875 when people were told that they were free to worship any religion.

Sunday Market 日曜市

This weekly Sunday Market is one of the most well-known in Japan. It features local agricultural products, potted plants, antiques, everyday items, and other special local products. The nearby Hirome Market is a street filled with restaurants and shops.

16
FamilyMart
Kakegawa Jinja
掛川神社
44
4.4km
Azōno
薊野
Red Cross Hosp
Katsuo GH
070-5352-1167
かつおゲストハウス

Pokapoka Onsen
ぽかぽか温泉
Sushi
44
16
FamilyMart
Anrakuji 30
安楽寺
5.6km to No.31
★ユースホステル
088-823-0858
Kōchi YH
(700m ahead)
Iriake
入明
コンフォート Comfort BH 088-884-2811
楽家櫻舘 BH Gakuya 088-804-1122
タウン駅前 BH Town 088-884-0066
Bus Terminal (Intercity)
Tourist Information
Kōchi
1.0km
Volver
(Vegan)
mont bell
BH Los Inn 088-884-1110 ロスイン
Sakura BH 088-882-5021 さくら
高知 Kōchi BH 088-822-8008
スーパー Super BH 088-802-9000
ツーリストイン Tourist Inn 088-820-5151
0.7km
タウンセンター BH Town Center 088-824-1800
グリーン BH Kōchi Green 088-822-1800
BH First 088-861-6688 ファースト
BH AreaOne 088-880-1919 エリアワン
EN Hostel 088-855-9888 (booking.com)
GH Tosa 090-5272-9341 GH土佐
Tomarigi Hostel 080-2979-4212
Harimayabashi GH (booking.com) はりまや橋
高知城 Kōchi Castle
ひろめ市場 Hirome Market
Sunday Market
Shopping Street
Pref. Office
City Office
33
Harimaya-bashi
高野寺 Kōyaji
Sakai-machi
Bus Stop
堺町バス停
CUL-PORT
かるぽーと
32
サンライズ Sunrise BH 088-822-1281
タウン本町 BH Town Honmachi 088-825-0055
高知ビジネス Kōchi BH 088-875-3121
Harimayabashi Bus Stop
(Inter-City) はりまやばしバス停
patagonia
BH Avest Kōchi
088-885-0077
アベスト
General Sports Ground
総合運動場
FamilyMart
2.3km
BH Best Price
088-861-1223
ベストプライス
Sushi
Kagami River
鏡川
Sambashi Line
Street Car
とさでん桟橋線
Aoyagi-bashi-higashizume Bus Stop
青柳橋東詰バス停

CUL-PORT かるぽーと
(Yokoyama Memorial Manga Museum)

O 9:00am-6:00pm
C Mon. F ¥410-

Manga artist, Ryūichi Yokoyama (1909-2001) was born in Kōchi prefecture, so the city built this museum in his name. The prefecture has produced several other well-known manga artists, and actively promotes development of manga culture.

Makino Botanical Garden 牧野植物園

O 9:00am-4:30pm C 12/27-1/1 F ¥730-

Materials once owned by Tomitarō Makino (1862-1957), a botanist from Kōchi prefecture are stored here. This multi-purpose botanical garden is also a great place to relax and take a break.

31 Chikurinji 三十一番 竹林寺

H Monju Bosatsu
☎ 088-882-3085
3577 Godaisan, Kōchi City
S None
Free of charge (70)
A By bus bound for Maehama Shako bus stop from Harimaya-bashi bus stop (N2). Get off at Aoyagi-bashi-higashizume Bus Stop, about 30 min. walk.

According to legend, Emperor Shōmu was told by Monju Bosatsu to find a place similar to Mt. Godai-san in China. He commanded Gyōki to search for such a place and founded this temple in 724. Originally, there was a 3-storey pagoda, but it was blown down by a typhoon in 1899. The present 5-storey one was built in 1980.

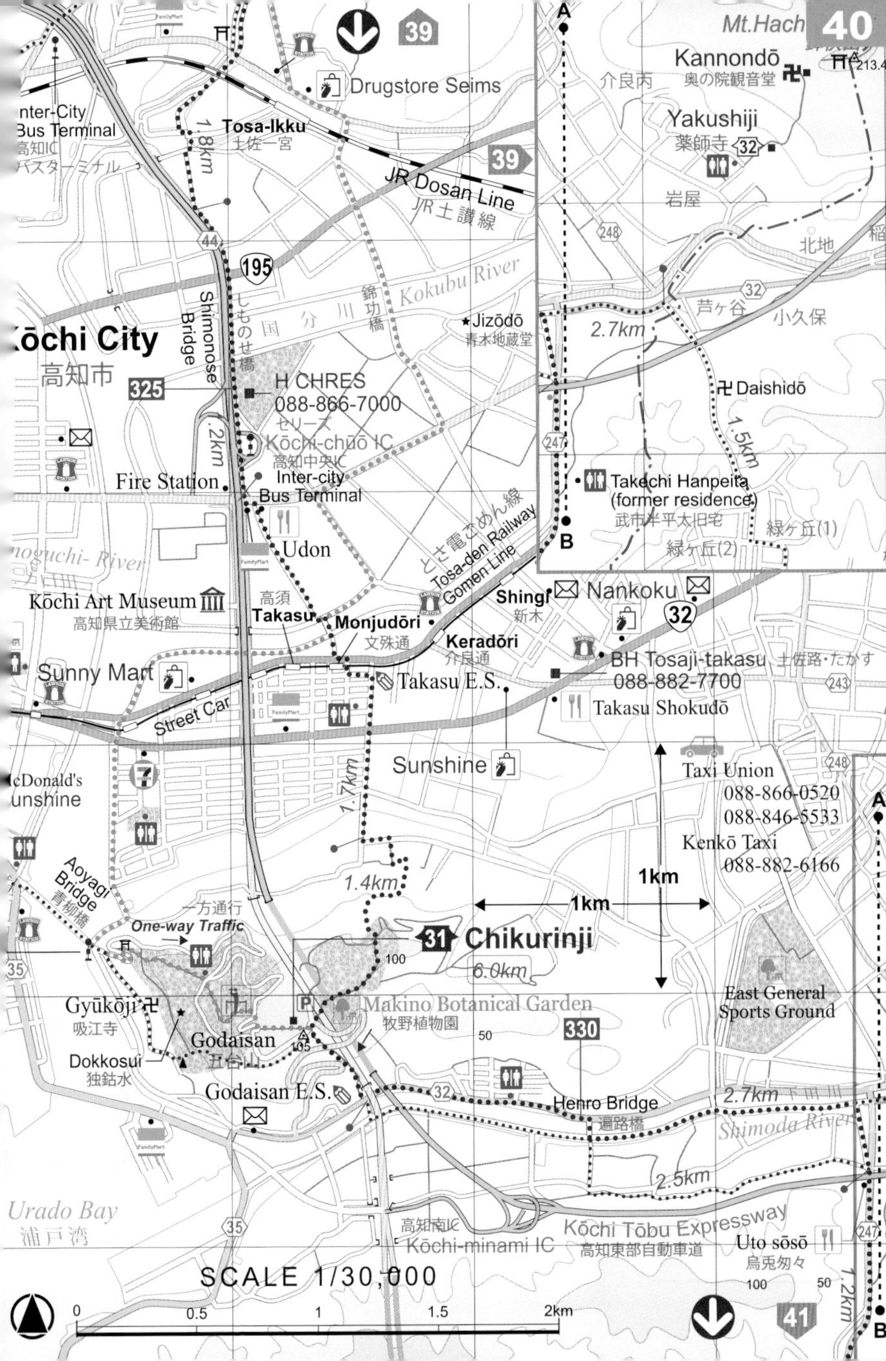

Mt.Hach
Kannondō
奥の院観音堂
213.4
介良丙
Yakushiji
薬師寺
岩屋
北地
芦ヶ谷
小久保
2.7km
Daishidō
1.5km
Takechi Hanpeita (former residence)
武市半平太旧宅
緑ヶ丘(1)
緑ヶ丘(2)
Drugstore Seims
Inter-City Bus Terminal
高知IC バスターミナル
Tosa-Ikku
土佐一宮
1.8km
JR Dosan Line
JR土讃線
Kokubu River
国分川
錦功橋
Shimonose Bridge
しものせ橋
Jizōdō
青木地蔵堂
Kōchi City
高知市
H CHRES
088-866-7000
セリーズ
Kōchi-chūō IC
高知中央IC
Inter-city Bus Terminal
1.2km
Fire Station
Udon
とさ電さめん線
Tosa-den Railway Gomen Line
Kōchi Art Museum
高知県立美術館
高須
Takasu
Monjudōri
文殊通
Keradōri
介良通
Shingi
新木
Nankoku
BH Tosaji-takasu
土佐路・たかす
088-882-7700
Sunny Mart
Takasu E.S.
Takasu Shokudō
Street Car
Sunshine
1.7km
McDonald's
Sunshine
Taxi Union
088-866-0520
088-846-5533
Kenkō Taxi
088-882-6166
1km
1km
Aoyagi Bridge
青柳橋
1.4km
一方通行
One-way Traffic
Chikurinji
6.0km
Gyūkōji
吸江寺
Makino Botanical Garden
牧野植物園
East General Sports Ground
Godaisan
五台山
105
Dokkosui
独鈷水
Godaisan E.S.
Henro Bridge
遍路橋
2.7km
Shimoda River
2.5km
Urado Bay
浦戸湾
高知南IC
Kōchi-minami IC
Kōchi Tōbu Expressway
高知東部自動車道
Uto sōsō
烏兎匆々
1.2km
SCALE 1/30,000
0
0.5
1
1.5
2km

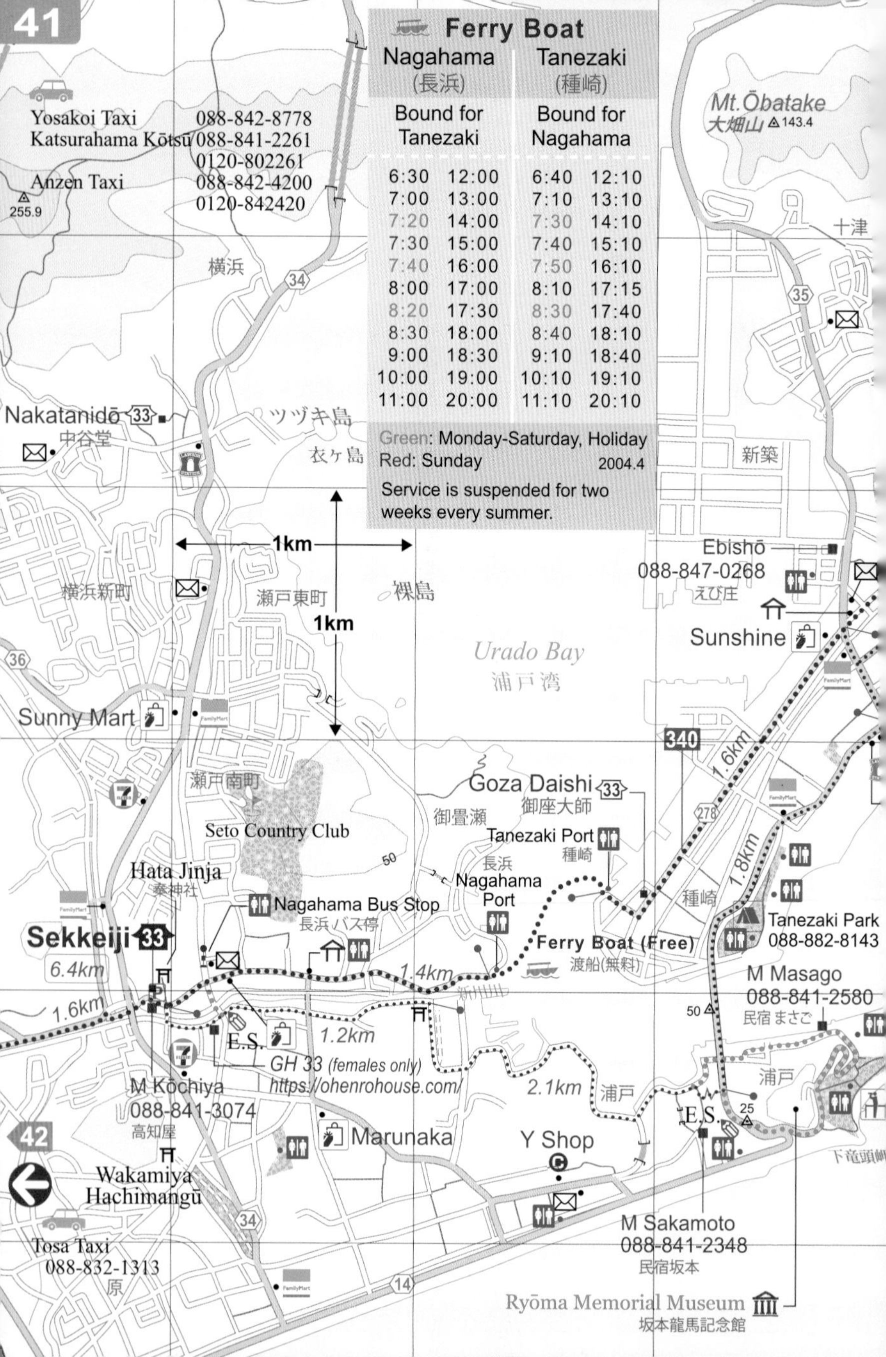

Ferry Boat

Nagahama (長浜) Bound for Tanezaki		Tanezaki (種崎) Bound for Nagahama	
6:30	12:00	6:40	12:10
7:00	13:00	7:10	13:10
7:20	14:00	7:30	14:10
7:30	15:00	7:40	15:10
7:40	16:00	7:50	16:10
8:00	17:00	8:10	17:15
8:20	17:30	8:30	17:40
8:30	18:00	8:40	18:10
9:00	18:30	9:10	18:40
10:00	19:00	10:10	19:10
11:00	20:00	11:10	20:10

Green: Monday-Saturday, Holiday
Red: Sunday 2004.4
Service is suspended for two weeks every summer.

41
Yosakoi Taxi 088-842-8778
Katsurahama Kōtsū 088-841-2261
0120-802261
Anzen Taxi 088-842-4200
0120-842420
255.9
横浜
34
Mt.Ōbatake
大畑山 143.4
十津
35
Nakatanidō 33
中谷堂
ツヅキ島
衣ヶ島
新築
1km
1km
Ebishō
088-847-0268
えび庄
横浜新町
瀬戸東町
裸島
Sunshine
Urado Bay
浦戸湾
36
Sunny Mart
340
1.6km
瀬戸南町
Goza Daishi 33
御座大師
御畳瀬
Seto Country Club
Tanezaki Port
種崎
278
1.8km
50
長浜
Nagahama Port
Hata Jinja
秦神社
Nagahama Bus Stop
長浜バス停
種崎
Tanezaki Park
088-882-8143
Sekkeiji 33
6.4km
Ferry Boat (Free)
渡船(無料)
1.4km
M Masago
088-841-2580
民宿まさご
1.6km
50
1.2km
E.S.
GH 33 (females only)
https://ohenrohouse.com/
2.1km
浦戸
浦戸
M Kōchiya
088-841-3074
高知屋
E.S.
25
42
Marunaka
Y Shop
下竜頭岬
Wakamiya Hachimangū
34
M Sakamoto
088-841-2348
民宿坂本
Tosa Taxi
088-832-1313
原
14
Ryōma Memorial Museum
坂本龍馬記念館

osakai Festival
さこい祭り

This festival occurs annually between the 9th and the 12th of August. The only requirement is that dancing groups incorporate the naruko hand-held wooden clappers into their dance; choreography, costuming, and music are all up to the individual group.

40

1.2km
1.5km
Sun Plaza
Midorigaoka-3chōme
Bus Stop
緑ケ丘
35
Ige Jinja
Zenjibuji 32
85.4
Toochi
E.S.
8.1km
1.3km
1.4km
十市
247
248

Sekido Jinja
石土神社

Ike Park
池公園

池

376

Kōchi City
高知市

Ōhirayama Tunnel
大平山

2.3km

Sumiyoshi Jinja

Mt.Ōhira
大平山 142.3

100
50

Misato E.S.
三里小

1.7km

J.H.S.

三井田

14

335

Nankoku City
南国市

Shimoda Taxi 088-865-8432

SCALE 1/30,000

0 0.5 1 1.5 2km

Sango (coral) Center

Katsuo-bune
かつお船

Misato Taxi
088-847-3651
Kenkō Taxi
088-847-2926

Kōchi-shin Port
高知新港

上竜頭岬

Katsurahama
桂浜

土佐湾
Tosa Bay

太平洋
Pacific Ocean

Katsurahama 桂浜

Katsurahama is a particularly beautiful Kōchi beach, well known as a moon-viewing spot as well as popular song. The region features an aquarium, and a Ryōma Memorial Museum in city park.

Ryōma Memorial Museum 坂本龍馬記念館

O 9:00am-4:30pm **C** None **F** ¥700-

Ryōma Sakamoto (1836-1867), a native of Kōchi City, was a hero of the mid-nineteenth century who played a big role in Japan's modernization at the end of the Edo era. This museum, the building itself a marvel of modern architecture, tells the story of Ryōma's life and accomplishments.

32 Zenjibuji 三十二番 禅師峰寺

H Jūichimen Kannon Bosatsu
3084 Toochi, Nankoku City
Free of charge (20)
A By bus bound for Maehama Shako bus stop from Harimaya-bashi bus stop (N2). Get off at Midorigaoka-3chōme bus stop, about 15 min. walk.

☎ 088-865-8430
S None

In the early 9th century, Kōbō Daishi visited here and while praying for the safety of those on water, carved the main deity. This Jūichimen Kannon Bosatsu statue was called *funadama kannon* (spririt of the boat kannon) and the temple became known as a place to pray for the safety of sailors and fisherman.

56
37
Sunshine
Haruno Terrace
Haruno H.S.
Haruno Spa
088-894-5400
はるのの湯
36
Hydrangea Street (May)
アジサイ街道
Haruno J.H.S.
Folk Museum
Haruno-kōminkan-mae Bus Stop
(to Central Kōchi City)
春野公民館前バス停
Dept time (weekday)
7:22
16:28
City Office Branc
Nishi E.S.
350
1.2km
43
279
2.8km
2.1km
Hydrangea Street (May)
アジサイ通り
Tanemaji 34
9.8km
Mt.Sampō
95.8 三宝山
Ajisai Taxi
088-803-2228
0120-152228

34 Tanemaji 三十四番 種間寺

H Yakushi Nyorai ☎ 088-894-2234

72 Akiyama, Haruno-chō, Kōchi City **S** None

Free of charge (15)

A By bus bound for JA Haruno from Sakai-machi Bus Stop. Get off Haruno-kōminkan-mae Bus Stop, about 10 min. walk.

The name of this temple comes from a legend that Kūkai planted here five kinds of seeds (rice, wheat, 2 types of millet and bean) that he brought back from China. In front of the Daishi hall, there is a statue of "Kosodate Kannon" (child-rearing Kannon) to which people pray to for safe childbirth. If a birth is problem-free then a ladle with the bottom punched out is hung near the Kannon statue.

33 Sekkeiji 三十三番 雪蹊寺

H Yakushi Nyorai ☎ 088-837-2233

857-3 Nagahama, Kōchi City **S** None

Free of charge (10)

A By bus bound for Nagahama-shucchōsho from Sakai-machi (Harimaya-bashi crossing) Bus Terminal. Get off at the last stop, about 5 min. walk.

Sekkeiji, Temple 11 and 15 are the only Zen temples along the route. It was first founded as a Shingon temple by Kūkai during the Enryaku period (782-806). During the Tenshō period (1573-1591), a priest Geppō took over as abbot and changed the temple to Rinzai sect.

NOTE Motochika Chōsokabe 長宗我部元親

He was the provincial feudal lord of Tosa (Kōchi prefecture) during part of the 16th century. He invaded each province in Shikoku and had control of all of Shikou until 1585 however, as a result of the numerous battles, many temples along the Shikoku pilgrimage route were destroyed. It was a difficult period for each temple until the buildings could be reconstructed. Sekkeiji is the Chōsokabe's family temple.

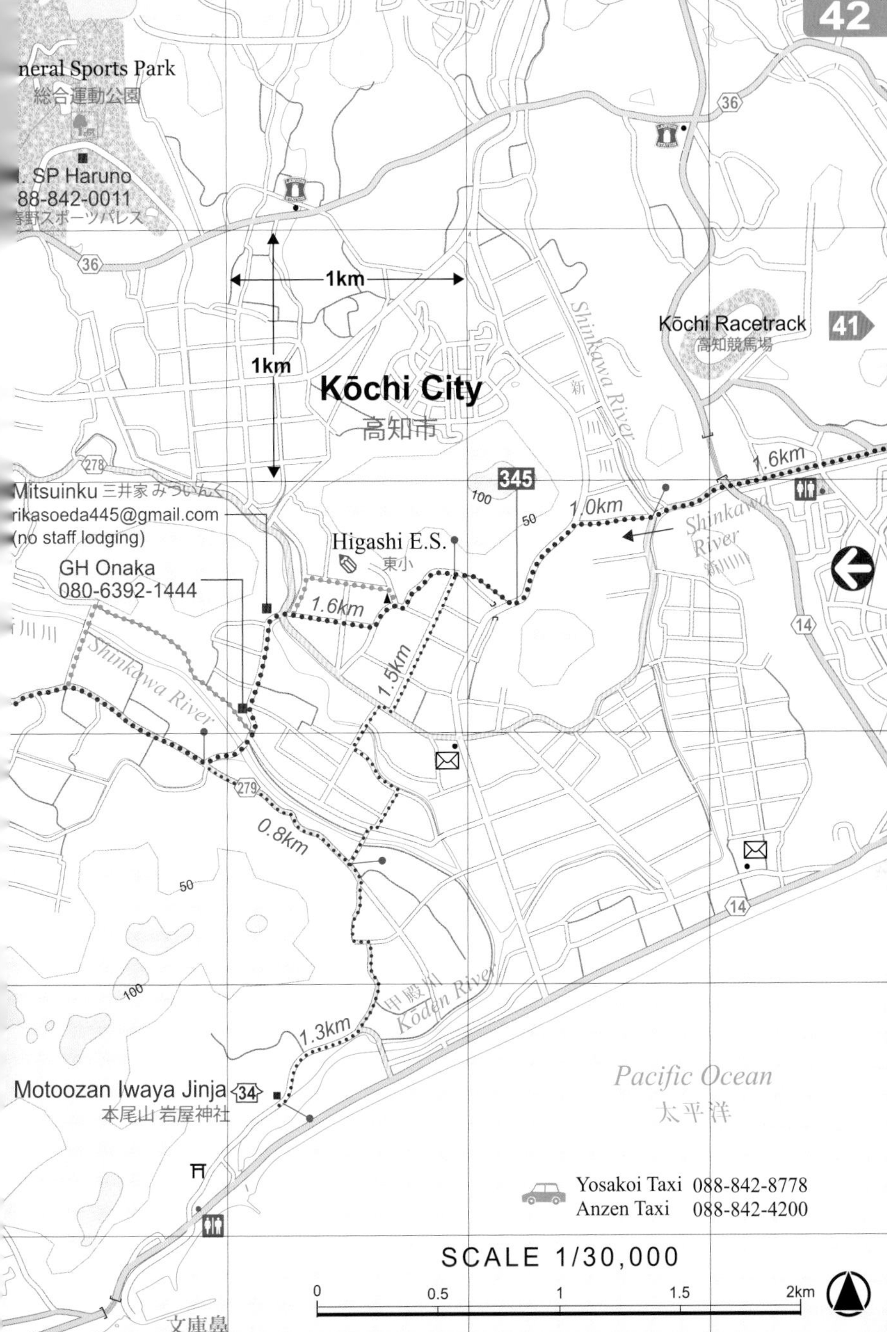

neral Sports Park
総合運動公園
. SP Haruno
88-842-0011
春野スポーツパレス
36
1km
1km
Kōchi City
高知市
Shinkawa River
新川川
Kōchi Racetrack
高知競馬場
41
278
345
1.6km
1.0km
Shinkawa River
新川川
Mitsuinku 三井家 みついんく
rikasoeda445@gmail.com
(no staff lodging)
Higashi E.S.
東小
GH Onaka
080-6392-1444
1.6km
1.5km
14
Shinkawa River
279
0.8km
50
100
14
甲殿川
Kōden River
1.3km
Motoozan Iwaya Jinja
34
本尾山 岩屋神社
Pacific Ocean
太平洋
Yosakoi Taxi 088-842-8778
Anzen Taxi 088-842-4200
SCALE 1/30,000
0
0.5
1
1.5
2km
文庫鼻

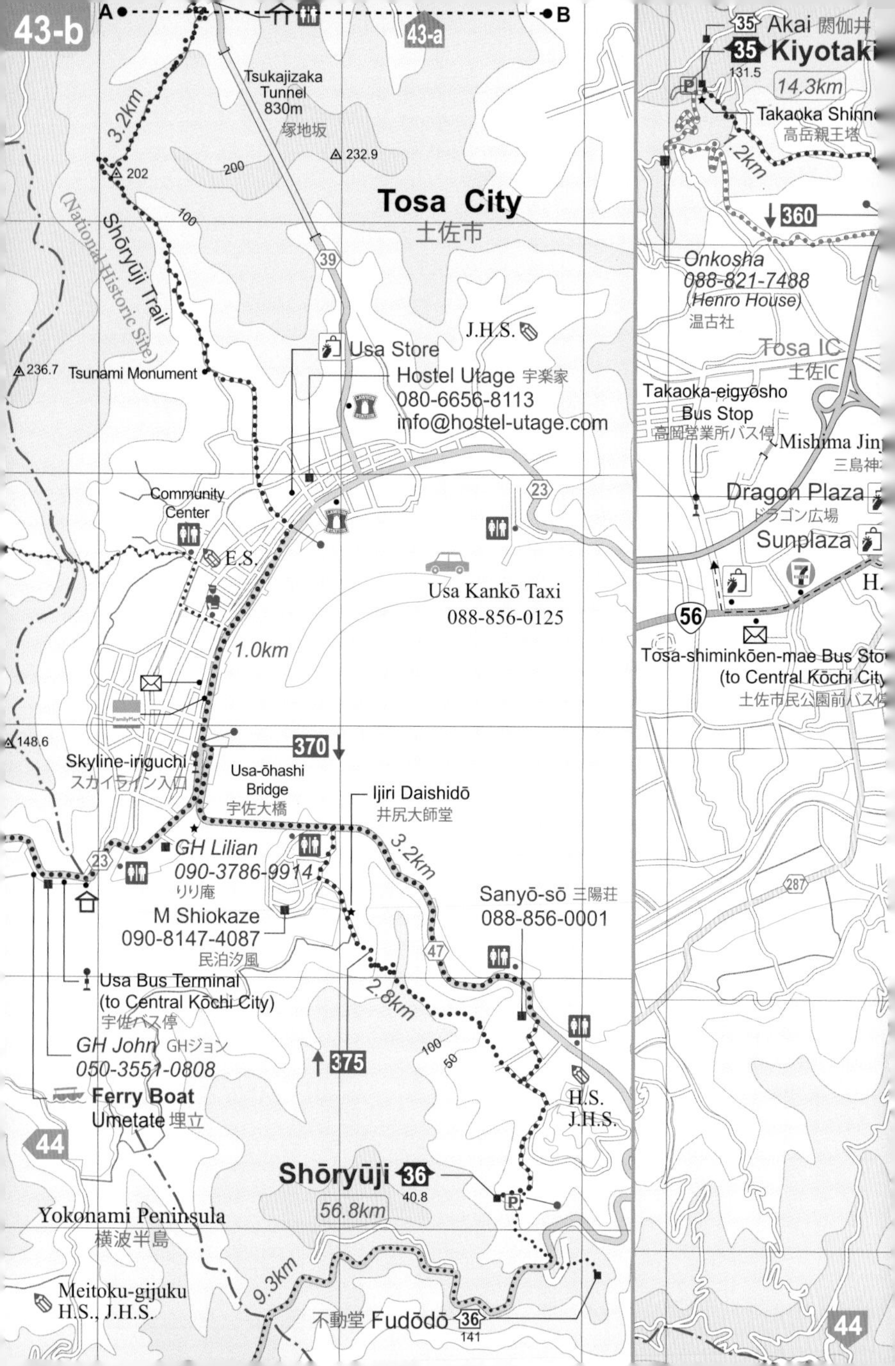
A
B
43-a
Tsukajizaka Tunnel 830m
塚地坂
232.9
202
200
100
3.2km
Tosa City
土佐市
39
(National Historic Site)
Shōryūji Trail
236.7
Tsunami Monument
J.H.S.
Usa Store
Hostel Utage 宇楽家
080-6656-8113
info@hostel-utage.com
Community Center
E.S.
23
Usa Kankō Taxi
088-856-0125
1.0km
148.6
370
Skyline-iriguchi
スカイライン入口
Usa-ōhashi Bridge
宇佐大橋
Ijiri Daishidō
井尻大師堂
3.2km
GH Lilian
090-3786-9914
りり庵
M Shiokaze
090-8147-4087
民泊汐風
Sanyō-sō 三陽荘
088-856-0001
47
2.8km
Usa Bus Terminal
(to Central Kōchi City)
宇佐バス停
GH John GHジョン
050-3551-0808
375
Ferry Boat
Umetate 埋立
H.S.
J.H.S.
44
Shōryūji 36
40.8
56.8km
Yokonami Peninsula
横波半島
9.3km
Meitoku-gijuku
H.S., J.H.S.
不動堂 Fudōdō 36
141
35 Akai 閼伽井
35 Kiyotaki
131.5
14.3km
Takaoka Shinno
高岳親王塔
1.2km
360
Onkosha
088-821-7488
(Henro House)
温古社
Tosa IC
土佐IC
Takaoka-eigyōsho Bus Stop
高岡営業所バス停
Mishima Jin
三島神
Dragon Plaza
ドラゴン広場
Sunplaza
56
Tosa-shiminkōen-mae Bus Stop
(to Central Kōchi City)
土佐市民公園前バス停
287
44

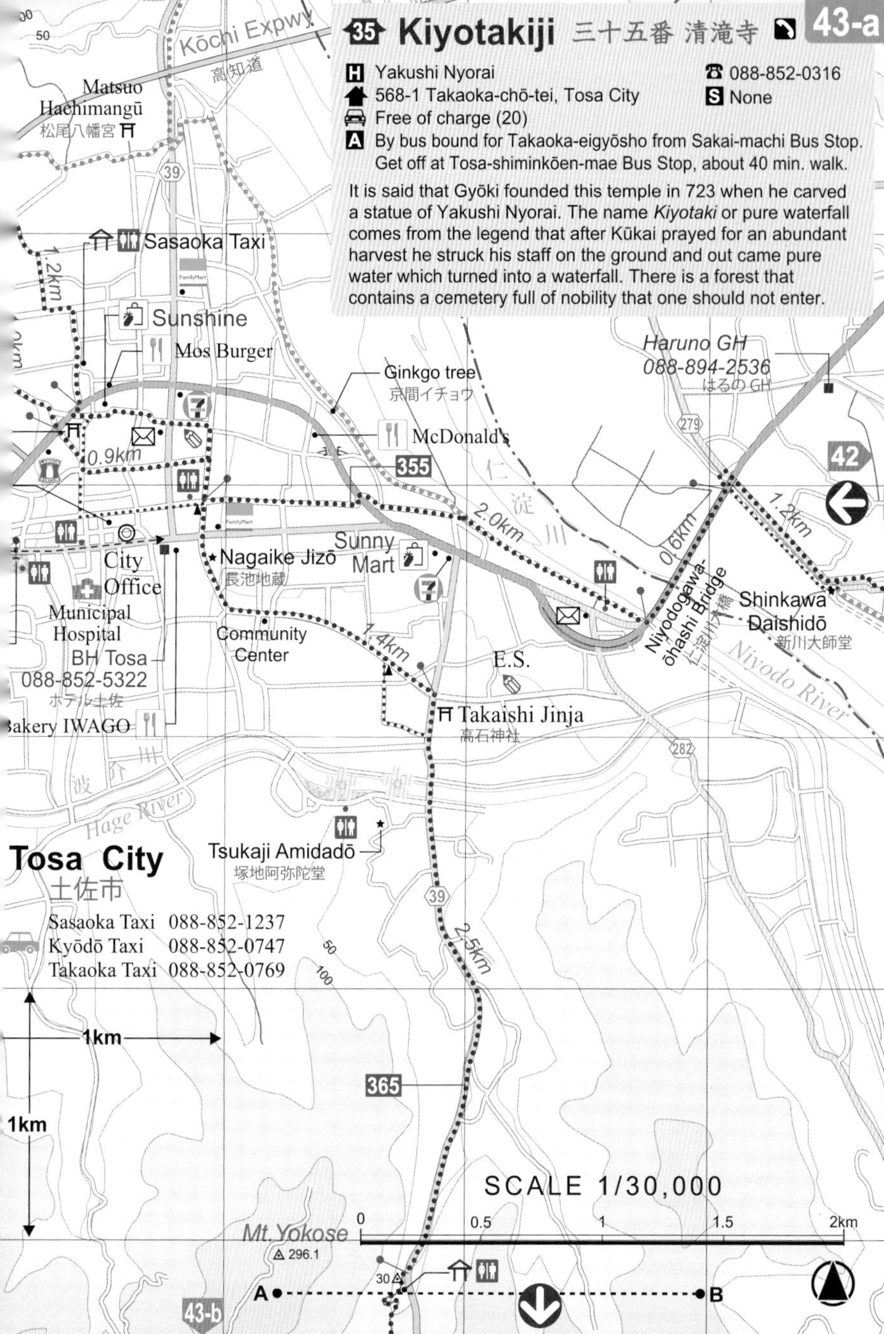

35 Kiyotakiji 三十五番 清滝寺
43-a
Yakushi Nyorai
568-1 Takaoka-chō-tei, Tosa City
Free of charge (20)
By bus bound for Takaoka-eigyōsho from Sakai-machi Bus Stop. Get off at Tosa-shiminkōen-mae Bus Stop, about 40 min. walk.
088-852-0316
None
It is said that Gyōki founded this temple in 723 when he carved a statue of Yakushi Nyorai. The name Kiyotaki or pure waterfall comes from the legend that after Kūkai prayed for an abundant harvest he struck his staff on the ground and out came pure water which turned into a waterfall. There is a forest that contains a cemetery full of nobility that one should not enter.
Kōchi Expwy
高知道
Matsuo Hachimangū
松尾八幡宮
Sasaoka Taxi
Sunshine
Mos Burger
Ginkgo tree
京間イチョウ
McDonald's
355
0.9km
1.2km
2.0km
0.6km
1.2km
1.4km
2.5km
City Office
Municipal Hospital
BH Tosa
088-852-5322
ホテル土佐
Bakery IWAGO
Nagaike Jizō
長池地蔵
Sunny Mart
Community Center
E.S.
Takaishi Jinja
高石神社
Haruno GH
088-894-2536
はるのGH
279
282
39
42
仁淀川
Niyodogawa-ōhashi Bridge
仁淀川大橋
Shinkawa Daishidō
新川大師堂
Niyodo River
波介川
Hage River
Tsukaji Amidadō
塚地阿弥陀堂
Tosa City
土佐市
Sasaoka Taxi 088-852-1237
Kyōdō Taxi 088-852-0747
Takaoka Taxi 088-852-0769
1km
1km
365
SCALE 1/30,000
0 0.5 1 1.5 2km
Mt.Yokose
296.1
A
B
43-b

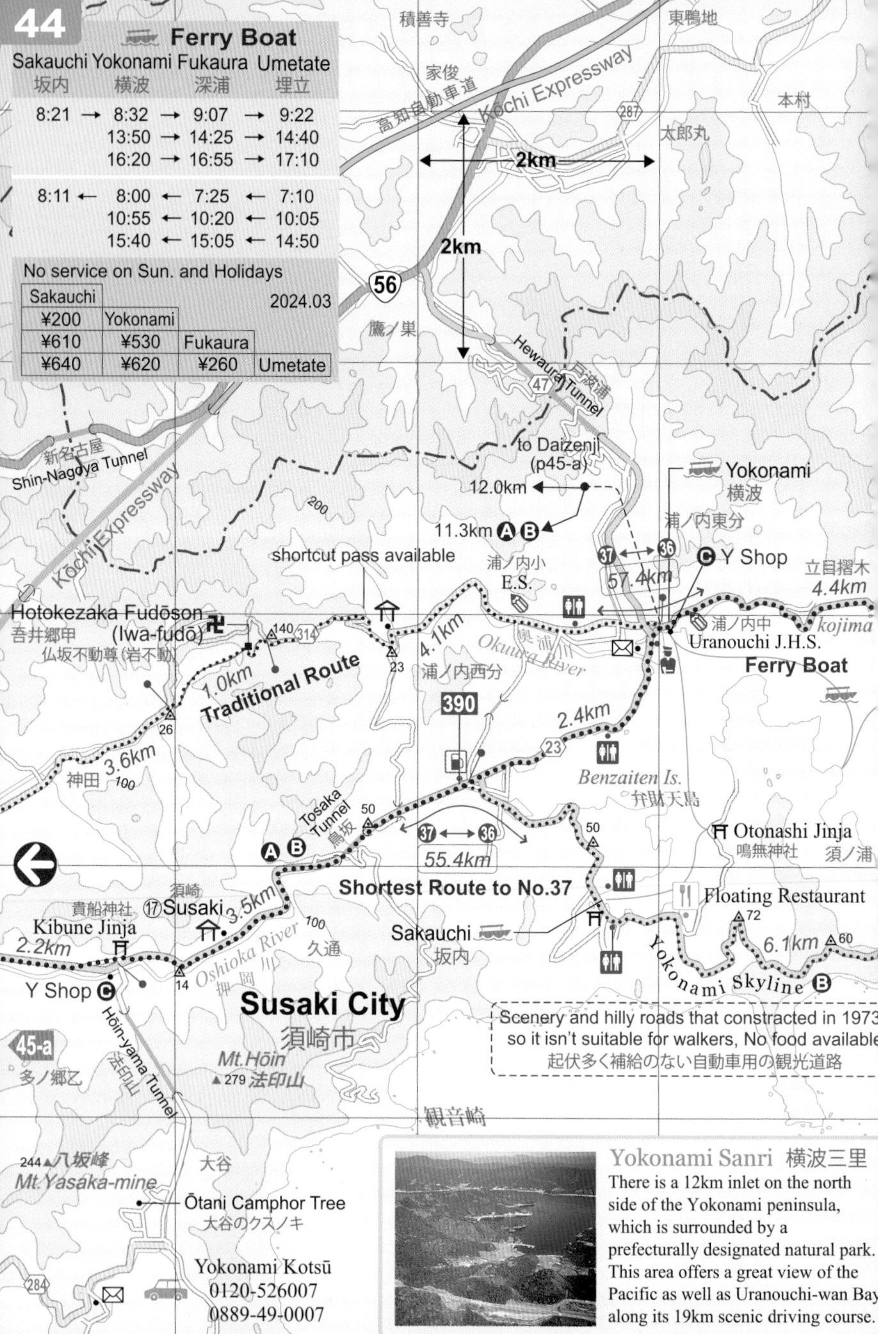

Ferry Boat

Sakauchi 坂内	Yokonami 横波	Fukaura 深浦	Umetate 埋立
8:21 →	8:32 →	9:07 →	9:22
	13:50 →	14:25 →	14:40
	16:20 →	16:55 →	17:10
8:11 ←	8:00 ←	7:25 ←	7:10
	10:55 ←	10:20 ←	10:05
	15:40 ←	15:05 ←	14:50

No service on Sun. and Holidays

2024.03

Sakauchi			
¥200	Yokonami		
¥610	¥530	Fukaura	
¥640	¥620	¥260	Umetate

44
積善寺
東鴨地
家俊
高知自動車道
Kochi Expressway
287
本村
太郎丸
2km
2km
56
鷹ノ巣
Hewaura Tunnel
戸波浦
47
新名古屋
Shin-Nagoya Tunnel
Kochi Expressway
200
to Daizenji (p45-a)
12.0km
11.3km A B
Yokonami
横波
浦ノ内東分
37 36
57.4km
shortcut pass available
浦ノ内小
E.S.
C Y Shop
立目摺木
4.4km
kojima
浦ノ内中
Uranouchi J.H.S.
Ferry Boat
Hotokezaka Fudōson
吾井郷甲
(Iwa-fudō)
仏坂不動尊(岩不動)
140
314
23
4.1km
奥浦川
Okuura River
浦ノ内西分
1.0km
Traditional Route
26
390
2.4km
23
3.6km
神田
100
Benzaiten Is.
弁財天島
Tosaka Tunnel
鳥坂
50
37 36
55.4km
A B
50
Otonashi Jinja
鳴無神社
須ノ浦
Shortest Route to No.37
須崎
貴船神社
17 Susaki
3.5km
Floating Restaurant
Kibune Jinja
100
Sakauchi
坂内
72
6.1km
60
2.2km
Oshioka River
押岡川
久通
Yokonami Skyline B
Y Shop C
14
Susaki City
須崎市
Hōin-yama Tunnel
法印山
45-a
Scenery and hilly roads that constracted in 1973 so it isn't suitable for walkers, No food available
起伏多く補給のない自動車用の観光道路
多ノ郷乙
Mt.Hōin
279 法印山
観音崎
244 八坂峰
Mt.Yasaka-mine
大谷
Ōtani Camphor Tree
大谷のクスノキ
284
Yokonami Kotsū
0120-526007
0889-49-0007

Yokonami Sanri 横波三里

There is a 12km inlet on the north side of the Yokonami peninsula, which is surrounded by a prefecturally designated natural park. This area offers a great view of the Pacific as well as Uranouchi-wan Bay along its 19km scenic driving course.

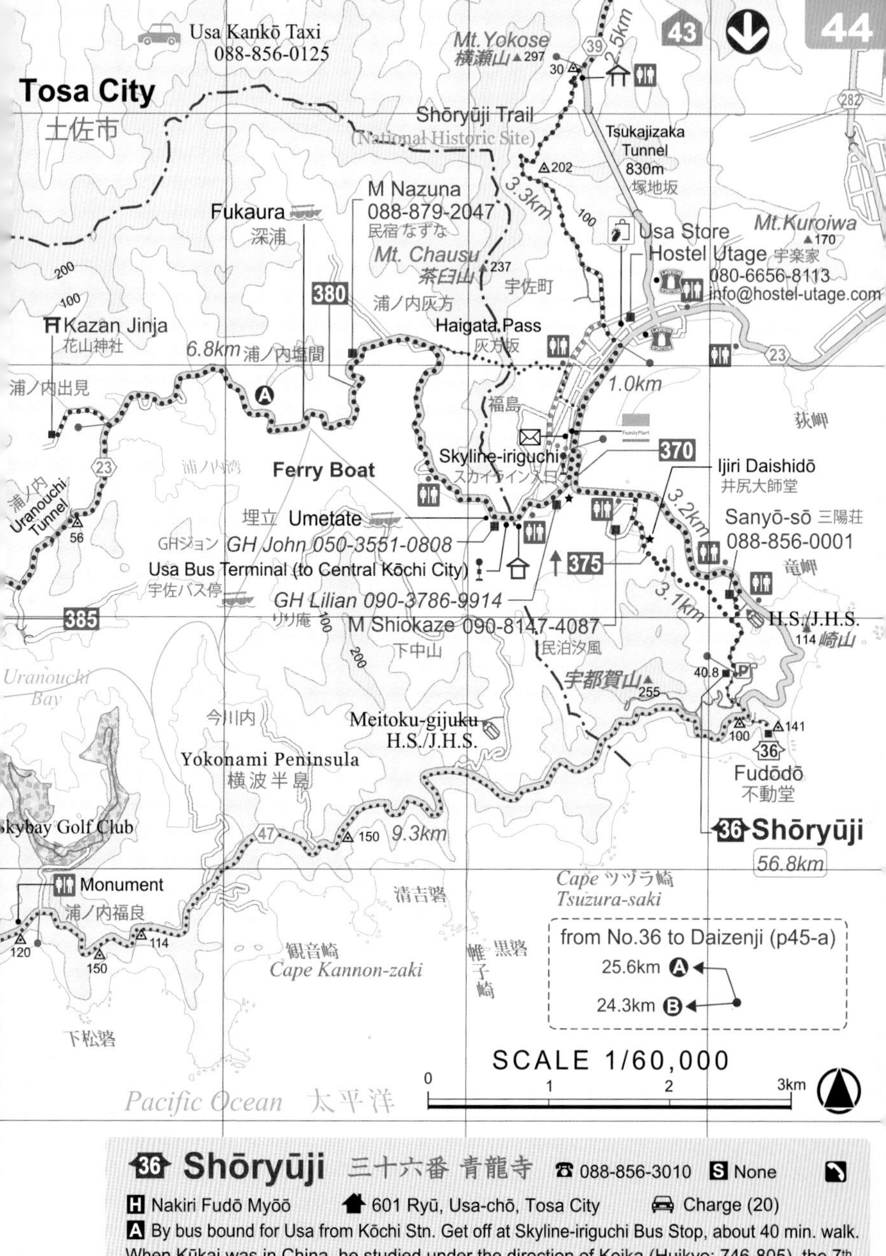
Usa Kankō Taxi
088-856-0125
Tosa City
土佐市
Mt.Yokose
横瀬山 297
2.5km
Shōryūji Trail
(National Historic Site)
Tsukajizaka
Tunnel
830m
塚地坂
3.3km
M Nazuna
088-879-2047
民宿なずな
Fukaura
深浦
Mt. Chausu
茶臼山 237
宇佐町
Usa Store
Hostel Utage 宇楽家
080-6656-8113
info@hostel-utage.com
Mt.Kuroiwa
170
浦ノ内灰方
Haigata Pass
灰方坂
Kazan Jinja
花山神社
6.8km 浦ノ内塩間
浦ノ内出見
1.0km
福島
Skyline-iriguchi
スカイライン入口
Ferry Boat
浦ノ内湾
Ijiri Daishidō
井尻大師堂
Uranouchi
Tunnel
埋立 Umetate
GHジョン GH John 050-3551-0808
Usa Bus Terminal (to Central Kōchi City)
宇佐バス停
GH Lilian 090-3786-9914
リリ庵
M Shiokaze 090-8147-4087
民泊汐風
3.2km
Sanyō-sō 三陽荘
088-856-0001
竜岬
3.1km
H.S./J.H.S.
崎山
下中山
宇都賀山 255
Uranouchi
Bay
今川内
Meitoku-gijuku
H.S./J.H.S.
Yokonami Peninsula
横波半島
Fudōdō
不動堂
Skybay Golf Club
9.3km
36 Shōryūji
56.8km
Monument
浦ノ内福良
清吉鼻
Cape ツヅラ崎
Tsuzura-saki
観音崎
Cape Kannon-zaki
帷子崎
黒碆
from No.36 to Daizenji (p45-a)
25.6km A
24.3km B
下松碆
SCALE 1/60,000
Pacific Ocean 太平洋

36 Shōryūji 三十六番 青龍寺

☎ 088-856-3010 S None

H Nakiri Fudō Myōō
601 Ryū, Usa-chō, Tosa City
Charge (20)

A By bus bound for Usa from Kōchi Stn. Get off at Skyline-iriguchi Bus Stop, about 40 min. walk.

When Kūkai was in China, he studied under the direction of Keika (Huikyo: 746-805), the 7th patriarch of Shingon Buddhism, at Shōryuji. Before Kūkai left to return to Japan, he threw a vajra (single-pronged ritual object) towards the east and later found it at this spot. He founded this temple giving it the same name as the one in China in memory of his master.

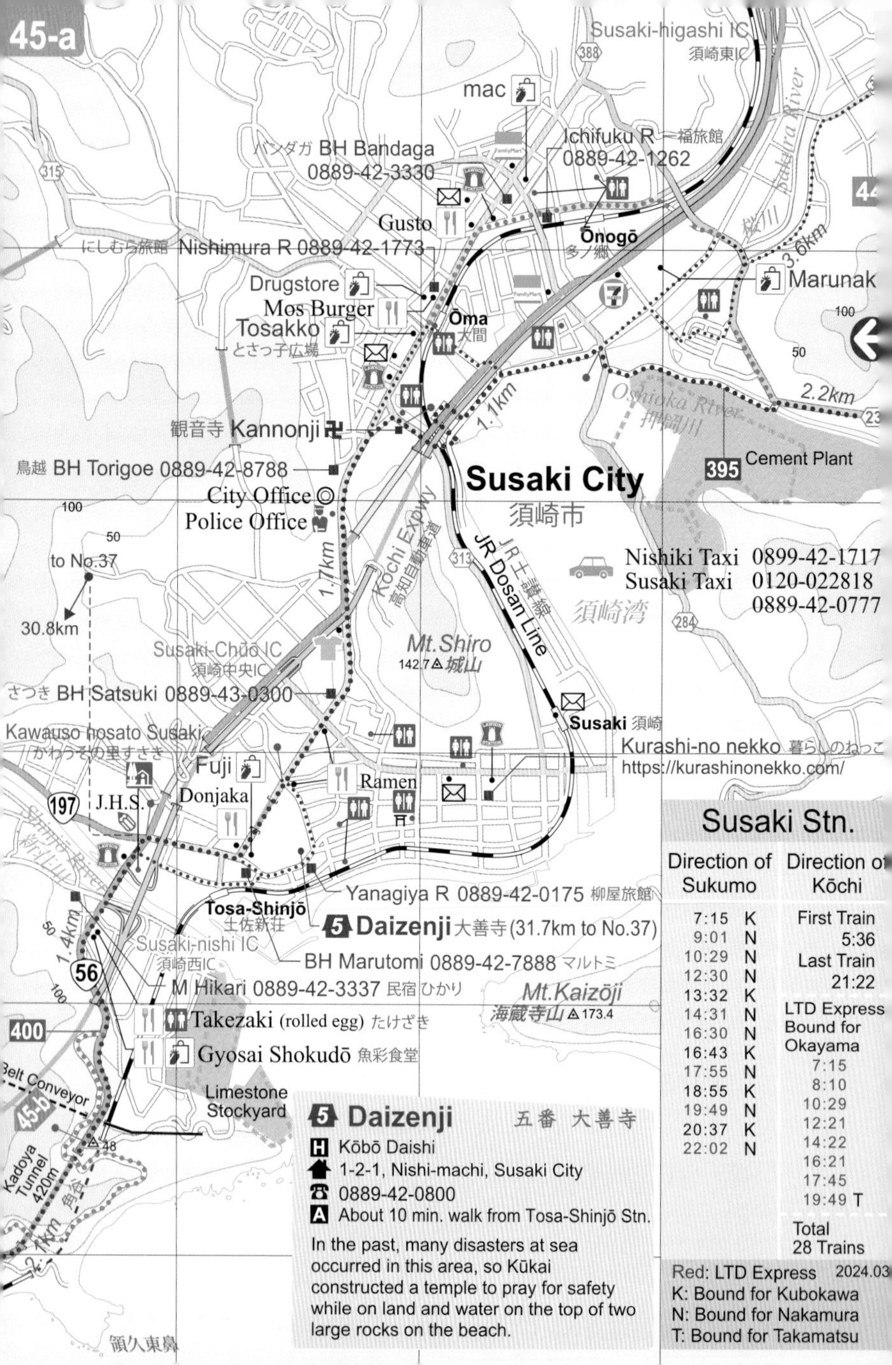
Susaki-higashi IC
須崎東IC
388
mac
Sakura River
桜川
Ichifuku R 福旅館
0889-42-1262
バンダガ BH Bandaga
0889-42-3330
315
Gusto
Ōnogō
多ノ郷
にしむら旅館 Nishimura R 0889-42-1773
3.6km
Marunak
Drugstore
Mos Burger
Tosakko
とさっ子広場
Ōma
大間
100
50
2.2km
Oshioka River
押岡川
1.1km
観音寺 Kannonji
鳥越 BH Torigoe 0889-42-8788
395
Cement Plant
Susaki City
須崎市
City Office
Police Office
100
50
to No.37
30.8km
1.7km
Kochi Expwy
高知自動車道
313
JR土讃線
JR Dosan Line
Nishiki Taxi 0899-42-1717
Susaki Taxi 0120-022818
0889-42-0777
須崎湾
284
Mt.Shiro
142.7 城山
Susaki-Chūō IC
須崎中央IC
さつき BH Satsuki 0889-43-0300
Susaki 須崎
Kawauso hosato Susaki
かわうその里すさき
Kurashi-no nekko 暮らしのねっこ
https://kurashinonekko.com/
Fuji
Ramen
197
J.H.S.
Donjaka
Yanagiya R 0889-42-0175 柳屋旅館
Tosa-Shinjō
土佐新荘
5 Daizenji 大善寺(31.7km to No.37)
Susaki-nishi IC
須崎西IC
BH Marutomi 0889-42-7888 マルトミ
1.4km
56
M Hikari 0889-42-3337 民宿 ひかり
Mt.Kaizōji
海蔵寺山 173.4
400
Takezaki (rolled egg) たけざき
Gyosai Shokudō 魚彩食堂
Belt Conveyor
45-b
Limestone
Stockyard
48
Kadoya Tunnel 420m
角谷
2.1km
須久東鼻

5 Daizenji 五番 大善寺

H Kōbō Daishi
1-2-1, Nishi-machi, Susaki City
0889-42-0800
A About 10 min. walk from Tosa-Shinjō Stn.

In the past, many disasters at sea occurred in this area, so Kūkai constructed a temple to pray for safety while on land and water on the top of two large rocks on the beach.

Susaki Stn.

Direction of Sukumo		Direction of Kōchi
7:15	K	First Train 5:36
9:01	N	Last Train 21:22
10:29	N	LTD Express Bound for Okayama
12:30	N	7:15
13:32	K	8:10
14:31	N	10:29
16:30	N	12:21
16:43	K	14:22
17:55	N	16:21
18:55	K	17:45
19:49	N	19:49 T
20:37	K	
22:02	N	Total 28 Trains

Red: LTD Express 2024.03
K: Bound for Kubokawa
N: Bound for Nakamura
T: Bound for Takamatsu

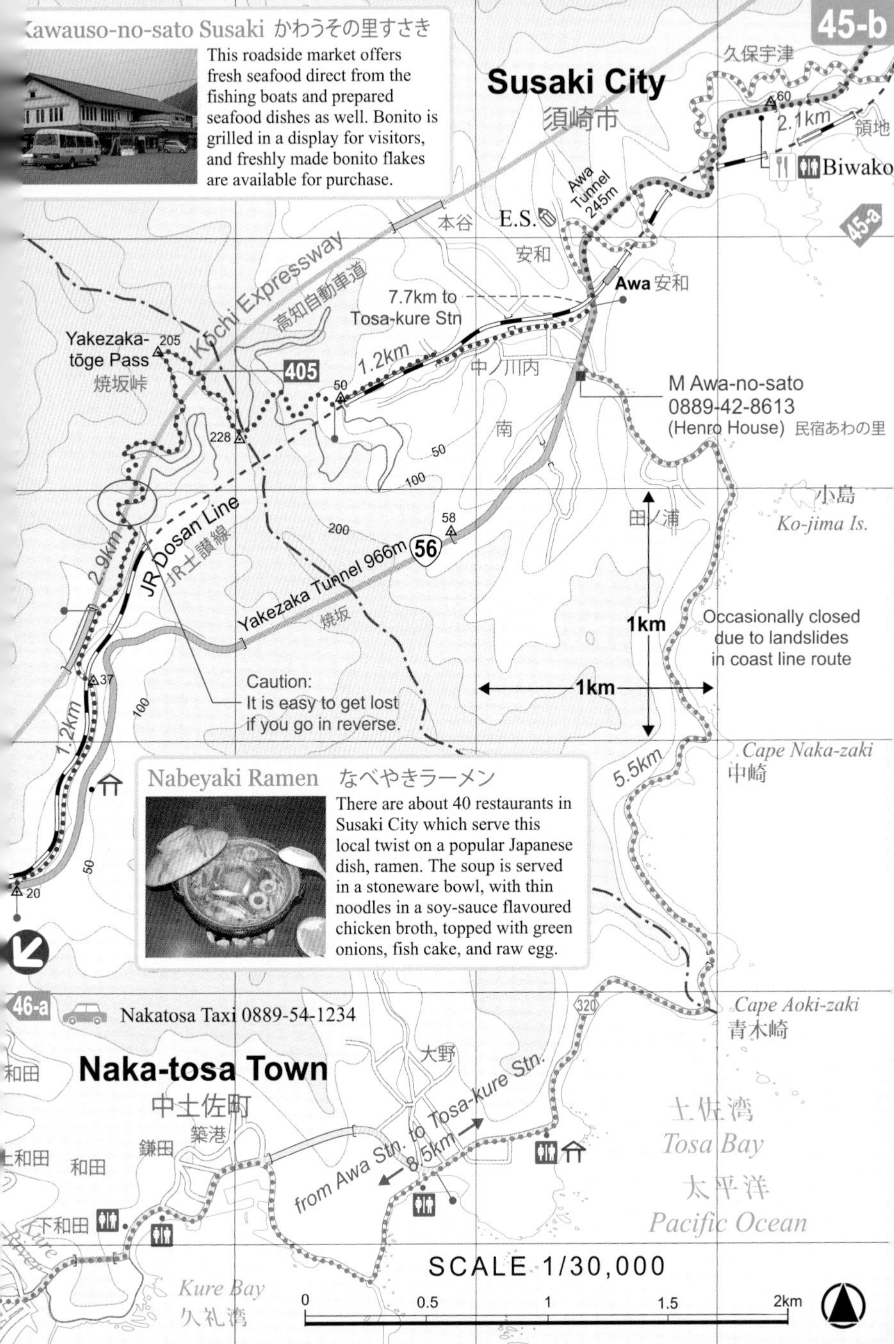
45-b
Kawauso-no-sato Susaki かわうその里すさき
This roadside market offers fresh seafood direct from the fishing boats and prepared seafood dishes as well. Bonito is grilled in a display for visitors, and freshly made bonito flakes are available for purchase.
Susaki City
須崎市
久保宇津
60
2.1km
領地
Biwako
Awa Tunnel 245m
E.S.
本谷
安和
45-a
Kōchi Expressway
高知自動車道
7.7km to Tosa-kure Stn
Awa 安和
Yakezaka-tōge Pass
焼坂峠
205
405
1.2km
中ノ川内
50
228
M Awa-no-sato
0889-42-8613
(Henro House) 民宿あわの里
南
50
100
小島
Ko-jima Is.
JR Dosan Line
JR土讃線
200
58
田ノ浦
2.9km
56
Yakezaka Tunnel 966m
焼坂
1km
Occasionally closed due to landslides in coast line route
1km
37
Caution:
It is easy to get lost if you go in reverse.
100
1.2km
Cape Naka-zaki
中崎
5.5km
Nabeyaki Ramen なべやきラーメン
There are about 40 restaurants in Susaki City which serve this local twist on a popular Japanese dish, ramen. The soup is served in a stoneware bowl, with thin noodles in a soy-sauce flavoured chicken broth, topped with green onions, fish cake, and raw egg.
50
20
46-a
Nakatosa Taxi 0889-54-1234
320
Cape Aoki-zaki
青木崎
大野
和田
Naka-tosa Town
中土佐町
築港
鎌田
上和田
和田
from Awa Stn. to Tosa-kure Stn.
8.5km
土佐湾
Tosa Bay
太平洋
Pacific Ocean
下和田
Kure River
SCALE 1/30,000
Kure Bay
久礼湾
0
0.5
1
1.5
2km

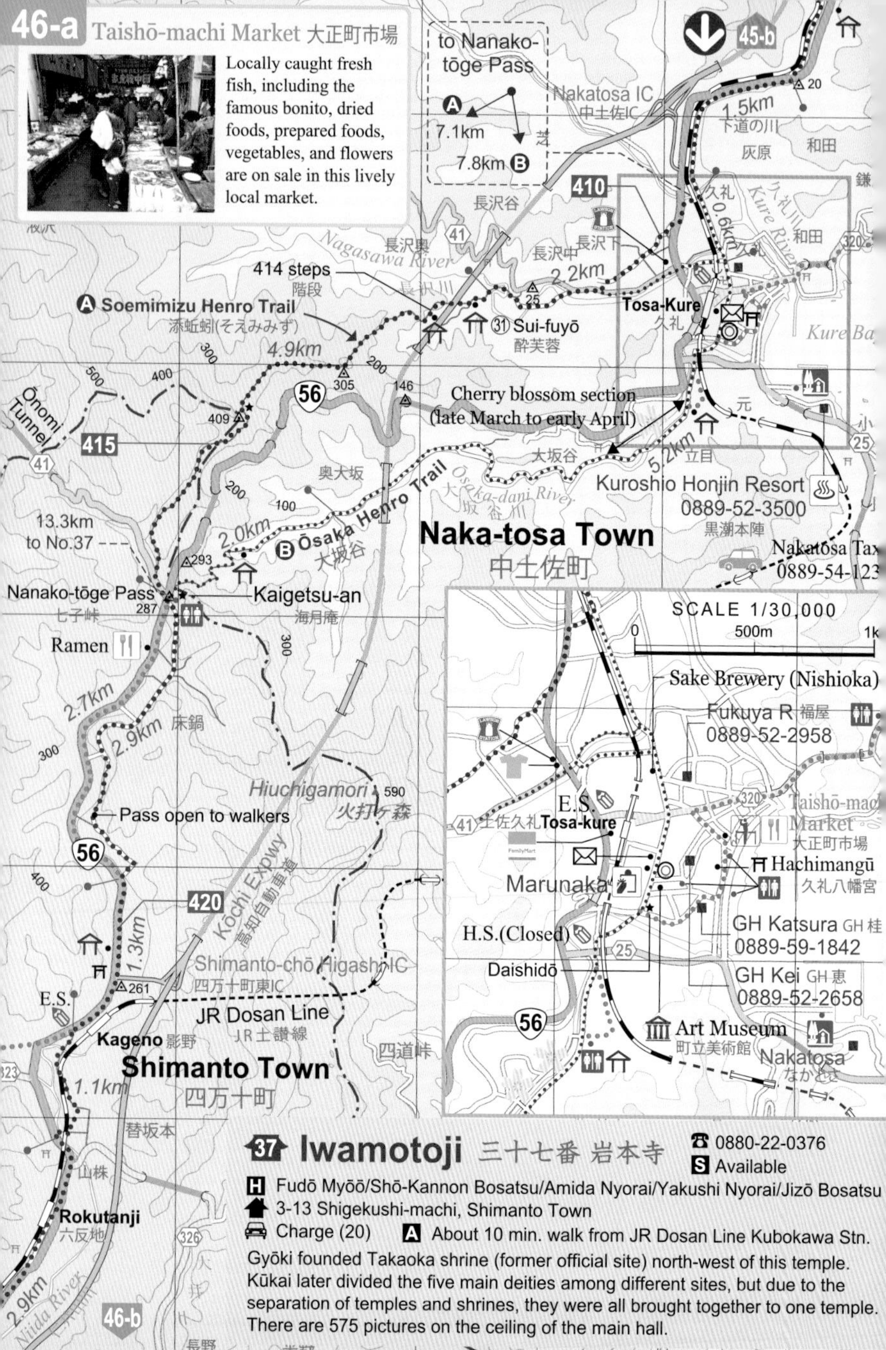
46-a
Taishō-machi Market 大正町市場
Locally caught fresh fish, including the famous bonito, dried foods, prepared foods, vegetables, and flowers are on sale in this lively local market.
to Nanako-tōge Pass
A 7.1km
7.8km B
45-b
Nakatosa IC
中土佐IC
1.5km
下道の川
灰原
和田
410
久礼
Kure River
久礼川
0.6km
和田
320
長沢谷
Nagasawa River
長沢奥
長沢中
長沢下
長沢川
2.2km
414 steps
階段
A Soemimizu Henro Trail
添蚯蚓(そえみみず)
Tosa-Kure
久礼
Kure Bay
31 Sui-fuyō
酔芙蓉
4.9km
Ōnomi Tunnel
415
41
56
Cherry blossom section
(late March to early April)
大坂谷
立目
5.2km
Kuroshio Honjin Resort
0889-52-3500
黒潮本陣
奥大坂
Ōsaka-dani River
大坂谷川
B Ōsaka Henro Trail
大坂谷
2.0km
Naka-tosa Town
中土佐町
Nakatosa Taxi
0889-54-123
13.3km
to No.37
Nanako-tōge Pass
七子峠
Kaigetsu-an
海月庵
Ramen
2.7km
2.9km
床鍋
Hiuchigamori
火打ヶ森
Pass open to walkers
SCALE 1/30,000
0
500m
Sake Brewery (Nishioka)
Fukuya R 福屋
0889-52-2958
E.S.
土佐久礼
Tosa-kure
Taishō-machi Market
大正町市場
Hachimangū
久礼八幡宮
Marunaka
H.S.(Closed)
GH Katsura GH 桂
0889-59-1842
Daishidō
GH Kei GH 恵
0889-52-2658
Art Museum
町立美術館
Nakatosa
なかとさ
420
Kōchi Expwy
高知自動車道
1.3km
Shimanto-chō Higashi IC
四万十町東IC
JR Dosan Line
JR土讃線
E.S.
Kageno 影野
Shimanto Town
四万十町
四道峠
1.1km
替坂本
山株
Rokutanji
六反地
326
2.9km
Niida River
46-b
長野
37 Iwamotoji 三十七番 岩本寺
0880-22-0376
S Available
H Fudō Myōō/Shō-Kannon Bosatsu/Amida Nyorai/Yakushi Nyorai/Jizō Bosatsu
3-13 Shigekushi-machi, Shimanto Town
Charge (20)
A About 10 min. walk from JR Dosan Line Kubokawa Stn.
Gyōki founded Takaoka shrine (former official site) north-west of this temple. Kūkai later divided the five main deities among different sites, but due to the separation of temples and shrines, they were all brought together to one temple. There are 575 pictures on the ceiling of the main hall.

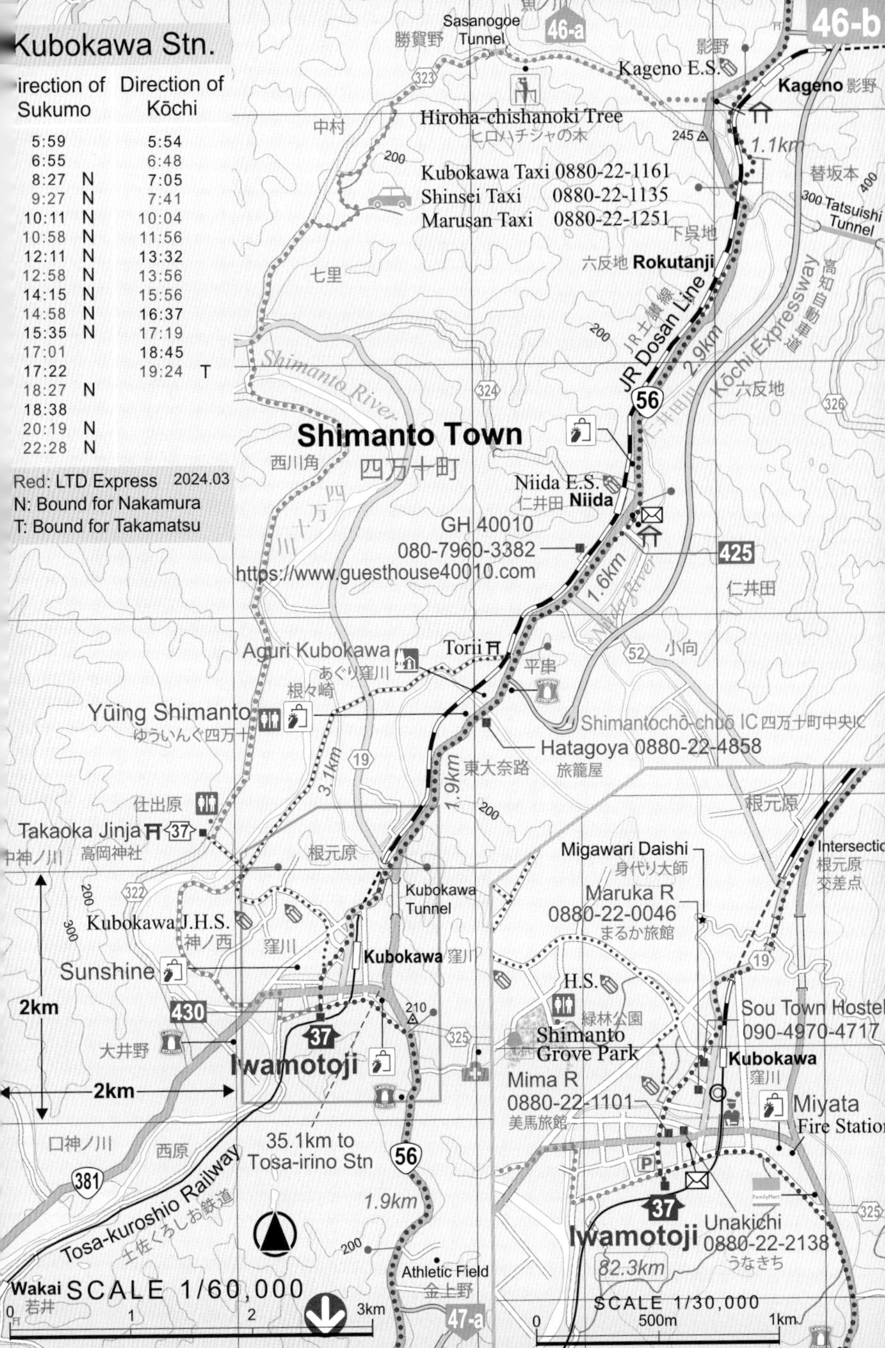

Kubokawa Stn.

irection of Sukumo		Direction of Kōchi	
5:59		5:54	
6:55		6:48	
8:27	N	7:05	
9:27	N	7:41	
10:11	N	10:04	
10:58	N	11:56	
12:11	N	13:32	
12:58	N	13:56	
14:15	N	15:56	
14:58	N	16:37	
15:35	N	17:19	
17:01		18:45	
17:22		19:24	T
18:27	N		
18:38			
20:19	N		
22:28	N		

Red: LTD Express 2024.03
N: Bound for Nakamura
T: Bound for Takamatsu

魚ノ川
Sasanogoe Tunnel
勝賀野
46-a
影野
Kageno E.S.
Kageno 影野
Hiroha-chishanoki Tree
ヒロハチシャの木
中村
323
245
1.1km
替坂本
400
300 Tatsuishi Tunnel
200
Kubokawa Taxi 0880-22-1161
Shinsei Taxi 0880-22-1135
Marusan Taxi 0880-22-1251
下呉地
六反地 Rokutanji
七里
高知自動車道
Kōchi Expressway
JR土讃線
JR Dosan Line
2.9km
200
Shimanto River
324
56
六反地
326
仁井田川
Shimanto Town
四万十町
西川角
四万十川
Niida E.S.
仁井田 Niida
GH 40010
080-7960-3382
https://www.guesthouse40010.com
425
1.6km
Niida River
仁井田
Aguri Kubokawa
あぐり窪川
Torii
平串
52
小向
根々崎
Yūing Shimanto
ゆういんぐ四万十
Shimantochō-chūō IC 四万十町中央IC
Hatagoya 0880-22-4858
旅籠屋
3.1km
19
1.9km
東大奈路
200
根元原
仕出原
Takaoka Jinja
37
高岡神社
中神ノ川
根元原
322
200
300
Kubokawa Tunnel
Kubokawa J.H.S.
神ノ西
窪川
Kubokawa 窪川
Sunshine
2km
430
210
325
大井野
Iwamotoji
2km
口神ノ川
西原
35.1km to Tosa-irino Stn
56
381
Tosa-kuroshio Railway
土佐くろしお鉄道
1.9km
200
Athletic Field
金上野
Wakai
若井
SCALE 1/60,000
0
1
2
3km
47-a
Migawari Daishi
身代り大師
Maruka R
0880-22-0046
まるか旅館
Intersection
根元原交差点
19
H.S.
緑林公園
Shimanto Grove Park
Sou Town Hostel
090-4970-4717
Kubokawa
窪川
Mima R
0880-22-1101
美馬旅館
Miyata Fire Station
P
FamilyMart
37
325
Unakichi
0880-22-2138
うなきち
Iwamotoji
82.3km
SCALE 1/30,000
0
500m
1km

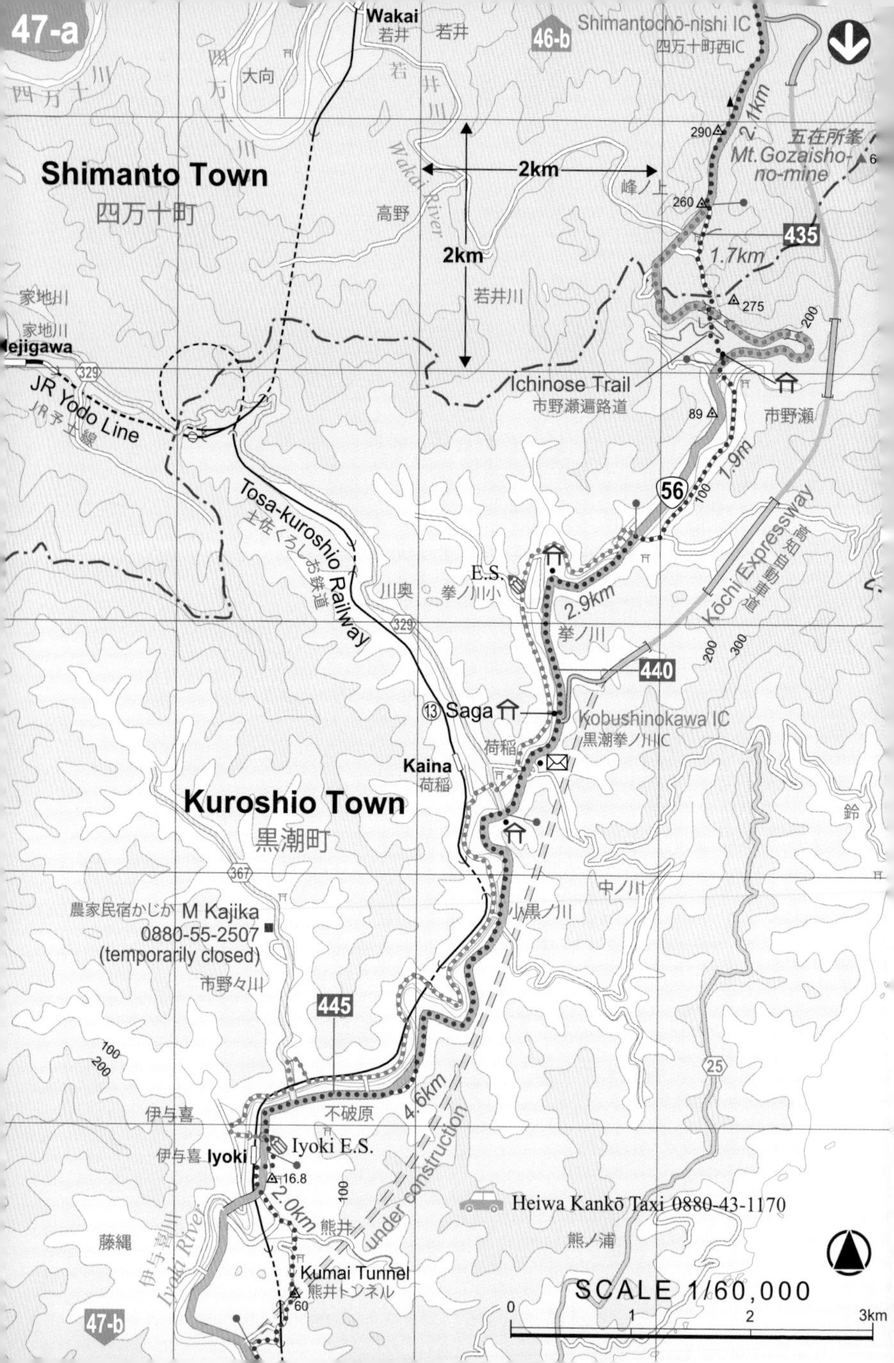

47-a
Wakai
若井
若井
46-b
Shimantochō-nishi IC
四万十町西IC
四万十川
四万十川
大向
若井川
Wakai River
2km
2km
2.1km
290
五在所峯
Mt. Gozaisho-no-mine
Shimanto Town
四万十町
高野
峰ノ上
260
435
1.7km
若井川
275
家地川
家地川
Iejigawa
329
JR Yodo Line
JR予土線
200
Ichinose Trail
市野瀬遍路道
市野瀬
89
1.9m
56
100
Tosa-kuroshio Railway
土佐くろしお鉄道
E.S.
川奥
拳ノ川小
2.9km
Kōchi Expressway
329
拳ノ川
200
300
440
⑬ Saga
Kobushinokawa IC
黒潮拳ノ川IC
荷稲
Kaina
荷稲
Kuroshio Town
黒潮町
鈴
367
中ノ川
小黒ノ川
農家民宿かじか M Kajika
0880-55-2507
(temporarily closed)
市野々川
445
100
200
4.6km
伊与喜
不破原
under construction
Iyoki E.S.
伊与喜 Iyoki
16.8
2.0km
100
熊井
Heiwa Kankō Taxi 0880-43-1170
伊与喜川
Iyoki River
藤縄
熊ノ浦
25
Kumai Tunnel
熊井トンネル
60
SCALE 1/60,000
0
1
2
3km
47-b

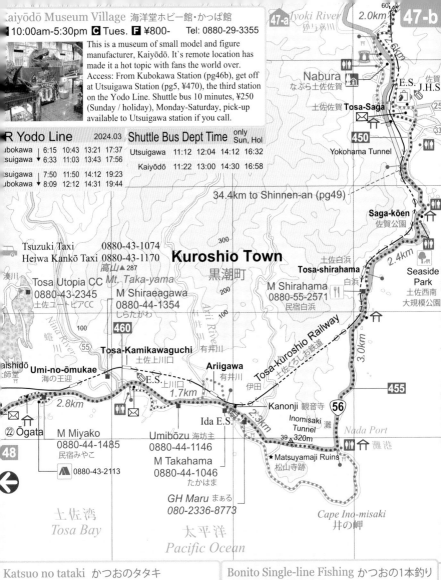

Kaiyōdō Museum Village 海洋堂ホビー館・かっぱ館

10:00am-5:30pm C Tues. F ¥800- Tel: 0880-29-3355

This is a museum of small model and figure manufacturer, Kaiyōdō. It`s remote location has made it a hot topic with fans the world over. Access: From Kubokawa Station (pg46b), get off at Utsuigawa Station (pg5, ¥470), the third station on the Yodo Line. Shuttle bus 10 minutes, ¥250 (Sunday / holiday), Monday-Saturday, pick-up available to Utsuigawa station if you call.

JR Yodo Line 2024.03

Kubokawa	↓	6:15	10:43	13:21	17:37
Utsuigawa		6:33	11:03	13:43	17:56
Utsuigawa	↓	7:50	11:50	14:12	19:23
Kubokawa		8:09	12:12	14:31	19:44

Shuttle Bus Dept Time only Sun, Hol

Utsuigawa	11:12	12:04	14:12	16:32
Kaiyōdō	11:22	13:00	14:30	16:58

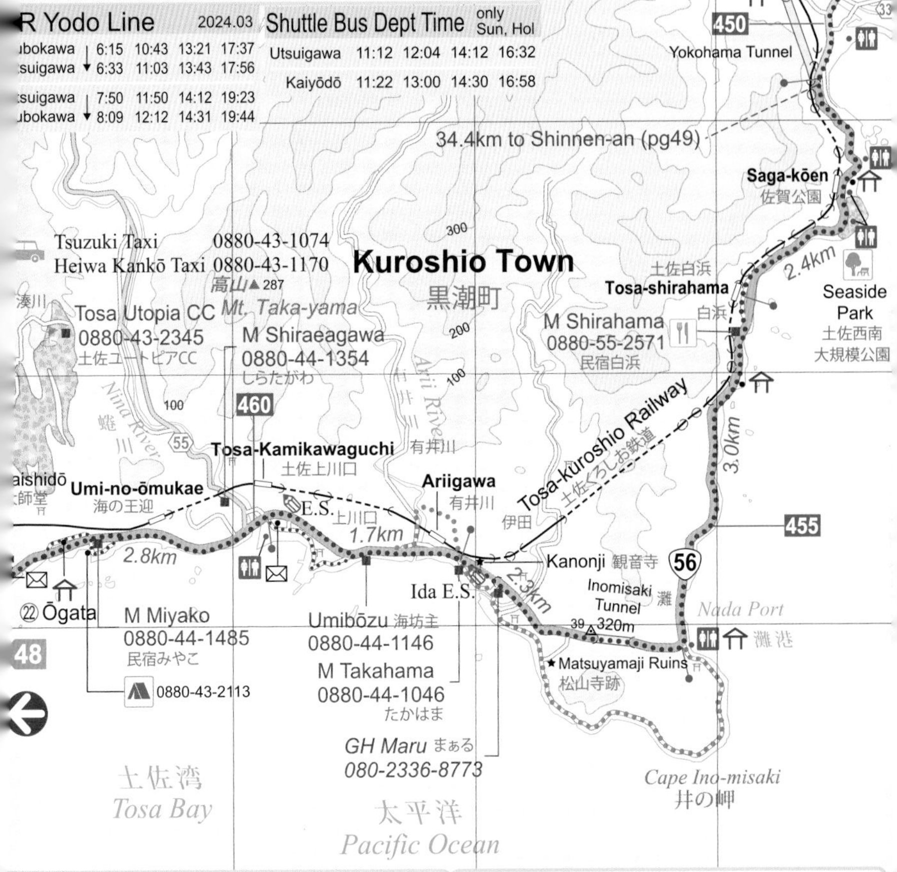

Iyoki River 伊与喜川
2.0km
2.6km
Nabura なぶら土佐佐賀
E.S.
J.H.S. 佐賀
土佐佐賀 Tosa-Saga
450
Yokohama Tunnel
34.4km to Shinnen-an (pg49)
Saga-kōen 佐賀公園
2.4km
Seaside Park 土佐西南大規模公園
Tosa-shirahama 土佐白浜
白浜
M Shirahama 0880-55-2571 民宿白浜

Kuroshio Town 黒潮町

Tsuzuki Taxi 0880-43-1074
Heiwa Kankō Taxi 0880-43-1170

高山 ▲287 Mt. Taka-yama
湊川
Tosa Utopia CC 0880-43-2345 土佐ユートピアCC
M Shiraeagawa 0880-44-1354 しらたがわ
Nina River 蜷川
Arii River 有井川
460
55
Tosa-Kamikawaguchi 土佐上川口
Tosa-Kuroshio Railway 土佐くろしお鉄道
Daishidō 大師堂
Umi-no-ōmukae 海の王迎
E.S. 上川口
1.7km
Ariigawa 有井川
伊田
2.8km
3.0km
455
56
Kanonji 観音寺
2.3km
Ida E.S.
Inomisaki Tunnel 320m
Nada Port 灘港
㉒ Ōgata
M Miyako 0880-44-1485 民宿みやこ
Umibōzu 海坊主 0880-44-1146
M Takahama 0880-44-1046 たかはま
0880-43-2113
GH Maru まぁる 080-2336-8773
Matsuyamaji Ruins 松山寺跡
Cape Ino-misaki 井の岬
土佐湾 Tosa Bay
太平洋 Pacific Ocean

48

Katsuo no tataki かつおのタタキ

Bonito is grilled over a straw fire to make Katsuo no tataki, a well-known local dish. The outside of the fish is grilled while the inside is left rare, then sliced and served with a tangy citrus shoyu dip (ponzu) and various strongly-flavoured herbs.

Bonito Single-line Fishing かつおの1本釣り

Bonito, a fish with a huge presence in Kōchi, is caught mainly by single-line fishing. Kōchi fishermen take their boats far into the ocean to chase after schools of bonito. Saga Port is the most well-known spot.

Blue: Mon. - Fri. Green: Mon. - Sat. Red: Sun., Hol.

Stop	Page	Fare											
Nakamura Stn	(pg 48)				8:20		10:14	11:42		12:35	13:39		15:
Ichinose	(pg 49)	¥700			8:42		10:36	12:04		12:57	14:01		16:
Shimonokae-shimoura	(pg 49)	¥900			8:51		10:45	12:13		13:06	14:10		16:
Shimizu Plaza Pal	(pg 50)	¥1400	8:05	8:46	9:21	10:25	11:15	12:50	13:32	13:36	14:40	16:37	16:
Ashizuri-misaki	(pg 51)	¥1900	8:37	9:18	10:05	10:57	11:59	13:34	14:04	14:20	15:24	17:09	17:

Stop	Page	Fare											
Ashizuri-misaki	(pg 51)		6:15	7:05	7:14	9:10	9:37	9:45	11:03	11:08	13:12	14:13	14:
Shimizu Plaza Pal	(pg 50)	¥800	7:00	8:07	7:56	10:00	10:10	10:35	12:00	11:41	14:02	14:46	15:
Shimonokae-shimoura	(pg 49)	¥1300	7:24	8:31		10:24		10:59	12:24		14:26		15:
Ichinose	(pg 49)	¥1400	7:30	8:37		10:30		11:05	12:30		14:32		16:
Nakamura Stn	(pg 48)	¥1900	7:55	9:02		10:55		11:30	12:55		14:57		16:

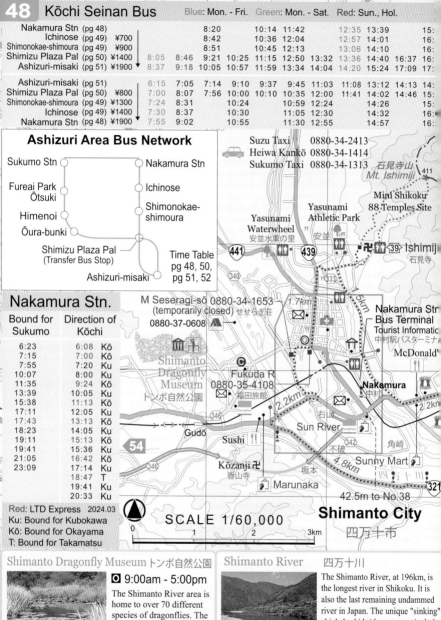

Ashizuri Area Bus Network

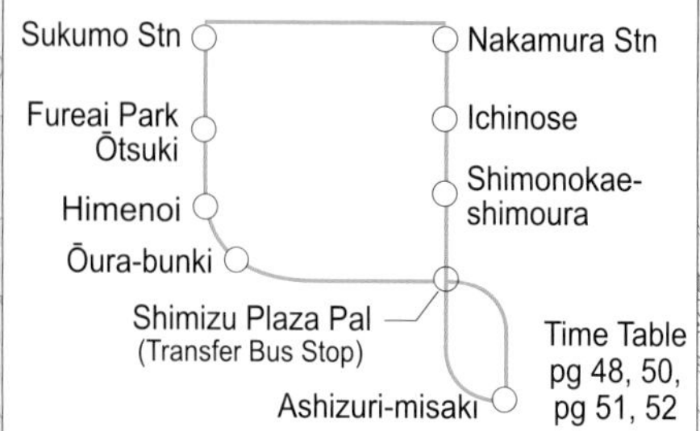

Sukumo Stn
Fureai Park Ōtsuki
Himenoi
Ōura-bunki
Shimizu Plaza Pal (Transfer Bus Stop)
Ashizuri-misaki
Nakamura Stn
Ichinose
Shimonokae-shimoura

Time Table pg 48, 50, pg 51, 52

Nakamura Stn.

Bound for Sukumo	Direction of Kōchi	
6:23	6:08	Kō
7:15	7:00	Kō
7:55	7:20	Ku
10:07	8:00	Ku
11:35	9:24	Kō
13:39	10:05	Ku
15:38	11:13	Kō
17:11	12:05	Ku
17:43	13:13	Kō
18:23	14:05	Ku
19:11	15:13	Kō
19:41	15:36	Ku
21:05	16:42	Kō
23:09	17:14	Ku
	18:47	T
	19:41	Ku
	20:33	Ku

Red: LTD Express 2024.03
Ku: Bound for Kubokawa
Kō: Bound for Okayama
T: Bound for Takamatsu

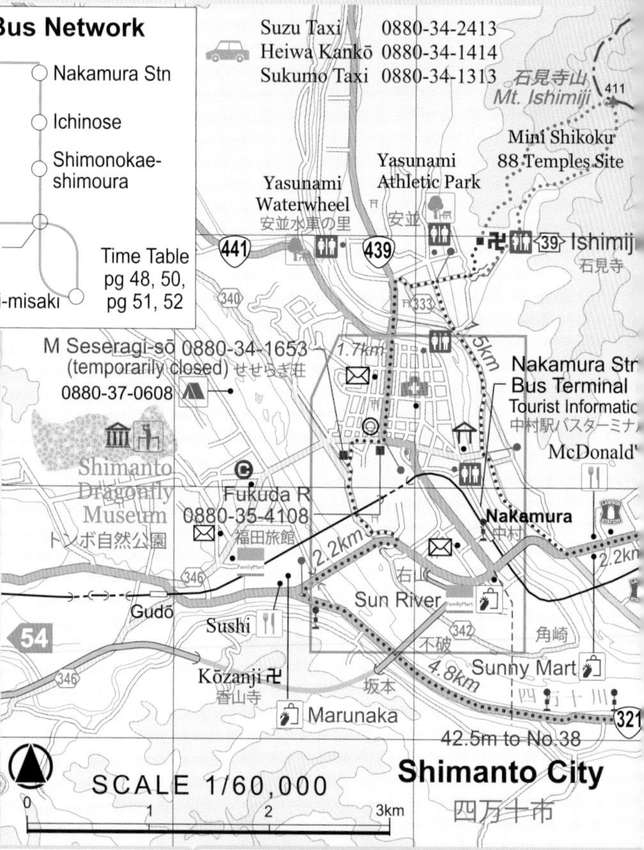

Suzu Taxi 0880-34-2413
Heiwa Kankō 0880-34-1414
Sukumo Taxi 0880-34-1313

石見寺山 Mt. Ishimiji
Mini Shikoku 88 Temples Site
Yasunami Athletic Park
Yasunami Waterwheel 安並水車の里
安並
Ishimiji 石見寺
M Seseragi-sō 0880-34-1653 (temporarily closed) せせらぎ荘
0880-37-0608
Shimanto Dragonfly Museum トンボ自然公園
Fukuda R 0880-35-4108 福田旅館
Nakamura Stn Bus Terminal Tourist Information 中村駅バスターミナル
McDonald's
Nakamura 中村
Gudō
Sushi
Sun River
右山
不破
角崎
Sunny Mart
Kōzanji 香山寺
坂本
Marunaka
四万十川
1.7km 5km 2.2km 2.2km 4.8km
42.5m to No.38

Shimanto City
四万十市

SCALE 1/60,000
0 1 2 3km

Shimanto Dragonfly Museum トンボ自然公園

9:00am - 5:00pm

The Shimanto River area is home to over 70 different species of dragonflies. The Shimanto Dragonfly Museum is a place to study about dragonflies and other wildlife from the river.

Shimanto River 四万十川

The Shimanto River, at 196km, is the longest river in Shikoku. It is also the last remaining undammed river in Japan. The unique "sinking" chinkabashi bridges are particularly scenic, with sightseeing boats from which visitors can watch fish swimming in the clear river water.

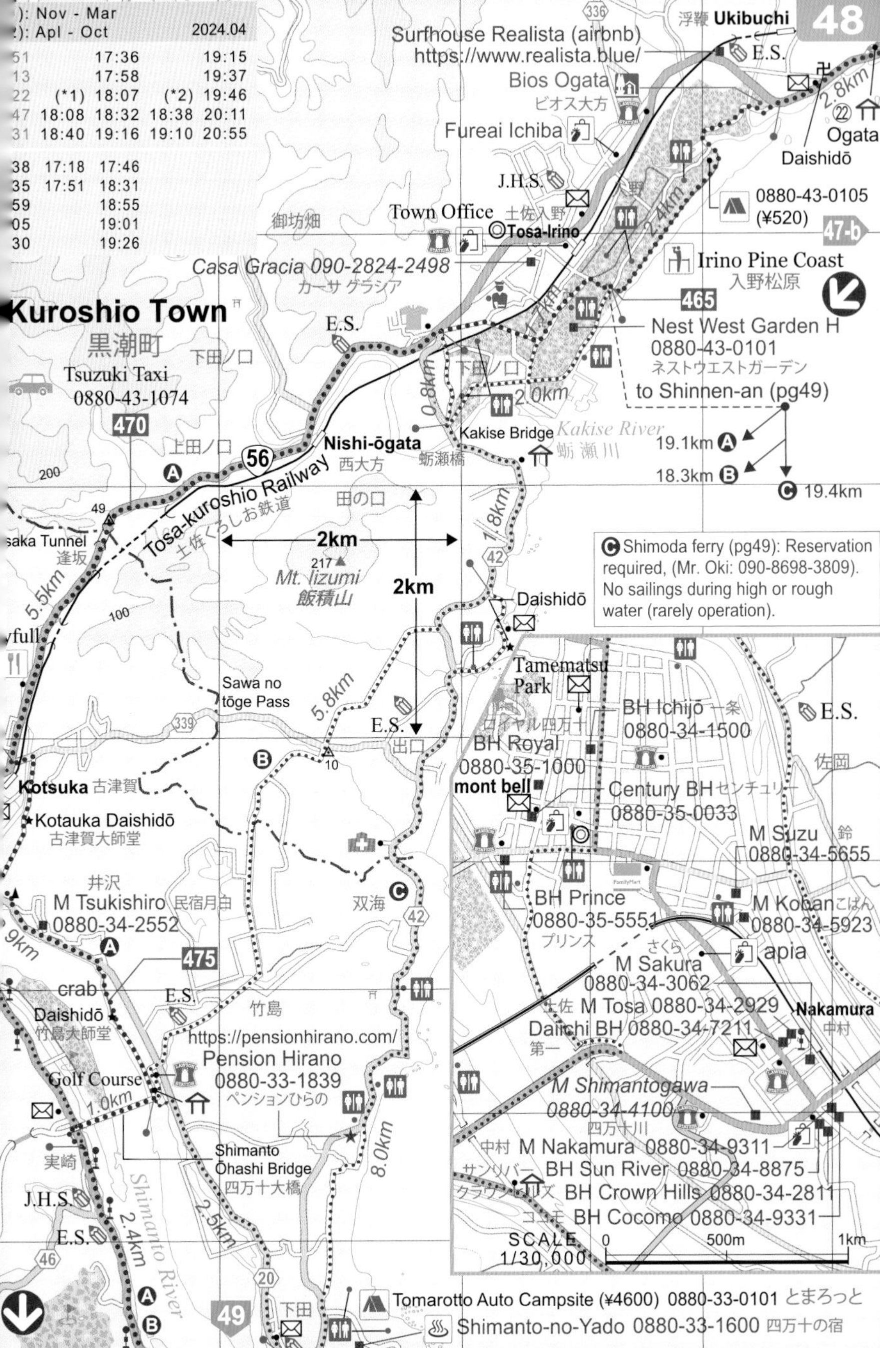

): Nov - Mar
): Apl - Oct
2024.04
51 17:36 19:15
13 17:58 19:37
22 (*1) 18:07 (*2) 19:46
47 18:08 18:32 18:38 20:11
31 18:40 19:16 19:10 20:55
38 17:18 17:46
35 17:51 18:31
59 18:55
05 19:01
30 19:26
Kuroshio Town
黒潮町
Tsuzuki Taxi
0880-43-1074
470
浮鞭 Ukibuchi
Surfhouse Realista (airbnb)
https://www.realista.blue/
E.S.
Bios Ogata
ビオス大方
Fureai Ichiba
2.8km
Ogata
Daishidō
J.H.S.
0880-43-0105
(¥520)
Town Office
土佐入野
Tosa-Irino
47-b
Casa Gracia 090-2824-2498
カーサ グラシア
Irino Pine Coast
入野松原
465
Nest West Garden H
0880-43-0101
ネストウエストガーデン
to Shinnen-an (pg49)
19.1km A
18.3km B
C 19.4km
2.4km
1.7km
0.8km
2.0km
Kakise Bridge
蛎瀬橋
Kakise River
蛎瀬川
Nishi-ōgata
西大方
上田ノ口
下田ノ口
田の口
Tosa-kuroshio Railway
土佐くろしお鉄道
2km
Mt. Iizumi
飯積山
217
Saka Tunnel
逢坂
5.5km
1.8km
Daishidō
C Shimoda ferry (pg49): Reservation required, (Mr. Oki: 090-8698-3809). No sailings during high or rough water (rarely operation).
Sawa no tōge Pass
5.8km
E.S.
出口
Kotsuka 古津賀
Kotauka Daishidō
古津賀大師堂
井沢
M Tsukishiro 民宿月白
0880-34-2552
双海
475
crab
Daishidō
竹島大師堂
竹島
https://pensionhirano.com/
Pension Hirano
0880-33-1839
ペンションひらの
Golf Course
1.0km
Shimanto Ōhashi Bridge
四万十大橋
実崎
J.H.S.
E.S.
2.4km
Shimanto River
2.5km
8.0km
Tamematsu Park
BH Ichijō 一条
0880-34-1500
ロイヤル四万十
BH Royal
0880-35-1000
mont bell
Century BH センチュリー
0880-35-0033
E.S.
佐岡
M Suzu 鈴
0880-34-5655
BH Prince
0880-35-5551
プリンス
M Koban こばん
0880-34-5923
さくら
M Sakura
0880-34-3062
apia
土佐 M Tosa 0880-34-2929
Daiichi BH 0880-34-7211
第一
Nakamura
中村
M Shimantogawa
0880-34-4100
四万十川
中村 M Nakamura 0880-34-9311
サンリバー BH Sun River 0880-34-8875
クラウンヒルズ BH Crown Hills 0880-34-2811
ココモ BH Cocomo 0880-34-9331
SCALE 1/30,000
0 500m 1km
49
下田
Tomarotto Auto Campsite (¥4600) 0880-33-0101 とまろっと
Shimanto-no-Yado 0880-33-1600 四万十の宿

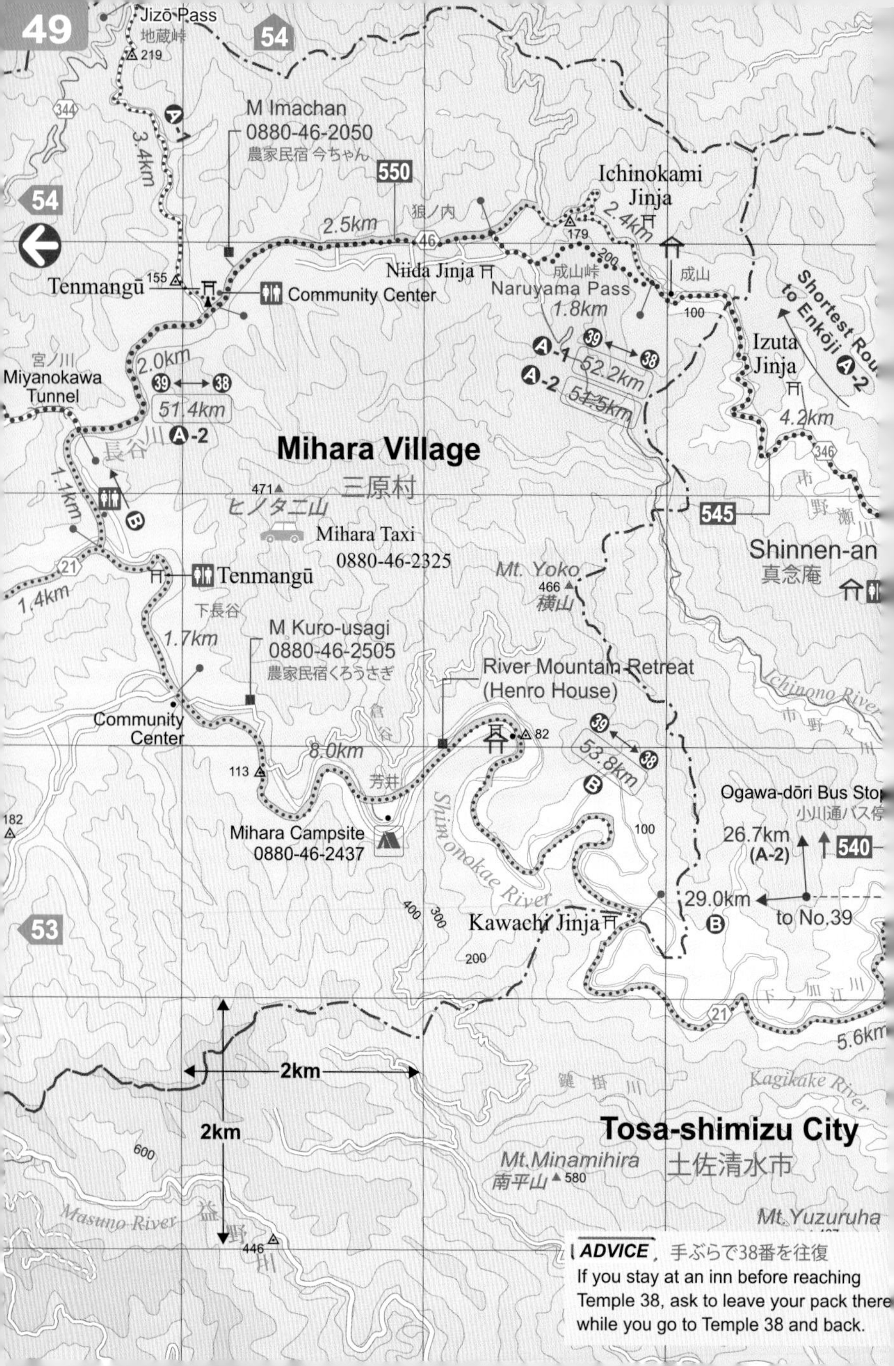

Jizō Pass
地蔵峠
219
54
344
3.4km
A-1
M Imachan
0880-46-2050
農家民宿 今ちゃん
550
狼ノ内
2.5km
46
Ichinokami
Jinja
179
2.4km
200
成山峠
成山
Naruyama Pass
1.8km
100
Niida Jinja
Tenmangū
155
Community Center
Shortest Route to Enkōji A-2
Izuta
Jinja
宮ノ川
Miyanokawa
Tunnel
2.0km
39 38
51.4km
A-2
A-1
52.2km
A-2
51.5km
4.2km
346
長谷川
Mihara Village
三原村
471
ヒノタニ山
1.1km
B
Mihara Taxi
0880-46-2325
545
市野瀬川
21
Tenmangū
Shinnen-an
真念庵
1.4km
Mt. Yoko
466
横山
下長谷
1.7km
M Kuro-usagi
0880-46-2505
農家民宿くろうさぎ
River Mountain Retreat
(Henro House)
Ichinono River
市野々川
倉谷
Community
Center
82
53.8km
B
113
8.0km
芳井
Ogawa-dōri Bus Stop
小川通バス停
182
Mihara Campsite
0880-46-2437
Shimonokae River
100
26.7km
(A-2)
540
400
300
29.0km
to No.39
53
Kawachi Jinja
B
200
下ノ加江川
21
5.6km
2km
Kagikake River
鍵掛川
2km
Tosa-shimizu City
土佐清水市
600
Mt.Minamihira
南平山
580
Masuno River
益野川
446
Mt.Yuzuruha

ADVICE 手ぶらで38番を往復

If you stay at an inn before reaching Temple 38, ask to leave your pack there while you go to Temple 38 and back.

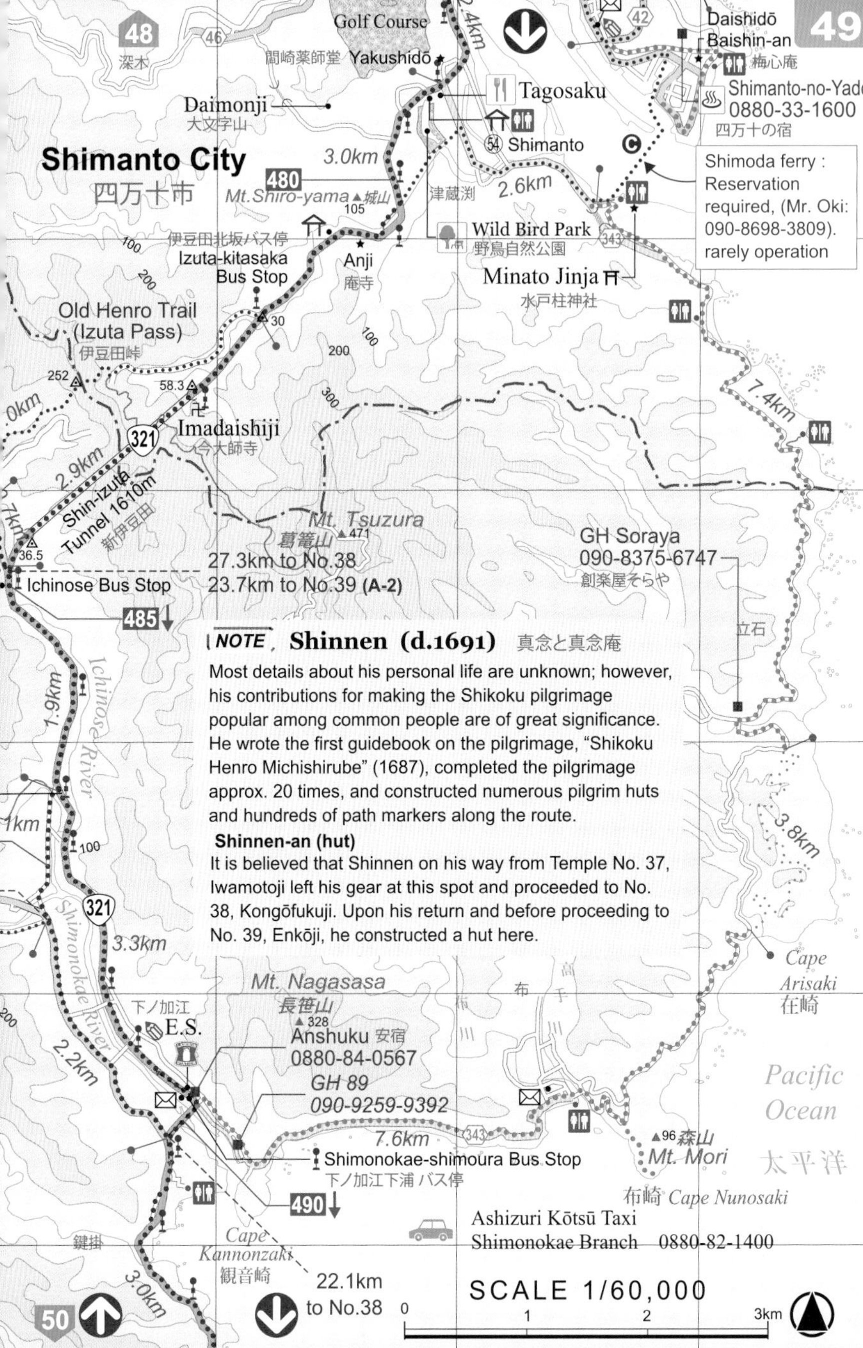

48
深木
46
Golf Course
間崎薬師堂 Yakushidō
2.4km
42
Daishidō
Baishin-an
梅心庵
Shimanto-no-Yado
0880-33-1600
四万十の宿
Daimonji
大文字山
Tagosaku
Shimanto City
四万十市
3.0km
480
Mt.Shiro-yama 城山
105
54 Shimanto
津蔵渕
2.6km
Shimoda ferry : Reservation required, (Mr. Oki: 090-8698-3809). rarely operation
Wild Bird Park
野鳥自然公園
343
伊豆田北坂バス停
Izuta-kitasaka Bus Stop
Anji
庵寺
Minato Jinja
水戸柱神社
Old Henro Trail (Izuta Pass)
伊豆田峠
30
252
58.3
321
Imadaishiji
今大師寺
7.4km
2.9km
Shin-izuta Tunnel 1610m
新伊豆田
Mt. Tsuzura
葛篭山
471
36.5
GH Soraya
090-8375-6747
創楽屋そらや
27.3km to No.38
23.7km to No.39 (A-2)
Ichinose Bus Stop
485
立石
1.9km
Ichinose River
3.8km
321
3.3km
Shimonokae River
Cape Arisaki
在崎
Mt. Nagasasa
長笹山
328
下ノ加江
E.S.
Anshuku 安宿
0880-84-0567
2.2km
GH 89
090-9259-9392
7.6km
343
Shimonokae-shimoura Bus Stop
下ノ加江下浦 バス停
96 森山
Mt. Mori
Pacific Ocean
太平洋
490
布崎 Cape Nunosaki
Ashizuri Kōtsū Taxi
Shimonokae Branch 0880-82-1400
鍵掛
Cape Kannonzaki
観音崎
3.0km
22.1km to No.38
SCALE 1/60,000
0 1 2 3km
50

NOTE Shinnen (d.1691) 真念と真念庵

Most details about his personal life are unknown; however, his contributions for making the Shikoku pilgrimage popular among common people are of great significance. He wrote the first guidebook on the pilgrimage, “Shikoku Henro Michishirube” (1687), completed the pilgrimage approx. 20 times, and constructed numerous pilgrim huts and hundreds of path markers along the route.

Shinnen-an (hut)

It is believed that Shinnen on his way from Temple No. 37, Iwamotoji left his gear at this spot and proceeded to No. 38, Kongōfukuji. Upon his return and before proceeding to No. 39, Enkōji, he constructed a hut here.

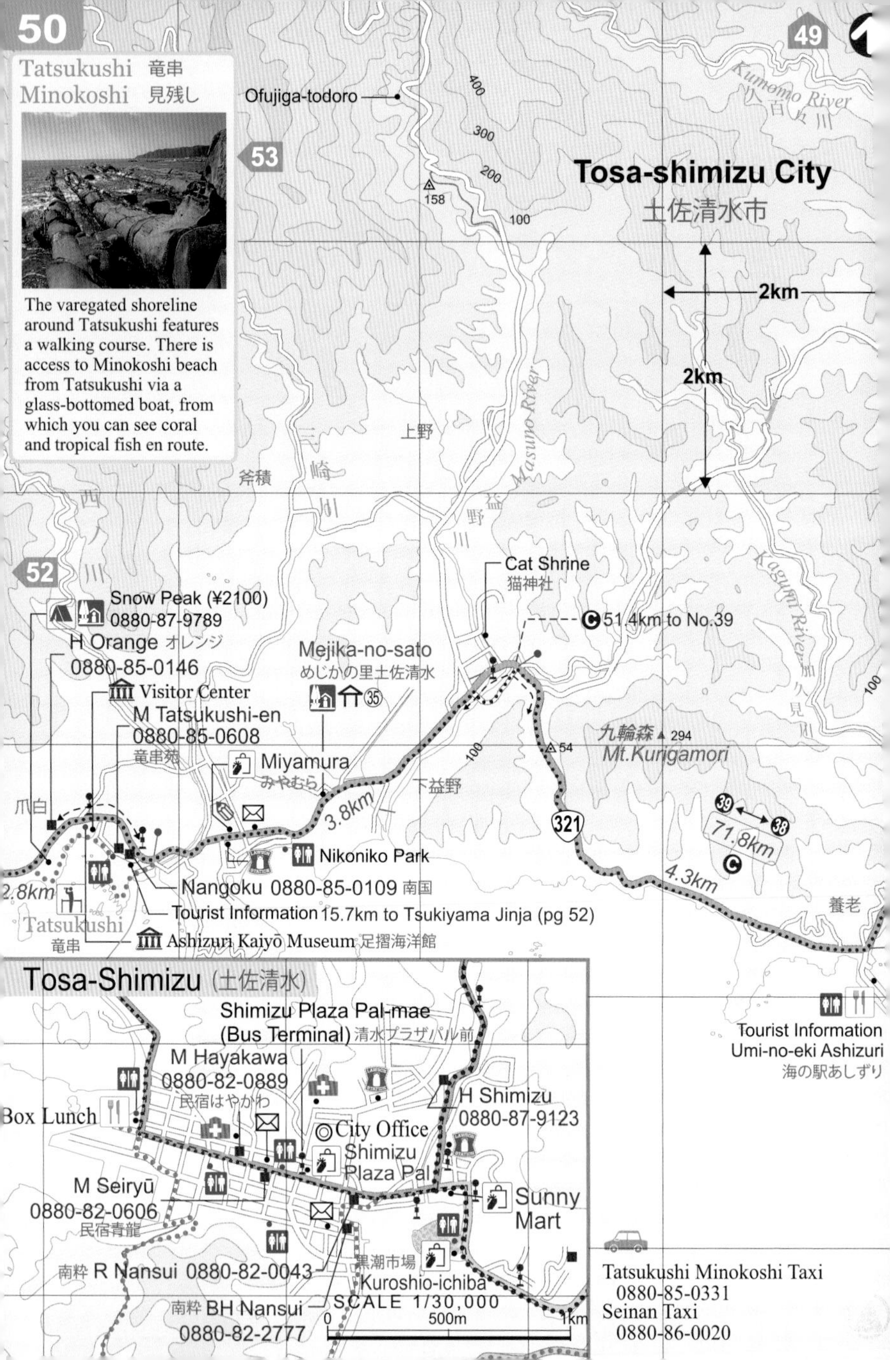

50
49
Tatsukushi 竜串
Minokoshi 見残し
The varegated shoreline around Tatsukushi features a walking course. There is access to Minokoshi beach from Tatsukushi via a glass-bottomed boat, from which you can see coral and tropical fish en route.
53
Ofujiga-todoro
400
300
200
158
100
Kumomo River
八百々川
Tosa-shimizu City
土佐清水市
2km
2km
Masuno River
上野
三崎川
斧積
西ノ川
益野川
52
Snow Peak (¥2100)
0880-87-9789
H Orange オレンジ
0880-85-0146
Visitor Center
M Tatsukushi-en
0880-85-0608
竜串苑
Mejika-no-sato
めじかの里土佐清水
35
Cat Shrine
猫神社
51.4km to No.39
Kagumi River
加久見川
九輪森 294
Mt.Kurigamori
54
100
Miyamura
みやむら
下益野
3.8km
爪白
321
39
38
71.8km
4.3km
Nikoniko Park
Nangoku 0880-85-0109 南国
2.8km
Tourist Information 15.7km to Tsukiyama Jinja (pg 52)
Tatsukushi
竜串
Ashizuri Kaiyō Museum 足摺海洋館
養老
Tosa-Shimizu (土佐清水)
Shimizu Plaza Pal-mae
(Bus Terminal) 清水プラザパル前
M Hayakawa
0880-82-0889
民宿はやかわ
Box Lunch
H Shimizu
0880-87-9123
City Office
Shimizu
Plaza Pal
M Seiryū
0880-82-0606
民宿青龍
Sunny
Mart
黒潮市場
Kuroshio-ichiba
南粋 R Nansui 0880-82-0043
南粋 BH Nansui
0880-82-2777
SCALE 1/30,000
0
500m
1km
Tourist Information
Umi-no-eki Ashizuri
海の駅あしずり
Tatsukushi Minokoshi Taxi
0880-85-0331
Seinan Taxi
0880-86-0020

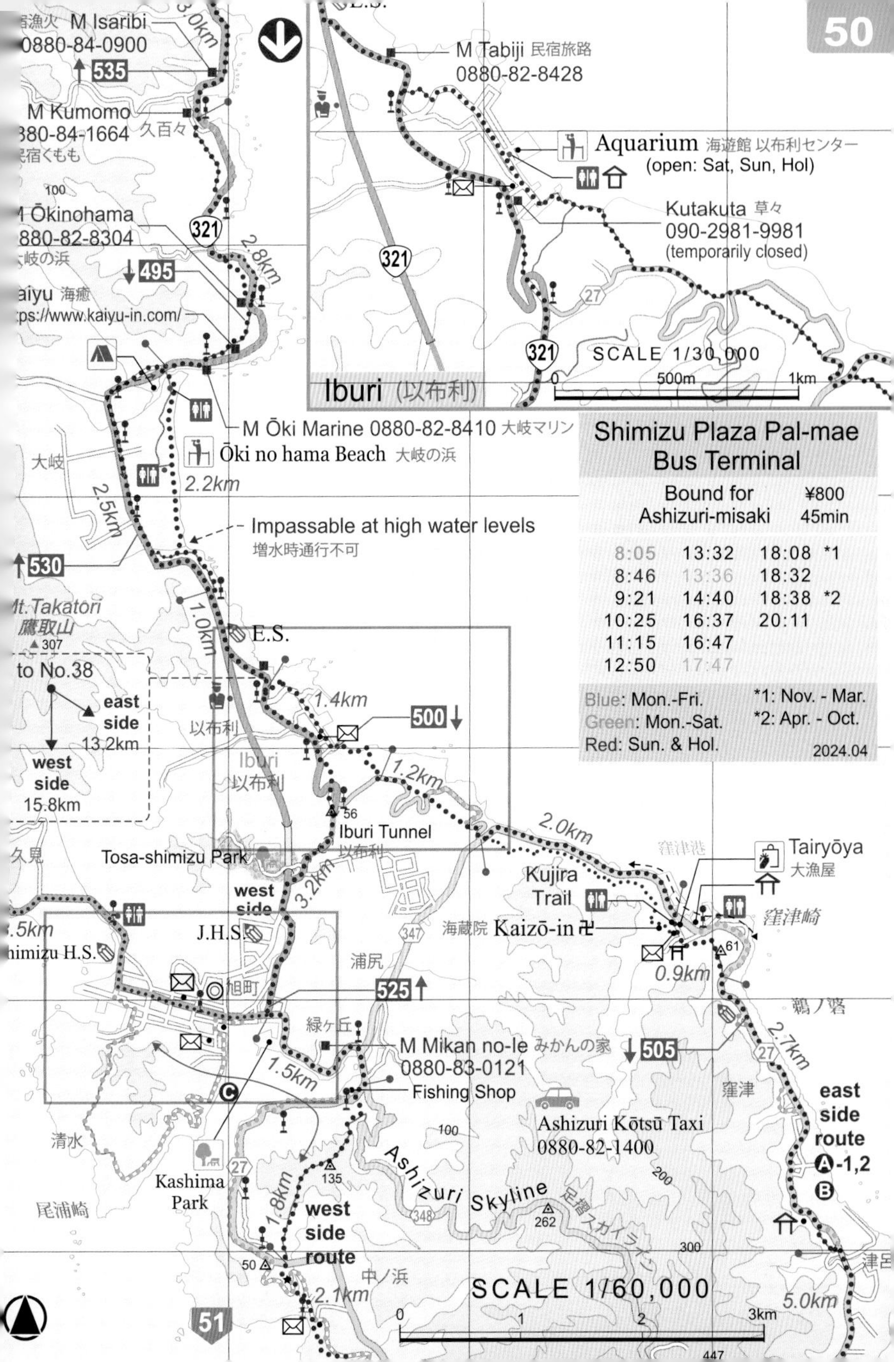

M Isaribi
0880-84-0900
535
3.0km
M Kumomo
880-84-1664
民宿くもも
久百々
M Ōkinohama
880-82-8304
大岐の浜
321
2.8km
495
Kaiyu 海癒
https://www.kaiyu-in.com/
M Ōki Marine 0880-82-8410 大岐マリン
Ōki no hama Beach 大岐の浜
大岐
2.5km
2.2km
Impassable at high water levels
増水時通行不可
530
Mt.Takatori
鷹取山
307
1.0km
E.S.
to No.38
east side 13.2km
west side 15.8km
1.4km
500
以布利
Iburi 以布利
1.2km
56
Iburi Tunnel 以布利
2.0km
Tosa-shimizu Park
3.2km
久見
west side
J.H.S.
Shimizu H.S.
旭町
525
緑ケ丘
M Mikan no-Ie みかんの家
0880-83-0121
Fishing Shop
1.5km
505
浦尻
347
海蔵院 Kaizō-in
Kujira Trail
窪津港
Tairyōya 大漁屋
窪津崎
61
0.9km
鶴ノ碆
2.7km
27
窪津
east side route
A-1,2
B
Ashizuri Kōtsū Taxi
0880-82-1400
清水
Kashima Park
尾浦崎
27
135
1.8km
west side route
Ashizuri Skyline 足摺スカイライン
348
262
100
200
300
50
中ノ浜
2.1km
51
5.0km
津呂
SCALE 1/60,000
0 1 2 3km
447
M Tabiji 民宿旅路
0880-82-8428
Aquarium 海遊館 以布利センター
(open: Sat, Sun, Hol)
Kutakuta 草々
090-2981-9981
(temporarily closed)
321
27
SCALE 1/30,000
0 500m 1km
Iburi (以布利)

Shimizu Plaza Pal-mae Bus Terminal

Bound for Ashizuri-misaki		¥800 45min	
8:05	13:32	18:08	*1
8:46	13:36	18:32	
9:21	14:40	18:38	*2
10:25	16:37	20:11	
11:15	16:47		
12:50	17:47		

Blue: Mon.-Fri.
Green: Mon.-Sat.
Red: Sun. & Hol.

*1: Nov. - Mar.
*2: Apr. - Oct.

2024.04

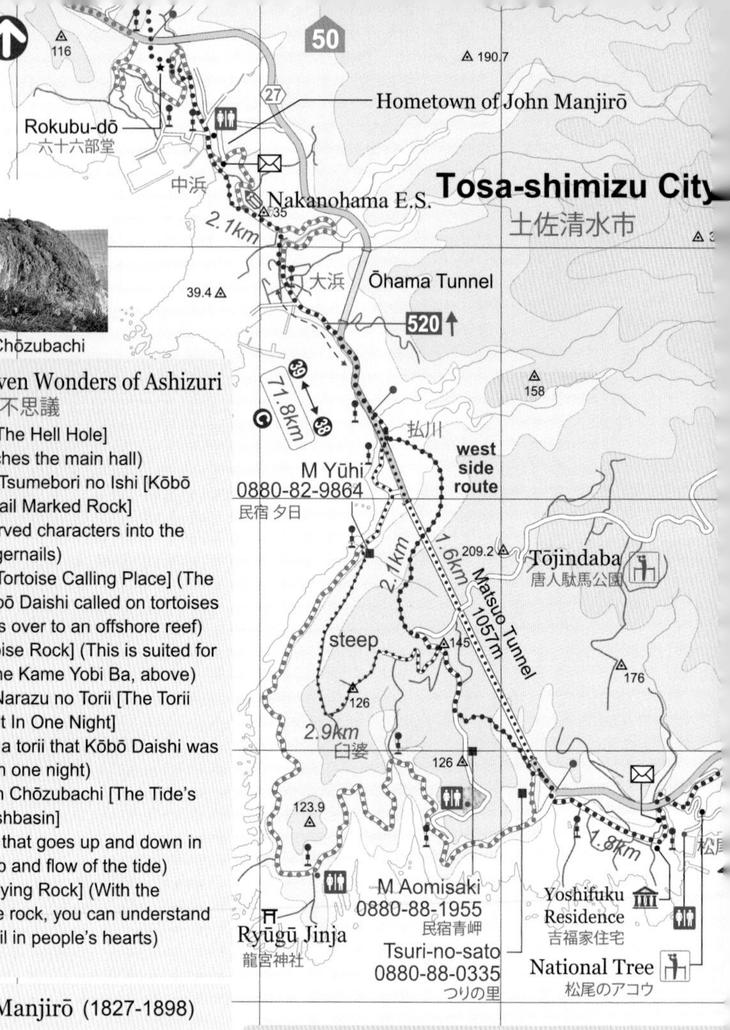

116
50
190.7
27
Hometown of John Manjirō
Rokubu-dō
六十六部堂
中浜
Nakanohama E.S.
Tosa-shimizu City
土佐清水市
35
2.1km
39.4
大浜
Ōhama Tunnel
520
39
71.8km
38
158
払川
M Yūhi
0880-82-9864
民宿 夕日
west side route
209.2
Tōjindaba
唐人駄馬公園
2.1km
1.6km
Matsuo Tunnel 1057m
steep
145
126
176
2.9km
臼婆
126
123.9
1.8km
M Aomisaki
0880-88-1955
民宿青岬
Yoshifuku Residence
吉福家住宅
Ryūgū Jinja
龍宮神社
Tsuri-no-sato
0880-88-0335
つりの里
National Tree
松尾のアコウ

Shio no Kanman Chōzubachi

NOTE The Seven Wonders of Ashizuri
足摺七不思議

- Jigoku no Ana [The Hell Hole] (A hole that reaches the main hall)
- Kōbō Daishi no Tsumebori no Ishi [Kōbō Daishi's Fingernail Marked Rock] (Kōbo Daishi carved characters into the rock with his fingernails)
- Kame Yobi Ba [Tortoise Calling Place] (The place where Kōbō Daishi called on tortoises to help him cross over to an offshore reef)
- Kame Ishi [Tortoise Rock] (This is suited for a compass for the Kame Yobi Ba, above)
- Ichi Ya Konryū Narazu no Torii [The Torii That Wasn't Built In One Night] (The remains of a torii that Kōbō Daishi was unable to build in one night)
- Shio no Kanman Chōzubachi [The Tide's Ebb & Flow Washbasin] (Water in a rock that goes up and down in time with the ebb and flow of the tide)
- Yurugi Ishi [Swaying Rock] (With the movement of the rock, you can understand the good and evil in people's hearts)
- And others.

NOTE John Manjirō (1827-1898)
ジョン万次郎

In 1841, he and four friends left the port of Tosa-shimizu city to go fishing, but they got caught in a storm and landed on an unhabitated island. After 143 days, they were rescued by an American whaling ship and taken to Hawaii. John went to the mainland US where he learned English, shipbuilding and navigation etc. In 1851, he returned to Japan and later acted as an interpreter and translator for the government when Commodore Perry arrived in Japan to force the opening of Japan.

38 Kongōfukuji 三十八番 金剛福寺

H Senju Kannon Bosatsu — S None

214-1 Ashizuri-misaki,Tosashimizu City

Free of charge (40) — ☎ 0880-88-0038

A By bus bound for Ashizuri-misaki from Nakamura Stn, about 105 min. Get off at the last stop.

In 822, Kōbō Daishi followed the wish of Emperor Saga, carved a statue of Senju Kannon and founded this temple. It is believed one can set off for the land of paradise *(fudaraku)* where Kannon lives from here because Kōbō Daishi saw Kannon when he looked out into the sea.

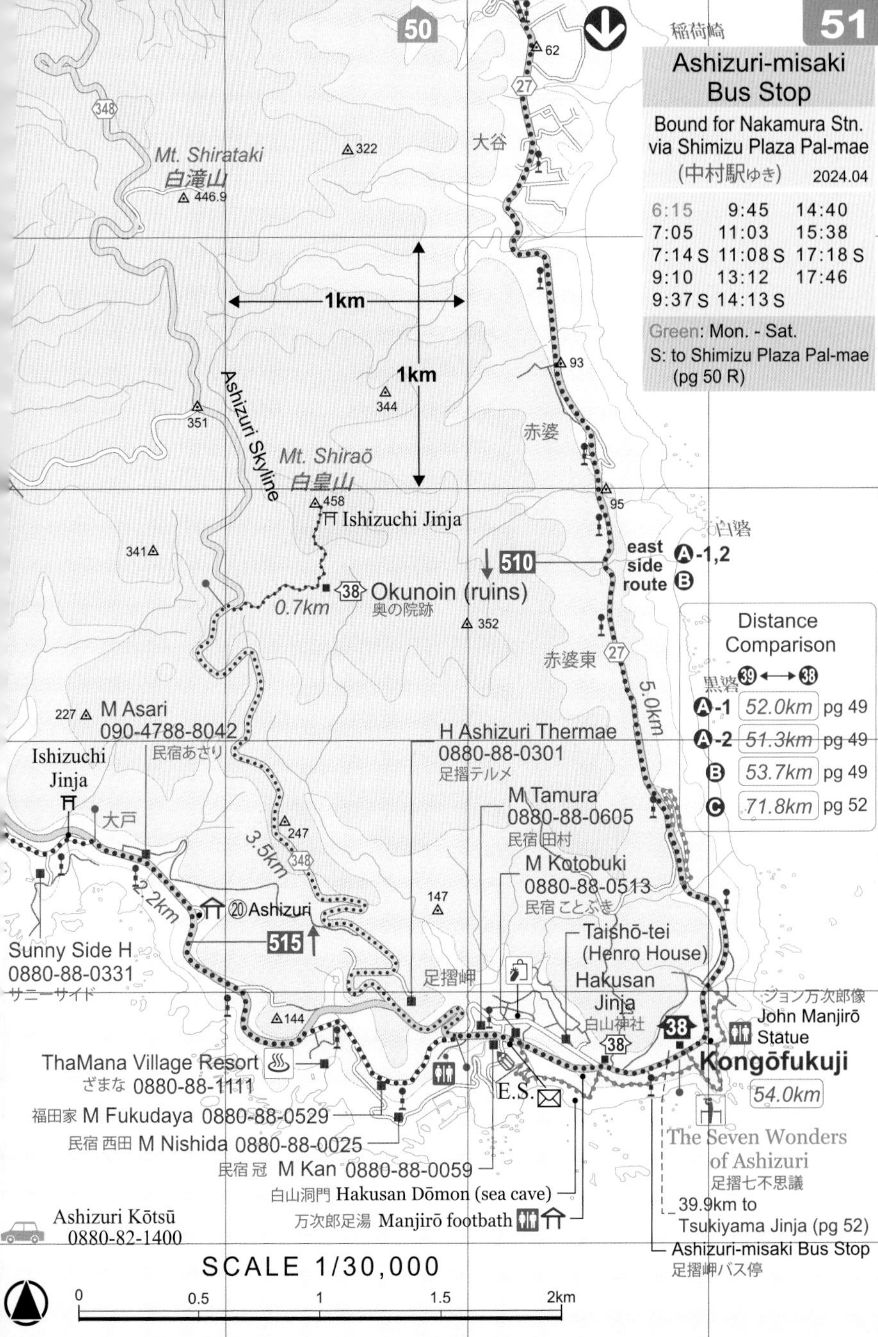

50
稲荷崎
Ashizuri-misaki Bus Stop
Bound for Nakamura Stn. via Shimizu Plaza Pal-mae
(中村駅ゆき) 2024.04
6:15 9:45 14:40
7:05 11:03 15:38
7:14 S 11:08 S 17:18 S
9:10 13:12 17:46
9:37 S 14:13 S
Green: Mon. - Sat.
S: to Shimizu Plaza Pal-mae (pg 50 R)
Mt. Shirataki
白滝山
446.9
322
大谷
62
27
348
1km
1km
344
351
93
Ashizuri Skyline
Mt. Shiraō
白皇山
赤婆
458
Ishizuchi Jinja
95
白碆
341
510
east side route A-1,2 B
Okunoin (ruins)
奥の院跡
0.7km
38
352
Distance Comparison
黒碆 39 ↔ 38
A-1 52.0km pg 49
A-2 51.3km pg 49
B 53.7km pg 49
C 71.8km pg 52
赤婆東
5.0km
227
M Asari
090-4788-8042
民宿あさり
H Ashizuri Thermae
0880-88-0301
足摺テルメ
Ishizuchi Jinja
大戸
M Tamura
0880-88-0605
民宿田村
247
3.5km
M Kotobuki
0880-88-0513
民宿 ことぶき
2.2km
⑳ Ashizuri
147
Taishō-tei (Henro House)
515
Sunny Side H
0880-88-0331
サニーサイド
足摺岬
Hakusan Jinja
白山神社
ジョン万次郎像
John Manjirō Statue
144
Kongōfukuji
54.0km
ThaMana Village Resort
ざまな 0880-88-1111
福田家 M Fukudaya 0880-88-0529
民宿 西田 M Nishida 0880-88-0025
E.S.
The Seven Wonders of Ashizuri
足摺七不思議
民宿 冠 M Kan 0880-88-0059
白山洞門 Hakusan Dōmon (sea cave)
39.9km to Tsukiyama Jinja (pg 52)
Ashizuri Kōtsū
0880-82-1400
万次郎足湯 Manjirō footbath
Ashizuri-misaki Bus Stop
足摺岬バス停
SCALE 1/30,000
0 0.5 1 1.5 2km

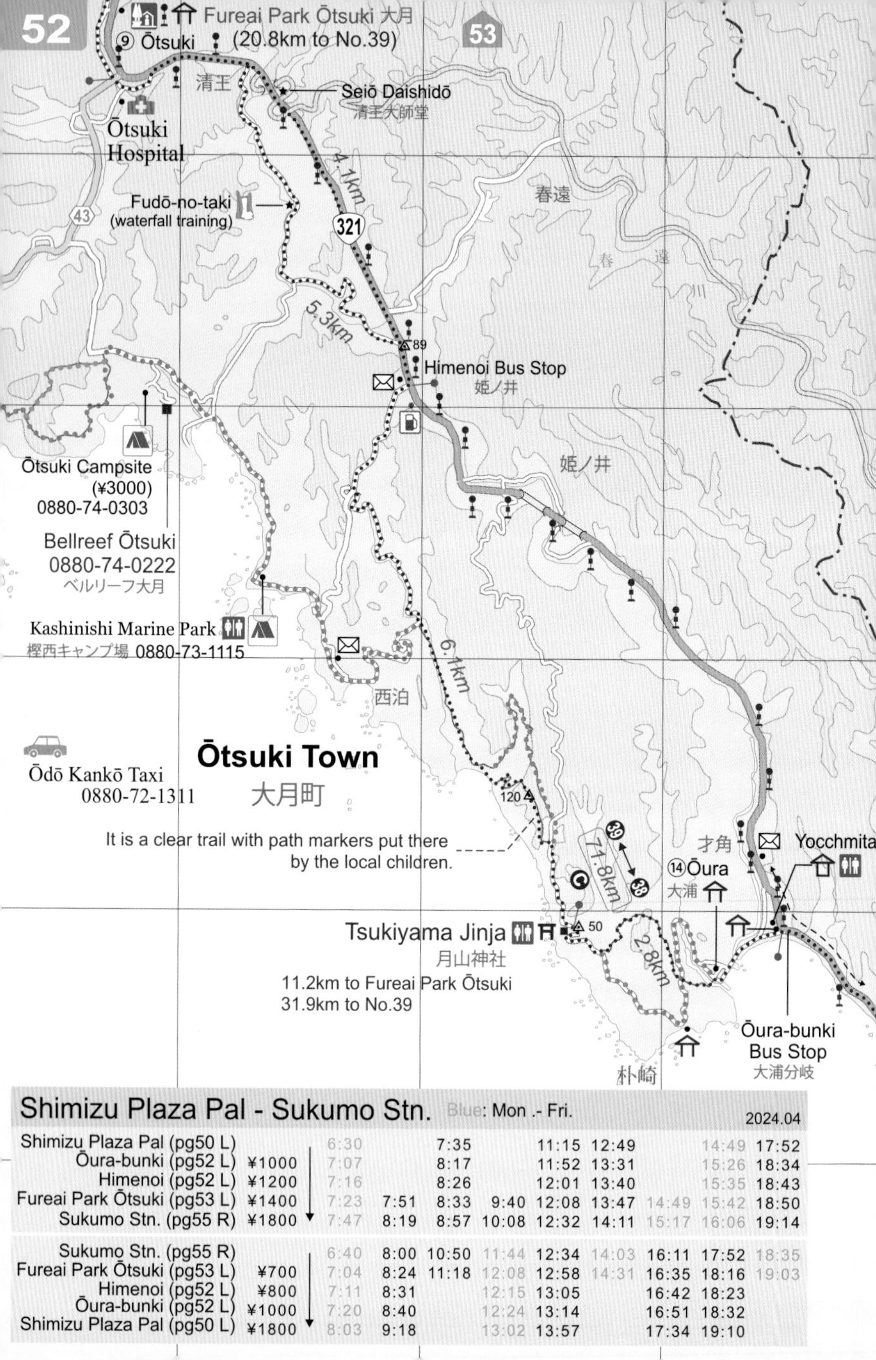

53
Fureai Park Ōtsuki 大月
(20.8km to No.39)
⑨ Ōtsuki
清王
Seiō Daishidō
清王大師堂
Ōtsuki Hospital
4.1km
Fudō-no-taki
(waterfall training)
43
321
春遠
春 遠 川
5.3km
89
Himenoi Bus Stop
姫ノ井
姫ノ井
Ōtsuki Campsite
(¥3000)
0880-74-0303
Bellreef Ōtsuki
0880-74-0222
ベルリーフ大月
Kashinishi Marine Park
樫西キャンプ場 0880-73-1115
6.1km
西泊
Ōdō Kankō Taxi
0880-72-1311
Ōtsuki Town
大月町
120
It is a clear trail with path markers put there by the local children.
39
71.8km
38
才角
Yocchmita
⑭Ōura
大浦
Tsukiyama Jinja
月山神社
50
2.8km
11.2km to Fureai Park Ōtsuki
31.9km to No.39
Ōura-bunki Bus Stop
大浦分岐
朴崎

Shimizu Plaza Pal - Sukumo Stn.

Blue: Mon .- Fri. 2024.04

Stop	Fare									
Shimizu Plaza Pal (pg50 L)		6:30		7:35		11:15	12:49		14:49	17:52
Ōura-bunki (pg52 L)	¥1000	7:07		8:17		11:52	13:31		15:26	18:34
Himenoi (pg52 L)	¥1200	7:16		8:26		12:01	13:40		15:35	18:43
Fureai Park Ōtsuki (pg53 L)	¥1400	7:23	7:51	8:33	9:40	12:08	13:47	14:49	15:42	18:50
Sukumo Stn. (pg55 R)	¥1800	7:47	8:19	8:57	10:08	12:32	14:11	15:17	16:06	19:14

Stop	Fare									
Sukumo Stn. (pg55 R)		6:40	8:00	10:50	11:44	12:34	14:03	16:11	17:52	18:35
Fureai Park Ōtsuki (pg53 L)	¥700	7:04	8:24	11:18	12:08	12:58	14:31	16:35	18:16	19:03
Himenoi (pg52 L)	¥800	7:11	8:31		12:15	13:05		16:42	18:23	
Ōura-bunki (pg52 L)	¥1000	7:20	8:40		12:24	13:14		16:51	18:32	
Shimizu Plaza Pal (pg50 L)	¥1800	8:03	9:18		13:02	13:57		17:34	19:10	

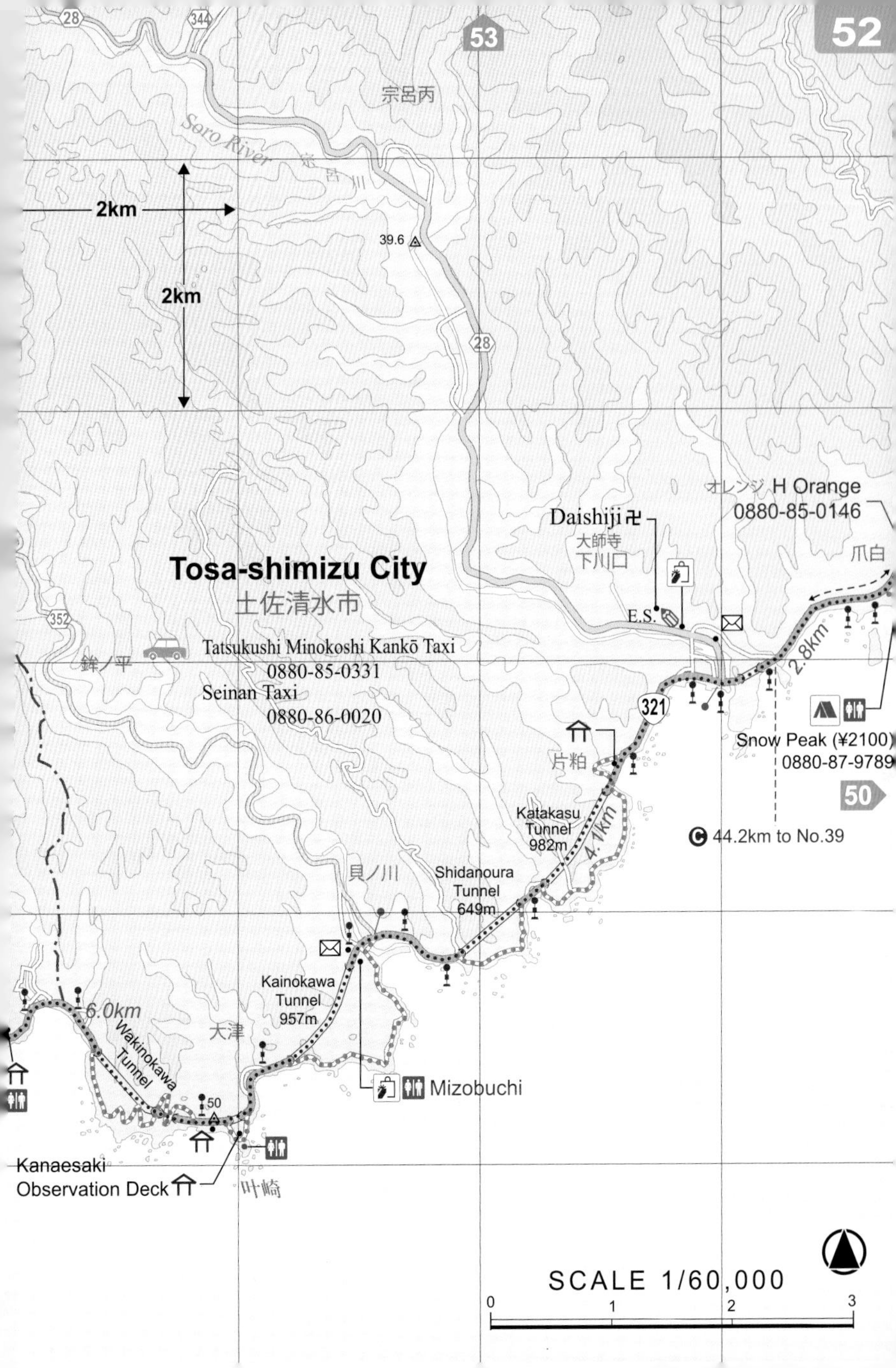
53
宗呂丙
Soro River
宗呂川
2km
2km
39.6
28
344
352
Tosa-shimizu City
土佐清水市
Tatsukushi Minokoshi Kankō Taxi
0880-85-0331
Seinan Taxi
0880-86-0020
鋒ノ平
Daishiji
大師寺
下川口
E.S.
オレンジ H Orange
0880-85-0146
爪白
2.8km
321
Snow Peak (¥2100)
0880-87-9789
50
片粕
Katakasu Tunnel 982m
4.1km
44.2km to No.39
貝ノ川
Shidanoura Tunnel 649m
Kainokawa Tunnel 957m
6.0km
Wakinokawa Tunnel
大津
Mizobuchi
50
Kanaesaki Observation Deck
叶崎
SCALE 1/60,000
0
1
2
3

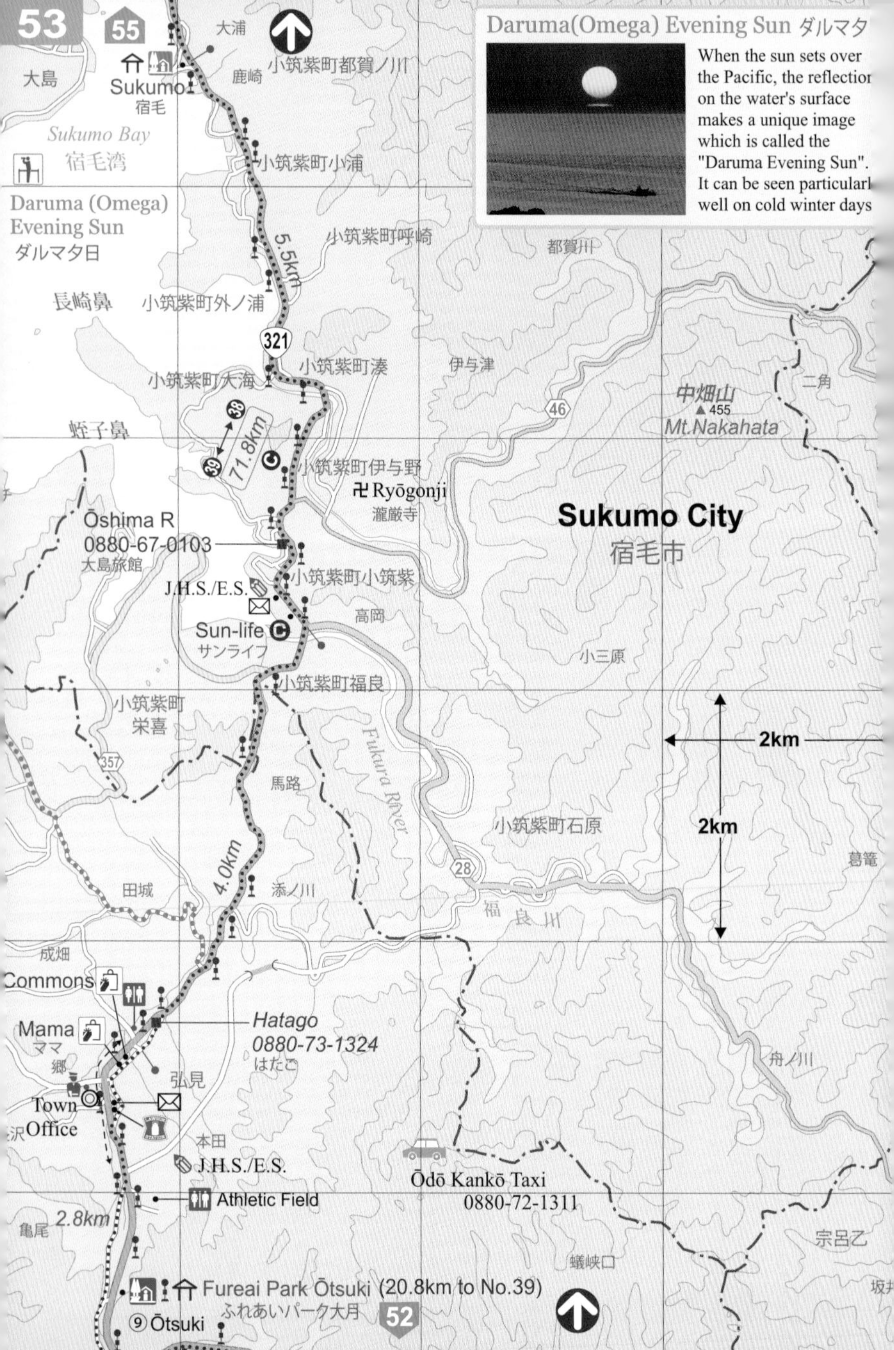

55
大浦
大島
Sukumo
宿毛
鹿崎
小筑紫町都賀ノ川
Sukumo Bay
宿毛湾
小筑紫町小浦
Daruma (Omega) Evening Sun
ダルマタ日
5.5km
小筑紫町呼崎
都賀川
長崎鼻
小筑紫町外ノ浦
321
小筑紫町湊
伊与津
小筑紫町大海
38
71.8km
39
中畑山
455
Mt.Nakahata
二角
46
蛭子鼻
小筑紫町伊与野
Ryōgonji
瀧厳寺
Sukumo City
宿毛市
Ōshima R
0880-67-0103
大島旅館
J.H.S./E.S.
小筑紫町小筑紫
Sun-life
サンライフ
高岡
小三原
小筑紫町福良
小筑紫町
栄喜
2km
357
馬路
Fukura River
2km
小筑紫町石原
28
葛篭
4.0km
田城
添ノ川
福良川
成畑
Commons
Hatago
0880-73-1324
はたご
Mama
ママ
郷
弘見
舟ノ川
Town Office
沢
本田
J.H.S./E.S.
Ōdō Kankō Taxi
0880-72-1311
Athletic Field
2.8km
亀尾
宗呂乙
蟻峡口
Fureai Park Ōtsuki (20.8km to No.39)
ふれあいパーク大月
⑨ Ōtsuki
52

Daruma(Omega) Evening Sun ダルマタ

When the sun sets over the Pacific, the reflectior on the water's surface makes a unique image which is called the "Daruma Evening Sun". It can be seen particularl well on cold winter days

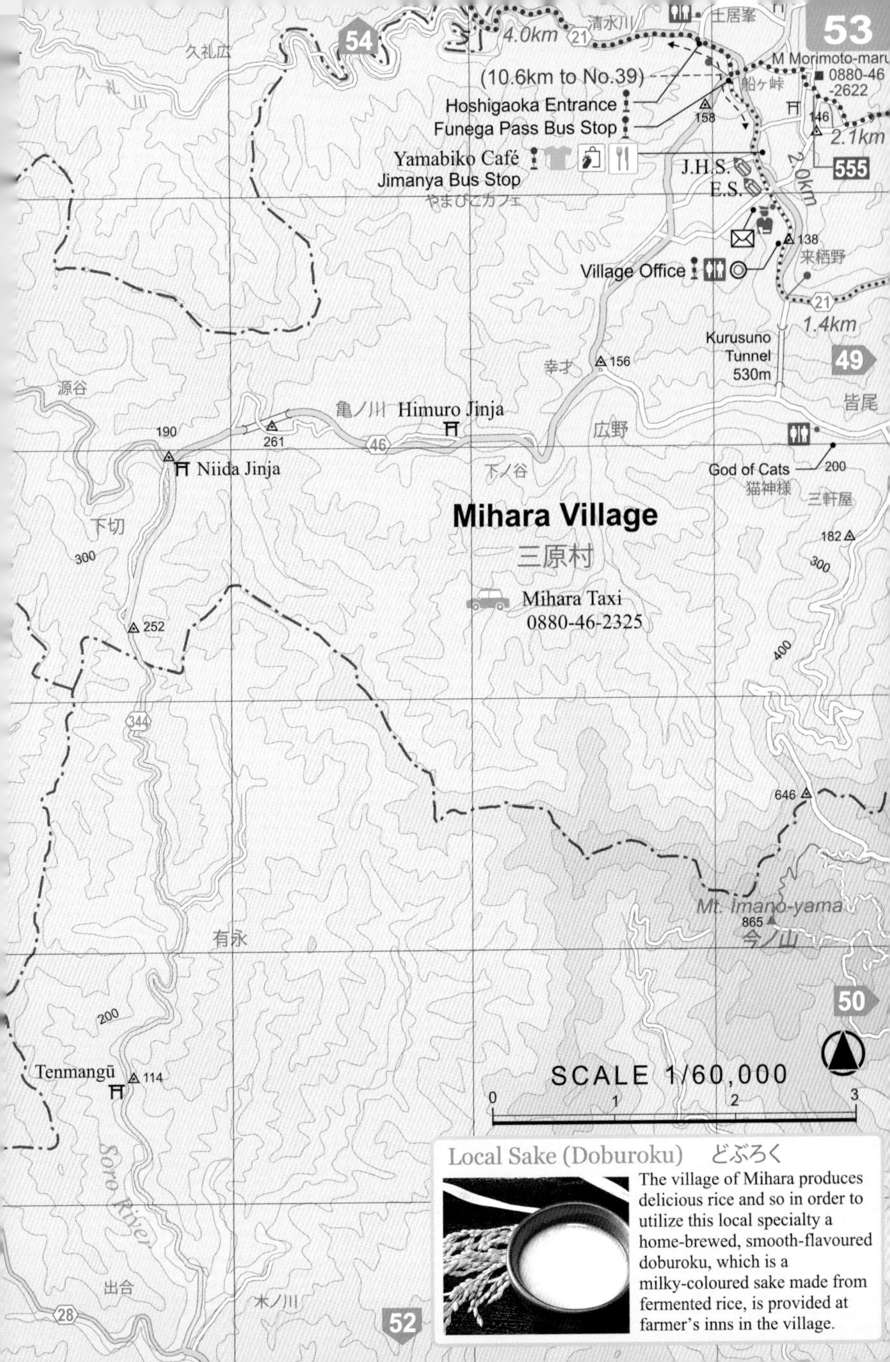

53
54
4.0km
21
清水川
土居峯
久礼広
M Morimoto-maru
0880-46-2622
(10.6km to No.39)
船ヶ峠
Hoshigaoka Entrance
158
146
Funega Pass Bus Stop
2.1km
Yamabiko Café
Jimanya Bus Stop
やまびこカフェ
J.H.S.
E.S.
2.0km
555
138
来栖野
Village Office
21
1.4km
Kurusuno
Tunnel
530m
49
幸才
156
源谷
亀ノ川
Himuro Jinja
皆尾
190
261
46
広野
Niida Jinja
下ノ谷
God of Cats
猫神様
200
三軒屋
Mihara Village
三原村
下切
300
182
300
Mihara Taxi
0880-46-2325
252
400
344
646
Mt. Imano-yama
865
今ノ山
有永
50
200
Tenmangū
114
SCALE 1/60,000
0
1
2
3
Soro River
出合
木ノ川
28
52

Local Sake (Doburoku) どぶろく

The village of Mihara produces delicious rice and so in order to utilize this local specialty a home-brewed, smooth-flavoured doburoku, which is a milky-coloured sake made from fermented rice, is provided at farmer's inns in the village.

39 Enkōji 三十九番 延光寺

☎ 0880-66-0225
S None

H Yakushi Nyorai
Free of charge (50)
390 Nakayama, Hirata-chō, Sukumo City
A About 40 min. walk from Tosa-kuroshio Railway Hirata Stn.

Gyōki founded this temple in 724 and carved a statue of Yakushi Nyorai. To the right of the Main hall is the "eye-washing well" *(mearai-ido)* claimed to cure eye sickness. In 911, it is believed that a turtle with a red bell on its back came to this temple from the ocean.

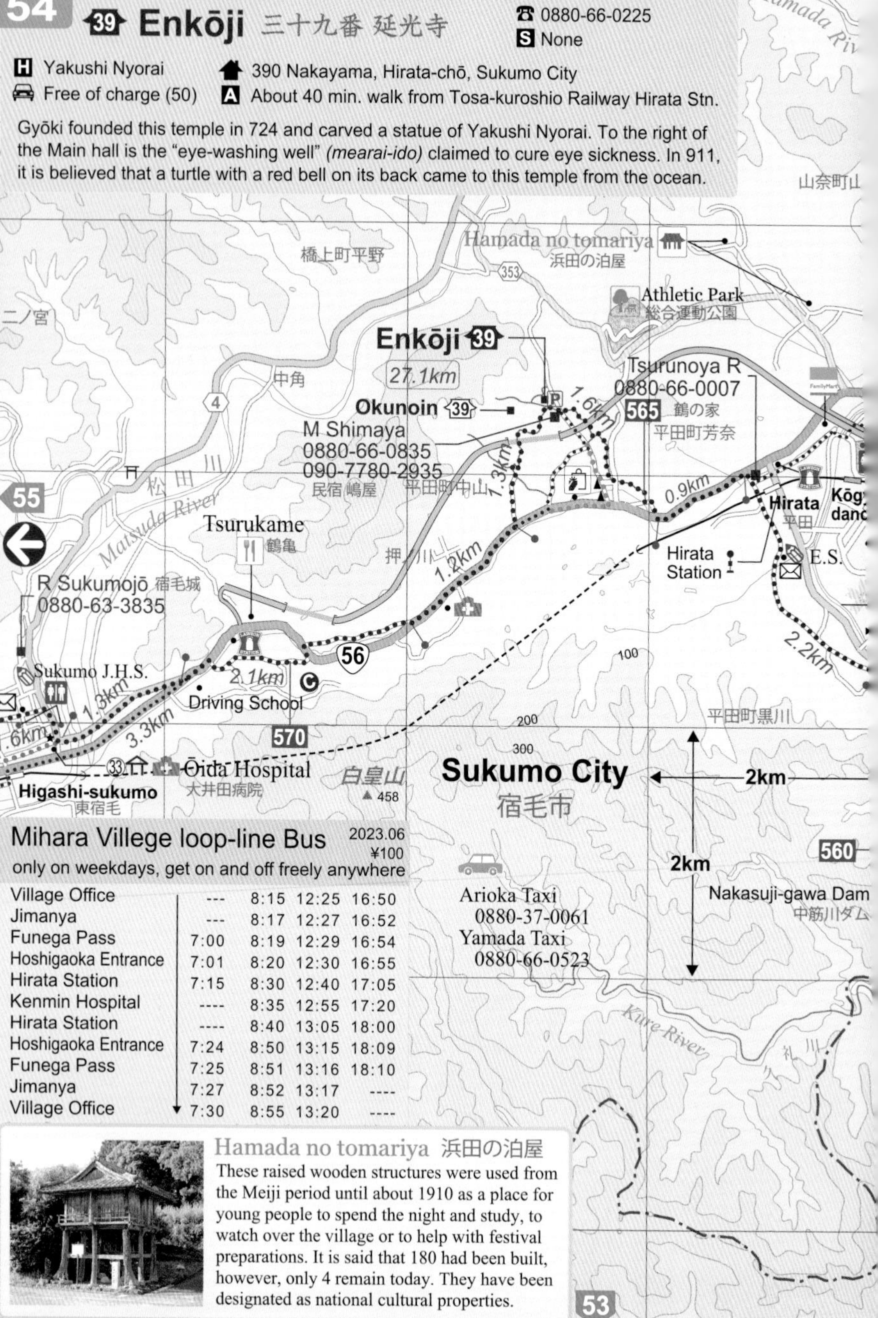

Yamada River
山奈町山
Hamada no tomariya
浜田の泊屋
353
橋上町平野
Athletic Park
総合運動公園
二ノ宮
Enkōji 39
27.1km
Tsurunoya R
0880-66-0007
鶴の家
565
平田町芳奈
中角
4
Okunoin 39
M Shimaya
0880-66-0835
090-7780-2935
民宿 嶋屋
平田町中山
1.6km
1.3km
0.9km
Hirata
平田
55
松田川
Matsuda River
Tsurukame
鶴亀
押ノ川
1.2km
Hirata Station
E.S.
R Sukumojō 宿毛城
0880-63-3835
56
2.2km
100
Sukumo J.H.S.
2.1km
Driving School
1.3km
3.3km
1.6km
570
200
平田町黒川
300
33
Ōida Hospital
大井田病院
白皇山
458
Sukumo City
宿毛市
2km
2km
Higashi-sukumo
東宿毛
560
Arioka Taxi
0880-37-0061
Yamada Taxi
0880-66-0523
Nakasuji-gawa Dam
中筋川ダム
Kure River
53

Mihara Villege loop-line Bus

2023.06 ¥100
only on weekdays, get on and off freely anywhere

Village Office	---	8:15	12:25	16:50
Jimanya	---	8:17	12:27	16:52
Funega Pass	7:00	8:19	12:29	16:54
Hoshigaoka Entrance	7:01	8:20	12:30	16:55
Hirata Station	7:15	8:30	12:40	17:05
Kenmin Hospital	----	8:35	12:55	17:20
Hirata Station	----	8:40	13:05	18:00
Hoshigaoka Entrance	7:24	8:50	13:15	18:09
Funega Pass	7:25	8:51	13:16	18:10
Jimanya	7:27	8:52	13:17	----
Village Office	7:30	8:55	13:20	----

Hamada no tomariya 浜田の泊屋

These raised wooden structures were used from the Meiji period until about 1910 as a place for young people to spend the night and study, to watch over the village or to help with festival preparations. It is said that 180 had been built, however, only 4 remain today. They have been designated as national cultural properties.

54
Inkstone of 三原硯石
Mihara Village
The small Village of Mihara produces high quality inkstone made from black slate rock, which are highly recommended by calligraphers throughout Japan.
国見
荒川
Kunimi
国見
生ノ川
Nakasuji River
中筋川
48
56
土佐くろしお鉄道
Kenmin Hostpital
横瀬川
50
磯ノ川
間
Nakamura Sukumo Expwy
Higashi J.H.S.
Tosa-kuroshio Railway
Arioka
有岡
江ノ村
Daishidō
大師堂
6.8km
上ノ土居
Shimanto City
四万十市
Industrial Park
工業団地
九樹
Shinnen Henro Trail
真念遍路道
2.6km
Cherry blossom trees along the river
100
344
200
300
Jizō Pass
地蔵峠
219
100
貝ヶ森
Mt.Kaigamori
455
2.0km
A-2
B
200
Mihara Village
三原村
(10.6km to No.39)
300
A-1
3.4km
M. Imachan
0880-46-2050
農家民宿 今ちゃん
49
100
M Morimoto-maru
0880-46-2622
農家民宿 森本まる
2.5km
46
555
Tenmangū
155
Community Center
Shortest Route to Enkōji A-2
4.0km
21
Umenoki Park
梅の木公園
2.1km
宮ノ川
Miyanokawa Tunnel
2.0km
39
38
51.5km
Hoshigaoka Entrance
Funega Pass Bus Stop
158
146
135
A-2
Yamabiko Café
やまびこカフェ
Jimanya Bus Stop
柚ノ木
J.H.S.
E.S.
Cemetery
上下長谷
1.1km
471
Mt. Hinotani
ヒノタニ山
B
Mihara Taxi
0880-46-2325
2.0km
138
200
1.4km
Village Office
21
Tenmangū
1.7km
下長谷
21
SCALE 1/60,000
0
1
2
3km
53
亀ノ川

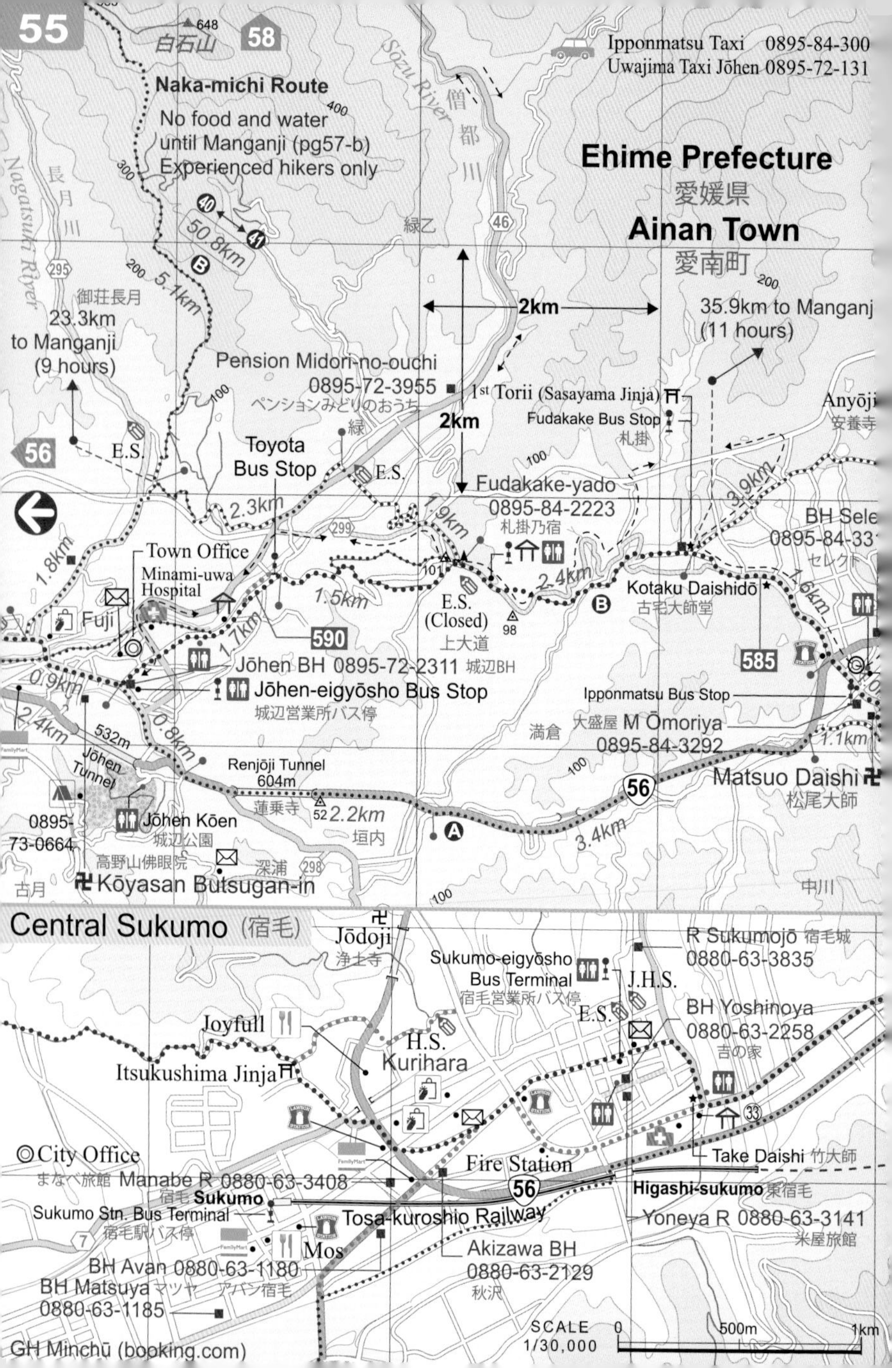
58
白石山
648
Naka-michi Route
No food and water
until Manganji (pg57-b)
Experienced hikers only
Ipponmatsu Taxi 0895-84-300
Uwajima Taxi Jōhen 0895-72-131
Sōzu River
僧都川
Ehime Prefecture
愛媛県
Ainan Town
愛南町
Nagatsuki River
長月川
50.8km
5.1km
緑乙
御荘長月
23.3km
to Manganji
(9 hours)
2km
35.9km to Manganj
(11 hours)
Pension Midori-no-ouchi
0895-72-3955
ペンションみどりのおうち
1st Torii (Sasayama Jinja)
Fudakake Bus Stop
札掛
Anyōji
安養寺
56
E.S.
Toyota
Bus Stop
Fudakake-yado
0895-84-2223
札掛乃宿
2.3km
1.9km
3.9km
BH Sele
0895-84-33
セレクト
1.8km
Town Office
Minami-uwa
Hospital
Fuji
1.5km
E.S.
(Closed)
上大道
2.4km
Kotaku Daishidō
古宅大師堂
1.6km
1.7km
590
585
Jōhen BH 0895-72-2311 城辺BH
Jōhen-eigyōsho Bus Stop
城辺営業所バス停
0.9km
2.4km
532m
Jōhen
Tunnel
0.8km
Ipponmatsu Bus Stop
満倉
大盛屋 M Ōmoriya
0895-84-3292
1.1km
Renjōji Tunnel
604m
蓮乗寺
2.2km
垣内
Matsuo Daishi
松尾大師
0895-
73-0664
Jōhen Kōen
城辺公園
3.4km
高野山佛眼院
Kōyasan Butsugan-in
深浦
古月
中川
Central Sukumo (宿毛)
Jōdoji
浄土寺
Sukumo-eigyōsho
Bus Terminal
宿毛営業所バス停
R Sukumojō 宿毛城
0880-63-3835
J.H.S.
E.S.
BH Yoshinoya
0880-63-2258
吉の家
Joyfull
H.S.
Kurihara
Itsukushima Jinja
City Office
まなべ旅館 Manabe R 0880-63-3408
Fire Station
Take Daishi 竹大師
宿毛 Sukumo
Higashi-sukumo 東宿毛
Sukumo Stn. Bus Terminal
宿毛駅バス停
Tosa-kuroshio Railway
Yoneya R 0880-63-3141
米屋旅館
Mos
Akizawa BH
0880-63-2129
秋沢
BH Avan 0880-63-1180
BH Matsuya マツヤ アバン宿毛
0880-63-1185
GH Minchū (booking.com)
SCALE
1/30,000
0
500m
1km

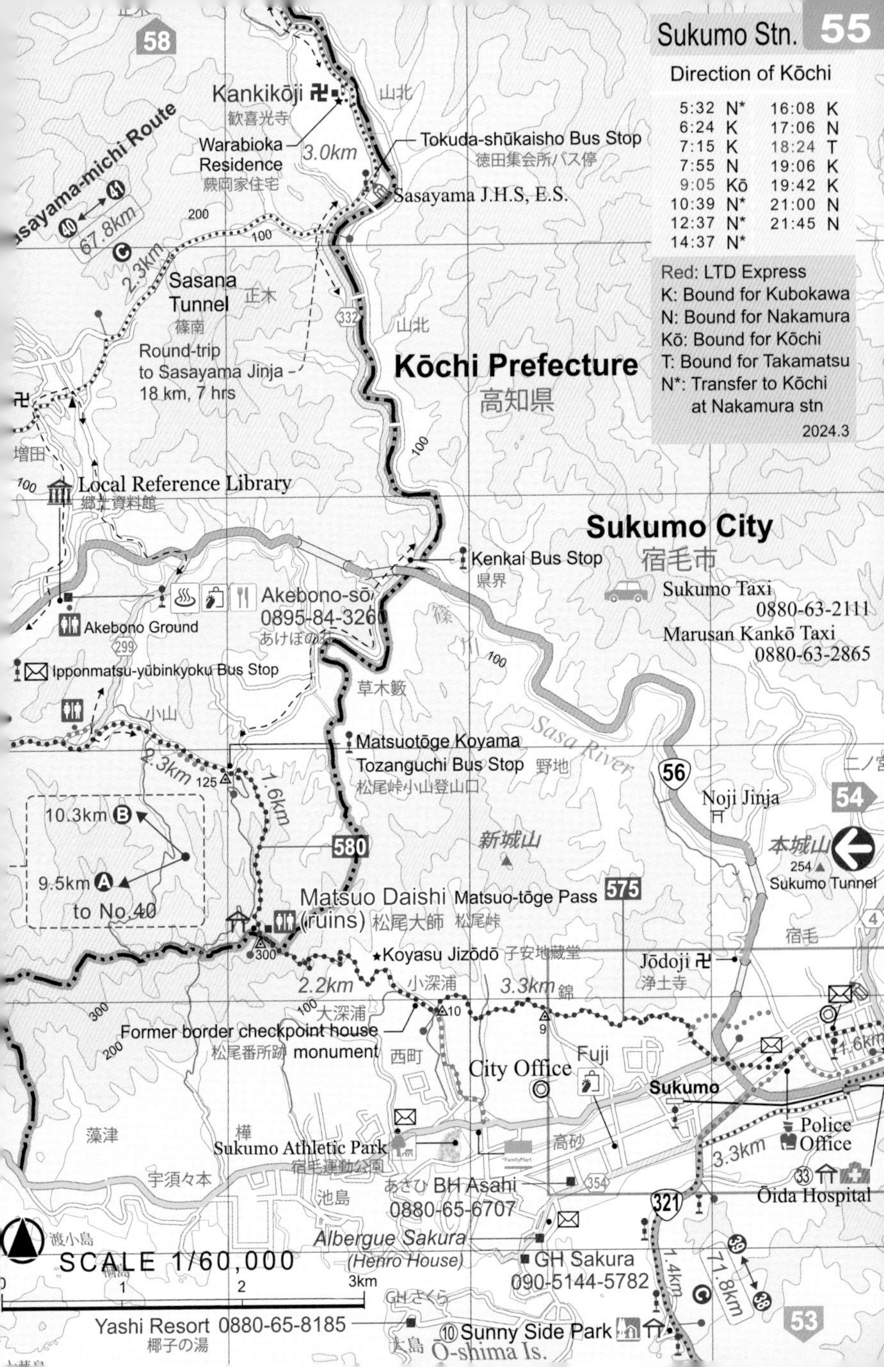
Sukumo Stn.
Direction of Kōchi
5:32 N* 16:08 K
6:24 K 17:06 N
7:15 K 18:24 T
7:55 N 19:06 K
9:05 Kō 19:42 K
10:39 N* 21:00 N
12:37 N* 21:45 N
14:37 N*
Red: LTD Express
K: Bound for Kubokawa
N: Bound for Nakamura
Kō: Bound for Kōchi
T: Bound for Takamatsu
N*: Transfer to Kōchi at Nakamura stn
2024.3
58
Kankikōji
歓喜光寺
山北
Warabioka Residence
蕨岡家住宅
3.0km
Tokuda-shūkaisho Bus Stop
徳田集会所バス停
Sasayama J.H.S, E.S.
Sasayama-michi Route
40 41
67.8km
2.3km
Sasana Tunnel
篠南
正木
332
山北
Round-trip to Sasayama Jinja - 18 km, 7 hrs
Kōchi Prefecture
高知県
増田
Local Reference Library
郷土資料館
Sukumo City
宿毛市
Kenkai Bus Stop
県界
Sukumo Taxi
0880-63-2111
Marusan Kankō Taxi
0880-63-2865
Akebono-sō
0895-84-3260
あけぼの荘
Akebono Ground
299
Ipponmatsu-yūbinkyoku Bus Stop
草木籔
小山
Sasa River
Matsuotōge Koyama Tozanguchi Bus Stop
松尾峠小山登山口
野地
56
Noji Jinja
54
2.3km
1.6km
10.3km B
9.5km A
to No.40
580
新城山
本城山
254
Sukumo Tunnel
Matsuo Daishi (ruins)
松尾大師
Matsuo-tōge Pass
松尾峠
575
宿毛
Koyasu Jizōdō 子安地蔵堂
Jōdoji
浄土寺
2.2km
小深浦
3.3km
錦
大深浦
Former border checkpoint house monument
松尾番所跡
西町
City Office
Fuji
Sukumo
1.6km
Police Office
藻津
樺
Sukumo Athletic Park
宿毛運動公園
高砂
3.3km
宇須々本
池島
あさひ BH Asahi
0880-65-6707
354
33
Ōida Hospital
321
Albergue Sakura
(Henro House)
GH Sakura
090-5144-5782
GH さくら
渡小島
SCALE 1/60,000
0 1 2 3km
39
71.8km
38
1.4km
Yashi Resort 0880-65-8185
椰子の湯
10 Sunny Side Park
大島 Ō-shima Is.
53

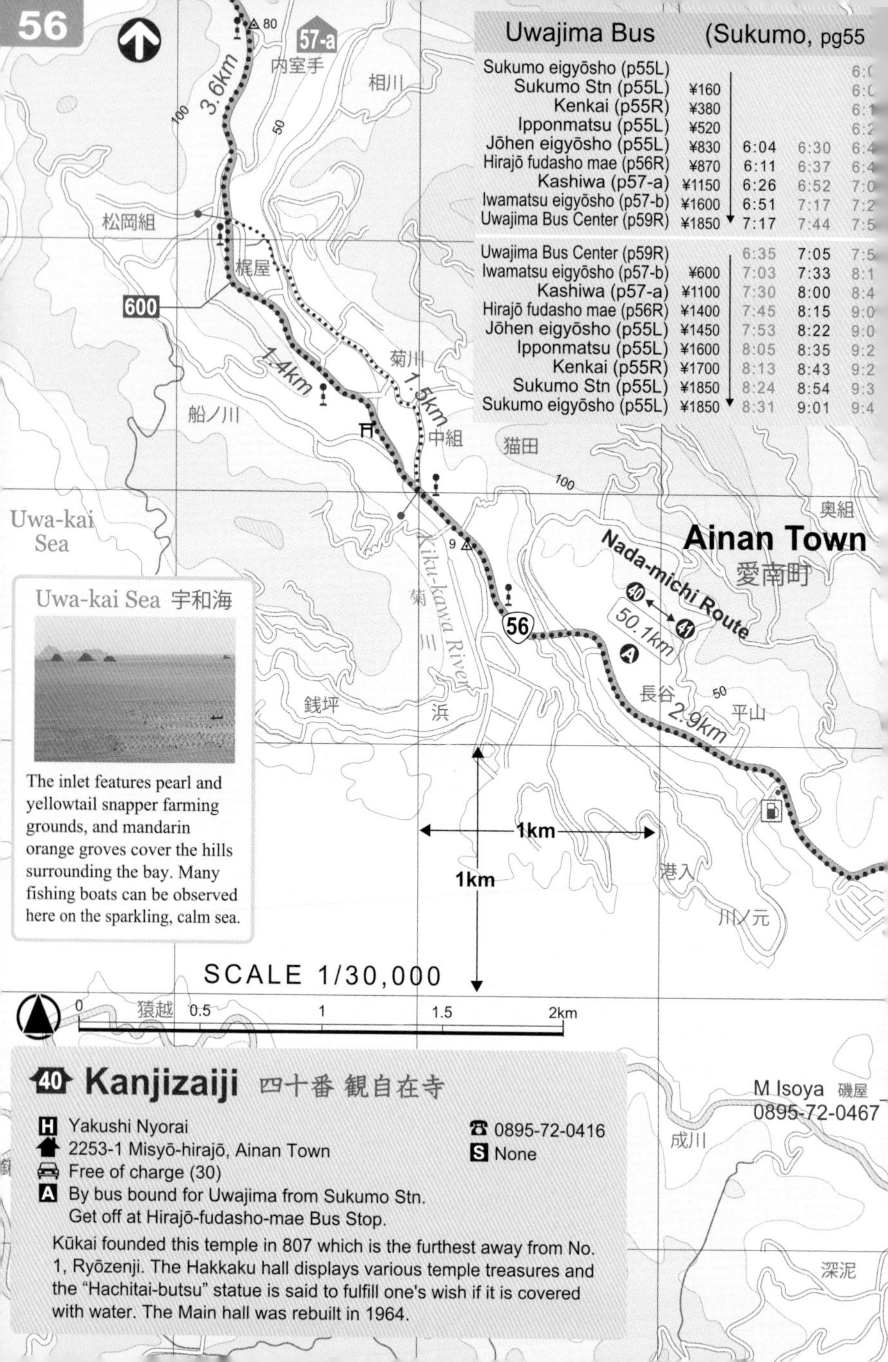

57-a
内室手
相川
3.6km
80
100
50
松岡組
梶屋
600
1.4km
1.5km
菊川
船ノ川
中組
猫田
100
Uwa-kai
Sea
奥組
Ainan Town
愛南町
Nada-michi Route
40
41
50.1km
A
9
菊
Kiku-kawa River
川
56
銭坪
浜
長谷
50
2.9km
平山
1km
1km
港入
川ノ元
SCALE 1/30,000
0
猿越
0.5
1
1.5
2km
M Isoya 磯屋
0895-72-0467
成川
深泥

Uwajima Bus (Sukumo, pg55

Sukumo eigyōsho (p55L)				6:(
Sukumo Stn (p55L)	¥160			6:(
Kenkai (p55R)	¥380			6:1
Ipponmatsu (p55L)	¥520			6:2
Jōhen eigyōsho (p55L)	¥830	6:04	6:30	6:4
Hirajō fudasho mae (p56R)	¥870	6:11	6:37	6:4
Kashiwa (p57-a)	¥1150	6:26	6:52	7:0
Iwamatsu eigyōsho (p57-b)	¥1600	6:51	7:17	7:2
Uwajima Bus Center (p59R)	¥1850	7:17	7:44	7:5
Uwajima Bus Center (p59R)		6:35	7:05	7:5
Iwamatsu eigyōsho (p57-b)	¥600	7:03	7:33	8:1
Kashiwa (p57-a)	¥1100	7:30	8:00	8:4
Hirajō fudasho mae (p56R)	¥1400	7:45	8:15	9:0
Jōhen eigyōsho (p55L)	¥1450	7:53	8:22	9:0
Ipponmatsu (p55L)	¥1600	8:05	8:35	9:2
Kenkai (p55R)	¥1700	8:13	8:43	9:2
Sukumo Stn (p55L)	¥1850	8:24	8:54	9:3
Sukumo eigyōsho (p55L)	¥1850	8:31	9:01	9:4

Uwa-kai Sea 宇和海

The inlet features pearl and yellowtail snapper farming grounds, and mandarin orange groves cover the hills surrounding the bay. Many fishing boats can be observed here on the sparkling, calm sea.

40 Kanjizaiji 四十番 観自在寺

H Yakushi Nyorai
2253-1 Misyō-hirajō, Ainan Town
Free of charge (30)
A By bus bound for Uwajima from Sukumo Stn. Get off at Hirajō-fudasho-mae Bus Stop.

☎ 0895-72-0416
S None

Kūkai founded this temple in 807 which is the furthest away from No. 1, Ryōzenji. The Hakkaku hall displays various temple treasures and the “Hachitai-butsu” statue is said to fulfill one's wish if it is covered with water. The Main hall was rebuilt in 1964.

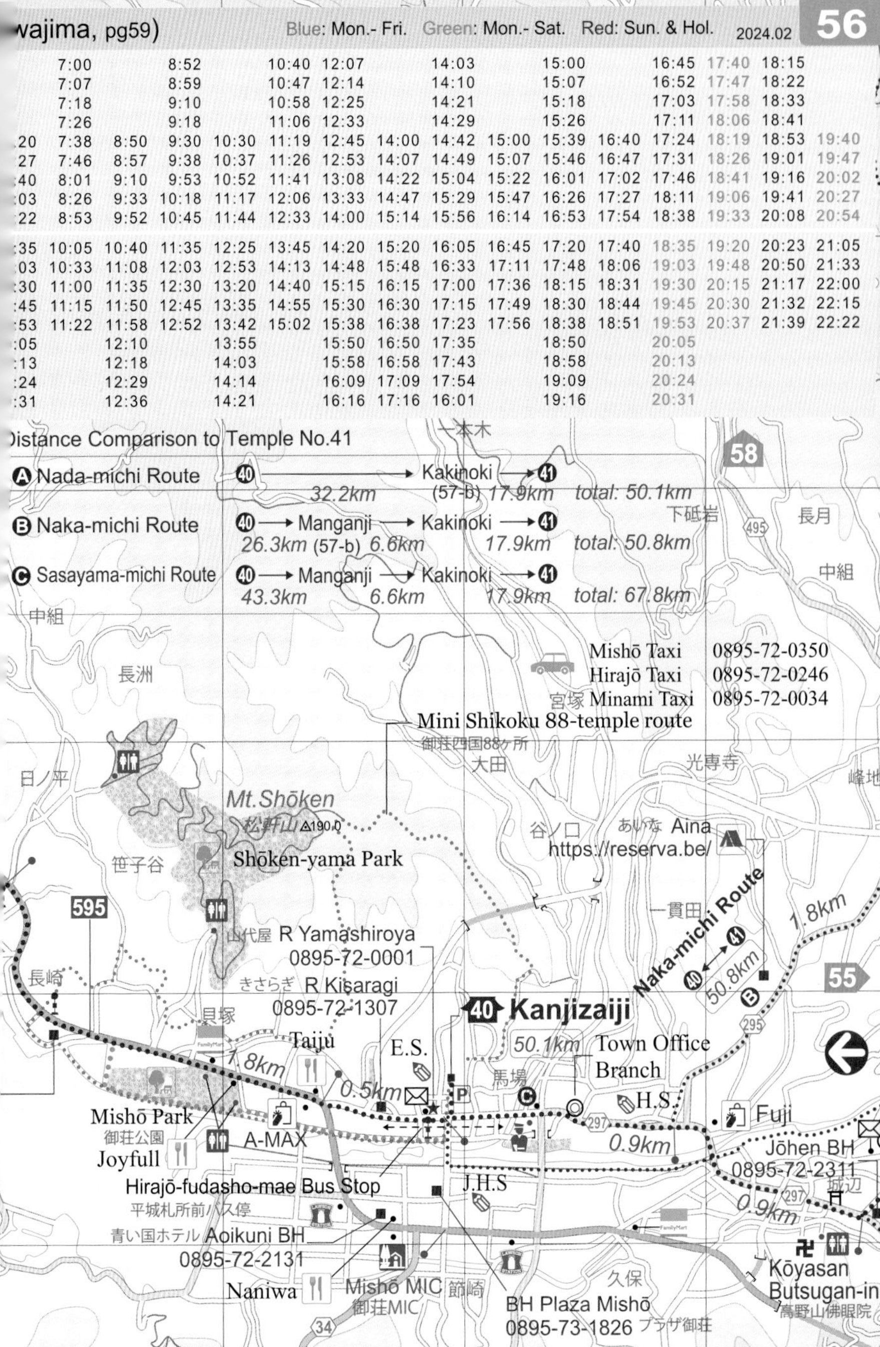

	7:00		8:52		10:40	12:07		14:03		15:00		16:45	17:40	18:15	
	7:07		8:59		10:47	12:14		14:10		15:07		16:52	17:47	18:22	
	7:18		9:10		10:58	12:25		14:21		15:18		17:03	17:58	18:33	
	7:26		9:18		11:06	12:33		14:29		15:26		17:11	18:06	18:41	
:20	7:38	8:50	9:30	10:30	11:19	12:45	14:00	14:42	15:00	15:39	16:40	17:24	18:19	18:53	19:40
:27	7:46	8:57	9:38	10:37	11:26	12:53	14:07	14:49	15:07	15:46	16:47	17:31	18:26	19:01	19:47
:40	8:01	9:10	9:53	10:52	11:41	13:08	14:22	15:04	15:22	16:01	17:02	17:46	18:41	19:16	20:02
:03	8:26	9:33	10:18	11:17	12:06	13:33	14:47	15:29	15:47	16:26	17:27	18:11	19:06	19:41	20:27
:22	8:53	9:52	10:45	11:44	12:33	14:00	15:14	15:56	16:14	16:53	17:54	18:38	19:33	20:08	20:54

:35	10:05	10:40	11:35	12:25	13:45	14:20	15:20	16:05	16:45	17:20	17:40	18:35	19:20	20:23	21:05
:03	10:33	11:08	12:03	12:53	14:13	14:48	15:48	16:33	17:11	17:48	18:06	19:03	19:48	20:50	21:33
:30	11:00	11:35	12:30	13:20	14:40	15:15	16:15	17:00	17:36	18:15	18:31	19:30	20:15	21:17	22:00
:45	11:15	11:50	12:45	13:35	14:55	15:30	16:30	17:15	17:49	18:30	18:44	19:45	20:30	21:32	22:15
:53	11:22	11:58	12:52	13:42	15:02	15:38	16:38	17:23	17:56	18:38	18:51	19:53	20:37	21:39	22:22
:05		12:10		13:55		15:50	16:50	17:35		18:50		20:05			
:13		12:18		14:03		15:58	16:58	17:43		18:58		20:13			
:24		12:29		14:14		16:09	17:09	17:54		19:09		20:24			
:31		12:36		14:21		16:16	17:16	16:01		19:16		20:31			

Distance Comparison to Temple No.41

A Nada-michi Route	40 → 32.2km	Kakinoki (57-b) → 17.9km	41	total: 50.1km
B Naka-michi Route	40 → 26.3km (57-b)	Manganji → 6.6km	Kakinoki → 17.9km 41	total: 50.8km
C Sasayama-michi Route	40 → 43.3km	Manganji → 6.6km	Kakinoki → 17.9km 41	total: 67.8km

一本木
58
下砥岩
長月
495
中組
中組
長洲
Mishō Taxi 0895-72-0350
Hirajō Taxi 0895-72-0246
宮塚 Minami Taxi 0895-72-0034
Mini Shikoku 88-temple route
御荘四国88ヶ所
大田
光専寺
峰地
日ノ平
Mt.Shōken
松野山 △190.0
谷ノ口
あいな Aina
https://reserva.be/
笹子谷
Shōken-yama Park
595
一貫田
Naka-michi Route
40 ↔ 41
50.8km
B
1.8km
山代屋 R Yamashiroya
0895-72-0001
長崎
きさらぎ R Kisaragi
0895-72-1307
55
貝塚
40 Kanjizaiji
295
50.1km
Town Office Branch
Taiju
1.8km
E.S.
馬場
0.5km
H.S.
C
Mishō Park
御荘公園
A-MAX
297
Fuji
Joyfull
0.9km
Jōhen BH
0895-72-2311
城辺
Hirajō-fudasho-mae Bus Stop
平城札所前バス停
J.H.S
297
0.9km
青い国ホテル Aoikuni BH
0895-72-2131
久保
Kōyasan
Butsugan-in
高野山佛眼院
Naniwa
Mishō MIC
御荘MIC
節崎
BH Plaza Mishō
0895-73-1826 プラザ御荘
34

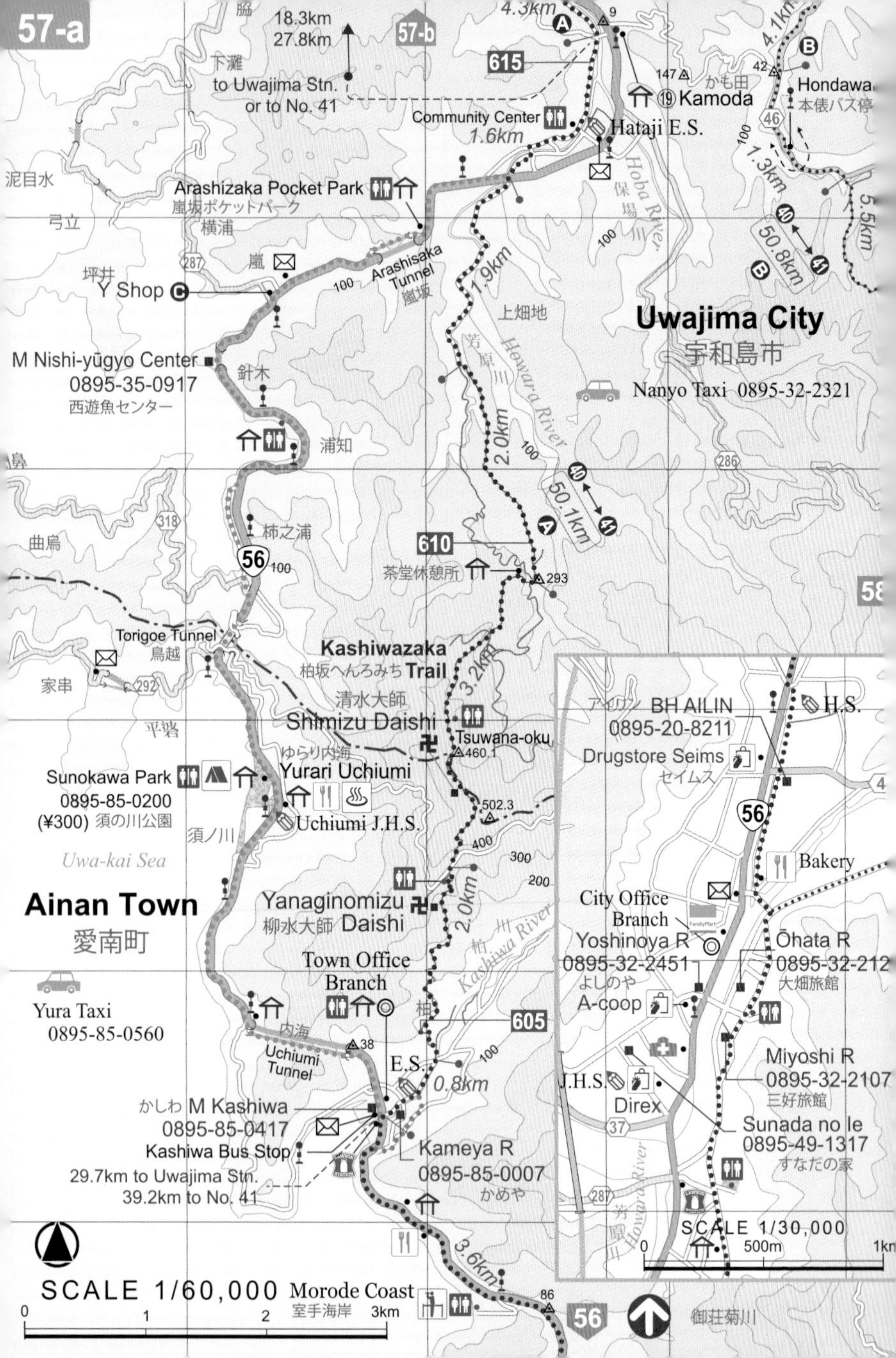
57-b
18.3km
27.8km
下灘
to Uwajima Stn.
or to No. 41
615
Kamoda
Community Center
Hataji E.S.
1.6km
Hondawa
本俵バス停
1.3km
5.5km
50.8km
泥目水
Arashizaka Pocket Park
嵐坂ポケットパーク
横浦
弓立
Hoba River
保場川
嵐
Arashisaka Tunnel
嵐坂
坪井
Y Shop
1.9km
上畑地
Uwajima City
宇和島市
M Nishi-yūgyo Center
0895-35-0917
西遊魚センター
針木
芳原川
Howara River
Nanyo Taxi 0895-32-2321
浦知
2.0km
50.1km
曲烏
柿之浦
610
茶堂休憩所
Torigoe Tunnel
鳥越
Kashiwazaka
柏坂へんろみち Trail
3.2km
家串
清水大師
Shimizu Daishi
平碆
Tsuwana-oku
ゆらり内海
Yurari Uchiumi
Sunokawa Park
0895-85-0200
(¥300) 須の川公園
Uchiumi J.H.S.
須ノ川
Uwa-kai Sea
Ainan Town
愛南町
Yanaginomizu Daishi
柳水大師
2.0km
Kashiwa River
Town Office Branch
Yura Taxi
0895-85-0560
605
内海
Uchiumi Tunnel
E.S.
0.8km
かしわ M Kashiwa
0895-85-0417
Kashiwa Bus Stop
29.7km to Uwajima Stn.
39.2km to No. 41
Kameya R
0895-85-0007
かめや
3.6km
SCALE 1/60,000
0 1 2 3km
Morode Coast
室手海岸
御荘菊川
BH AILIN
アイリン
0895-20-8211
H.S.
Drugstore Seims
セイムス
Bakery
City Office Branch
Yoshinoya R
0895-32-2451
よしのや
Ōhata R
0895-32-212
大畑旅館
A-coop
Miyoshi R
0895-32-2107
三好旅館
J.H.S.
Direx
Sunada no Ie
0895-49-1317
すなだの家
Howara River
芳原川
SCALE 1/30,000
0 500m 1km

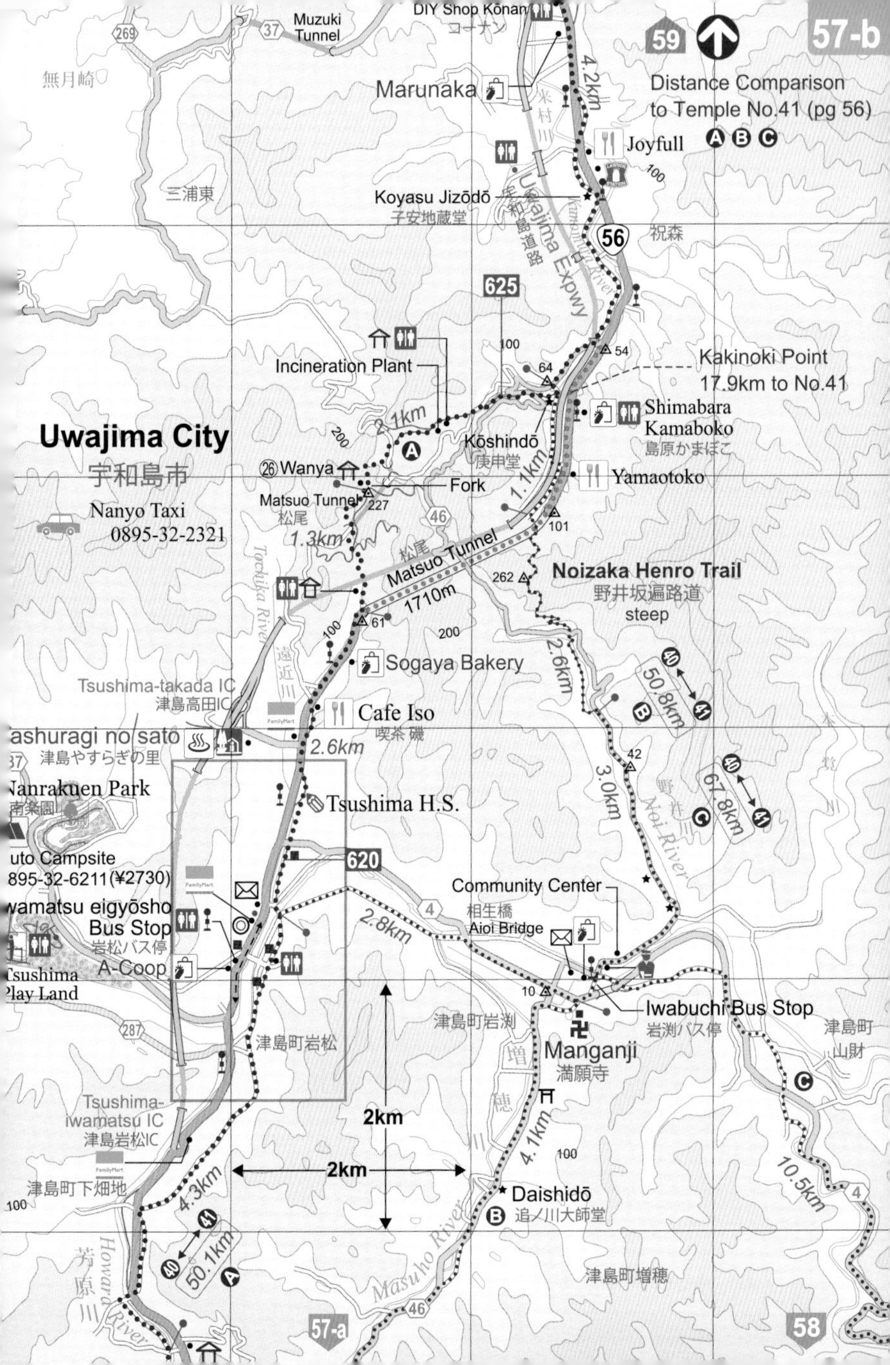

59
DIY Shop Kōnan
コーナン
Muzuki Tunnel
無月崎
Marunaka
Distance Comparison to Temple No.41 (pg 56)
A B C
Joyfull
4.2km
三浦東
Koyasu Jizōdō
子安地蔵堂
Uwajima Expwy
宇和島道路
祝森
56
625
Incineration Plant
Kakinoki Point
17.9km to No.41
Shimabara Kamaboko
島原かまぼこ
2.1km
Uwajima City
宇和島市
Kōshindō
庚申堂
26 Wanya
Fork
Yamaotoko
1.1km
Matsuo Tunnel
松尾
Nanyo Taxi
0895-32-2321
1.3km
Matsuo Tunnel
1710m
Noizaka Henro Trail
野井坂遍路道
steep
Sogaya Bakery
2.6km
Tsushima-takada IC
津島高田IC
Cafe Iso
喫茶 礒
50.8km
ashuragi no sato
津島やすらぎの里
2.6km
Nanrakuen Park
南楽園
Tsushima H.S.
67.8km
3.0km
Noi River
uto Campsite
895-32-6211(¥2730)
620
wamatsu eigyōsho Bus Stop
岩松バス停
A-Coop
Tsushima Play Land
Community Center
相生橋
Aioi Bridge
2.8km
Iwabuchi Bus Stop
岩渕バス停
津島町岩渕
Manganji
満願寺
津島町山財
津島町岩松
Tsushima-iwamatsu IC
津島岩松IC
2km
2km
4.1km
10.5km
津島町下畑地
4.3km
Daishidō
追ノ川大師堂
50.1km
Howard River
芳原川
Masuho River
津島町増穂
57-a
58

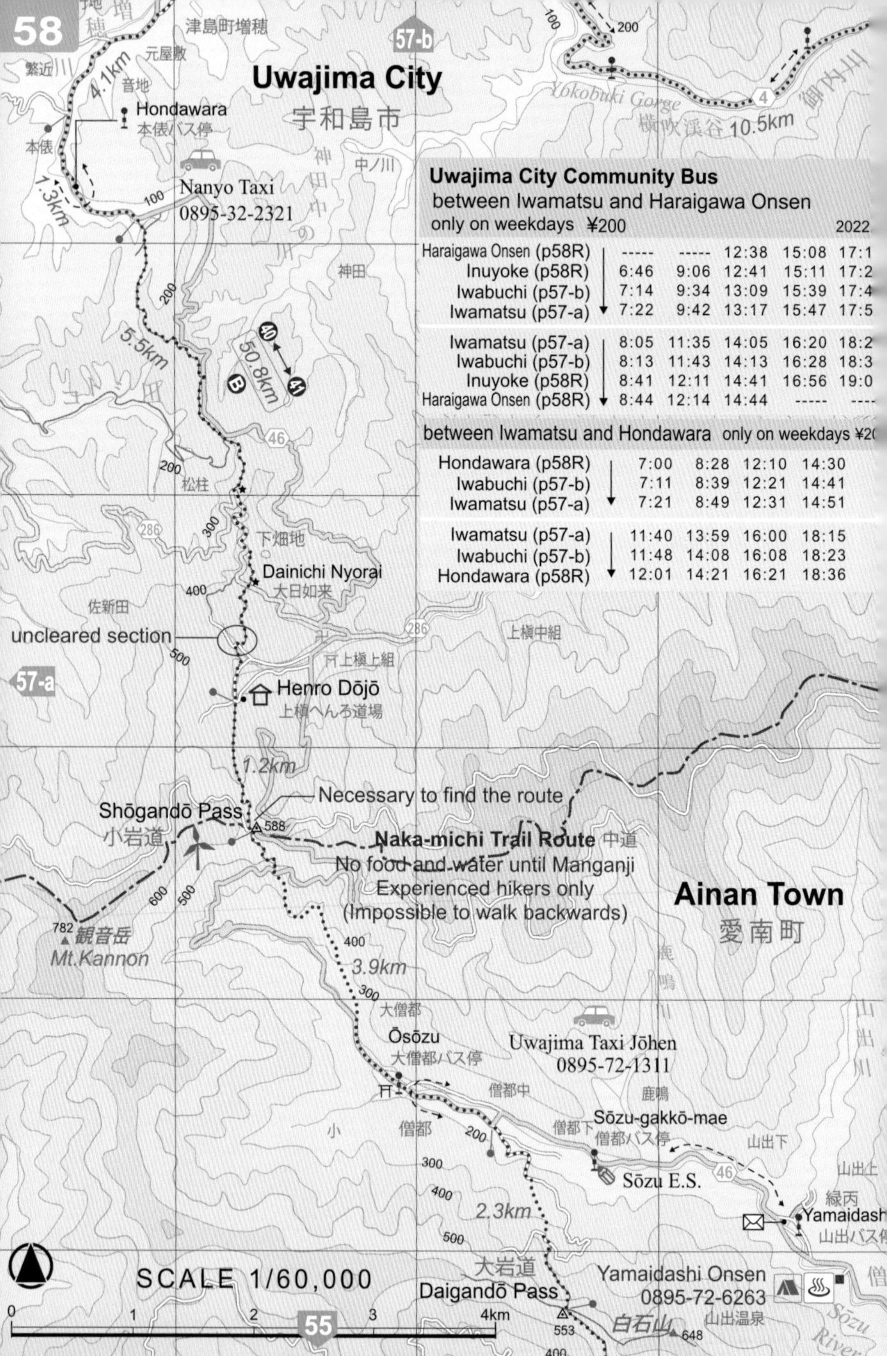
57-b
Uwajima City
宇和島市
津島町増穂
元屋敷
繁近
音地
4.1km
Hondawara
本俵バス停
本俵
1.3km
Nanyo Taxi
0895-32-2321
100
神田川
中ノ川
神田
200
5.5km
40
41
50.8km
B
46
200
松柱
286
300
下畑地
Dainichi Nyorai
大日如来
400
佐新田
uncleared section
500
286
上槇中組
上槇上組
57-a
Henro Dōjō
上槇へんろ道場
1.2km
Necessary to find the route
Shōgandō Pass
小岩道
588
Naka-michi Trail Route 中道
No food and water until Manganji
Experienced hikers only
(Impossible to walk backwards)
Ainan Town
愛南町
600
500
782 観音岳
Mt.Kannon
400
3.9km
300
鹿鳴川
大僧都
Ōsōzu
大僧都バス停
Uwajima Taxi Jōhen
0895-72-1311
僧都中
鹿鳴
山出川
小
僧都
200
僧都下
Sōzu-gakkō-mae
僧都バス停
山出下
300
46
Sōzu E.S.
山出上
400
緑丙
2.3km
Yamaidash
山出バス停
500
大岩道
Daigandō Pass
Yamaidashi Onsen
0895-72-6263
山出温泉
553
白石山 648
400
Sōzu River
SCALE 1/60,000
0 1 2 3 4km
55
Yokobuki Gorge
横吹渓谷 10.5km
4
御内川
200
100

Uwajima City Community Bus
between Iwamatsu and Haraigawa Onsen
only on weekdays ¥200 2022

Haraigawa Onsen (p58R)	-----	-----	12:38	15:08	17:1
Inuyoke (p58R)	6:46	9:06	12:41	15:11	17:2
Iwabuchi (p57-b)	7:14	9:34	13:09	15:39	17:4
Iwamatsu (p57-a)	7:22	9:42	13:17	15:47	17:5

Iwamatsu (p57-a)	8:05	11:35	14:05	16:20	18:2
Iwabuchi (p57-b)	8:13	11:43	14:13	16:28	18:3
Inuyoke (p58R)	8:41	12:11	14:41	16:56	19:0
Haraigawa Onsen (p58R)	8:44	12:14	14:44	-----	----

between Iwamatsu and Hondawara only on weekdays ¥20

Hondawara (p58R)	7:00	8:28	12:10	14:30
Iwabuchi (p57-b)	7:11	8:39	12:21	14:41
Iwamatsu (p57-a)	7:21	8:49	12:31	14:51

Iwamatsu (p57-a)	11:40	13:59	16:00	18:15
Iwabuchi (p57-b)	11:48	14:08	16:08	18:23
Hondawara (p58R)	12:01	14:21	16:21	18:36

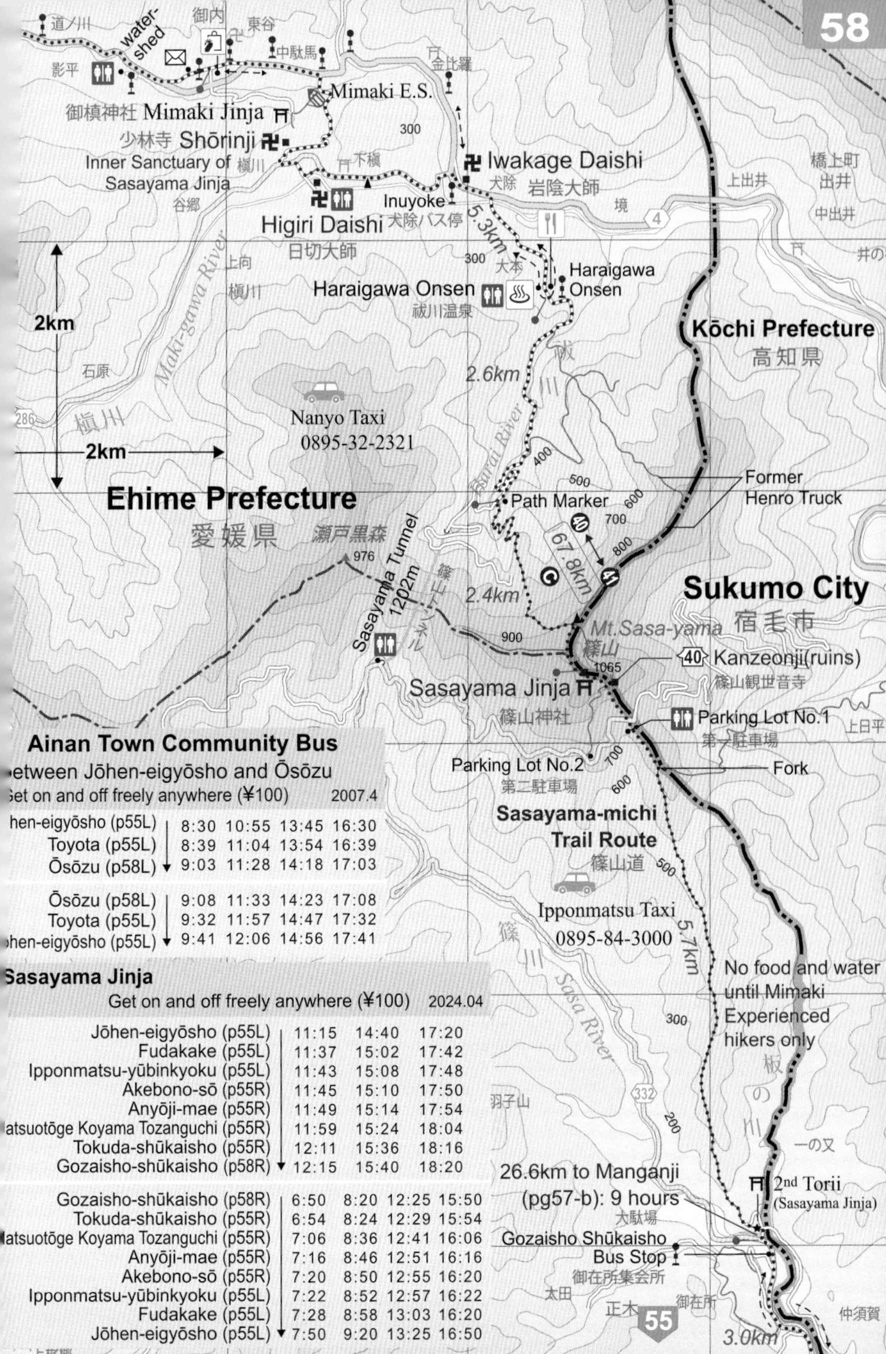

道ノ川
water-shed
御内
東谷
中駄馬
影平
金比羅
Mimaki E.S.
御槙神社 Mimaki Jinja
300
少林寺 Shōrinji
Iwakage Daishi
Inner Sanctuary of
Sasayama Jinja
槇川
下槇
犬除
岩陰大師
谷郷
Inuyoke
犬除バス停
Higiri Daishi
日切大師
5.3km
境
4
上出井
橋上町
出井
中出井
井の
上向
槇川
300
大本
Haraigawa
Onsen
Haraigawa Onsen
祓川温泉
Maki-gawa River
2km
Kōchi Prefecture
高知県
石原
2.6km
祓
川
Nanyo Taxi
0895-32-2321
286
槇川
2km
Harai River
400
500
Former
Henro Truck
Ehime Prefecture
愛媛県
Path Marker
600
700
40
67.8km
800
瀬戸黒森
976
Sasayama Tunnel
1202m
篠山トンネル
2.4km
41
Sukumo City
宿毛市
Mt.Sasa-yama
篠山
900
40 Kanzeonji(ruins)
篠山観世音寺
1065
Sasayama Jinja
篠山神社
Parking Lot No.1
第一駐車場
上日平
Parking Lot No.2
第二駐車場
700
600
Fork
Sasayama-michi
Trail Route
篠山道
500
Ipponmatsu Taxi
0895-84-3000
5.7km
篠
川
Sasa River
No food and water
until Mimaki
Experienced
hikers only
300
板
の
川
羽子山
332
200
一の又
26.6km to Manganji
(pg57-b): 9 hours
大駄場
2nd Torii
(Sasayama Jinja)
Gozaisho Shūkaisho
Bus Stop
御在所集会所
太田
正木
御在所
55
仲須賀
3.0km

Ainan Town Community Bus

etween Jōhen-eigyōsho and Ōsōzu

et on and off freely anywhere (¥100) 2007.4

hen-eigyōsho (p55L)	8:30	10:55	13:45	16:30
Toyota (p55L)	8:39	11:04	13:54	16:39
Ōsōzu (p58L)	9:03	11:28	14:18	17:03

Ōsōzu (p58L)	9:08	11:33	14:23	17:08
Toyota (p55L)	9:32	11:57	14:47	17:32
hen-eigyōsho (p55L)	9:41	12:06	14:56	17:41

Sasayama Jinja

Get on and off freely anywhere (¥100) 2024.04

Jōhen-eigyōsho (p55L)	11:15	14:40	17:20
Fudakake (p55L)	11:37	15:02	17:42
Ipponmatsu-yūbinkyoku (p55L)	11:43	15:08	17:48
Akebono-sō (p55R)	11:45	15:10	17:50
Anyōji-mae (p55R)	11:49	15:14	17:54
atsuotōge Koyama Tozanguchi (p55R)	11:59	15:24	18:04
Tokuda-shūkaisho (p55R)	12:11	15:36	18:16
Gozaisho-shūkaisho (p58R)	12:15	15:40	18:20

Gozaisho-shūkaisho (p58R)	6:50	8:20	12:25	15:50
Tokuda-shūkaisho (p55R)	6:54	8:24	12:29	15:54
atsuotōge Koyama Tozanguchi (p55R)	7:06	8:36	12:41	16:06
Anyōji-mae (p55R)	7:16	8:46	12:51	16:16
Akebono-sō (p55R)	7:20	8:50	12:55	16:20
Ipponmatsu-yūbinkyoku (p55L)	7:22	8:52	12:57	16:22
Fudakake (p55L)	7:28	8:58	13:03	16:20
Jōhen-eigyōsho (p55L)	7:50	9:20	13:25	16:50

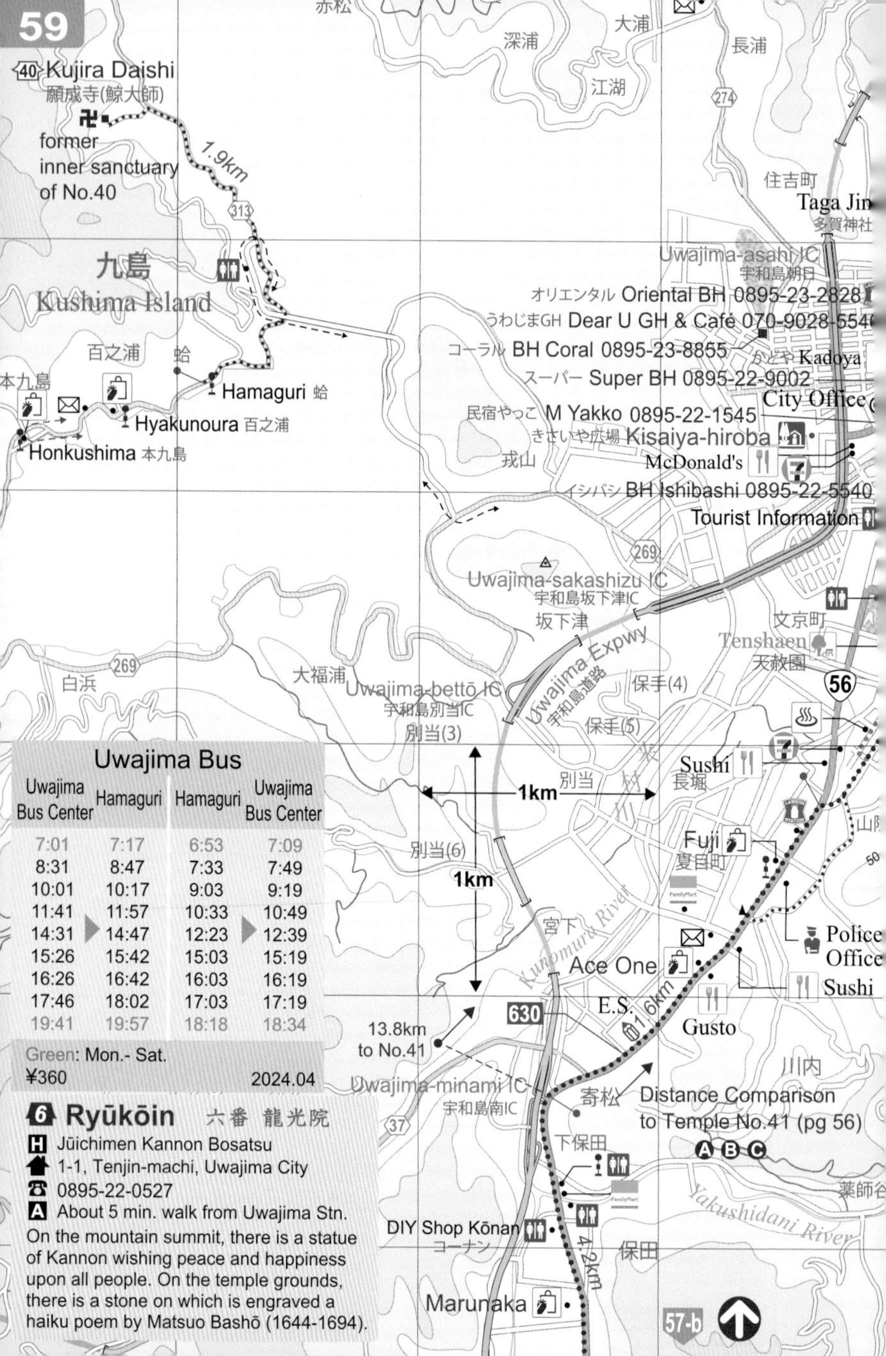
40 Kujira Daishi
願成寺(鯨大師)
former inner sanctuary of No.40
1.9km
313
九島
Kushima Island
百之浦
蛤
本九島
Hamaguri 蛤
Hyakunoura 百之浦
Honkushima 本九島
赤松
深浦
大浦
長浦
江湖
274
住吉町
Taga Jin
多賀神社
Uwajima-asahi IC
宇和島朝日
オリエンタル Oriental BH 0895-23-2828
うわじまGH Dear U GH & Café 070-9028-5546
コーラル BH Coral 0895-23-8855
かどや Kadoya
スーパー Super BH 0895-22-9002
City Office
民宿やっこ M Yakko 0895-22-1545
きさいや広場 Kisaiya-hiroba
McDonald's
戎山
イシバシ BH Ishibashi 0895-22-5540
Tourist Information
269
Uwajima-sakashizu IC
宇和島坂下津IC
坂下津
文京町
Tenshaen
天赦園
Uwajima Expwy
宇和島道路
56
269
白浜
大福浦
Uwajima-bettō IC
宇和島別当IC
別当(3)
保手(4)
保手(5)
別当
長堀
Sushi
1km
1km
別当(6)
Fuji
夏目町
FamilyMart
Police Office
宮下
Kunomura River
Ace One
Sushi
630
E.S.
1.6km
Gusto
13.8km to No.41
Uwajima-minami IC
宇和島南IC
寄松
川内
Distance Comparison to Temple No.41 (pg 56)
A B C
37
下保田
薬師谷
Yakushidani River
DIY Shop Kōnan
コーナン
4.2km
保田
Marunaka
57-b

Uwajima Bus

Uwajima Bus Center	Hamaguri	Hamaguri	Uwajima Bus Center
7:01	7:17	6:53	7:09
8:31	8:47	7:33	7:49
10:01	10:17	9:03	9:19
11:41	11:57	10:33	10:49
14:31	14:47	12:23	12:39
15:26	15:42	15:03	15:19
16:26	16:42	16:03	16:19
17:46	18:02	17:03	17:19
19:41	19:57	18:18	18:34

Green: Mon.- Sat.
¥360 2024.04

6 Ryūkōin 六番 龍光院

H Jūichimen Kannon Bosatsu
1-1, Tenjin-machi, Uwajima City
☎ 0895-22-0527
A About 5 min. walk from Uwajima Stn.

On the mountain summit, there is a statue of Kannon wishing peace and happiness upon all people. On the temple grounds, there is a stone on which is engraved a haiku poem by Matsuo Bashō (1644-1694).

60-a

56
Hachiman Jinja 八幡神社
Fuji GRAND
伊吹町
Suka River 須賀川
KFC
635
JR Yosan Line
2.4km
Matsunoyu 松の湯
320
Yano
50
arei Jinja 和霊神社
Maruyama Park 丸山公園
Pension Service
Bull Fight Field 闘牛場
Uwajima
BH Clement 0895-23-6111 クレメント
Terminal BH 0895-22-2280 ターミナル
6 40 Ryūkōin 龍光院 (9.7km to No.41)
Uwajima-ekimae Bus Stop 宇和島駅前バス停
Hozumi-tei ほづみ亭
Wabisuke 和日輔
Station
Daiichi BH 0895-25-0001 第1
Cherry blossom trees
Uwajima Bus Center 宇和島バスセンター
wajima Castle
Regent BH 0895-23-0808 リージェント
野川
Atago Park 宇和津町
愛宕公園
神田川 賀古町
Jinden River
5km
Date Museum 伊達博物館
Taiheiji 泰平寺
結掛
大超寺奥
40 Mameki Daishi 馬目木大師

Uwajima City
宇和島市

Uwajima Taxi	0895-22-5454
Shikoku Jidōsha	0895-22-2345
Marunouchi Taxi	0895-22-3131

本川内

SCALE 1/30,000
0 0.5 1 1.5 2km

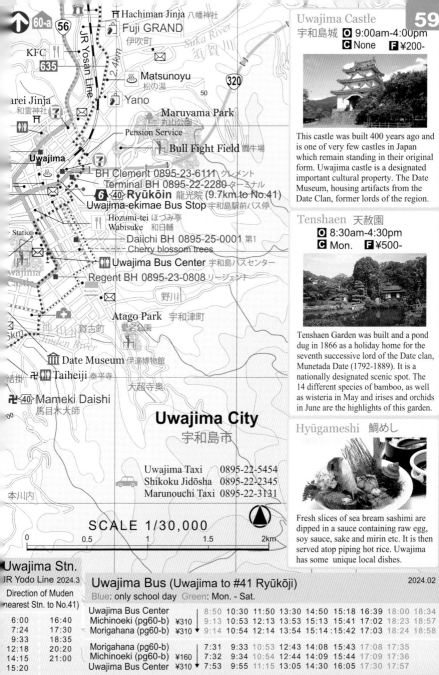

Uwajima Castle
宇和島城 O 9:00am-4:00pm
C None F ¥200-

This castle was built 400 years ago and is one of very few castles in Japan which remain standing in their original form. Uwajima castle is a designated important cultural property. The Date Museum, housing artifacts from the Date Clan, former lords of the region.

Tenshaen 天赦園
O 8:30am-4:30pm
C Mon. F ¥500-

Tenshaen Garden was built and a pond dug in 1866 as a holiday home for the seventh successive lord of the Date clan, Munetada Date (1792-1889). It is a nationally designated scenic spot. The 14 different species of bamboo, as well as wisteria in May and irises and orchids in June are the highlights of this garden.

Hyūgameshi 鯛めし

Fresh slices of sea bream sashimi are dipped in a sauce containing raw egg, soy sauce, sake and mirin etc. It is then served atop piping hot rice. Uwajima has some unique local dishes.

Uwajima Stn.
JR Yodo Line 2024.3

Direction of Muden (nearest Stn. to No.41)

6:00	16:40
7:24	17:30
9:33	18:35
12:18	20:20
14:15	21:00
15:20	

Uwajima Bus (Uwajima to #41 Ryūkōji)
2024.02

Blue: only school day Green: Mon. - Sat.

Stop	Fare									
Uwajima Bus Center		8:50	10:30	11:50	13:30	14:50	15:18	16:39	18:00	18:34
Michinoeki (pg60-b)	¥310	9:13	10:53	12:13	13:53	15:13	15:41	17:02	18:23	18:57
Morigahana (pg60-b)	¥310	9:14	10:54	12:14	13:54	15:14	15:42	17:03	18:24	18:58

Stop	Fare								
Morigahana (pg60-b)		7:31	9:33	10:53	12:43	14:08	15:43	17:08	17:35
Michinoeki (pg60-b)	¥160	7:32	9:34	10:54	12:44	14:09	15:44	17:09	17:36
Uwajima Bus Center	¥310	7:53	9:55	11:15	13:05	14:30	16:05	17:30	17:57

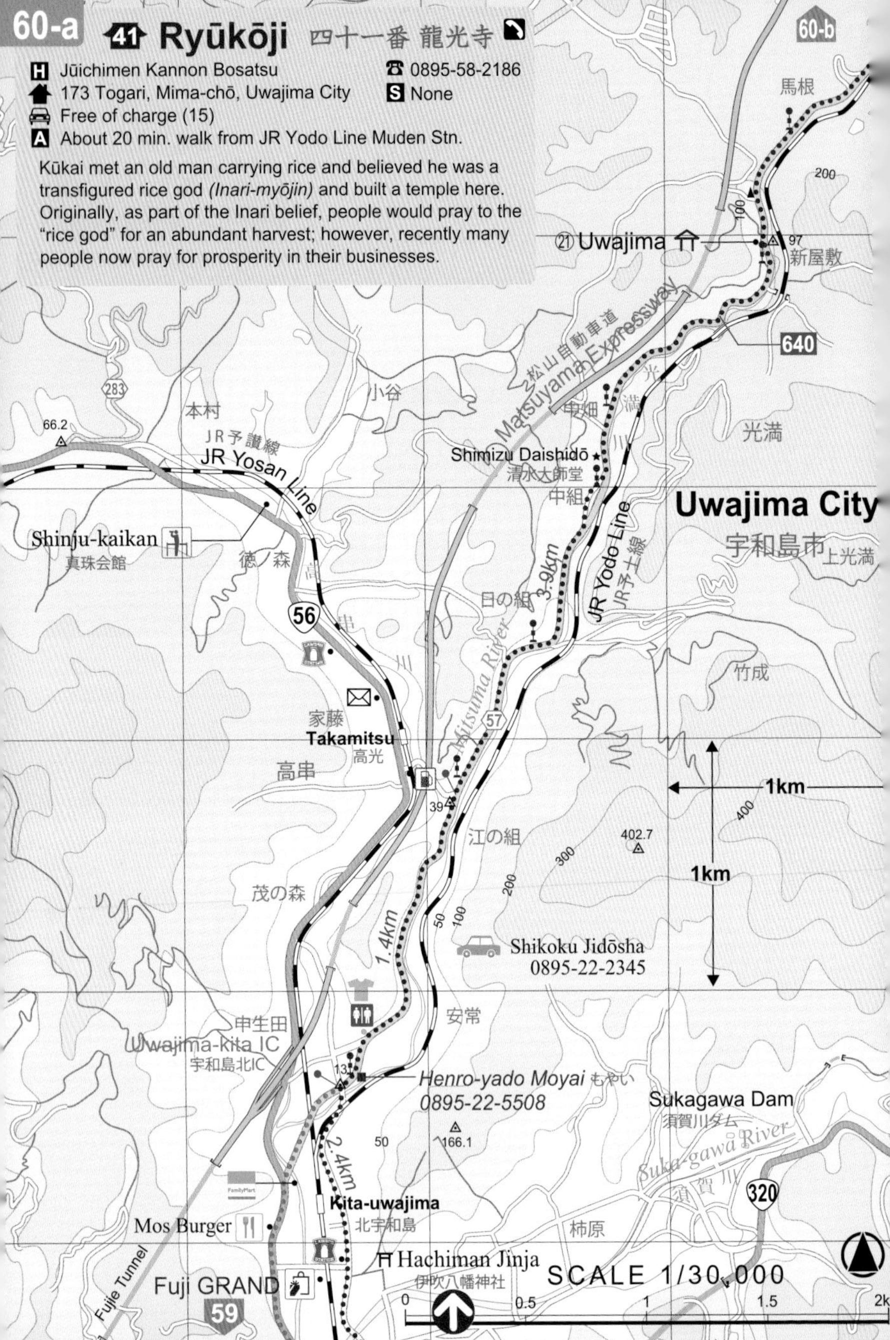
60-a
41 Ryūkōji 四十一番 龍光寺
Jūichimen Kannon Bosatsu
173 Togari, Mima-chō, Uwajima City
Free of charge (15)
About 20 min. walk from JR Yodo Line Muden Stn.
0895-58-2186
None
Kūkai met an old man carrying rice and believed he was a transfigured rice god (Inari-myōjin) and built a temple here. Originally, as part of the Inari belief, people would pray to the "rice god" for an abundant harvest; however, recently many people now pray for prosperity in their businesses.
60-b
馬根
200
100
㉑ Uwajima
97
新屋敷
松山自動車道
Matsuyama Expressway
640
小谷
本村
283
66.2
JR予讃線
JR Yosan Line
光満
Shimizu Daishidō
清水大師堂
中組
Uwajima City
宇和島市
上光満
JR Yodo Line
JR予土線
3.9km
Shinju-kaikan
真珠会館
徳ノ森
56
日の組
Mitsuma River
竹成
家藤
Takamitsu
高光
57
高串
1km
1km
39
江の組
402.7
400
300
200
茂の森
1.4km
50
100
Shikoku Jidōsha
0895-22-2345
安常
申生田
Uwajima-kita IC
宇和島北IC
13
Henro-yado Moyai もやい
0895-22-5508
2.4km
50
166.1
Sukagawa Dam
須賀川ダム
Suka-gawa River
須賀川
320
FamilyMart
Kita-uwajima
北宇和島
柿原
Mos Burger
Hachiman Jinja
伊吹八幡神社
Fuji GRAND
59
Fujie Tunnel
SCALE 1/30,000
0
0.5
1
1.5
2km

42 Butsumokuji 四十二番 佛木寺

H Dainichi Nyorai
1683 Sunawachi, Mima-chō, Uwajima City
Free of charge (15)
A About 60 min. walk from JR Yodo Line Muden Stn.

☎ 0895-58-2216
S None

An old man suggested that Kūkai ride on the back of a cow and after a while, they came upon a camphor tree in which was the jewel *(hōshu)* that Kūkai had thrown from China. In this tree, Kūkai carved a Dainichi Nyorai statue, placed the jewel between its eyes and constructed a temple. At first, people came to pray for prosperity at home, but lately many people visit here in memory of lost pets.

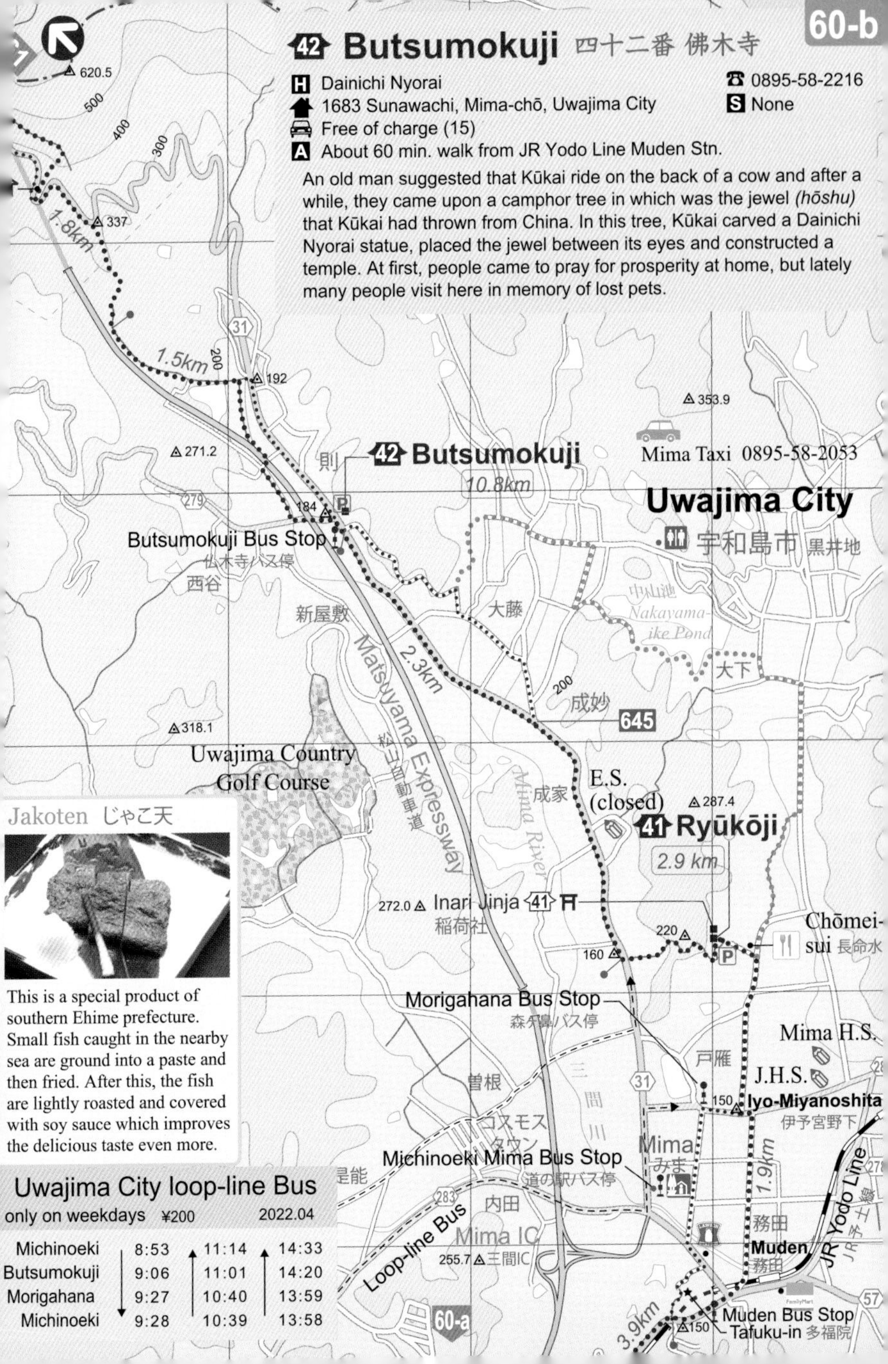

620.5
500
400
300
337
1.8km
31
1.5km
200
192
353.9
271.2
42 Butsumokuji
10.8km
Mima Taxi 0895-58-2053
279
184
Uwajima City
Butsumokuji Bus Stop
仏木寺バス停
宇和島市 黒井地
西谷
中山池
Nakayama-ike Pond
新屋敷
大藤
大下
Matsuyama Expressway
松山自動車道
2.3km
200
成妙
645
318.1
Uwajima Country Golf Course
E.S. (closed)
287.4
成家
Mima River
41 Ryūkōji
2.9 km
272.0
Inari Jinja 41
稲荷社
220
160
Chōmei-sui 長命水
Morigahana Bus Stop
森ケ鼻バス停
Mima H.S.
J.H.S.
戸雁
曽根
三間川
31
150
Iyo-Miyanoshita
伊予宮野下
コスモスタウン
Mima みま
Michinoeki Mima Bus Stop
道の駅バス停
是能
1.9km
283
内田
務田
Loop-line Bus
Mima IC
255.7 三間IC
Muden 務田
JR Yodo Line JR予土線
57
3.9km
150
Muden Bus Stop
Tafuku-in 多福院

60-a

Jakoten じゃこ天

This is a special product of southern Ehime prefecture. Small fish caught in the nearby sea are ground into a paste and then fried. After this, the fish are lightly roasted and covered with soy sauce which improves the delicious taste even more.

Uwajima City loop-line Bus

only on weekdays ¥200 2022.04

	↓	↑	↑
Michinoeki	8:53	11:14	14:33
Butsumokuji	9:06	11:01	14:20
Morigahana	9:27	10:40	13:59
Michinoeki	9:28	10:39	13:58

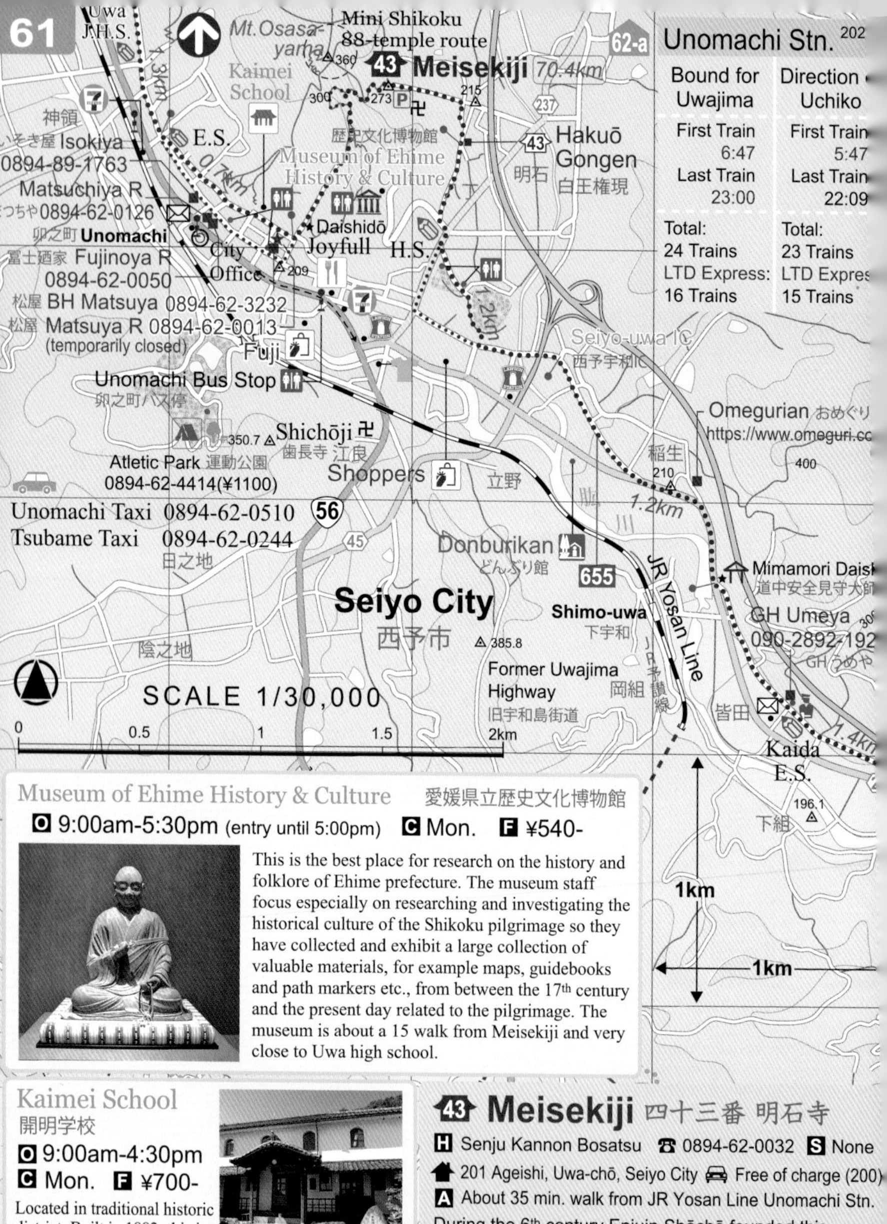

62-a
Unomachi Stn. 202
Bound for Uwajima
First Train 6:47
Last Train 23:00
Total: 24 Trains
LTD Express: 16 Trains
Direction Uchiko
First Train 5:47
Last Train 22:09
Total: 23 Trains
LTD Express: 15 Trains
Uwa J.H.S.
Mt.Osasa-yama
Mini Shikoku 88-temple route
360
Kaimei School
43 Meisekiji 70.4km
300
273
215
1.3km
神領
いそき屋 Isokiya 0894-89-1763
E.S.
0.7km
歴史文化博物館
Museum of Ehime History & Culture
Hakuō Gongen
明石
白王権現
Matsuchiya R
まつちや 0894-62-0126
Daishidō
卯之町 Unomachi
City Office
Joyfull
H.S.
冨士廼家 Fujinoya R 0894-62-0050
209
松屋 BH Matsuya 0894-62-3232
松屋 Matsuya R 0894-62-0013
(temporarily closed)
1.2km
Fuji
Seiyo-uwa IC
西予宇和IC
Unomachi Bus Stop
卯之町バス停
Omegurian おめぐり
https://www.omeguri.co
Shichōji
歯長寺
江良
350.7
稲生
400
Atletic Park 運動公園
0894-62-4414(¥1100)
Shoppers
立野
210
1.2km
Unomachi Taxi 0894-62-0510
Tsubame Taxi 0894-62-0244
56
45
田之地
Donburikan
どんぶり館
655
Mimamori Daishi
道中安全見守大師
Seiyo City
西予市
Shimo-uwa
下宇和
GH Umeya
090-2892-192
GHうめや
陰之地
385.8
JR Yosan Line
JR予讃線
Former Uwajima Highway
旧宇和島街道
岡組
皆田
1.4km
SCALE 1/30,000
0
0.5
1
1.5
2km
Kaida E.S.
196.1
下組
1km
1km

Museum of Ehime History & Culture 愛媛県立歴史文化博物館

O 9:00am-5:30pm (entry until 5:00pm) **C** Mon. **F** ¥540-

This is the best place for research on the history and folklore of Ehime prefecture. The museum staff focus especially on researching and investigating the historical culture of the Shikoku pilgrimage so they have collected and exhibit a large collection of valuable materials, for example maps, guidebooks and path markers etc., from between the 17th century and the present day related to the pilgrimage. The museum is about a 15 walk from Meisekiji and very close to Uwa high school.

Kaimei School 開明学校

O 9:00am-4:30pm
C Mon. **F** ¥700-

Located in traditional historic district. Built in 1882, this is the oldest wooden school structure standing in Western Japan. This designated important cultural property has a unique modern design with white walls and arched windows. Education-related materials from the time of construction are on display.

43 Meisekiji 四十三番 明石寺

H Senju Kannon Bosatsu ☎ 0894-62-0032 **S** None
201 Ageishi, Uwa-chō, Seiyo City Free of charge (200)
A About 35 min. walk from JR Yosan Line Unomachi Stn.

During the 6th century Enjuin Shōchō founded this temple and built various facilities here. The name of this temple, "Daybreak and Stone" derives from the legend of a beautiful goddess who until daybreak carried large rocks while praying; however, when she saw the sun coming up she disappeared.

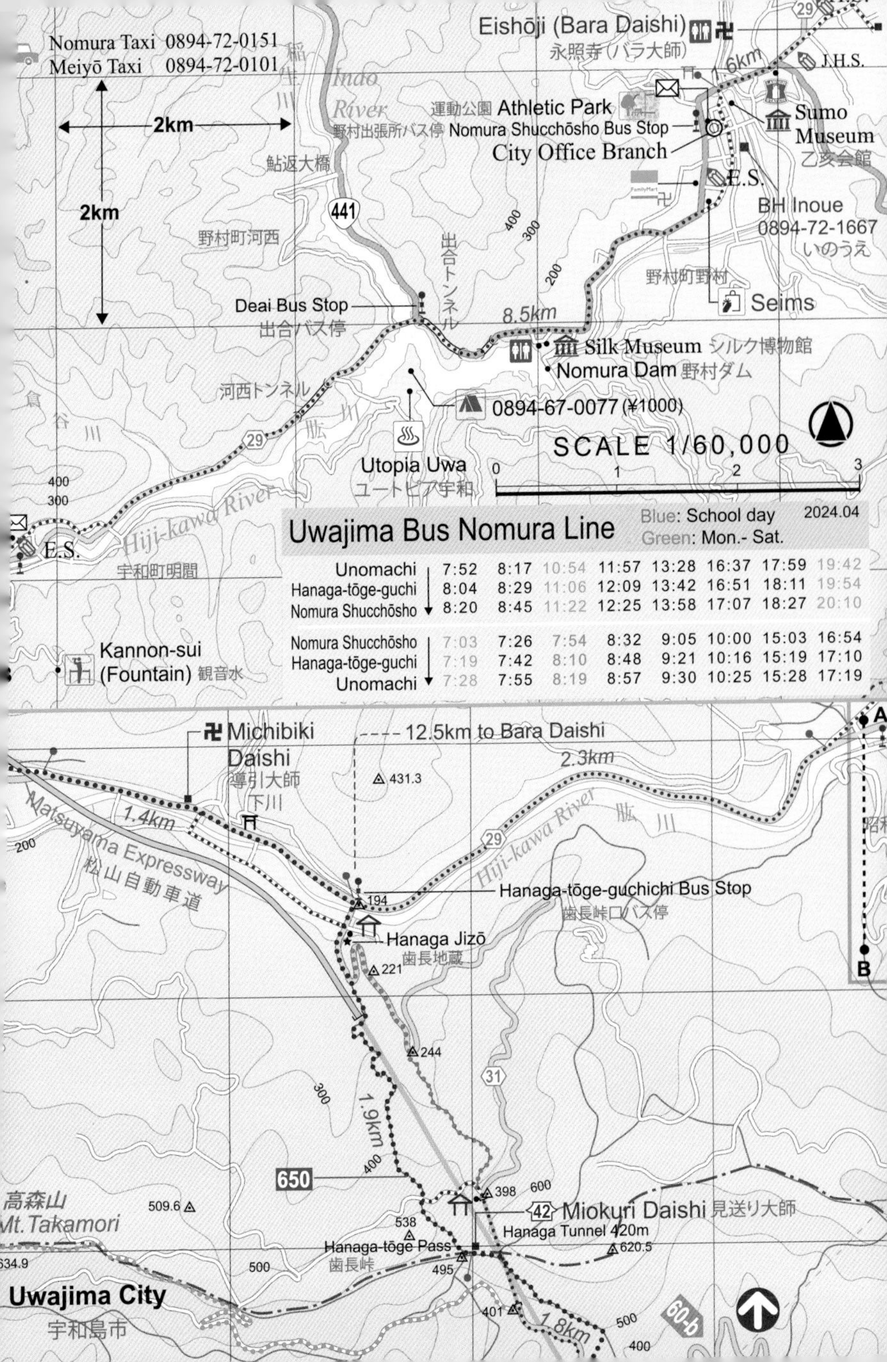
Nomura Taxi 0894-72-0151
Meiyō Taxi 0894-72-0101
2km
2km
稲生川
Indo River
鮎返大橋
441
野村町河西
出合トンネル
Deai Bus Stop
出合バス停
8.5km
河西トンネル
29
Eishōji (Bara Daishi)
永照寺(バラ大師)
6km
J.H.S.
運動公園 Athletic Park
野村出張所バス停 Nomura Shucchōsho Bus Stop
City Office Branch
Sumo Museum
乙亥会館
E.S.
BH Inoue
0894-72-1667
いのうえ
野村町野村
Seims
Silk Museum シルク博物館
Nomura Dam 野村ダム
0894-67-0077 (¥1000)
Utopia Uwa
ユートピア宇和
SCALE 1/60,000
0
1
2
3
肱川
Hiji-kawa River
E.S.
宇和町明間
Kannon-sui
(Fountain) 観音水
Michibiki Daishi
導引大師
下川
12.5km to Bara Daishi
431.3
2.3km
1.4km
Matsuyama Expressway
松山自動車道
Hiji-kawa River
肱川
29
Hanaga-tōge-guchichi Bus Stop
歯長峠口バス停
194
Hanaga Jizō
歯長地蔵
221
244
31
1.9km
650
高森山
Mt.Takamori
509.6
398
Miokuri Daishi 見送り大師
42
Hanaga Tunnel 420m
538
Hanaga-tōge Pass
歯長峠
495
620.5
634.9
Uwajima City
宇和島市
401
1.8km
60-b
A
B

Uwajima Bus Nomura Line

Blue: School day
Green: Mon.- Sat.
2024.04

↓								
Unomachi	7:52	8:17	10:54	11:57	13:28	16:37	17:59	19:42
Hanaga-tōge-guchi	8:04	8:29	11:06	12:09	13:42	16:51	18:11	19:54
Nomura Shucchōsho	8:20	8:45	11:22	12:25	13:58	17:07	18:27	20:10

↓								
Nomura Shucchōsho	7:03	7:26	7:54	8:32	9:05	10:00	15:03	16:54
Hanaga-tōge-guchi	7:19	7:42	8:10	8:48	9:21	10:16	15:19	17:10
Unomachi	7:28	7:55	8:19	8:57	9:30	10:25	15:28	17:19

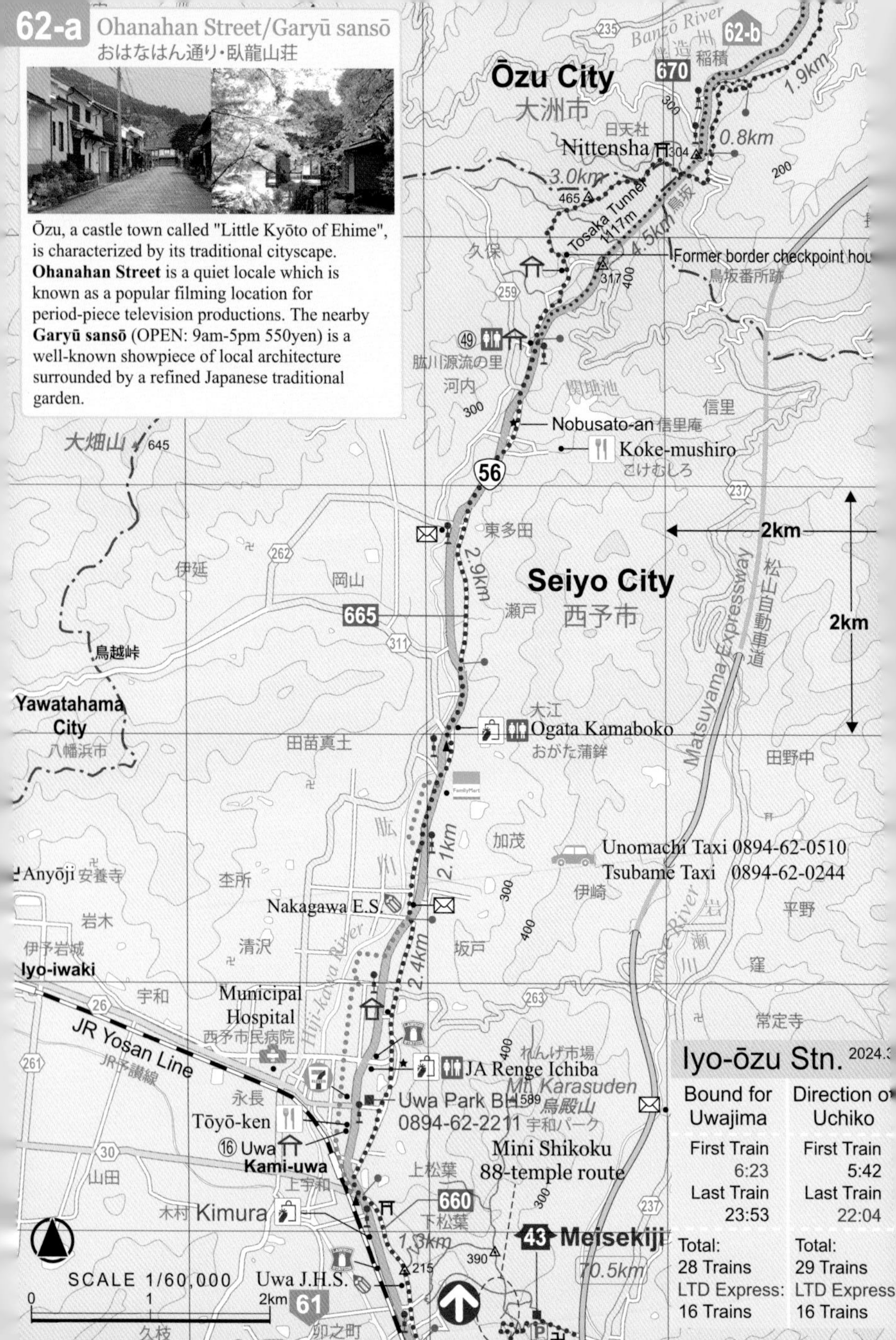
62-a
Ohanahan Street/Garyū sansō
おはなはん通り・臥龍山荘
Ōzu, a castle town called "Little Kyōto of Ehime", is characterized by its traditional cityscape. Ohanahan Street is a quiet locale which is known as a popular filming location for period-piece television productions. The nearby Garyū sansō (OPEN: 9am-5pm 550yen) is a well-known showpiece of local architecture surrounded by a refined Japanese traditional garden.
62-b
Banzō River
Ōzu City
大洲市
670
稲積
1.9km
0.8km
日天社
Nittensha
304
3.0km
465
Tosaka Tunnel 1117m
4.5km
鳥坂
久保
Former border checkpoint hou
鳥坂番所跡
317
259
49
肱川源流の里
河内
関地池
信里
Nobusato-an 信里庵
Koke-mushiro
こけむしろ
大畑山
645
56
237
東多田
2km
2.9km
262
伊延
岡山
Seiyo City
西予市
瀬戸
665
311
松山自動車道
Matsuyama Expressway
鳥越峠
Yawatahama City
八幡浜市
大江
Ogata Kamaboko
おがた蒲鉾
田苗真土
田野中
FamilyMart
加茂
2.1km
Unomachi Taxi 0894-62-0510
Tsubame Taxi 0894-62-0244
Anyōji 安養寺
杢所
伊崎
Nakagawa E.S.
岩木
伊予岩城
Iyo-iwaki
清沢
坂戸
平野
2.4km
Hiji-kawa River
Municipal Hospital
西予市民病院
26
宇和
263
常定寺
JR Yosan Line
JR予讃線
261
れんげ市場
JA Renge Ichiba
Mt. Karasuden
烏殿山
589
永長
Uwa Park BH
0894-62-2211 宇和パーク
Tōyō-ken
16 Uwa
Kami-uwa
30
山田
上宇和
上松葉
Mini Shikoku 88-temple route
660
木村 Kimura
下松葉
237
1.3km
43 Meisekiji
70.5km
390
215
SCALE 1/60,000
0 1 2km
Uwa J.H.S.
61
久枝
卯之町
Iyo-ōzu Stn. 2024.3
Bound for Uwajima
First Train 6:23
Last Train 23:53
Total: 28 Trains
LTD Express: 16 Trains
Direction of Uchiko
First Train 5:42
Last Train 22:04
Total: 29 Trains
LTD Express 16 Trains

62-b
Niiya Taxi 0893-25-0828
Uwajima Taxi 0893-24-7734
JR Yosan Line
JR予讃線
Gorō
五郎
Furusato R
0893-25-0928
ふるさと
新谷町
685
Zuianji
瑞安寺
H.S.
2.3km
Kitayama
喜多山
Niiya
橋の下、必見 Toyogahashi 8
(See Kōbō Daishi sleeping under the bridge)
Ōzu IC
大洲IC
Super BH 0893-37-9000
スーパーホテル
Ōzu Plaza BH
オオズプラザ 0893-25-1100
1.6km
Mos Burger
Umetako R
0893-25-0826
うめたこ旅館
JR Uchiko Line
JR内子線
680
240
1.4km
3.3km
徳森
McDonald's
Joyfull
OZ Messe
Marunaka
63
Ōzu-kita IC
大洲北IC
232
伊予大洲
Iyo-Ōzu
2.7km
2.6km
Tokiwa R 0893-24-3634
(Regional Trail Information Center)
市木
49.0km to No.44
大洲
Tomisu-yama Park
197
320
富士山
0893-23-2384
(¥2200)
City Office
Hiji-kawa River
44
菅田町
菅田
63
Joyfull
大洲南IC
Ōzu-minami IC
Ōzu-kōnan IC
大洲肱南IC
3.1km
Sukunahikona
Jinja
少彦名神社
Shoppers
Ōzu City
大洲市
24
大洲北只IC
Ōzu-kitatada IC
675
56
Kōnan Taxi
0893-24-2010
Ōzu GC
2.5km
Detour
Fudakake Parking
ポケットパーク札掛
松尾
Vending Machine
野佐来
Fudakakeji
(Fudakake Daishi)
仏陀懸寺(札掛大師)
441
62-a
4.5km
1.9km
梅川
SCALE 1/60,000
0 1 2km
8 Toyogahashi 八番 十夜ケ橋
H Miroku Bosatsu
Toyogahashi, Ōzu City
0893-25-2530
A By bus bound for Nagahama-ekimae from Iyo-Ōzu Stn. Get off at Toyogahashi Bus Stop
The tradition of not tapping one's staff while on a bridge comes from the story of Kūkai when he had to to spend a long, cold night under the bridge here.
Central Ōzu (大洲)
0 0.5 1km
BH West River
0893-24-4046
ウエストリバー
Koyasu-Kannon
子安観音
Iyo-Ōzu
伊予大洲
H.S.
Tourist Information
Fuji GRAND
BH Ōta オータ
0893-24-3533
Tokiwa R (ときわ) 常磐旅館
0893-24-3634
(Henro House, booking.com)
Yoshino-yu
56
Hatagoya Muchū はたご屋 霧中
hostel.muchuu1111@gmail.com
Ōzu Castle
大洲城
Hiji-kawa River
197
松楽 Shōraku R
0893-24-4143
City Office
Garyū sansō
臥竜山荘
Ohanahan Street
Tourist Information
Asamoya あさもや
臥龍の湯 Garyū-no-yu

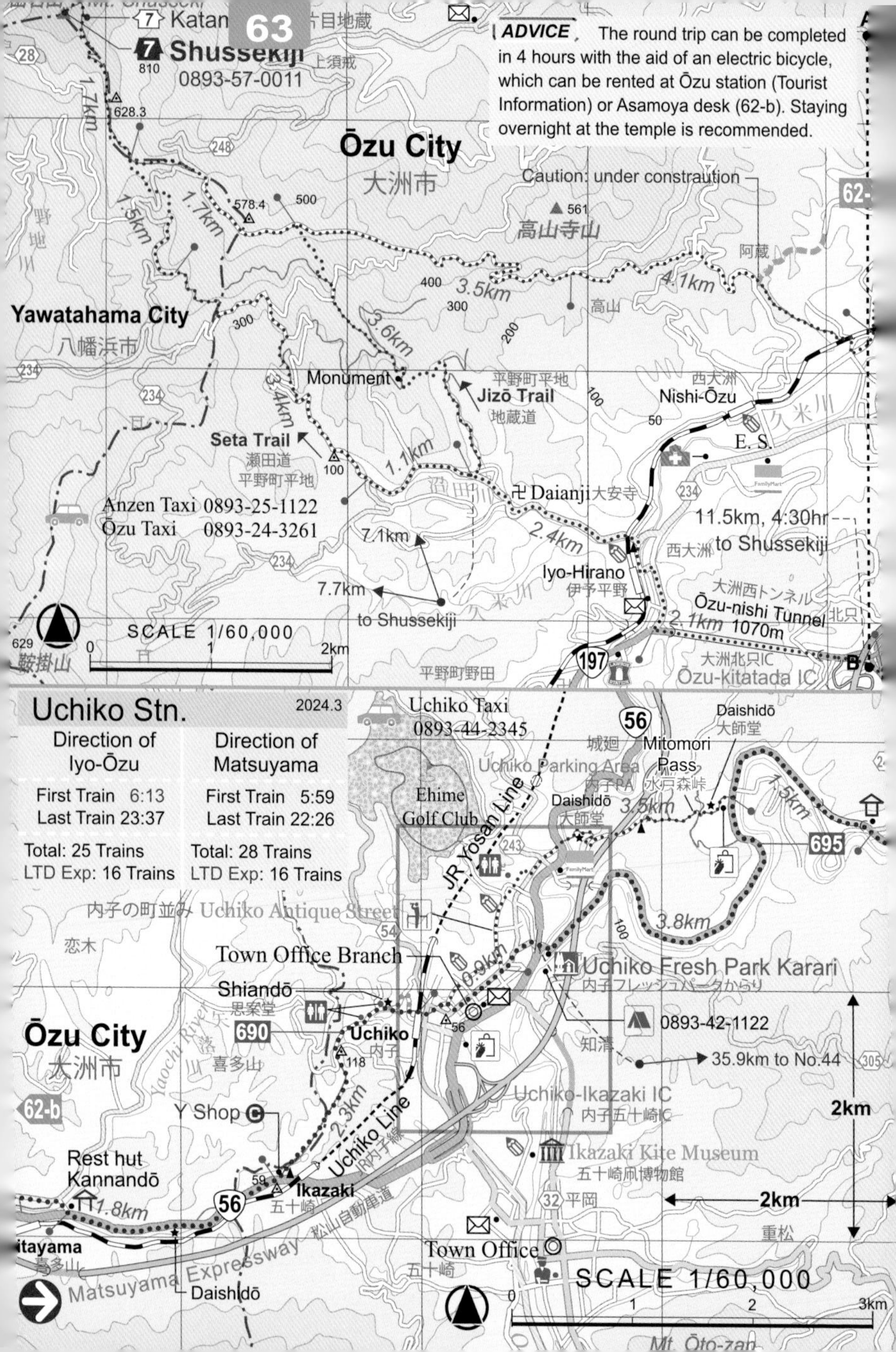
ADVICE The round trip can be completed in 4 hours with the aid of an electric bicycle, which can be rented at Ōzu station (Tourist Information) or Asamoya desk (62-b). Staying overnight at the temple is recommended.
7 Katan
7 Shussekiji
810
0893-57-0011
上須戒
Ōzu City
大洲市
Caution: under constrаution
62-
561
高山寺山
阿蔵
3.5km
4.1km
高山
1.7km
1.5km
1.7km
628.3
578.4
500
400
300
200
100
50
Yawatahama City
八幡浜市
3.6km
3.4km
Monument
Jizō Trail
地蔵道
平野町平地
Seta Trail
瀬田道
平野町平地
100
1.1km
Nishi-Ōzu
西大洲
久米川
E. S.
FamilyMart
Daianji大安寺
Anzen Taxi 0893-25-1122
Ōzu Taxi 0893-24-3261
7.1km
7.7km
to Shussekiji
2.4km
11.5km, 4:30hr to Shussekiji
西大洲
Iyo-Hirano
伊予平野
大洲西トンネル
Ōzu-nishi Tunnel 1070m
2.1km
北只
SCALE 1/60,000
0 1 2km
629
鞍掛山
197
平野町野田
大洲北只IC
Ōzu-kitatada IC
B
Uchiko Stn.
2024.3
Direction of Iyo-Ōzu
First Train 6:13
Last Train 23:37
Total: 25 Trains
LTD Exp: 16 Trains
Direction of Matsuyama
First Train 5:59
Last Train 22:26
Total: 28 Trains
LTD Exp: 16 Trains
Uchiko Taxi
0893-44-2345
56
城廻
Uchiko Parking Area
内子PA
Daishidō
大師堂
Mitomori Pass
水戸森峠
1.5km
Ehime Golf Club
Daishidō
大師堂
3.5km
JR Yosan Line
243
695
内子の町並み Uchiko Antique Street
54
恋木
3.8km
100
Town Office Branch
0.9km
Uchiko Fresh Park Karari
内子フレッシュパークからり
Shiandō
思案堂
690
Uchiko
内子
56
118
0893-42-1122
知清
35.9km to No.44
305
Ōzu City
大洲市
Yaochi River
喜多山
Uchiko-Ikazaki IC
内子五十崎IC
2km
62-b
Y Shop
2.3km
Uchiko Line
JR内子線
Ikazaki Kite Museum
五十崎凧博物館
Rest hut Kannandō
59
Ikazaki
五十崎
56
1.8km
松山自動車道
32 平岡
2km
重松
itayama
喜多山
Matsuyama Expressway
Town Office
五十崎
Daishidō
SCALE 1/60,000
0 1 2 3km
Mt. Ōto-zan

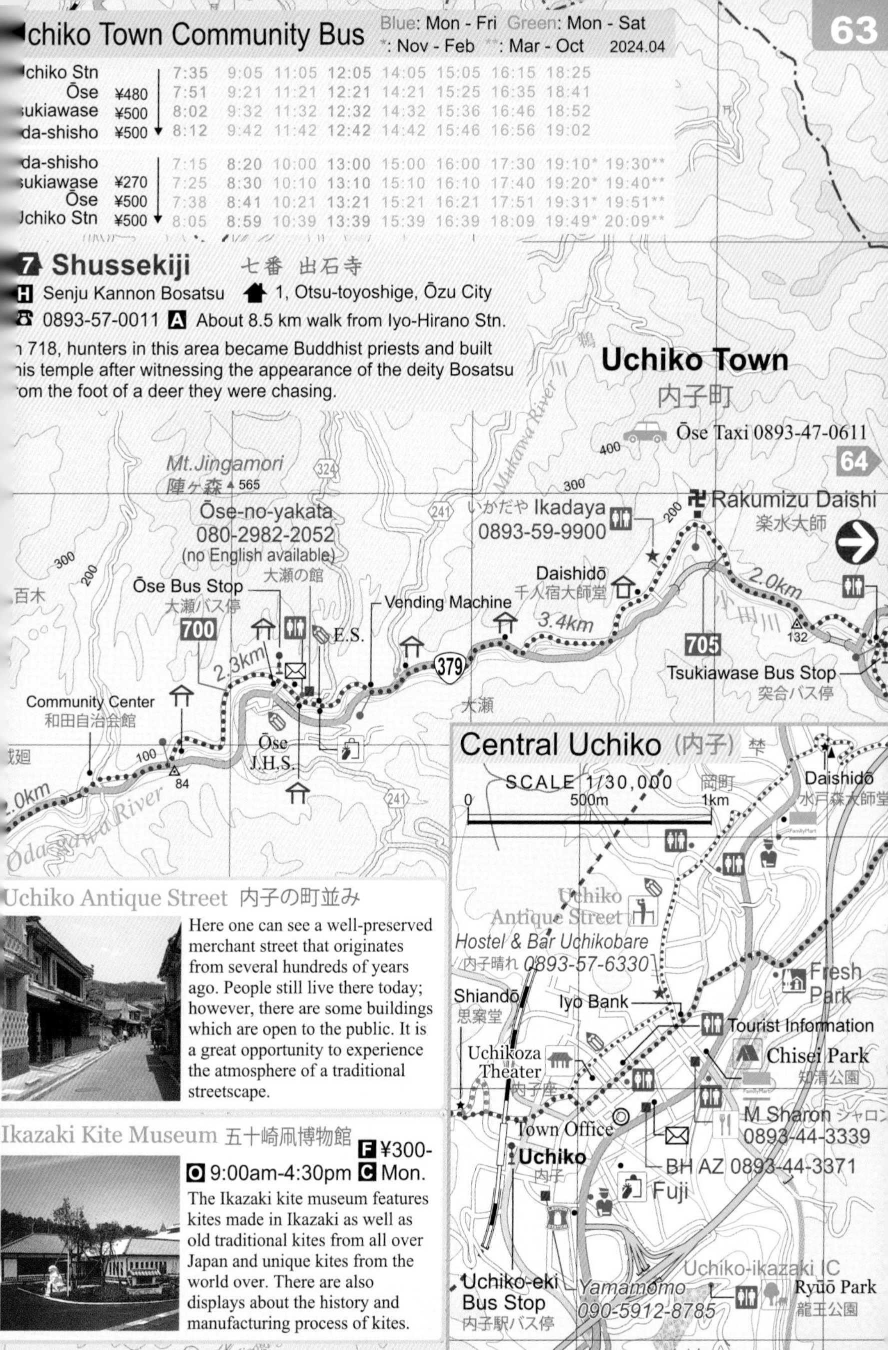

chiko Town Community Bus

Blue: Mon - Fri Green: Mon - Sat
*: Nov - Feb **: Mar - Oct 2024.04

chiko Stn		7:35	9:05	11:05	12:05	14:05	15:05	16:15	18:25
Ōse	¥480	7:51	9:21	11:21	12:21	14:21	15:25	16:35	18:41
ukiawase	¥500	8:02	9:32	11:32	12:32	14:32	15:36	16:46	18:52
da-shisho	¥500	8:12	9:42	11:42	12:42	14:42	15:46	16:56	19:02

da-shisho		7:15	8:20	10:00	13:00	15:00	16:00	17:30	19:10*	19:30**
ukiawase	¥270	7:25	8:30	10:10	13:10	15:10	16:10	17:40	19:20*	19:40**
Ōse	¥500	7:38	8:41	10:21	13:21	15:21	16:21	17:51	19:31*	19:51**
chiko Stn	¥500	8:05	8:59	10:39	13:39	15:39	16:39	18:09	19:49*	20:09**

7 Shussekiji 七番 出石寺

H Senju Kannon Bosatsu 1, Otsu-toyoshige, Ōzu City

☎ 0893-57-0011 A About 8.5 km walk from Iyo-Hirano Stn.

n 718, hunters in this area became Buddhist priests and built his temple after witnessing the appearance of the deity Bosatsu rom the foot of a deer they were chasing.

Uchiko Town
内子町
Ōse Taxi 0893-47-0611
64
Mt.Jingamori
陣ヶ森 565
Ōse-no-yakata
080-2982-2052
(no English available)
大瀬の館
いかだや Ikadaya
0893-59-9900
Rakumizu Daishi
楽水大師
Daishidō
千人宿大師堂
Ōse Bus Stop
大瀬バス停
700
Vending Machine
E.S.
3.4km
2.0km
2.3km
705
Tsukiawase Bus Stop
突合バス停
Community Center
和田自治会館
Ōse
J.H.S.
大瀬
Mukawa River
Odagawa River
Central Uchiko (内子)
SCALE 1/30,000
0 500m 1km
Daishidō
水戸森大師堂
Uchiko
Antique Street
Hostel & Bar Uchikobare
内子晴れ 0893-57-6330
Shiandō
思案堂
Iyo Bank
Fresh Park
Tourist Information
Chisei Park
知清公園
Uchikoza Theater
内子座
Town Office
M Sharon シャロン
0893-44-3339
Uchiko
内子
BH AZ 0893-44-3371
Fuji
Uchiko-ikazaki IC
Uchiko-eki Bus Stop
内子駅バス停
Yamamomo
090-5912-8785
Ryūō Park
龍王公園

Uchiko Antique Street 内子の町並み

Here one can see a well-preserved merchant street that originates from several hundreds of years ago. People still live there today; however, there are some buildings which are open to the public. It is a great opportunity to experience the atmosphere of a traditional streetscape.

Ikazaki Kite Museum 五十崎凧博物館

F ¥300-
O 9:00am-4:30pm C Mon.

The Ikazaki kite museum features kites made in Ikazaki as well as old traditional kites from all over Japan and unique kites from the world over. There are also displays about the history and manufacturing process of kites.

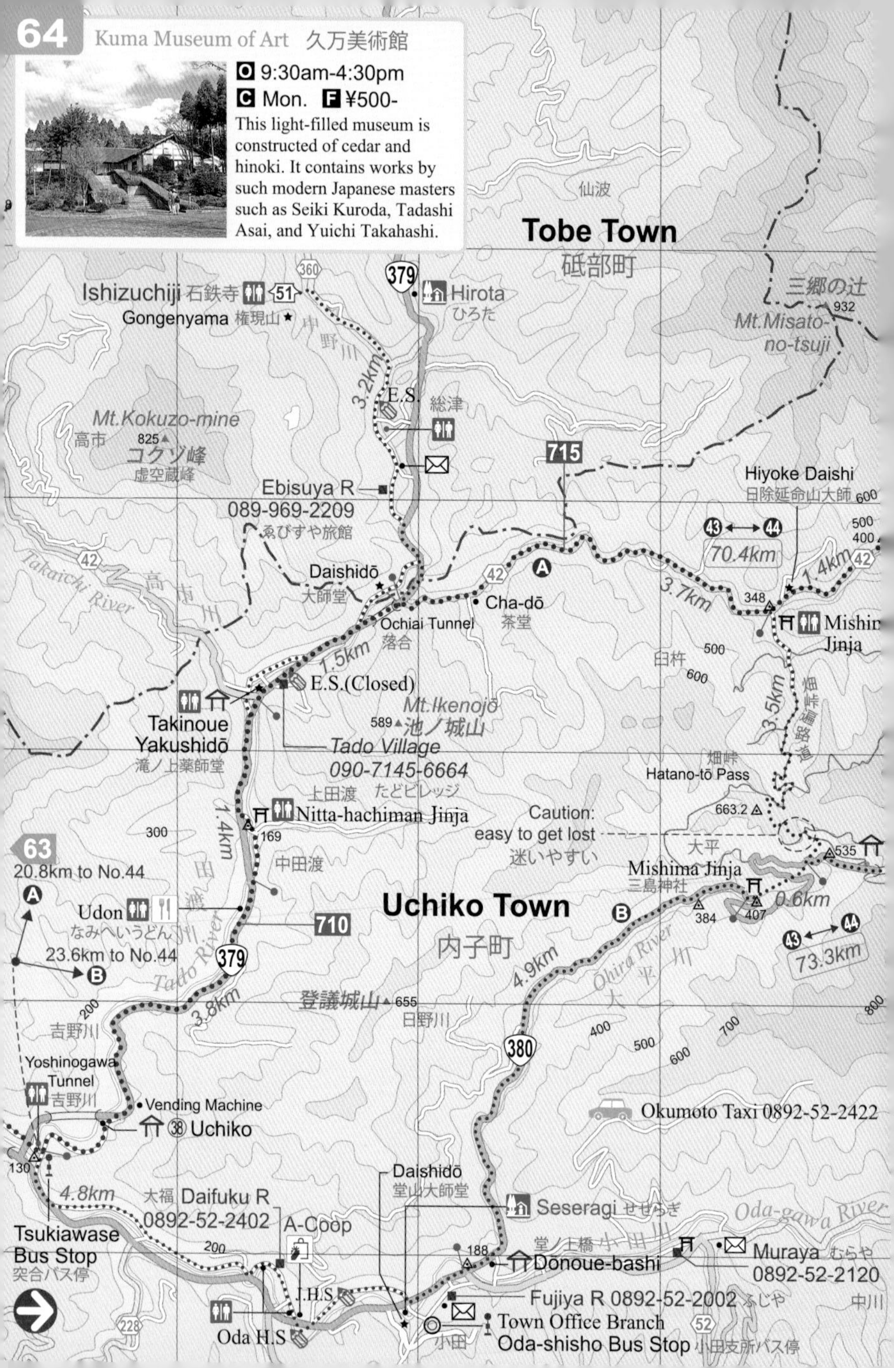
64
Kuma Museum of Art 久万美術館
O 9:30am-4:30pm
C Mon. F ¥500-
This light-filled museum is constructed of cedar and hinoki. It contains works by such modern Japanese masters such as Seiki Kuroda, Tadashi Asai, and Yuichi Takahashi.
Tobe Town
砥部町
仙波
三郷の辻
932
Mt.Misato-no-tsuji
360
379
51
Ishizuchiji 石鉄寺
Gongenyama 権現山
Hirota
ひろた
中野川
3.2km
E.S.
総津
Mt.Kokuzo-mine
高市
825
コクゾ峰
虚空蔵峰
715
Ebisuya R
089-969-2209
ゑびすや旅館
Hiyoke Daishi
日除延命山大師
600
500
400
43 44
70.4km
42
Takaichi River
高市川
Daishidō
大師堂
Cha-dō
茶堂
3.7km
1.4km
348
Mishin
Jinja
Ochiai Tunnel
落合
1.5km
E.S.(Closed)
臼杵
500
600
Takinoue Yakushidō
滝ノ上薬師堂
Mt.Ikenojō
589 池ノ城山
Tado Village
090-7145-6664
たどビレッジ
上田渡
3.5km
畑峠遍路道
畑峠
Hatano-tō Pass
663.2
Nitta-hachiman Jinja
169
1.4km
300
Caution:
easy to get lost
迷いやすい
大平
535
63
20.8km to No.44
A
Mishima Jinja
三島神社
中田渡
田渡川
Uchiko Town
内子町
B
384
407
0.6km
Udon
なみへいうどん
710
23.6km to No.44
B
43 44
73.3km
Tado River
379
4.9km
Ōhira River
大平川
3.8km
登議城山 655
日野川
200
吉野川
380
400
500
600
700
800
Yoshinogawa Tunnel
吉野川
Vending Machine
38 Uchiko
Okumoto Taxi 0892-52-2422
130
4.8km
Tsukiawase Bus Stop
突合バス停
大福 Daifuku R
0892-52-2402
A-Coop
200
Daishidō
堂山大師堂
Seseragi せせらぎ
Oda-gawa River
小田川
188
堂ノ上橋
Donoue-bashi
Muraya むらや
0892-52-2120
J.H.S
Fujiya R 0892-52-2002 ふじや
中川
228
Oda H.S
Town Office Branch
Oda-shisho Bus Stop 小田支所バス停
小田
52

Mt.Katsuragamori
桂ヶ森 1224
66
Okuma Daishi 於久万大師
Sansan
Kuma J.H.S.
久万中学前(JRバス停) Kuma-chūgaku-mae Bus Stop
久万営業所(伊予鉄バス停) Kuma-eigyōsho Bus Stop
(Transfer Bus Stop to Iwayaji)
4km
2.0km
492
489
久万
44
Daihōji
9.3km
E.S.
H.S.
65
2.5km
900
鴨田峠 Hiwada-tō Pass
Danjiri Rock
だんじり岩
800
700
600
790
725
2.8km
Tentsuki Place GH
080-6382-8896
Daishidō
森田大師堂
Shimosakaba-
tōge Pass
下坂場峠
3.0km
600
Katsuragi
葛城神社 Jinja
二名
570
527
2.3km
Fountain
Fire Station
473
下野尻
3.3km
153
1.8km
Nōsono-tō Pass
農祖峠 651
33
Kuma River
Kuma-kōgen Town
久万高原町
Omogo Taxi 0892-21-1220
9.3km to No.48
720
412
600
1.3km
497
Nimyō River
2km
2km
1.2km
Ōmoto-
hachiman
Jinja
露峰
380
Hōrenji
Iyo-ochiai Bus Stop
伊予落合 バス停
484
Fujimine E.S.
Cha-dō
茶堂
Mt.Uchikoshi
打越山
860
父野川
700
5.1km
594
554
Mayumi Tunnel
真弓峠 710m
Mayumi-Tōge Pass
SCALE 1/60,000
1
2
3km
Central Kuma-kōgen (久万高原)
SCALE
1/30,000
0
500m
1km
Kuma Museum of Art
久万美術館
でんこ Denko
0892-21-0092
M Ichiriki 一里木
0892-21-0505
mac
Seims
Sansan
さんさん
Kuma J.H.S.
12
Kuma-chūgaku mae Bus Stop
Kuma-eigyōsho Bus Stop
Okuma Daishi
於久万大師
Town Office
Fureai Road
Kuma-kōgen
Bus Stop
M Oheso
090-4970-5851
Garden Time
0892-21-0005
Kuma
E.S.

44 Daihōji 四十四番 大寶寺

- H Jūichimen Kannon Bosatsu ☎ 0892-21-0044
- 1173 Sugō, Kuma-kōgen Town
- S Available (group only)
- Free of charge (20) 5 min. walk
- A By bus bound for Ochide from Matsuyama Stn. Get off at Kuma-chūgaku-mae Bus Stop, about 20 min. walk.

In 701, a priest who had returned from Korea placed a statue of Jūichimen Kannon Bosatsu in the mountain. This was later found by a couple of hunter brothers who started this temple. At the main gate, there are huge straw sandals which are remade every hundred years.

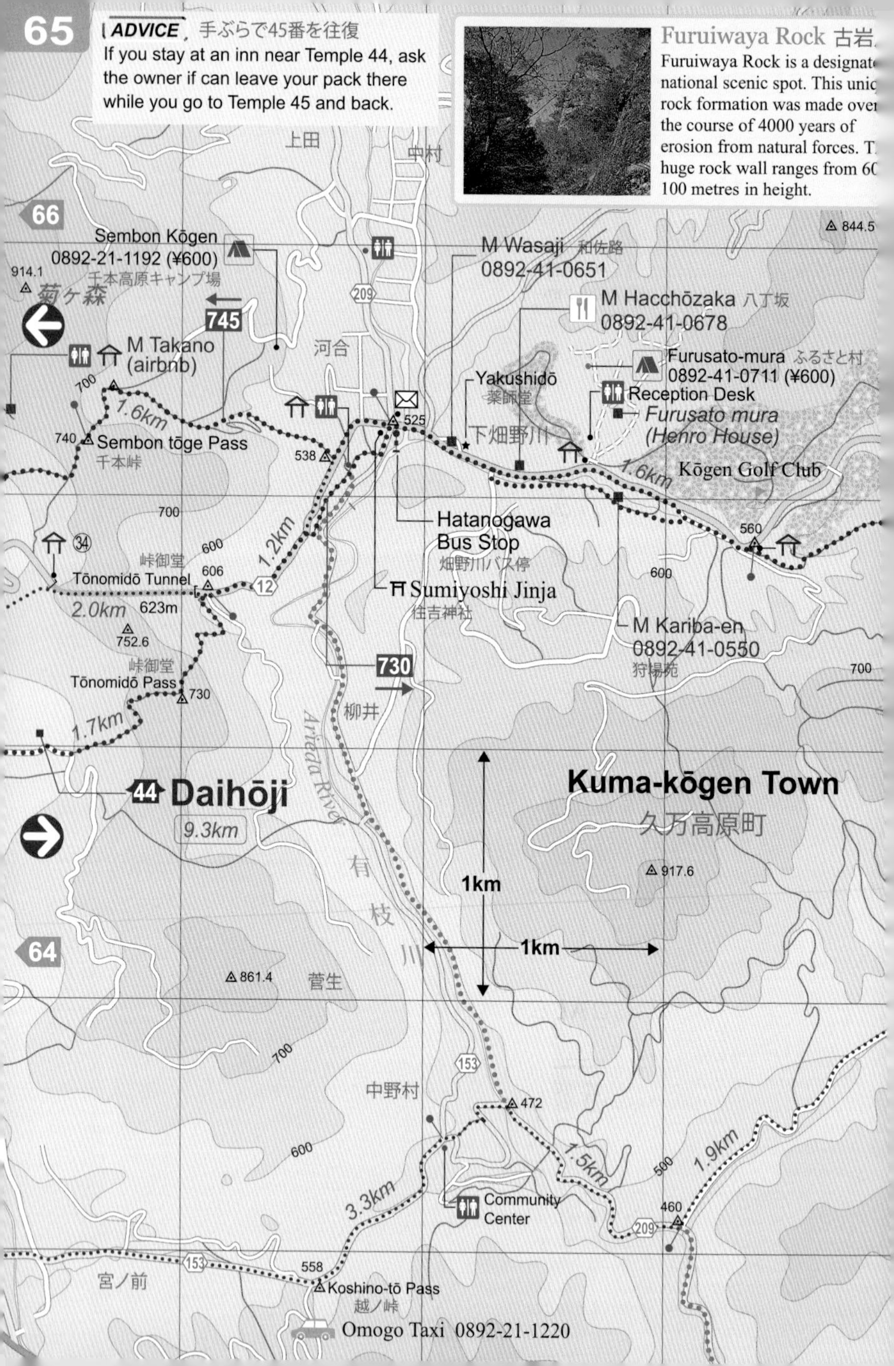
65
ADVICE 手ぶらで45番を往復
If you stay at an inn near Temple 44, ask the owner if can leave your pack there while you go to Temple 45 and back.
Furuiwaya Rock 古岩
Furuiwaya Rock is a designat
national scenic spot. This uniq
rock formation was made over
the course of 4000 years of
erosion from natural forces. T
huge rock wall ranges from 60
100 metres in height.
上田
中村
66
844.5
Sembon Kōgen
0892-21-1192 (¥600)
千本高原キャンプ場
914.1
菊ケ森
745
M Wasaji 和佐路
0892-41-0651
209
M Hacchōzaka 八丁坂
0892-41-0678
M Takano
(airbnb)
河合
Furusato-mura ふるさと村
0892-41-0711 (¥600)
Yakushidō
薬師堂
Reception Desk
Furusato mura
(Henro House)
700
1.6km
525
下畑野川
740
Sembon tōge Pass
千本峠
538
1.6km
Kōgen Golf Club
700
Hatanogawa
Bus Stop
畑野川バス停
560
34
1.2km
峠御堂
600
Tōnomidō Tunnel
606
12
600
Sumiyoshi Jinja
住吉神社
2.0km
623m
752.6
M Kariba-en
0892-41-0550
狩場苑
峠御堂
Tōnomidō Pass
730
730
700
柳井
1.7km
Arieda River
44 Daihōji
9.3km
Kuma-kōgen Town
久万高原町
917.6
有
枝
川
1km
1km
64
861.4
菅生
700
153
中野村
472
600
1.5km
500
1.9km
3.3km
Community
Center
460
209
153
558
宮ノ前
Koshino-tō Pass
越ノ峠
Omogo Taxi 0892-21-1220

45 Iwayaji 四十五番 岩屋寺

☎ 0892-57-0417 S None

Fudō Myōō 1468 Nanatori, Kuma-kōgen Town Charge (100) 20 min. walk

By bus bound for Kuma from Matsuyama Stn. Get off at Kuma-chūgaku-mae Bus Stop. Change bus for Omogo from Kuma-eigyōsho. Get off at Iwayaji-mae Bus Stop, about 20 min. walk.

According to legend, Kūkai was told about this place by a mysterious female recluse, Hokke-sennin. Kūkai carved two Fudō Myōō statues and created this temple which is considered a *"nansho"* (difficult place). Here you can try visiting Seriwari-zenjō, a place where Kōbō Daishi trained. It is reached by passing thirty-six stone Buddhist statues of immortal youths, going through a wooden gate, and then climbing up a steep rock face with ropes, chains and ladders. If you ask at the temple office, the staff will give you the key to open the gate and special osamefuda to place at each statue along the way. (¥300) It will take less than two hours to go from the temple to the summit and back.

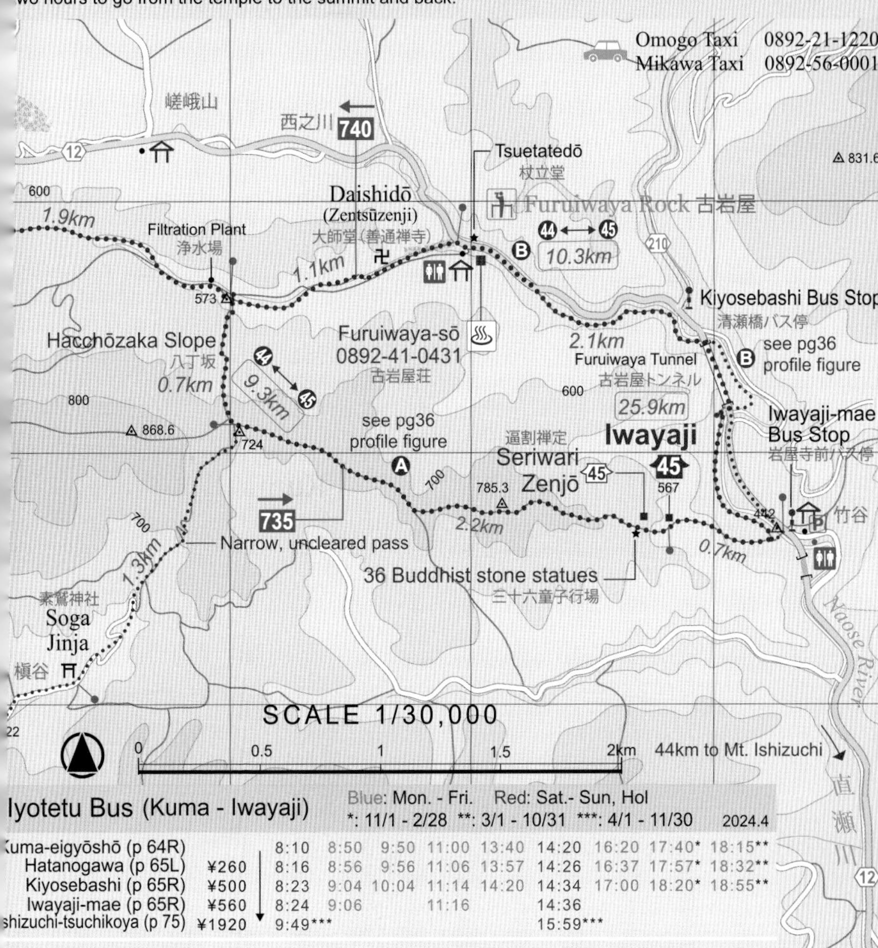

Omogo Taxi 0892-21-1220
Mikawa Taxi 0892-56-0001
嵯峨山
西之川
740
12
Tsuetatedō
杖立堂
831.6
600
Daishidō
(Zentsūzenji)
大師堂（善通禅寺）
Furuiwaya Rock 古岩屋
1.9km
Filtration Plant
浄水場
1.1km
44 ↔ 45
10.3km
210
573
Kiyosebashi Bus Stop
清瀬橋バス停
Hacchōzaka Slope
八丁坂
0.7km
Furuiwaya-sō
0892-41-0431
古岩屋荘
44 ↔ 45
9.3km
2.1km
Furuiwaya Tunnel
古岩屋トンネル
see pg36
profile figure
800
600
25.9km
Iwayaji-mae
Bus Stop
岩屋寺前バス停
868.6
724
see pg36
profile figure
逼割禅定
Seriwari
Zenjō
Iwayaji
45
700
785.3
567
竹谷
735
700
2.2km
Narrow, uncleared pass
0.7km
1.3km
36 Buddhist stone statues
三十六童子行場
素鵞神社
Soga
Jinja
槙谷
Naose River
直瀬川
SCALE 1/30,000
0
0.5
1
1.5
2km
44km to Mt. Ishizuchi
七鳥

Iyotetu Bus (Kuma - Iwayaji)

Blue: Mon. - Fri. Red: Sat.- Sun, Hol

*: 11/1 - 2/28 **: 3/1 - 10/31 ***: 4/1 - 11/30 2024.4

Stop	Fare									
Kuma-eigyōshō (p 64R)		8:10	8:50	9:50	11:00	13:40	14:20	16:20	17:40*	18:15**
Hatanogawa (p 65L)	¥260	8:16	8:56	9:56	11:06	13:57	14:26	16:37	17:57*	18:32**
Kiyosebashi (p 65R)	¥500	8:23	9:04	10:04	11:14	14:20	14:34	17:00	18:20*	18:55**
Iwayaji-mae (p 65R)	¥560	8:24	9:06		11:16		14:36			
Ishizuchi-tsuchikoya (p 75)	¥1920	9:49***					15:59***			

Stop	Fare							
Ishizuchi-tsuchikoya (p 75)					10:20***			16:35***
Iwayaji-mae (p 65R)	¥1570			11:05	11:35***	13:05	16:15	17:45***
Kiyosebashi (p 65R)	¥1610	7:07	10:27	11:07	11:37***	13:07	16:17	17:47***
Hatanogawa (p 65L)	¥1780	7:31	10:36	11:16	11:46***	13:16	16:26	17:56***
Kuma-eigyōshō (p 64R)	¥1920	7:48	10:43	11:23	11:53***	13:23	16:33	18:03***

67-a
Yasakaji 47
4.4km
Jōruriji 46
1.0km
R Chōchinya 長珍屋
089-963-0280
E.S.
1.6km
207
1.9km
川井
219
33
宮内
Town Office
Mura River 村川
Tobe River 砥部川
407
Mt. Ōtomo
砥部焼観光センター
Tobe-yaki Kankō Center
久谷町
100
88
Tobe-yaki Pottery Museum
砥部焼伝統産業会館
大南
五本松
大角蔵
外山
岩谷口
Shiogamori Bus Stop
塩ケ森バス停
Accessible Bus Stop from No.45 to No.46
200
岩谷
Tobe Town
砥部町
Matsuyama City
松山市
379
53
2km
2km
33

NOTE **The Legend of Emon Saburō** 衛門三郎伝説

Emon Saburō was a wealthy yet cruel man from Ehime prefecture who is considered by some to be the founder of the pilgrimage. Emon, in order to seek forgiveness from Kūkai for smashing his begging bowl, set out on the pilgrimage. On his 22nd circuit, Emon collapsed near Temple 12 and it is here that Kūkai appeared, forgave Emon and allowed him to be reborn as a human again. Many years later, a boy was born clutching a 5.4cm stone in his hand on which was written Emon Saburō. This stone can be seen at Temple 51, Ishiteji (Stone Hand Temple).

46 Jōruriji 四十六番 浄瑠璃寺

☎ 089-963-0279
S None
H Yakushi Nyorai
282 Jōruri-machi, Matsuyama City — Free of charge (10)
A By bus bound for Tobe from Matsuyama-shieki Stn. Get off at Nishino Bus Stop, about 45 min. walk.

Founded by 708 by Gyōki who carved a statue of Yakushi Nyorai. In 812, Kūkai came and restored the dilapidated buildings. From this time, it was considered a sacred site. Within the precincts there is a tree which is over 1,000 years old, a footprint stone and handprint stone of Buddha.

47 Yasakaji 四十七番 八坂寺

☎ 089-963-0271
S None
H Amida Nyorai
773 Yasaka, Jōruri-machi, Matsuyama City — Free of charge (30)
A By bus bound for Tobe from Matsuyama-shieki Stn. Get off at Nishino Bus Stop, about 30 min. walk.

In 701, the Lord of Iyo, Tamaoki, built the temple and later, Kūkai restored it. It is said that there were eight paths leading here, thus the name eight slope *(yasaka)*. It prospered as a place for Shugendō training.

Tobe-yaki Pottery
砥部焼

The clay used to produce china ware can be found in Tobe and there are over 100 kilns in the area. The traditional white-on-blue designs and the relatively heavy construction is a feature of Tobe-yaki. This local pottery is a nationally designated traditional craft.

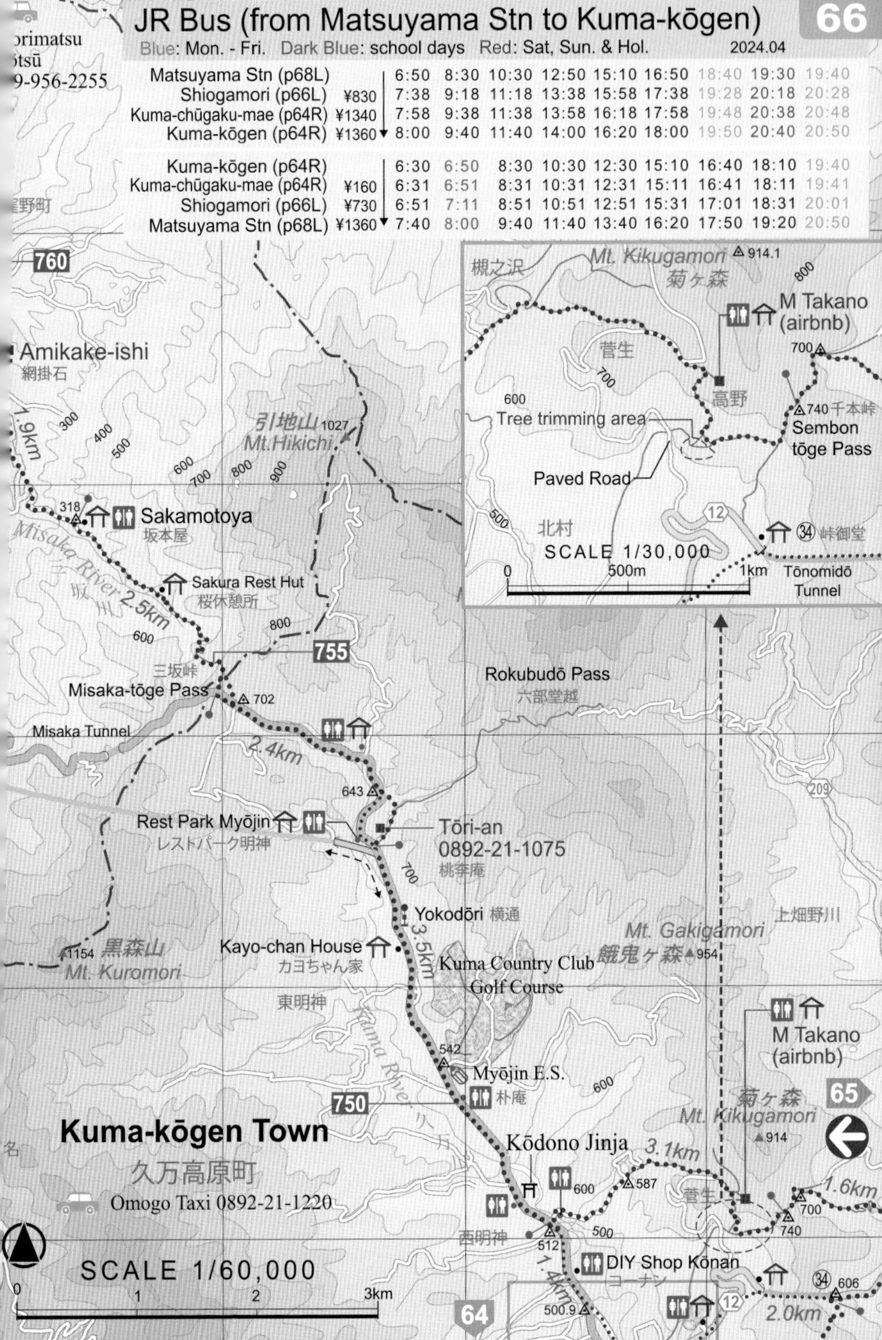

JR Bus (from Matsuyama Stn to Kuma-kōgen)

Blue: Mon. - Fri. Dark Blue: school days Red: Sat, Sun. & Hol. 2024.04

Stop	Fare									
Matsuyama Stn (p68L)		6:50	8:30	10:30	12:50	15:10	16:50	18:40	19:30	19:40
Shiogamori (p66L)	¥830	7:38	9:18	11:18	13:38	15:58	17:38	19:28	20:18	20:28
Kuma-chūgaku-mae (p64R)	¥1340	7:58	9:38	11:38	13:58	16:18	17:58	19:48	20:38	20:48
Kuma-kōgen (p64R)	¥1360	8:00	9:40	11:40	14:00	16:20	18:00	19:50	20:40	20:50

Stop	Fare									
Kuma-kōgen (p64R)		6:30	6:50	8:30	10:30	12:30	15:10	16:40	18:10	19:40
Kuma-chūgaku-mae (p64R)	¥160	6:31	6:51	8:31	10:31	12:31	15:11	16:41	18:11	19:41
Shiogamori (p66L)	¥730	6:51	7:11	8:51	10:51	12:51	15:31	17:01	18:31	20:01
Matsuyama Stn (p68L)	¥1360	7:40	8:00	9:40	11:40	13:40	16:20	17:50	19:20	20:50

orimatsu
ōtsū
9-956-2255
760
Amikake-ishi
網掛石
1.9km
引地山 1027
Mt.Hikichi
318
Sakamotoya
坂本屋
Misaka River
三坂川
2.5km
Sakura Rest Hut
桜休憩所
755
三坂峠
Misaka-tōge Pass
702
Misaka Tunnel
2.4km
643
Rest Park Myōjin
レストパーク明神
Tōri-an
0892-21-1075
桃李庵
Yokodōri 横通
3.5km
Kayo-chan House
カヨちゃん家
1154 黒森山
Mt. Kuromori
東明神
Kuma Country Club
Golf Course
Kuma River
542
Myōjin E.S.
朴庵
750
Kuma-kōgen Town
久万高原町
Omogo Taxi 0892-21-1220
SCALE 1/60,000
0
1
2
3km
Kōdono Jinja
3.1km
587
512
西明神
1.4km
DIY Shop Kōnan
コーナン
500.9
64
Rokubudō Pass
六部堂越
209
上畑野川
Mt. Gakigamori
餓鬼ヶ森 954
M Takano
(airbnb)
65
菊ヶ森
Mt. Kikugamori
914
菅生
1.6km
700
740
606
2.0km
槻之沢
Mt. Kikugamori 914.1
菊ヶ森
M Takano
(airbnb)
菅生
高野
Tree trimming area
Paved Road
740 千本峠
Sembon
tōge Pass
北村
峠御堂
SCALE 1/30,000
0
500m
1km
Tōnomidō
Tunnel

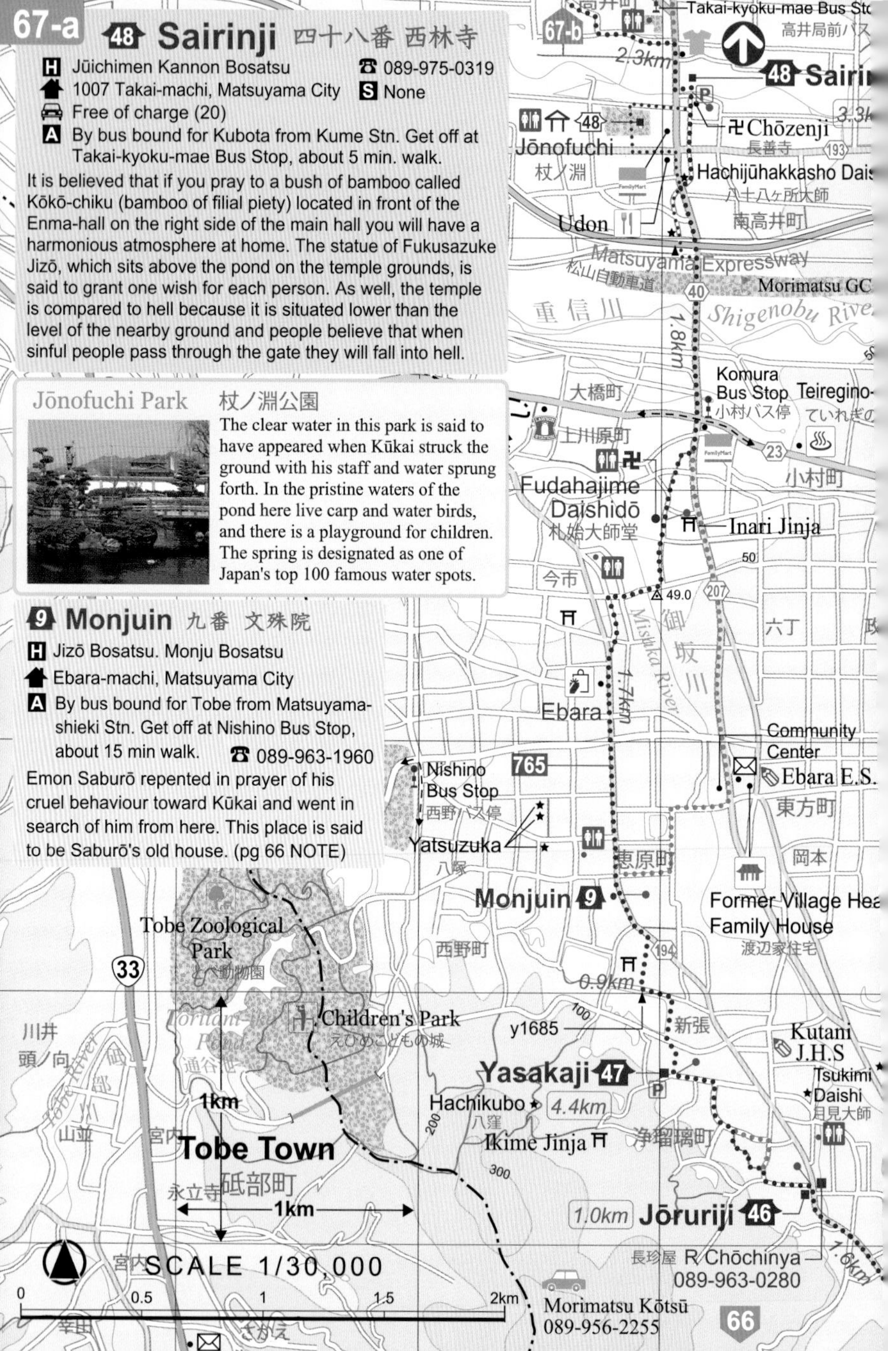

48 Sairinji 四十八番 西林寺

- H Jūichimen Kannon Bosatsu
- ☎ 089-975-0319
- 1007 Takai-machi, Matsuyama City
- S None
- Free of charge (20)
- A By bus bound for Kubota from Kume Stn. Get off at Takai-kyoku-mae Bus Stop, about 5 min. walk.

It is believed that if you pray to a bush of bamboo called Kōkō-chiku (bamboo of filial piety) located in front of the Enma-hall on the right side of the main hall you will have a harmonious atmosphere at home. The statue of Fukusazuke Jizō, which sits above the pond on the temple grounds, is said to grant one wish for each person. As well, the temple is compared to hell because it is situated lower than the level of the nearby ground and people believe that when sinful people pass through the gate they will fall into hell.

Jōnofuchi Park 杖ノ淵公園

The clear water in this park is said to have appeared when Kūkai struck the ground with his staff and water sprung forth. In the pristine waters of the pond here live carp and water birds, and there is a playground for children. The spring is designated as one of Japan's top 100 famous water spots.

9 Monjuin 九番 文殊院

- H Jizō Bosatsu. Monju Bosatsu
- Ebara-machi, Matsuyama City
- A By bus bound for Tobe from Matsuyama-shieki Stn. Get off at Nishino Bus Stop, about 15 min walk.
- ☎ 089-963-1960

Emon Saburō repented in prayer of his cruel behaviour toward Kūkai and went in search of him from here. This place is said to be Saburō's old house. (pg 66 NOTE)

67-b
Takai-kyoku-mae Bus Stop
高井局前バス
2.3km
48 Sairinji
3.3km
Jōnofuchi
杖ノ淵
卍 Chōzenji
長善寺
193
Hachijūhakkasho Daishi
八十八ヶ所大師
南高井町
Udon
Matsuyama Expressway
松山自動車道
Morimatsu GC
40
重信川
Shigenobu River
1.8km
Komura Bus Stop
小村バス停
Teiregino-
ていれぎの
大橋町
上川原町
23
小村町
Fudahajime Daishidō
札始大師堂
Inari Jinja
50
今市
49.0
207
御坂川
Misaka River
六丁
Ebara
1.7km
765
Community Center
Nishino Bus Stop
西野バス停
Ebara E.S.
東方町
Yatsuzuka
八塚
恵原町
岡本
Monjuin 9
Former Village Head Family House
渡辺家住宅
Tobe Zoological Park
とべ動物園
33
西野町
194
0.9km
Children's Park
えひめこどもの城
y1685
新張
Kutani J.H.S
川井
頭ノ向
Tobe River
通谷
Yasakaji 47
Tsukimi Daishi
月見大師
1km
Hachikubo
八窪
4.4km
山並
宮内
Tobe Town
砥部町
Ikime Jinja
浄瑠璃町
永立寺
1km
1.0km
Jōruriji 46
1.6km
宮内
SCALE 1/30,000
0 0.5 1 1.5 2km
長珍屋 R Chōchinya
089-963-0280
Morimatsu Kōtsū
089-956-2255

50 Hantaji 五十番 繁多寺

- H Yakushi Nyorai
- ☎ 089-975-0910
- 32 Hatadera-machi Matsuyama City
- S None
- Free of charge (5)
- A By bus bound for Tsuda-danchi-mae from Kume Stn. Get off at Hantaji-guchi Bus Stop, about 10 min. walk.

Gyōki founded this temple around 750 and later, Kūkai as well as Ippen Shōnin (1239-1289), the founder of Jishū Sect also trained and studied here. Within the Shōten Hall there is a Kangiten (protective deity) which is said to help with passing exams, having a prosperous business, warding off misfortune and assuring a good relationship between husband and wife. The bell was made in 1696 due to the contributions from a wide range of people.

49 Jōdoji 四十九番 浄土寺

- H Shaka Nyorai
- ☎ 089-975-1730
- 1198 Takanoko-machi Matsuyama City
- S None
- Charge (20)
- A About 5 min. walk from Iyotetsu Railway Kume Stn.

This temple was founded during the Tenpyō era (729-749) by a Buddhist priest, Emyō, and consisted of numerous buildings; however, it was totally destroyed in the 14th century. Kūya (903-962) stayed here for three years and when he left, the people of the village asked that he carve a statue of himself. "Jōdo" is a pure land where the Buddha lives.

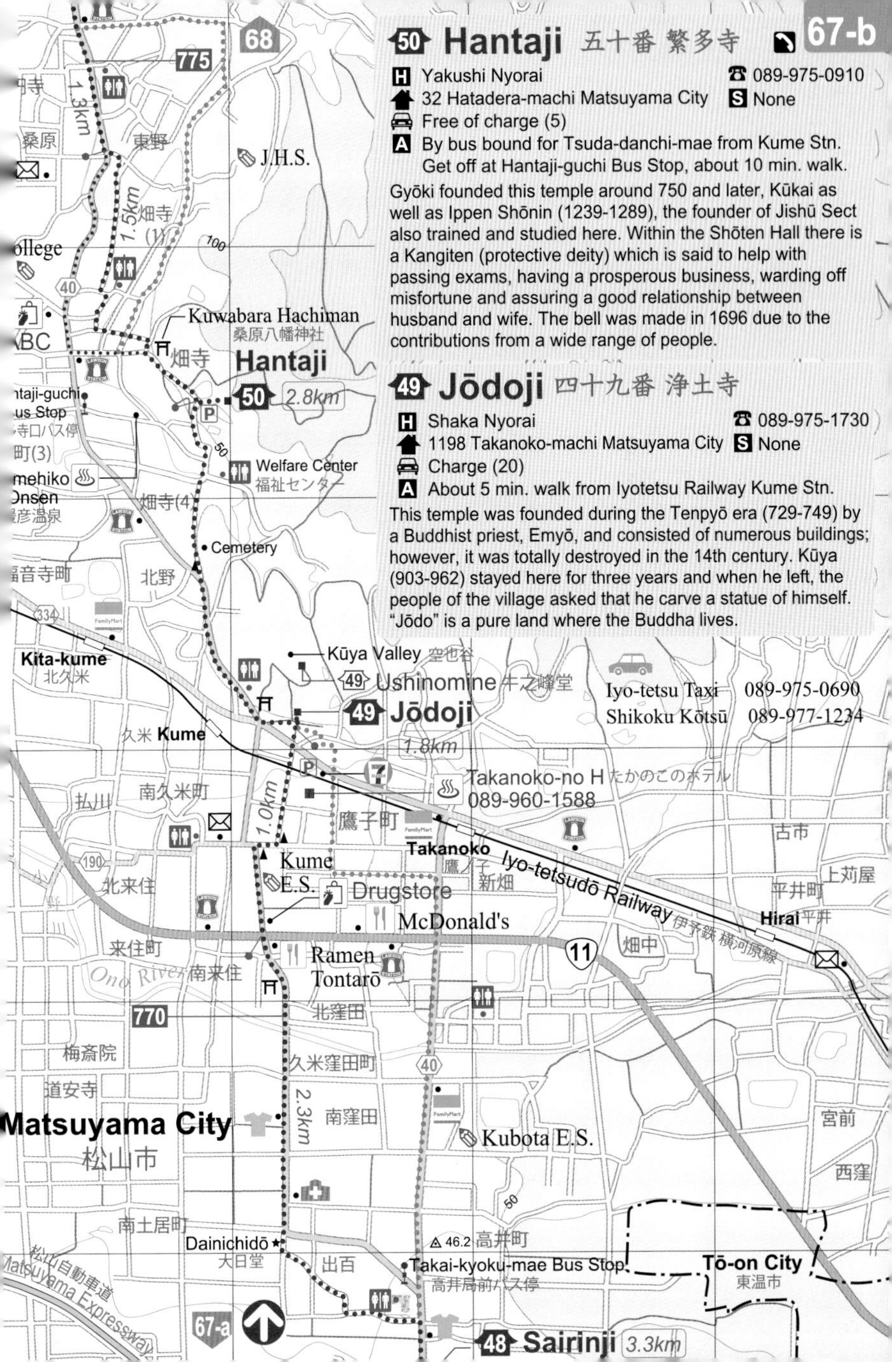

68
775
1.3km
1.5km
東野
桑原
J.H.S.
College
40
Kuwabara Hachiman
桑原八幡神社
畑寺
Hantaji
50 2.8km
Hantaji-guchi Bus Stop
繁多寺口バス停
Umehiko Onsen
梅彦温泉
Welfare Center
福祉センター
Cemetery
北野
334
Kita-kume
北久米
Kūya Valley 空也谷
49 Ushinomine 牛之峰堂
49 Jōdoji
1.8km
Iyo-tetsu Taxi 089-975-0690
Shikoku Kōtsū 089-977-1234
久米 Kume
南久米町
Takanoko-no H たかのこのホテル
089-960-1588
鷹子町
1.0km
Takanoko
鷹ノ子
Kume E.S.
Drugstore
McDonald's
Iyo-tetsudō Railway 伊予鉄 横河原線
190
北来住
来住町
Ramen Tontarō
Ono River
南来住
11
畑中
Hirai 平井
平井町
上苅屋
古市
新畑
770
北窪田
久米窪田町
梅斎院
道安寺
40
2.3km
南窪田
Matsuyama City
松山市
Kubota E.S.
宮前
西窪
南土居町
Dainichidō 大日堂
46.2 高井町
出百
Takai-kyoku-mae Bus Stop
高井局前バス停
Tō-on City
東温市
松山自動車道
Matsuyama Expressway
67-a
48 Sairinji 3.3km

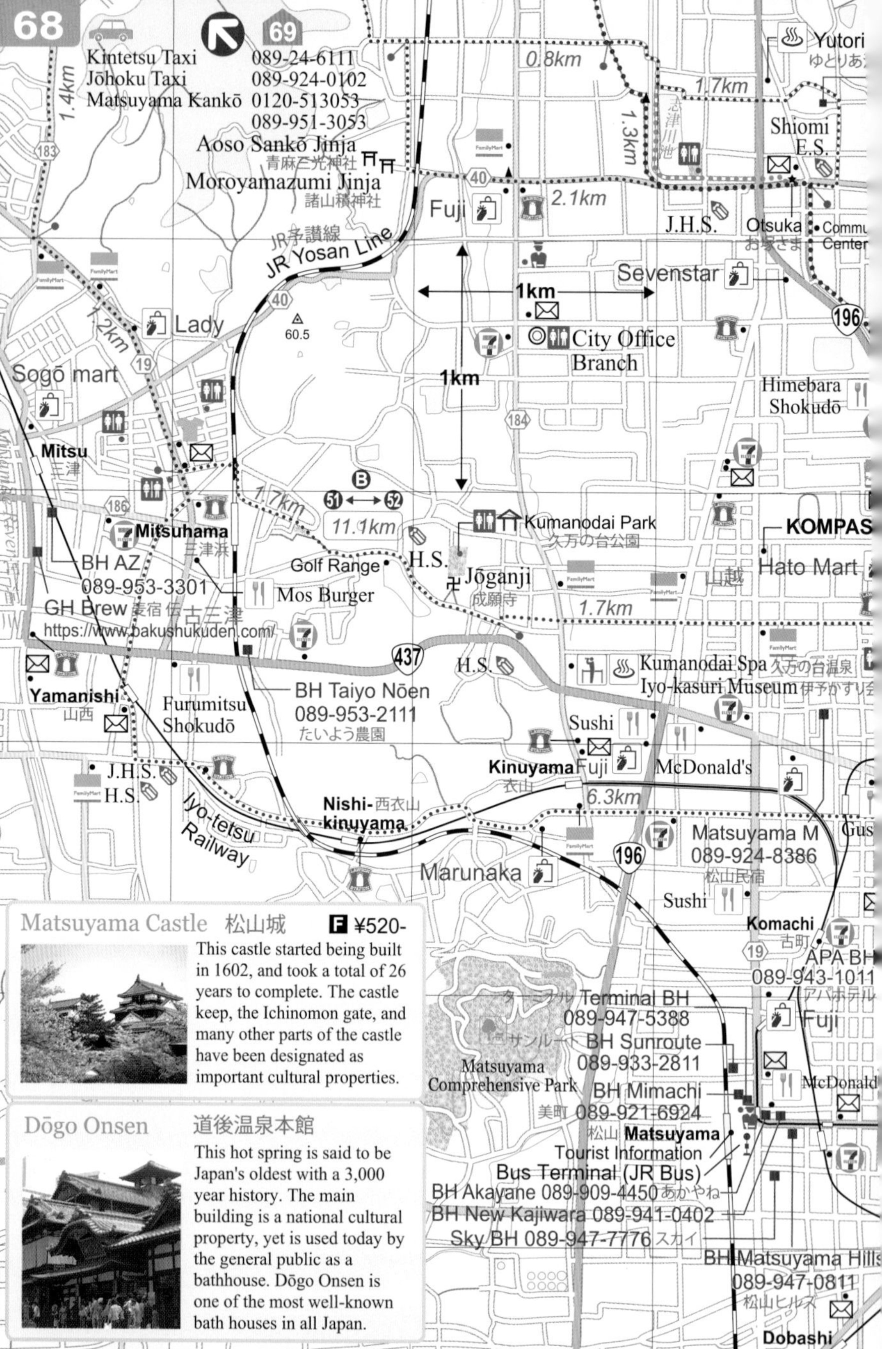
69
Kintetsu Taxi 089-24-6111
Jōhoku Taxi 089-924-0102
Matsuyama Kankō 0120-513053
089-951-3053
Aoso Sankō Jinja
青麻三光神社
Moroyamazumi Jinja
諸山積神社
JR予讃線
JR Yosan Line
0.8km
1.7km
1.3km
2.1km
1.4km
1.2km
1.7km
11.1km
1.7km
6.3km
Yutori
ゆとりあ
Shiomi E.S.
Fuji
J.H.S.
Otsuka
お塚さま
Commu Center
Sevenstar
1km
1km
60.5
City Office Branch
Lady
Sogō mart
Himebara Shokudō
Mitsu
三津
Mitsuhama
三津浜
BH AZ
089-953-3301
GH Brew 麦宿 伝 古三津
https://www.bakushukuden.com/
Mos Burger
Golf Range
H.S.
Kumanodai Park
久万の台公園
Jōganji
成願寺
KOMPAS
Hato Mart
山越
Yamanishi
山西
Furumitsu Shokudō
BH Taiyo Nōen
089-953-2111
たいよう農園
H.S.
Kumanodai Spa 久万の台温泉
Iyo-kasuri Museum 伊予かすり会
Sushi
Kinuyama
衣山
Fuji
McDonald's
J.H.S.
H.S.
Iyo-tetsu Railway
Nishi-kinuyama
西衣山
Marunaka
Matsuyama M
089-924-8386
松山民宿
Sushi
Komachi
古町
APA BH
089-943-1011
アパホテル
Fuji
Terminal BH
ターミナル
089-947-5388
サンルート
BH Sunroute
089-933-2811
Matsuyama Comprehensive Park
BH Mimachi
美町 089-921-6924
松山 Matsuyama
Tourist Information
Bus Terminal (JR Bus)
BH Akayane 089-909-4450 あかやね
BH New Kajiwara 089-941-0402
Sky BH 089-947-7776 スカイ
BH Matsuyama Hills
089-947-0811
松山ヒルズ
McDonald
Dobashi
183
19
186
437
196
40
184

Matsuyama Castle 松山城

F ¥520-

This castle started being built in 1602, and took a total of 26 years to complete. The castle keep, the Ichinomon gate, and many other parts of the castle have been designated as important cultural properties.

Dōgo Onsen 道後温泉本館

This hot spring is said to be Japan's oldest with a 3,000 year history. The main building is a national cultural property, yet is used today by the general public as a bathhouse. Dōgo Onsen is one of the most well-known bath houses in all Japan.

51 Ishiteji 五十一番 石手寺

☎ 089-977-0870
S None

H Yakushi Nyorai
2-9-21 Ishite, Matsuyama City
Charge (80)

A By bus bound for Oku-dōgo from Matsuyama Stn. Get off at Ishiteji-mae Bus Stop.

In 729, Gyōki founded this temple and Kūkai later changed the temple to Shingon. In 892, the name was changed to "Ishite-ji" (Rock Hand Temple) which originates from the legend of Emon Saburō and a child being born here with a rock in his hand. The grilled *mochi* that is on sale here is well known and in olden times used to be given out for free to pilgrims.

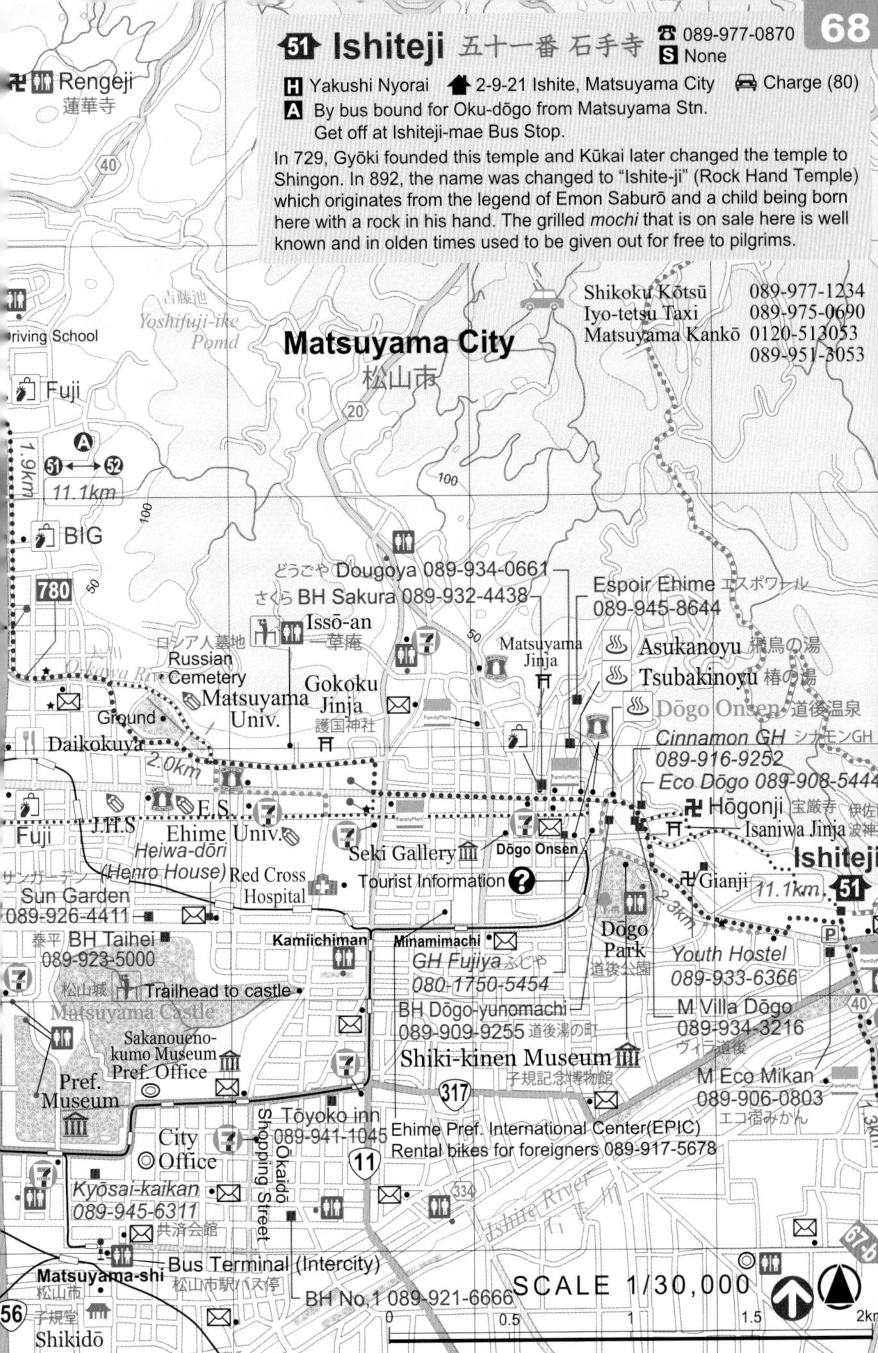

Rengeji
蓮華寺
40
吉藤池
Yoshifuji-ike Pond
Driving School
Matsuyama City
松山市
Shikoku Kōtsū 089-977-1234
Iyo-tetsu Taxi 089-975-0690
Matsuyama Kankō 0120-513053
089-951-3053
Fuji
20
1.9km
51 ↔ 52
11.1km
100
BIG
780
50
どうごや Dougoya 089-934-0661
さくら BH Sakura 089-932-4438
Espoir Ehime エスポワール
089-945-8644
Issō-an
一草庵
ロシア人墓地
Russian Cemetery
大川
Okawa River
Matsuyama Jinja
Asukanoyu 飛鳥の湯
Tsubakinoyu 椿の湯
Dōgo Onsen 道後温泉
Matsuyama Univ.
Gokoku Jinja
護国神社
Ground
Daikokuya
2.0km
Cinnamon GH シナモンGH
089-916-9252
Eco Dōgo 089-908-5444
Hōgonji 宝厳寺
Isaniwa Jinja
伊佐爾波神社
E.S.
J.H.S
Fuji
Ehime Univ.
Heiwa-dōri
(Henro House)
Seki Gallery
Dōgo Onsen
Ishiteji
サンガーデン
Sun Garden
089-926-4411
Red Cross Hospital
Tourist Information
Gianji
11.1km
51
2.3km
泰平 BH Taihei
089-923-5000
Kamiichiman
Minamimachi
GH Fujiya ふじや
080-1750-5454
Dōgo Park
道後公園
Youth Hostel
089-933-6366
松山城
Trailhead to castle
Matsuyama Castle
BH Dōgo-yunomachi
089-909-9255 道後湯の町
M Villa Dōgo
089-934-3216
ヴィラ道後
40
Sakanoueno-kumo Museum
Pref. Office
Shiki-kinen Museum
子規記念博物館
M Eco Mikan
089-906-0803
エコ宿みかん
Pref. Museum
317
Tōyoko inn
089-941-1045
Ōkaidō Shopping Street
Ehime Pref. International Center(EPIC)
Rental bikes for foreigners 089-917-5678
1.3km
City Office
11
Kyōsai-kaikan
089-945-6311
共済会館
334
Ishite River
石手川
67-b
Bus Terminal (Intercity)
松山市駅バス停
Matsuyama-shi
松山市
BH No,1 089-921-6666
SCALE 1/30,000
0 0.5 1 1.5 2km
56
子規堂
Shikidō

52 Taisanji 五十二番 太山寺

☎ 089-978-0329 | S None

H Jūichimen Kannon Bosatsu | 1730 Taisanji-chō, Matsuyama City | Free of charge (50)

A By bus bound for Taisanji from Mitsuhama Stn. Get off at the last stop (Taisanji), about 10 min. walk.

In 586, when Mano Kogorō was travelling by boat from Kyūshū to Ōsaka City a severe storm came and the sailors prayed to Kannon for protection. It is said that to show his gratitude, he constructed a temple here in one night. The main hall was built in 1305 and is designated as a National Treasure.

53 Enmyōji 五十三番 円明寺

☎ 089-978-1129 | S None

H Amida Nyorai | 1-182 Wake-machi, Matsuyama City | Free of charge (10)

A About 5 min. walk from JR Yosan Line Iyo-Wake Stn.

This temple was founded by Gyōki during the mid-8th century; however, it was moved to its present location in 1633. In 1921, Frederick Starr, an anthropologist professor from the University of Chicago, visited this temple and was shown the oldest bronze nameplate (osamefuda) that exists along the Shikoku Pilgrimage route. (Not available for public viewing) To the left of the Daishi hall is a lantern on which is carved a statue of Mary, disguised as Kannon, which would have been worshipped by the hidden Christians.

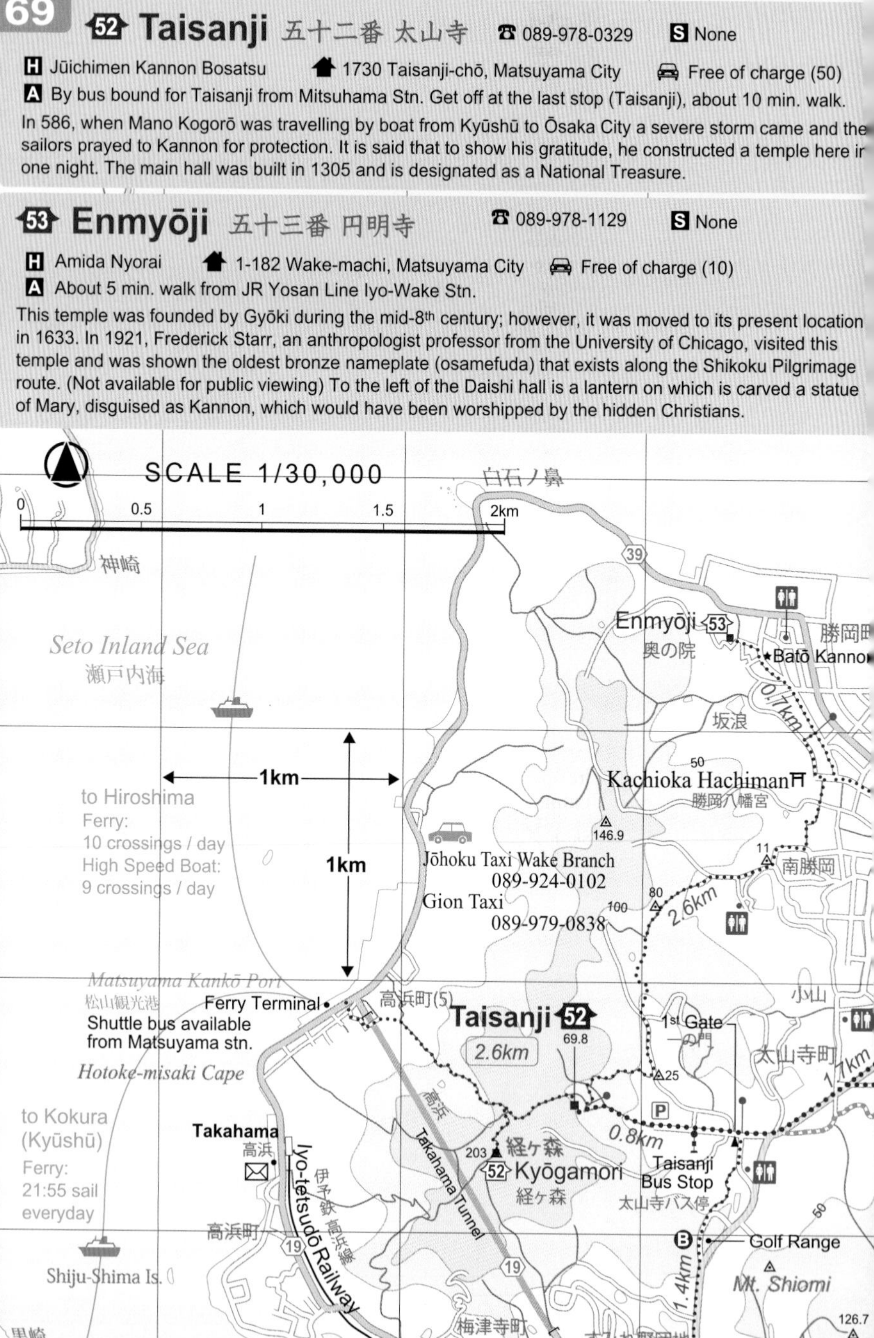

SCALE 1/30,000
0
0.5
1
1.5
2km
白石ノ鼻
神崎
39
Seto Inland Sea
瀬戸内海
Enmyōji 53
奥の院
勝岡町
★Batō Kannon
0.7km
坂浪
50
Kachioka Hachiman
勝岡八幡宮
1km
1km
to Hiroshima
Ferry:
10 crossings / day
High Speed Boat:
9 crossings / day
146.9
Jōhoku Taxi Wake Branch
089-924-0102
Gion Taxi
089-979-0838
11
南勝岡
80
100
2.6km
Matsuyama Kankō Port
松山観光港
Ferry Terminal
Shuttle bus available
from Matsuyama stn.
高浜町(5)
Taisanji 52
69.8
2.6km
1st Gate
一の門
小山
太山寺町
1.7km
Hotoke-misaki Cape
25
P
to Kokura
(Kyūshū)
Ferry:
21:55 sail
everyday
Takahama
高浜
高浜
Takahama Tunnel
203
経ケ森
52 Kyōgamori
経ケ森
0.8km
Taisanji
Bus Stop
太山寺バス停
Iyo-tetsudō Railway
伊予鉄高浜線
高浜町
19
19
60
B
Golf Range
Shiju-Shima Is.
1.4km
Mt. Shiomi
126.7
黒崎
梅津寺町

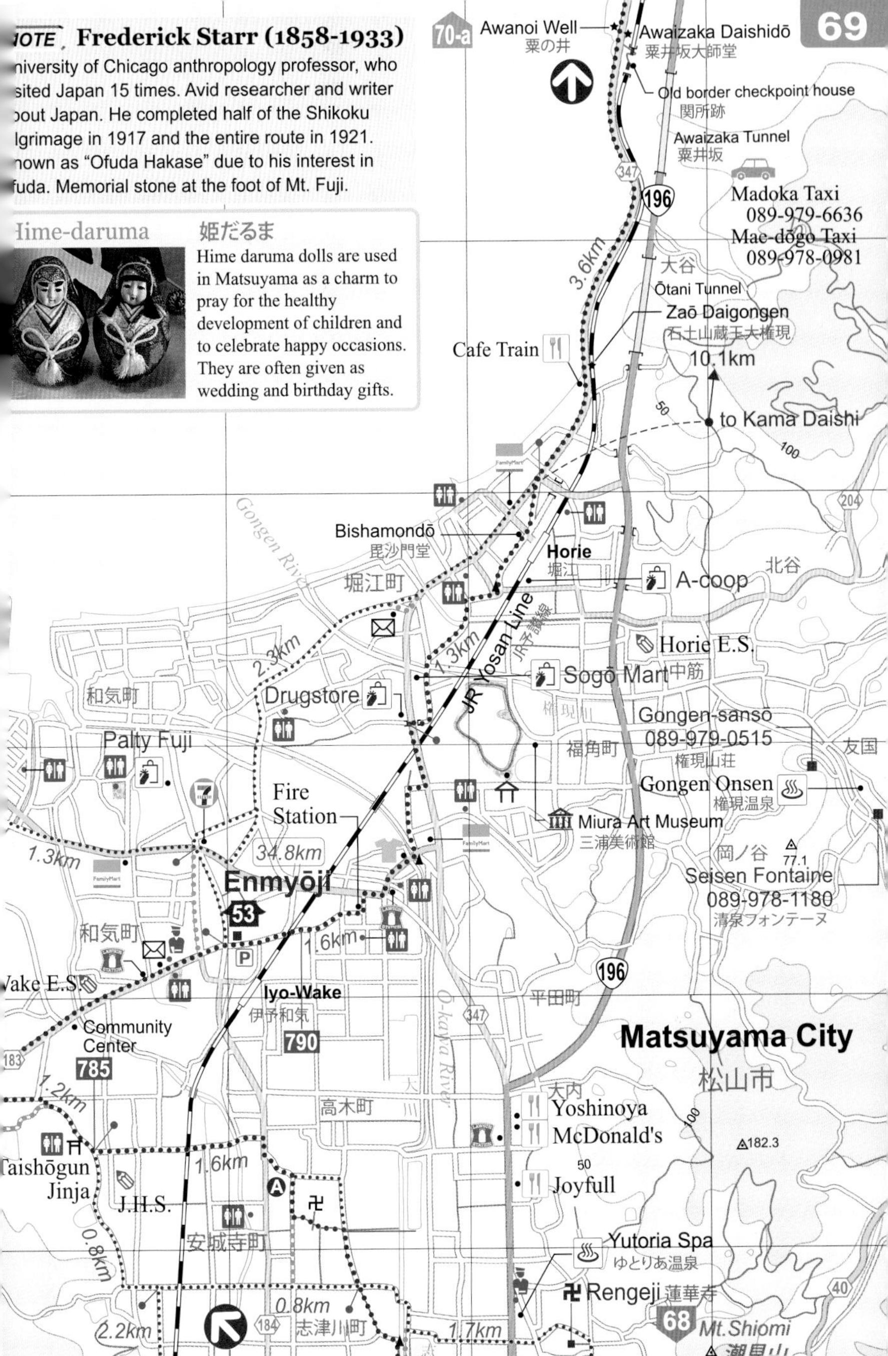

NOTE Frederick Starr (1858-1933)
niversity of Chicago anthropology professor, who
sited Japan 15 times. Avid researcher and writer
bout Japan. He completed half of the Shikoku
lgrimage in 1917 and the entire route in 1921.
nown as "Ofuda Hakase" due to his interest in
fuda. Memorial stone at the foot of Mt. Fuji.
Hime-daruma
姫だるま
Hime daruma dolls are used in Matsuyama as a charm to pray for the healthy development of children and to celebrate happy occasions. They are often given as wedding and birthday gifts.
70-a
Awanoi Well
粟の井
Awaizaka Daishidō
粟井坂大師堂
Old border checkpoint house
関所跡
Awaizaka Tunnel
粟井坂
347
196
Madoka Taxi
089-979-6636
Mae-dōgo Taxi
089-978-0981
3.6km
大谷
Ōtani Tunnel
Zaō Daigongen
石土山蔵王大権現
10.1km
Cafe Train
to Kama Daishi
50
100
204
Bishamondō
毘沙門堂
Gongen River
Horie
堀江
堀江町
A-coop
北谷
JR Yosan Line
JR予讃線
Horie E.S.
2.3km
1.3km
Sogō Mart
中筋
Drugstore
和気町
権現山
Gongen-sansō
089-979-0515
権現山荘
Palty Fuji
福角町
友国
Gongen Onsen
権現温泉
Fire Station
Miura Art Museum
三浦美術館
1.3km
34.8km
岡ノ谷
77.1
Enmyōji
53
Seisen Fontaine
089-978-1180
清泉フォンテーヌ
和気町
1.6km
P
Wake E.S.
196
Iyo-Wake
伊予和気
平田町
Community Center
790
347
O-kawa River
Matsuyama City
松山市
183
785
1.2km
大内
高木町
Yoshinoya
McDonald's
Taishōgun Jinja
1.6km
182.3
J.H.S.
50
Joyfull
0.8km
安城寺町
Yutoria Spa
ゆとりあ温泉
Rengeji 蓮華寺
0.8km
40
2.2km
184
志津川町
1.7km
68
Mt. Shiomi
潮見山

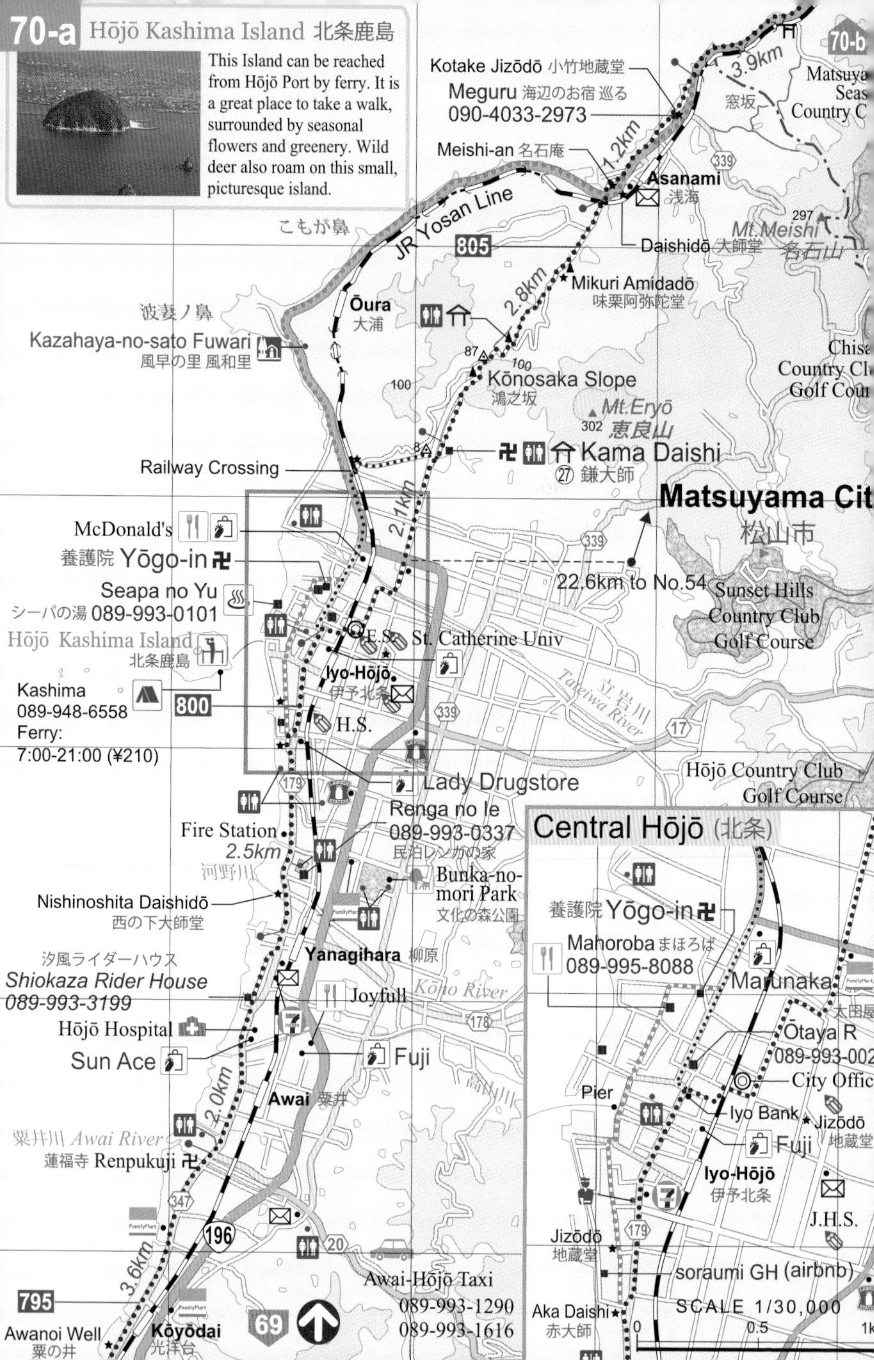
70-a
Hōjō Kashima Island 北条鹿島
This Island can be reached from Hōjō Port by ferry. It is a great place to take a walk, surrounded by seasonal flowers and greenery. Wild deer also roam on this small, picturesque island.
70-b
Kotake Jizōdō 小竹地蔵堂
Meguru 海辺のお宿 巡る
090-4033-2973
3.9km
Matsuya
Seas
Country C
窓坂
Meishi-an 名石庵
1.2km
339
Asanami
浅海
297
Mt.Meishi
名石山
Daishidō 大師堂
JR Yosan Line
805
こもが鼻
2.8km
Mikuri Amidadō
味栗阿弥陀堂
Ōura
大浦
波妻ノ鼻
Kazahaya-no-sato Fuwari
風早の里 風和里
87
100
Kōnosaka Slope
鴻之坂
Chisa
Country Cl
Golf Cour
Mt.Eryō
302
恵良山
Kama Daishi
㉗ 鎌大師
Railway Crossing
Matsuyama Cit
松山市
2.1km
McDonald's
養護院 Yōgo-in
339
22.6km to No.54
Seapa no Yu
シーパの湯 089-993-0101
Sunset Hills
Country Club
Golf Course
Hōjō Kashima Island
北条鹿島
E.S.
St. Catherine Univ
Iyo-Hōjō
伊予北条
Kashima
089-948-6558
Ferry:
7:00-21:00 (¥210)
800
H.S.
339
立岩川
Tateiwa River
17
Hōjō Country Club
Golf Course
179
Lady Drugstore
Renga no Ie
089-993-0337
民泊レンガの家
Fire Station
2.5km
河野川
Central Hōjō (北条)
Bunka-no-mori Park
文化の森公園
Nishinoshita Daishidō
西の下大師堂
養護院 Yōgo-in
Mahoroba まほろば
089-995-8088
汐風ライダーハウス
Shiokaza Rider House
089-993-3199
Yanagihara 柳原
Marunaka
Joyfull
Kōno River
太田屋
Ōtaya R
089-993-002
Hōjō Hospital
178
Sun Ace
Fuji
City Office
Pier
Iyo Bank
Jizōdō
地蔵堂
2.0km
Awai 粟井
Fuji
粟井川 Awai River
蓮福寺 Renpukuji
Iyo-Hōjō
伊予北条
347
J.H.S.
196
20
179
Jizōdō
地蔵堂
3.6km
Awai-Hōjō Taxi
089-993-1290
089-993-1616
soraumi GH (airbnb)
SCALE 1/30,000
795
Aka Daishi
赤大師
0
0.5
1km
Awanoi Well
粟の井
Kōyōdai
光洋台
69

Tile Museum かわら館

F ¥210- C Mon.
O 9:00am-5:00pm

The area of Kikuma is well-known for making roof tiles and this 4-storey facility explains the history and manufacture of tiles as well as displays various tiles from around the world.

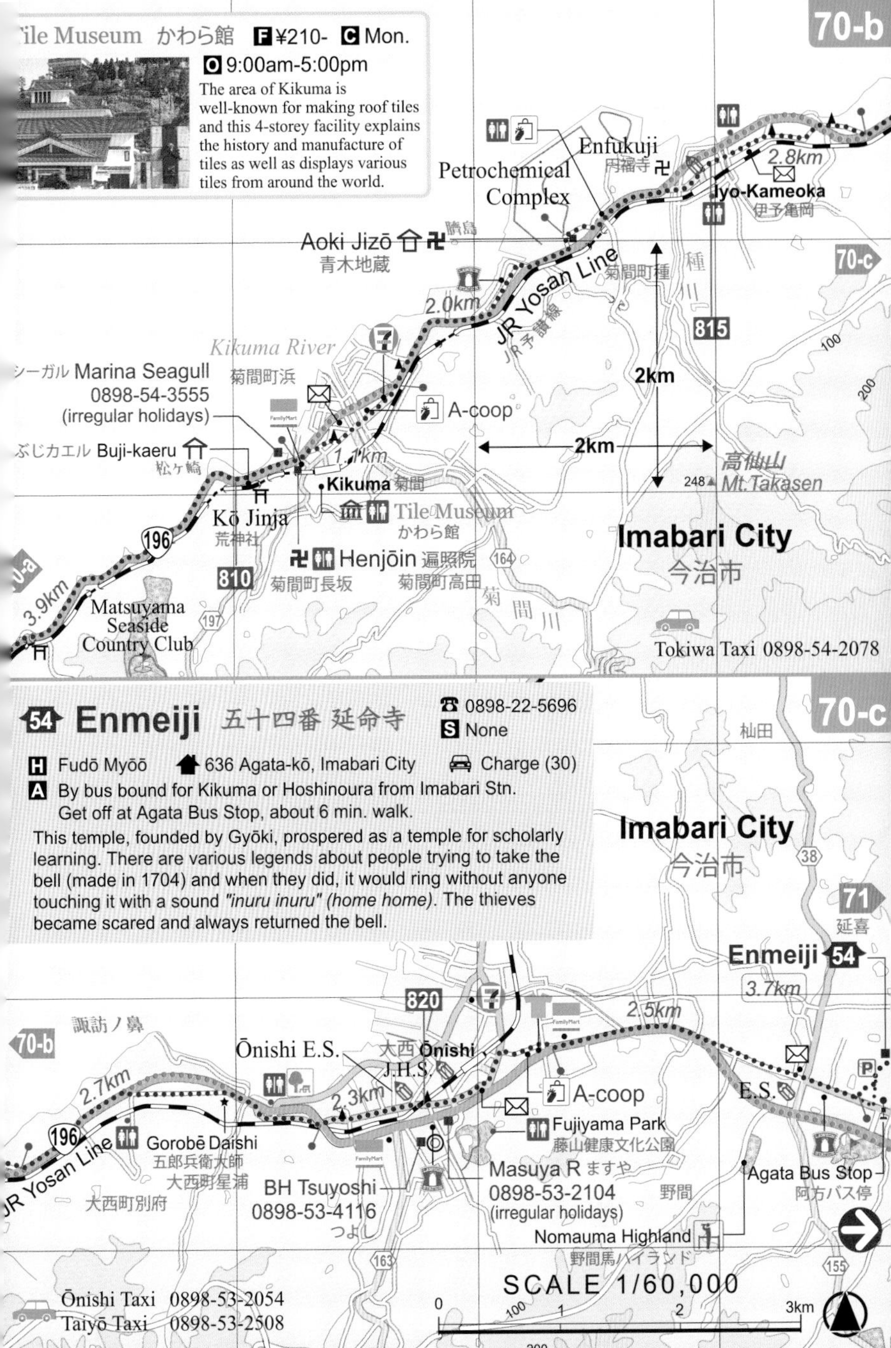

Enfukuji
円福寺
Petrochemical Complex
Iyo-Kameoka
伊予亀岡
2.8km
Aoki Jizō
青木地蔵
鴨島
菊間町種
種川
70-c
JR Yosan Line
JR予讃線
2.0km
815
Kikuma River
シーガル Marina Seagull
0898-54-3555
(irregular holidays)
菊間町浜
A-coop
2km
2km
ぶじカエル Buji-kaeru
松ヶ崎
1.1km
高仙山
248
Mt.Takasen
Kikuma 菊間
Kō Jinja
荒神社
Tile Museum
かわら館
196
Imabari City
今治市
Henjōin 遍照院
810
菊間町長坂
菊間町高田
164
菊間川
3.9km
Matsuyama Seaside Country Club
197
Tokiwa Taxi 0898-54-2078

54 Enmeiji 五十四番 延命寺

☎ 0898-22-5696
S None

H Fudō Myōō
636 Agata-kō, Imabari City
Charge (30)

A By bus bound for Kikuma or Hoshinoura from Imabari Stn. Get off at Agata Bus Stop, about 6 min. walk.

This temple, founded by Gyōki, prospered as a temple for scholarly learning. There are various legends about people trying to take the bell (made in 1704) and when they did, it would ring without anyone touching it with a sound *"inuru inuru" (home home)*. The thieves became scared and always returned the bell.

杣田
Imabari City
今治市
38
71
延喜
Enmeiji 54
3.7km
820
2.5km
諏訪ノ鼻
70-b
Ōnishi E.S.
大西 Ōnishi J.H.S.
2.7km
2.3km
A-coop
E.S.
Fujiyama Park
藤山健康文化公園
196
JR Yosan Line
Gorobē Daishi
五郎兵衛大師
大西町星浦
大西町別府
BH Tsuyoshi
0898-53-4116
つよし
Masuya R ますや
0898-53-2104
(irregular holidays)
野間
Agata Bus Stop
阿方バス停
Nomauma Highland
野間馬ハイランド
163
155
SCALE 1/60,000
0 1 2 3km
100
200
Ōnishi Taxi 0898-53-2054
Taiyō Taxi 0898-53-2508

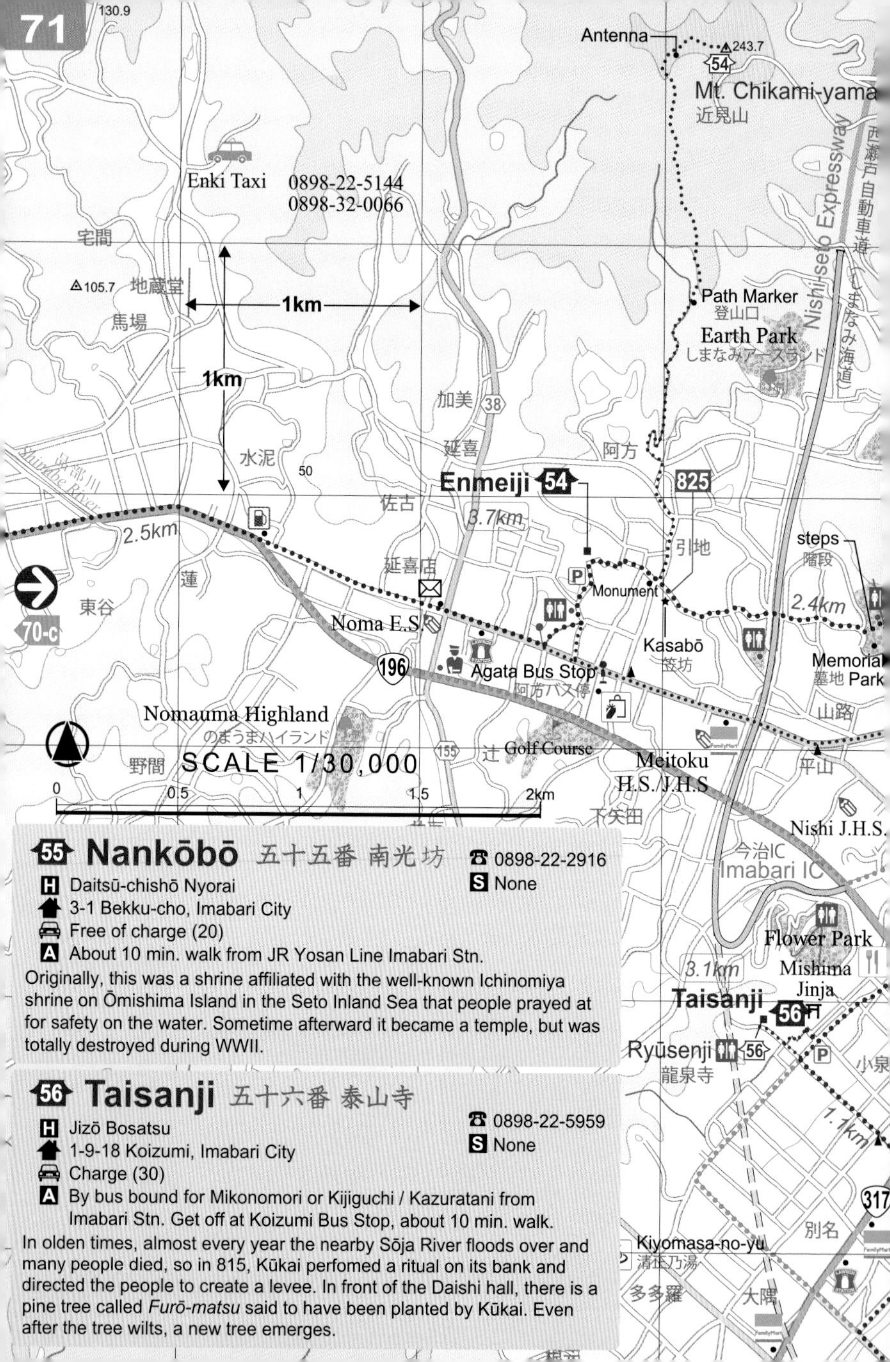

130.9
Antenna
243.7
54
Mt. Chikami-yama
近見山
Nishi-seto Expressway
西瀬戸自動車道（しまなみ海道）
Enki Taxi
0898-22-5144
0898-32-0066
宅間
105.7
地蔵堂
馬場
1km
1km
Path Marker
登山口
Earth Park
しまなみアースランド
加美
38
延喜
阿方
水泥
50
Shirabe River
Enmeiji 54
825
佐古
3.7km
2.5km
引地
steps
階段
延喜店
Monument
2.4km
蓮
東谷
70-c
Noma E.S.
Kasabō
笠坊
196
Agata Bus Stop
阿方バス停
Memorial Park
墓地
山路
Nomauma Highland
のまうまハイランド
155
辻
Golf Course
Meitoku H.S./J.H.S
平山
野間
SCALE 1/30,000
0
0.5
1
1.5
2km
下矢田
Nishi J.H.S.
今治IC
Imabari IC
Flower Park
3.1km
Mishima Jinja
Taisanji
56
Ryūsenji
56
龍泉寺
小泉
1.1km
317
別名
Kiyomasa-no-yu
清正乃湯
多多羅
大隅

55 Nankōbō 五十五番 南光坊

☎ 0898-22-2916
S None

H Daitsū-chishō Nyorai
3-1 Bekku-cho, Imabari City
Free of charge (20)
A About 10 min. walk from JR Yosan Line Imabari Stn.

Originally, this was a shrine affiliated with the well-known Ichinomiya shrine on Ōmishima Island in the Seto Inland Sea that people prayed at for safety on the water. Sometime afterward it became a temple, but was totally destroyed during WWII.

56 Taisanji 五十六番 泰山寺

☎ 0898-22-5959
S None

H Jizō Bosatsu
1-9-18 Koizumi, Imabari City
Charge (30)
A By bus bound for Mikonomori or Kijiguchi / Kazuratani from Imabari Stn. Get off at Koizumi Bus Stop, about 10 min. walk.

In olden times, almost every year the nearby Sōja River floods over and many people died, so in 815, Kūkai perfomed a ritual on its bank and directed the people to create a levee. In front of the Daishi hall, there is a pine tree called *Furō-matsu* said to have been planted by Kūkai. Even after the tree wilts, a new tree emerges.

ADVICE 横峰寺の打ち方

Going to Yokomineji

It takes about three hours to reach Yokomineji (p73-b) from the intersection at Route 11 and since it takes just less than three hours to go from Yokomineji to Kōonji (No. 61), many people visit Kōonji and Hōjuji (no.62) one day and go to Yokomineji the next morning.

Imabari Hospital
Shimanami-kaidō しまなみ海道
JR Yosan Line JR予讃線
Seto Inland Sea 瀬戸内海
Jinkuji 神供寺
Ōyamazumi Jinja 大山祇神社
55 Nankōbō 3.1km
Kōyasan Imabari Branch 高野山今治別院
GH Orenge no kaze 0898-52-8758 オレンジの風
BR Shōfuku 0898-32-7555 笑福
Komechō R 0898-32-0554 米長
Imabari Plaza BH 0898-25-2500 今治プラザ
City Office
BH Port side 0898-32-1515 ポートサイド
Imabari Dai-ichi BH 0898-22-1320 今治第一
Imabari Castle 今治城
BH Crown Hills 0898-23-0005 クラウンヒルズ
Imabari Kokusai H 0898-36-1111 国際ホテル
BH Urban 0898-22-5311 今治アーバン
Cyclo-no-Ie 0898-35-4496 シクロの家
Tourist Information, Rental bikes
Kisuke-no-yado キスケの宿 0898-22-0026
GH the Doors 090-3185-2211
Shin-nihon Kōtsū 0898-24-1111
Dai-ichi Taxi 0898-22-1250
Shimanami Taxi 0898-22-0555
Sōja River 蒼社川
Bekku E.S.
Imabari-kita H.S.
Himesaka Jinja
Imabari 今治
Gusto
Imabari-nishi H.S.
Imabari City 今治市
McDonald's
Fuji
Koizumi Bus Stop 小泉バス停
Henro Tomb
41 Imabari-hidaka 今治日高
(Old ferry crossing monument)
Sushi
Saisaikiteya さいさいきて屋
72 中寺

Ship-building town 造船の町

The largest ship-building companies in Japan are located in Imabari-city.

Shimanami-kaidō しまなみ海道

This highway is a 60-kilometer route consisting of seven bridges over six islands in the Seto Inland Sea which allows one to travel from Onomichi city, Hiroshima prefecture to Imabari city, Ehime prefecture.

71
Shoppers
Saisai-kiteya
さいさいきて屋
Sogō Mart
Mos Burger
BH BARI Inn
0898-33-0909
バリ・イン
Sushi
Yoshinoya
Iyo-Tomita
伊予富田
秋元
317
156
Sōja River
蒼社川
1.1km
四村
徳重
Ōsugi Bus Stop
大須木バス停
Ikanashi Jinja五十嵐
Shimizu E.S.
川崎
Mt. Futō
府頭山
57 Iwashimizu Hachiman Jinja
岩清水八幡神社
Jōjakuji 浄寂寺
0.8km
57 Eifukuji
2.5km
八幡
別所
1.4km
835
40
under construction until 2026
五十嵐台団地
Inuzuka Reservoir
大塚池
Detour Route
82
Kichishōzenji
吉祥禅寺
23 Senyūji
仙遊寺
100
1.0km
谷
0.9km
0.5km
180
281.1
58
252.0
Senyūji
6.3km
5.4km
to No.59
5.4km
Chikurinji
竹林寺
上居
50
155
長山
新谷
大野
新田
1.8km
Ryūto River
龍登川
中寺
J.H.S.
松木
0.7km
Community Center
松木集会所
Bakery
Drugstore
840
高市
196
Imabari City
今治市
平山
鹿ノ子池
町谷
Kankiji
歓喜寺
川筋
Kanokoike Park
鹿ノ子池公園
本郷
Udon Yamabiko
1.9km
2.6km
Expressway (under construction)
古谷
155
1km
1km
200
SCALE 1/30,000
0
0.5
1
1.5
2km

57 Eifukuji 五十七番 栄福寺

- H Amida Nyorai
- 200 Yawata-kō, Tamagawa-chō, Imabari City
- Free of charge (15)
- A By bus bound for Mikomori or Kijiguchi / Kazuratani from Imabari Stn. Get off at Ōsugi Bus Stop, about 20 min. walk.
- ☎ 0898-55-2432 S None

At the summit of Mt. Futō, Kūkai held a fire ritual (goma) in order to prevent accidents at sea. On the last day of this ritual, Amida Nyorai appeared from the ocean. On each side of the Main Hall, there are copies of the "Buddhist feet rocks" from the temple in India where Shaka achieved enlightenment.

58 Senyūji 五十八番 仙遊寺

- H Senju Kannon Bosatsu
- 483 Bessho-kō, Tamagawa-chō, Imabari City
- Charge (10)
- A By bus bound for Mikomori or Kijiguchi / Kazuratani from Imabari Stn. Get off at Ōsugi Bus Stop, about 60 min. walk.
- ☎ 0898-55-2141 S Available

During the mid-7th century, a local ruler, Ochi Morioki, built this temple. One legends states that the statue of Senju Kannon Bosatsu was carved by a female dragon which came up the Ryūto River from the sea. The temple fell into disuse, but was restored by Kūkai and prospered.

NOTE Kokubunji 国分寺

In 741, Emperor Shōmu (701-756) who believed that the Buddhist faith was a means to ensure both the happiness of the individual and peace for the country as a whole decreed that a monastery (kokubunji) and a nunnery (kokubun-niji) should be built in each province in Japan. Generally temples in Japan operate by receiving financial donations from local, pious people called *"danka"*, who affiliate themselves with that temple. On the other hand, kokubunji, which were established and operated through a top-down approach, received a national budget and thus had no *danka*. So, by the time there was a transition from an aristocratic to a feudal political system in the late 10th century all kokubunji had disappeared. When there is a political change temples lose their support base. Some time afterward several kokubunji were restored, but it depended on the regional consensus. In various places around Japan kokubunji remains as a place name but there are very few examples outside Shikoku where the temple actually exists.

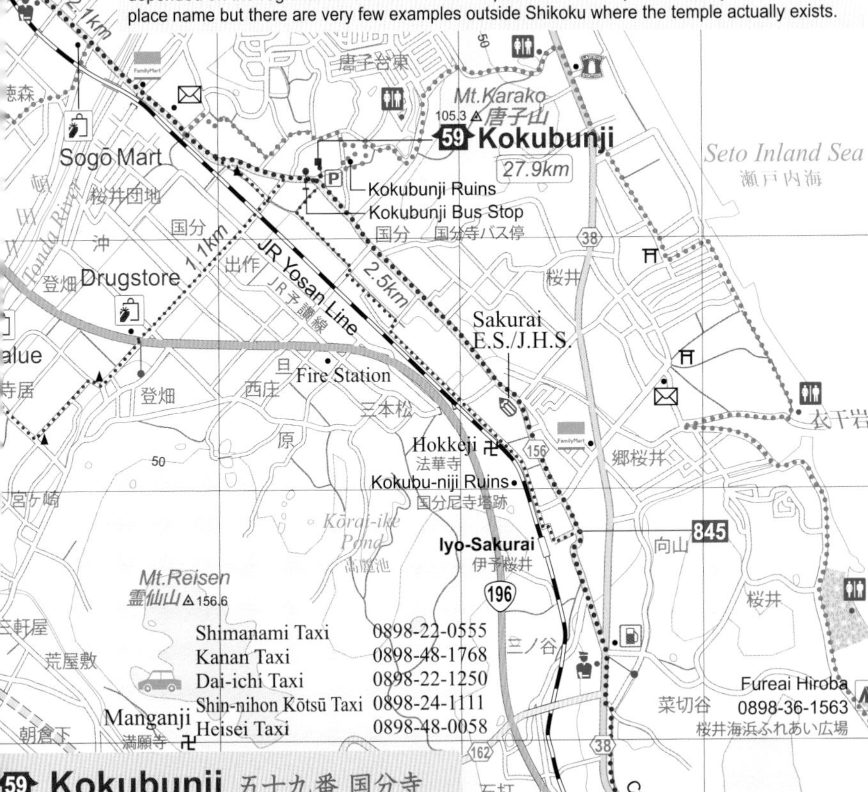
Mt.Karako
105.3 唐子山
59 Kokubunji
27.9km
Seto Inland Sea
瀬戸内海
Kokubunji Ruins
Kokubunji Bus Stop
国分 国分寺バス停
Sogō Mart
桜井団地
Tonda River
Drugstore
2.1km
1.1km
2.5km
JR Yosan Line
JR予讃線
Sakurai
E.S./J.H.S.
Fire Station
西庄
登畑
三本松
Hokkeji
法華寺
Kokubu-niji Ruins
国分尼寺塔跡
Kōrai-ike Pond
高麗池
Iyo-Sakurai
伊予桜井
845
向山
Mt.Reisen
霊仙山 156.6
衣干岩
郷桜井
桜井
Manganji
満願寺
Fureai Hiroba
0898-36-1563
桜井海浜ふれあい広場
菜切谷
石打
長沢
1.9km
Cycling Road
Sakurai-Shikki Kaikan
桜井漆器会館
Hot Spring Source
Imabari-yunoura IC
今治湯ノ浦IC
今治湯ノ浦温泉
Imabari-yunoura Onsen
73-a

Shimanami Taxi	0898-22-0555
Kanan Taxi	0898-48-1768
Dai-ichi Taxi	0898-22-1250
Shin-nihon Kōtsū Taxi	0898-24-1111
Heisei Taxi	0898-48-0058

59 Kokubunji 五十九番 国分寺

H Yakushi Nyorai
4-1-33 Kokubu, Imabari City
Charge (45)
A By bus bound for Sakurai-danchi-junkan from Imabari Stn. Get off at Kokubunji Bus Stop.
☎ 0898-48-0533 S None

This is the provincial temple of Ehime prefecture founded by Gyōki in 741. There are many cultural properties displayed in the *shoin* (study hall). There is also a statue of Kōbō Daishi with which you can shake hands and make a wish. As well, if you touch the vase of Yakushi while praying, it is believed that you will be cured of any sickness.

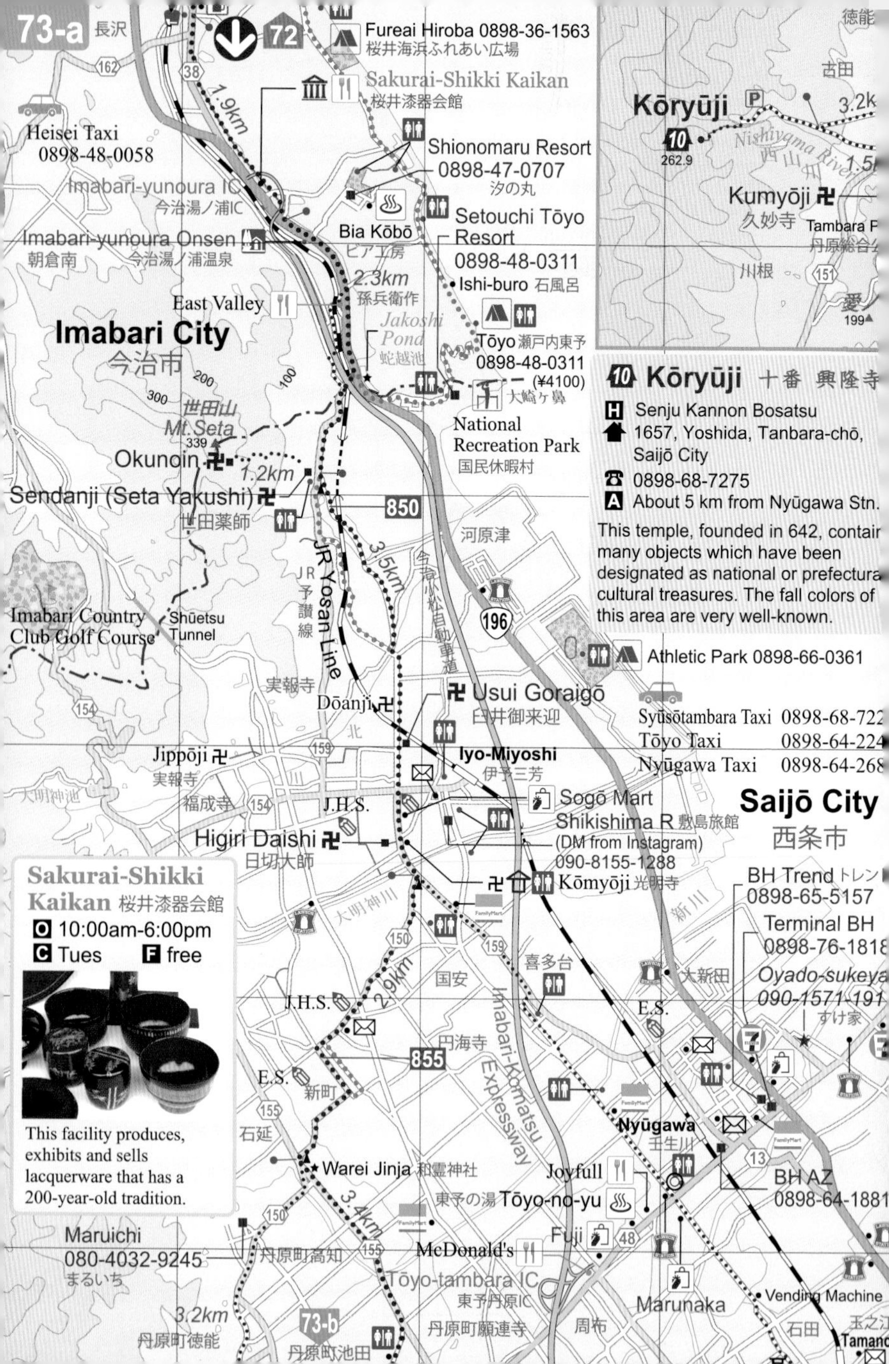

73-a
長沢
72
Fureai Hiroba 0898-36-1563
桜井海浜ふれあい広場
Sakurai-Shikki Kaikan
桜井漆器会館
1.9km
Heisei Taxi
0898-48-0058
Shionomaru Resort
0898-47-0707
汐の丸
Imabari-yunoura IC
今治湯ノ浦IC
Bia Kōbō
ビア工房
Setouchi Tōyo Resort
0898-48-0311
Imabari-yunoura Onsen
今治湯ノ浦温泉
朝倉南
2.3km
孫兵衛作
Ishi-buro 石風呂
East Valley
Jakoshi Pond
蛇越池
Imabari City
今治市
Tōyo 瀬戸内東予
0898-48-0311
(¥4100)
大崎ケ鼻
世田山
Mt.Seta
339
National Recreation Park
国民休暇村
Okunoin
1.2km
Sendanji (Seta Yakushi)
世田薬師
850
河原津
Kōryūji
262.9
Nishiyama River
西山川
3.2km
1.5km
古田
徳能
Kumyōji
久妙寺
Tambara P
丹原総合公
川根
199
10 Kōryūji 十番 興隆寺
H Senju Kannon Bosatsu
1657, Yoshida, Tanbara-chō, Saijō City
0898-68-7275
A About 5 km from Nyūgawa Stn.
This temple, founded in 642, contain many objects which have been designated as national or prefectura cultural treasures. The fall colors of this area are very well-known.
3.5km
JR予讃線
JR Yosan Line
今治小松自動車道
196
Imabari Country Club Golf Course
Shūetsu Tunnel
Athletic Park 0898-66-0361
実報寺
Dōanji
Usui Goraigō
臼井御来迎
Syūsōtambara Taxi 0898-68-722
Tōyo Taxi 0898-64-224
Nyūgawa Taxi 0898-64-268
Jippōji
実報寺
Iyo-Miyoshi
伊予三芳
大明神池
福成寺
J.H.S.
Sogō Mart
Shikishima R 敷島旅館
(DM from Instagram)
090-8155-1288
Saijō City
西条市
Higiri Daishi
日切大師
Kōmyōji 光明寺
BH Trend トレン
0898-65-5157
Terminal BH
0898-76-1818
Oyado-sukeya
090-1571-191
すけ家
Sakurai-Shikki Kaikan 桜井漆器会館
O 10:00am-6:00pm
C Tues
F free
This facility produces, exhibits and sells lacquerware that has a 200-year-old tradition.
大明神川
新川
喜多台
国安
2.9km
大新田
J.H.S.
E.S.
Imabari-Komatsu Expressway
円海寺
855
E.S.
新町
石延
Nyūgawa
壬生川
Warei Jinja 和霊神社
Joyfull
BH AZ
0898-64-1881
3.4km
東予の湯 Tōyo-no-yu
Fuji
Maruichi
080-4032-9245
まるいち
丹原町高知
McDonald's
Tōyo-tambara IC
東予丹原IC
Marunaka
Vending Machine
3.2km
73-b
丹原町徳能
丹原町池田
丹原町願連寺
周布
石田
玉之江
Tamanoe

Ishizuchi Andō
0898-68-0181
080-4999-1955
いしづち安藤家
Drugstore
City Office
H.S.
E.S.
Shōzenji 正善寺
GH Bekku
090-7578-7053
J.H.S.
Kuramitsu Jinja 闇罔神社
Tamanoe 玉之江
Imabari-Komatsu Expwy
Nakayama River
Seirakuji 清楽寺
62 Hōjuji
Iyo-Komatsu 伊予小松
Hōanji 法安寺
Iyo-komatsu-kita IC 伊予小松北IC
61 Kōonji
BR Komatsu
0898-72-5881
旅館小松
Nonaka Daishi 野中大師
Ikiki Jizō
Takagamo Jinja 高鴨神社
Ishizuchi-san SA 石鎚山SA
0898-76-3111 (¥1000)
9.5km to No. 60
Community Center
Ayanobu Jinja
Iwane E.S.
Komatsu Oasis 小松オアシス
Iyo-komatsu IC/JCT いよ小松IC/JCT
Myōunji 妙雲寺
Shirataki (waterfall training) 白滝
Saijō City 西条市
Matsuyama Expressway
Komachi Onsen Shikokuya
0898-76-3388
小町温泉しこくや
Tambara Taxi 0898-68-7222
Komatsu Taxi 0898-72-2124
Daishidō 大師堂
SCALE 1/60,000
Toll Gate 料金所
Toll Road (¥1850) free for walkers
Caution: Path slippery after rainfall
雨天時は滑りやすい
Jizōdō
Hoshigamori 星ヶ森
60 Yokomineji
薬師堂 Yakushidō
モエ坂 Moe-zaka Slope
Occasionally closed due to landslides
Kōguchi Bus Stop
Itazuri 虎杖
to Mt. Ishizuchi-san
石鎚山へ至る

11 Ikiki Jizō 十一番 生木地蔵

H Ikiki Jizō Bosatsu

Imai, Tanbara-chō, Saijō City

☎ 0898-68-7371

A About 5.4 km from Nyūgawa Stn.

A statue of Jizō Bosatsu has been carved right into the camphor tree which blooms green leaves, thus this main deity has been given the name of Ikiki or living tree Jizō.

60 Yokomineji 六十番 横峰寺

H Dainichi Nyorai 2253 Ishizuchi, Komatsu-chō, Saijō City

Charge (50) 5 min. walk ☎ 0897-59-0142 S None

A By bus bound for Ropeway-mae from Iyo-Saijō Stn. Get off at Yokomine-tozanguchi Bus Stop. Change bus for the last stop about 10 min. walk.

This temple (740m) was founded in 651 by En-no-Gyōja. Later, Kūkai spent time in training here and enshrined a statue of Dainichi Nyorai. It is said that through prayers given here, the brain illness of Emperor Kanmu (781-806) was cured. During the early Meiji period, the temple fell into disuse, but in 1909 it was restored. This temple is the *sekishoji* (spiritual barrier temple) of Iyo (Ehime) prefecture.

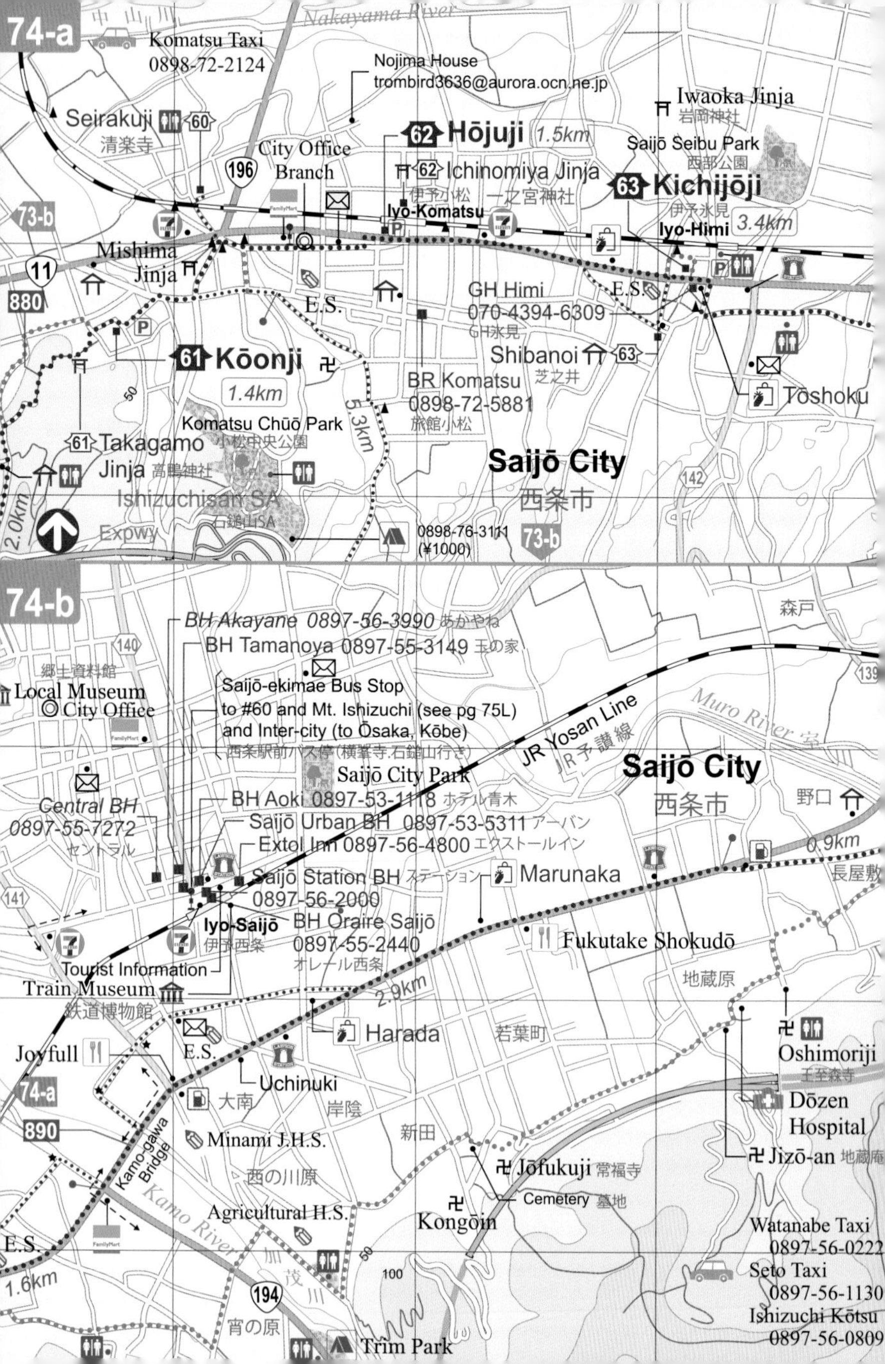

74-a
Nakayama River
中山川
Komatsu Taxi
0898-72-2124
Nojima House
trombird3636@aurora.ocn.ne.jp
Seirakuji
清楽寺
60
196
City Office
Branch
62 Hōjuji 1.5km
62 Ichinomiya Jinja
伊予小松 一之宮神社
Iyo-Komatsu
Iwaoka Jinja
岩岡神社
Saijō Seibu Park
西部公園
63 Kichijōji
伊予氷見
Iyo-Himi
3.4km
73-b
11
880
Mishima
Jinja
E.S.
GH Himi
070-4394-6309
GH氷見
E.S.
61 Kōonji
1.4km
Shibanoi
芝之井
63
BR Komatsu
0898-72-5881
旅館小松
5.3km
Tōshoku
Komatsu Chūō Park
小松中央公園
61 Takagamo
Jinja 高鴨神社
Saijō City
西条市
142
Ishizuchisan SA
石鎚山SA
Expwy
2.0km
0898-76-3111
(¥1000)
73-b
74-b
森戸
BH Akayane 0897-56-3990 あかやね
BH Tamanoya 0897-55-3149 玉の家
140
139
郷土資料館
Local Museum
City Office
Saijō-ekimae Bus Stop
to #60 and Mt. Ishizuchi (see pg 75L)
and Inter-city (to Ōsaka, Kōbe)
西条駅前バス停（横峯寺.石鎚山行き）
JR Yosan Line
JR予讃線
Muro River
Saijō City Park
Saijō City
西条市
野口
Central BH
0897-55-7272
セントラル
BH Aoki 0897-53-1118 ホテル青木
Saijō Urban BH 0897-53-5311 アーバン
Extol Inn 0897-56-4800 エクストールイン
0.9km
Saijō Station BH ステーション
0897-56-2000
Marunaka
長屋敷
141
Iyo-Saijō
伊予西条
BH Oraire Saijō
0897-55-2440
オレール西条
Fukutake Shokudō
Tourist Information
Train Museum
鉄道博物館
2.9km
地蔵原
Harada
若葉町
Joyfull
E.S.
Uchinuki
Oshimoriji
王至森寺
74-a
890
大南
岸陰
Dōzen
Hospital
新田
Kamo-gawa
Bridge
Minami J.H.S.
西の川原
Jōfukuji 常福寺
Jizō-an 地蔵庵
Cemetery 墓地
Kongōin
Agricultural H.S.
Kamo River
加茂川
E.S.
Watanabe Taxi
0897-56-0222
Seto Taxi
0897-56-1130
1.6km
194
Ishizuchi Kōtsu
0897-56-0809
宵の原
Trim Park

61 Kōonji 六十一番 香園寺 ☎ 0898-72-3861 S None

Dainichi Nyorai 19 Minamikawa-kō, Komatsu-chō, Saijō City

Free of charge (100) A About 20 min. walk from JR Yosan Line Iyo-Komatsu Stn.

is temple was founded during the 6th century by Shōtoku Taishi 73-621). When Kūkai came here, he found a pregnant woman who was pain so he lit incense and prayed for her. As a result a boy was safely orn. This temple is widely known as "Koyasu Daishi" - Daishi of protecting ildren. The modern concrete Main Hall is a unique feature of this temple.

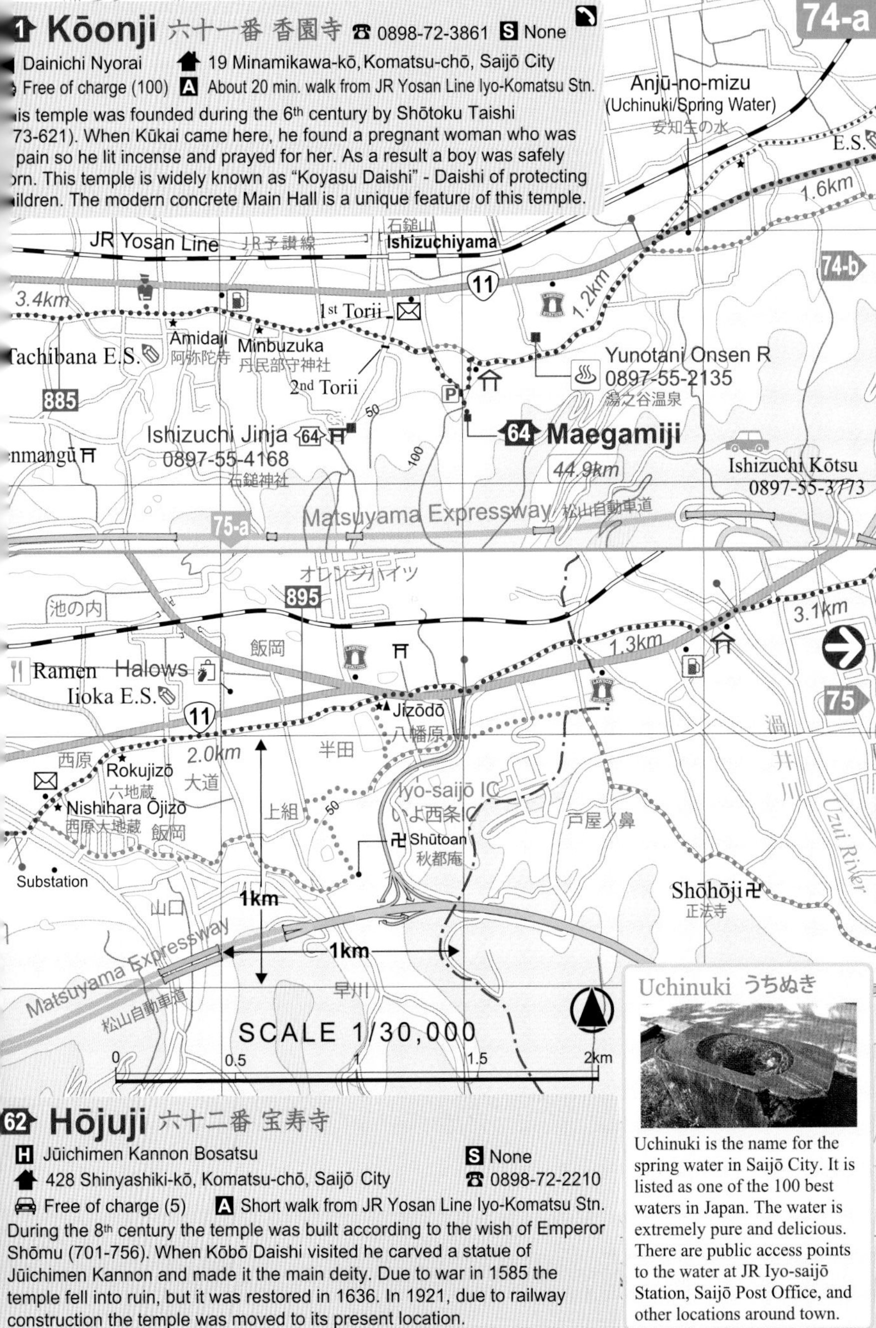
Anjū-no-mizu
(Uchinuki/Spring Water)
安知生の水
E.S.
1.6km
JR Yosan Line
JR予讃線
石鎚山
Ishizuchiyama
74-b
11
3.4km
1st Torii
1.2km
Amidaji
阿弥陀寺
Minbuzuka
丹民部守神社
Tachibana E.S.
2nd Torii
Yunotani Onsen R
0897-55-2135
湯之谷温泉
885
50
Ishizuchi Jinja
64
0897-55-4168
石鎚神社
64 Maegamiji
nmangū
100
44.9km
Ishizuchi Kōtsu
0897-55-3773
Matsuyama Expressway 松山自動車道
75-a
オレンジハイツ
895
池の内
3.1km
1.3km
飯岡
Ramen Halows
Iioka E.S.
75
Jizōdō
八幡原
11
2.0km
半田
西原
Rokujizō
六地蔵
大道
Nishihara Ōjizō
西原大地蔵
飯岡
Iyo-saijō IC
いよ西条IC
上組
50
戸屋ノ鼻
Uzui River
渦井川
Shūtoan
秋都庵
Substation
Shōhōji
正法寺
1km
山口
1km
Matsuyama Expressway
松山自動車道
早川
SCALE 1/30,000
0
0.5
1
1.5
2km

62 Hōjuji 六十二番 宝寿寺

H Jūichimen Kannon Bosatsu S None

428 Shinyashiki-kō, Komatsu-chō, Saijō City ☎ 0898-72-2210

Free of charge (5) A Short walk from JR Yosan Line Iyo-Komatsu Stn.

During the 8th century the temple was built according to the wish of Emperor Shōmu (701-756). When Kōbō Daishi visited he carved a statue of Jūichimen Kannon and made it the main deity. Due to war in 1585 the temple fell into ruin, but it was restored in 1636. In 1921, due to railway construction the temple was moved to its present location.

Uchinuki うちぬき

Uchinuki is the name for the spring water in Saijō City. It is listed as one of the 100 best waters in Japan. The water is extremely pure and delicious. There are public access points to the water at JR Iyo-saijō Station, Saijō Post Office, and other locations around town.

Mt. Ishizuchi 石鎚山

Mt. Ishizuchi, where Kūkai spent time in training, is the highest mountain in Western Japan (1982m) and is considered to be one of 7 sacred mountains in Japan. During the 7th century, the priest En no Gyōja chose this mountain as a sacred site for those who believe in Shugendō or mountain worship. Today, many tourists and followers of Shugendō visit this mountain. For those who wish to test their physical and mental strength, try using the four climbing chains (48m, 33m, 65m and 68m) to reach the summit. Otherwise, there is also a long and somewhat steep detour route.

If you have an extra day and the weather is good, I recommend taking the bus from Saijō train station and then the ropeway to reach the mountain summit. The path to the top is well-maintained. If you plan to make a return trip in one day between May and October, you should be okay with just wearing your pilgrim coat plus a t-shirt, but if you plan to stay the night at the top, you will need warm clothes.
When you decide to climb this 1982-meter mountain, carefully consider what to take and what to wear as the weather can change very quickly.

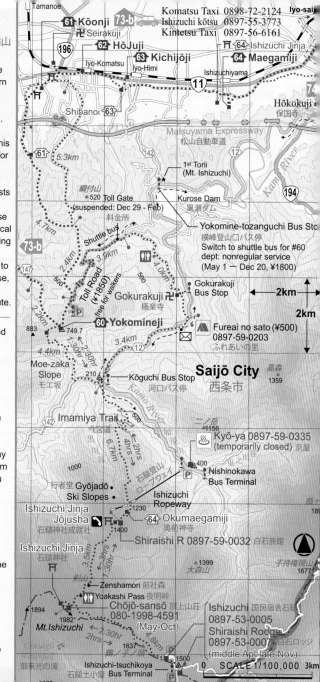

Detailed Map

Komatsu Taxi 0898-72-2124
Ishizuchi kōtsu 0897-55-3773
Kintetsu Taxi 0897-56-6161

61 Kōonji
62 HōJuji
63 Kichijōji
64 Maegamiji
64 Ishizuchi Jinja
60 Yokomineji
64 Okumaegamiji
Tamanoe
Seirakuji
Iyo-Komatsu
Iyo-Himi
Ishizuchiyama
Iyo-saij
Shibanoi 63
Hōkokuji 保国寺
Matsuyama Expressway 松山自動車道
1st Torii (Mt. Ishizuchi)
Kurose Dam 黒瀬ダム
Kamo River
網付山 520 Toll Gate (suspended: Dec 29 - Feb) 料金所
Shuttle bus
Yokomine-tozanguchi Bus Sto
横峰登山口バス停
Switch to shuttle bus for #60
dept: nonregular service
(May 1 ー Dec 20, ¥1800)
Toll Road (¥1850) free for walkers
Gokurakuji 極楽寺
Gokurakuji Bus Stop
2km
Fureai no sato (¥500)
0897-59-0203
ふれあいの里
5.3km
4.7km
2.4km
3.9km
4.0km
2.2km
4.4km
3.4km
1:30hr
2:30hr
883
749.7
Moe-zaka Slope モエ坂
210
Kōguchi Bus Stop 河口バス停
Saijō City 西条市
高森 1359
Imamiya Trail 今宮道
黒川谷
6.7km
4hrs
2hrs
二ノ岳 1156
Kyō-ya 0897-59-0335
(temporarily closed) 京屋
400
Nishinokawa Bus Terminal
石鎚登山ロープウェイ
Ishizuchi Ropeway
1000
行者堂 Gyōjadō
Ski Slopes
1230
Ishizuchi Jinja Jōjusha
石鎚神社成就社
1400
Shiraishi R 0897-59-0032 白石旅館
Ishizuchi Jinja 石鎚神社
3.5km
3hrs
1:30hr
1399 大森山
子持権現山 1677
剣山
Zenshamori 前社森
Yoakashi Pass 夜明峠
Chōjō-sansō 頂上山荘
080-1998-4591
(May-Oct)
1894
1982
Mt.Ishizuchi
2:30hr
2hrs
4.8km
1637
鶴ノ子ノ頭
Ishizuchi 国民宿舎石鎚
0897-53-0005
Shiraishi Rodge
0897-53-0007 白石ロッジ
(middle Apl-late Nov)
1500
Goraikō Waterfall 御来光の滝
Ishizuchi-tsuchikoya Bus Terminal
石鎚土小屋
SCALE 1/100,000
0 3km

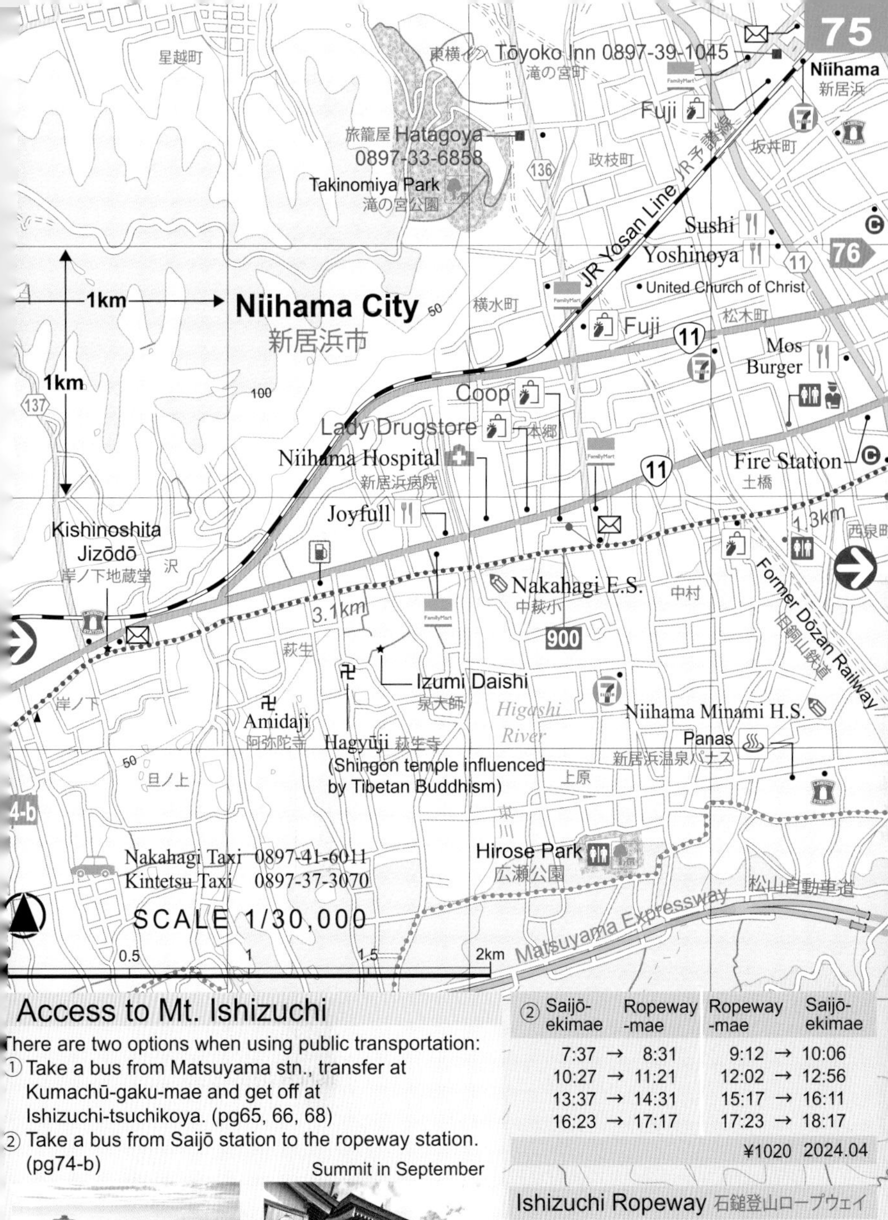

Niihama City
新居浜市
1km
1km
SCALE 1/30,000
0.5
1
1.5
2km
東横イン Tōyoko Inn 0897-39-1045
滝の宮町
Niihama
新居浜
Fuji
旅籠屋 Hatagoya
0897-33-6858
Takinomiya Park
滝の宮公園
星越町
政枝町
坂井町
JR Yosan Line JR予讃線
Sushi
Yoshinoya
United Church of Christ
76
横水町
松木町
Fuji
Mos Burger
Coop
Lady Drugstore
本郷
Niihama Hospital
新居浜病院
Fire Station
土橋
Joyfull
1.3km
西泉町
Kishinoshita Jizōdō
岸ノ下地蔵堂
沢
Nakahagi E.S.
中萩小
中村
Former Dōzan Railway
旧銅山鉄道
3.1km
900
萩生
Izumi Daishi
泉大師
岸ノ下
Amidaji
阿弥陀寺
Hagyūji 萩生寺
(Shingon temple influenced by Tibetan Buddhism)
Higashi River
Niihama Minami H.S.
Panas
新居浜温泉パナス
上原
旦ノ上
4-b
Nakahagi Taxi 0897-41-6011
Kintetsu Taxi 0897-37-3070
Hirose Park
広瀬公園
松山自動車道
Matsuyama Expressway

Access to Mt. Ishizuchi

There are two options when using public transportation:

1. Take a bus from Matsuyama stn., transfer at Kumachū-gaku-mae and get off at Ishizuchi-tsuchikoya. (pg65, 66, 68)
2. Take a bus from Saijō station to the ropeway station. (pg74-b)

Summit in September

② Saijō-ekimae	Ropeway-mae	Ropeway-mae	Saijō-ekimae
7:37 →	8:31	9:12 →	10:06
10:27 →	11:21	12:02 →	12:56
13:37 →	14:31	15:17 →	16:11
16:23 →	17:17	17:23 →	18:17
		¥1020	2024.04

Ishizuchi Ropeway 石鎚登山ロープウェイ

O Mon - Fri 8:40am-5:00pm
Sat / Sun / Hol 7:40am-6:00pm
20 minute intervals (depends on season)

C None (except periods for maintenance)

F round-trip: ¥2200- one-way: ¥1100-

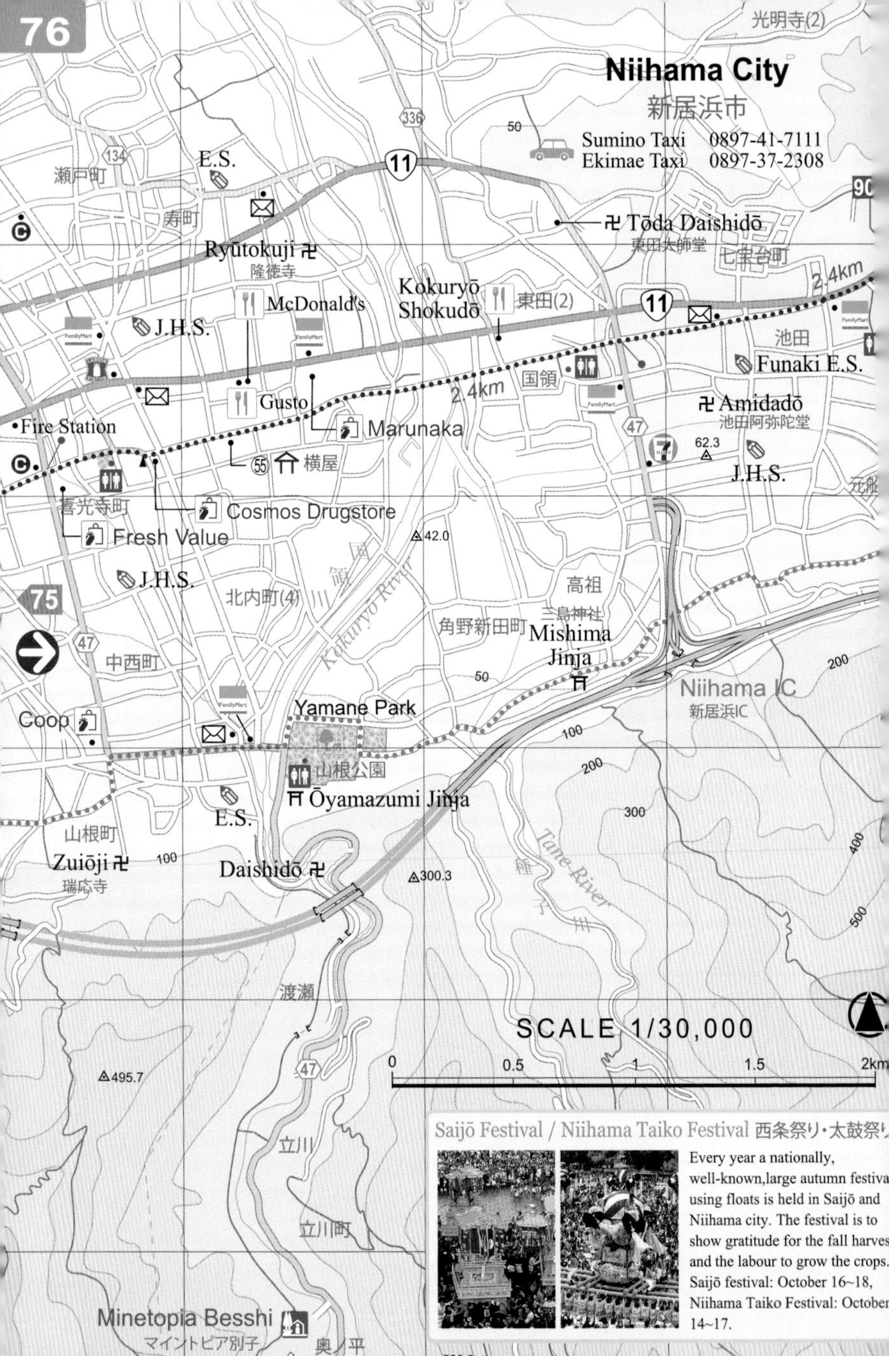
Niihama City
新居浜市
Sumino Taxi 0897-41-7111
Ekimae Taxi 0897-37-2308
光明寺(2)
336
134
11
50
90
瀬戸町
E.S.
寿町
Ryūtokuji 卍
隆徳寺
Tōda Daishidō 卍
東田大師堂
七宝台町
2.4km
Kokuryō Shokudō
McDonald's
東田(2)
J.H.S.
池田
Funaki E.S.
国領
Gusto
Marunaka
Amidadō 卍
池田阿弥陀堂
Fire Station
47
62.3
55
横屋
J.H.S.
喜光寺町
Cosmos Drugstore
Fresh Value
42.0
J.H.S.
北内町(4)
国領川
Kokuryō River
高祖
三島神社
Mishima Jinja
角野新田町
75
中西町
200
Niihama IC
新居浜IC
Coop
Yamane Park
山根公園
100
Ōyamazumi Jinja
E.S.
山根町
Zuiōji 卍
瑞応寺
Daishidō 卍
300.3
300
400
種子川
Tane River
500
渡瀬
SCALE 1/30,000
0
0.5
1
1.5
2km
495.7
立川
立川町
Minetopia Besshi
マイントピア別子
奥ノ平

Saijō Festival / Niihama Taiko Festival 西条祭り・太鼓祭り

Every year a nationally, well-known,large autumn festival using floats is held in Saijō and Niihama city. The festival is to show gratitude for the fall harvest and the labour to grow the crops. Saijō festival: October 16~18, Niihama Taiko Festival: October 14~17.

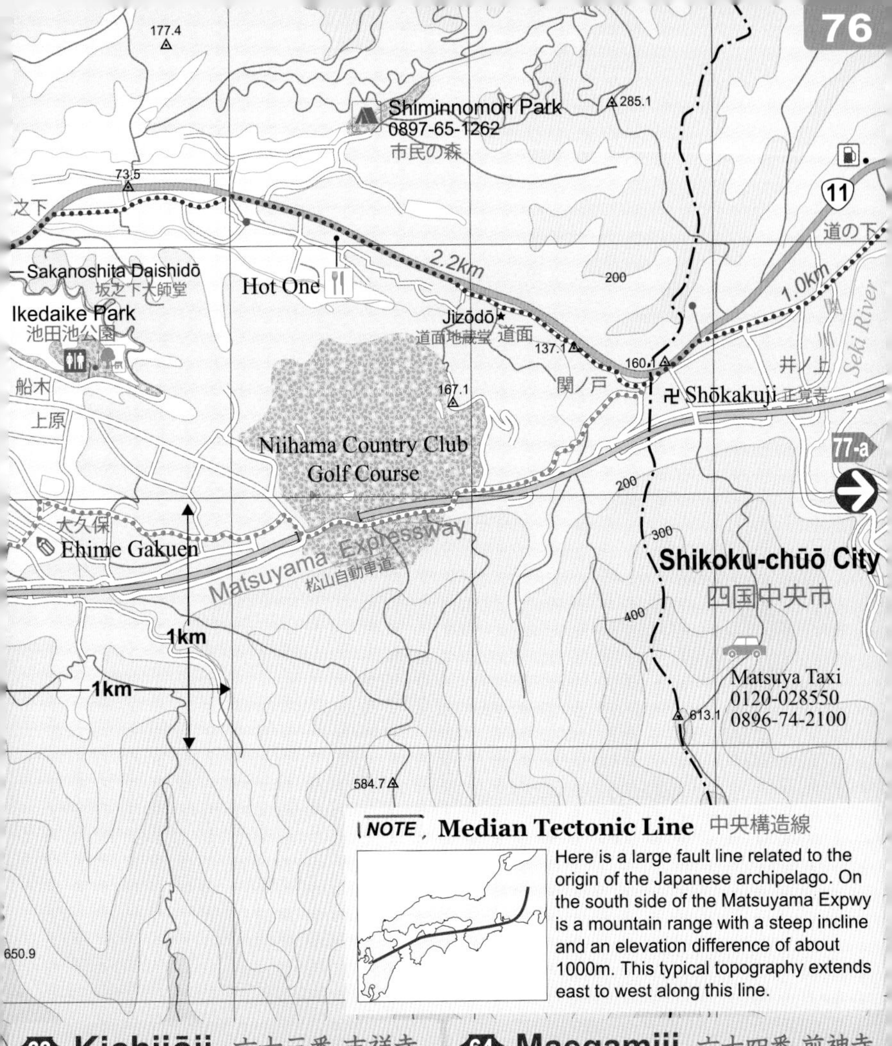
177.4
Shiminnomori Park
0897-65-1262
市民の森
285.1
73.5
之下
11
道の下
2.2km
1.0km
Seki River
—Sakanoshita Daishidō
坂之下大師堂
Hot One
200
Ikedaike Park
池田池公園
Jizōdō★
道面地蔵堂 道面
137.1
160.1
井ノ上
船木
167.1
関ノ戸
卍 Shōkakuji 正覚寺
上原
Niihama Country Club
Golf Course
77-a
200
大久保
Ehime Gakuen
Matsuyama Expressway
松山自動車道
300
Shikoku-chūō City
四国中央市
400
1km
1km
Matsuya Taxi
0120-028550
0896-74-2100
613.1
584.7
650.9

NOTE Median Tectonic Line 中央構造線

Here is a large fault line related to the origin of the Japanese archipelago. On the south side of the Matsuyama Expwy is a mountain range with a steep incline and an elevation difference of about 1000m. This typical topography extends east to west along this line.

63 Kichijōji 六十三番 吉祥寺

H Bishamonten
☎ 0897-57-8863
1048 Himi-otsu, Saijō City
S None
Charge (10)
A About 3 min. walk from JR Yosan Line Iyo-Himi Stn.

This is the only temple along the Shikoku pilgrimage route that has Bishamon-ten as its main deity which was made by Kūkai. Within the precincts there is a rock with a round hole in the middle. It is said if you can walk from the main hall with your eyes closed while saying your wish and put your staff through the hole that your prayer will come true.

64 Maegamiji 六十四番 前神寺

H Amida Nyorai
☎ 0897-56-6695
1426 Sunouchi-kō, Saijō City
S None
Free of charge (30)
A About 10 min. walk from JR Yosan Line Ishizuchisan Stn.

En no Gyōja (634- around 700) founded this temple and it was a place of deep faith for nobles and military families. On the 20th of every month, the three Zaō Gongen statues are opened for public viewing and it is believed that if one rubs a part of your body on it that the sickness will be healed.

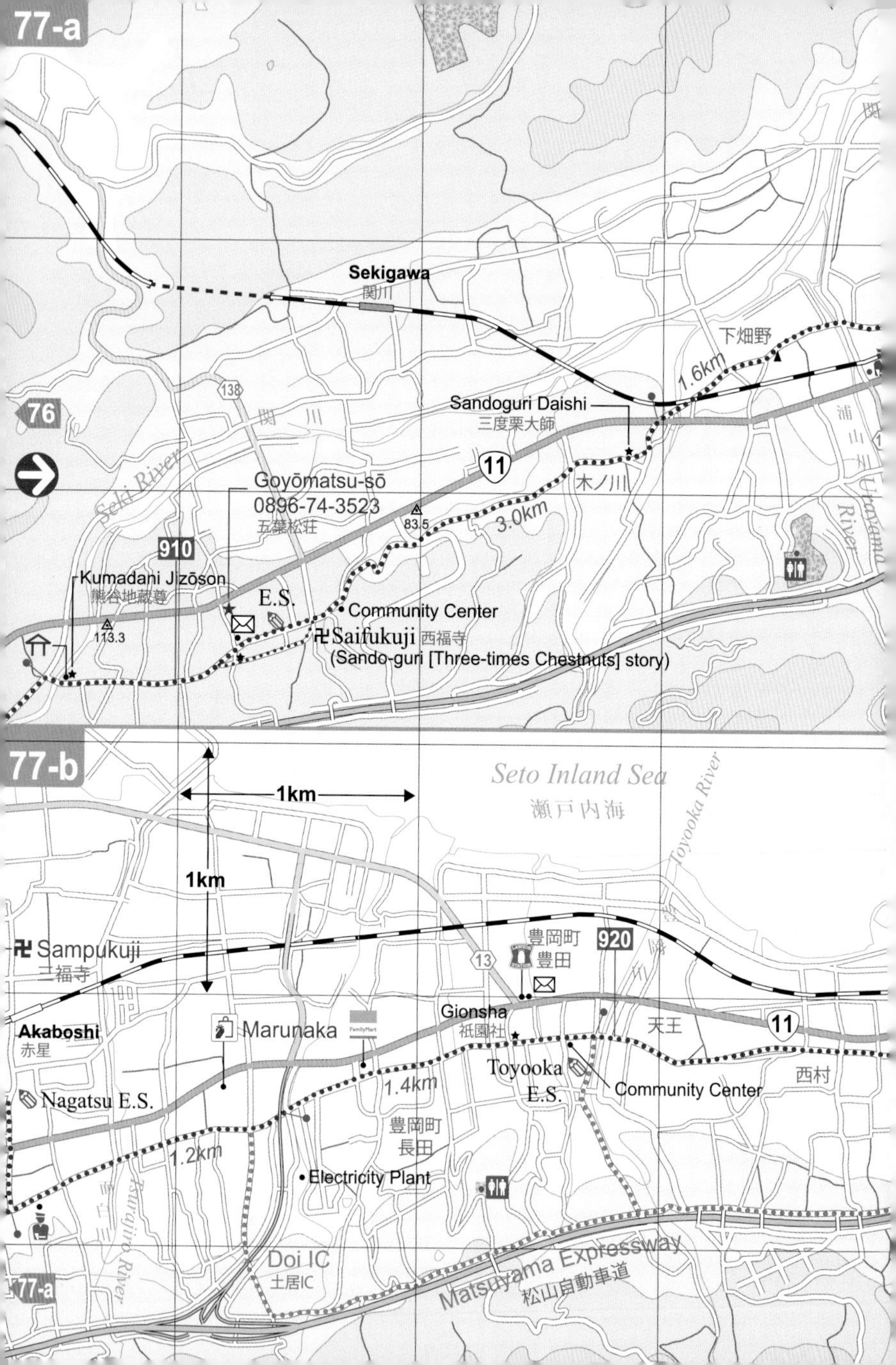

77-a
Sekigawa
関川
下畑野
1.6km
Sandoguri Daishi
三度栗大師
76
138
関 川
Seki River
11
Goyōmatsu-sō
0896-74-3523
五葉松荘
木ノ川
83.5
3.0km
浦山川
Urayama River
910
Kumadani Jizōson
熊谷地蔵尊
E.S.
113.3
Community Center
Saifukuji 西福寺
(Sando-guri [Three-times Chestnuts] story)
77-b
Seto Inland Sea
瀬戸内海
1km
1km
Toyooka River
Sampukuji
三福寺
920
豊岡町
豊田
13
Akaboshi
赤星
Marunaka
FamilyMart
Gionsha
祇園社
天王
11
Toyooka
E.S.
Community Center
西村
Nagatsu E.S.
1.4km
豊岡町
長田
1.2km
Electricity Plant
Tsuraijiro River
Doi IC
土居IC
Matsuyama Expressway
松山自動車道
77-a

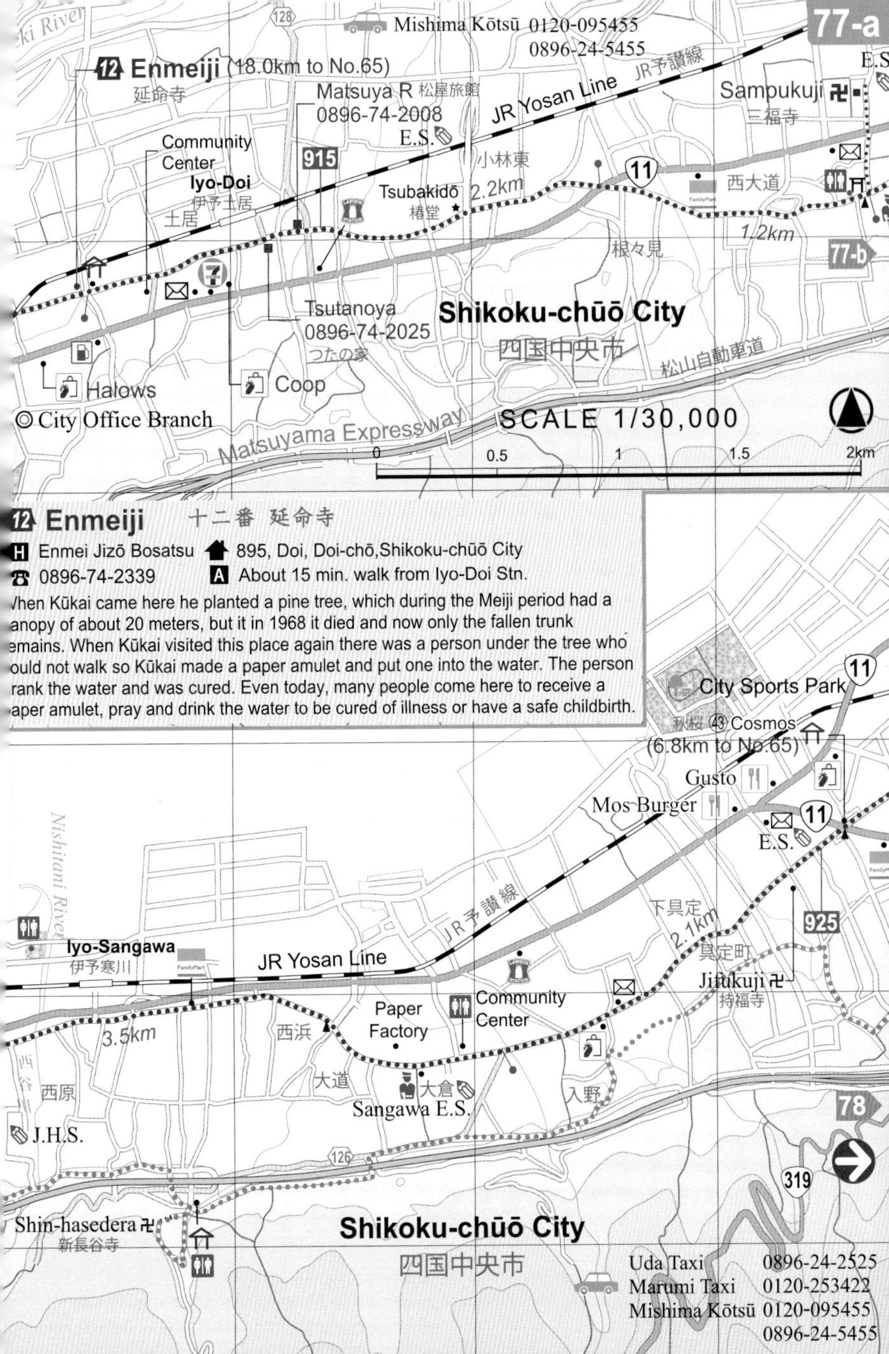
Mishima Kōtsū 0120-095455
0896-24-5455
12 Enmeiji (18.0km to No.65)
延命寺
Matsuya R 松屋旅館
0896-74-2008
E.S.
JR Yosan Line
JR予讃線
Sampukuji
三福寺
E.S.
Community Center
915
Iyo-Doi
伊予土居
土居
小林東
11
Tsubakidō
椿堂
2.2km
西大道
1.2km
77-b
根々見
Tsutanoya
0896-74-2025
つたの家
Shikoku-chūō City
四国中央市
松山自動車道
Halows
Coop
City Office Branch
SCALE 1/30,000
Matsuyama Expressway
0 0.5 1 1.5 2km
12 Enmeiji 十二番 延命寺
H Enmei Jizō Bosatsu
895, Doi, Doi-chō,Shikoku-chūō City
0896-74-2339
A About 15 min. walk from Iyo-Doi Stn.
Vhen Kūkai came here he planted a pine tree, which during the Meiji period had a anopy of about 20 meters, but it in 1968 it died and now only the fallen trunk emains. When Kūkai visited this place again there was a person under the tree who ould not walk so Kūkai made a paper amulet and put one into the water. The person rank the water and was cured. Even today, many people come here to receive a aper amulet, pray and drink the water to be cured of illness or have a safe childbirth.
City Sports Park
11
秋桜 43 Cosmos
(6.8km to No.65)
Gusto
Mos Burger
11
E.S.
Nishitani River
下具定
2.1km
925
具定町
Jifukuji
持福寺
Iyo-Sangawa
伊予寒川
JR Yosan Line
JR予讃線
Paper Factory
Community Center
3.5km
西浜
大道
大倉
Sangawa E.S.
入野
西谷
西原
J.H.S.
78
126
319
Shin-hasedera
新長谷寺
Shikoku-chūō City
四国中央市
Uda Taxi 0896-24-2525
Marumi Taxi 0120-253422
Mishima Kōtsū 0120-095455
0896-24-5455

Uda Taxi 0896-24-2525
Marumi Taxi 0120-253422
0896-23-2323
Mishima Kōtsū 0120-095455
Kūkai
090-2784-9004
(females only)
村松町
妻鳥町
Fuji GRAND
本村
紙屋町
JR予讃線
JR Yosan Line
E.S.
Sushi
BH Route I
050-5211-57
Fire Station
Mishimano-yu 三島乃湯
朝日
Joyfu
Aeon
BH Live Max リブマックス
0896-23-2011
Kōganji
興願寺
H Grandforet 0896-23-3355
グランフォーレ
Super BH
0896-22-9000
スーパーホテル
E.S.
Fuji
BH Mild マイルド
0896-24-3090
Ōnaru 御宿大成
0896-23-2122
City Office
3.1km
Zenpōji
善法寺
Iyo-Mishima 16.2
伊予三島
McDonald's
Halows
Mishima-kawanoe
三島川之江IC
Fresh Value
Akano-i River
赤野井川
(last store to pg 81)
J.H.S.
真庄
Police Station
1.8km
中田井
50
0.5km
E.S.
上柏町
2.7km
62
93
Hachiman Jinja
Togawa Park
戸川疎水公園
六塚
横尾
0.8km
柱尾
121
3.3km
野々首
100
319
Power Plant
77-b
Mishima Park
三島公園
Conduit pipe
SCALE 1/30,000
0 0.5 1 1.5 2km
J.H.S.

65 Sankakuji

☎ 0896-56-3065

S None

六十五番 三角寺

H Jūichimen Kannon Bosatsu

75 Sankakuji-kō, Kanada-chō, Shikoku-chūō City

Charge (40)

A By bus bound for Kirinomori from Iyo-Mishima Stn. Get off at Sankakuji-guchi Bus Stop, about 45 min. walk.

During the early 8th century, Gyōki founded this temple. The name of this temple is "triangular temple" which originates from the triangular goma altar used by Kūkai to exterminate a troublesome ghost which lived in this area. People believe that the main deity will ward off misfortune and allow for easy childbirth. People give a rice paddle if their prayers come true.

Paper City 四国中央市

There are a lot of paper-manufacturing companies along the coast of this city. A museum about paper-making is located near Kawanoe train station.

13 Senryūji 十三番 仙龍寺

H Kōbō Daishi

Umatate Shingū-mura Shikoku-chūō City

☎ 0896-72-2033

A By bus bound for Shingu from Kawanoe Stn. Get off at Horikiri-tunnel-guchi BusStop, about 3.6 km walk

Kūkai constructed a goma ritual altar in the cave and trained here for 21 days. There is a statue of Fudō Myōō in the deepest part of the cave in the Main hall.

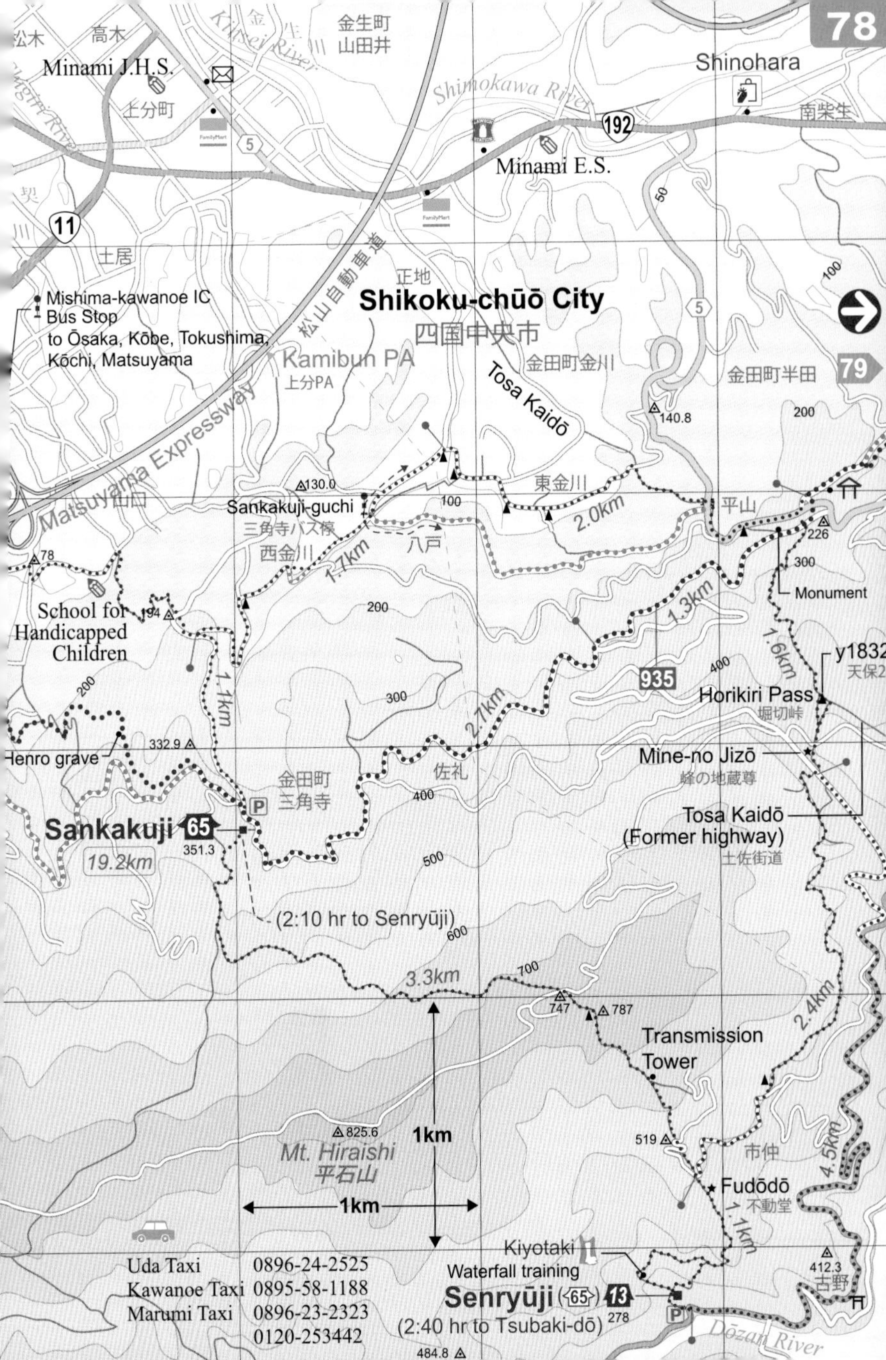

Minami J.H.S.
上分町
Kinsei River
金生町
山田井
Shimokawa River
Shinohara
南柴生
192
5
11
Minami E.S.
土居
正地
松山自動車道
Shikoku-chūō City
四国中央市
Mishima-kawanoe IC
Bus Stop
to Ōsaka, Kōbe, Tokushima, Kōchi, Matsuyama
Kamibun PA
上分PA
金田町金川
金田町半田
79
Tosa Kaidō
Matsuyama Expressway
140.8
130.0
Sankakuji-guchi
三角寺バス停
東金川
平山
2.0km
八戸
西金川
1.7km
226
300
Monument
78
School for Handicapped Children
194
1.3km
1.6km
935
y1832
天保2
Horikiri Pass
堀切峠
1.1km
2.7km
332.9
Henro grave
Mine-no Jizō
峰の地蔵尊
金田町
三角寺
佐礼
Sankakuji
65
351.3
19.2km
Tosa Kaidō
(Former highway)
土佐街道
(2:10 hr to Senryūji)
3.3km
747
787
Transmission Tower
2.4km
825.6
1km
Mt. Hiraishi
平石山
519
市仲
Fudōdō
不動堂
4.5km
1.1km
Uda Taxi 0896-24-2525
Kawanoe Taxi 0895-58-1188
Marumi Taxi 0896-23-2323
0120-253442
Kiyotaki
Waterfall training
Senryūji
65
13
278
(2:40 hr to Tsubaki-dō)
412.3
古野
Dōzan River
484.8

79
15 Hashikuraji 十五番 箸蔵寺
H Konpira Daigongen
Shūzu, Ikeda-chō, Miyoshi City
0883-72-0812 A About 10 min. walk from Hashikura Stn. Change the Ropeway.
The origin of this temple's name comes from the oath spoken by the deity Konpira Daigongen to Kūkai that all people will be saved. This temple is the inner sanctum of Kotohira Shrine.
12.3km
Aikurushidani River
Hashikuraji 15
Tsubojiri
つぼじり
4.5km
Miyoshi City
三好市
JR Dosan Line
Sankyō Taxi
0883-72-3300
Hashikuraji Ropeway
Round-trip ¥1700-
1.9km
Sushiroku R 寿司六旅館
0883-72-7422
Fukuya R ふくや旅館
0883-72-0868
池田町西山
E.S.
1.6km
6.0km
BH Awa-Ikeda
0883-72-1010
阿波池田いれぶん2
Ikeda Dam
Yoshino River
吉野川
徳島道
Tokushima Expressway
池田町白地
Awa-Ikeda
阿波池田
JR Dosan Line
Ikawa-Ikeda IC
井川池田IC
西井川
Intercity Bus Terminal
(Osaka, Kobe)
Frespo
Miyoshi Hospital
7.9km
1.9km
Awanoshō Resort 0883-74-1414 あわの抄
Konishi R 0883-74-0311 小西
M Hakuchi-sō 0883-74-0487 (pick-up available) 白地荘
M Tabibito-yado 0883-76-4727 旅人宿
090-5275-1951
SCALE 1/60,000
0 1 2km
Access to Hashikuraji (箸蔵寺)
大野原町
海老済
Unpenji Ropeway 2019.04
O Mar-Nov 7:20-17:00
Dec-Feb 8:00-17:00
C None
F Round-trip ¥2200-
One-way ¥1200-
Service every 20min (00,20,40)
Ehime Prefecture
愛媛県
Shikoku-chūō City
四国中央市
Manda Tunnel
4.2km
Manda Trail
曼陀道
Kawanoe-higashi JCT
川之江東JCT
柴生町
Nitta Jinja
14 Jōfukuji (Tsubaki-dō)
常福寺(椿堂)
2.8km
855m
Sakaime Tunnel
2.2km
0.6km
3.1km
Narutaki Fudō
成瀧不動
E.S.
Hichida Bus Stop
七田バス停
Kinsei River 金生川
川滝町下山
3.2km
78
金田町半田
Kawanoe Taxi 0120-818823
Uda Taxi 0896-24-2525
Maruha Taxi 0896-58-2121
SCALE 1/60,000
0 1 2 3km
0.6km
3.1km
Mōri-sō 毛利荘
(Henro House)
Yuki Kōbō

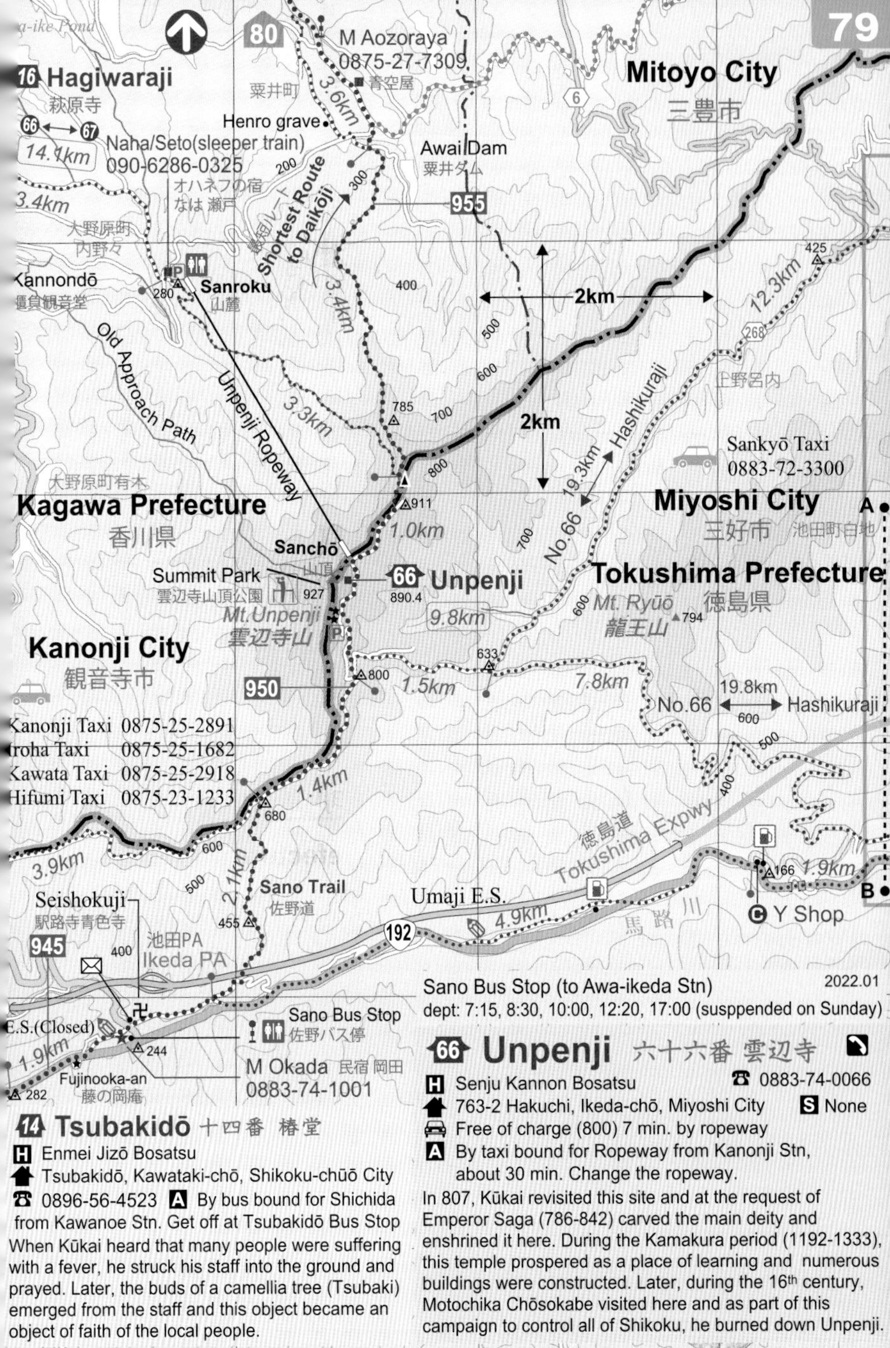
80
16 Hagiwaraji
萩原寺
66 ↔ 67
14.1km
3.4km
M Aozoraya
0875-27-7309
青空屋
粟井町
3.6km
Henro grave
Naha/Seto(sleeper train)
090-6286-0325
オハネフの宿
なは 瀬戸
Mitoyo City
三豊市
6
Awai Dam
粟井ダム
955
Shortest Route to Daikōji
最短ルート
大野原町
内野々
Kannondō
櫃負観音堂
280
Sanroku
山麓
3.4km
400
2km
2km
425
12.3km
268
500
600
Old Approach Path
Unpenji Ropeway
3.3km
785
700
800
上野呂内
Hashikuraji
19.3km
No.66
Sankyō Taxi
0883-72-3300
大野原町有木
Kagawa Prefecture
香川県
911
1.0km
Miyoshi City
三好市
池田町白地
A
Sanchō
山頂
Summit Park
雲辺寺山頂公園
927
66 Unpenji
890.4
Tokushima Prefecture
徳島県
Mt. Ryūō
龍王山
794
Mt. Unpenji
雲辺寺山
9.8km
Kanonji City
観音寺市
633
950
800
1.5km
7.8km
No.66
19.8km
Hashikuraji
Kanonji Taxi 0875-25-2891
Iroha Taxi 0875-25-1682
Kawata Taxi 0875-25-2918
Hifumi Taxi 0875-23-1233
1.4km
680
3.9km
徳島道
Tokushima Expwy
166
1.9km
B
Seishokuji
駅路寺青色寺
945
2.1km
Sano Trail
佐野道
455
Umaji E.S.
4.9km
192
馬路川
Y Shop
池田PA
Ikeda PA
E.S.(Closed)
1.9km
244
Sano Bus Stop
佐野バス停
M Okada 民宿 岡田
0883-74-1001
Fujinooka-an
藤の岡庵
282

Sano Bus Stop (to Awa-ikeda Stn) 2022.01
dept: 7:15, 8:30, 10:00, 12:20, 17:00 (susppended on Sunday)

66 Unpenji 六十六番 雲辺寺

H Senju Kannon Bosatsu ☎ 0883-74-0066
763-2 Hakuchi, Ikeda-chō, Miyoshi City S None
Free of charge (800) 7 min. by ropeway
A By taxi bound for Ropeway from Kanonji Stn, about 30 min. Change the ropeway.

In 807, Kūkai revisited this site and at the request of Emperor Saga (786-842) carved the main deity and enshrined it here. During the Kamakura period (1192-1333), this temple prospered as a place of learning and numerous buildings were constructed. Later, during the 16th century, Motochika Chōsokabe visited here and as part of this campaign to control all of Shikoku, he burned down Unpenji.

14 Tsubakidō 十四番 椿堂

H Enmei Jizō Bosatsu
Tsubakidō, Kawataki-chō, Shikoku-chūō City
☎ 0896-56-4523 A By bus bound for Shichida from Kawanoe Stn. Get off at Tsubakidō Bus Stop

When Kūkai heard that many people were suffering with a fever, he struck his staff into the ground and prayed. Later, the buds of a camellia tree (Tsubaki) emerged from the staff and this object became an object of faith of the local people.

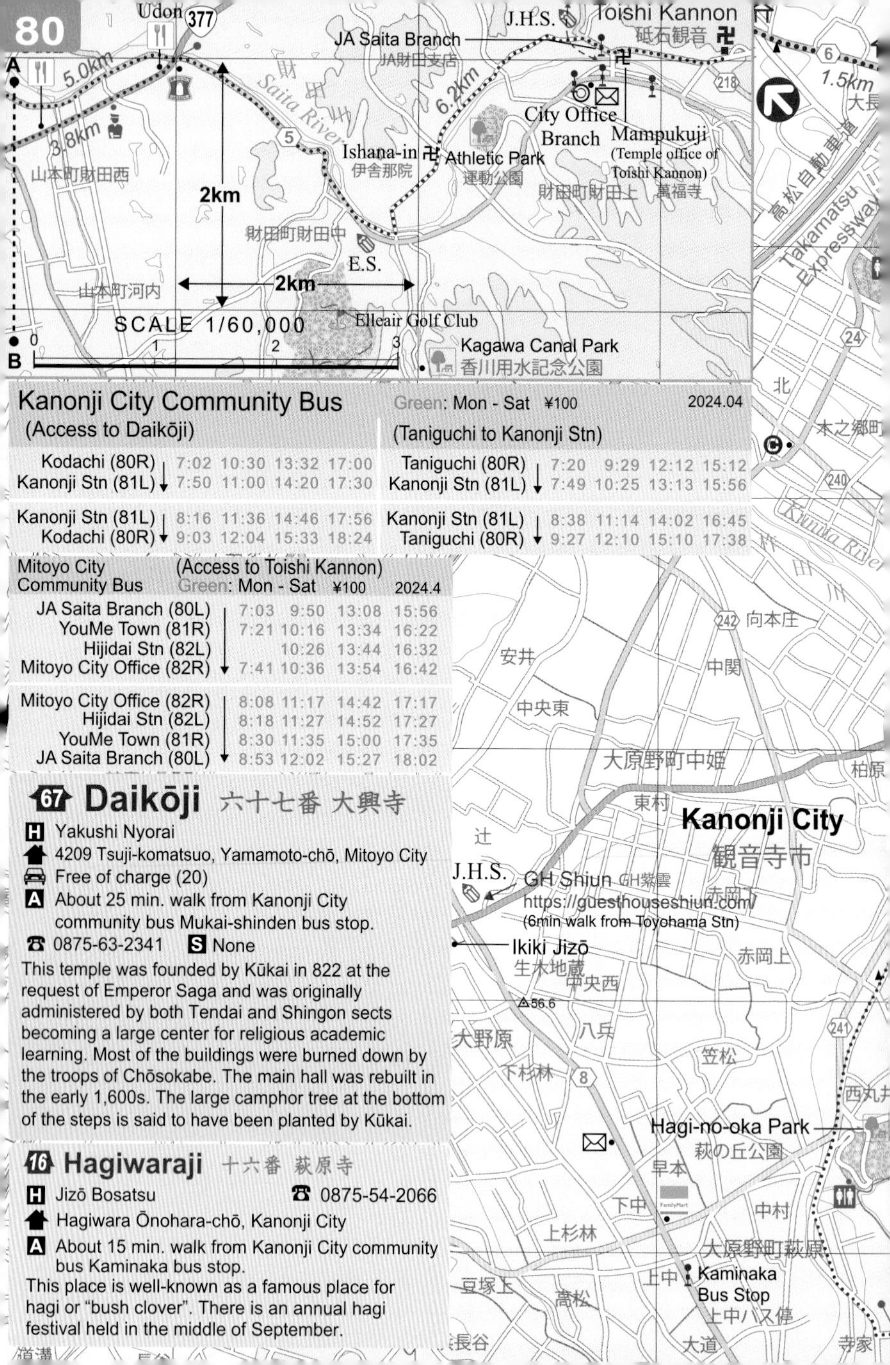
Udon
377
JA Saita Branch
JA財田支店
J.H.S.
Toishi Kannon
砥石観音
5.0km
3.8km
6.2km
1.5km
Saita River
山本町財田西
Ishana-in
伊舎那院
Athletic Park
運動公園
City Office Branch
Mampukuji
(Temple office of Toishi Kannon)
萬福寺
財田町財田上
2km
財田町財田中
E.S.
山本町河内
2km
SCALE 1/60,000
Elleair Golf Club
Kagawa Canal Park
香川用水記念公園
高松自動車道
Takamatsu Expressway
北
木之郷町
Kunita River
安井
向本庄
中関
中央東
大原野町中姫
柏原
東村
辻
Kanonji City
観音寺市
J.H.S.
GH Shiun GH紫雲
https://guesthouseshiun.com/
(6min walk from Toyohama Stn)
赤岡下
Ikiki Jizō
生木地蔵
中央西
赤岡上
56.6
大野原
八兵
笠松
下杉林
西丸井
Hagi-no-oka Park
萩の丘公園
早本
下中
中村
上杉林
大原野町萩原
豆塚上
上中
Kaminaka Bus Stop
上中バス停
高松
大道
寺家

Kanonji City Community Bus

(Access to Daikōji) — Green: Mon - Sat ¥100 — 2024.04

Kodachi (80R) ↓	7:02	10:30	13:32	17:00
Kanonji Stn (81L)	7:50	11:00	14:20	17:30
Kanonji Stn (81L) ↓	8:16	11:36	14:46	17:56
Kodachi (80R)	9:03	12:04	15:33	18:24

(Taniguchi to Kanonji Stn)

Taniguchi (80R) ↓	7:20	9:29	12:12	15:12
Kanonji Stn (81L)	7:49	10:25	13:13	15:56
Kanonji Stn (81L) ↓	8:38	11:14	14:02	16:45
Taniguchi (80R)	9:27	12:10	15:10	17:38

Mitoyo City Community Bus

(Access to Toishi Kannon) Green: Mon - Sat ¥100 2024.4

JA Saita Branch (80L) ↓	7:03	9:50	13:08	15:56
YouMe Town (81R)	7:21	10:16	13:34	16:22
Hijidai Stn (82L)		10:26	13:44	16:32
Mitoyo City Office (82R)	7:41	10:36	13:54	16:42
Mitoyo City Office (82R) ↓	8:08	11:17	14:42	17:17
Hijidai Stn (82L)	8:18	11:27	14:52	17:27
YouMe Town (81R)	8:30	11:35	15:00	17:35
JA Saita Branch (80L)	8:53	12:02	15:27	18:02

67 Daikōji 六十七番 大興寺

H Yakushi Nyorai

4209 Tsuji-komatsuo, Yamamoto-chō, Mitoyo City

Free of charge (20)

A About 25 min. walk from Kanonji City community bus Mukai-shinden bus stop.

☎ 0875-63-2341 S None

This temple was founded by Kūkai in 822 at the request of Emperor Saga and was originally administered by both Tendai and Shingon sects becoming a large center for religious academic learning. Most of the buildings were burned down by the troops of Chōsokabe. The main hall was rebuilt in the early 1,600s. The large camphor tree at the bottom of the steps is said to have been planted by Kūkai.

16 Hagiwaraji 十六番 萩原寺

H Jizō Bosatsu ☎ 0875-54-2066

Hagiwara Ōnohara-chō, Kanonji City

A About 15 min. walk from Kanonji City community bus Kaminaka bus stop.

This place is well-known as a famous place for hagi or "bush clover". There is an annual hagi festival held in the middle of September.

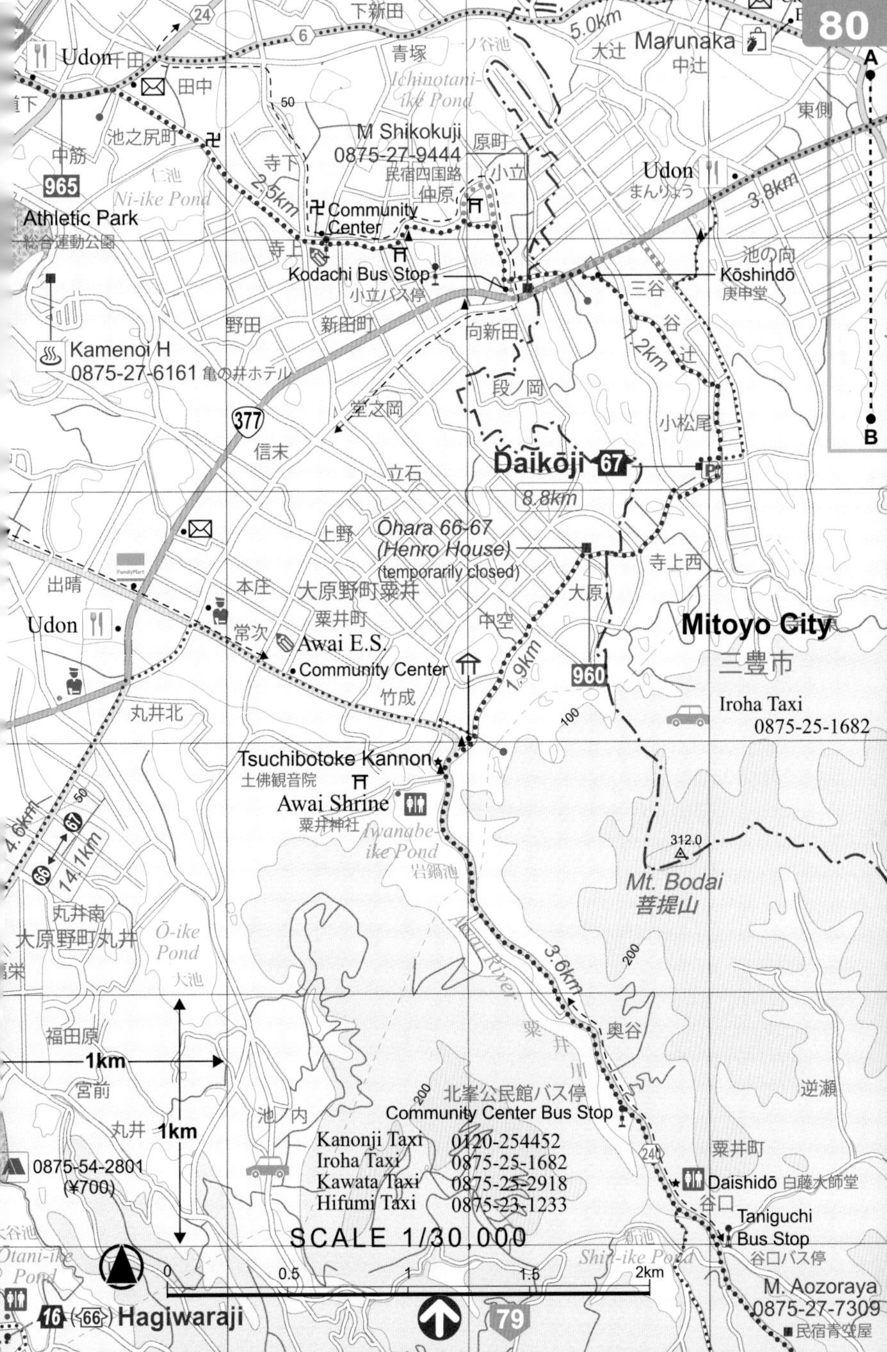

Udon
Marunaka
M Shikokuji
0875-27-9444
民宿四国路
Ichinotani-ike Pond
Ni-ike Pond
Athletic Park
総合運動公園
Community Center
Kodachi Bus Stop
小立バス停
Kōshindō
庚申堂
Kamenoi H
0875-27-6161 亀の井ホテル
5.0km
2.5km
3.8km
1.2km
Daikōji 67
8.8km
Ōhara 66-67
(Henro House)
(temporarily closed)
Udon
Awai E.S.
Community Center
Mitoyo City
三豊市
Iroha Taxi
0875-25-1682
1.9km
Tsuchibotoke Kannon
土佛観音院
Awai Shrine
粟井神社
Iwanabe-ike Pond
岩鍋池
Mt. Bodai
菩提山
312.0
4.6km
14.1km
Ō-ike Pond
大池
Awai River
3.6km
1km
1km
北峯公民館バス停
Community Center Bus Stop
Kanonji Taxi 0120-254452
Iroha Taxi 0875-25-1682
Kawata Taxi 0875-25-2918
Hifumi Taxi 0875-23-1233
0875-54-2801
(¥700)
Daishidō 白藤大師堂
Taniguchi Bus Stop
谷口バス停
SCALE 1/30,000
0 0.5 1 1.5 2km
Ōtani-ike Pond
Shin-ike Pond
M. Aozoraya
0875-27-7309
民宿青空屋
16 (66) Hagiwaraji
79
A
B

68 Jinnein 六十八番 神恵院

☎ 0875-25-3871
S None

H Amida Nyorai
1-2-7 Yahata-chō, Kanonji City
Free of charge (20)
A About 20 min. walk. from Kanonji Stn.

This temple was founded in 703 by a Buddhist priest, Nisshō. Gyōki came here in 722 and when Kūkai came in 807 he drew a picture of Amida Nyorai and enshrined it as the main deity. During the 19th century the picture was moved to Kannonji.
Originally, Kotohiki Hachiman shrine was the 68th sacred site, but due to the separation of Buddhism and Shintoism in 1868, Jinnein, which was managing the shrine, took over. However, Jinnein could not survive because it did not have any money so the Main hall was moved to the temple grounds of Kannonji.

69 Kannonji 六十九番 観音寺

☎ 0875-25-3871
S None

H Shō Kannon Bosatsu
3875 Yahata-chō,Kanonji City
Free of charge (20)
A About 20 min. walk. from Kanonji Stn.

Nisshō also founded this temple which is beside Temple 68 (Kotohiki Hachimangū). When Kūkai came in 807, he carved a statue of Shō Kannon Bosatsu and built a sanctuary to enshrine it on the hillside of the mountain. Kūkai increased the number of buildings and changed the name to Kannonji.

Kotohiki Park 琴弾公園

A huge, 17th century-style coin (called *"Kan-ei-tsū-hō"*) made of sand is the feature of this park. The coin is 345m in circumference. It is said that by looking at this coin, the viewer can ensure good health, a long life, and freedom from financial worry.

Kōryūji Ruins
興隆寺跡
(石塔群)
Fudō-no-taki Falls
Country Park
不動の滝カントリーパーク
Setouchi Base
(Henro House)
瀬戸内ベース
FamilyMart
200
100
50
Udon
かなくま餅
Saita River
財田川
1.9km
Kannonji 69
Jinnein 68
4.6km
970
Marunaka
Ichiya-an
一夜庵
M Yasuragi 銭形やすらぎ
080-3167-7311
八幡町
Kamara Jinja
加麻良神社
流岡町
Cafe
Kotohiki Park
68
Kotohiki Hachimangū
Sanka Bridge
三架橋
H.S.
BH Kanonji 観音寺
0875-23-1251
村黒町
Kotohiki
ことひき
R Bansui 旅館晩翠
Coop
JR Yosan Line
JR予讃線
30
Zenigata
銭形
藤川旅館 Fujikawa R
0875-25-3548
1.2km
Chūō H.S.
Gusto
City Office
坂本町
R Wakamatsuya Bekkan
若松家別館 0875-25-3277
237
JA
E.S.
植田町
Tourist Information
BH Sunny-inn
サニーイン 0875-23-3210
Hyper inn
ハイパーイン 0875-25-2818
Kanonji
観音寺
Joyfull
Hatagoya
0875-25-1858
旅籠屋
Ueda Tenmangu
植田天満宮
Driving School
240
6
1.8km
Kanonji City Community Bus Stop
Mitoyo City Community Bus Stop
Kanonji Grand BH
0875-25-5151
グランド
Okunobō Ido
奥の坊井戸
Marunaka
21
8
1.5km

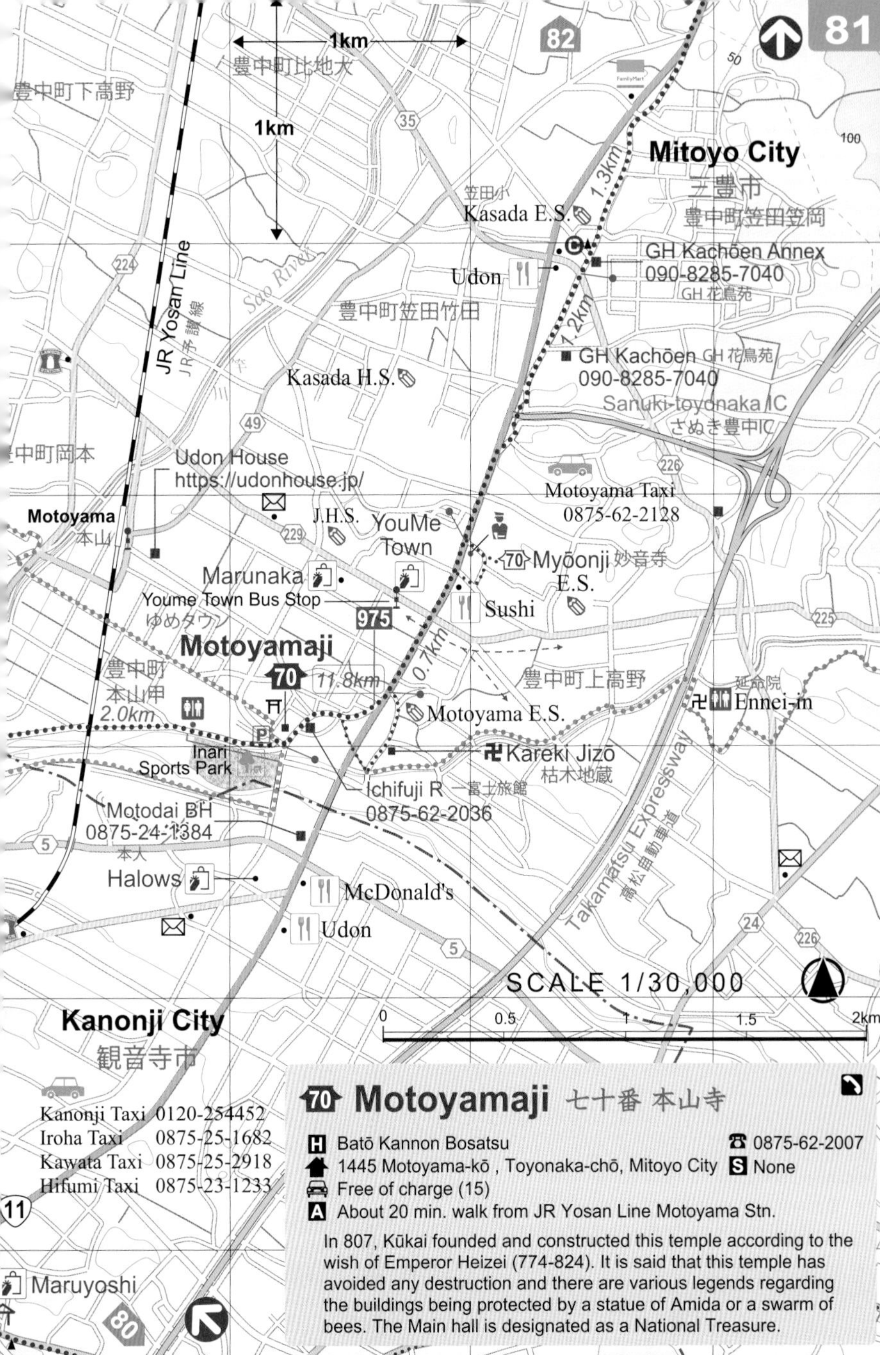
1km
1km
82
豊中町比地大
豊中町下高野
FamilyMart
35
Mitoyo City
三豊市
豊中町笠田笠岡
笠田小
Kasada E.S.
1.3km
GH Kachōen Annex
090-8285-7040
GH 花鳥苑
Udon
224
JR Yosan Line
JR予讃線
Sao River
豊中町笠田竹田
1.2km
GH Kachōen GH 花鳥苑
090-8285-7040
Kasada H.S.
Sanuki-toyonaka IC
さぬき豊中IC
49
中町岡本
Udon House
https://udonhouse.jp/
226
Motoyama Taxi
0875-62-2128
Motoyama
本山
J.H.S.
YouMe Town
229
Myōonji 妙音寺
E.S.
Marunaka
Youme Town Bus Stop
ゆめタウン
975
Sushi
225
Motoyamaji
0.7km
豊中町本山甲
70
11.8km
2.0km
豊中町上高野
延命院
Ennei-in
Motoyama E.S.
Inari Sports Park
Kareki Jizō
枯木地蔵
Ichifuji R 一富士旅館
0875-62-2036
Motodai BH
0875-24-1384
5
本大
Takamatsu Expressway
高松自動車道
Halows
McDonald's
Udon
24
226
5
SCALE 1/30,000
0
0.5
1
1.5
2km
Kanonji City
観音寺市
Kanonji Taxi 0120-254452
Iroha Taxi 0875-25-1682
Kawata Taxi 0875-25-2918
Hifumi Taxi 0875-23-1233
11
Maruyoshi
80

70 Motoyamaji 七十番 本山寺

H Batō Kannon Bosatsu
☎ 0875-62-2007
1445 Motoyama-kō , Toyonaka-chō, Mitoyo City
S None
Free of charge (15)
A About 20 min. walk from JR Yosan Line Motoyama Stn.

In 807, Kūkai founded and constructed this temple according to the wish of Emperor Heizei (774-824). It is said that this temple has avoided any destruction and there are various legends regarding the buildings being protected by a statue of Amida or a swarm of bees. The Main hall is designated as a National Treasure.

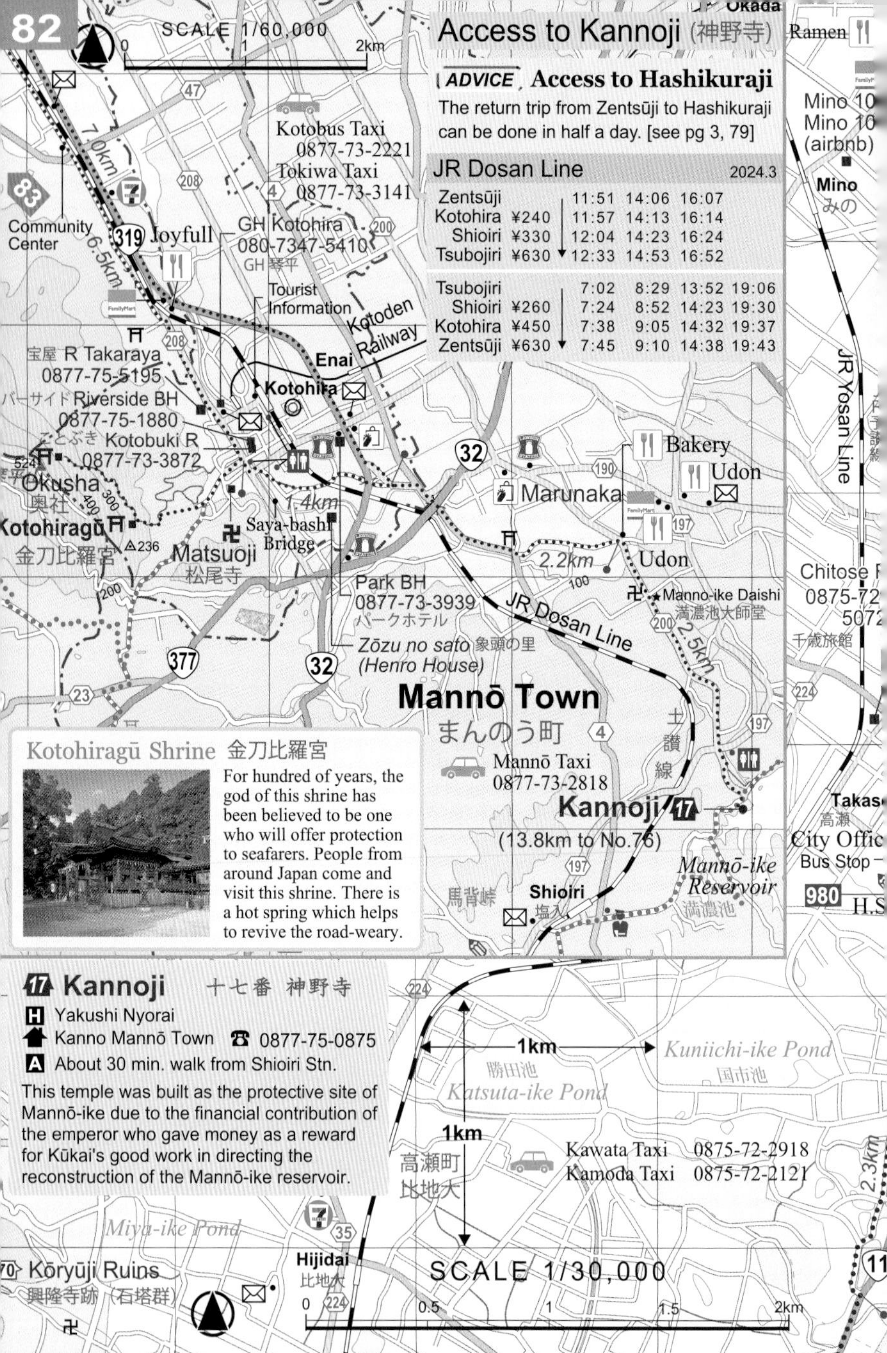
SCALE 1/60,000
0 1 2km
Access to Kannoji (神野寺)
ADVICE Access to Hashikuraji
The return trip from Zentsūji to Hashikuraji can be done in half a day. [see pg 3, 79]
JR Dosan Line 2024.3
Zentsūji 11:51 14:06 16:07
Kotohira ¥240 11:57 14:13 16:14
Shioiri ¥330 12:04 14:23 16:24
Tsubojiri ¥630 12:33 14:53 16:52
Tsubojiri 7:02 8:29 13:52 19:06
Shioiri ¥260 7:24 8:52 14:23 19:30
Kotohira ¥450 7:38 9:05 14:32 19:37
Zentsūji ¥630 7:45 9:10 14:38 19:43
Okada
Ramen
Mino 10
Mino 10
(airbnb)
Mino
みの
JR Yosan Line
Kotobus Taxi
0877-73-2221
Tokiwa Taxi
0877-73-3141
7.0km
Community Center
Joyfull
GH Kotohira
080-7347-5410
GH 琴平
6.5km
Tourist Information
Kotoden Railway
Enai
Kotohira
宝屋 R Takaraya
0877-75-5195
リバーサイド Riverside BH
0877-75-1880
ことぶき Kotobuki R
0877-73-3872
Okusha
奥社
Kotohiragū
金刀比羅宮
236
1.4km
Saya-bashi Bridge
Matsuoji
松尾寺
Park BH
0877-73-3939
パークホテル
Zōzu no sato 象頭の里
(Henro House)
Bakery
Udon
Marunaka
Udon
2.2km
Manno-ike Daishi
満濃池大師堂
2.5km
JR Dosan Line
Chitose
0875-72
5072
千歳旅館
Mannō Town
まんのう町
Mannō Taxi
0877-73-2818
Kannoji 17
(13.8km to No.76)
土讃線
Shioiri
塩入
馬背峠
Mannō-ike Reservoir
満濃池
Takase
高瀬
City Office
Bus Stop
H.S
Kotohiragū Shrine 金刀比羅宮
For hundred of years, the god of this shrine has been believed to be one who will offer protection to seafarers. People from around Japan come and visit this shrine. There is a hot spring which helps to revive the road-weary.
17 Kannoji 十七番 神野寺
Yakushi Nyorai
Kanno Mannō Town 0877-75-0875
About 30 min. walk from Shioiri Stn.
This temple was built as the protective site of Mannō-ike due to the financial contribution of the emperor who gave money as a reward for Kūkai's good work in directing the reconstruction of the Mannō-ike reservoir.
1km
1km
Kuniichi-ike Pond
国市池
Katsuta-ike Pond
勝田池
高瀬町
比地大
Kawata Taxi 0875-72-2918
Kamoda Taxi 0875-72-2121
2.3km
Miya-ike Pond
70 Kōryūji Ruins
興隆寺跡（石塔群）
Hijidai
比地大
SCALE 1/30,000
0 0.5 1 1.5 2km

Sakura Taxi 0120-225048 0875-72-5048

GH Shippōya 090-4970-1654 七宝屋

Hoshikawa R. 0875-72-5041 ほ志川旅館

Mannō-ike Reservoir 満濃池

Since olden times, rain has been scarce in Kagawa prefecture and the local people have had to worry about the lack of water. To solve this problem a reservoir called Mannō-ike was built in present day Mannō town between 701-704. However, during a flood in 818 the retaining wall broke and it was decided that Kūkai should act as supervisor for its reconstruction. He took on the job and completed the project in an unexpected fast period of only three months because the local people were so eager to work under his direction.

71 Iyadaniji 七十一番 弥谷寺

H Senju Kannon Bosatsu
70 Omi-otsu, Mino-chō, Mitoyo City
Charge (30) A 3.3 km from Mino Stn.
☎ 0875-72-3446 S None

Gyōki founded this temple and it was originally called "Eight Province Temple" *(Yakuni-dera)* because from here one can see eight surrounding provinces. When Kūkai revisited here in 807, he participated in the gumonji-hō rite and changed its name. This temple is attributed with many miracle cures.

72 Mandalaji 七十二番 曼荼羅寺

H Dainichi Nyorai
1380-1 Yoshiwara-chō, Zentsūji City
Charge (10)
A By community bus from Shiyakusho-mae (City hall). Get off at Mandalaji-mae.
☎ 0877-63-0072 S None

This temple, built in 596 and originally called Yozakaji, was the clan temple for the Saeki family the ancestors of Kūkai. After his return from China, Kūkai dedicated the Kongōkai and Taizōkai Mandala and changed the name of the temple to Mandalaji.

73 Shusshakaji 七十三番 出釈迦寺

H Shaka Nyorai
1091 Yoshiwara-chō, Zentsūji City
Free of charge (20)
A By community bus from Shiyakusho-mae (City hall). Get off at Mandalaji-mae, about 10 min. walk.
☎ 0877-63-0073 S None

According to legend, Kūkai, at the age of seven, climbed the mountain (481m) and said, "I want to enter the world of Buddhism and save many people. If it is not possible for this wish to come true, I command that Shaka Nyorai appear. If not, I will throw away my life." He then jumped off a cliff and Shaka Nyorai and a heavenly being appeared and saved his life. As a result, he carved a statue, constructed temple buildings, and founded this temple.

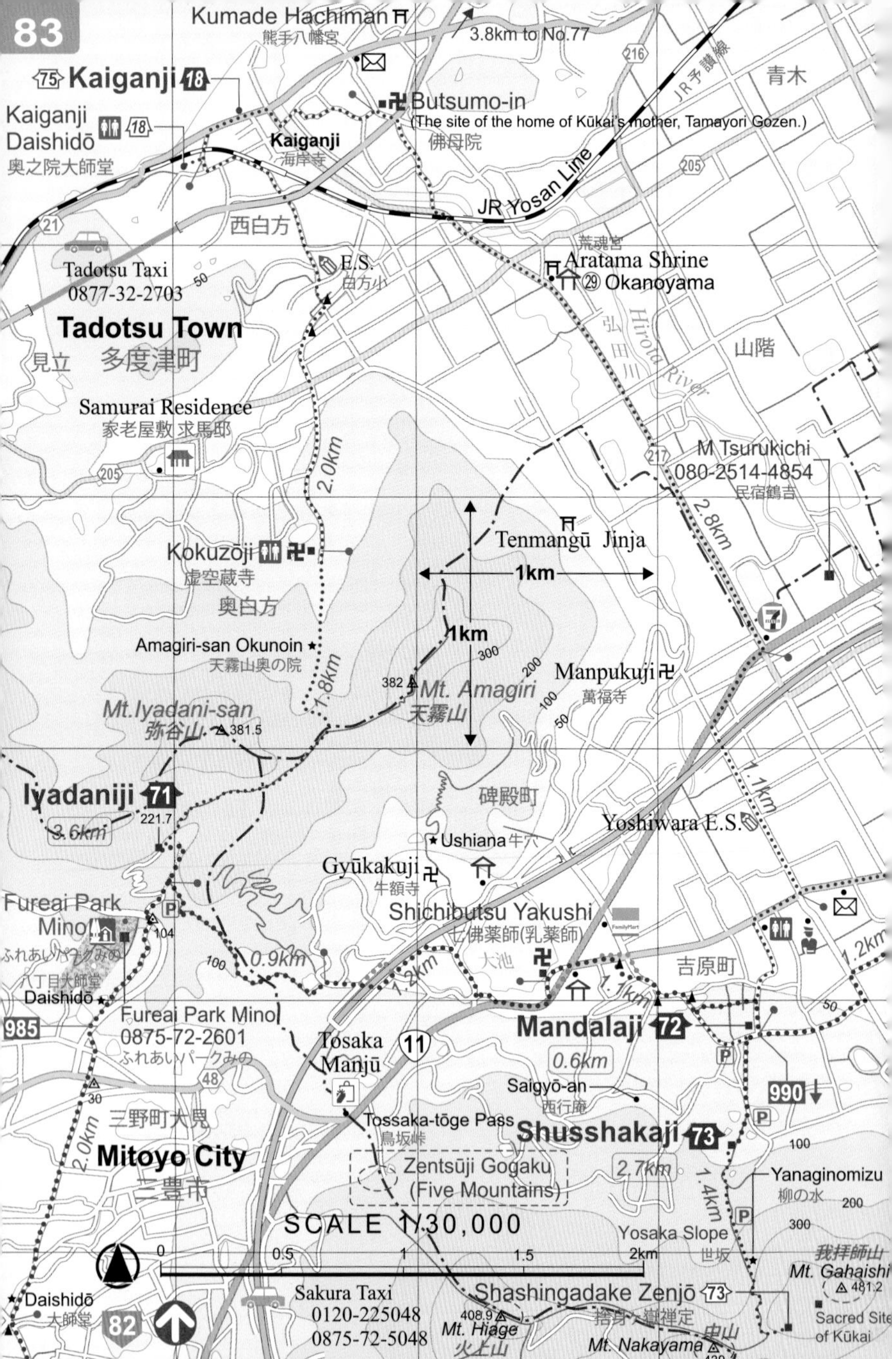

Kumade Hachiman
熊手八幡宮
3.8km to No.77
75 Kaiganji 18
Kaiganji Daishidō 18
奥之院大師堂
Butsumo-in
(The site of the home of Kūkai's mother, Tamayori Gozen.)
佛母院
Kaiganji
海岸寺
JR予讃線
青木
JR Yosan Line
西白方
荒魂宮
Aratama Shrine
29 Okanoyama
Tadotsu Taxi
0877-32-2703
E.S.
白方小
Tadotsu Town
見立
多度津町
弘田川
Hirota River
山階
Samurai Residence
家老屋敷 求馬邸
2.0km
M Tsurukichi
080-2514-4854
民宿鶴吉
2.8km
Tenmangū Jinja
1km
Kokuzōji
虚空蔵寺
奥白方
Amagiri-san Okunoin
天霧山奥の院
1.8km
382
Mt. Amagiri
天霧山
Manpukuji
萬福寺
Mt.Iyadani-san
弥谷山
381.5
Iyadaniji 71
3.6km
221.7
碑殿町
1.1km
Yoshiwara E.S.
Ushiana 牛穴
Gyūkakuji
牛額寺
Fureai Park Mino
ふれあいパークみの
104
Shichibutsu Yakushi
七佛薬師(乳薬師)
大池
吉原町
1.2km
八丁目大師堂
Daishidō
0.9km
1.2km
1.1km
Fureai Park Mino
0875-72-2601
ふれあいパークみの
Mandalaji 72
0.6km
Tosaka Manjū
11
48
Saigyō-an
西行庵
990
三野町大見
Tossaka-tōge Pass
鳥坂峠
Shusshakaji 73
2.7km
1.4km
Yanaginomizu
柳の水
Mitoyo City
三豊市
2.0km
Zentsūji Gogaku
(Five Mountains)
SCALE 1/30,000
Yosaka Slope
世坂
我拝師山
Mt. Gahaishi
481.2
Daishidō
大師堂
Sakura Taxi
0120-225048
0875-72-5048
Shashingadake Zenjō 73
捨身ヶ嶽禅定
408.9
Mt. Hiage
火上山
中山
Mt. Nakayama
Sacred Site of Kūkai

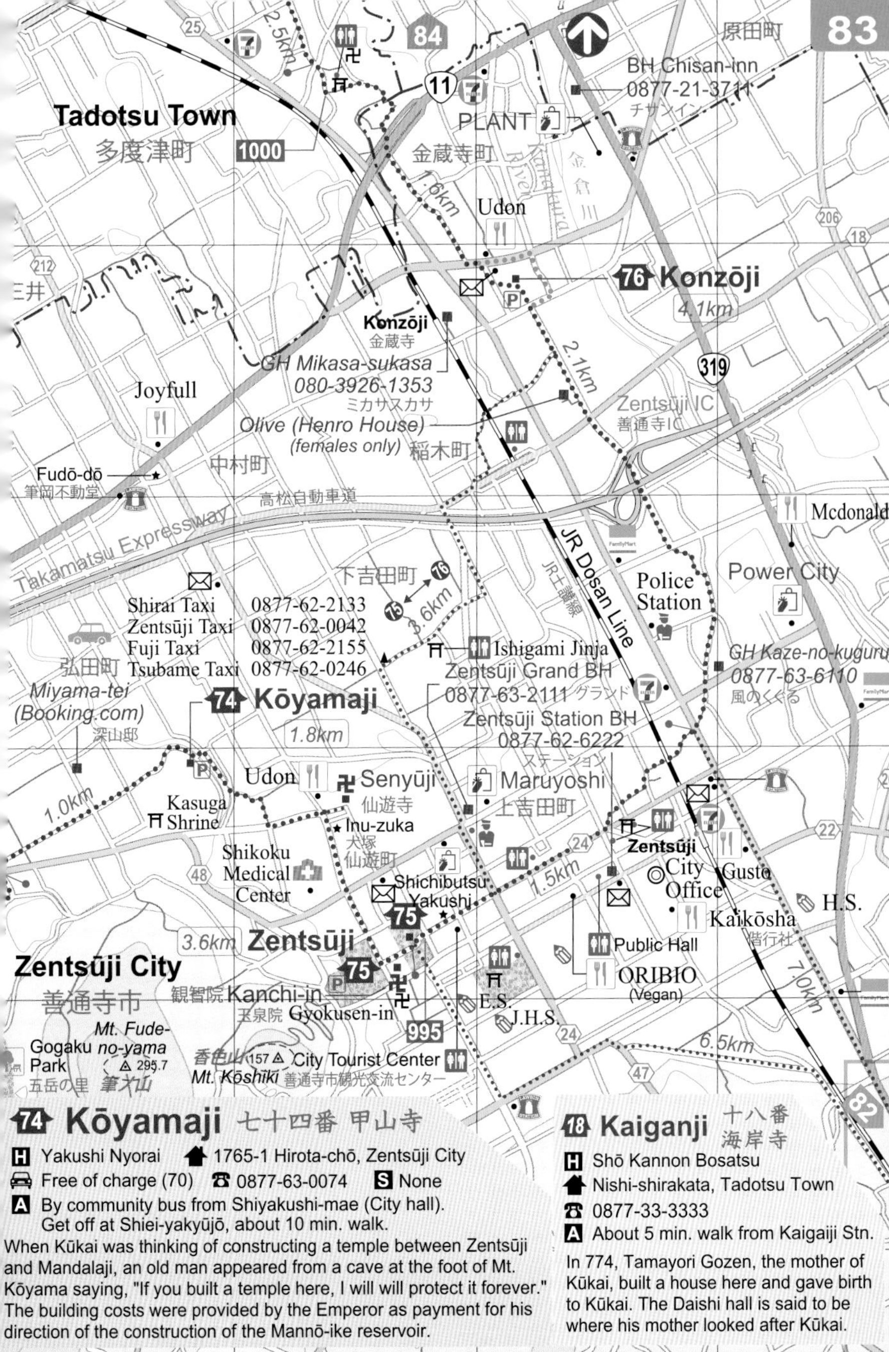

Tadotsu Town
多度津町
84
1000
2.5km
11
25
BH Chisan-inn
0877-21-3711
チサンイン
原田町
PLANT
金蔵寺町
Kanakura River
金倉川
1.6km
Udon
206
18
212
三井
76 Konzōji
4.1km
Konzōji
金蔵寺
GH Mikasa-sukasa
080-3926-1353
ミカサスカサ
2.1km
319
Zentsūji IC
善通寺IC
Joyfull
Olive (Henro House)
(females only)
稲木町
中村町
Fudō-dō
筆岡不動堂
高松自動車道
Takamatsu Expressway
Mcdonald
JR Dosan Line
JR土讃線
下吉田町
3.6km
Police Station
Power City
Shirai Taxi 0877-62-2133
Zentsūji Taxi 0877-62-0042
Fuji Taxi 0877-62-2155
Tsubame Taxi 0877-62-0246
弘田町
Ishigami Jinja
Zentsūji Grand BH
0877-63-2111 グランド
GH Kaze-no-kuguru
0877-63-6110
風のくぐる
Miyama-tei
(Booking.com)
深山邸
74 Kōyamaji
1.8km
Zentsūji Station BH
0877-62-6222
ステーション
1.0km
Udon
Senyūji
仙遊寺
Maruyoshi
上吉田町
Kasuga Shrine
Inu-zuka
犬塚
仙遊町
24
22
Zentsūji
Gusto
Shikoku Medical Center
48
1.5km
City Office
Shichibutsu Yakushi
H.S.
Kaikōsha
偕行社
75
3.6km
Zentsūji
Public Hall
7.0km
Zentsūji City
善通寺市
75
観智院 Kanchi-in
E.S.
ORIBIO
(Vegan)
玉泉院 Gyokusen-in
J.H.S.
995
Mt. Fude-no-yama
295.7
筆ノ山
Gogaku Park
五岳の里
香色山 157
Mt. Kōshiki
City Tourist Center
善通寺市観光交流センター
6.5km
47
82

74 Kōyamaji 七十四番 甲山寺

H Yakushi Nyorai
🏠 1765-1 Hirota-chō, Zentsūji City
🚗 Free of charge (70) ☎ 0877-63-0074 S None
A By community bus from Shiyakushi-mae (City hall). Get off at Shiei-yakyūjō, about 10 min. walk.

When Kūkai was thinking of constructing a temple between Zentsūji and Mandalaji, an old man appeared from a cave at the foot of Mt. Kōyama saying, "If you built a temple here, I will will protect it forever." The building costs were provided by the Emperor as payment for his direction of the construction of the Mannō-ike reservoir.

18 Kaiganji 十八番 海岸寺

H Shō Kannon Bosatsu
🏠 Nishi-shirakata, Tadotsu Town
☎ 0877-33-3333
A About 5 min. walk from Kaigaiji Stn.

In 774, Tamayori Gozen, the mother of Kūkai, built a house here and gave birth to Kūkai. The Daishi hall is said to be where his mother looked after Kūkai.

76 Konzōji 七十六番 金倉寺

☎ 0877-62-0845
S None

H Yakushi Nyorai
1160 Konzōji-chō, Zentsūji City
Charge (80)

A About 5 min. walk from JR Dosan Line Konzōji Stn.

In 774, Wake no Michimaro (Dōzen) founded this temple and named it Dōzenji. Enchin (794-864), cousin of Kūkai, after returning from China in 858 lived here for awhile and remodeled the buildings to resemble Shōryūji in China. The buildings were destroyed during the 16th century; however, they were rebuilt during the Kanei era (1624-1644).

75 Zentsūji 七十五番 善通寺

H Yakushi Nyorai
3-3-1 Zentsūji-chō, Zentsūji City
Charge (200)
☎ 0877-62-0111
S Available

A About 20 min. walk from JR Dosan Line Zentsūji Stn.

Zentsūji Temple is the birthplace of Kūkai (774-835) and Zentsūji City has developed to meet the needs of visitors to this site. Along with Kongōbuji on Mt. Kōya (Wakayama pref.) and Tōji temple in Kyōto, it is one of the three most important sites related to Kūkai. The temple grounds are large and there are many interesting sites to see. For example, the Kaidan-meguri (¥500) is a 90 meter path under the Main hall which must be walked in total darkness.

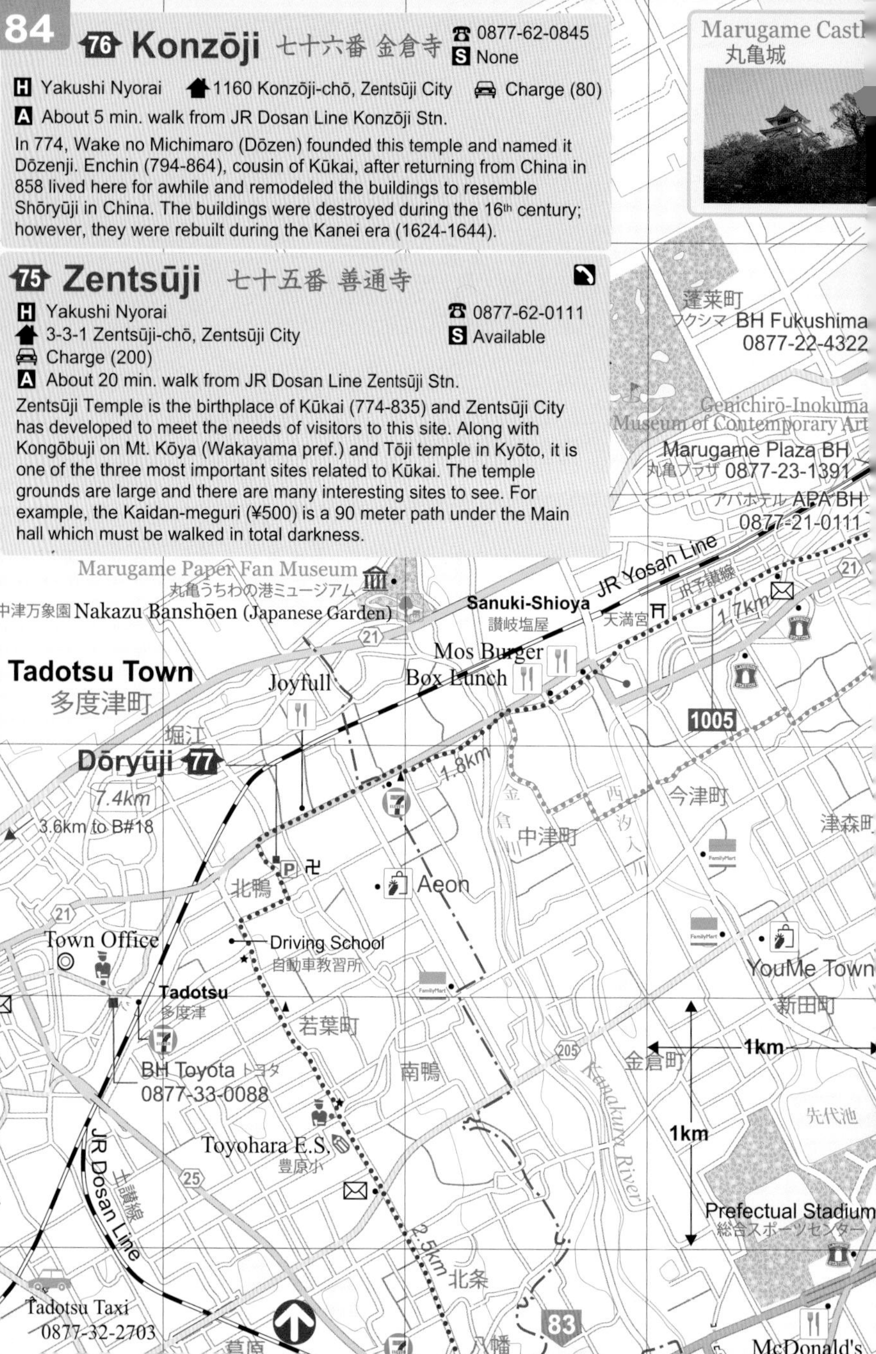

Marugame Castle
丸亀城
蓬莱町
フクシマ BH Fukushima
0877-22-4322
Genichirō-Inokuma
Museum of Contemporary Art
Marugame Plaza BH
丸亀プラザ 0877-23-1391
アパホテル APA BH
0877-21-0111
Marugame Paper Fan Museum
丸亀うちわの港ミュージアム
中津万象園 Nakazu Banshōen (Japanese Garden)
Sanuki-Shioya
讃岐塩屋
JR Yosan Line
JR予讃線
天満宮
1.7km
21
Mos Burger
Box Lunch
Tadotsu Town
多度津町
Joyfull
堀江
Dōryūji 77
1005
1.8km
7.4km
3.6km to B#18
金倉川
中津町
西汐入川
今津町
津森町
北鴨
Aeon
Town Office
Driving School
自動車教習所
Tadotsu
多度津
YouMe Town
新田町
若葉町
1km
南鴨
金倉町
BH Toyota トヨタ
0877-33-0088
205
Kanakura River
先代池
Toyohara E.S.
豊原小
25
JR Dosan Line
土讃線
2.5km
Prefectual Stadium
総合スポーツセンター
北条
Tadotsu Taxi
0877-32-2703
83
八幡
McDonald's

…was constructed under the direction of Ikoma Chikamasa (1526-1603), lord of the Sanuki (Kagawa) domain, over a period of five years from 1597. The castle keep stills remains today and it is a symbol of Marugame City. The fan-shaped rocks are well-known and the gate and castle keep are considered important cultural properties.

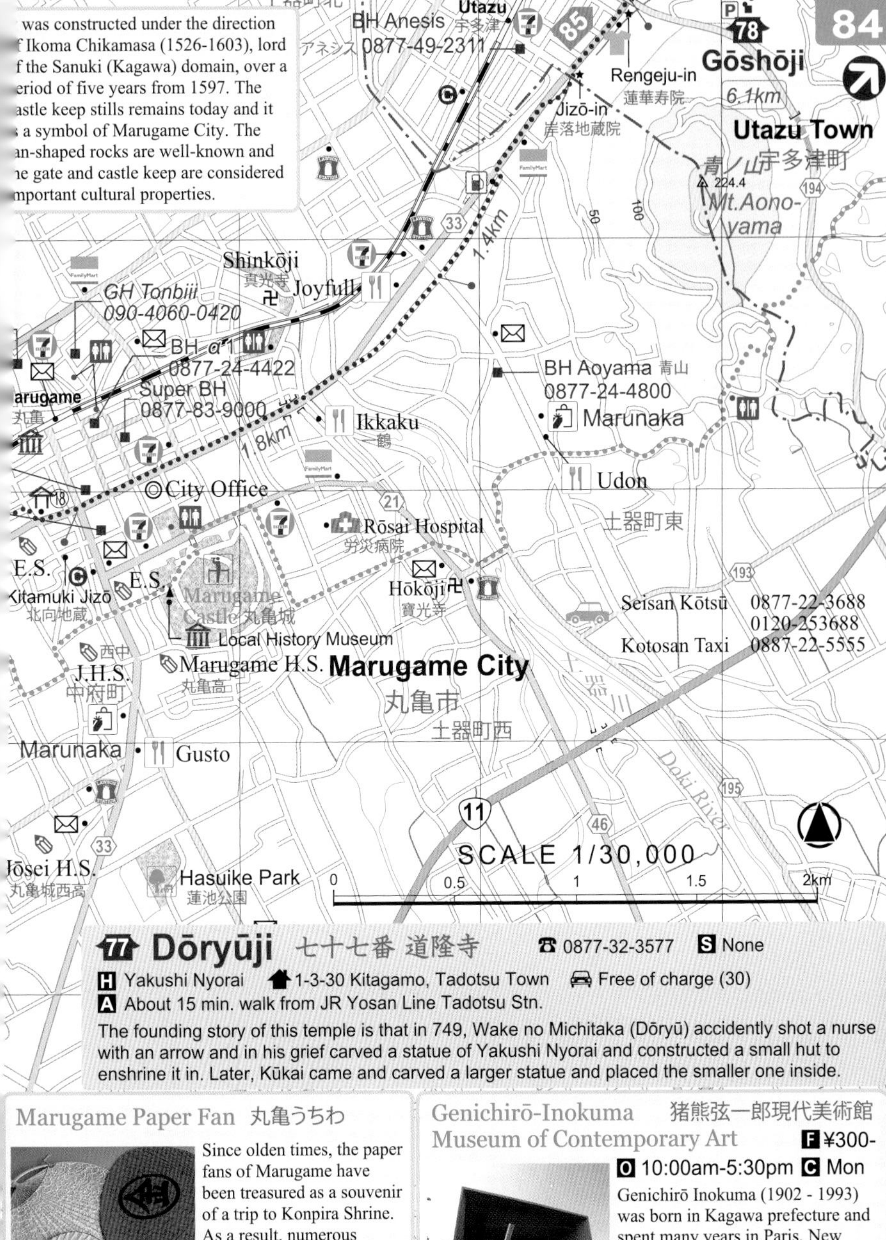
Utazu
宇多津
BH Anesis
アネシス 0877-49-2311
85
78
Gōshōji
6.1km
Rengeju-in
蓮華寿院
Jizō-in
岸落地蔵院
Utazu Town
宇多津町
青ノ山
224.4
Mt.Aono-yama
194
33
1.4km
Shinkōji
真光寺
Joyfull
GH Tonbiii
090-4060-0420
BH α'1
0877-24-4422
Super BH
0877-83-9000
Marugame
丸亀
1.8km
Ikkaku
一鶴
BH Aoyama 青山
0877-24-4800
Marunaka
Udon
City Office
18
21
Rōsai Hospital
労災病院
土器町東
E.S.
Kitamuki Jizō
北向地蔵
Marugame Castle 丸亀城
Local History Museum
Hōkōji
寶光寺
193
Seisan Kōtsū 0877-22-3688
0120-253688
Kotosan Taxi 0887-22-5555
西中
J.H.S.
中府町
Marugame H.S.
丸亀高
Marugame City
丸亀市
土器町西
土器川
Marunaka
Gusto
Doki River
195
11
46
33
Jōsei H.S.
丸亀城西高
Hasuike Park
蓮池公園
SCALE 1/30,000
0 0.5 1 1.5 2km

77 Dōryūji 七十七番 道隆寺

☎ 0877-32-3577 **S** None

H Yakushi Nyorai 1-3-30 Kitagamo, Tadotsu Town Free of charge (30)

A About 15 min. walk from JR Yosan Line Tadotsu Stn.

The founding story of this temple is that in 749, Wake no Michitaka (Dōryū) accidently shot a nurse with an arrow and in his grief carved a statue of Yakushi Nyorai and constructed a small hut to enshrine it in. Later, Kūkai came and carved a larger statue and placed the smaller one inside.

Marugame Paper Fan 丸亀うちわ

Since olden times, the paper fans of Marugame have been treasured as a souvenir of a trip to Konpira Shrine. As a result, numerous manufacturers of fans have sprung up and now this area holds 90% of the national production share.

Genichirō-Inokuma Museum of Contemporary Art 猪熊弦一郎現代美術館

F ¥300-

O 10:00am-5:30pm **C** Mon

Genichirō Inokuma (1902 - 1993) was born in Kagawa prefecture and spent many years in Paris, New York and Hawaii. His artworks are on display in this museum, and there is also a cafe-restaurant onsite and a hall which hosts films and concerts.

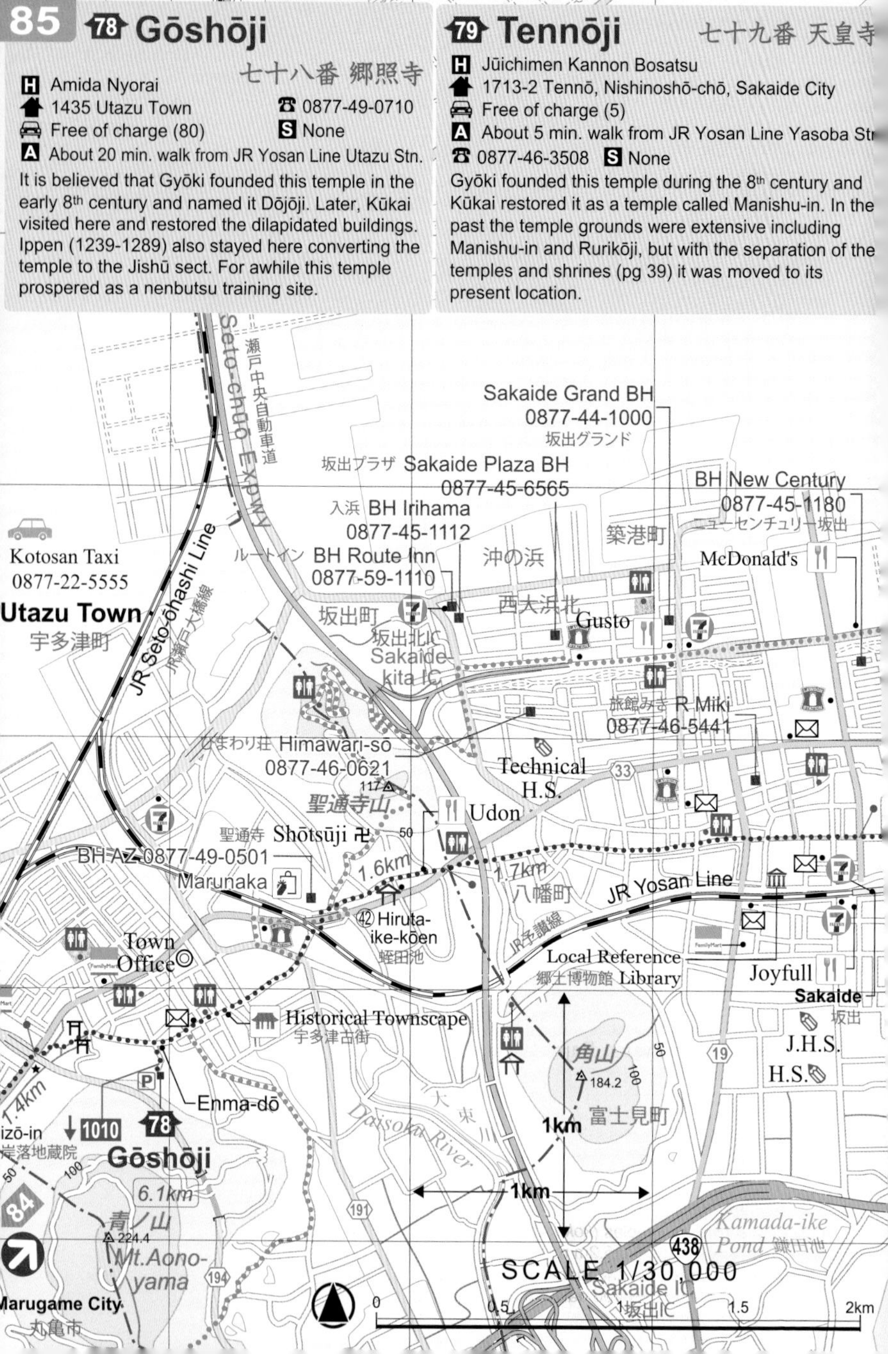

78 Gōshōji 七十八番 郷照寺

H Amida Nyorai
🏠 1435 Utazu Town ☎ 0877-49-0710
🚗 Free of charge (80) S None
A About 20 min. walk from JR Yosan Line Utazu Stn.

It is believed that Gyōki founded this temple in the early 8th century and named it Dōjōji. Later, Kūkai visited here and restored the dilapidated buildings. Ippen (1239-1289) also stayed here converting the temple to the Jishū sect. For awhile this temple prospered as a nenbutsu training site.

79 Tennōji 七十九番 天皇寺

H Jūichimen Kannon Bosatsu
🏠 1713-2 Tennō, Nishinoshō-chō, Sakaide City
🚗 Free of charge (5)
A About 5 min. walk from JR Yosan Line Yasoba Stn
☎ 0877-46-3508 S None

Gyōki founded this temple during the 8th century and Kūkai restored it as a temple called Manishu-in. In the past the temple grounds were extensive including Manishu-in and Rurikōji, but with the separation of the temples and shrines (pg 39) it was moved to its present location.

Seto-chūō Expwy
瀬戸中央自動車道
Sakaide Grand BH
0877-44-1000
坂出グランド
坂出プラザ Sakaide Plaza BH
0877-45-6565
BH New Century
0877-45-1180
ニューセンチュリー坂出
入浜 BH Irihama
0877-45-1112
ルートイン BH Route Inn
0877-59-1110
築港町
沖の浜
McDonald's
Kotosan Taxi
0877-22-5555
Utazu Town
宇多津町
JR Seto-ōhashi Line
JR瀬戸大橋線
坂出町
西大浜北
Gusto
坂出北IC
Sakaide-kita IC
旅館みき R.Miki
0877-46-5441
ひまわり荘 Himawari-sō
0877-46-0621
Technical H.S.
33
117
聖通寺山
Udon
聖通寺 Shōtsūji
50
BH AZ 0877-49-0501
Marunaka
1.6km
1.7km
八幡町
JR Yosan Line
JR予讃線
42 Hiruta-ike-kōen
蛭田池
Town Office
Local Reference Library
郷土博物館
Joyfull
Sakaide
坂出
Historical Townscape
宇多津古街
J.H.S.
H.S.
角山
184.2
19
Enma-dō
富士見町
1.4km
1km
1010
78
Gōshōji
大束川
Daisoku River
6.1km
84
青ノ山
224.4
Mt.Aono-yama
1km
191
194
Kamada-ike Pond 鎌田池
438
SCALE 1/30,000
Sakaide IC
坂出IC
0
0.5
1
1.5
2km
Marugame City
丸亀市

NOTE Sutoku Jōkō (1119-1164) Story 崇徳上皇

ōkō" is the official title given to an emperor (Tennō) who has retired. From 1123 to 1142 Sutoku reigned as e 75th emperor of Japan, but in 1156 he was exiled to Sanuki after losing the Hōgen rebellion and lived a e of confinement in the town of Sakaide until his murder in the summer of 1164. But to prevent his body om decomposing while they waited for an order from Kyōto the authorities put his body in the Yasoba pond. nce they received a reply they cremated his body and buried his ashes close to temple no. 81, Shiromineji. or this reason No. 79 became Tennōji (Temple of the Emperor) and people worship him at the neighbouring hrine, Shirominegu. In later generations Sutoku appears in many pictures and stories as a vengeful spirit om his unfortunate life.

Distance Comparison
79 → 81 → 82 → 80 → 83
7.7km 5.0km 6.8km 9.1km total: 28.6km
79 → 80 → 81 → 82 → 83
6.7km 6.6km 5.0km 12.4km total: 30.7km
NOTE Enma 閻魔
He is the god of hell who judges the dead based on their actions while alive and decides whether they will go heaven or hell. A building with a statue of Enma is located at the entrance of Temple No. 78.
Sakaide City
坂出市
Sanuki-hama-kaidō Road
さぬき浜街道
Aya-gawa River
林田町
E.S.
81 ↔ 79
7.7km
2.5km
Kumoi Gosho
(Sutoku residence ruins)
雲井御所
to No.81
久米町
江尻町
Ryūkōin 龍光院
1015
86
Kaisei Hosp
回生病院
City Office
Marunaka
Police Office
Drugstore
Community Center
1.9km
西庄小
E.S.
E.S.
1.7km
八十場
Yasoba
坂出江尻
1.0km
Kiyomizu-ya
清水屋
Yasoba-no-mizu
八十場の水
0.6km
1.6km
E.S.
Shiraminegū 79
Rurikōji 79
瑠璃光寺
白峰宮
Tennōji 79
Yasoba
(Henro House)
八十場
to No.80
Kanayama Jinja
6.7km
79 Fudōnotaki
Manishuin
不動の滝・魔尼珠院

80 Kokubunji 八十番 国分寺

☎ 087-874-0033
S None

H Jūichimen Senju Kannon Bosatsu
2065 Kokubunji-chō-kokubu,Takamatsu City
Free of charge (20)
A About 5 min. walk from JR Yosan Line Kokubu Stn.

This is the fourth provincial temples *(kokubunji)* on Shikoku and was founded by Gyōki who carved the 5.2m main deity statue. Later, Kūkai came, repaired the statue and made this temple a sacred site. The bell and Main hall have escaped damage over the centuries and are Important Cultural Treasures. (Admission Fee: ¥200)

S-K Taxi	0877-44-1111
Shikoku Taxi	0877-44-0001
Kotosan Taxi	0800-100-5103
	0877-46-3805

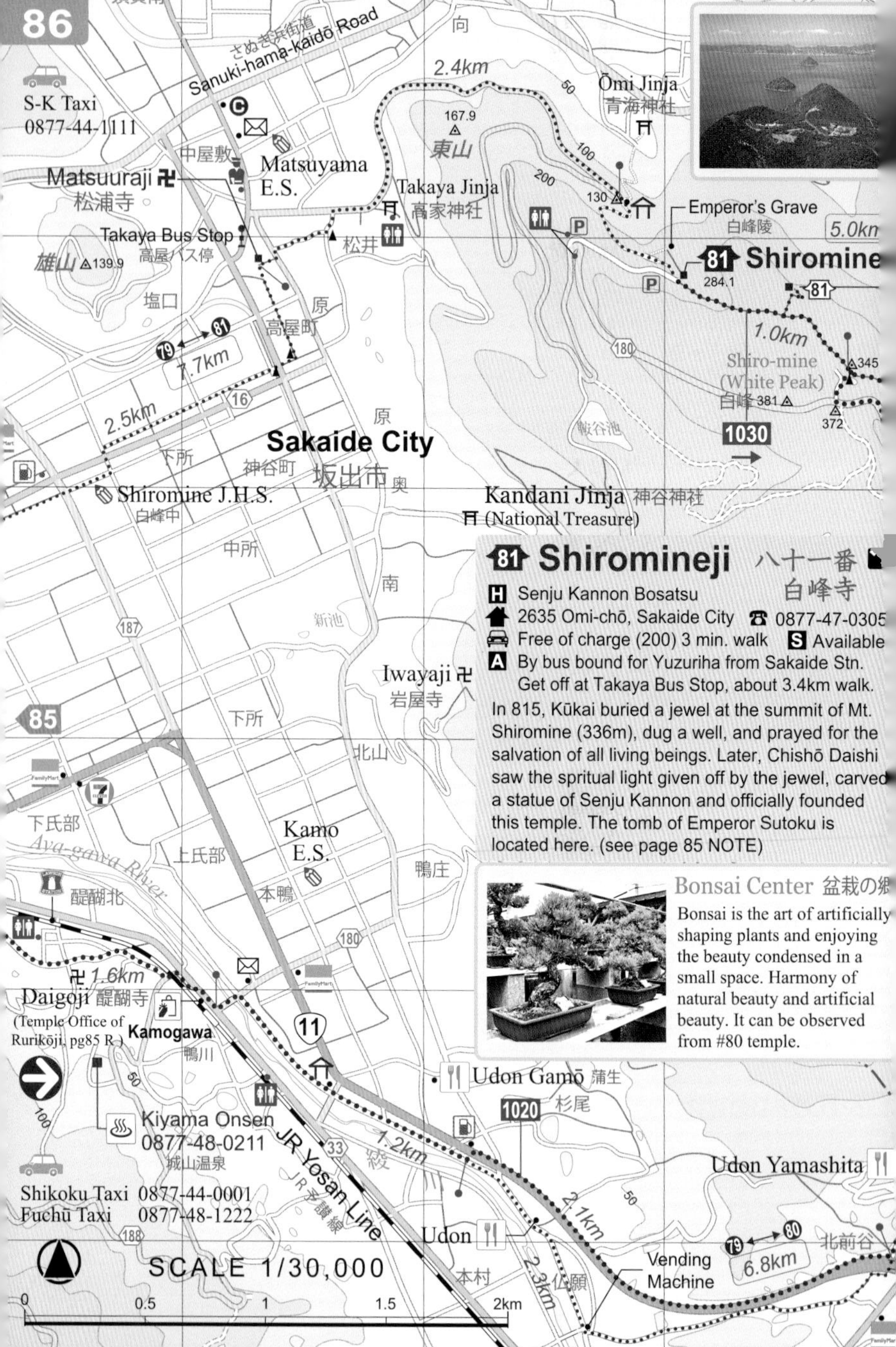

S-K Taxi
0877-44-1111
さぬき浜街道
Sanuki-hama-kaidō Road
向
2.4km
Ōmi Jinja
青海神社
167.9
東山
中屋敷
Matsuuraji
松浦寺
Matsuyama
E.S.
Takaya Jinja
高家神社
Takaya Bus Stop
高屋バス停
松井
雄山
139.9
塩口
原
高屋町
Emperor's Grave
白峰陵
5.0km
81 Shiromine
284.1
1.0km
Shiro-mine
(White Peak)
白峰 381
345
372
79 81
7.7km
2.5km
原
Sakaide City
坂出市
神谷町
下所
奥
綾谷池
1030
Shiromine J.H.S.
白峰中
Kandani Jinja 神谷神社
(National Treasure)
中所
南
新池
Iwayaji
岩屋寺
85
下所
北山
下氏部
Aya-gawa River
上氏部
Kamo
E.S.
鴨庄
醍醐北
本鴨
1.6km
Daigoji 醍醐寺
(Temple Office of
Rurikōji, pg85 R)
Kamogawa
鴨川
Kiyama Onsen
0877-48-0211
城山温泉
JR Yosan Line
JR予讃線
1.2km
綾
Udon Gamō 蒲生
杉尾
1020
Udon Yamashita
2.1km
Udon
2.3km
本村
仏願
Vending
Machine
79 80
6.8km
北前谷
Shikoku Taxi 0877-44-0001
Fuchū Taxi 0877-48-1222
SCALE 1/30,000
0 0.5 1 1.5 2km
81 Shiromineji 八十一番 白峰寺
Senju Kannon Bosatsu
2635 Omi-chō, Sakaide City 0877-47-0305
Free of charge (200) 3 min. walk S Available
By bus bound for Yuzuriha from Sakaide Stn. Get off at Takaya Bus Stop, about 3.4km walk.
In 815, Kūkai buried a jewel at the summit of Mt. Shiromine (336m), dug a well, and prayed for the salvation of all living beings. Later, Chishō Daishi saw the spritual light given off by the jewel, carved a statue of Senju Kannon and officially founded this temple. The tomb of Emperor Sutoku is located here. (see page 85 NOTE)
Bonsai Center 盆栽の郷
Bonsai is the art of artificially shaping plants and enjoying the beauty condensed in a small space. Harmony of natural beauty and artificial beauty. It can be observed from #80 temple.

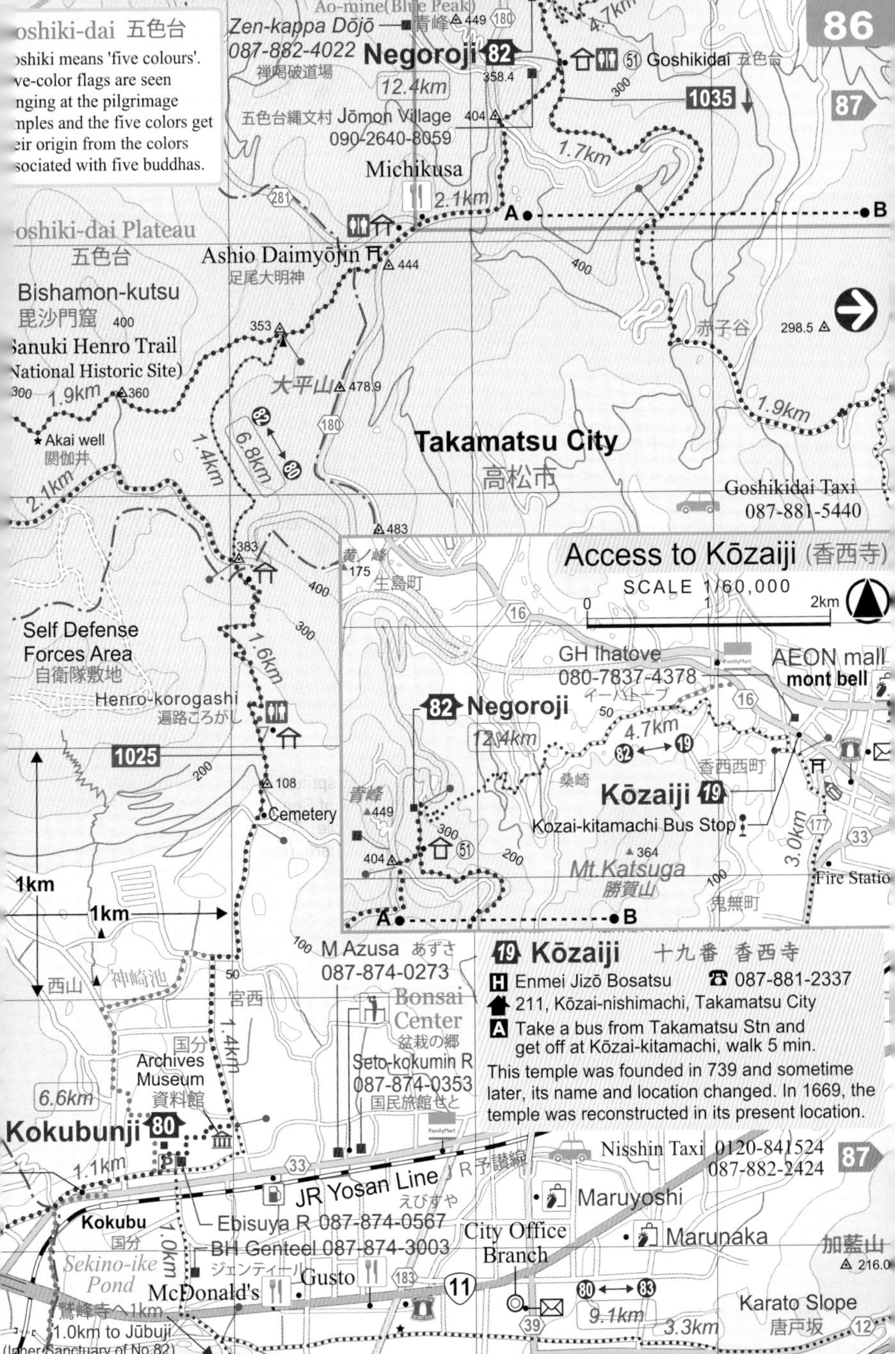
oshiki-dai 五色台
oshiki means 'five colours'. ve-color flags are seen nging at the pilgrimage mples and the five colors get eir origin from the colors sociated with five buddhas.
Ao-mine(Blue Peak)
Zen-kappa Dōjō 青峰 449
087-882-4022
禅喝破道場
Negoroji 82
12.4km
358.4
Goshikidai 五色台
1035
87
五色台縄文村 Jōmon Village 404
090-2640-8059
Michikusa
1.7km
2.1km
281
A
B
oshiki-dai Plateau
五色台
Ashio Daimyōjin
足尾大明神
444
400
Bishamon-kutsu
毘沙門窟 400
353
Sanuki Henro Trail
National Historic Site)
赤子谷
298.5
大平山 478.9
1.9km
360
300
1.9km
Akai well
閼伽井
180
1.4km
6.8km
Takamatsu City
高松市
2.1km
Goshikidai Taxi
087-881-5440
483
383
黄ノ峰
175
生島町
400
Access to Kōzaiji (香西寺)
SCALE 1/60,000
0
1
2km
16
300
Self Defense
Forces Area
自衛隊敷地
1.6km
GH Ihatove
080-7837-4378
イーハトーブ
AEON mall
mont bell
Henro-korogashi
遍路ころがし
82 Negoroji
12.4km
4.7km
1025
200
香西西町
桑崎
Kōzaiji 19
108
青峰
449
Cemetery
Kozai-kitamachi Bus Stop
177
33
300
364
404
51
200
Mt.Katsuga
勝賀山
3.0km
100
Fire Statio
1km
1km
鬼無町
A
B
100
M Azusa あずさ
087-874-0273
19 Kōzaiji 十九番 香西寺
Enmei Jizō Bosatsu 087-881-2337
211, Kōzai-nishimachi, Takamatsu City
Take a bus from Takamatsu Stn and get off at Kōzai-kitamachi, walk 5 min.
This temple was founded in 739 and sometime later, its name and location changed. In 1669, the temple was reconstructed in its present location.
西山
神崎池
50
宮西
Bonsai
Center
盆栽の郷
国分
Archives
Museum
資料館
1.4km
Seto-kokumin R
087-874-0353
国民旅館せと
6.6km
Kokubunji 80
1.1km
33
Nisshin Taxi 0120-841524
087-882-2424
87
JR Yosan Line
JR予讃線
えびすや
Maruyoshi
Kokubu
国分
Ebisuya R 087-874-0567
City Office
Branch
Marunaka
1.0km
BH Genteel 087-874-3003
ジェンティール
加藍山
216.0
Sekino-ike
Pond
Gusto
183
McDonald's
11
鷲峰寺へ1km
9.1km
Karato Slope
1.0km to Jūbuji
3.3km
唐戸坂
39
12
(Inner Sanctuary of No.82)

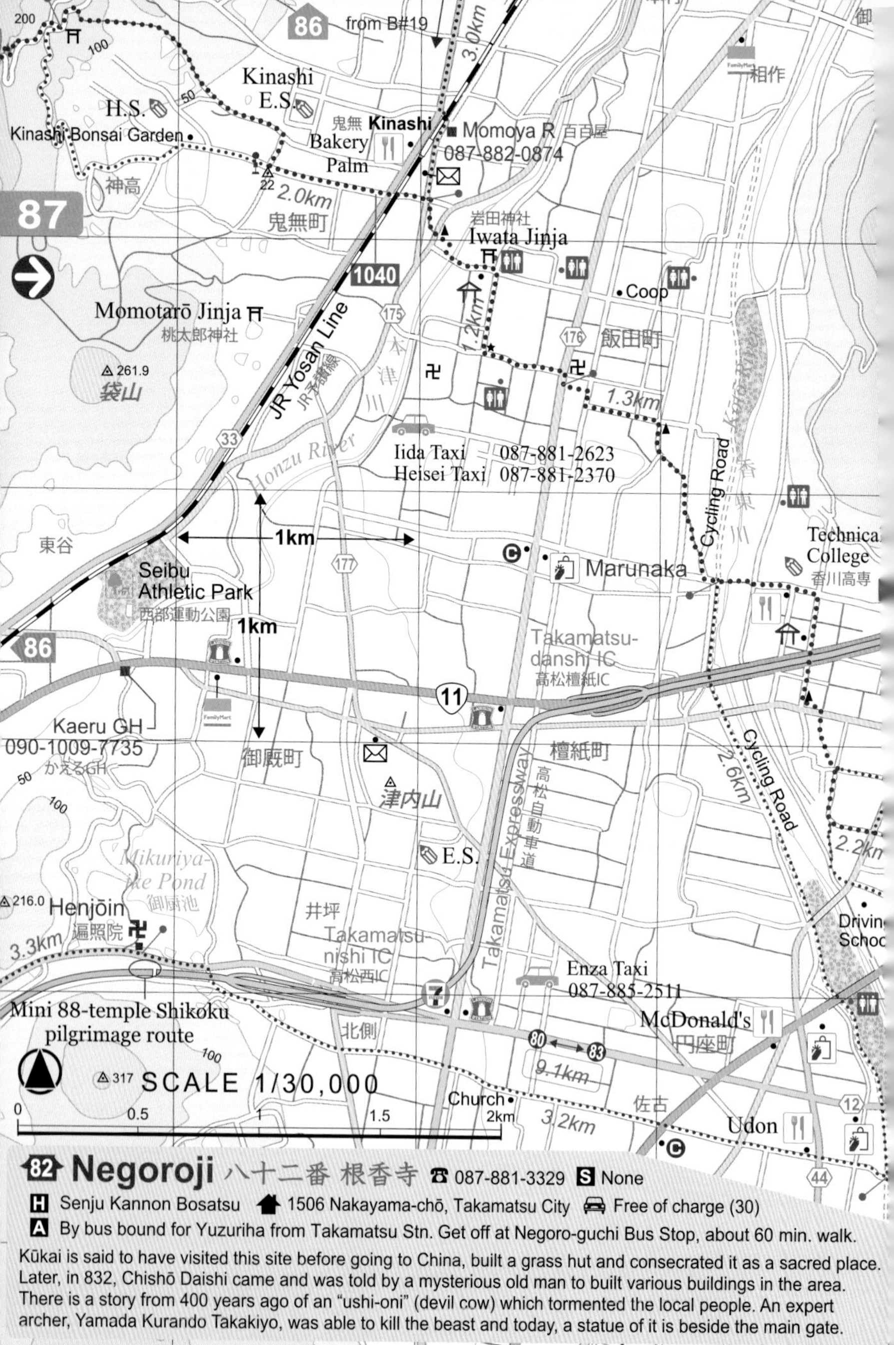
86
from B#19
3.0km
87
Kinashi E.S.
H.S.
Kinashi Bonsai Garden
鬼無 Kinashi
Bakery Palm
Momoya R 百百屋
087-882-0874
神高
2.0km
鬼無町
岩田神社
Iwata Jinja
1040
Coop
Momotarō Jinja
桃太郎神社
261.9
袋山
JR Yosan Line
JR予讃線
175
本津川
1.2km
176
飯田町
1.3km
33
Honzu River
Iida Taxi 087-881-2623
Heisei Taxi 087-881-2370
Cycling Road
香東川
Kotō River
1km
東谷
177
Marunaka
Technical College
香川高専
Seibu Athletic Park
西部運動公園
86
Takamatsu-danshi IC
高松檀紙IC
11
Kaeru GH
090-1009-7735
かえるGH
御厩町
檀紙町
2.6km
高松自動車道
津内山
Takamatsu Expressway
E.S.
2.2km
Mikuriya-ike Pond
御厨池
216.0
Henjōin
遍照院
3.3km
井坪
Takamatsu-nishi IC
高松西IC
Driving School
Enza Taxi
087-885-2511
Mini 88-temple Shikoku pilgrimage route
北側
McDonald's
円座町
80
83
9.1km
317
SCALE 1/30,000
0 0.5 1 1.5 2km
Church
佐古
3.2km
Udon
12
44
相作
御

82 Negoroji 八十二番 根香寺

☎ 087-881-3329 S None

H Senju Kannon Bosatsu 1506 Nakayama-chō, Takamatsu City Free of charge (30)

A By bus bound for Yuzuriha from Takamatsu Stn. Get off at Negoro-guchi Bus Stop, about 60 min. walk.

Kūkai is said to have visited this site before going to China, built a grass hut and consecrated it as a sacred place. Later, in 832, Chishō Daishi came and was told by a mysterious old man to built various buildings in the area. There is a story from 400 years ago of an "ushi-oni" (devil cow) which tormented the local people. An expert archer, Yamada Kurando Takakiyo, was able to kill the beast and today, a statue of it is beside the main gate.

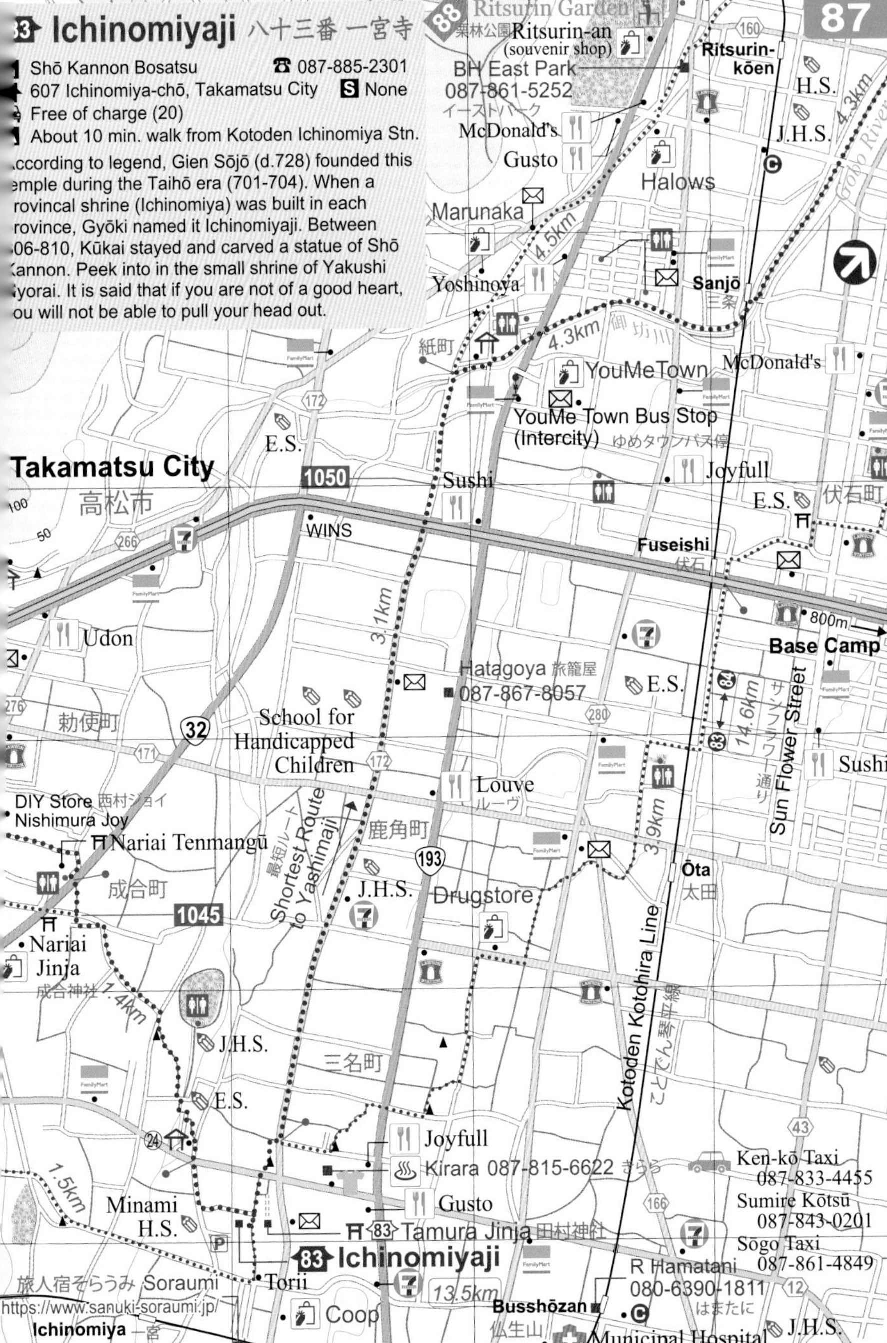

83 Ichinomiyaji 八十三番 一宮寺

Shō Kannon Bosatsu ☎ 087-885-2301
607 Ichinomiya-chō, Takamatsu City S None
Free of charge (20)
About 10 min. walk from Kotoden Ichinomiya Stn.

According to legend, Gien Sōjō (d.728) founded this temple during the Taihō era (701-704). When a provincal shrine (Ichinomiya) was built in each province, Gyōki named it Ichinomiyaji. Between 806-810, Kūkai stayed and carved a statue of Shō Kannon. Peek into in the small shrine of Yakushi Nyorai. It is said that if you are not of a good heart, you will not be able to pull your head out.

88
Ritsurin Garden
栗林公園
Ritsurin-an
(souvenir shop)
Ritsurin-kōen
BH East Park
087-861-5252
イーストパーク
McDonald's
Gusto
Halows
H.S.
J.H.S.
4.3km
Gobo River
Marunaka
4.5km
Yoshinoya
Sanjō
三条
4.3km
御坊川
紙町
YouMeTown
McDonald's
YouMe Town Bus Stop
(Intercity) ゆめタウンバス停
E.S.
172
Takamatsu City
高松市
1050
Sushi
Joyfull
E.S.
伏石町
WINS
266
Fuseishi
伏石
800m
Base Camp
Udon
3.1km
Hatagoya 旅籠屋
087-867-8057
E.S.
84
14.6km
83
School for
Handicapped
Children
280
276
勅使町
32
171
172
Sun Flower Street
サンフラワー通り
Sushi
Louve
ルーヴ
DIY Store 西村ジョイ
Nishimura Joy
Nariai Tenmangū
最短ルート
Shortest Route
to Yashimaji
鹿角町
193
3.9km
Ōta
太田
成合町
J.H.S.
Drugstore
1045
Nariai
Jinja
成合神社
1.4km
Kotoden Kotohira Line
ことでん琴平線
J.H.S.
三名町
E.S.
43
24
Joyfull
Kirara 087-815-6622 きらら
Ken-kō Taxi
087-833-4455
1.5km
Gusto
166
Sumire Kōtsū
087-843-0201
Minami
H.S.
Tamura Jinja 田村神社
83
Sōgo Taxi
087-861-4849
83 Ichinomiyaji
R Hamatani
080-6390-1811
はまたに
旅人宿そらうみ Soraumi
https://www.sanuki-soraumi.jp/
Torii
13.5km
Busshōzan
仏生山
12
Coop
Ichinomiya 一宮
Municipal Hospital
J.H.S.

to Shōdoshima
Naoshima
Clement Inn
087-811-1200
Tamamo Park 玉藻公園
手荷物預かり所 Baggage Storage Office
レンタサイクル Rental bikes Station
Kagawa Museum
県立ミュージアム
Tourist Information
Udon
マリンパレス H Marine Palace
087-851-6677
Bus Terminal (Intercity)
GH BJ Station 080-3775-9044
Takamatsu-chikkō
高松築港
パール Pearl BH 087-822-3382
パールガーデン Parl Garden
087-821-8500
Takamatsu
First Inn
087-822-1919
Pref Hosp
清恵 BH Kiyoe 087-851-4713
月光園 New Gekkōen 087-822-0953
BH Chateau-est シャトーエス
087-823-8100
センチュリー Century BH 087-851-0558
Palace Takamatsu 087-851-3232
159
Kataharamachi
Celecton BH 087-821-2222
セレクトン
30
Sakika Youth GH 087-822-2111 サキカ
昭和町
Shōwa-chō
高松市美術館
City Art Museum
BH Patio
087-823-2320
パティオ
History Museum
歴史資料館
City Office
Kōyasan Sanuki Branch
高野山讃岐別院
I-PAL Kagawa 087-837-5908
(International Exchange Center)
Imabashi
Red Cross Hospital
WeBase
087-851-5500
Matsushima nichōme
33
Pref. Office
H.S.
BH City Hotel
087-834-3345
シティホテル
Kawaramachi
瓦町
Round1
Iwaseo-hachiman
Udon
Traditional Apt
090-2893-2640
Hulaton Cabin
087-802-2070
Sushi
Sushi
Ritsurin-kōen-kitaguchi
173
Hanazono
Capital Hotel 087-831-3330
11
Hostel JAQ 087-813-4075
Ritsurin
栗林
E.S.
GH Wakabaya 若葉屋
070-5683-5335
Park Side BH 087-837-5555
パークサイド
Ritsurin Garden
栗林公園
JR高徳線
4.5km
BH Sunshine
087-837-6161
サンシャイン
Ritsurin-an souvenir shop
160
163
BH East Park
087-861-5252
イーストパーク
Ritsurin-kōen
H.S.
172
Kotoden Nagao Line
ことでん長尾線
43
Ritsurin Kōtsū
0120-612933
McDonald's
Sumire Kōtsū
087-843-0201
Gusto
J.H.S.
4.3km
Gobo River
Sun Flower Street
サンフラワー通り
Rainbow Street
レインボー通り
280
Sōgo Taxi
087-861-4849
Footbridge
Halows
Kotoden Kotohira Line
ことでん琴平線
御坊川
100
50
Yoshinoya
Marunaka
KFC
266
Sanjō
三条
43
5.9km
84
83
14.6km
McDonald's
YouMeTown
YouMe Town Bus Stop
(Intercity) ゆめタウンバス停
3.1km
Gusto
SCALE 1/30,000
1050
0
0.5
1
1.5
2km
Joyfull
87

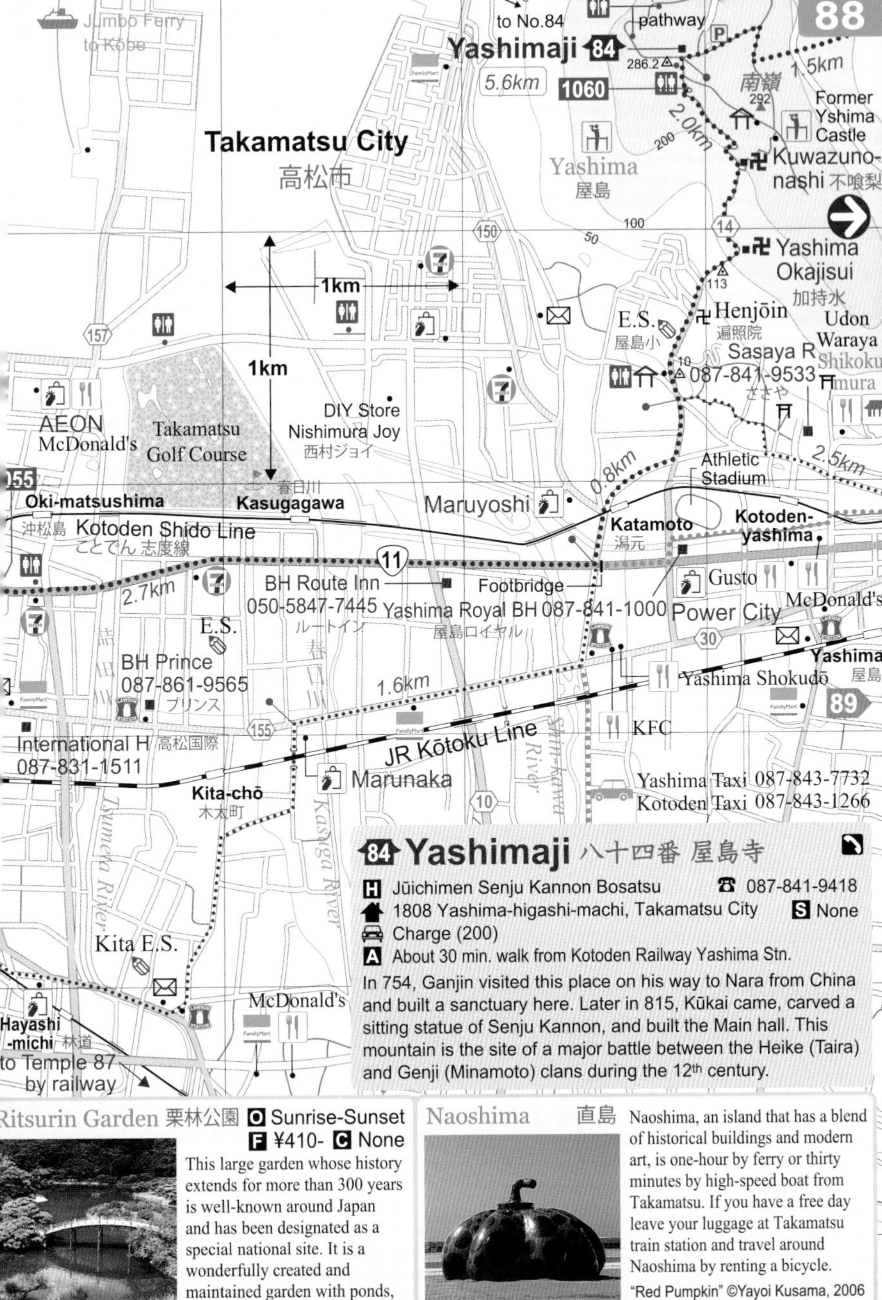

Jumbo Ferry to Kōbe
to No.84
pathway
Yashimaji 84
5.6km
1060
286.2
1.5km
南嶺
292
2.0km
Former Yshima Castle
200
Kuwazuno-nashi 不喰梨
Yashima
屋島
Takamatsu City
高松市
100
50
150
14
Yashima Okajisui
加持水
113
1km
1km
157
E.S.
屋島小
Henjōin
遍照院
Udon Waraya
Shikoku Mura
Sasaya R 087-841-9533
ささや
10
AEON
McDonald's
Takamatsu Golf Course
DIY Store Nishimura Joy
西村ジョイ
2.5km
0.8km
Athletic Stadium
春日川
Oki-matsushima
Kasugagawa
Maruyoshi
Katamoto
潟元
Kotoden-yashima
沖松島
Kotoden Shido Line
ことでん 志度線
11
BH Route Inn
050-5847-7445
ルートイン
Footbridge
Yashima Royal BH 087-841-1000
屋島ロイヤル
Gusto
Power City
McDonald's
2.7km
E.S.
BH Prince
087-861-9565
プリンス
30
Yashima
屋島
Yashima Shokudō
1.6km
89
155
International H 高松国際
087-831-1511
JR Kōtoku Line
Shin-kawa River
KFC
Marunaka
Kita-chō
木太町
10
Yashima Taxi 087-843-7732
Kotoden Taxi 087-843-1266
Tsumeda River
Kasuga River
Kita E.S.
McDonald's
Hayashi-michi 林道
to Temple 87 by railway

84 Yashimaji 八十四番 屋島寺

H Jūichimen Senju Kannon Bosatsu ☎ 087-841-9418

1808 Yashima-higashi-machi, Takamatsu City S None

Charge (200)

A About 30 min. walk from Kotoden Railway Yashima Stn.

In 754, Ganjin visited this place on his way to Nara from China and built a sanctuary here. Later in 815, Kūkai came, carved a sitting statue of Senju Kannon, and built the Main hall. This mountain is the site of a major battle between the Heike (Taira) and Genji (Minamoto) clans during the 12th century.

Ritsurin Garden 栗林公園

O Sunrise-Sunset

F ¥410- C None

This large garden whose history extends for more than 300 years is well-known around Japan and has been designated as a special national site. It is a wonderfully created and maintained garden with ponds, bridges, stones, and tea houses.

Naoshima 直島

Naoshima, an island that has a blend of historical buildings and modern art, is one-hour by ferry or thirty minutes by high-speed boat from Takamatsu. If you have a free day leave your luggage at Takamatsu train station and travel around Naoshima by renting a bicycle.

"Red Pumpkin" ©Yayoi Kusama, 2006
Naoshima Miyanoura Port Square

Isamu Noguchi Garden Museum
イサム・ノグチ庭園美術館
open: Tue, Thu, Sat,
Reservation Required
087-870-1500
Historic spots of the Gempei War
Mt.Goken 五剣山
Yakuriji 85
223.0
6.9km
1065
御宿 鷹柳
Takayamagi
087-845-1573
1.6km
Yakuri Cable Car
Round-trip: ¥1000
7:30 - 17:15
282
1.5km
150
屋島東町
36
50
100
1.2km
Yashima-higashi E.S.
屋島東小
Udon Yamadaya
61
145
200
Mt.Gen gamine
217
源氏ケ
1.9km
Marunaka
1.3km
Stone Museum
石の民俗資料館
88
E.S.
牟礼
100
GH Ryū-chan House
087-841-7276
Susakiji (Tomb of Shinnen) 洲崎寺
Rokumanji
六萬寺
Shikoku-mura
Udon Waraya
四国村
Kur Onsen
Yakuri
Maruyoshi
Maru
H.S.
J.H.S
Kotoden
Coop
Rokumanji
六万寺
相引川
2.5km
11
ことでん志度線
Shido Line
Furu-takamatsu
Furu-takamatsu-minami
古高松南
Tomb of Dōkyū
道休墓
J.H.S.
3.2km
八栗新道
Yakuri-shinmichi
Yakuri-guchi
八栗口
Ōmachi
大町
GH Yashima
(booking.com, airbnb)
Murekara
(airbnb)
ムレカラ
Yashima
屋島
Takamatsu City
高松市
City Office Branch
Sanuki-Mure
讃岐牟礼
Yakuri Taxi 0120-451177
087-845-1177
Yashima Taxi 087-843-7732
Motoi Musubi
元結
SCALE 1/30,000
0
0.5
1
1.5
2km
272
高松町

85 Yakuriji 八十五番 八栗寺

H Shō Kannon Bosatsu

3416 Mure, Mure-Chō, Takamatsu City

Free of charge (200) 4 min. by cable car

A About 25 min. walk from Kotoden Railway Yakuri Stn. And take the cable car.

☎ 087-845-9603 S None

Before Kūkai departed for China, it is said that he came here, planted eight chestnuts *(ya-kuri)* and prayed that his journey would be safe. Returning to Japan, he revisited this site and participated in ascetic training. At that time, 5 swords fell from heaven and a mountain God appeared declaring that this land was sacred. The eight chestnut seeds had grown into large trees.

86 Shidoji 八十六番 志度寺

H Jūichimen Kannon Bosatsu

1102 Shido, Sanuki City

Free of charge (50)

A About 5 min. walk from JR Kōtoku Line Shido Stn.

☎ 087-894-0086 S None

In 626, a Buddhist nun called Ōshi Sonoko carved a statue of Jūichimen Kannon Bosatsu from a piece of driftwood in the bay of Shido. In 693, Gyōki and the son of Fujiwara no Fuhito visited this place and constructed several buildings. During the Muromachi period (1392-1573) the temple prospered, but later fell into ruin. In 1671 the main hall and Niōmon gate were rebuilt with support from the lord of Takamatsu.

Shikoku-mura Village 四国村

O 9:30am - 4:30pm **C** Tues **F** ¥1600-

This is an open air museum featuring various traditional buildings from the Edo or Meiji period. The structures have been collected from around Shikoku and reconstructed here. The udon restaurant near the entrance is very popular.

Aji Stone 庵治石

You can see many stone shops around Susakiji temple because this area is well known in Japan for its rocks of excellent quality, called aji-ishi, which are excavated north of Yakuriji.

Yashima 屋島

It is a plateau (elev 293m) which protrudes into the Seto Inland Sea and is known nationwide as being the place where the Genpei War occurred in 1185. Temple 86, Yashimaji is located here.

Sanuki City Communuty Bus
to No.87, 88 & Ōtakiji

Green: Mon - Fri
weekday: ¥200
Sat, Sun, Hol: ¥500

JR Shido Stn (p89 R)	7:50		12:17		17:20
Shido Bus Stop (p90-a)	8:00		12:27		17:30
Asahi-machi (p90-b)	8:41	11:31	13:01		18:01
Hellow work (p90-b)	8:42	11:32	13:02	15:12	18:02
Michinoeki Nagao (p91)	8:55	11:43	13:13	15:23	18:13
Ōkuboji (p91)	9:12	12:00	13:30	15:48	-----
Nakayama (p91)	[9:27]		[13:45]	[15:36]	18:26

Nakayama (p91)	6:48	[9:46]		[14:01]	
Ōkuboji (p91)	----	10:00	12:15	14:17	16:00
Michinoeki Nagao (p91)	7:01	10:17	12:32	14:32	16:17
Hellow work (p90-b)	7:08	10:24	12:39	14:39	16:26
Asahi-machi (p90-b)	7:19	10:41	12:46	15:01	16:44
Shido Bus Stop (p90-a)	7:33	10:55			16:58
JR Shido Stn (p89 R)	7:44	11:06			17:09

[ ] : Reservation required by phone (080-2990-4393) 2024.4

Tamaura Kōtsū 087-894-0143
0120-380143
Marusen Taxi 087-894-0888
0120-088856

牟礼町大町
2.6km
George Nakashima Memorial Gallery
ジョージナカシマ記念館
(Former grave of Shinnen)
真念旧墓
塩屋
Shioya
1070
Genpei-no-sato MURE
源平の里むれ
E.S.
Fusazaki 房前
Hachiman Jinja
Aizenji
愛染寺
Shido Bay 志度湾
Sanuki City
さぬき市
Udon
冨士屋 Fujiya R
087-894-1175
たいや旅館 Taiya R
087-894-0038
Gennai Hiraga 平賀源内記念館
Memorial Museum
JR Kōtoku Line
JR高徳線
牟礼町原
Hara 原
2.5km
Ishiya R 087-894-0021 いしや
R Iseda 旅館いせだ
087-894-7778
City Office
Jizōji
地蔵寺
1km
1km
Fork
分岐
86 Shidoji
7.1km
Henro grave
College of Health Sciences
Gusto
JR Shido Station Bus Stop
(Direction of Nagaoji, Ōkuboji & Ōtakiji)
志度駅バス停(長尾寺、大窪寺、大瀧寺方面)
Shido
志度
GH Tsushima
(airbnb)
民泊對馬
McDonald's
3.7km
Coop
1.4km
90-a

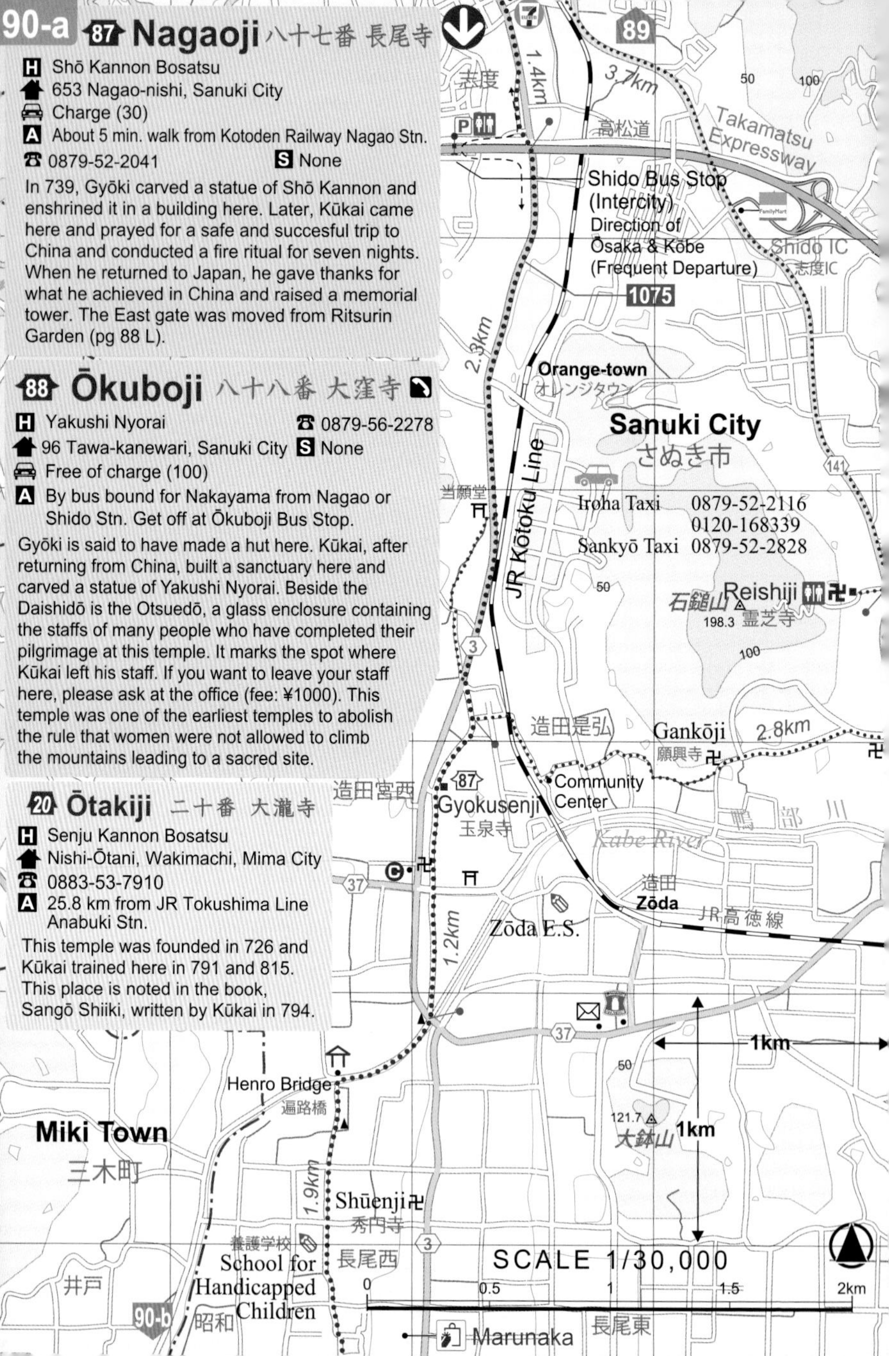

87 Nagaoji 八十七番 長尾寺

H Shō Kannon Bosatsu

653 Nagao-nishi, Sanuki City

Charge (30)

A About 5 min. walk from Kotoden Railway Nagao Stn.

☎ 0879-52-2041 S None

In 739, Gyōki carved a statue of Shō Kannon and enshrined it in a building here. Later, Kūkai came here and prayed for a safe and succesful trip to China and conducted a fire ritual for seven nights. When he returned to Japan, he gave thanks for what he achieved in China and raised a memorial tower. The East gate was moved from Ritsurin Garden (pg 88 L).

88 Ōkuboji 八十八番 大窪寺

H Yakushi Nyorai ☎ 0879-56-2278

96 Tawa-kanewari, Sanuki City S None

Free of charge (100)

A By bus bound for Nakayama from Nagao or Shido Stn. Get off at Ōkuboji Bus Stop.

Gyōki is said to have made a hut here. Kūkai, after returning from China, built a sanctuary here and carved a statue of Yakushi Nyorai. Beside the Daishidō is the Otsuedō, a glass enclosure containing the staffs of many people who have completed their pilgrimage at this temple. It marks the spot where Kūkai left his staff. If you want to leave your staff here, please ask at the office (fee: ¥1000). This temple was one of the earliest temples to abolish the rule that women were not allowed to climb the mountains leading to a sacred site.

20 Ōtakiji 二十番 大瀧寺

H Senju Kannon Bosatsu

Nishi-Ōtani, Wakimachi, Mima City

☎ 0883-53-7910

A 25.8 km from JR Tokushima Line Anabuki Stn.

This temple was founded in 726 and Kūkai trained here in 791 and 815. This place is noted in the book, Sangō Shiiki, written by Kūkai in 794.

89
1.4km
3.7km
志度
高松道
Takamatsu Expressway
Shido Bus Stop (Intercity)
Direction of Ōsaka & Kōbe (Frequent Departure)
FamilyMart
Shido IC
志度IC
1075
2.3km
Orange-town
オレンジタウン
Sanuki City
さぬき市
JR Kōtoku Line
当願堂
Iroha Taxi 0879-52-2116
0120-168339
Sankyō Taxi 0879-52-2828
141
50
石鎚山
198.3
Reishiji
霊芝寺
100
3
造田是弘
Gankōji
願興寺
2.8km
Community Center
造田宮西
87
Gyokusenji
玉泉寺
鴨部川
Kabe River
37
造田
Zōda
JR高徳線
Zōda E.S.
1.2km
1km
1km
Henro Bridge
遍路橋
Miki Town
三木町
121.7
大鉢山
1.9km
Shūenji
秀円寺
養護学校
School for Handicapped Children
長尾西
SCALE 1/30,000
0
0.5
1
1.5
2km
井戸
90-b
昭和
長尾東
Marunaka

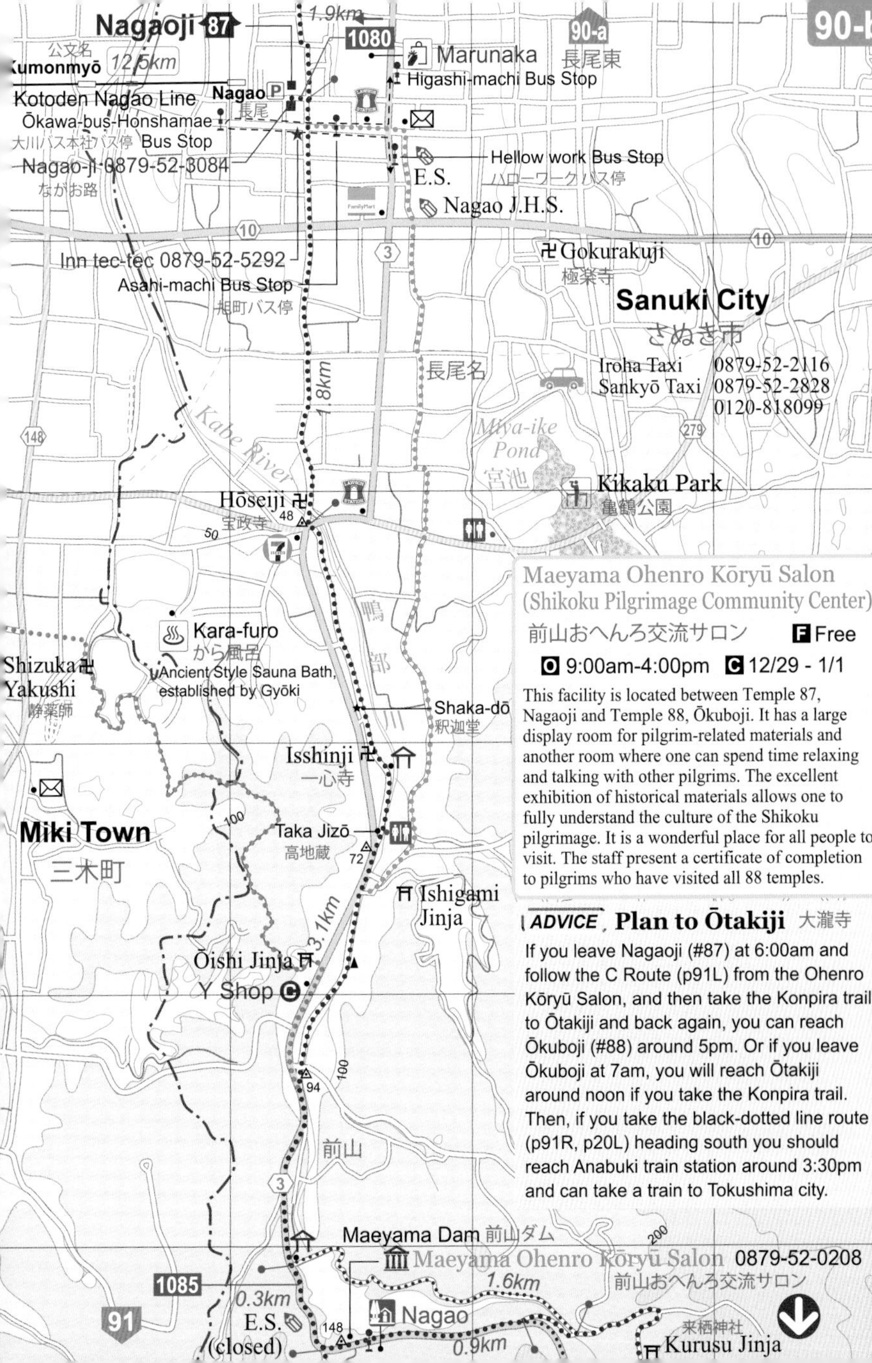
Nagaoji 87
公文名
Kumonmyō 12.5km
1.9km
1080
90-a
長尾東
Marunaka
Higashi-machi Bus Stop
Kotoden Nagao Line
Nagao
長尾
Ōkawa-bus-Honshamae
大川バス本社バス停 Bus Stop
Nagao-ji 0879-52-3084
ながお路
Hellow work Bus Stop
ハローワークバス停
E.S.
Nagao J.H.S.
10
3
Inn tec-tec 0879-52-5292
Asahi-machi Bus Stop
旭町バス停
Gokurakuji
極楽寺
Sanuki City
さぬき市
長尾名
1.8km
Iroha Taxi 0879-52-2116
Sankyō Taxi 0879-52-2828
0120-818099
Miya-ike Pond
宮池
279
148
Kabe River
Kikaku Park
亀鶴公園
Hōseiji
宝政寺
48
50
鴨部川
Maeyama Ohenro Kōryū Salon
(Shikoku Pilgrimage Community Center)
前山おへんろ交流サロン
Free
9:00am-4:00pm
12/29 - 1/1
This facility is located between Temple 87, Nagaoji and Temple 88, Ōkuboji. It has a large display room for pilgrim-related materials and another room where one can spend time relaxing and talking with other pilgrims. The excellent exhibition of historical materials allows one to fully understand the culture of the Shikoku pilgrimage. It is a wonderful place for all people to visit. The staff present a certificate of completion to pilgrims who have visited all 88 temples.
Kara-furo
から風呂
Ancient Style Sauna Bath, established by Gyōki
Shizuka Yakushi
静薬師
Shaka-dō
釈迦堂
Isshinji
一心寺
Miki Town
三木町
100
Taka Jizō
高地蔵
72
Ishigami Jinja
3.1km
ADVICE Plan to Ōtakiji 大瀧寺
If you leave Nagaoji (#87) at 6:00am and follow the C Route (p91L) from the Ohenro Kōryū Salon, and then take the Konpira trail to Ōtakiji and back again, you can reach Ōkuboji (#88) around 5pm. Or if you leave Ōkuboji at 7am, you will reach Ōtakiji around noon if you take the Konpira trail. Then, if you take the black-dotted line route (p91R, p20L) heading south you should reach Anabuki train station around 3:30pm and can take a train to Tokushima city.
Ōishi Jinja
Y Shop
94
100
前山
3
Maeyama Dam 前山ダム
Maeyama Ohenro Kōryū Salon 0879-52-0208
前山おへんろ交流サロン
200
1085
1.6km
0.3km
91
E.S. (closed)
148
Nagao
0.9km
来栖神社
Kurusu Jinja

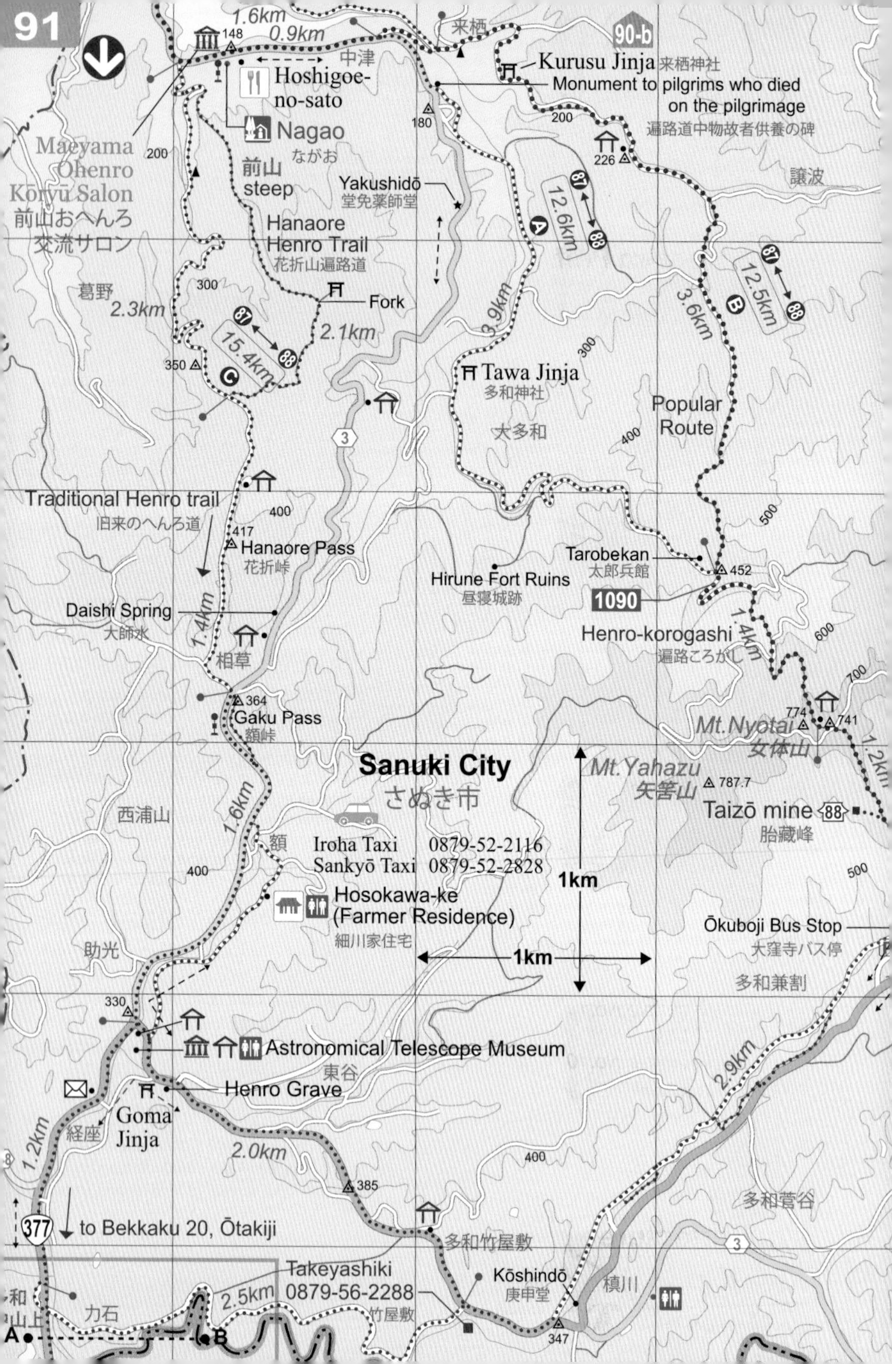
90-b
1.6km
0.9km
来栖
Kurusu Jinja 来栖神社
Monument to pilgrims who died on the pilgrimage
遍路道中物故者供養の碑
中津
Hoshigoe-no-sato
Nagao
ながお
Maeyama Ohenro Kōryū Salon
前山おへんろ交流サロン
前山 steep
Yakushidō 堂免薬師堂
Hanaore Henro Trail
花折山遍路道
Fork
2.1km
2.3km
葛野
87 ↔ 88 15.4km C
87 ↔ 88 12.6km A
87 ↔ 88 12.5km B
3.9km
3.6km
譲波
Tawa Jinja
多和神社
大多和
Popular Route
Traditional Henro trail
旧来のへんろ道
Hanaore Pass
花折峠
Tarobekan
太郎兵館
Hirune Fort Ruins
昼寝城跡
1090
Henro-korogashi
遍路ころがし
1.4km
Daishi Spring
大師水
相草
Gaku Pass
額峠
Mt.Nyotai
女体山
1.2km
Sanuki City
さぬき市
Mt.Yahazu
矢筈山
Taizō mine
胎藏峰
88
西浦山
1.6km
額
Iroha Taxi 0879-52-2116
Sankyō Taxi 0879-52-2828
1km
1km
Hosokawa-ke (Farmer Residence)
細川家住宅
Ōkuboji Bus Stop
大窪寺バス停
多和兼割
助光
Astronomical Telescope Museum
東谷
Henro Grave
Goma Jinja
経座
1.2km
2.0km
2.9km
多和菅谷
377
to Bekkaku 20, Ōtakiji
多和竹屋敷
Takeyashiki 0879-56-2288
竹屋敷
Kōshindō
庚申堂
槙川
2.5km
力石
A
B

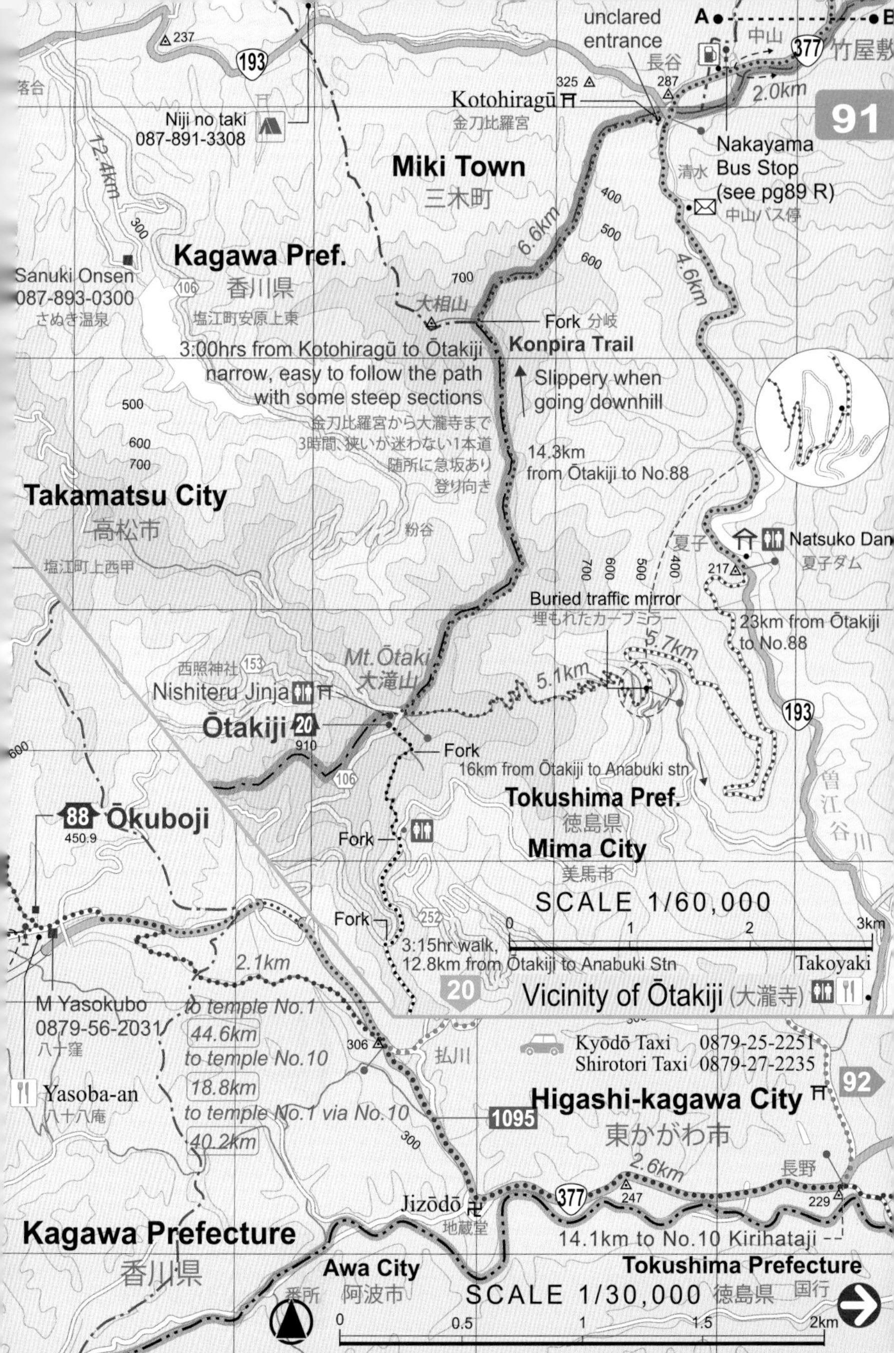

unclared entrance
A
B
中山
377
竹屋敷
長谷
2.0km
91
193
237
落合
Niji no taki
087-891-3308
325
287
Kotohiragū
金刀比羅宮
Nakayama Bus Stop (see pg89 R)
中山バス停
清水
Miki Town
三木町
12.4km
300
Kagawa Pref.
香川県
6.6km
4.6km
400
500
600
700
Sanuki Onsen
087-893-0300
さぬき温泉
106
塩江町安原上東
大相山
Fork 分岐
Konpira Trail
3:00hrs from Kotohiragū to Ōtakiji
narrow, easy to follow the path
with some steep sections
金刀比羅宮から大瀧寺まで
3時間、狭いが迷わない1本道
随所に急坂あり
登り向き
Slippery when going downhill
14.3km from Ōtakiji to No.88
Takamatsu City
高松市
塩江町上西甲
粉谷
夏子
Natsuko Dam
夏子ダム
217
Buried traffic mirror
埋もれたカーブミラー
23km from Ōtakiji to No.88
5.7km
5.1km
Mt.Ōtaki
大滝山
西照神社
153
Nishiteru Jinja
Ōtakiji
20
910
Fork
16km from Ōtakiji to Anabuki stn
193
Tokushima Pref.
徳島県
曽江谷川
88
Ōkuboji
450.9
Fork
Mima City
美馬市
SCALE 1/60,000
0
1
2
3km
Fork
252
3:15hr walk, 12.8km from Ōtakiji to Anabuki Stn
Takoyaki
2.1km
20
Vicinity of Ōtakiji (大瀧寺)
M Yasokubo
0879-56-2031
八十窪
to temple No.1
44.6km
to temple No.10
18.8km
to temple No.1 via No.10
40.2km
306
払川
Kyōdō Taxi 0879-25-2251
Shirotori Taxi 0879-27-2235
92
Yasoba-an
八十八庵
1095
Higashi-kagawa City
東かがわ市
300
2.6km
長野
Jizōdō
地蔵堂
377
247
229
14.1km to No.10 Kirihataji
Kagawa Prefecture
香川県
Awa City
阿波市
番所
Tokushima Prefecture
徳島県
国行
SCALE 1/30,000
0
0.5
1
1.5
2km

NOTE After Ōkuboji 大窪寺のあとは3通り

Visiting all 88 temples is called 'kechigan' (結願) (the fulfillment of one's wish). Regardless of the order in which the temples are visited the last one is the kechigan temple. Others think that kechigan occurs when the circle is completed. In other words, when one returns to the temple from which the journey began. In any case, it is common that after one finishes the pilgrimage to go to Kōyasan and report to Kōbō Daishi of the successful journey.

三殿
松崎
Yodaji
与田寺
Toramaru Park
0879-24-1810 (¥500)
Ōuchi Bus Stop (Inter-city)
Direction of Ōsaka & Kōbe
(Frequent Departure)
Mt. Nachi
那智山 271
Yoda River
風呂
水主
3.4km
与田川
Monument
former
Kōkaiji
旧弘海寺
Mizushi Jinja
水主神社
虎丸山 417
Mt. Toramaru
Sanuki City
さぬき市
2km
2km
560 笠ヶ峰
本宮山
346
Mt. Hongū
Ōuchi Dam
大内ダム
Mizushi Sanzan
(mizushi 3 mountains)
Influenced by Kumano Sanzan
(Wakayama Prefecture)
3.4km
109
Hoshigoe-tōge Pass
星越峠
1105
Higashi-kagawa City
東かがわ市
E.S.
(closed)
Sanpōji
三宝寺
75
61
3.5km
与田山
入野山
Hachimangū
377
五名
E.S.
(Closed)
1.7km
100
Henro Grave
1100
91
200
1.6km
五明
Gomyō
Tunnel
Ginkgo
tree
2.0km
Kagawa Prefecture
香川県
229
1.3km
218
UTA GH
utagest@gmail.com
Path
Marker
1.7km
Hacchō-zaka Slope
八丁坂
SCALE 1/60,000
0
1
2
3km
Tokushima
Prefecture
徳島県
Awa City
阿波市
191
to No.10, Kirihataji
5.3km
A
城王山 598
B

NOTE Mizushi Sanzan 水主三山

This area includes three small mountains (417m, 346m and 271m) [sanzan] and the Mizushi shrine. Saichō prayed at this shrine in 790, Kūkai dug a well called Akai here, and in the 12th century Minamoto Yoshitsune visited here to pray for victory in battle. During the Muromachi period (1392-1573) it is believed that Zōun (1366-1449), a priest from Yodaiji, put the sacred symbol of the deities from the three major shrines in Kumano here. On the way to Yodaiji near Kōkaiji there is a stone monument marking the spot of an ancient stone bath.

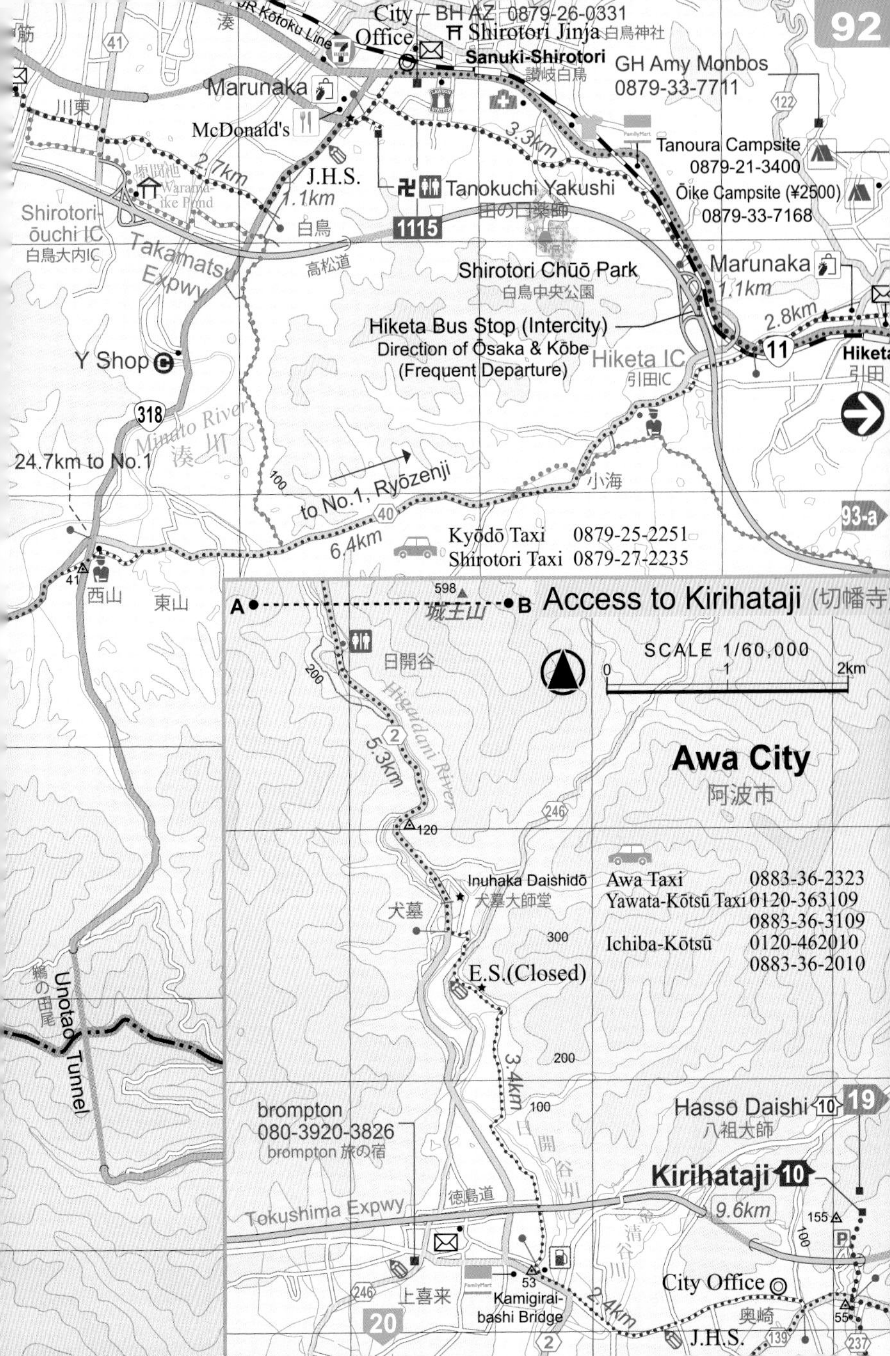

JR Kōtoku Line
City Office
BH AZ 0879-26-0331
Shirotori Jinja 白鳥神社
Sanuki-Shirotori
讃岐白鳥
GH Amy Monbos
0879-33-7711
Marunaka
McDonald's
川東
J.H.S.
Tanokuchi Yakushi
田の口薬師
Tanoura Campsite
0879-21-3400
Ōike Campsite (¥2500)
0879-33-7168
Waramaike Pond
Shirotori-ōuchi IC
白鳥大内IC
白鳥
1115
高松道
Takamatsu Expwy
Shirotori Chūō Park
白鳥中央公園
Marunaka
Hiketa Bus Stop (Intercity)
Direction of Ōsaka & Kōbe
(Frequent Departure)
Hiketa IC
引田IC
Hiketa
引田
Y Shop
318
Minato River
湊川
24.7km to No.1
to No.1, Ryōzenji
小海
Kyōdō Taxi 0879-25-2251
Shirotori Taxi 0879-27-2235
西山
東山
Access to Kirihataji (切幡寺)
城王山
日開谷
SCALE 1/60,000
Higaidani River
Awa City
阿波市
Inuhaka Daishidō
犬墓大師堂
犬墓
Awa Taxi 0883-36-2323
Yawata-Kōtsū Taxi 0120-363109
0883-36-3109
Ichiba-Kōtsū 0120-462010
0883-36-2010
E.S.(Closed)
Unotao Tunnel
Hasso Daishi
八祖大師
brompton
080-3920-3826
brompton 旅の宿
Kirihataji
Tokushima Expwy
徳島道
上喜来
Kamigirai-bashi Bridge
City Office
奥崎
J.H.S.

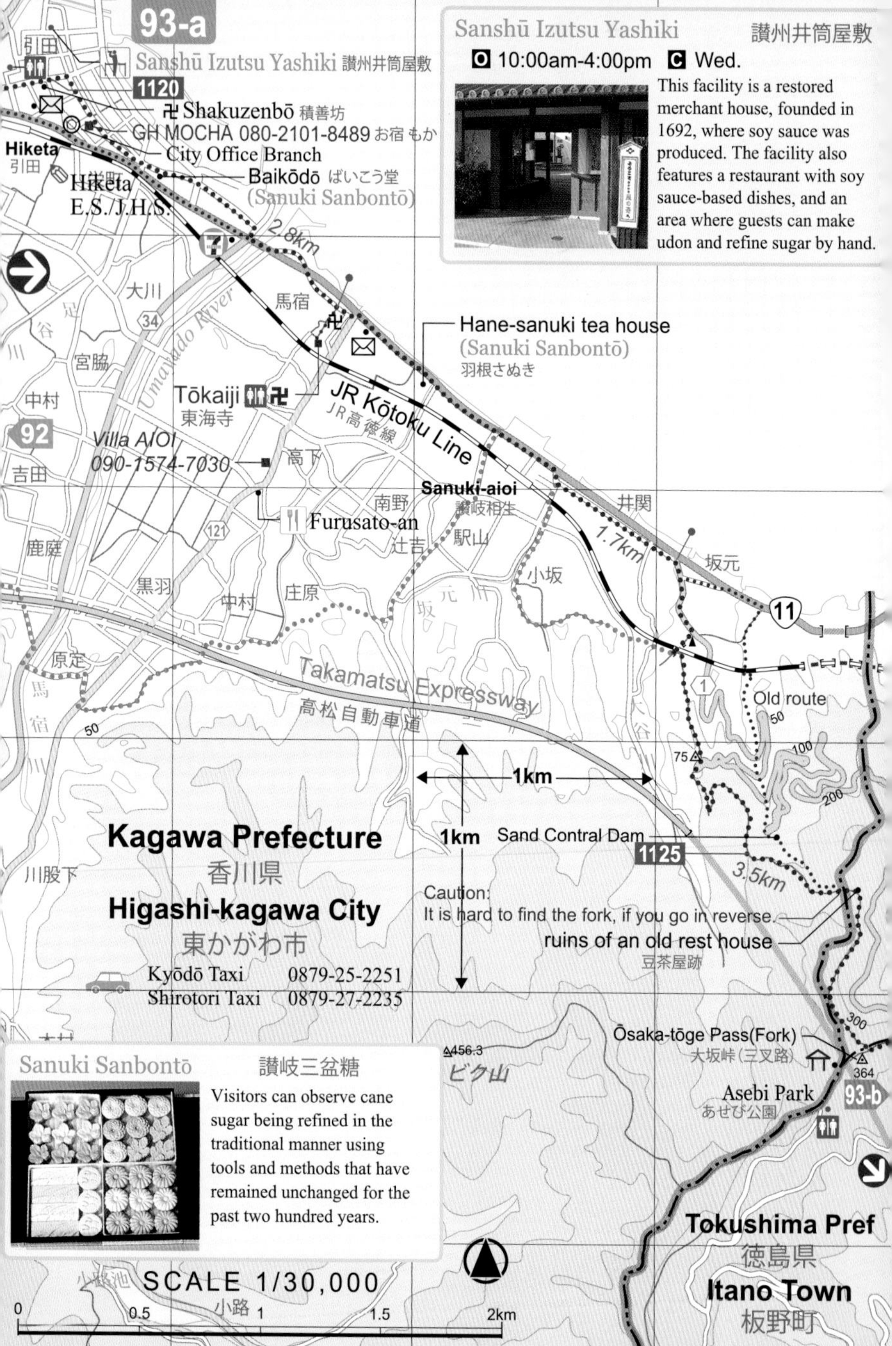
93-a
Sanshū Izutsu Yashiki 讃州井筒屋敷
1120
Shakuzenbō 積善坊
GH MOCHA 080-2101-8489 お宿 もか
City Office Branch
Baikōdō ばいこう堂
(Sanuki Sanbontō)
Hiketa
引田
Hiketa E.S./J.H.S.
2.8km
大川
Umayado River
馬宿
Hane-sanuki tea house
(Sanuki Sanbontō)
羽根さぬき
宮脇
中村
Tōkaiji
東海寺
JR Kōtoku Line
JR高徳線
92
Villa AIOI
090-1574-7030
高下
吉田
Sanuki-aioi
讃岐相生
南野
井関
Furusato-an
辻吉
駅山
1.7km
鹿庭
坂元
小坂
黒羽
中村
庄原
11
原定
Takamatsu Expressway
高松自動車道
Old route
75
1km
1km
Kagawa Prefecture
香川県
Higashi-kagawa City
東かがわ市
Sand Contral Dam
1125
3.5km
Caution:
It is hard to find the fork, if you go in reverse.
ruins of an old rest house
豆茶屋跡
Kyōdō Taxi 0879-25-2251
Shirotori Taxi 0879-27-2235
Ōsaka-tōge Pass(Fork)
大坂峠(三叉路)
456.3
ビク山
364
Asebi Park
あせび公園
93-b
Tokushima Pref
徳島県
Itano Town
板野町
SCALE 1/30,000
0 0.5 1 1.5 2km
Sanshū Izutsu Yashiki 讃州井筒屋敷
O 10:00am-4:00pm C Wed.
This facility is a restored merchant house, founded in 1692, where soy sauce was produced. The facility also features a restaurant with soy sauce-based dishes, and an area where guests can make udon and refine sugar by hand.
Sanuki Sanbontō 讃岐三盆糖
Visitors can observe cane sugar being refined in the traditional manner using tools and methods that have remained unchanged for the past two hundred years.

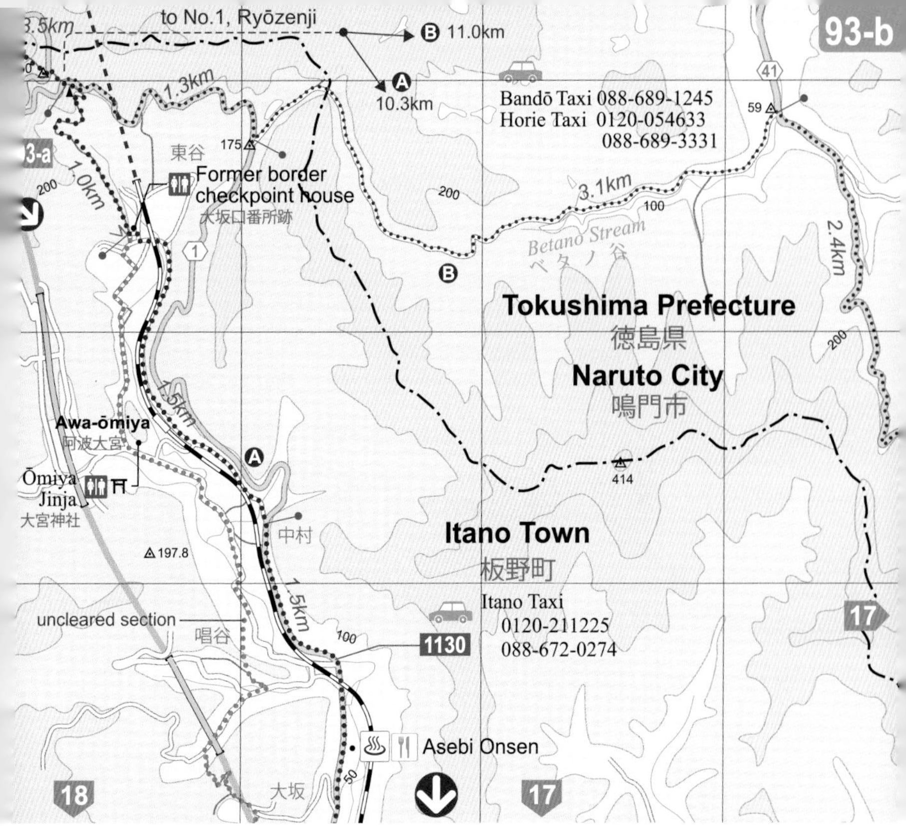

to No.1, Ryōzenji
3.5km
B 11.0km
A 10.3km
1.3km
Bandō Taxi 088-689-1245
Horie Taxi 0120-054633
088-689-3331
41
59
175
東谷
1.0km
Former border checkpoint house
大坂口番所跡
200
3.1km
100
Betano Stream
ベタノ谷
1
B
Tokushima Prefecture
徳島県
Naruto City
鳴門市
2.4km
200
1.5km
Awa-ōmiya
阿波大宮
A
Ōmiya Jinja
大宮神社
414
中村
Itano Town
板野町
197.8
1.5km
Itano Taxi
0120-211225
088-672-0274
uncleared section
唱谷
100
1130
17
Asebi Onsen
50
大坂
18
17

Going to Mt. Kōya

Access to Mt. Kōya

Nankai Electric Railway

One starting point is Namba station at the Nankai Railway Line in Osaka. It takes 110 minutes (price: one way 2190yen) on the express train from Namba to Kōyasan station. (A reduced fare return ticket is available at principal Nankai Railway stations. It includes a bus ticket for Kōyasan.) Tourist information is available at Namba station. The route is the same if leaving from Kansai airport.

Access to Mt. Kōya from various places in Shikoku

(see pg 16)

- **Going by bus:**

1. There are highway buses offering a direct service on the 5th floor of Nankai Namba bus terminal (Namba station) from Tokushima (Toku Bus) and Takamatsu (Foot Bus). (A discounted return ticket is available from Namba to Kōyasan). The Foot Bus stops at Naruto Nishi PA bus stop, which is a 25-minute walk from Temple 1, Ryōzenji (see pg 17)

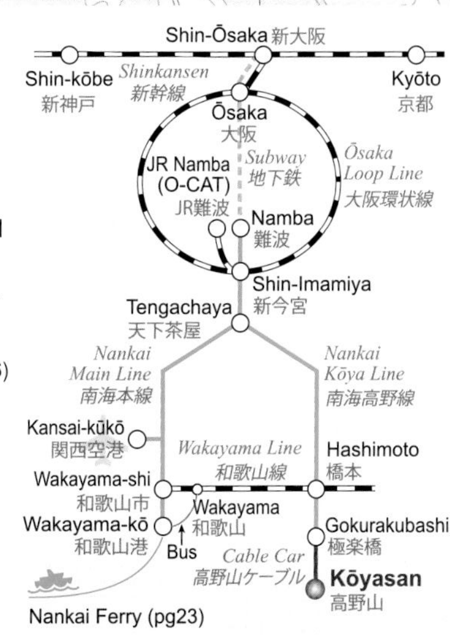

Shin-Ōsaka 新大阪
Shin-kōbe 新神戸
Shinkansen 新幹線
Kyōto 京都
Ōsaka 大阪
JR Namba (O-CAT) JR難波
Subway 地下鉄
Ōsaka Loop Line 大阪環状線
Namba 難波
Shin-Imamiya 新今宮
Tengachaya 天下茶屋
Nankai Main Line 南海本線
Nankai Kōya Line 南海高野線
Kansai-kūkō 関西空港
Wakayama Line 和歌山線
Hashimoto 橋本
Wakayama-shi 和歌山市
Wakayama 和歌山
Wakayama-kō 和歌山港
Gokurakubashi 極楽橋
Bus
Cable Car 高野山ケーブル
Kōyasan 高野山
Nankai Ferry (pg23)

The discount return ticket for Kōyasan includes return transportation along with the bus on Kōyasan and discounted tickets for various sites.

2. There are buses for Ōsaka from Tokushima, Kōchi, Matusyama and Takamatsu that stop at Ōsaka City Air Terminal (O-CAT), which is a 10-minute walk from Namba station.
(see pg 23, 40, 68, 88)

- **Going by rail:**

The bullet train from Okayama station stops at Shin-Ōsaka station. From there, you can travel to Ōsaka station and then to Shin-Imamiya station by the JR Line, then change to the Nankai line. Or you can take the subway from Shin-Ōsaka to Namba station.

- **Going by Nankai Ferry:** (see pg 15, 23)

Recommended route: Take the ferry from Tokushima port to Wakayama port (2:10 hr, 2,500yen); take th train from Wakayama port to Tengachaya stn, switch trains for Gokurakubashi stn, then take the funicula up to Kōyasan stn. (about 3hrs, 1,900yen). * Special one-way price ticket from Tokushima port to Kōyasan stn: 2,500yen. Or you can take a train and bus from Wakayama port station to Hashimoto (2hrs 250yen and 860yen) and then transfer to the Nankai Kōya line to go to Kōyasan station (1hr, 990yen)

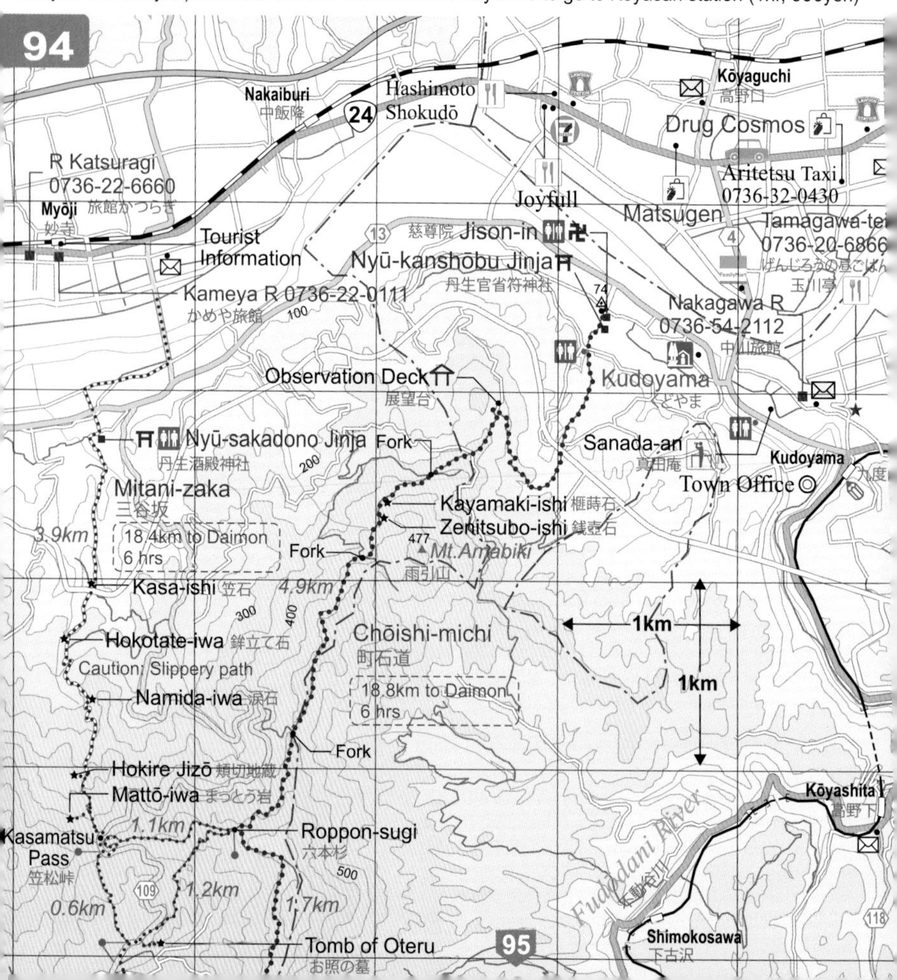
94
Nakaiburi
中飯降
24
Hashimoto Shokudō
Kōyaguchi
高野口
Drug Cosmos
Aritetsu Taxi
0736-32-0430
R Katsuragi
0736-22-6660
Myōji
妙寺
旅館かつらぎ
Joyfull
Matsugen
Tamagawa-te
0736-20-6866
玉川亭
Tourist Information
13
慈尊院 Jison-in
Nyū-kanshōbu Jinja
丹生官省符神社
4
Kameya R 0736-22-0111
かめや旅館
100
74
Nakagawa R
0736-54-2112
中山旅館
Observation Deck
展望台
Kudoyama
くどやま
Nyū-sakadono Jinja
丹生酒殿神社
Fork
200
Sanada-an
真田庵
Kudoyama
Town Office
Mitani-zaka
三谷坂
Kayamaki-ishi 榧蒔石
Zenitsubo-ishi 銭壺石
3.9km
18.4km to Daimon
6 hrs
Fork
477
Mt.Amabiki
雨引山
Kasa-ishi 笠石
4.9km
300
400
1km
Hokotate-iwa 鉾立て石
Chōishi-michi
町石道
Caution: Slippery path
1km
18.8km to Daimon
6 hrs
Namida-iwa 涙石
Fork
Hokire Jizō 頬切地蔵
Mattō-iwa まっとう岩
Kōyashita
高野下
1.1km
Kasamatsu Pass
笠松峠
Roppon-sugi
六本杉
500
109
1.2km
0.6km
1.7km
Fudōdani River
不動谷川
118
Tomb of Oteru
お照の墓
95
Shimokosawa
下古沢

Approach Route to Mt. Kōya

Advice: The place where the most persimmons grow in Japan is along the Kinokawa river, which flows at the foot of the northern side of Mt. Kōya. So, along the way not only are there other narrow routes as marked on the map, but there are also many forks in the path, but if you follow the markers there is little chance that you will get lost.

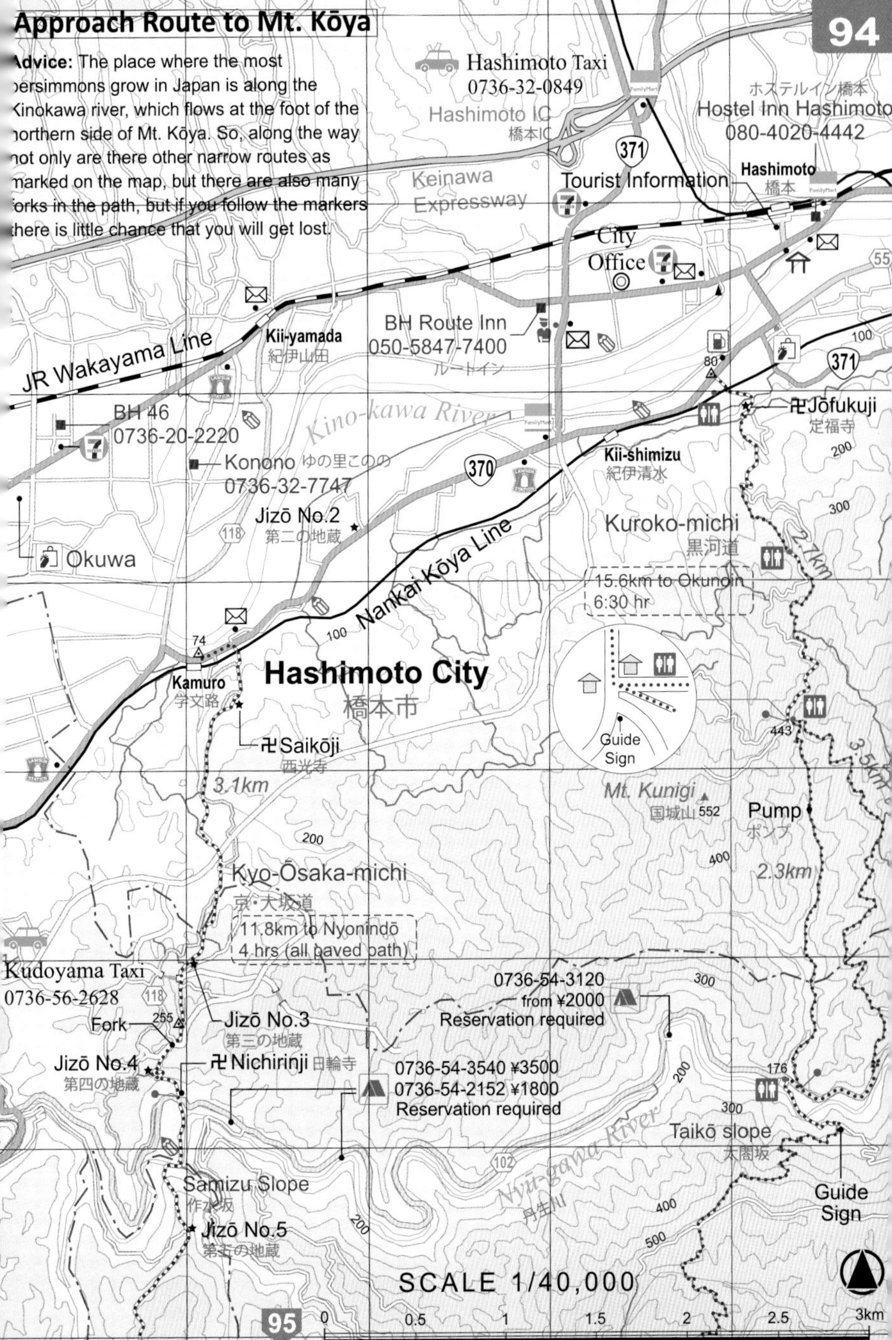
Hashimoto Taxi
0736-32-0849
Hashimoto IC
橋本IC
ホステルイン橋本
Hostel Inn Hashimoto
080-4020-4442
371
Keinawa Expressway
Tourist Information
Hashimoto
橋本
City Office
55
JR Wakayama Line
Kii-yamada
紀伊山田
BH Route Inn
050-5847-7400
ルートイン
100
80
Kino-kawa River
Jōfukuji
定福寺
BH 46
0736-20-2220
Konono ゆの里このの
0736-32-7747
370
Kii-shimizu
紀伊清水
200
Jizō No.2
第二の地蔵
118
Okuwa
Kuroko-michi
黒河道
300
2.7km
15.6km to Okunoin
6:30 hr
Nankai Kōya Line
100
74
Kamuro
学文路
Hashimoto City
橋本市
Guide Sign
Saikōji
西光寺
443
3.5km
3.1km
Mt. Kunigi
国城山 552
Pump
ポンプ
200
400
2.3km
Kyo-Ōsaka-michi
京・大坂道
11.8km to Nyonindō
4 hrs (all paved path)
Kudoyama Taxi
0736-56-2628
118
0736-54-3120
from ¥2000
Reservation required
300
Fork
255
Jizō No.3
第三の地蔵
Jizō No.4
第四の地蔵
Nichirinji 日輪寺
0736-54-3540 ¥3500
0736-54-2152 ¥1800
Reservation required
176
200
300
Taikō slope
太閤坂
Nyū-gawa River
丹生川
102
Samizu Slope
作水坂
Guide Sign
Jizō No.5
第五の地蔵
200
400
500
SCALE 1/40,000
0 0.5 1 1.5 2 2.5 3km

95

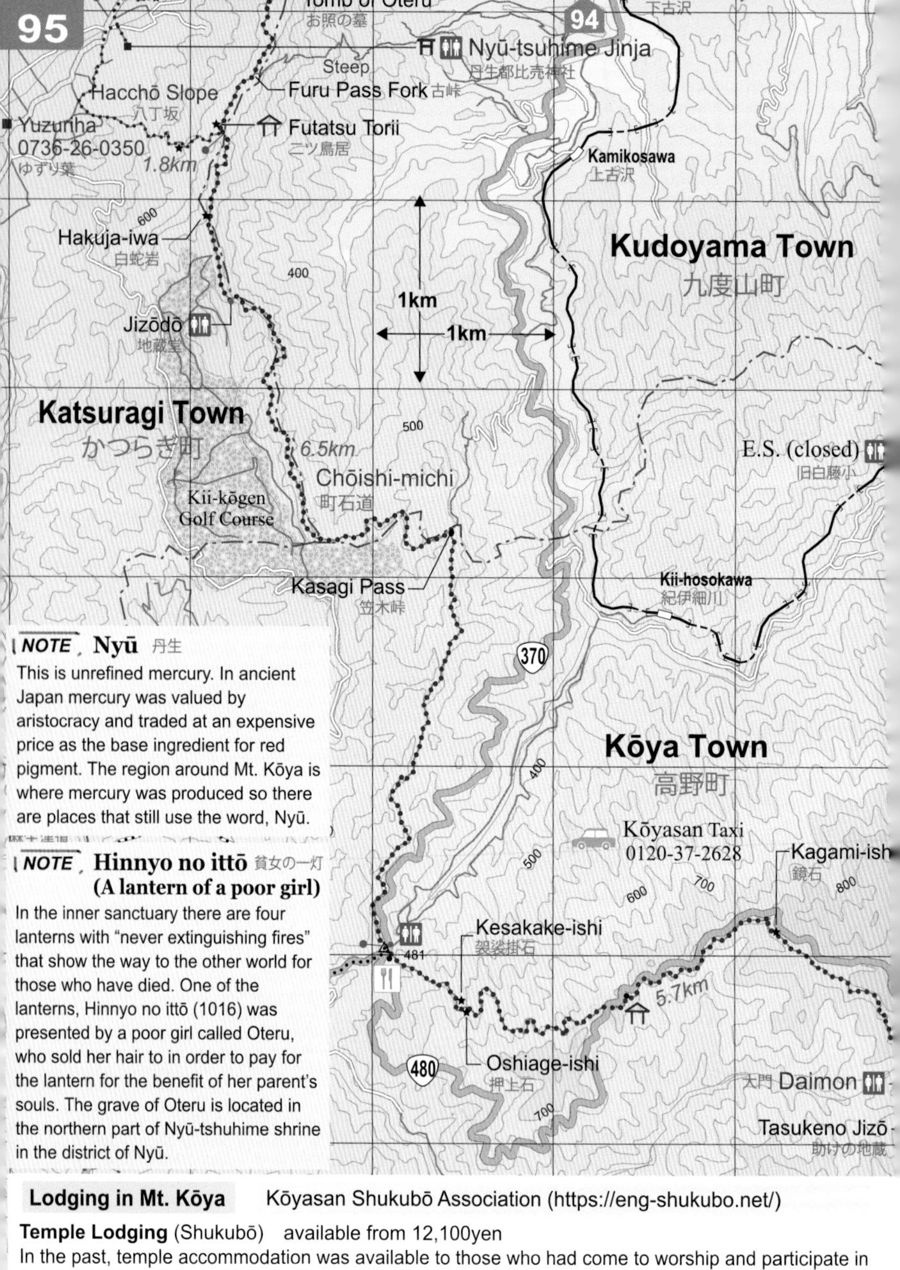

Tomb of Oteru
お照の墓
94
下古沢
Nyū-tsuhime Jinja
丹生都比売神社
Steep
Furu Pass Fork 古峠
Hacchō Slope
八丁坂
Yuzuriha
0736-26-0350
ゆずり葉
Futatsu Torii
二ツ鳥居
1.8km
Kamikosawa
上古沢
600
Hakuja-iwa
白蛇岩
400
Kudoyama Town
九度山町
1km
1km
Jizōdō
地蔵堂
Katsuragi Town
かつらぎ町
500
6.5km
E.S. (closed)
旧白藤小
Chōishi-michi
町石道
Kii-kōgen
Golf Course
Kasagi Pass
笠木峠
Kii-hosokawa
紀伊細川
370
Kōya Town
高野町
400
Kōyasan Taxi
0120-37-2628
500
600
700
800
Kagami-ish
鏡石
Kesakake-ishi
袈裟掛石
481
5.7km
480
Oshiage-ishi
押上石
700
大門 Daimon
Tasukeno Jizō
助けの地蔵

NOTE Nyū 丹生

This is unrefined mercury. In ancient Japan mercury was valued by aristocracy and traded at an expensive price as the base ingredient for red pigment. The region around Mt. Kōya is where mercury was produced so there are places that still use the word, Nyū.

NOTE Hinnyo no ittō 貧女の一灯
(A lantern of a poor girl)

In the inner sanctuary there are four lanterns with "never extinguishing fires" that show the way to the other world for those who have died. One of the lanterns, Hinnyo no ittō (1016) was presented by a poor girl called Oteru, who sold her hair to in order to pay for the lantern for the benefit of her parent's souls. The grave of Oteru is located in the northern part of Nyū-tshuhime shrine in the district of Nyū.

Lodging in Mt. Kōya Kōyasan Shukubō Association (https://eng-shukubo.net/)

Temple Lodging (Shukubō) available from 12,100yen

In the past, temple accommodation was available to those who had come to worship and participate in training. Today, while maintaining their original function and solemnity, temples now offer services similar seen at other lodging facilities to cater to the wide variety of people who chose to spend the night.

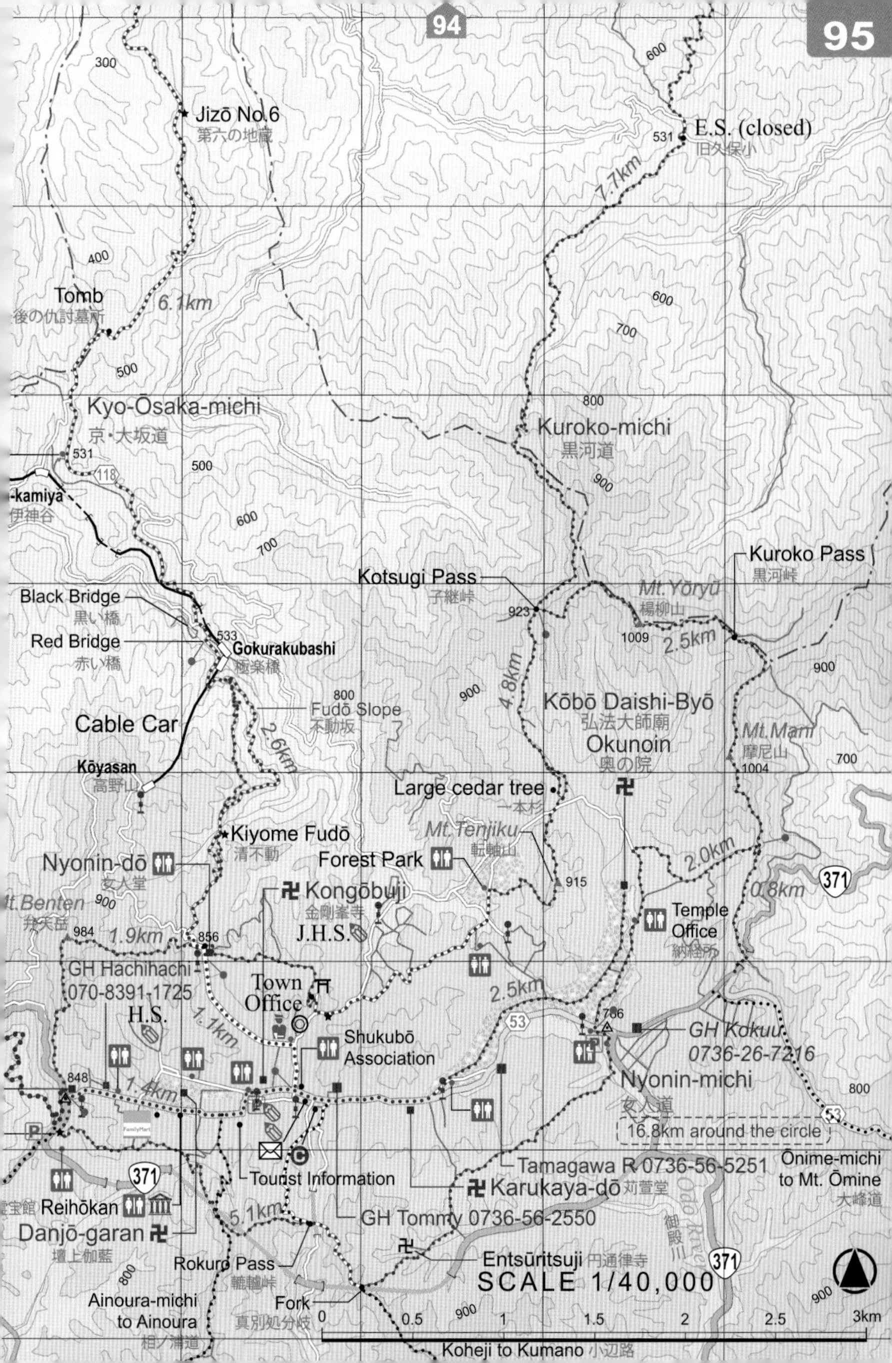
94
Jizō No.6
第六の地蔵
E.S. (closed)
旧久保小
7.7km
Tomb
後の仇討墓所
6.1km
Kyo-Ōsaka-michi
京・大坂道
Kuroko-michi
黒河道
-kamiya
伊神谷
Kotsugi Pass
子継峠
Kuroko Pass
黒河峠
Mt.Yōryū
楊柳山
2.5km
Black Bridge
黒い橋
Red Bridge
赤い橋
Gokurakubashi
極楽橋
Fudō Slope
不動坂
2.6km
4.8km
Cable Car
Kōbō Daishi-Byō
弘法大師廟
Okunoin
奥の院
Mt.Mani
摩尼山
Kōyasan
高野山
Large cedar tree
一本杉
Kiyome Fudō
清不動
Mt.Tenjiku
転軸山
Nyonin-dō
女人堂
Forest Park
2.0km
Mt.Benten
弁天岳
Kongōbuji
金剛峯寺
0.8km
J.H.S.
Temple Office
納経所
1.9km
GH Hachihachi
070-8391-1725
Town Office
2.5km
H.S.
1.1km
Shukubō Association
GH Kokuu
0736-26-7216
Nyonin-michi
女人道
1.4km
16.8km around the circle
Tamagawa R 0736-56-5251
Ōnime-michi to Mt. Ōmine
大峰道
Tourist Information
Karukaya-dō 苅萱堂
Reihōkan
霊宝館
5.1km
GH Tommy 0736-56-2550
Danjō-garan
壇上伽藍
Odo River
御殿川
Entsūritsuji 円通律寺
Rokuro Pass
轆轤峠
SCALE 1/40,000
Ainoura-michi to Ainoura
相ノ浦道
Fork
真別処分岐
0 0.5 1 1.5 2 2.5 3km
Koheji to Kumano 小辺路

Practical Phrases

Pronunciation Key:

a =`ah` sound as in father　*e* =`eh` sound as in end　*i* =`ee` sound as in eat
o =`oh` sound as in Ohio　*u* =`oo` sound as in food

Long vowels〔for example:(ō are simply longer in duration) the sound does not change.〕

Basics

Yes / No	*hai / iie*	はい / いいえ
Please	*onegai shimasu*	お願いします
Thank you	*arigatō gozaimasu*	ありがとうございます
You're welcome	*dō itashimashite*	どういたしまして
Excuse me	*sumimasen*	すみません
Sorry	*gomennasai*	ごめんなさい
Good morning	*ohayō gozaimasu*	おはようございます
Good afternoon	*konnichiwa*	こんにちは
Good evening	*konban wa*	こんばんは
Good night	*oyasumi nasai*	おやすみなさい
Goodbye	*sayonara*	さようなら
Mr./Mrs./Miss	*.....san*	～～さん

Numbers / Time / Days of the Week / Days of the Month

1	*ichi*	いち	(一)	5	*go*	ご	(五)	9	*kyū*	きゅう	(九)
2	*ni*	に	(二)	6	*roku*	ろく	(六)	10	*jū*	じゅう	(十)
3	*san*	さん	(三)	7	*nana*	なな	(七)	11	*jū ichi*	じゅういち	(十一)
4	*yon*	よん	(四)	8	*hachi*	はち	(八)	12	*jū ni*	じゅうに	(十二)

Minute	*fun*	ふん	afternoon	*gogo*	ごご	Wed	*suiyōbi*	水曜日
O'clock	*ji*	じ	Sun	*nichiyōbi*	日曜日	Thurs	*mokuyōbi*	木曜日
Month	*gatsu*	がつ	Mon	*getsuyōbi*	月曜日	Fri	*kinyōbi*	金曜日
Morning	*gozen*	ごぜん	Tues	*kayōbi*	火曜日	Sat	*doyōbi*	土曜日

1 st	*tsuitachi*	一日	6 th	*muika*	六日	11 th	*jū-ichi-nichi*	十一日
2 nd	*futsuka*	二日	7 th	*nanuka*	七日	12 th	*jū-ni-nichi*	十二日
3 rd	*mikka*	三日	8 th	*yōka*	八日	20 th	*Hatsuka*	二十日
4 th	*yokka*	四日	9 th	*kokonoka*	九日	21 th	*nijū-ichi-nichi*	二十一日
5 th	*itsuka*	五日	10 th	*tōka*	十日	22 th	*nijū-ni-nichi*	二十二日

June 27= *roku gatsu ni jū nana nichi*　5:35 PM= *gogo go ji san jū go fun*

Useful Expressions

Do you speak English?	*eigo ga wakari masu ka*	えいごがわかりますか
I don't speak Japanese.	*nihongo ga wakari masen*	にほんごがわかりません
I understand./ I don't understand.	*wakari mashita / wakari masen*	わかりました / わかりません
I'm (American).	*watashi wa (amerika) jin desu*	わたしは(アメリカ)じんです
What's your name?	*namae wa nan desu ka*	なまえはなんですか

What time is it?	*ima nanji desu ka*	いまなんじですか
Yesterday / today / tomorrow	*kinō / kyō / ashita*	きのう/きょう/あした
I am lost.	*michi ni mayoi mashita*	みちにまよいました
I would like to use restroom.	*toire wo kashite kudasai*	トイレを貸してください
Left/right	*hidari / migi*	ひだり/みぎ
Turn to the left / right .	*hidari(migi) e magaru*	ひだり(みぎ)へ曲がる
East/West/North/South	*higashi/nishi/kita/minami*	東・西・北・南
Where is.........?	*......wa doko desu ka*	～～はどこですか
Please contact	*....ni renraku shite kudasai*	～～に連絡してください
Please call a doctor(the police).	*isha(keisatu) wo yonde kudasai*	医者(警察)を呼んでください
I have a stomachache.	*onaka ga itai desu*	おなかが痛いです
I have a fever.	*netsu ga arimasu*	熱があります
I have lost (my)	*....wo nakushi mashita*	～～をなくしました

ticket	*kippu*	きっぷ	signal	*shingō*	信号	charge	*jūden*	充電
station	*eki*	えき	box lunch	*obentō*	おべんとう	hand / leg	*te / ashi*	手/足
bus stop	*basutei*	バス停	water / tea	*mizu / ocha*	みず/お茶	shoe	*kutsu*	くつ
crossing	*kōsaten*	交差点	smartphone	*sumaho*	スマートフォン	medicine	*kusuri*	薬

At Lodging

I'd like to make a reservation.	*yoyaku onegai shimasu*	予約お願いします
I'd like to cancel a reservation.	*sumimasen cansel shimasu*	キャンセルします
tonight / tomorrow	*konban / ashita*	こんばん / あす
the day after tomorrow	*asatte*	あさって
For one / For two	*hitori desu / futari desu*	ひとりです / ふたりです
My name is	*namae wa .....desu*	なまえは～～です
I will arrive at (six) o'clock.	*(roku) ji ni tsukimasu*	(6) 時に着きます
I am at .... now.	*ima .....ni imasu*	いま～～にいます
breakfast / dinner	*chōshoku / yūshoku*	朝食 / 夕食
I would like dinner.	*yūshoku onegai shimasu*	夕食お願いします
without meals	*sudomari desu*	素泊まりです
How much is it?	*ikura desuka*	いくらですか
Can I use a credit card?	*kado wa tsukae masu ka*	カードはつかえますか
Can I use the Internet?	*internet wa tsukae masu ka*	インターネットはつかえますか
bath / bathroom	*ofuro / toire*	おふろ / トイレ
Can I do a wash?	*sentaku dekimasu ka*	せんたくできますか
It's delicious.	*oishii desu*	おいしいです
I am vegetarian.	*watashi wa vegetarian desu*	私はベジタリアンです
Fish and vegetable are OK.	*sakana to yasai wa daijōbu*	魚と野菜は大丈夫
I don’t eat fish and meat.	*sakana mo niku mo dame*	魚と肉の両方ダメ
I would like another helping.	*okawari onegai shimasu*	おかわりお願いします

one stay	*i ppaku*	一泊	no room available	*manshitsu*	満室
two stay	*ni haku*	二泊	share a room	*aibeya*	相部屋

information
Tourist Information

List of Public Information Offices *English speaking staff on duty*

Explanatory notes O Open Hours ☎ Phone C Closed Days

Tourist Information Center (TIC) O 9:00 - 17:00 ☎ 03-3201-3331 C Jan 1 https://www.jnto.go.j
3-3-1 Marunouchi Chiyoda-ku Tokyo 100-0005 (Shin-Tokyo Bldg 1F, JR Keiyō Line Tokyo Stn. Exit No.6

Narita Airport Terminal 1 Arrival Lobby 1F O 8:00 - 20:00 ☎ 0476-30-3383

Narita Airport Terminal 2 Arrival Lobby 1F O 8:00 - 20:00 ☎ 0476-34-5877

Kansai Int'l Airport Terminal 1 Arrival Lobby 1F O 7:00 - 19:00 ☎ 072-456-6160

Information Center Namba (see page 93-b) O 9:00 - 19:00 C Jan. 1, 2
NANKAI Railway Namba Station 2F

Tokushima Welcome Center O 10:00 - 18:30 ☎ 088-635-9002 C Jan. 1
Amico Shopping Center 1F, in front of JR Tokushima Station (see page 23)

Kōchi Tourist Information O 8:30 - 18:00 ☎ 088-879-6400
In front of JR Kōchi Station (see page 40)

Dōgo Tourist Information O 8:30 - 17:00 ☎ 089-921-3708
In front of Iyotetsu Streetcar Dōgo Onsen Stn (see page 68)

Takamatsu Tourist Information O 9:00 - 20:00 ☎ 087-826-0170
In JR Takamatsu Station (see page 88)

Hiking & Outdoor Shops

Ōsaka City

There are some large outdoor shops around Osaka Station, Namba Station, and Tennoji Station.
ex:

mont-bell: JR Tennōji Stn Bldg Mio 6F (pg 15 R) https://www.montbell.com/
Kōjitsu-sansō: Grand Front 5F nearby Ōsaka Stn (pg 15 L) https://www.kojitusanso.jp/
Ishii Sports: Links Umeda 6F next to Ōsaka Stn (pg 15 L) https://www.ici-sports.com/

Tokushima City

mont-bell: 1400m east of Yoshinari Stn, or By bus bound for Youme Town from Tokushima Stn, 1400m west of Youme Town.
ALEX Sports: along the Route 55 (pg 23 R)
Kōjitsu-sansō: along the Route 55 (pg 23 R)

Kōchi City

mont-bell: 900m east of Kōchi Stn (pg 40 L)
Patagonia: 1500m west of Harimayabashi Stn (pg 40 L)

Shimanto City

mont-bell: in BH Royal (pg 48 L)

Matsuyama City

KOMPAS: (pg 68 L)

Takamatsu City

Base Camp: 1500m west of Fuseishi Stn (pg 87 L)
mont-bell: in AEON mall, shuttle bus available from Takamatsu Stn (pg 86 R)

ADVICE Full-fledged mountain climbing shoes are too rugged and not suitable for paved roads so some foreign pilgrims regret using the type of footwear they brought from their country. Waterproof walking shoes are preferable. NOTE: It is difficult to buy shoes larger than size 12 (30cm) in Japan.